Economics of Agricultural Commodities SERIES

Sugar

Sugarcane, Sugar Beet, Honey Sugar By-Product, Sugar Substitute and Sugar Policy

Economics of Agricultural Commodities

Other Volumes in the Series

- Spices and Medicinal Plants
- Plantation Crops
- Vegetables
- Fruits and Nuts
- Fiber, Cotton and Jute
- Tobacco and Other Small Crops
- Oil Seeds
- Cereals
- Pulses

Economics of Agricultural Commodities SERIES

Sugar

PC Bansil PhD

Director
Techno Economic Research Institute
New Delhi

CBS Publishers & Distributors Pvt Ltd

New Delhi • Bengaluru • Chennai • Kochi • Mumbai • Pune
Hyderabad • Kolkata • Nagpur • Patna • Vijayawada

Disclaimer

Science and technology are constantly changing fields. New research and experience broaden the scope of information and knowledge. The author has tried his best in giving information available to him while preparing the material for this book. Although, all efforts have been made to ensure optimum accuracy of the material, yet it is quite possible some errors might have been left uncorrected. The publisher, the printer and the author will not be held responsible for any inadvertent errors, or inaccuracies.

ISBN: 978-81-239-2622-3

First Edition: 2015

Published by Satish Kumar Jain and produced by Varun Jain for
CBS Publishers & Distributors Pvt Ltd
4819/XI Prahlad Street, 24 Ansari Road, Daryaganj, New Delhi 110 002, India.
Ph: 23289259, 23266861, 23266867 Website: www.cbspd.com
Fax: 011-23243014 e-mail: delhi@cbspd.com; cbspubs@airtelmail.in.
Corporate Office: 204 FIE, Industrial Area, Patparganj, Delhi 110 092
Ph: 4934 4934 Fax: 4934 4935 e-mail: publishing@cbspd.com; publicity@cbspd.com

Branches

- **Bengaluru:** Seema House 2975, 17th Cross, K.R. Road, Banasankari 2nd Stage, Bengaluru 560 070, Karnataka
  Ph: +91-80-26771678/79 Fax: +91-80-26771680 e-mail: bangalore@cbspd.com
- **Chennai:** 7, Subbaraya Street, Shenoy Nagar, Chennai 600 030, Tamil Nadu
  Ph: +91-44-26260666, 26208620 Fax: +91-44-42032115 e-mail: chennai@cbspd.com
- **Kochi:** Ashana House, No. 39/1904, A.M. Thomas Road, Valanjambalam, Ernakulam 682016, Kochi, Kerala
  Ph: +91-484-4059061-65, 67 Fax: +91-484-4059065 e-mail: kochi@cbspd.com
- **Mumbai:** 83-C, Dr E Moses Road, Worli, Mumbai-400018, Maharashtra
  Ph: +91-22-24902340/41 Fax: +91-22-24902342 e-mail: mumbai@cbspd.com
- **Pune:** Bhuruk Prestige, Sr. No. 52/12/2+1+3/2 Narhe, Haveli (Near Katraj-Dehu Road Bypass), Pune 411 041, Maharashtra
  Ph: +91-20-64704058, 64704059, 32392277 Fax: +91-20-24300160 e-mail: pune@cbspd.com

Representatives

- **Hyderabad** 0-9885175004
- **Kolkata** 0-9831437309, 0-9051152362
- **Nagpur** 0-9021734563
- **Patna** 0-9334159340
- **Vijayawada** 0-9000660880

Printed at: India Binding House, Noida, UP

to

Sundeep

My grandson—a person with guts—is very fond of cars from young age. When he was in Libya with us during the late seventies, he could recognize the make of every car that passed by. It is perhaps no coincidence that after trying his hand at various activities, he has returned to his childhood passion by taking a car dealership, which he now manages as his full time job. Today, he has his own showrooms for Hyundai and Polaris, two entirely different types of vehicles. Unlike common cars, Polaris is meant for running off the road in hilly regions. I am sure that he will achieve great hights as a businessman. I wish him a long, happy, healthy and prosperous life.

Preface

The book *Sugar* is one of the volumes in the Series, **Economics of Agricultural Commodities**. It consists of 6 chapters: Sugarcane, •Sugar Beet, •Honey, • Sugar By-products, • Sugar Substitutes and •Sugar Policy. Each chapter deals in depth of the topic concerned. Starting with a historical approach, each section covers in details of the various economic aspects along with the benefits and other relevant issues. Then in the final situation world issues are discussed in detail.

The entire work depends on secondary sources of data including the net. Although every possible source has been studied to provide data, there are a number of difficulties one faces. For example, the FAO and the USDA are primary sources for international production and trade. But both of these sources provide widely different data. We have provided the original data from all possible sources since we have no way to screen this vast source.

During the course of our studies, we observed that information available on various aspects of sugar is scattered. It is difficult at present to lay one's hand at a specific publication which supplies relevant information. We thought to fill this gap, hence this series.

The study is the result of innumerable sources—published / unpublished, quite a large number of daily newspapers, journals, magazines and books. The final presentation, however, is in a specific order so as to give the reader the required information at one place. We are grateful to a large number of authors whose work or research formed the base of this study. Thanks are due to Dr ML Srivastava and Mr Ravi Shankar without whose contribution the book would not have been able to see the light of the day. Our faculty members, Dr PN Radhakrishnan and Dr SR Mohnot, were always available to guide and contribute their bit. Last but not the least is the major contribution of our staff members Mrs Vasantha Krishnan and Mrs Ajitha Ganagadharan who never got tired to type and retype the material.

I do hope that the book in its updated form will prove useful to students of agricultural economics, researchers, educated farmers, administrators, policymakers and bankers alike. I shall very much welcome any comments for further improvement of the volume.

I must, however, say that none of them is responsible for any errors or omissions from which this work may suffer as at present. I am personally responsible for all this.

PC Bansil

Contents

2 Sugar Beet 207

3 Honey 257

4 Sugar By-Products 291

5 Sugar Substitutes 319

6 Sugar Policy 335

1

Sugarcane

HISTORY OF SUGARCANE

The historical and mythological evidences clearly show that the original home of sugarcane and sugar manufacturing is India. "The soldiers of Alexander the Great who invaded India around 327 BC were the first Europeans to see sugarcane in India. Although they took sugarcane to Europe it was not actually cultivated there until 700 AD". Evidently, sugarcane was there in India long before it was cultivated in Europe and it was from India that Europe came to know about sugarcane. However, the process of making sugar was invented between the 4th and the 6th centuries. About 600 AD, Tsai-Hang, the Chinese Emperor sent a mission to Bihar to understand the art of sugar manufacturing. It is evident from these facts that the original home of sugarcane and sugar manufacturing is India.

Indian economy is an agrarian economy. Seventy percent of the descendants of this country rely on agriculture. Geographically, the Indian subcontinent prostrates to the north of the equator and hence the climatic conditions are conducive to sugarcane cultivation. The States lying south of the Narmada River, i.e. Maharashtra, Andra Pradesh, Karnataka and Tamil Nadu are the best-suited area for sugarcane growing.

Sugar (sucrose) is a carbohydrate that occurs naturally in every fruit and vegetable. It is a major product of photosynthesis—the process by which plants transform the suns energy into food. Sugar occurs in greatest quantities in sugarcane and sugar beets from which it is separated for commercial use. The natural sugar stored in the cane stalk or beet root is separated from rest of the plant material through a process known as refining. Sugarcane originated in New Guinea where it has been known for thousands of years sugar's long history has included its spread from New Guinea to South Asia, then with Arab farmers to the Mediterranean, and most notoriously as the foundation of the Caribbean slave trade. Here in India, it cross-bred with some wild sugarcane relatives to produce the commercial sugarcane we know today.

The historical and mythological evidences clearly show that the original home of sugarcane and sugar manufacturing is India. "The process of making sugar was invented between the 4th century and the 6th century". About 600 AD, Tsai-Hang, the Chinese Emperor sent a mission to Bihar to understand the art of sugar manufacturing. It is evident from these facts that the original home of sugarcane and sugar manufacturing is India.

ORIGIN

There is another story according to which cultivation of sugarcane probably originated on the island of New Guinea in the South Pacific about 8,000 years ago and spread to the nearby Solomon Islands, the New Hebrides and then to New Caledonia. In one Polynesian account of the origin of mankind, two fishermen, the only people on earth, 1 day, found a piece of cane in their net. At first, thinking it useless, they threw it away, but after catching it by chance for 3 days running, they planted it in the ground. It grew and after a while it burst and a woman appeared from it. She cooked for the men by day and hid by night in the cane. How the two men got there in the first place is not explained?

- Modern sugarcane is a complex hybrid of two or more of five species of the genus *Saccharum*.
- It belongs to family *Gramineae*, class monocotyledons and order glumaceae sub-family panicoidae, tribe andripogoneae and subtribe saccharininea.
- The cultivated canes belong to two main groups: (1) thin, hardy north Indian types *S. barberi* and the Chinese *S. sinense* and (b) thick, juicy noble canes *S. officinarum*.
- Highly prized cane is *S. officinarum*. It is probably evolved from *S. robustum* by introgression from other genera.
- Thus, *S. robustum* is the closest wild relative and putative ancestor of *S. officinarum*.
- It is agreed that the origin of *S. officinarum* is the Indo-Myanmar China border with New Guinea as the main center of diversity.
- The *officinarums* are called the "noble canes" due to thick, juicy, low-fibered canes of high sucrose content.
- The process of nobilization in sugarcane is the modified back crossing of wild cane.
- *S. spontaneum* with *S. officinarum* and a repeated back crossing to the noble parent (*S. officinarum*).
- Some of the important noble cane cultivars were Otaheita, Cheribon, Calodonia, Badila, etc.
- However, by 1975, the noble cane era ended due to serious diseases like mosaic, sereh, smut and red rot.
- It is stated that the cradle of cultivated sugarcane is the region where two wild species, i.e. *Saccharum spontaneum* and *S. robustum* are found. *S. robustum* is derived from natural crossing between *S. spontaneum* and *Miscanthis floridulus* and the origin is New Guinea.
- The origin of *S. spontaneum* is subtropical India. The habitat of these two wild canes is swamps, river banks, water courses, etc.
- One small group of canes is *S. edule* which is related to *S. robustum* and the aborted inflorescences of these species are used as food by the natives of Melanesia.
- Cultivation of sugarcane in India dates back to the Vedie period.
- The earliest mention of sugarcane cultivation is found in Indian writings of the period 1400–1000 BC the word "sugar" is derived from the Sanskrit word "sankkara" or "sarkara".
- Barber (1931) was of the opinion that the thin Indian canes probably originated in the moist parts of north eastern Indian, from some plant closely related to Saccharum spontaneum. (Kans). Tropical cane might have originated in some of the larger islands of Occania, most probably in New Guinea.
- Brandes (1956) also concluded that it originated in New Guinea where various forms of thick, tall, tropical cane have been grown from ancient times.

About 2000 years later, sugarcane had moved westward reaching Indonesia, the Philippines, and then Northern India. Its Eastward spread has been traced to the migrations of the Pacific Islanders when it arrived in Hawaii between 600 AD and 1100 AD. Captain Cook saw indigenous cane still growing in Polynesia when he was there just over 200 years ago. Then, it was being used for making a kind of beer.

The word "sugar" is thought to derive from the ancient Sanskrit *sharkara*. By the 6th century BC, sharkara was frequently referred to in Sanskrit texts which even distinguished superior and inferior varieties of sugarcane. The Susrutha Samhita listed 12 varieties; the best types were supposed to be the vamshika with thin reeds and the paundraka of Bengal. It was also being called guda, a term which is still used in India to denote jaggery. A Persian account from the 6th century BC gives the first account of solid sugar and describes it as coming from the Indus Valley. This early sugar would have resembled what is known as "raw" (sugar: Indian dark brown sugar or gur).

At this time, honey was the only sweetener in the countries beyond Asia and all visitors to India were much taken with the "reed which produced honey without bees". The Greek historian Herodotus knew of the sugarcane in the 5th century BC and Alexander is said to have sent some home when he came to the Punjab region in 326 BC. Practically every traveler to India over the centuries mentions sugarcane; the Moroccan Ibn Battuta wrote of the sugarcanes of Kerala which excelled every other in the 14th century; Francois Bernier, in India from 1658–1659, wrote of the extensive fields of sugarcane in Bengal.

- Caraka reported in 100 BC about the existence of two sugarcane types: (1) Iksh and (2) Paundra.
- In 200 BC, Patanjali mentioned that by about 400 BC sugarcane was familiar at Takshasila. There were citations on sugarcane during 800 BC in Atharva Veda and Manu in 1000 BC.
- Sugarcane was first mentioned in China during 286 AD (Bashan) and it was reported to be known in the period of Su-ma-siang Ju.
- After the time of Buddha, Indian sailors who possibly had contacts with Myammar, Indonesia and Malaysia would have brought *Saccharum officinarum* to India from Indonesia.
- *Saccharum* is the Latin name proposed by Linne in 1753 as a derivation from Karkara and Sakkara from Sanskrit and Prakrit.
- It is the opinion of many explorers that sugarcane had its origin in *Saccharum barberi* Jesweit of North India, and that *Saccharum officinarum* had Polynesian origin.
- Barber and Jesweit (1930) indicated that *Saccharum officinarum* evolved in Malaysia, Indonesia, Papua-New Guinea region or in the islands of Polynesia or Melanesia groups.

Brandes et al. have mentioned in records of their expedition during 1928 that maximum diversity was noted in New Guinea from where *Saccharum officnarum* might have evolved and since *S. robustum* was endemic to this area, the latter may be the ancestor of the former. It was accepted then as both the species had chromosome number of 2n=80. Warner and Grassl also confirmed it after the expedition in 1957.

From about 1000 BC its cultivation gradually spread along human migration routes to Southeast Asia and India and east into the Pacific. It is thought to have hybridized with wild sugarcanes of India and China, to produce the "thin" canes. It spread westwards to the Mediterranean between 600 AD and 1400 AD.

Sugarcane was introduced into China from India around 800 BC. Crude sugar was being produced by 400 BC and by 700 AD, it was being commercially exploited by Indians in the subcontinent. In China, the boiled down and sun-dried juice of sugarcane was called "stone honey", and the most expensive, highly prized luxury items were the white cakes of stone honey imported from India. In 510 BC, a Persian military expedition recorded finding sugarcane in that subcontinent, and later, Alexander the Great also found it there. His Admiral, Nearchos, is recorded as describing "a reed which makes honey without bees". Theophrastus in 287 BC described it as "honey which is in a cane", and Dioscoredes described it as "a kind of concentrated honey, called saccharon, found in canes in India and Arabia, like in consistence to salt, and brittle to be broken between the teeth".

Sugarcane culture slowly spread Westward reaching Persia by 500 AD. The next migration was started by the Prophet Mohammed who, a few years before his death in 632 AD, began a Holy War for the conversion of the world to Islam. When his armies conquered Persia, they found sugarcane and adopted its cultivation, carrying it with them in their conquests, now calling it "the Persian Reed".

Arabs were responsible for much of its spread as they took it to Egypt around 640 AD during their conquests. They carried it with them as they advanced around the Mediterranean. Sugarcane spread by this means to Syria, Cyprus and Crete, eventually reaching Spain around 715 AD. Around 1,420 the Portuguese introduced sugarcane into Madeira, from where it soon reached the Canary Islands, the Azores and West Africa. Columbus transported sugarcane from the Canary Islands to what is now the Dominican Republic in 1493. The crop was taken to Central and South America from the 1520s onwards, and later to the British and French West Indies.

Sugarcane was introduced to Egypt after their defeat by the Arabs in 710 AD. Using their highly developed skills in agriculture and chemistry, the Egyptians developed clarification, crystallization, and refining processes. From there, sugarcane continued its Westward journey across Northern Aftica reaching Morocco. Then, crossing the Mediterranean to Southern Spain by 755 AD and to Sicily in 950 AD, it progressed along the southern littoral of the Mediterranean, where in time it reached the islands off the Atlantic coast of Africa. An example of the extreme costliness of sugar in those days was the construction of the Badii palace in Marrakech by Ahmed el Mansour. The building materials including gold, Italian marble and onyx were all traded for their weight in sugar.

But, the method was crude beyond imagination. Cane was cut in pieces-crushed under heavy weight-juice thus obtained was boiled and stirred till it turned solids. Solids of uneven shape and size were called sarkaran, a Sanskrit term of "gravel". Modern word "sugar" is derived from the word Sarkara. Thus, it could be rightly said that India has been the original home for sugarcane as well as sugar manufacture.

Production of sugar then was a primitive process. A blindfolded mule or ox treading in a circle drove a vertical grinding mill or a pestle in a mortar to crush the cane, and the juice was evaporated by boiling to a sticky mixture of crystals and syrup. Such a method is still in use in India where the product is called gur or jaggery. Although it tastes good on bread, it does not keep well. The original word for sugar is probably the Sanskrit "sarkar" meaning grain. The East Indian word for sugar was "shekar"; in Arabic, it was "al zucar", adopted in Spanish as "azucar", French as "sucre", German as "Zucker" and in English as "sugar".

In the middle ages, similar equipment was used to produce sugar. In Sicily, the grinding stone was powered as a rule by men. There is a painting dating from about 1580 by Hans van der Straat, of a sugar factory near Palermo. A contemporary description says that going into the place was like entering the Forge of Vulcan: "the men who worked there being blackened by the smoke from the fires, dirty, sweaty, and scorched, more like demons than men". It goes on to describe all of the various jobs: cutting cane, crushing, boiling the juice, even planting cane tops in manure as seed for the following year.

In 10th century Europe, sugar was considered a valuable medicine. Later, it was considered a rare spice and its price was as high as that of pepper, saffron and cinnamon. Like those spices, the Arabs also controlled the European sugar trade. Because of its exalted status, sugar was used to season things to a degree that today we would consider excessive and unappetizing. Meats were often cooked in a heavy syrup of sugar with almonds and fruit.

Further knowledge in Europe about sugar was spread during the Crusades of the 11th to 13th centuries. Many people from various European nations and social levels fought in this series of 28 campaigns. Some records show that large cane plantations belonged to various Christian orders in the region. Shipping and trade between the Mideast and the Europe during this period was almost exclusively in the hands of Venetian merchants. There are indications that, besides raw sugar trade, the Venetians also developed some primitive form of sugar refining. There is evidence that in the middle of the 14th century the Venetians were manufacturing and trading "sugar loaves" with their customers. Sugar was one of the first pharmaceutical ingredients, as it is still used today, to mask the bitter or unpleasant taste of medicines. Special jars of "rose" and "violet" sugars, flavored with aromatic substances and extremely expensive, were made for sickly royal children. Sugar was so rare that a teaspoon of it in the 16th century commanded the equivalent of $5. According to English records from the 17th century, one could purchase a calf for £4 of sugar.

England, because of its separation from the continent of Europe, saw very little sugar before the early 14 century. Its scarcity is indicated by an order, written in Norman French, from King Henry III to the Mayor of Winchester in 1226, to provide 3 lbs of Alexandrian sugar for a banquet" if so much is to be had". The first regular seabome trade to England began in 1319 when Venetian traders sold some 50 tons of sugar for $3,000—the modem equivalent of over 11 million (at today's prices, that amount of sugar could be purchased for $23,650).

From the mid-16th century much of the sugar consumed in England was bought from "Barbary", now called Morocco. The Barbary Company was created in 1551; one of its founders was Thomas Wyndham, a Vice-Admiral in King Henry VIII's Navy, who traded in a vessel called the Lion to the port of Agadir. Barbary sugar had a very bad name for quality; queen Elizabeth I's Secretary of State, Lord Burleigh, actually complained about it to the Grocers' Company. Before it ceased to exist, the Barbary Company became the stepping stone for later British ventures afield. It pioneered the West Indian Trade which began to develop the 17th century and later became of very important in the 18th century.

On his second voyage to the New World, Columbus brought cane cuttings from the Canary Islands to Hispaniola, the island now composed of the Dominican Republic and The Republic of Haiti. The first attempt to grow cane there faded, but by 1509 sugar was being produced in profitable amounts.

Sugar shaped a good deal of history of the New World. By 1520, cane was growing in Mexico, and the Spanish explorer Cortez established the first North American sugar mill there in 1535. Cultivation soon spread to Peru, Brazil, Columbia and Venezuela. Puerto Rico had a mill by 1547. By the year 1600, sugar production in the subtropical and tropical Americas had become the world's largest and most lucrative industry. The "sugar islands" of the West Indies brought great wealth to England and France. Queen Elizabeth displayed her wealth by putting a sugar bowl on her table and using sugar as an everyday food and seasoning. Great Britain took a commanding position in the sugar trade, and consumption of tea in the English diet increased tremendously with the use of sugar. By the end of the 17th century, this new beverage was in general use. By the eighteenth century, the demand for sugar was so great that it became a matter of active public interest.

Sugar was a minor, expensive luxury until the 16th century, when two things happened to change this:

1. Supplies of honey, the regular sweetener, declined because of the reformation campaign against the monasteries. They were the major honey producers although honey was a by-product of beeswax production, used for making candles.
2. The supply of sugar became more available, although not necessarily cheap. Two discoveries soon followed which greatly increased the demand for sugar in Europe: the discovery that fruit could be preserved in sugar, and the making of jam with sugar. These uses of sugar had been known by the ancient Indians, Chinese and Arabs who had greater access to crystalline sugar.

When sugar became more plentiful, but was still very expensive, a new passion arose—sugar sculpture. In 16th century Italy, intricate spun-sugar sculpture became the rage for the tables of the rich. Majestic set pieces of sugar icing were a part of the ostentatious display of wealth throughout Mediterranean Europe.

While the often futile scramble for gold and treasure in the New World was going on, wealth of another kind was slowly being developed in the West Indies and southward into South America sugar, at first, mainly from the Spanish. In the early years from 1620 to 1640 of the British colonization in Barbados, for example, sugar was of no importance, only tobacco, indigo and cotton were planted. In 1700, after sugarcane was introduced, although the population was then only about 30,000, there were some 1,300 sugarcane plantations and nearly 500 factories driven either by windmills or by animals. Barbados was soon producing about 8,000 tons a year (15 tons per factory on average. Today, a single factory in Brazil produces 30,000 tons per day). The newer captures and acquisitions, like Antigua and Jamaica, became important sources of sugar. The French also began to produce sugar in their colonial islands of Martinique and Guadeloupe.

British and French sea captains brought in new varieties of cane to replace the original strains introduced by Columbus. One of these men, Captain Bligh, only 3 years after the mutiny against him in HMS Bounty, sailed into St. Vincent carrying a cargo of cane plants and breadfruit trees from Oceania.

There was, however, a sinister reason for the breadfruit: it was intended as a form of food suited to Africans living and working as slaves in the plantations. Earlier settlers had tried importing agricultural workers from England. As the demand for sugar grew so did the demand for labor, and it became the custom to "transport" political dissidents, felons, and other undesirables as an alternative to hanging. Oliver Cromwell barbadoed" hundreds, and these were later joined by the remnants of the Army of the Duke of Monmouth, sent there after the Battle of Sedgemoor by Judge Jeffreys in 1686. Few survived in the climate, and although some of their descendants can still be seen in Barbados, where they are called "redlegs". Another source of labor was sought, and it was found in Africa.

There was nothing new about slavery in the New World. Columbus is traditionally reported to have taken slaves with him, and by 1526 the use of slaves in Cuba was officially approved, a licence or *asiento* being granted by the King of Spain. This *asiento* later became a British monopoly in 1713 after the Treaty of Utrecht, as one of the spoils of Marlborough's Wars. The practice was finally abolished in 1789. If the growth of the sugar industry paralleled that of the slave trade in the Caribbean, then so did the antislavery movement. There were many plantation owners who objected to the trade, partly for humanitarian reasons and partly because of fears that the importation of large numbers of Africans would upset the balance of the local population. However, as the Council of the island of St. Kitts wrote to the House of Lords: "it is as great a bondage for us to cultivate our plantations without Negroes as for the Egyptians to make bricks without straw".

The sugar planter was only one link in a chain, and not the most profitable; he bore the risk of drought, heat, hurricane, insurrection, plague, and insect pests as well as isolation from home. The trade in fact was triangular. Ships left Europe with goods such as textiles, hardware, and toys, which were bartered in West Africa for gold dust and slaves. The coastal tribes would supply the latter from among their opposite numbers or enemies inland. On arrival in the West Indies, these would be sold and the money used to buy sugar and rum for Europe.

Early on there were movements, particularly in England, against the slave trade. John Locke, the philosopher, described the practice in 1689 as being "opposed to the generous temper and courage of our nation". Thanks to the efforts of William Wilhefforce, begun in 1789, the Royal Assent was ended by a Parliamentary Bill abolishing slavery in 1833. Afterward, the affranchised slaves were often unwilling to work on the sugarcane plantations although there was still a huge labor demand. There was another search for labor, this time from Portugal, China and India. In the end, the major replacement became the "indentured" labor from India, imported in "Companies" under regulated conditions (the Portuguese and Chinese soon contrived to escape from sugar and setup shops and businesses). South Africa today, has the largest population of Indians outside of India, brought in to work the cane fields.

In the Far East, slavery continued long after 1833 and this created a certain amount of "negative press" in the early 19th century. An advertisement in England offered for sale an Assortment of Sugar Basins, handsomely labelled in gold letters "East India sugar, not made by slaves". It is hard to exaggerate the importance of sugar in history two centuries ago. It was no longer a luxury as it had been in the Middle Ages, although it still cost six or seven times as much as it does now, and then it was only readily available from the Caribbean. So, for nearly a century, that area became the Cockpit of Neptune, the naval equivalent of Flanders among those islands, the Navies of France and England fought for control.

Horatio Nelson spent much of his naval career in the West Indies. In 1805, he pursued the French fleet from the Mediterranean to the Caribbean just missing it. The French Admiral, Villeneuve, although posing a threat to the British sugar islands, was very nervous and sailed back to Europe just before Nelson reached the Windward Islands. The Battle of Trafalgar was nearly fought off the island of Barbados. Admiral Vernon, also known as "Old Grog" because be always wore a boat cloak of grosgrain, a French material anglicized as grogram, found while serving in the West Indies that sailors, issued with half a pint of neat rum every day were quite incapable of manning the ship. Therefore, he introduced a Fleet Order in 1740 that the rum must be diluted with three parts of water ("grog" is still rationed in the British Navy today).

Admiral Sir George Rodney, whose statue in the robes of a Roman Senator, stands in Spanish Town Square, Jamaica. The end of his first period of service in 1762 coincided with the end of the Seven Years War England had won, capturing Cuba, Martinique, Guadeloupe and Canada from France.

When the terms of peace in the Treaty of Paris were under discussion, there was much argument about what should be retained as spoils of war. Lord Bute, the Prime Minister, said "Some want me to keep Guadeloupe and some Canada. No one will tell me which I shall be hanged for not keeping". In the end, the enormous land mass of Canada was kept, not the tiny sugar island of Guadeloupe. Sugar was still an expensive luxury in the early 19th century in Europe, when the famous chef-historian, Brillat-Savarin made the observation that "Sugar won't hurt you, but it will make a hole in your pocket".

The genus *Saccharum* has five important species:

1. *Saccharum officinarum*
2. *S. sinense*
3. *S. barberi*
4. *S. robustum*
5. *S. spontanuem.*

The first three species are the cultivated species and the last two are wild ones.

Saccharum Officinarum

- This is the species usually referred to when we speak of sugarcane.
- This is one of the original cultivated species, although none of the original *officinarums* is industrially grown at present.
- Several *officinarum* varieties were under cultivation before the advent of hybrid varieties. It is rich in sucrose.
- Its stalks are vigorous and long with low fiber content. The Dutch scientists called them "noble canes". It has 2n=80 chromosomes. At present, they are grown for chewing purpose.

Saccharum Sinense

- This is known as "Chinese Cane" as its place of origin is central and South East China.
- It is thin stalked with long internodes, and long and narrow leaves.

- They are low and in sucrose and purity, high in fiber and starch.
- The chromosome number is 2n=111 to 120. "Uba" is one of the notable varieties under this species which was in cultivation in several countries.
- At present, the species is considered unsuitable for commercial cultivation.

Saccharum Barberi

- This species derives its name from the scientist Dr CA Barber who described these original canes of subtropical India.
- This is known as "Indian species". It has chromosome numbers 2n=81 to 124.
- These were under large scale cultivation in the subtropical India for manufacture of gur and Khandsari sugar.
- These are sturdier and disease resistant and have higher sugar and fiber contents. They are thin stalked.
- The clones of this species are highly tolerant to high and low temperatures, problem soils and water logged conditions.
- However, because of their very poor yields, they are not under commercial cultivation at present.

Saccharum Robustum

- This species was discovered in New Guinea Islands. The stalks are long, thick and vigorous growing.
- It is rich in fiber and poor in sugar. The chromosome number is 2n=60 and 80.
- This is a wild species and not suitable for agricultural production.

Saccharum Spontaneum

- This is also known as "wild cane". Its varieties have varying number of chromosomes (2n=40 to 128). Considerable variation is noticed in the morphology of the species.
- In general, the cane is very thin and short, the leaves are narrow and hard.
- The plant is very sturdy and resistant to most diseases.
- The species is not useful for sugar production.
- The sugar content is very low.
- This species is useful for evolving hybrid varieties particularly to obtain disease and stress resistant types.
- Both the Chinese and Indian canes were carried by Arab traders to Persia, Syria, Cyprus, Malta and Sicily in the Mediterranean.
- Alexander the great took this "honey reed" to Africa after the conquest of India. By the 15th centruty, it reached Europe via Egypt and Marocco and in the 17th century, it moved to the "Sugar isles" of the Caribbean and North East Brazil.
- By the 19th century, sugar beet got established as an industrial crop.
- But, 60% of sugar comes from sugarcane and is distributed in 37 North and South of Equator.
- Presently, this giant grass is grown in over 79 countries.
- Sugarcane is intimately associated with Indian mythology.
- The word saccharum seems to originate from Sanskrit word "Sarkara". It symbolizes prosperity for it adorns Goddess of wealth "Sri Lakshmi".

- The most ancient reference to sugarcane is in Athervaveda which is 5,000 years old.
- It is also referred extensively in Buddhist literature. During Alexander's invasion, hig generals observed sugarcane as a closely managed garden crop.
- Now, India has been widely accepted as the original home of this sugarcane that were under cultivation in North India.

Ancient Greek doctors referred it as "Indian salt".

CLASSIFICATION

- Sugarcane belongs to the genus *Saccharum* in the family *Gramineae,*
- Cultivated sugarcane is classified into three species.

Saccharum Officinarum

- These are thick and juicy canes good for chewing purpose also.
- This species includes the tropical canes indigenous to the New Guinea.
- These canes contain high sugar content, low fiber and produce high tonnage.
- These are generally resistant to smut but are susceptible to red rot and mosaic diseases.
- The cultivation of this species is limited to tropical areas. But in recent years, these canes have been succeeded by hybridization among *Officianarum, Spontaneum* and other species in subtropical regions.

Saccharum Sinense

- This species of cultivated sugarcane is indigenous to north-eastern India.
- This species is characterized by long and thin stalks, broad leaves, low to medium sucrose content and early maturity.
- This species includes "Pansahi", "Nargori" and "Mungo" groups of sugarcane.
- Internodes of these canes are long and more or less zigzag and nodes are prominent.

Saccharum Barberi

- This species is also indigenous to North-Eastern India.
- It characterized by short mid thin stalks, narrow leaves, low to medium sucrose content, and early maturity.
- This species includes "Sarethe" and "Sunnabile" groups of sugarcane. Both the above mentioned species, indigenous to North-Eastern India were in cultivation for many centuries but nowadays canes of these species have been replaced by complex hybrid clones.

In addition to the above three cultivated species there are two wild species *S. spontaneum* and *S. robustum.*

However, there is considerable potential to be exported.

- Sugarcane and sugar beet are the main sources of sugar in the world.
- Out of total sugar produced in the world 60% is obtained only from sugarcane.
- Asia is the largest producer of sugar followed by Europe
- Most of the sugar in Asia comes from sugarcane whereas in Europe from sugar beet.
- Presently, sugarcane is grown on an area of 16 million tons in over 79 countries.
- The global production of raw sugar is 112 million tons.
- The consumption is anticipated at 110 million tons with a little carryover stocks. India stands first in area (3.93 million hectares) and production (167 million tons) among the sugarcane growing countries of the world.
- However, per hectare yields (68 tons/hectare) are less than many important countries.

DISTRIBUTION

- Sugarcane is grown over the land surface of the earth between latitudes 35°N and 35°S.
- The important sugarcane producing countries in the world are India, Cuba, Brazil, Mexico, Pakistan, China, Philippines and Thailand.
- It is one of the important crops of the world cultivated over on Modern Techniques of Raising Field Crops area of 13.46 million hectares with a total production of 754.13 million tons of cane (1979).
- In India, area and production of sugarcane has been fluctuating from year to year depending upon pricing policy and climatic conditions.
- It occupies about 3.1 million hectares. The total production of cane is 156.45 million tons.
- UP has the largest acreage under sugarcane, and accounts for about 52% of the area under this crop in whole of India and also accounts for 40% of the total annual production.
- Productivity is the highest in Tamil Nadu followed by Maharashtra and Karnataka.
- India ranks first among sugarcane growing countries of the world in both extent of area and production of cane. Along with white sugar, khandsari (indigenous) sugar and gur (jaggery) are also consumed in the country.
- Parthasarathy (1946) referred to Tamil classics of the Sangam period (2000 BC) Pattirrup-pattu where references were made to growth, arrowing and cultivation.

CANE SUGAR AND THE ENVIRONMENT

Cane Agriculture

The various cane varieties cultivated for commercial purposes world-wide are species or hybrids of the *Saccharum* genus, which in turn belongs to the grass family.

Its geographical origin remains a controversial subject, but in general it is acknowledged that it originated in the South Pacific region, Java and New Guinea, and subsequently spread out from there.

One of the outstanding features of sugarcane is, among others, its extraordinary capacity for growth. It is not unusual to find agricultural yields exceeding 100 tons per hectare annually on commercial acreages. Its genetic potential is much greater. When varieties are selected and agrotechnical handlings are carried on, with the objective of maximizing biomass production, it is possible to obtain yields as high as 300 tons/hectare and even exceeding this volume. Theoretical potential of up to 400 tons/hectare is estimated. This high productivity rate is the result of a high photosynthetic efficiency, compared to other commercial crops, which permits an increased utilization of solar energy and, consequently, a higher coefficient for fixing atmospheric carbon dioxide.

Further, cane agriculture can be practiced with a minimum consumption of chemical products and highly compatible with the environment and soil conservation. An issue of the utmost importance, from an ecological as well as economic standpoint, is the harvest of green cane; that is, without previous burning the foliage for harvest. Harvesting green cane is a widespread practice that has been used for many years in Cuba, and which has been gradually extended to other countries such as Australia and Brazil. The issue is not only the pollution problems generated during burning, but most important, improved soil fertility conservation, lower consumption of herbicides and the possibility of using part of the residues as fuel, animal feed or raw material.

Further, the use of fertilizers can be reduced significantly, and in some cases even eliminated, under advantageous economic conditions (4). Noteworthy examples of alternatives that contribute to reducing input of chemical fertilizers include those recycling in the field the wastes and residues of the industry such as filter mud, and the liquid effluents as irrigation water.

In Cuba, it has been a widespread practice for many years to use residuals in cane irrigation, a practice referred to as ferti-irrigation. Likewise, irrigation of cane fields with the vinasse obtained as a waste from alcohol distilleries is a generalized practice in Brazil. These practices, handled with adequate control, not only solve the problem of how to dispose of liquid wastes but also make an important contribution of both the organic and mineral materials required by the soil. Both filter mud and agricultural crop wastes may be improved considerably with regard to their value as fertilizer through relatively simple compost processes whereby ashes from bagasse furnaces and other elements contributing phosphorous and potassium—of great importance to the crop—are added. The application of minimum tilling methods or localized tilling in cane acreages has been another element of significant economic importance and contribution to improved soil conservation. Several specially-designed alternatives or techniques have been used on a widespread basis in the various types of soils, with highly beneficial results.

The struggle to combat pests that attack sugarcane is carried out entirely through biological methods. Control of the sugarcane borer (*Diatrea saccharilis*) is achieved through the systematic reproduction and release of a natural enemy, the Cuban fly, *Lixophaga diatrea*. Cane diseases are confronted through the ongoing development and inclusion of new commercial varieties, a well-established practice in most of the principal sugarcane-producing countries. Crop rotation and inter-cropping, although practised only to a limited extent at present, have shown an excellent economic possibility and positive effect for cane, basically when used with beans, peanuts and the leguminous genus in general.

Industrial Processing: Diversification

Cane is not only a plant that grows at a faster rate than other commercial crops and can be cultivated with sustainable techniques. The structural and chemical composition of sugarcane makes it particularly appealing for transformation into valuable products through industrial processing. For years, sugar has been the principal, and virtually only commercial product obtained from cane. Probably the only exception, and then only fairly recently, is the Brazilian alcohol fuel program. The objective is both, to take advantage of cane for other purposes different from sugar, such as use of the by-products of the sugar industry and sugar itself as raw materials to obtain products with a high aggregate value and of interest to the market. This is what the so-called diversification consists of. The concept of diversification mentioned above and its economic and strategic importance for cane-producing countries has been the focus of attention at several international fora in the past few years A study of the alternatives for diversification of sugarcane calls for an analysis of the different fractions that make up its vegetative structure which are shown in below:

Vegetative structure of sugarcane (% of dry matter)

Part above ground	*Total plant*	*Part growing*
Clean stalks	50	59
Tops	10	12
Leaves	25	29
Roots	15	–
Total	**100**	**100**

These fractions in turn have the average composition shown in below:

Cane components (%)

Components	*Clean stalks*	*Tops + leaves*
Total sugars	15,43	2,18
Sucrose	14,10	–
Lignocelullose (fiber)	12,21	19,80
Ashes	0,54	2,31
Other	0,82	2,43
Total dry matter	29,00	26,00
Water	71,00	74,00

A study of the tables above clearly shows the importance of bearing in mind the potential use of the so-called agricultural wastes (tops + leaves), which represent nearly 40% of the total weight.

Likewise, the clean stalks are made up mainly of soluble sugars; and bagasse constitutes the lignocellulose portion. Soluble sugars, both those taken directly from cane juice and those extracted during the intermediate currents of the sugar process (filter juice, A or B molasses) or from final molasses may be transformed into products with a high value and market interest through chemical or biotechnical processes. Some of the principal products manufactured today on a commercial scale reshown in below.

Some derivatives of cane sugars

Product	*Process*	*Use*
Sugar	C	Food industry, domestic consumption
Glucose/fructose	C	Food and pharmaceutical industries
Ethyl alcohol	B	Fuel beverages, chemical and pharmaceutical industries
Yeasts	B	Fodders bakery products and the biotechnology industry
L—lysine	B	Fodders food industry
Citric acid	B	Food and pharmaceutical industries
Lactic acid	B	Chemical and pharmaceutical industries
Acetic acid	B	Direct consumption, several industries
Monosodium glutamate	B	Food industry
Acetone and butanol	B	Chemical industry
Oxalic acid	C	Chemical and construction industries
Dextran and/or xantane	B	Chemical and food industries
Sorbitol and/or manitol	C	Food and pharmaceutical industries
Tensoactive products	C	Several industries, domestic use

The main advantage of using cane juice for these products, rather than molasses, is the possibility of having the bagasse as an energy source capable of satisfying the thermal and electrical demands of the industrial process. This is the case of the traditional sugar industry and of alcohol production as carried out in Brazil, directly from cane. As will be seen further on, with this system it is not only possible to satisfy the energy requirements of the process but to obtain significant surplus electricity as well.

For its part, cane bagasse represents a renewable source of fibrous raw material, which can replace wood in many of its applications. Various types and selections of top quality agglomerated boards are produced from cane bagasse at present. It is estimated that world installed capacity for bagasse boards of different types total approximately 800.000 cubic meters annually; nonetheless, this still represents only 2% of the total production volume. In Cuba, there are five bagasse board factories, which produce the so-called particle board (low density). One of them has a double production line where the mende or medium density type is also manufactured.

Likewise, paper and cardboard of excellent quality may be obtained from bagasse, capable of competing with equivalent products obtained from wood. The only area in which bagasse is at a disadvantage compared to wood is the type of paper used for industrial purposes, which calls for high tenacity. This is impossible to achieve with bagasse due to the features of its fiber, which is shorter than soft woods.

The ever-increasing awareness at the international level of the need to preserve the forests that still exist in tropical and subtropical regions, and the restrictions on further development the extraction of commercial areas in temperate regions, open up interesting prospects for products made from bagasse fiber, which in addition to being an annually renewable source, may be processed through less intensive, and therefore less aggressive to the environment technologies, than traditional wood sources.

Cane for Animal Feed

In countries with tropical and subtropical climates, which is where sugar is produced, animal feed availabilities are one of the most crucial economic problems. For many years, the attempts to transfer models based on the use of grains and cereals have proven not to be economically feasible.

Sugarcane and the by-products of the sugar industry can, nonetheless, represent fundamental feed support for both rumiants and swine, as shown by international experience. For cattle feed, there is a wide range of experience in the comprehensive use of cane, with good production indicators and economic results, when combined with an adequate supply of cane pieces or chopped cane. Glucogenic precursors such as those obtained from grain residues (rice for example), and small amounts of genuine protein, both vegetable and animal (a significant part of assimilable nitrogen requirements can be furnished through urea) must also be added. Bagasse or its pith has been used in cattle feed, for both dairy cattle and fattening. For many years, a treatment for pith was used in Cuba to increase its digestibility, using sodium hydroxide and adding final molasses and urea. More recently, this technology has been replaced by a more economical alternative, in which the fiber is predigested using lime.

In Brazil, there is a wide range of experience in fattening cattle using bagasse hydrolized with steam as a base. Although this option requires a larger investment for building treatment facilities, it has the advantage that chemicals are not needed.

Compared to grains and cereals, the principal restriction of sugarcane as feed for monogastric animals is the fact that it has virtually no protein. Nonetheless, by-products of the sugar industry are perfect as a cheap source of metabolizable energy in swine feed diets. A solution must be found to contribute protein in diets, which may be achieved through protein concentrates such as soybean or fish flours Fodder (torula) yeast has been used on a large scale in Cuba as a protein concentrate for swine feed. It is produced at industrial plants through aerobic fermentation of final molasses. *Saccharomyces* yeast, another sugarcane derivative, obtained as a by-product of alcohol distilleries, is another highly economically feasible alternative. Brazil is unquestionably the country with the greatest potential for this option; and in fact, yeast recovery has been on the rise over the past few years. The technical and economic feasibility of swine rations based on intermediate molasses from sugar factories, and yeast from alcohol distilleries has been proven on a commercial scale in both Cuba and Brazil.

Sugarcane and Energy

The high photosynthetic capacity of sugarcane makes it an important source of energy. A comparison of the energy value of the cane biomass and the energy consumed in its harvest and cultivation shows a ratio of 20:1. This makes sugarcane a biomass of enormous interest at present, as alternatives are under study to reduce the rate of gas accumulation and consequent global warming, as a result of the use of fossil fuels. The cane sugar industry creates its own fuel, bagasse, which is not only capable of satisfying the energy demands of the factory but generating surplus electricity, with the consequent ecological and economic benefits.

The traditional sugar mill is highly inefficient from an energy standpoint, since it was designed to not be forced to have bagassesurpluses. On average, steam consumption for the process ranges between 450 kg and 550 kg of steam per ton of cane processed. Nonetheless, consumption of under 300 kg / ton is possible to achieve, with schemes and equipment well-known and widely used in the beet sugar industry.

Likewise, the furnaces in which the bagasse has traditionally been burned for steam production have energy efficiency rates of approximately 60–65%; whereas it is possible to achieve efficiency rates of nearly 90%, with heat-recovery designs and systems to reduce the final temperature of combustion gases. These traditional energy schemes were designed to obtain precisely the electrical power required by the factory as the steam produced by low-pressure turbogenerators passes through. In order to produce surplus electricity at the sugar factory, steam consumption must be reduced in the process, furnace efficiency must be improved; and at the same time, steam generation pressure must be increased. In this case, it is possible to obtain surpluses of up to 100 kw-hour / ton of milled cane, as proven by experiences on a large scale in Hawaii, Reunion Island and Florida. New technologies currently in the development stage, based on gasification of the biomass and use of gas turbines and combined cycles, would make it possible to increase the generation potential of the sugar industry to levels approximately twice those mentioned above.

Further, the use of agricultural residues of the cane harvest to produce energy would also make it possible to double the factory potential and use facilities during the between crop periods. In Cuba, there are experiences on a commercial scale with use of cane straw as fuel in mill furnaces; and work is currently underway on studies to perfect this and storage methods. And lastly, from an energy and environmental standpoint, it is absolutely essential to mention the strategic importance of ethyl alcohol production from cane for use as automotive fuel. The experience of Brazil is well-known and has been discussed in depth at the international level.

Environmental Standards and Legislation

The inclusion of environmental issues in domestic legislation in countries introduces legal control as a guarantee for compliance with the standards provided for in each case.

Policies aimed at correcting failure to comply with environmental legislation may be divided basically into two general types: (1) those using incentives (or policies based on market operation), whereby taxes or charges are collected according to the damages caused by those who pollute and (2) those calling for quantitative restrictions (or "official control mechanisms"), which do not have this flexibility.

The status of environmental legislation in our region presents a wide range of features and stages: some nations include it in their Constitution, and even have ministries, secretariats and / or institutions devoted to the environment. Most have general legislation at the state level (implemented or in the implementation stage). And those with the least provisions include specific standards applicable to the sugar agroindustry and others are in the process of preparing legislative bills. Our countries are also unequal insofar as drafting, implementation, demands and compliance of environmental laws and standards, in accordance with existing differences in legislation, ecological awareness and status of economic development. The existence of environmental legislation has promoted research projects as well as the search and development of ecologically compatible options in the industry.

The most comprehensive legislation and / or regulations spellout both qualitative and quantitative issues, reflecting the parameters to be evaluated, analytical methods, benchmarks, frequency of sampling, spillage standards, quality criteria and penalties, among other specifications. They also include citizens" right to a healthy and ecologically balanced environment, and therefore provide for the legitimate power to denounce acts that violate this right and to claim redress of damages caused. Laws provide for methods of determining liability and penalties. Some legislation also covers environmental education, research and development and incentives for environmental activities.

Within the regional sphere, our countries have adopted comprehensive multilateral and bilateral instruments pertaining to the environment; at the international level, conventions on the environment and natural resources have been entered into, which are included in legal ordinances of countries. To an ever-increasing extent, ecological issues are being reflected in international treaties, such as in funding projects and international co-operation projects. The regional sugar agroindustry is adopting measures aimed in some cases at facing the demands of environmental legislation in effect; and in others, at preparing for imminent reality of implementation in the respective nations of standards and controls to prevent environmental pollution.

General and Specific Environmental Standards

National, state and federal environmental standards related to the sugar agroindustry are those dealing with conservation of water resources, pollution and emission released into the air, disposal of liquid wastes or waste waters and solid wastes, noise and odors. As follows are the general parameters used world-wide for characterization, standardization and control:

Measurement units for sources of pollution

Pollutant	*Measurement unit*
Waste waters	DBO_5, DQO, pH, electrical conductivity, t°Q
Air emissions	SO_2, CO, CO_2 particles, NO_2, NO
Sound wastes	DQO, DBO_5, t°Q
Noise	Decibels (dBA)
Odor	Sensorial tests

In the member countries of Group of Latin American and Caribbean Sugar Exporting Countries [Spanish: Grupo de Países Latinoamericanos y del Caribe Exportadores de Azúcar (GEPLACEA)] although implementation levels and compliance with environmental legislation are in different stages, the interest and need to search for and develop ecologically compatible technological options for the sugar agroindustry are increasingly evident.

In this respect, the activities involved in production of "organic sugar" and "cleaner production techniques", which characterize the technologies and processes using natural (as opposed to chemical) inputs and preventive, rather than corrective, measures are being adopted to an ever-increasing extent within the environmental policies of the agroindustry in several sugar producing countries. This is one of fastest, more economical means of contributing to improving the environment.

SUGAR PLANTATIONS

Sugar plantations were highly valued in the Caribbean by the British and French colonists in the 19th and 20th centuries and the use of sugar in Europe rose during this period. Sugarcane is still an important crop in Cuba. Sugar plantations also arose in countries such as Barbados and Cuba because of the natural endowments that they had. These natural endowments included soil that was conducive to growing sugar and a high marginal product of labor realized through the increasing number of slaves.

Sugarcane That's Less Thirsty

A farmer had the cushion to compromise with his harvest, having already attained higher than the average sugarcane harvest of 32 tons per acre for the region. Adopting techniques developed by soil-structure interaction (SSI), a collaborative program of sugar retailers, investors, traders, producers and the civil society, some 1,000 farmers in and around Aurangabad could more than double their yields from an average of 25 tons from an acre. The farmer had gone a step ahead in optimising water use by taking intercrop of tomato amidst rows of sugarcane.

Bilda has been a village worth 12,000 tons of sugarcane each season. Located in the village is a community center where farmers frequently meet to exchange experiences on the better management practices initiated under SSI. A series of posters on the wall depict "how to" of the practices. The visuals cover subjects like bud selection and treatment, nursery raising, main field preparation, transplantation, weeding, mulching, fertilizer application, water management, earthing up, de-trashing, propping, plant protection, intercropping and harvesting.

A cocktail of 17 such practices, grouped under what has been known as "better management practices (BMP)", helped farmers achieve 50% reduction in seeding material alongside no less than 30% increase in yield. Consequent increase in sugar recovery got farmers a better price for their produce from the sugar mills. Notable among the practices has been a shift from flood to furrow system of irrigation which could save as much as 50% water. For a crop that consumes 2,500 liters water for each kg of sugarcane, the gain is indeed substantial.

Co-financed by the European Union, the 3-year initiative reached around 1,000 hectares of sugarcane growing area in 13 villages before it came to a close in 2011. Despite irrigation waters from the Jayakwadi dam reaching Bhivdhanora village, some farmers have persisted with growing sugarcane the manner in which they were trained by the SSI team led by the World Wide Fund for Nature.

That only 3% of land area growing sugarcane in the State takes away 60% of irrigation water has come under scanner during the current drought. Together with the current controversy around the failure of irrigation infrastructure to supply water, the issue being debated relates to whether dry districts with low per capita water availability should have been cultivating sugarcane at all. It was in anticipation to such vexed questions that initiative to improve water productivity at the primary production level was started.

Reducing the crop's water footprint cushioned sugarcane farmers in Maharashtras's Bild village from the damaging consequences of the current drought.

Together with paddy, sugarcane consumes maximum proportion of water utilized in agriculture, and hence also of the total water consumed, since agriculture itself as a sector consumes about 70–80% *vis-à-vis* other sectors. Given the fact that sugarcane is grown on 4 lakh hectares, reduction in its water footprint can contribute significantly to reducing irrigation water consumption. Further, it is Rs 30,000 crore sector accounting for principal livelihood of 35 million farmers, and 50 million others who are employed in 571 sugar-related industries.

Maharashtra has been a progressive state in terms of enacting policies and regulations pertaining to management of water resources. In such an environment, results from the 3-year pilot project could have been easily mainstreamed for improving livelihoods of sugarcane growers Ironically, when it comes to engineering water use efficiency at the farm level, the focus largely has been on increasing subsidy for drip and sprinkler irrigation and not as much on promotion of no-cost techniques like "better management practices".

Had drip and sprinkler irrigation system been effective, for which the state had doled out subsidy to cover 8 lakh hectares since 2005, the impact would have been visible. Conversely, the demand for irrigation only shot up resulting in absurd political statement being made to "fill" the dams. It is time the value of water use efficiency through better management practices gets realized. Not only does it help to increase crop harvests without additional costs, the sugar industry reportedly pays better price for such sugarcane because it reduces their processing costs!

Sugar in South Asia

Sugarcane has a very long history of cultivation in the Indian subcontinent. The earliest reference to it is in the Atharva Veda (c. 1500–800 BC) where it is called *ikshu* and mentioned as an offering in sacrificial rites. The Atharva Veda uses it as a symbol of sweet attractiveness.

INDIAN SCENARIO

Sugar in Literature

Indian literature abounds in references to the sugarcane: early Tamil literature describes sugarcane along the banks of the River Kaveri, and indeed sugarcane was usually cultivated in river valleys. Early Indian kings set aside land for pleasure gardens, groves and public parks, and gardens were attached to palaces and grand mansions. The Kamasutra, an early erotic treatize written by Vatsyayana (c. 2nd century AD to c. 4th century AD), recommended that a cultivated and wealthy man should surround his house with a garden.

The garden would be under the care of his wife who would dictate the layout of the garden and it is planting while the physical labor was left to professional gardeners. The Kamasutra spoke of pleasure gardens and practical gardens and was specific about what should be planted in the gardens. The practical garden had to include beds of green vegetables, sugarcane, fig trees, mustard, parsley and fennel. The great goddess Kamakshi of Tamil Nadu is portrayed in art holding in her four hands lotus blossom, sugarcane stalks, elephant goad and noose.

For all practical purposes, scientific sugar processing by vaccum pan method may have started sometimes in 20s. The development process was slow. Country met its sugar requirement through imports. The first sugar mill in India was setup in 1903 Bengal with a modest crushing capacity. In mid-20s, number of sugar mills sprang up in Uttar Pradesh (UP) and Bihar. By 1930–1931, there were 29 sugar factories producing just 1,000 thousand million tons of sugar and they found adverse competition from Japanese sugar which was ruling the Indian market.

Industry took up the matter with "Tariff Board" and Sugar Industry Protection Act was passed by the Indian Legislature in 1932. Under this act, protection was granted to the indigenous sugar industry. Salient features of Act are:

- The act shall be for a period of 14 years ending on 1 March, 1946.
- Performance was to be reviewed before 31 March, 1938.
- Government to identify measures for next 8 years.
- The main reason for low productivity of sugarcane in the country is that this crop is grown in very small holdings by millions of farmers under extremely diverse growing conditions—most favorable ones to least favorable ones.
- Therefore, our sugarcane production problems are quiet different from other countries and hence, require specific production technologies that could be adopted by our farming situations.
- UP has the largest area almost 50% of the cane area in the country, followed by Maharashtra, Karnataka, Tamil Nadu, Andhra Pradesh, Gujarat, Bihar, Haryana and Punjab. These nine are most important sugarcane producing states.
- Sugarcane production is also highest in UP followed by Maharashtra. Productivity wise, Tamil Nadu stands first with over 100 tons/hectare followed by Karnataka, Maharashtra. Bihar has the lowest productivity amount the major sugarcane growing states.
- The sugar Industry is the second largest agro-based industry, next only to textiles, in the country.
- There were 444 sugar factories (1995–1996) which utilize around 40–50% of the cane produced manufacturing 16.45 million tons of sugar with an average crushing capacity of 2,452 tons per day and a crushing duration of 161 days.
- The sugar industry contributes over 1,000 crores to the Central Exchequer as excise duty and taxes annually.
- Besides, almost an equal amount is realized by the state Governments through purchase taxes, cess, etc.

- At present sugarcane price, total value of sugarcane produced in the country is around 15,000 crores per year.
- The domestic sugar consumption is 13.2 million tons with an export of 1.0 million tons.
- The per capita consumption of white sugar is 14.1 kg and that of gur and khand sari is 8.1 kg.
- Sugar factories, being located in rural areas, supporting huge economic activities in the rural India. This sugar industry generates rural employment.

However, anytime during the period of the Act, if it was found that sugar was being imported at prices to make domestic industry ineffective, Government should have power to levy additional duty on imports. With enforcement of Sugar Protection Act within a period of 4 years country became self-sufficient in sugar. It was indeed a great beginning. The Industrial Policy Resolution of 1956 gave priority to cooperative segment in the sugar industry. About 60% of sugar factories are today in this sector. Capacity utilization is also very high in the cooperative sector.

Until the 1930s, the main types of sugarcane grown in India were the "thin" canes. They were well suited to the north Indian climate, although yields were fairly low. In the southern or tropical zone of the country, where the climate was more suitable for sugarcane cultivation, thicker "noble" canes were more important. Thicker varieties of sugarcane were brought in from the West Indies and the area under sugarcane was greatly expanded. Various hybrids were developed leading to a doubling of cane production in the Indian subcontinent.

Sugar industry was initially setup in the subtropical region: UP, Bihar, Punjab and Haryana. Till 1950, 90% of area under sugarcane was in this region. With commencement of planning process, sugarcane found its route in tropical area: Maharashtra, Gujarat, Tamil Nadu, Andhra Pradesh and Karnataka. Sugarcane being a tropical crop, finds favorable agroclimatic conditions for its growth in this region giving higher yields. Growth after 1950 was more in this region and by 1994–1995 the subtropical region, sugarcane area was 65% and cane production 55% of the total cane produced.

Now, the tropical region is already developed and reached near saturation level. The biggest state in this region: Maharashtra faces acute problem of lack of water which affects cultivation of sugarcane. The subtropical belt, with fertile land, high water table and irrigation, appears to be the area for future growth.

It was in mid-1960s that sugar became a priority and Government setup task force to plan requirement and growth. Policy was to focus on cane production, utilization and processing capabilities. Remunerative cane prices led the farmer shift to sugarcane and oilseeds. The growth in sugarcane production has been both in acreage and yield. Whether this trend will continue and will depend upon crop economics as farmer has been adopting commercial approach.

There is a need for rationalization of sugarcane policy to encourage farmers to improve yield and the mills have to build up rapport with the farmers and also build up trust and commitment for assured supplies of clean and freshly cut cane (improve extraction). In return, farmer would get better and quick return.

Sugar is a large, volatile agro-industry. It is capable of creating large scale rural income across the country. The industry consists of 200 cooperatives and corporations, 150 private millers and about a thousand unorganized khandsari producers. Nearly 50 million farmers are engaged in cane cultivation. Cane farming supports almost 7% of the country's rural population. Fifty million farmers are directly involved in the cultivation of sugarcane and several more are indirectly employed by the industry. About 4.25 million hectares are under sugarcane cultivation.

Sectorwise sugar factories in operation

1 year	*Private/government sector*	*Cooperative sector*	*Total*
1997–1998	178	222	400
1998–1999	178	249	427
1999–2000	172	251	423
2000–2001	177	259	436
2001–2002	184	250	434
2002–2003	184	269	453
2003–2004	187	235	422
2004–2005	197	203	400
2005–2006	216	239	455
2006–2007	252	252	504
2007–2008	267	249	516
2008–2009	260	229	489

India is the only country in the world which produces plantation white sugar. All other countries are producing either raw sugar or refined sugar or both. Thus, the processing capacities are quite different and so also is the quality of sugar. In terms of number of mills, India ranks first with 448 Mills, followed by China 241, Brazil 231, world total being 2,500. Average size is 2,150 TCD, much lower than world average. In India, we are still starting up 2,500 TCD mills. Mill capacity is calculated on the basis of normal crushing period.

Recovery: The quantum of sugar produced by a mill is determined by factors like daily crushing capacity, duration of crushing season in India and percentage of sugar recovery. The crushing season in India starts from October and reaches its peak in January before finally ending in March or April of the next year. But based on cane availability, starting of the crushing season may be postponed by one to one-and-a-half months in different states of the country. For example, in eastern UP crushing season starts only in November every year-about a month later than normal.

The recovery rate for sugar mills varies widely across the country. Maharashtra, Gujarat and Karnataka the rate is above 10%. In the past, the average recovery rate for the country ranged between 9.25% and 10.5%. The November–March (150-day) period is ideal for sugar recovery in general, more particularly in Bihar and UP. From April onward sugar recovery shows a downward trend and in June the percentage of sugar recovery comes down to lowest levels. The months of April, May and June are very hot in UP, Bihar and Punjab. This period would thus accentuate the drying of sucrose content and lead to lesser recovery of sugar.

Challenges before Sugar Technologists

Sugar production material balance: If we crush 100 tons of sugarcane on an average, in India we get only 10 tons of processed sugar whereas globally, the recovery in Brazil is 14.6, Australia 13.5 and Mexico 12.2. It is a challenge for the sugar technologists of India to progressively improve the sugar recovery from 10 to 15 in stages by application of the appropriate technology compatible for the particular area and the particular type of sugarcane. This may involve adoption of latest techniques in milling, juice clarification, evaporation, crystallization, centrifugation and overall process optimization, leading to enhanced results.

> We have to see how the industry can strike a balance between production of sugar, ethanol and alcohol which will lead to revenue maximization for the farmer and the sugar industry.

Sugar technology mission under taken Technology Information Forecasting and Assessment Council (TIFAC) for technical up gradation of Indian sugar industries has led to 20% reduction in sugar losses in certain demonstration cases. If the techniques and other research results and experiences are applied in all the states and in all the sugar factories, Indian sugar industries should be able to increase the sugar recovery to 14 from the existing 10.

> Department of Biotechnology and *Indian Council of Agricultural Research* (ICAR) may promote the use of biotechnology for improvement in quality and productivity of sugarcane.

Product diversification: If we study the Amul model of cooperative milk industry, we find that the white revolution had increased the quantum of milk produce in the country substantially. That has not resulted in reduction of the revenue to the farmer who is supplying milk to the dairy. This has been achieved by product diversification, such as production and marketing of butter, ghee, cheese, flavored milk, butter milk, curd icecream and in big cities even pizza by Amul Diary Corporation.

We require such a diversification system for sugar industry also, so that we can fully utilize the capacity of the sugar industries, which is around 28 million tons per year of sugar. The product mix in this case could be raw sugar, while sugar, ethanol and alcohol. Ethanol has multiple industrial and pharmaceutical applications apart from its use in blending of petrol for automotive applications.

A Bitter Sweet Story

The first cycle of reversal was seen during the period 1939–1944 and it continued till 1950–1951 for various reasons when the output fluctuated between 0.89 million tons and 1.1 million tons mainly on account of instability of cane supplies caused by weather conditions, preference of farmers to essential food crops which gave them higher return. Food production became a priority during the war period.

India's household consumption of sugar is barely 25% of what is produced; the remaining 75% goes into commercial produces, like your can of Coke. And, the sweetener passes through controls at every step from farm to factory, before being sold. After 3 years or so of a glut, sugar production tanked due to the "cyclical nature" of the cane crop. The storage, coupled with faulty government policy, experts say, is driving up prices in a manner that has caused much discomfort among consumers.

India is the world's largest sugar producer after Brazil, but also the largest consumer. In 2006–2007, India harvested a record 355 million tons of cane, producing

28 million tons of sugar. Domestic consumption stood at 20–22 million tons. This feat was repeated in 2007–2008 with India producing 26 million tons of sugar. India exported roughly 8 million tons of sugar together in 2007–2008 and 2008–2009, worth around $2 billion, and also reduced much of the sugar stocks by doling out a freight subsidy (Rs 1,350–1,450 per ton) for exports.

In India, inefficient or loss-making manufacturers were politically influential and push for more sops and higher prices. Market forces balance things out in the case of other commodities. But sugar is tightly controlled, resulting in wild price swings. Factories are required to compulsorily sell 10% of sugar (called levy sugar) they manufacture to the government at below-market prices for strategic stocks. The rest, "non-levy sugar", is for "free sale", but the government decides how much each mill can sell each month. For example, sensing a shortage in August 2009, the government allowed factories to sell 1.377 million tons, raising the quota slightly.

Farmers in UP would say this of sugarcane: *Ganna sab phaslon ka tau hai, yeh to bada kamau hai* (sugarcane is the chief of all crops, it brings in riches). This is no longer true. With government offering far better price for grains, cane-growers are increasingly switching to rice and wheat. "Sugarcane has brought us misery", said a farmer, who has stopped growing sugarcane on his land in Marakpur, 30 km from Meerut, in Uttar Pradesh. Sugarcane also involves more investment than other crops. In addition, it would mean the land cannot be used for any other purpose for about 20 months after cane is grown, a period during which paddy can be grown four times.

"There is a need to help maintain a balance between both manufacturer and consumer interest. The government should stop doling out a discriminatory higher "conversion price"—the cost paid for turning cane into levy sugar—for inefficient millers "if you do away with such protectionism, some inefficient players may die but at least that will kick in efficiency". A KPMG-AC Nielsen report states that complete deregulation of the sugar industry will "expose farmers, millers and consumers to significant risks". UP farmers are now demanding a minimum cane price of Rs 280 per quintal. This could lead to their growing cane again and a deadly shortage of grains. The government needs to break the cyclical nature of the crop by "reforming" the administrative price regime and making it market friendly.

Sugar in Punjab

From a humble beginning on a couple of acres 5 years ago, a technique for sugarcane cultivation is now in practice across 800–900 acres in Phagwara, with a further 1,000 acres booked for the September–October season. The "vertical single-bud Phagwara technique" is an innovation developed by two farmers, Avtar Singh of Phagwara and Jujhar Singh of Bhonki village, and is being promoted by the Wahid Sandhar Sungar Mill of Phagwara. This season alone, the mill brought 475 acres under the technique, apart from getting booking orders for 1,000 acres land from 400 farmers.

Avtar Singh explains the difference, "this technique is different in many ways from the method of cane cultivation traditionally followed in the state. We promote a nature-friendly concept. Rather than horizontally as in the traditional method, we plant the seeds vertically, because cane grows in that direction. Also, we set the plants north to south so that they can get more sunlight and air",

"Here, we make 45 parallel rows with trenches between every two, rather than 95 rows as in the traditional method. We keep a four-foot gap between rows and one of two feet between plants; in the traditional method the plants are sown only a few inches apart", says Avtar Singh, who is cultivating on 90 acres and was awarded Rs 51,000 by the Phagwara sugar mill for his innovation.

The technique saves about 85% of the seeds required on a field of given size, still doubles the yield, and saves nearly 50% water while helping recharge water and protecting the water table, say those who are promoting it. So far, 190 farmers of Phagwara have taken it up. This is a turnaround from the initial years, when most had spurned the option.

The sugar mill, which is providing the seeds and farm implements, is drawing farmers in with a bargain. If a farmer gets a yield under 250 quintals per acre (which they would have got had they gone with their traditional methods), the sugar mill bears the losses. If the farmer gets more then 250 quintals, he and the mill share 50% of his profit from that extra yield, says Dr Charanjit Singh, cane development officer, Phagwara.

"Farmers may not be able to increase their land holdings but they can definitely increase their yield from the land they have if they adopt this technique", says JS Wahid, owner of Wahid Sandhar Sugar Mill. "With the traditional method we get 250 quintals cane from one acre, but with this method one can get even 500–600 quintals from the same acre".

Dr Singh says, "in the traditional method, one plant has seven to eight offshoots; in this one, we get 40–45 and finally 25–30 canes at the maturing stage. On every acre, the traditional method would have required 35 quintals of seed at Rs 10,000, but the new method uses only six quintals at Rs 2,000 because of the wider spacing. And we need to fill only 22 rows with water, against 45", Dr Singh says.

Dr Singh says the same method is ideal for inter-cropping of potato, cauliflower, pea, tomato, cucumber, lady's finger and other vegetables. A farmer can earn a minimum Rs 1 lakh from one acre, he adds.

"I wanted to do something new and Jujhar Singh supported me in developing this nature-friendly method of cane cultivation on my couple of fields", says Avtar Singh, who is an MSc in biochemistry, and who gets over 600 quintals cane per acre.

"We first experimented with this technique on just one acre on our sugarcane farm, but now we have brought our entire 25 acres in Khanaura village under this technique", says Wahid, who is also the chairman of the marketing federation. "We have motivated other farmers, who have taken it up on 475 acres. Farmers who were reluctant earlier are now contacting us and getting bookings done".

Jaswinder Singh of Rawalpindi village says that until 3 years ago, he had not been interested. Even when he started, it was with some doubt. Now, he uses only the vertical method over 40 acres.

Crop Diversification in Punjab

Inter-cropping with sugarcane is not new to Punjab but only a few progressive farmers had taken it up, until this season. Punjab having adopted a diversification policy in 2013 to decrease the area under paddy, cane is one of the key targets with the government targeting a threefold increase in the area under it. It is not anywhere as popular as wheat or paddy, however. It is to deal with farmers' reluctance that the government has been promoting inter-cropping, so that the combination ends up more remunerative than paddy. Through district officials and sugar mills, it has taken up an aggressive campaign.

It does have some results to show. Progressive farmers in certain areas have reported they are earning three times what they did earlier after they started inter-cropping their cane with garlic, potato and turmeric. In inter-cropping, cane rows are sown three to four feet apart and this space is used for the other crop. According to estimates of the cane department, around 40–50% of the farmers already growing cane have taken to inter-cropping this autumn. At a few places, up to 80% farmers have gone for inter-cropping. It demands fewer seeds of cane, and yet gives a high yield, besides bringing in an additional income from the other crops.

The area under cane is not even 2% area of the states total agricultural land. Only 81,000 hectares was under it in 2012–2013 and that is now up to 96,000 hectares. This is out of 42 lakh hectares under agriculture. Under the diversification policy, Punjab wants to enhance the area under cane to 6% (2.60 lakh hectares) in 4–5 years. The overall plan is to divert 12 lakh hectares from paddy to various crops.

Currently, out of 24 sugar mills, only 16 are running, nine cooperative and seven private. To run even these 16 mills at full capacity for 180 days, the state needs 2.60 lakh hectares under cane, says cane commissioner Dr Ranjit Singh, stressing the need to promote inter-cropping.

"Inter-cropping was not very popular among cane growers because of lack of awareness but this year we have organized various seminars, camps for farmers and even sugar mills have sown on demonstration plots to encourage farmers. A farmer of Adrahman village (Jalandhar) experimented with garlic and earned around Rs 3 lakh per acre including the returns from cane from his 18 acres sugarcane farm. "He have made 55 rows separated by four feet on a one-acre field, and the space in between was used for garlic".

"In inter-cropping we need just 6–10 quintals seed against 35–40 quintals in the traditional method, which left hardly any room for inter-cropping. There is huge saving on seed and the yield is better and high. Against 350 quintals cane per acre, the farmer got 585 quintals per acre from his field. Because of better spacing, cane gets air and sunlight and grows thicker. From one acre I have earned Rs 1.69 lakh from cane and Rs 1.35 lakh from garlic".

Amarjit Singh of Bhogapur, Jalandhar, grows cane in paired rows eight feet apart, sowing potato and turmeric in between. "Potato is just a 2-month crop which I harvest in January. In May turmeric is sown, which is a round-the-year crop". The farmer earned Rs 1.5 lakh from cane and Rs 1.5 lakh from the other crops.

Inter-cropping increases productivity and gives higher returns than mono-cropping. For spring cane, he recommends 2-month crops such as moong and mah pulses are recommended.

Vital in Shift from Paddy

- **Sugarcane** is key to Punjab's plants to diversify from paddy with the government planning to treble the area under it in 4–5 years.
- Percent of Punjab's agricultural area or 81,000 hectares of 42 lakh was under sugarcane until last 2013. The targets are 2.60 lakh hectares.
- 1,500 hectares added during 2014 taking total area under cane to 96,000 hectares.
- Garlic potato, turmeric being promoted to inter-cropping with sugarcane.
- Inter-cropping's many benefits includes saving on seeds, a higher yield from cane, and additional income from the other crop. A farmer's income can go up to double with inter-cropping.

Sugar Mills Get over Rs 4,000 Crore in Interest-free Loans

Banks have so far disbursed over Rs 4,000 crore interest-free loans of the total Rs 6,600 crore approved by the government to cash-starved sugar mills for clearing dues to cane farmers.

In December, the Cabinet Committee on Economic Affairs (CCEA) had approved Rs 6,600 crore interest-free loans to the sugar industry exclusively for clearing sugarcane arrears. It decided to give loans via banks equivalent to the excise duty paid by the mills in the past 3 years.

"As on June 3, banks have disbursed Rs 4,072 crore interest-free loans to sugar mills", a senior Food Ministry official said.

Of which, Rs 1,412 crore and Rs 1,461 crore have been disbursed to mills located in Maharashtra and UP, the country's top-two sugar-producing states, he said.

The total interest burden, estimated at Rs 2,750 crore over the next 5 years, is being borne by the government. The Rs 80,000 crores sugar industry have been facing a cash crunch due to higher cost of production and lower selling prices in the wake of surplus output over the past few years.

Sweet Pill

- In December last, the CCEA had approved 6,600 crores interest-free loans to the sugar industry exclusively for clearing sugarcane arrears.
- The total interest burden, estimated at 2,750 crores over the next 5 years will be borne by the government.
- At present, sugarcane arrears stand at about ~11,000 crores, with the maximum of Rs 7,200 crores in UP.

Cut Sugar Consumption by Half: World Health Organization (WHO)

"Five percent of total calorie intake, which is around 6 teaspoons a day, should be target".

The WHO has recommended that sugar intake be reduced globally. Recommended levels of sugar should stay below 10% of total calorie intake a day but below 5% should be the target, the WHO.

The WHO launched the first ever public consultation on sugar intake. When finalized, the guideline will provide countries with recommendations on limiting the consumption of sugar to reduce public health problems like obesity and dental caries (commonly referred to as tooth decay).

The new draft guideline proposes that sugar should be less than 10% of total energy intake per day. It further suggests that a reduction to below 5% of total energy intake per day which is equivalent to around 25 gram (around 6 teaspoons) of sugar for an adult of normal body mass index (BMI) will have additional benefits. The suggested limits on intake of sugar apply to all monosaccharides (such as glucose, fructose) and disaccharides (such as sucrose or table sugar) that are added to food by the manufacturer, the cook or the consumer as well as sugar that are naturally present in honey, syrups, fruit juices and fruit concentrates.

Much of the sugar consumed today are "hidden" in processed foods that are not usually seen as sweet. For example, one tablespoon of ketchup contains around 4 gram (around 1 teaspoon) of sugars. A single can of sugar-sweetened soda contains up to 40 gram (around 10 teaspoons) of sugar.

The draft guideline was formulated based on analyzes of all published scientific studies on the consumption of sugar and how that relates to excess weight gain and tooth decay in adults and children.

Sugar-based Battery can Run a Mobile for 10 Days

It works like human body.

Washington: Scientists have developed a battery that uses sugar to generate electricity enough to power a smartphone for 10 days. The bio-battery designed by researchers at Virginia Polytechnic Institute and State University has a greater output per weight than the typical lithium ion batteries used in most electronic gadgets. The prototype has the potential to be lighter and more powerful than the batteries typically found in today's portable electronic devices including smartphones.

In the body, sugar is converted into energy in a process called metabolism, which decomposes sugar into carbon dioxide and water while releasing electrons. Bio-batteries produce energy though the same conversion process by capturing the electrons that are generated in the decomposition of sugar with the same tools that the body uses.

As bio-batteries use materials that are biologically based, they are renewable and nontoxic, making them an attractive alternative to traditional batteries that need metals and chemicals to operate. "By using the lithium ion batery, for example, your phone can only last for 1 day, but in the future it will use sugar as fuel and then the phone could last 10 days, said Zhiguang Zhu, a researcher at Virginia Tech.

The new bio-battery gets its efficiency by using a unique system based on enzymes which are proteins that help the reaction to take place.

Straight Up and Farther Apart

From a humble beginning on a couple of acres 5 years ago, a technique for sugarcane cultivation is now in practice across 800–900 acres in Phagwara, with a further 1,000 acres booked for the September–October season.

The "vertical single-bud Phagwara technique" is an innovation developed by two farmers, Avtar Singh of Phagwara and Jujhar Singh of Bhonki village, and is being promoted by the Wahid Sandhar Sungar Mill of Phagwara. This season alone, the mill brought 475 acres under the technique, apart from getting booking orders for 1,000 acres land from 400 farmers.

Avtar Singh explains the difference. "This technique is different in many ways from the method of cane cultivation traditionally followed in the state. We promote a nature-friendly concept. Rather than horizontally as in the traditional method, we plant the seeds vertically, because cane grows in that direction. Also, we set the plants north to south so that they can get more sunlight and air", he says.

"Here, we make 45 parallel rows with trenches between every two, rather than 95 rows as in the traditional method. We keep a four-foot gap between rows and one of two feet between plants; in the traditional method the plants are sown only a few inches apart", says Avtar Singh, who is cultivating on 90 acres and was awarded Rs 51,000 by the Phagwara sugar mill for his innovation.

A break from tradition allows sugarcane to grow uninhibited, says farmers better.

The technique saves about 85% of the seeds required on a field of given size, still doubles the yield, and saves nearly 50% water while helping recharge water and protecting the water table, say those who are promoting it. So far, 190 farmers of Phagwara have taken it up. This is a turnaround from the initial years, when most had spurned the option.

The sugar mill which is providing the seeds and farm implements is drawing farmers in with a bargain. If a farmer gets a yield under 250 quintals per acre (which they would have got had they gone with their traditional methods), the sugar mill bears the losses. If the farmer gets more then 250 quintals, he and the mill share 50% of his profit from that extra yield, says Dr Charanjit Singh, cane development officer, Phagwara.

"Farmers may not be able to increase their land holdings but they can definitely increase their yield from the land they have if they adopt this technique", says J S Wahid, owner of Wahid Sandhar Sugar Mill. "With the traditional method we get 250 quintals cane from one acre, but with this method one can get even 500–600 quintals from the same acre".

Dr Singh says, "in the traditional method, one plant has seven to eight offshoots; in this one, we get 40–45 and finally 25–30 canes at the maturing stage. On every acre, the traditional method would have required 35 quintals of seed at Rs 10,000, but the new method uses only six quintals at Rs 2,000 because of the wider spacing. And we need to fill only 22 rows with water, against 45", Dr Singh says.

> Vertical technique requires 85% fewer seeds than traditional method does on a field of same size, uses half as much water, yield is twice as much

Dr Singh says the same method is ideal for inter-cropping of potato, cauliflower, pea, tomato, cucumber, lady's finger and other vegetables. A farmer can earn a minimum Rs 1 lakh from one acre, he adds.

"I wanted to do something new and Jujhar Singh supported me in developing this nature-friendly method of cane cultivation on my couple of fields", says Avtar Singh, who is an MSc in biochemistry, and who gets over 600 quintals cane per acre.

"We first experimented with this technique on just one acre on our sugarcane farm, but now we have brought our entire 25 acres in Khanaura village under this technique", says Wahid, who is also the chairman of the marketing federation. "We have motivated other farmers, who have taken it up on 475 acres. Farmers who were reluctant earlier are now contacting us and getting bookings done".

Jaswinder Singh of Rawalpindi village says that until 3 years ago, he had not been interested. Even when he started, it was with some doubt. Now, he uses only the vertical method over 40 acres.

SUGAR PRODUCTION

During the reign of Akbar, Bengal occupied the first place in sugar production. Abu-I-Fazl mentions three kinds of sugarcane, viz. *paunda*, black and ordinary. These were grown in the provinces of Agra, Allahabad, Oudh, Lahore, Multan, Malwa, Malwa and Ajmer. Sugarcane is of various kinds, states Abu-I-Fazl, One species is so tender and so full of juice that a sparrow can make it flow out by pecking it; and it would break to pieces, if let fall. Sugarcane is either soft or hard. The latter is used for the preparation of brown sugarcandy, common sugarcandy, common sugar, white candy, and refined sugar, and thus becomes useful for all kinds of sweetmeats. In relative value terms indigo was the costliest crop (254) and sugarcane as number 2 at 2013.

India is the largest consumer of sugar in the world and Indian sugar industry is the 2nd largest agro-industry located in the rural India. Currently, there are 453 operating sugar mills in different parts of the country. There are about 50 million sugarcane farmers and about 2 million skilled/semi-skilled workers involved in ancillary activities, mostly from the rural areas. The industry not only generates power for its own requirement but surplus power for export to the grid based on by-product bagasse. It also produces ethanol, an eco-friendly and renewable energy for blending with petrol.[1] With sugarcane cultivation in around 4.25 million hectares of land, India produces around 280 million tons of sugarcane annually. The production of sugar has witnessed a dramatic increase of around 27.00 million tons during 2010–2011 against 1.10 million tons during 1950–1960. In spite of the improvement in the production of sugar over the years, this sector has not been nourished on sound lines.

The sugar production has been improving as modernization of facilities and better seeds and fertilizers are being used. The mills, which focus on the future, enable the farmers to obtain suitable aids to agricultures. The cumulative effects of non-payment to cane growers, drought and crop disease are a sharp decline in India's sugar production from 20,122 thousand tons in the previous year to 13,546 thousand tons during the 2007–2008 crushing season. However, during the year 2011–2012 it increased to 26,357 thousand tons.

Relative Value of Crops

According to Moreland, the statistics provided by Abu-Fazl in Ain-i-Akbari give us a rough idea of the relative value of the crops grown.

Crop value	*Comparative*	*Crop value*	*Comparative*
Wheat	100	Linseed	51
Barley	67	Rape	53
Gram (common)	60	Poppy	210
Jowar	59	Sugarcane (ordinary)	213
Bajra	42	Cotton	150
Mandua	44	Indigo	254
Sawan	22		

[1] Satheeskumar L and Selvaraj V "Sugar industry need of the hour", The Economic Challenger, October December 2007, No. 10, Issue. 37 pp. 61-63.

These figures are based on the average of the various assessment rates in force under Akbar in the provinces of Allahabad, Agra and Delhi. It will be noticed that the costliest crop was indigo, followed by sugarcane and poppy.

In India, sugarcane is the primary raw material required for the production of sugar. During the period 2000–2009, the average yield of sugarcane came down from 70 million tons per hectare to 60 million tons per hectare. In Tamil Nadu, average production is 135 million tons per hectare, whereas in Madhya Pradesh it is less than 40 million tons per hectare. The reasons for low yield appear to be:

1. Non-availability of high-yielding varieties
2. Dearth of good quality seed or saplings
3. Improper water management
4. Use of imbalanced fertilizer doses
5. Lack of plant protection
6. Non-implementation of improve cultivation practices.

The sugar technologies have to create a partnership between agricultural scientists, extension workers and farmers, so that there is persistent effort to increase the per hectare productivity in all the states of the country taking the experience of high-yielding varieties of different states. The suggestion is based on the experience of increase in productivity of seed cotton in Gheri Buttar village in Punjab where the productivity of seed cotton double from 460 kg/acre to 860 kg/acre through the partnership of farmers with a textile manufacturing company.

After two conservative years of decline in sugar production (2008–2009 and 2009–2010), production has started to resurge in 2010–2011 and is likely to gain strongly in 2011–2012. Sugarcane has a production cycle of 2–3 years, i.e. cane planted in a marketing years is harvested in the next marketing year, followed by one or two additional re-tune crops in the next 1–2 years About 60–70% of farmers take one-retune crop and the other 30–40% take two retune crops. The cane yield of a retune crop is normally lower than a retune crop is normally lower than that of a newly planted cane crop.

All India area production and yield of sugarcane (Tables 1.1, 1.1A and B) show that area under cane increased from 1.2 million hectares in 1930–1931 to 1.7 million hectates in 1950–1951, 2.6 million hectares in 1970–1971. It increased to 3.7 million hectare area in 2002–2003 and 5.25 million hectares in 2012–2013 (4.4 times), corresponding figures for cane production are 36.4, 69.2, 126.4, 241.0 and 365.0 million tons (10 times). Average area production and yield of sugarcane in statewise is shown in Table 1.2, and Scenario of Indian Sugar Industry over the years is in Table 1.2A. Statewise changes in the share of production of cane and sugar during TE 2002–2003 and 2012–2013 is shown in the graph of page number 48.

FY13 Cane Area Estimate Higher than Government Figures

The agriculture ministry's figures on crop estimates are always viewed with certain amount of cautiousness by experts, but now, using the satellite imagery, the sugar industry contradicts the government's estimates of sugarcane acreage for 2012–2013. With the help of satellite technology, the industry has estimated total cane acreage at 53.54 lakh hectares for the season, about 1.3% higher than the government's estimate for the same period.

1.1: Area, production and productivity of sugarcane in India

Year	*Area '000 hectares*	*Yield tons/hectares*	*Sugarcane (million tons)*	*Sugar (million tons)*	*Recovery (%)*
1930-31	1176	30.9	36.354	0.12	8.96
1940-41	1617	32.1	51.978	1.113	9.7
1950-51	1707	32.1	54.823	1.1	9.99
1960-61	2415	45.5	110.001	3.021	9.74
1970-71	2615	48.3	126.368	3.74	9.79
1980-81	2667	57.8	154.248	5.15	9.98
1981-82	3193	58.4	186.358	8.437	9.66
1982-83	3358	56.4	189.505	8.229	9.95
1983-84	3110	56	174.076	5.917	10.02
1984-85	2953	57.7	170.319	6.144	10.22
1985-86	2850	59.9	170.648	7.016	10.23
1986-87	3079	60.4	186.09	8.502	9.98
1987-88	3279	60	196.737	9.11	9.7
1988-89	3329	61	203.037	8.752	10.22
1989-90	3439	65.6	225.569	10.99	9.89
1990-91	3686	65.4	241.045	12.047	9.84
1991-92	3844	66.1	253.995	13.405	10.01
1992-93	3572	63.8	228.033	10.609	10.3
1993-94	3422	67.1	229.66	9.833	10
1994-95	3867	71.3	275.54	14.643	9.92
1995-96	4147	67.8	281.1	16.453	9.42
1996-97	4174	66.5	277.56	12.905	9.9
1997-98	3930	71.1	279.541	12.852	9.95
1998-99	4055	71.2	288.722	15.539	9.86
1999-00	4220	70.9	299.324	18.2	10.2
2000-01	4316	68.6	295.956	18.511	10.48
2001-02	4430	67.4	298.422	18.528	10.27
2002-03	4361	64.6	281.575	20.145	10.36
2003-04	3938	59.4	233.862	13.546	10.22
2004-05	3662	64.8	237.088	12.69	10.17
2005-06	4201	66.9	281.172	19.267	10.21
2006-07	5151	69	355.52	28.328	10.16
2007-08	5055	68.9	348.188	26.357	10.55
2008-09	4415	64.6	285.029	14.539	10.03
2009-10	4175	70	292.302	18.912	10.19
2010-11	4886	70.1	342.382	24.394	10.17
2011-12	5038	71.7	361.037	26.343	10.25
2012-13*	5064	66.9	338.963	25	n.a

Source: Cooperative Sugar Vol 45 (1), September 2013.
* Provisional.

Table 1.1A: Sugarcane: all India trends in area, production and yield

Area: '000 hectares
Production: '000 tons
Yield: Kg per hectare

Year	*Area*	*Production*	*Yield*
T.E.1992-93	3701	241025	65130
T.E.2002-03	4416	293516	66468
T.E.2012-13	4995	347460	69556
Compound Growth Rate			
1992-93 to 2002-03	1.78	1.99	0.20
2002-03 to 2012-13	1.24	1.70	0.46
1992-93 to 2012-13	1.51	1.85	0.33
Fitted Growth Rate			
1992-93 to 2002-03	2.33	2.43	0.04
2002-03 to 2012-13	2.07	3.25	1.16
1992-93 to 2012-13	1.44	1.44	0.04
Cofficient of Variation			
1992-93 to 2002-03	8.34	9.59	4.15
2002-03 to 2012-13	11.35	15.07	5.36
1992-93 to 2012-13	11.79	13.78	4.68

Every year the central government uses data sourced from states to take important policy decisions including on imports and exports. Officials, however, admit that it is not always that authentic. Advance information on crop conditions is forwarded to them by states. Forecasting is a scientific device involving systematic use of various parameters to foretell the future but there are times when state agencies forward crop coverage figures based on mere hearsay from village patwaris (accountants).

Now, according to an Indian Sugar Mills Association (ISMA) statement [shown in the page 48 (bottom graph)]the pan-India satellite-based area survey jointly commissioned by ISMA and the National Federation of Cooperative Sugar Factories has pegged total cane area for the season starting October at 53.54 lakh hectares - 2% more than the 2011–2012 crop area and about 1.3% higher than the government estimate of 52.88 lakh hectares for the FY 2013 crop year in its first advance estimation for the season (Table 1.2B).

Total cane produced in the country is utilized (Tables 1.3, 1.3A and B) for the production of sugar, seed, feed, chewing and gur/khandsari. While seed, feed and chewing is more or less a constant figure (12%), share of area under sugarcane was the highest in UP at 1.3 million hectares in 1970–1971, which increased to 2.2 million hectares by 2006–2007, but came down to 2.1 million hectares in 2010–2011. This was followed by Maharashtra at 1.0 million hectares in 2006–2007 and 0.96 million tons in 2010–2011 and Karnataka at 423 thousand hectares in 2010–2011.

Gur/Khandsari came down from 64.7% in 1958–1959 to 58% in 1970–1971 and further to 29.1% in 1999–2000. It was 16% in 2008–2009 and just 11% in 2012–2013 (Table 1.3). Basic parameters of the sugar industry at the all India level (Table 1.4) provides details about the number of working units, production of sugar, cane crushed, production of cane, molasses produced, etc from 1970–1971 to 2011–2012.

Table 1.1B: Relevant data on sugar

Year	*Area (000 ha)*	*Production (000 t)*	*Yield (t/ha)*	*Cane Crushed (000 t)*	*Sugar production (000 t)*	*Sugar factories*	*Average crushing duration (days)*	*Sugar consumption (000 t)*	*Recovery (%)*
1950-51	1707	69220	40.55	10971	1101	138	101	1204	10.03
1954-55	1620	70549	43.55	16267	1690	136	132	1750	9.92
1955-56	1846	72692	39.38	19241	1862	143	145	1971	9.83
1960-61	2456	110544	45.01	31109	3028	174	167	2126	9.74
1961-62	2413	103967	43.09	27937	2730	180	146	2588	9.77
1962-63	2242	91913	41.00	20765	2135	186	108	2486	10.24
1963-64	2249	104225	46.34	25632	2562	194	120	2307	9.68
1964-65	2603	121909	46.83	33459	3232	198	153	2469	9.64
1965-66	2836	123990	43.72	36404	3532	200	159	2810	9.68
1966-67	2301	92826	40.34	21659	2159	200	95	2601	9.91
1967-68	2046	95500	46.68	22599	2243	200	94	2215	9.94
1968-69	2532	124682	49.24	37455	3558	205	150	2605	9.46
1969-70	2749	135024	49.12	45672	4261	215	170	3264	9.33
1970-71	2615	126368	48.32	38204	3740	216	142	4025	9.78
1971-72	2390	113579	47.52	30997	3108	221	107	3795	10.03
1972-73	2452	124866	50.92	40407	3873	229	133	3514	9.57
1973-74	2752	140805	51.16	42278	3948	229	138	3518	9.34
1974-75	2894	144289	49.86	48435	4794	247	140	3476	9.90
1975-76	2762	140604	50.91	41849	4262	253	115	3689	10.19
1976-77	2866	153007	53.39	48819	4840	271	126	3757	9.92
1977-78	3151	176966	56.16	67329	6457	280	167	4482	9.66
1978-79	3088	151655	49.11	59717	5842	299	140	6214	9.78
1979-80	2610	128833	49.36	39050	3859	299	86	5108	9.88
1980-81	2667	154248	57.84	51584	5147	314	105	4901	9.98
1981-82	3193	186358	58.36	87342	8436	319	173	5500	9.66
1982-83	3358	189505	56.43	82695	8232	320	158	6479	9.95
1983-84	3110	174076	55.97	59022	5917	325	111	7546	10.03
1984-85	2953	170319	57.68	60092	6144	338	106	6981	10.22

Table 1.1B: Relevant data on sugar *(Contd.)*

Year	*Area (000 ha)*	*Production (000 t)*	*Yield (t/ha)*	*Cane Crushed (000 t)*	*Sugar production (000 t)*	*Sugar factories*	*Average crushing duration (days)*	*Sugar consumption (000 t)*	*Recovery (%)*
1985-86	2850	170648	59.88	68576	7016	341	116	6581	10.23
1986-87	3079	186090	60.44	85224	8502	353	141	7965	9.98
1987-88	3279	196737	60.00	93943	9110	357	153	9333	9.70
1988-89	3329	203037	60.99	85693	8752	366	133	9919	10.21
1989-90	3438	225569	65.61	111149	10988	377	158	10283	9.89
1990-91	3686	241045	65.39	122319	12046	385	166	10715	9.85
1991-92	3844	253965	66.07	133987	13404	392	173	11225	10.02
1992-93	3572	228033	63.84	103002	10609	393	123	12005	10.31
1993-94	3422	229659	67.11	98348	9833	394	111	11129	10.00
1994-95	3867	275540	71.25	147643	14643	408	159	11974	9.92
1995-96	4147	281099	67.78	174726	16452	416	181	13172	9.42
1996-97	4174	277560	66.50	130379	12905	412	130	13625	9.9
1997-98	3930	279541	71.13	129188	12855	400	123	13978	9.95
1998-99	4055	288722	71.20	157560	15539	426	141	14135	9.87
1999-00	4220	299324	70.93	178515	18200	423	152	15536	10.2
2000-01	4316	295956	68.57	176651	18511	436	139	16200	10.48
2001-02	4412	297208	67.36	180321	18527	434	140	16798	10.27
2002-03	4520	287383	63.58	194324	20140	453	141	17335	10.36
2003-04	3938	233862	59.39	132511	13546	423	100	–	10.22
2004-05	3661	237088	64.76	124771	12691	400	96	–	10.17
2005-06	4202	281172	66.91	188672	19267	453	126	–	10.22
2006-07	5151	355520	69.02	279249	28361	504	174	–	10.17
2007-08	5055	348188	68.88	249906	26356	516	149	–	10.55
2008-09	4415	285029	64.56	144978	14538	488	87	–	10.03
2009-10	4175	292302	70.01	185548	18912	490	108	–	10.2
2010-11	4886	342382	70.07	239807	24394	527	136	–	10.17
2011-12	5038	361037	71.66	256975	26343	529			10.25
2012-13	5063	334541	66.08						

(Contd.)

Table 1.2: Area, production and average yield statewise sugarcane

Area: in thousand hectares production: in thousand tons yield: per hectare in kg.

Year	Andhra Pradesh			Assam			Bihar			Goa			Gujarat		
	Area	Produ.	Yield	Area	Produ.	Yield	Area	Produ.	Yield	Area	Produ.	Yield	Area	Produ.	Yield
1970-71	119.6	9122.3	76273	32.2	1199.5	37252	161.9	6209.4	38353	0.6	40.0	83333	37.4	1936.7	51783
1971-72	119.1	10571.4	88761	33.8	1274.0	37692	141.9	4465.3	31468	0.8	50.0	62500	36.4	1849.0	50797
1972-73	134.3	9917.0	73842	34.3	1310.7	38213	134.3	4753.2	35392	0.8	50.0	82500	38.2	1801.1	47149
1973-74	143.6	10907.1	75955	39.2	1583.6	40398	138.8	5157.1	37155	0.9	66.0	56667	44.4	2227.1	50160
1974-75	195.1	11495.7	58922	41.9	1607.7	38370	140.7	5568.2	39575	1.0	51.0	57000	40.8	1999.2	49000
1975-76	146.6	10332.3	70480	41.2	1524.8	37010	133.7	4906.5	36698	1.2	57.0	50917	37.7	2079.6	55162
1976-77	146.1	10280.5	70366	46.5	1665.2	35811	127.8	4175.8	32674	1.3	61.1	49308	49.0	2716.8	55445
1977-78	169.0	12847.4	76020	45.4	1429.6	31489	138.5	4957.8	35796	1.4	64.1	45786	61.8	3486.7	56419
1978-79	142.3	9044.2	63557	47.9	1658.0	34614	131.1	3570.3	27233	1.4	64.1	50000	57.9	3286.6	56763
1979-80	113.6	8422.4	74141	47.4	1691.7	35690	119.6	3913.8	32724	1.5	70.0	38733	56.9	3191.6	56091
1980-81	132.4	10053.9	75936	48.1	1723.2	35825	110.8	3480.4	31412	1.2	58.1	49833	74.9	4435.2	59215
1981-82	179.7	14961.5	83258	49.4	2152.5	43573	123.6	4180.4	33822	1.2	59.8	53417	84.3	5022.8	59582
1982-83	169.7	12606.3	74286	49.0	2075.9	42365	130.4	4463.7	34231	1.5	64.1	44533	95.2	6695.4	70330
1983-84	141.5	9742.9	68854	49.2	2159.0	43882	127.6	3884.6	30444	1.5	66.8	53200	102.6	7746.3	75500
1984-85	137.7	9791.1	71105	53.0	2687.2	50702	111.8	3736.9	33425	1.6	79.8	42000	103.3	7582.3	73401
1985-86	133.2	9674.6	72632	47.8	1971.4	41243	119.0	4001.0	33622	1.6	67.2	50000	90.8	6489.6	71471
1986-87	137.8	8807.6	63916	46.5	2116.9	45525	112.0	3729.0	33295	1.7	80.0	50588	69.2	5565.9	80432
1987-88	143.3	9490.2	66226	43.2	1882.8	43583	119.6	4545.7	38008	1.7	86.0	35294	81.7	6077.8	74392
1988-89	153.9	10766.6	69958	41.7	1864.4	44710	126.9	5482.8	43206	1.7	60.0	48059	93.7	7907.1	84387

Table 1.2: Area, production and average yield statewise sugarcane *(Contd.)*

Area: in thousand hectares production: in thousand tons yield: per hectare in kg.

Year	Andhra Pradesh			Assam			Bihar			Goa			Gujarat		
	Area	Produ.	Yield	Area	Produ.	Yield	Area	Produ.	Yield	Area	Produ.	Yield	Area	Produ.	Yield
1989-90	158.0	11134.0	70468	38.8	1666.5	42951	124.6	6694.1	53725	1.9	81.7	44211	106.0	9159.8	86413
1990-91	182.1	12667.3	69562	35.8	1522.0	42514	148.7	7805.3	52490	1.8	84.0	48889	118.3	10599.7	89600
1991-92	202.2	15056.7	74464	37.8	1454.0	38466	144.9	7076.6	48838	1.9	88.0	42316	120.2	10239.4	85186
1992-93	171.1	12163.2	71088	39.9	1547.7	38789	132.9	6031.6	45384	1.9	80.4	37579	127.2	10872.1	85472
1993-94	175.6	13474.2	76732	35.8	1373.9	38377	119.9	4397.9	36680	1.6	71.4	33563	128.4	10232.0	79688
1994-95	209.2	16046.0	76702	35.6	1505.0	42275	123.2	5663.3	45968	1.4	53.7	39286	154.7	10785.0	69716
1995-96	213.8	15179.5	70999	35.9	1490.3	41513	125.1	5484.8	43843	1.4	55.0	41429	161.6	10511.2	65045
1996-97	199.3	15030.0	75414	35.9	1490.3	41513	129.6	5842.5	45081	1.3	58.0	48000	165.8	11404.3	68783
1997-98	192.2	13955.0	72607	31.3	1287.5	41134	108.0	4959.9	45925	1.3	62.4	49231	165.0	11836.2	71735
1998-99	213.7	16503.3	77226	30.6	1223.6	39987	106.9	5101.1	47718	1.3	64.0	52615	196.3	13566.3	69110
1999-00	231.0	18508.0	80121	29.0	1155.0	39828	97.3	4088.5	42020	1.3	68.4	56000	201.3	14066.2	69877
2000-01	217.4	17690.1	81371	27.0	988.0	36593	93.5	3987.6	42648	1.3	72.8	54308	177.7	12694.7	71439
2001-02	218.0	18082.0	82945	27.2	1011.4	37184	113.4	5211.1	45953	1.2	70.6	58833	175.8	12464.6	70902
2002-03	232.5	15387.2	66182	26.0	916.0	35231	107.3	4520.5	42130	1.2	65.5	54583	202.9	14071.3	69351
2003-04	209.0	15070.0	72105	25.0	981.0	39240	103.6	4285.9	41370	1.2	57.6	48000	176.4	12669.1	71820
2004-05	210.0	15739.0	74948	23.9	883.9	36983	104.2	4111.7	39460	1.2	60.6	50500	196.7	14570.0	74072
2005-06	230.0	17656.0	76765	23.4	871.2	37231	101.3	4337.9	42822	1.1	55.9	50818	197.0	14580.0	74010
2006-07	264.0	21692.0	82167	27.0	1055.0	39074	129.6	5955.5	45953	1.1	58.0	52727	214.0	15630.0	73037
2007-08	247.0	20296.0	82170	26.0	980.0	37692	108.6	3854.9	35496	1.0	56.0	56000	211.0	15190.0	71991

(Contd.)

Table 1.2: Area, production and average yield statewise sugarcane

Area: in thousand hectares production: in thousand tons yield: per hectare in kg.

Year	Haryana			Himachal Pradesh			Jammu & Kashmir			Karnataka			Kerala		
	Area	Produ.	Yield	Area	Produ.	Yield	Area	Produ.	Yield	Area	Produ.	Yield	Area	Produ.	Yield
1970-71	155.0	6980.0	45032	3.4	44.8	13176	2.1	22.3	10619	96.7	8482.8	87723	7.7	376.3	48870
1971-72	114.0	5140.0	45088	2.6	38.4	14769	2.1	21.8	10381	106.8	8775.9	82171	7.6	391.1	51461
1972-73	136.0	6000.0	44118	3.7	46.3	12514	1.3	15.3	11769	104.2	8458.3	81174	7.8	400.2	51308
1973-74	149.7	5930.0	39613	3.4	47.6	14000	1.1	13.5	12273	109.6	8562.7	78127	9.5	513.5	54053
1974-75	161.4	5910.0	36617	3.8	52.6	13842	1.1	27.8	25273	124.1	8629.0	69533	9.5	539.1	56747
1975-76	157.8	6870.0	43536	3.7	66.3	17919	1.1	13.4	12182	128.6	9718.6	75572	9.4	506.3	53862
1976-77	168.0	7280.0	43333	4.0	41.9	10475	2.1	14.9	7095	143.5	9985.3	69584	7.2	404.6	56194
1977-78	195.7	8970.0	45835	3.8	72.0	18947	1.0	29.9	29900	159.0	11605.8	72992	6.6	377.6	57212
1978-79	189.8	6890.0	36301	3.9	87.4	22410	1.1	35.1	31909	153.7	10972.7	71390	6.6	376.4	57030
1979-80	127.0	3950.0	31102	3.2	76.7	23969	1.0	37.9	37900	135.3	9670.5	71475	8.5	487.5	57353
1980-81	115.0	4660.0	40522	3.1	48.5	15645	0.8	29.7	37125	156.5	12421.0	79367	7.8	461.6	59179
1981-82	147.0	5840.0	39728	3.0	43.1	14367	0.8	22.8	28500	175.3	14286.0	81495	8.0	479.5	59938
1982-83	147.0	5500.0	37415	3.1	28.8	9290	0.8	22.1	27625	187.1	14916.0	79722	7.8	821.4	105308
1983-84	134.0	5930.0	44254	3.7	57.8	15622	0.7	22.8	32571	172.7	12820.0	74233	8.1	870.6	107481
1984-85	124.0	5190.0	41855	3.4	48.3	14206	0.7	24.1	34429	172.0	13392.0	77860	7.8	427.5	54808
1985-86	106.0	5150.0	48585	2.7	27.1	10037	0.6	18.0	30000	171.5	13815.0	80554	7.8	425.6	54564
1986-87	124.0	6740.0	54355	2.7	27.2	10074	0.6	17.0	28333	180.8	14854.0	82157	7.6	411.8	54184
1987-88	142.0	5240.0	36901	2.8	20.1	7179	0.5	11.5	23000	202.5	17580.0	86815	8.5	562.5	66176
1988-89	131.0	6580.0	50229	3.0	20.1	6700	0.5	21.6	43200	239.6	18733.0	78184	8.2	537.7	65573

Table 1.2: Area, production and average yield statewise sugarcane *(Contd.)*

Area: in thousand hectares production: in thousand tons yield: per hectare in kg.

Year	Haryana			Himachal Pradesh			Jammu & Kashmir			Karnataka			Kerala		
	Area	Produ.	Yield	Area	Produ.	Yield	Area	Produ.	Yield	Area	Produ.	Yield	Area	Produ.	Yield
1989-90	126.0	6750.0	53571	2.5	29.5	11800	0.4	18.2	45500	264.9	21210.0	80068	8.2	533.3	65037
1990-91	148.0	7800.0	52703	2.5	31.7	12680	0.4	18.2	45500	272.3	20964.0	76989	8.0	542.9	67863
1991-92	161.0	9000.0	55901	2.1	28.1	13381	0.4	11.9	29750	285.3	24117.0	84532	8.1	547.1	67543
1992-93	134.0	6550.0	48881	2.2	28.7	13045	0.3	11.2	37333	261.5	22479.6	85964	6.2	428.3	69081
1993-94	111.4	6420.0	57630	2.4	26.1	10875	0.3	11.2	37333	300.6	26602.9	88499	5.5	447.9	81436
1994-95	120.0	7010.0	58417	3.0	53.5	17833	0.3	7.4	24667	344.9	33092.7	95949	5.9	477.8	80983
1995-96	144.0	8090.0	56181	3.2	67.0	20938	0.3	7.7	25667	313.2	24917.9	79559	6.1	522.9	85721
1996-97	162.0	9020.0	55679	3.4	70.3	20676	0.2	6.5	32500	282.1	23374.4	82859	5.9	548.1	92898
1997-98	142.0	7550.0	53169	3.8	139.1	36605	0.2	6.5	32500	309.8	28332.7	91455	5.9	548.1	92898
1998-99	125.0	6880.0	55040	3.3	120.2	36424	0.2	6.0	30000	338.8	34770.9	102630	5.8	424.3	73155
1999-00	137.0	7640.0	55766	3.0	67.4	22467	0.1	0.4	4000	373.0	37566.9	100716	5.8	578.8	99793
2000-01	143.0	8170.0	57133	2.8	60.5	21607	0.1	–	0	417.1	42923.5	102909	3.4	275.6	81059
2001-02	161.0	9270.0	57578	3.0	82.7	27567	0.1	–	0	407.0	33016.6	81122	3.3	269.8	81758
2002-03	189.0	10650.0	56349	2.9	49.1	16931	0.2	0.6	3000	382.7	32485.3	84885	3.8	312.8	82316
2003-04	160.0	9280.0	58000	3.0	50.0	16667	0.2	0.6	3000	243.3	16015.4	65826	3.5	291.0	83143
2004-05	130.0	8060.0	62000	2.9	61.9	21345	0.1	0.5	5000	178.0	14276.0	80202	3.0	283.0	94333
2005-06	127.0	8180.0	64409	2.6	25.1	9654	0.2	0.8	4000	219.0	18267.0	83411	6.8	916.5	134779
2006-07	140.0	9580.0	68429	3.0	59.0	19667	0.2	0.8	4000	326.0	28669.7	87944	5.0	440.0	88000
2007-08	140.0	8860.0	63286	2.7	58.4	21630	0.1	0.2	2000	306.0	26240.0	85752	2.0	218.0	109000

(Contd.)

Table 1.2: Area, production and average yield statewise sugarcane

Area: in thousand hectares production: in thousand tons yield: per hectare in kg.

Year	Madhya Pradesh			Maharashtra			Manipur			Meghalaya			Mizoram		
	Area	Produ.	Yield	Area	Produ.	Yield	Area	Produ.	Yield	Area	Produ.	Yield	Area	Produ.	Yield
1970-71	60.7	1613.0	26573	217.2	14770.0	68002	–	–	–	0.2	6.5	32500	0.6	22.3	37167
1971-72	51.9	1437.7	27701	181.8	11494.5	63226	–	–	–	0.2	6.6	33000	0.6	24.6	41000
1972-73	51.9	1370.0	26397	146.0	11917.7	81628	–	–	–	0.2	7.0	35000	0.9	30.2	33556
1973-74	56.9	1518.0	26678	164.6	12943.0	78633	1.1	37.0	33636	0.2	7.0	35000	1.5	113.7	75800
1974-75	80.7	2000.1	24784	185.2	17178.1	92754	0.7	25.7	36714	0.2	7.1	35500	1.5	42.5	28333
1975-76	77.1	2465.2	31974	211.8	18869.6	89092	4.6	172.2	37435	0.2	8.0	40000	2.0	68.8	34400
1976-77	77.1	2317.9	30064	240.9	21498.9	89244	1.5	54.4	36267	0.2	9.4	47000	0.9	20.5	22778
1977-78	56.1	1681.7	29977	246.0	23319.6	94795	2.1	82.5	39286	0.2	9.7	48500	0.9	7.9	8778
1978-79	61.8	1790.3	28969	244.1	22482.0	92102	2.1	67.5	32143	0.2	9.7	48500	0.5	9.1	18200
1979-80	51.4	1111.4	21623	222.0	19819.3	89276	2.1	71.7	34143	0.2	9.1	45500	3.5	7.0	2000
1980-81	39.1	1071.2	27396	255.5	23590.6	92331	2.3	77.9	33870	0.2	9.3	46500	1.1	5.1	4636
1981-82	42.6	1209.6	28394	297.1	28779.6	96868	2.3	77.9	33870	0.2	9.0	45000	1.1	5.1	4636
1982-83	47.2	1356.4	28737	325.8	31360.3	96256	1.7	60.0	35294	0.2	9.0	45000	1.1	5.1	4636
1983-84	44.6	1476.5	33105	299.0	26549.1	88793	1.7	60.0	35294	0.1	5.6	56000	0.7	3.5	5000
1984-85	42.6	1390.2	32634	292.6	26367.4	90114	1.7	60.0	35294	0.2	7.2	36000	1.0	3.5	3500
1985-86	37.2	1217.6	32731	265.3	23705.6	89354	0.7	19.3	27571	0.2	5.5	27500	0.6	2.7	4500
1986-87	45.6	1645.9	36094	279.9	24091.3	86071	2.6	71.7	27577	0.1	4.6	46000	0.6	5.9	9833
1987-88	47.2	1603.9	33981	291.9	24983.6	85590	2.9	95.3	32862	0.1	4.0	40000	1.0	3.0	3000
1988-89	43.9	1644.2	37453	314.3	25499.6	81131	2.3	74.0	32174	0.1	3.0	30000	0.5	6.5	13000

Table 1.2: Area, production and average yield statewise sugarcane *(Contd.)*

Area: in thousand hectares production: in thousand tons yield: per hectare in kg.

Year	Madhya Pradesh			Maharashtra			Manipur			Meghalaya			Mizoram		
	Area	Produ.	Yield	Area	Produ.	Yield	Area	Produ.	Yield	Area	Produ.	Yield	Area	Produ.	Yield
1989-90	38.7	1371.6	35442	383.1	34008.3	88771	1.7	55.4	32588	0.1	2.4	24000	0.6	7.1	11833
1990-91	39.4	1391.6	35320	444.0	38416.2	86523	1.9	63.0	33158	0.1	2.0	20000	0.5	1.8	3600
1991-92	46.2	1646.3	35634	453.3	36186.6	79829	1.5	49.0	32667	0.1	2.1	21000	0.5	5.3	10600
1992-93	39.9	1324.6	33198	403.8	30853.5	76408	1.8	58.8	32667	0.1	2.2	22000	0.8	5.6	7000
1993-94	53.2	1084.0	20376	344.1	27891.5	81056	1.8	58.8	32667	0.1	2.3	23000	1.0	5.7	5700
1994-95	37.3	1377.0	36917	517.5	44260.3	85527	1.3	41.2	31692	0.1	2.1	21000	0.9	7.6	8444
1995-96	47.9	1914.1	39960	580.0	46656.1	80442	1.2	38.6	32167	0.1	2.3	23000	1.1	7.3	6636
1996-97	45.0	1761.4	39142	516.2	41804.8	80986	1.3	42.8	32923	0.1	2.2	22000	1.2	7.7	6417
1997-98	42.3	1631.7	38574	459.7	38174.3	83042	0.5	15.4	30800	0.1	2.3	23000	1.3	7.5	5769
1998-99	40.5	1621.0	40025	529.8	47151.1	88998	0.7	22.9	32714	0.1	0.3	3000	1.0	4.8	4800
1999-00	46.7	1991.0	42634	590.0	53143.0	90073	0.7	21.2	30286	0.1	0.2	2000	0.7	1.5	2143
2000-01	74.9	1660.4	22168	595.0	49589.0	83343	0.7	24.2	34571	0.1	0.2	2000	1.0	6.4	6400
2001-02	41.6	1616.0	38846	578.0	45140.0	78097	0.7	21.2	30286	0.1	0.2	2000	1.4	9.4	6714
2002-03	39.2	1563.0	39872	573.0	42617.0	74375	0.7	20.6	29429	0.1	0.2	2000	1.4	7.4	5286
2003-04	43.3	1873.7	43273	443.0	25668.0	57941	0.3	22.0	73333	0.1	0.2	2000	0.1	3.6	36000
2004-05	52.5	2148.0	40914	324.0	20475.0	63194	0.6	21.8	36333	0.1	0.2	2000	1.2	5.7	4750
2005-06	55.5	2425.0	43694	501.0	38853.0	77551	0.7	23.0	32857	0.1	0.2	2000	1.4	4.6	3286
2006-07	64.3	2806.0	43639	1049.0	78568.0	74898	0.7	23.0	32857	0.1	0.2	2000	1.4	4.6	3286
2007-08	75.2	3180.0	42287	1093.0	88437.0	80912	0.5	16.8	33600	0.1	0.3	3000	0.9	0.8	889

(Contd.)

Table 1.2: Area, production and average yield statewise sugarcane

Area: in thousand hectares production: in thousand tons yield: per hectare in kg.

Year	Nagaland			Orissa			Punjab			Rajasthan			Tamil Nadu			Tripura		
	Area	Produ.	Yield	Area	Produ.	Yield	Area	Produ.	Yield	Area	Produ.	Yield	Area	Produ.	Yield	Area	Produ.	Yield
1970-71	–	–	–	30.2	1626.9	53871	127.7	5270.0	41269	37.1	1214.7	32741	135.0	10443.4	77359	2.8	100.7	35964
1971-72	–	–	–	30.6	1916.9	62644	103.0	4030.0	39126	27.6	1203.2	43594	116.5	9625.9	82626	2.6	87.1	33500
1972-73	1.4	39.2	28000	30.7	2001.5	65195	102.5	4690.0	45756	34.0	1352.2	39771	143.9	12112.7	84174	2.1	65.4	31143
1973-74	1.4	50.0	35714	41.0	2406.3	58690	110.3	5820.0	52765	40.2	1946.1	48410	186.2	18297.7	98269	2.0	67.1	33550
1974-75	2.0	60.0	30000	44.0	2750.0	62500	123.0	6150.0	50000	51.3	2169.6	42292	160.4	14592.7	90977	2.2	86.0	39091
1975-76	2.7	81.0	30000	45.4	2973.8	65502	114.2	6130.0	53678	40.2	1558.2	38761	128.3	11936.0	93032	2.1	86.7	41286
1976-77	3.1	95.0	30645	45.0	2770.0	61556	113.0	6070.0	53717	44.2	1990.9	45043	154.5	14245.5	92204	2.2	93.4	42455
1977-78	3.5	105.0	30000	43.0	2600.0	60465	116.0	6520.0	56207	61.2	2828.1	46211	167.4	16994.7	101522	2.0	87.6	43800
1978-79	3.1	169.8	54774	46.0	2810.0	61087	110.0	6240.0	56727	59.6	2195.7	36841	154.4	15430.8	99940	2.0	77.2	38600
1979-80	4.3	137.6	32000	46.5	2823.0	60710	77.0	3930.0	51039	33.8	1159.6	34308	149.4	15393.4	103035	1.8	70.0	38889
1980-81	4.1	122.4	29854	48.6	3060.0	62963	71.0	3920.0	55211	29.5	1163.9	39454	183.0	18570.0	101475	1.7	65.0	38235
1981-82	4.3	136.8	31814	50.0	3220.0	64400	106.0	6120.0	57736	37.1	1436.8	38728	201.3	20208.1	100388	1.8	71.3	39611
1982-83	3.8	140.5	36974	51.2	3169.4	61902	104.0	6340.0	60962	38.1	1429.9	37530	174.5	15210.0	87163	2.0	80.0	40000
1983-84	3.0	90.0	30000	42.3	2861.9	67657	84.0	5530.0	65833	33.6	1485.4	44208	151.7	13258.2	87397	2.0	75.9	37950
1984-85	3.0	81.0	27000	57.0	3700.0	64912	78.7	4920.0	62516	30.8	1369.3	44458	169.5	17594.2	103801	2.0	72.8	36400
1985-86	3.2	96.0	30000	57.8	3700.0	64014	78.0	5050.0	64744	26.5	1009.5	38094	191.1	20004.8	104682	1.8	64.9	36056
1986-87	3.3	106.0	32121	45.5	2785.6	61222	97.0	6110.0	62990	29.3	1290.5	44044	196.4	21604.7	110004	1.8	69.4	38556
1987-88	3.4	119.0	35000	42.3	2785.7	65856	106.0	5820.0	54906	26.6	948.4	35654	194.5	20765.9	106766	1.9	72.5	38158
1988-89	3.5	129.0	36857	47.0	3200.2	68089	97.0	6000.0	61856	16.1	686.3	42627	220.9	23767.6	107594	1.9	80.5	42368

Table 1.2: Area, production and average yield statewise sugarcane *(Contd.)*

Area: in thousand hectares production: in thousand tons yield: per hectare in kg.

Year	Nagaland			Orissa			Punjab			Rajasthan			Tamil Nadu			Tripura		
	Area	Produ.	Yield	Area	Produ.	Yield	Area	Produ.	Yield	Area	Produ.	Yield	Area	Produ.	Yield	Area	Produ.	Yield
1989-90	3.8	130.0	34211	47.5	3325.0	70000	103.0	6500.0	63107	15.6	716.3	45917	231.6	23444.5	101228	2.0	87.9	43950
1990-91	3.8	130.0	34211	49.0	3549.0	72429	101.0	6000.0	59406	22.8	1203.1	52768	232.9	23480.2	100817	1.9	91.0	47895
1991-92	3.3	140.0	42424	42.5	2744.6	64579	109.0	6920.0	63486	31.2	1360.7	43612	238.0	24886.8	104566	1.6	76.8	48000
1992-93	4.0	200.0	50000	16.0	754.2	47138	112.0	6369.0	56866	24.3	1129.0	46461	215.6	23064.2	106977	1.5	69.0	46000
1993-94	4.2	193.4	46048	13.4	781.0	58284	77.0	4710.0	61169	20.6	1020.0	49515	249.4	25991.8	104217	1.6	72.2	45125
1994-95	3.8	125.0	32895	20.3	1198.6	59044	83.0	5160.0	62169	21.9	987.0	45068	327.8	36456.1	111214	1.7	74.3	43706
1995-96	2.5	120.0	48000	27.3	1594.2	58396	132.0	8620.0	65303	28.0	1410.8	50386	326.2	32944.2	100994	1.5	75.0	50000
1996-97	2.5	125.0	50000	23.5	1332.1	56685	173.0	11040.0	63815	26.7	1290.2	48322	259.6	25918.8	99841	1.1	55.0	50000
1997-98	1.0	50.0	50000	18.7	1144.0	61176	126.0	7150.0	56746	23.2	1158.7	49944	282.8	30183.6	106731	1.1	58.0	52727
1998-99	1.2	68.0	56667	22.3	1469.5	65897	103.0	6130.0	59515	22.6	1078.8	47735	306.2	33764.8	110270	1.1	51.3	46636
1999-00	0.6	30.0	50000	20.6	1080.3	52442	108.0	6770.0	62685	19.3	786.8	40767	316.4	34285.0	108360	1.0	51.3	51300
2000-01	0.8	35.0	43750	16.8	963.9	57375	121.0	7770.0	64215	13.5	561.3	41578	315.3	33188.0	105258	1.0	54.1	54100
2001-02	1.0	50.0	50000	11.0	644.0	58545	142.0	9250.0	65141	9.1	432.2	47495	321.0	32620.0	101620	1.0	52.7	52700
2002-03	2.0	80.0	40000	14.2	753.2	53042	154.0	9290.0	60325	10.0	421.7	42170	261.4	24165.4	92446	1.2	56.2	46833
2003-04	3.0	130.0	43333	14.6	858.1	58774	123.0	6620.0	53821	5.8	309.4	53345	192.1	17656.0	91910	1.1	47.5	43182
2004-05	3.0	142.1	47367	15.4	859.9	55838	86.0	5170.0	60116	5.7	276.6	48526	232.0	23396.0	100845	1.1	52.4	47636
2005-06	4.4	210.9	47932	16.3	1073.0	65828	84.0	4860.0	57857	7.9	482.6	61089	335.4	35106.5	104671	1.1	52.6	47818
2006-07	4.8	233.9	48729	20.1	1274.4	63403	99.0	6020.0	60808	10.9	629.7	57771	391.2	41124.0	105123	0.9	42.4	47111
2007-08	5.0	247.3	49460	19.8	1096.2	55364	110.0	6990.0	63545	10.4	593.8	57096	354.2	38071.0	107484	1.0	46.7	46700

(Contd.)

Table 1.2: Area, production and average yield statewise sugarcane

Area: in thousand hectares production: in thousand tons yield: per hectare in kg.

Year	Uttar Pradesh			West Bengal			A & N Islands			Pondicherry			All India		
	Area	Produ.	Yield	Area	Produ.	Yield	Area	Produ.	Yield	Area	Produ.	Yield	Area	Produ.	Yield
1970-71	1345.2	54672.3	40643	38.3	2075.2	54183	–	–	–	1.5	128.4	85600	2615.1	126368.0	48322
1971-72	1274.1	49354.2	38737	33.9	1656.8	48873	–	–	–	1.5	150.0	100000	2390.4	113569.5	47511
1972-73	1308.0	56727.3	43369	32.5	1643.7	50575	–	–	–	1.6	152.0	95000	2451.6	124866.7	50933
1973-74	1472.7	60772.7	41266	30.8	1626.8	52818	–	–	–	1.8	184.5	102500	2752.1	140804.5	51163
1974-75	1491.5	61479.2	41220	29.0	1682.3	58010	0.3	12.6	42000	1.9	167.6	88211	2894.2	144288.9	49855
1975-76	1440.7	58359.3	40508	29.3	1713.1	58468	0.3	12.6	42000	1.5	89.8	59867	2762.2	140603.5	50903
1976-77	1455.9	65215.5	44794	29.5	1812.4	61437	0.1	4.1	41000	2.1	179.7	85571	2866.2	153006.7	53383
1977-78	1636.5	76818.6	46941	31.4	1906.8	60726	0.1	1.9	19000	2.1	158.2	75333	3151.1	176965.5	56160
1978-79	1633.8	62324.2	38147	32.1	1884.9	58720	0.1	1.3	13000	2.0	176.1	88050	3087.8	151655.1	49114
1979-80	1372.8	51228.4	37317	29.3	1437.2	49051	0.1	0.5	5000	1.8	122.0	67778	2610.2	128833.4	49358
1980-81	1363.4	64204.9	47092	14.3	867.4	60657	0.1	0.3	3000	1.9	145.4	76526	2666.6	154248.0	57844
1981-82	1651.7	76440.1	46280	23.0	1410.8	61339	0.1	0.3	3000	2.2	183.6	83455	3193.3	186357.6	58359
1982-83	1782.7	81386.7	45654	31.1	1599.6	51434	0.1	1.3	13000	1.9	163.6	86105	3357.6	189505.6	56441
1983-84	1688.0	78243.8	46353	20.3	1022.4	50365	0.1	0.4	4000	1.9	112.6	59263	3109.7	174076.2	55978
1984-85	1543.2	70888.2	45936	13.4	769.9	57455	0.1	0.5	5000	2.0	135.8	67900	2953.2	170319.2	57673
1985-86	1490.0	73036.8	49018	12.9	812.1	62953	0.1	0.6	6000	2.9	283.2	97655	2849.4	170648.1	59889
1986-87	1677.7	84736.3	50507	12.5	757.4	60592	0.1	0.6	6000	3.3	460.2	139455	3078.7	186089.5	60444
1987-88	1801.0	93054.0	51668	11.0	691.5	62864	0.1	0.6	6000	3.5	293.0	83714	3278.6	196736.9	60006
1988-89	1761.3	88522.7	50260	16.4	1162.4	70878	0.6	15.5	25833	2.9	272.0	93793	3328.9	203036.8	60992
1989-90	1761.3	97422.3	55313	15.1	1031.0	68278	0.6	15.5	25833	1.9	174.8	92000	3437.9	225569.2	65612

Table 1.2: Area, production and average yield statewise sugarcane *(Contd.)*

Area: in thousand hectares production: in thousand tons yield: per hectare in kg.

Year	Uttar Pradesh			West Bengal			A & N Islands			Pondicherry			All India		
	Area	Produ.	Yield	Area	Produ.	Yield	Area	Produ.	Yield	Area	Produ.	Yield	Area	Produ.	Yield
1990-91	1855.6	103562.2	55811	12.2	859.3	70434	0.2	5.0	25000	2.8	256.0	91429	3686.0	241045.5	65395
1991-92	1932.6	111098.2	57486	17.0	969.3	57018	0.2	4.7	23500	3.5	285.9	81686	3844.4	253995.1	66069
1992-93	1857.5	102929.1	55413	15.4	888.7	57708	0.2	5.9	29500	2.6	186.8	71846	3571.8	228033.4	63843
1993-94	1760.8	104081.6	59110	10.3	542.4	52660	0.2	4.4	22000	2.4	162.7	67792	3421.6	229659.3	67120
1994-95	1839.1	110238.8	59942	10.6	648.9	61217	0.2	4.6	23000	3.3	264.0	80000	3867.0	275539.9	71254
1995-96	1974.4	119830.4	60692	17.2	1311.8	76267	0.3	6.6	22000	3.1	241.8	78000	4147.4	281099.5	67777
1996-97	2110.6	125348.4	59390	24.9	1810.3	72703	0.3	6.7	22333	2.6	170.2	65462	4174.1	277560.0	66496
1997-98	1985.2	129266.7	65115	25.8	1825.7	70764	0.2	4.8	24000	2.4	191.3	79708	3929.8	279541.4	71134
1998-99	1974.6	116483.4	58991	26.9	2001.9	74420	0.2	4.7	23500	2.8	210.2	75071	4054.9	288722.4	71203
1999-00	2011.0	115418.9	57394	22.9	1762.8	76978	0.1	4.7	47000	2.8	237.6	84857	4219.7	299323.9	70935
2000-01	1938.4	106067.5	54719	21.6	1465.6	67852	0.2	4.7	23500	2.5	200.4	80160	4315.7	295956.2	68577
2001-02	2035.0	117982.0	57976	23.3	1983.4	85124	0.1	2.4	24000	2.1	197.4	94000	4411.6	297207.8	67370
2002-03	2149.0	120948.0	56281	19.5	1281.3	65708	0.5	13.8	27600	2.3	209.5	91087	4520.3	287383.2	63576
2003-04	2030.1	112754.0	55541	16.9	1252.6	74118	0.3	2.9	9667	1.7	147.7	86882	3938.4	233861.8	59380
2004-05	1954.7	118715.6	60733	15.6	1033.2	66231	0.2	5.7	28500	1.5	127.3	84867	3661.5	237088.4	64752
2005-06	2155.8	125469.9	58201	15.0	1247.7	83180	0.3	5.9	19667	2.1	157.3	74905	4201.7	281171.8	66919
2006-07	2246.5	133949.4	59626	16.6	1266.7	76307	0.1	2.6	26000	2.1	157.3	74905	5150.8	355519.7	69022
2007-08	2179.0	124665.3	57212	16.9	1272.0	75266	0.2	3.5	17500	2.3	228.4	99304	5055.2	348187.9	68877

Source: Area and Production of Principal Crops in India (Various Issues), Directorate of Economics & Statistics, Department of Agriculture & Co-operation, Ministry of Agriculture.

Table 1.2A: Scenario of Indian sugar industry over the years

Year	*Number of factories in operation day)*	*Average duration (days) tons)*	*Average capacity (tons per day)*	*Sugar produced (million tons)*	*Recovery (%)*	*Molasses '000 tons*
1930-31	29	n.a	n.a	0.12	8.96	n.a
1935-36	135	126	644	0.934	9.29	336
1940-41	148	113	750	1.113	9.7	431
1945-46	145	93	768	0.959	10.09	333
1950-51	139	101	882	1.1	9.99	387
1955-56	143	145	980	1.834	9.83	736
1960-61	174	166	1172	3.021	9.74	1210
1965-66	200	159	1253	3.541	9.7	1530
1970-71	215	139	1394	3.74	9.79	1611
1975-76	252	116	1563	4.262	10.18	1703
1980-81	315	104	1718	5.15	9.98	2126
1981-82	320	173	1721	8.437	9.66	3837
1982-83	321	158	1179	8.229	9.95	3507
1983-84	326	111	1779	5.917	10.02	2436
1984-85	339	106	1824	6.144	10.22	2463
1985-86	342	116	1885	7.016	10.23	2857
1986-87	354	141	1862	8.502	9.98	3663
1987-88	357	152	1888	9.11	9.7	4205
1988-89	365	133	1925	8.752	10.22	3595
1989-90	377	158	2036	10.99	9.89	4881
1990-91	385	166	2088	12.047	9.84	5454
1991-92	392	172	2167	13.405	10.01	6056
1992-93	393	123	2325	10.609	10.3	4381
1993-94	394	114	2388	9.833	10	4227
1994-95	408	159	2483	14.643	9.92	6497
1995-96	416	181	2531	16.453	9.42	8297
1996-97	412	130	2656	12.905	9.9	5936
1997-98	400	123	2863	12.852	9.95	5547
1998-99	427	141	2855	15.539	9.86	6978
1999-00	423	151	3049	18.2	10.2	8013
2000-01	436	138	3203	18.511	10.48	7820
2001-02	434	138	3285	18.528	10.27	8073
2002-03	453	140	3343	20.145	10.36	8879
2003-04	422	99	3493	13.546	10.22	5905
2004-05	400	97	3508	12.69	10.17	5513
2005-06	455	125	3619	19.267	10.21	8549
2006-07	504	173	3561	28.328	10.16	13111
2007-08	516	149	3586	26.357	10.55	11313
2008-09	489	87	3751	14.539	10.03	6546
2009-10	490	109	3846	18.912	10.19	8400
2010-11	527	135	3744	24.394	10.17	10970
2011-12*	529	137	3877	26.243	10.25	11824

* Provisional

Source: Cooperative Sugar Vol 45 (1), September 2013.

Table 1.2B: Comparative position of 1st advance estimates for 2013-14 vis-à-vis 4th advance estimates (Kharif only) for 2012-13 and final estimates (Kharif only) for 2011-12

Sugarcane

State	*Production ('000 tons)*			*Area ('000 hectares)*			*Yield (kg hectare)*		
1st advance estimates 2013-14	*4th advance estimates 2012-13*	*Final 2011-12*	*1st advance estimates 2013-14*	*4th advance estimates 2012-13*	*Final 2011-12*	*1st advance estimates 2013-14*	*estimates 2012-13*	*4th advance 2011-12*	*Final*
Andhra Pradesh	14898.0	15680.0	16686.0	191.0	196.0	204.0	78000	80000	81794
Assam	1080.0	1036.0	993.5	29.0	28.0	25.7	37241	37000	38611
Bihar	15084.9	14737.8	11288.6	265.6	262.8	218.3	56800	56080	51714
Chhattisgarh	30.6	37.3	24.4	11.2	13.5	9.1	2732	2763	2681
Gujarat	11700.0	13350.0	12750.0	180.0	185.0	202.0	65000	72162	63119
Haryana	9490.0	7437.0	6959.0	130.0	101.0	95.0	73000	73634	73253
Himachal Pradesh	25.9	37.3	28.3	1.8	1.7	2.1	14142	22310	13714
Jharkhand	499.1	462.8	457.3	7.1	6.7	6.6	70197	69216	69216
Karnataka	3466.0	35732.0	38808.0	410.0	425.0	430.0	84551	84075	90251
Kerala	51.2	166.2	263.0	0.5	1.7	2.6	94889	97199	101165
Madhya Pradesh	3249.5	2516.1	2677.0	77.0	59.5	69.2	42201	42287	38685
Maharashtra	72404.0	62174.8	86733.1	936.0	937.0	1022.0	77355	66355	84866
Odisha	818.3	952.4	884.7	13.1	14.5	14.5	62319	65545	61014
Punjab	6720.0	4890.0	5653.0	96.0	83.0	80.0	70000	58916	70663
Rajasthan	342.9	401.8	451.3	5.1	5.5	6.4	67243	73056	70293
Tamil Nadu	24791.9	35187.5	38575.7	231.7	382.5	346.4	107000	92001	111378
Uttar Pradesh	135429.0	134851.3	128819.0	2172.0	2212.0	2162.0	62352	60964	59583
Uttarakhand	7466.0	6718.0	6311.0	122.0	110.0	108.0	61197	61073	58435
West Bengal	2100.0	1685.0	1681.4	20.0	16.1	16.1	105000	104808	104567
Others	926.0	909.8	992.3	21.7	22.2	17.7	42661	40982	56067
All India	**341773.4**	**338963.1**	**361036.6**	**4920.9**	**5063.7**	**5037.7**	**69453**	**66940**	**71668**

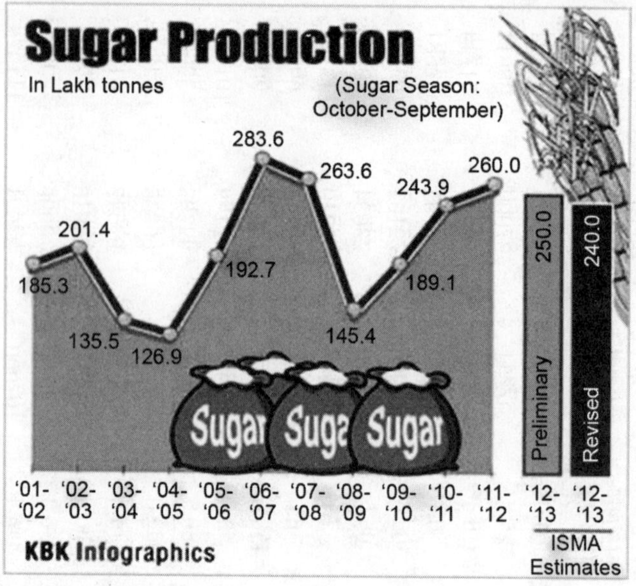

Source: ISMA.

Steps for production of sugar:

1. Extracting juice by pressing sugarcane.
2. Boiling the juice to obtain crystals.
3. Creating raw sugar by spinning crystals in extractors
4. Taking raw sugar to a refinery for the process of filtering and washing to discard remaining non-sugar elements and hue.
5. Crystallizing and drying sugar.
6. Packaging the ready sugar.

Registered installed capacity of sugar mills shows that in keeping with production levels of sugar, UP is at the top followed by Maharashtra (Table 1.5).

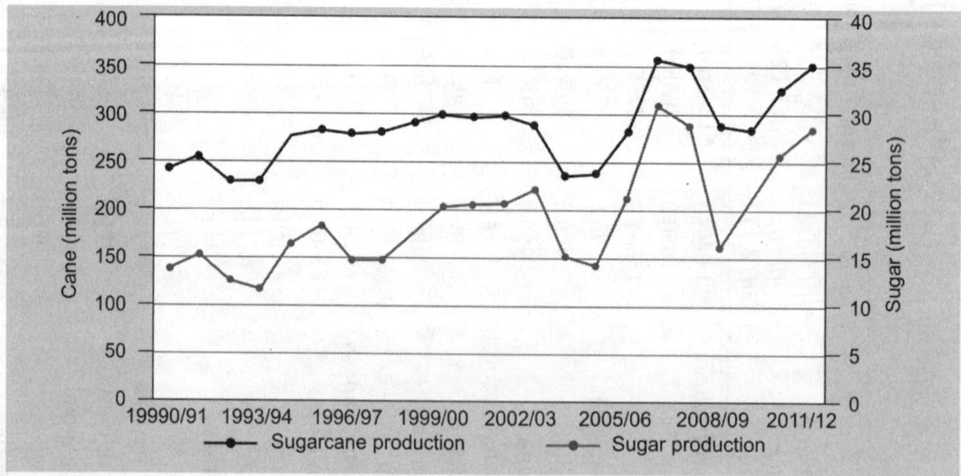

Source: 1. Ministry of agriculture, department of economics and statistics, government of India; 2. Indian Sugar Mills Association

Table 1.3: Area, production and utilization pattern of sugarcane in India

Sugarcane Years chewing***	Production area (million hectares)	sugarcane* (million tons)	Sugarcane used for (million tons)		
			*Production Sugar**	*Khandsari and Gur***	*Seed feed and*
2003-04	3.94	233.86	132.51 (56.66)	71.35 (30.51)	30.00 (12.83)
2004-05	3.66	237.09	124.77 (52.63)	83.87 (35.37)	28.45 (12.00)
2005-06	4.2	281.17	188.67 (67.10)	58.75 (20.90)	33.74 (12.00)
2006-07	5.15	355.52	279.24 (78.55)	33.60 (9.45)	42.66 (12.00)
2007-08	5.06	348.19	249.90 (71.77)	56.50 (16.23)	41.78 (12.00)
2008-09	4.4	285	145.00 (50.88)	105.8 (37.12)	34.20 (12.00)
2009-10	4.2	277.8	185.54 (60.79)	58.91 (21.21)	33.33 (12.00)
2010-11	4.94	342.38	240.00 (70.10)	61.30 (17.90)	41.08 (12.00)
2011-12	5.09	357.67	260.00 (74.74)	46.12 (13.26)	41.74 (12.00)
2012-13	5.25	365	270.00 (73.97)	51.20 (14.03)	43.80 (12.00)
CGR (%)	1.46***	1.54***			

(Figures shows in bracket are the percentage of sugarcane production utilized)
* Directorate of Economic and Statistics, Ministry of Agriculture.
** Indian Sugar Mills Association except 2011/12 and 2012/13.
*** FAS/New Delhi estimate.
Note: Figures for 2011/12 and 2012/13 are FAS estimates.

Irrigated area under sugarcane increased from 67.3% in 1950–1951 to 93% in 2007–2008 (Table 1.5A). Of the total sugar production of 48.7 million tons in 1980–1981, levy sugar was 31.1 million tons and free sugar as 18.7 million tons (Table 1.6). As against this corresponding figures for 2012–2013 were 120.2, 12.2 and 108 million tons. Wholesale free market price in October 1975–1976 at Bombay, Culcutta and Delhi were Rs 448,440 and 438 per quintal. The same in October 2012–2013 were Rs 3,423,760 and 3,750 per quintal in the corresponding cities (Table 1.7).

The first sugar mill was established during 1784 in Bengal on the banks of Hoogly. There are 529 mills today with an average crushing capacity 12.6 million tons during 2005–2006 of tons per day. Number of sugar mills in selected states is as in Tables 1.8 and 1.8A. UP was at the top upto 1996–1997. But thereafter, Maharashtra became the leader with regard to the number of mills. Major number of mills was in the Corporate sector upto 1980–1981 with corporate sector 166 as against co-operative 148. From 1985–1986 cooperative sector took the lead (Table 1.9). Capacity and production of cooperative sugar factories is as in Table 1.10. Palm gur production shows in Table 1.10A. Average sugar recovery and crushing period (Table 1.11) show that Maharashtra has the highest recovery of 10–11% followed by Karnataka, Gujarat and Andhra Pradesh. In the recent years, Rajasthan had the lowest recovery rate at below 8%. With regard to crushing period, Punjab was at the top in the earlier period. But, it has been taken over by Tamil Nadu – touched the highest number of days (267) during 2006–2007.

Production of sugar by states is as in Table 1.12. UP was the major producer till 2005–2006, but was taken over by Maharashtra from 2006–2007. During 2011–2012, while Maharashtra produced nearly 9.0 million tons of sugar, production UP was only 7.0 million tons.

Table 1.3A: Utilization of sugarcane for different purposes

Year utilized for (November to October	Production of sugarcane (in terms of cane (thousand tons)	Cane used for (thousand tons) percentage of sugarcane production					
		production of white sugar	Seed feed chewing, etc.	Gur and Khandsari	Production of white sugar	Seed,feed chewing etc.	Gur and khandsari
1956-57	82,908	21,197	10,411	51,300	25.5	12.5	61.9
1957-58	83,651	20,065	10,270	53,316	24.0	12.3	63.7
1958-59	86,149	19,804	10,590	35,755	23.0	12.3	64.7
1959-60	91,394	24,812	11,271	55,411	27.1	12.3	60.6
1960-61	110,544	31,113	13,620	65,811	27.2	12.3	59.5
1961-62	103,967	27,948	12,743	63,276	26.9	12.3	60.8
1962-63	94,470	20,743	11,419	623,008	22.0	12.1	65.9
1963-64	104,908	25,761	12,595	66,552	24.6	12.0	63.4
1964-65	119,598	33,420	14,539	71,639	27.9	12.2	59.9
1970-71	126368	38204	15173	72991	30.2	12.0	57.8
1971-72	113569	30974	13514	69081	27.3	11.9	60.8
1972-73	124867	40406	14999	69461	32.4	12.0	55.6
1973-74	140805	42283	16802	81720	30.0	11.9	58.1
1974-75	144289	48425	17188	78676	33.5	11.9	54.5
1975-76	140604	41849	16692	82063	29.8	11.9	58.3
1976-77	153007	48967	18317	85723	32.0	12.0	56.0
1977-78	176965	67288	21029	88648	38.0	11.9	50.1
1978-79	151655	59715	17957	73983	39.4	11.8	48.8
1979-80	128883	39048	15104	74681	30.3	11.7	58.0
1980-81	154248	51572	18201	84475	33.4	11.8	54.8
1981-82	186358	87360	21787	77211	46.9	11.7	41.4
1982-83	189506	82669	22304	84533	43.6	11.8	44.6
1983-84	174076	58970	20803	94283	33.9	11.9	54.2
1984-85	170319	60049	20115	90155	35.3	11.8	52.9
1985-86	170648	68560	20205	81883	40.2	11.8	48.0
1986-87	186090	85184	22242	78664	45.8	12.0	42.3
1987-88	196737	93910	23562	82477	47.7	12.0	41.9
1988-89	203037	85669	24114	93254	42.2	11.9	45.9
1989-90	225569	111116	26718	87735	49.3	11.8	38.9
1990-91	241046	122287	28552	93207	50.7	11.9	37.4
1991-92	253995	133999	26629	93367	52.8	10.5	36.7
1992-93	228033	102971	27098	97964	45.1	11.9	43.0
1993-94	229659	98052	27260	104347	42.7	11.9	45.4
1994-95	275540	147598	32706	95235	53.6	11.9	34.5
1995-96	281099	174169	32888	74042	62.0	11.7	26.3
1996-97	277560	130379	33104	114077	47.0	11.9	41.1
1997-98	279542	129049	33186	117307	46.2	11.8	42.0
1998-99	288722	156790	33469	98463	54.3	11.6	34.1
1999-2000	299324	178449	34380	86495	59.6	11.5	28.9
2000-01	295956	176648	33930	85378	59.7	11.5	29.8
2001-02	297208	180346	34724	82138	60.7	11.7	27.6
2002-03 (P)	281575	194365	33524	53686	69.0	11.9	19.1

Source: Indian Sugar, the complete sugar journal, Vol. No. LV, No. 9, December, 2005.

Table 1.3B: Estimates of area, production and yield of sugarcane

States/UTs	Area ('000 hectares)					Production ('000 tons)					Yied (kg/hectares)				
	2006-07	2007-08	2008-09	2009-10	2010-11	2006-07	2007-08	2008-09	2009-10	2010-11	2006-07	2007-08	2008-09	2009-10	2010-11
Andhra Pradesh	264.0	247.0	196.0	158.0	192.0	21692.0	20296.0	15380.0	11708.0	14964.0	82167	82170	78469	74101	77938
Arunachal Pradesh	1.0	1.2	1.4	1.5	1.5	16.8	21.8	23.4	27.1	29.0	16800	18167	16714	18067	19333
Assam	27.0	26.0	28.6	27.1	29.7	1055.0	980.0	1099.7	1059.0	1075.0	39074	37692	38451	39077	36196
Bihar	129.6	108.6	111.9	115.9	248.0	5955.5	3854.9	4959.9	5032.6	12763.6	45953	35496	44324	43422	51466
Chhattisgarh	7.2	11.1	10.6	12.4	8.3	18.7	27.5	25.4	29.2	21.8	2597	2477	2396	2355	2627
Gujarat	214.0	211.0	221.0	154.0	190.0	15630.0	15190.0	15510.0	12400.0	13760.0	73037	71991	70181	80519	72421
Goa	1.1	1.0	1.0	0.9	0.9	58.0	56.0	49.3	52.3	49.1	52727	56000	49300	58111	54556
Haryana	140.0	140.0	90.0	74.0	85.0	9580.0	8860.0	5130.0	5335.0	6042.0	68429	63286	57000	72095	71082
Himachal Pradesh	3.0	2.7	2.3	2.2	1.7	59.0	58.4	53.1	45.6	38.3	19667	21630	23087	20727	22529
Jammu & Kashmir	0.2	0.1	0.0	0.0	0.0	0.8	0.2	0.0	0.0	0.0	4000	2000		2000	1667
Jharkhand	4.0	6.0	5.7	6.5	6.6	142.0	150.0	348.8	447.0	457.3	35500	25000	61193	68769	69288
Karnataka	326.0	306.0	281.0	337.0	423.0	28669.7	26240.0	23328.0	30443.0	39657.0	87944	85752	83018	90335	93752
Kerala	5.0	2.0	2.2	3.0	2.8	440.0	218.0	275.5	285.0	271.8	88000	109000	125227	95000	95517
Madhya Pradesh	64.3	75.2	70.5	62.1	65.1	2806.0	3180.0	2975.0	2535.0	2667.0	43639	42287	42199	40821	40968
Maharashtra	1049.0	1093.0	768.0	756.0	965.0	78568.0	88437.0	60648.0	64159.0	81895.7	74898	80912	78969	84866	84866
Manipur	0.7	0.5	0.6	0.6	5.2	23.0	16.8	21.3	21.3	301.3	32857	33600	35500	35500	57944
Meghalaya	0.1	0.1	0.1	0.1	0.1	0.2	0.3	0.3	0.2	0.2	2000	3000	3000	2623	2000
Mizoram	1.4	0.9	1.3	1.4	1.4	4.6	0.8	13.7	12.4	7.9	3286	889	10538	8857	5643

(Contd.)

Table 1.3B: Estimates of area, production and yield of sugarcane

States/UTs	*Area ('000 hectares)*					*Production ('000 tons)*					*Yied (kg/hectares)*				
	2006-07	*2007-08*	*2008-09*	*2009-10*	*2010-11*	*2006-07*	*2007-08*	*2008-09*	*2009-10*	*2010-11*	*2006-07*	*2007-08*	*2008-09*	*2009-10*	*2010-11*
Nagaland	4.8	5.0	4.3	5.1	4.3	233.9	247.3	185.8	152.9	184.9	48729	49460	43209	29980	43000
Orissa	20.1	19.8	10.8	8.0	13.1	1274.4	1096.2	646.2	489.9	902.7	63403	55364	59833	61238	68908
Punjab	99.0	110.0	81.0	60.0	70.0	6020.0	6690.0	4670.0	3700.0	4170.0	60808	60818	57654	61667	59571
Rajasthan	10.9	10.4	6.5	6.0	5.5	629.7	593.8	388.2	344.5	367.9	57771	57096	59723	57417	66891
Tamil Nadu	391.2	354.2	308.9	293.2	316.0	41124.0	38071.0	32804.4	29745.6	34251.8	105123	107484	106197	101452	108392
Tripura	0.9	1.0	1.0	0.9	0.9	42.4	46.7	51.7	44.9	46.5	47111	46700	51700	51096	51646
Uttar Pradesh	2246.5	2179.0	2084.0	1977.0	2125.0	133949.4	124665.3	109048.0	117140.0	120545.0	59626	57212	52326	59251	56727
Uttaranchal	121.0	124.0	107.0	96.0	106.7	6100.0	7686.0	5590.0	5842.0	6497.6	50413	61984	52243	60854	60896
West Bengal	16.6	16.9	17.6	13.8	15.0	1266.7	1272.0	1638.3	1000.8	1134.1	76307	75266	93085	72522	75607
A & N Islands	0.1	0.2	0.2	0.1	0.2	2.6	3.5	3.0	2.0	2.3	26000	17500	15000	20000	11500
Pondicherry	2.1	2.3	1.9	1.8	1.8	157.3	228.4	162.3	247.3	277.7	74905	99304	85421	137389	157327
All India	**5150.8**	**5055.2**	**4415.4**	**4174.6**	**4884.8**	**355519.7**	**348187.9**	**285029.3**	**292301.6**	**342381.6**	**69022**	**68877**	**64553**	**70020**	**70091**

Table 1.4: Basic parameters of sugar industry

Parameters	*Unit*	*1970-71*	*1980-81*	*1984-85*	*1985-86*	*1986-87*	*1987-88*	*1988-89*	*1989-90*	*1990-91*	*1991-92*	*1992-93*	*1993-94*	*1994-95*	*1995-96*	*1996-97*
Working units	No	216	314	338	341	353	356	366	377	385	392	393	394	408	416	412
Sugar production	mn MT	3.7	5.1	6.1	7.0	8.5	9.1	8.8	11.0	12.0	13.4	10.6	9.8	14.6	16.5	12.9
Cane crushed	mn MT	38.2	51.6	6.0	6.9	8.5	940.0	85.7	111.1	122.3	134.0	103.0	98.3	147.6	174.8	130
Production of sugarcane	mn MT	126.0	154.0	170.0	172.0	180.0	197.0	204.0	226.0	241.0	254.0	228.0	229.7	275.5	281.1	278
Molasses produced	mn MT	1.6	2.1	2.5	2.8	3.7	4.2	3.6	4.9	5.4	6.0	4.4	4.2	6.5	8.3	6
Gur & Khandsari Prod	mn MT	73.0	84.5	90.2	81.9	78.7	82.5	93,3	87.7	93.2	93.4	98.0	104.3	95.2	74.0	114.1
Sugar recovery	%	9.8	10.0	10.2	10.2	10.0	9.7	9.9	9.9	9.9	10.0	10.3	10.0	9.9	9.4	10
Population	mn	551	684	737	751	765	780	816	833	848	868	884	895	911	916	932
Total consumption Sugar	mn MT	4.03	4.90	8.09	8.27	8.69	9.38	9.94	10.21	10.71	11.27	11.87	11.96	12.27	13.13	14.05
Per capita consumption																
- Sugar	kg/year	7.3	7.2	11.0	11.0	11.4	12.0	12.4	12.3	12.5	12.9	13.4	13.4	13.2	14.1	14.6
- Gur/khandsari	kg/year	13.5	12.6	12.2	11.0	10.7	10.2	12.4	10.3	10.4	9.6	8.9	9.1	10.2	9.3	9.8

(Contd.)

Table 1.4: Basic parameters of sugar industry

Parameters	*Unit*	*1997-98*	*1998-99*	*1999-2000*	*2000-01*	*2001-02*	*2002-03*	*2003-04*	*2004-05*	*2005-06*	*2006-07*	*2007-08*	*2008-09*	*2009-10*	*2010-11*	*2011-12*
Working units	No	400	426	423	436	434	453	423	400	453	504	516	488	490	527	529
Sugar production	mn MT	12.9	15.5	18.2	18.5	18.6	20.1	13.5	12.7	19.3	28.4	26.4	14.5	18.9	24.4	26.3
Cane crushed	mn MT	129	157.5	182.0	139.0	180.3	194.3	132.5	124.8	188.7	279.2	249.9	145.0	185.5	239.8	257.0
Production of sugarcane	mn MT	280	295.7	315.1	299.2	299.3	289.6	233.9	237.1	281.2	355.5	348.2	285.0	292.3	342.4	357.7
Molasses produced	mn MT	6	7.0	8.0	7.8	8.1	8.9	5.9	5.5	8.5	13.1	11.3	6.5	8.4	11.0	11.8
Gur & Khandsari Prod	mn MT	117.3	98.5	86.5	85.4	82.1	57.1	76.6	85.2	59.0	35.4	50.1	93.7	71.9	59.3	60.1
Sugar recovery	%	10	10.0	10.2	10.5	10.5	10.4	10.2	10.2	10.2	10.2	10.6	10.0	10.2	10.2	10.3
Population	mn	948	987	977	1019	1037	1055	1073	1089	1106	1122	1138	1154	1170	1186	1202
Total consumption Sugar	mn MT	14.84	15.22	16.10	16.25	16.52	18.38	17.28	18.50	18.50	20.00	22.20	22.50	21.33	20.77	22.00
Per capita consumption																
- Sugar	kg/year	14.5	14.9	16.5	16.5	17.00	17.3	18.1	17.0	16.7	17.8	19.8	19.9	17.9	17.5	18.3
- Gur/khandsari	kg/year	8.7	12.6	12.6	8.3	7.9	5.4	7.1	8.7	5.3	3.0	4.4	4.5	5.1	5.0	5.0

Table 1.5: Registered installed capacity of sugar mills by states

(Lakh or 0.1 mn MT)

States	*1970-71*	*80-81*	*84-85*	*85-86*	*86-87*	*87-88*	*88-89*	*90-91*	*91-92*	*92-93*	*93-94*	*94-95*	*95-96*	*96-97*	*97-98*	*98-99*	*99-00*	*00-01*	*01-02*	*02-03*	*03-04*	*04-05*	*09-10*	*10-11*	*11-12*
Andhra Pradesh	2.83	4.96	5.56	5.62	5.70	5.80	5.52	5.52	8.81	6.38	6.38	6.35	6.79	6.79	7.49	8.35	8.05	8.05	8.05	8.12	9.08	9.08	9.33	9.57	10.55
Bihar	3.39	3.39	3.47	3.51	3.50	3.50	3.27	3.42	4.12	3.92	6.38	4.12	4.12	4.12	4.01	4.27	4.05	4.05	4.05	3.19	4.84	4.85	4.85	4.85	4.84
Gujarat	1.42	3.91	4.96	5.15	5.10	5.30	5.81	6.53	13.39	7.47	3.92	8.11	8.54	8.54	8.96	9.60	10.00	10.00	10.00	9.64	10.71	10.71	10.79	11.30	12.37
Karnataka	2.36	5.51	7.13	7.29	7.90	7.90	7.70	7.70	6.53	8.37	7.47	8.37	8.37	8.37	8.37	8.93	9.00	9.20	9.20	12.84	14.46	14.60	20.48	21.16	28.35
Maharashtra	9.36	20.34	22.96	24.49	25.60	26.90	29.89	31.23	32.09	36.65	36.65	38.34	39.87	39.87	43.00	45.86	40.23	47.17	47.17	65.73	69.35	69.78	75.30	78.34	84.83
Madhya Pradesh	0.30	0.52	0.64	0.64	0.60	0.60	0.77	0.77	1.68	0.76	0.76	0.99	0.99	0.99	0.99	0.99	0.80	0.80	0.80	1.45	1.54	1.54	2.50	2.50	2.76
Punjab	0.55	0.77	0.88	1.10	1.20	1.40	2.48	3.95	4.30	9.69	5.20	6.25	6.25	6.25	6.25	6.25	6.25	5.25	5.25	6.49	6.84	6.84	6.84	7.19	4.74
Rajasthan	0.22	0.22	0.27	0.27	0.30	0.30	0.23	0.23	0.23	0.23	0.23	0.23	0.23	0.23	0.23	0.23	0.23	0.23	0.23	0.23	0.23	0.23	0.23	0.23	0.23
Tamil Nadu	2.90	5.74	6.19	6.66	6.80	6.90	8.32	10.05	10.28	11.93	11.93	11.84	12.63	12.63	12.73	13.12	14.63	14.63	14.63	15.24	15.24	15.24	19.03	19.49	23.17
Uttar Pradesh	12.33	15.56	17.61	18.22	18.70	19.30		24.49	25.35	29.00	29.00	32.06	34.79	34.79	36.39	38.99	38.99	38.99	38.99	40.6	44.11	45.37	74.72	74.72	66.06
Uttarakhand																					4.12	4.12	4.19	4.19	3.22
Total India	**37.01**	**63.12**	**72.74**	**75.95**	**78.60**	**81.20**	**90.87**	**98.48**	**102.39**	**109.41**	**115.45**	**122.20**	**128.46**	**128.46**	**134.59**	**142.25**	**146.28**	**148.72**	**148.90**	**176.85**	**188.03**	**189.81**	**236.25**	**242.10**	**243.03**

Table 1.5A: All India area, production and yield of sugarcane alongwith coverage under irrigation

Area - million hectares, Production - million tons, Yield - kg/hectare

Year	*Area*	*Production*	*Yield*	*Area under irrigation (%)*
1	2	3	4	5
1950-51	1.71	57.05	33422	67.3
1951-52	1.94	61.63	31786	68.8
1952-53	1.73	51.00	29495	66.3
1953-54	1.41	44.41	31497	67.7
1954-55	1.62	58.74	36303	68.8
1955-56	1.85	60.54	32779	67.2
1956-57	2.05	69.05	33683	64.9
1957-58	2.07	71.16	34325	65.2
1958-59	1.95	73.36	37658	67.4
1959-60	2.14	77.82	36414	67.9
1960-61	2.42	110.00	45549	69.3
1961-62	2.46	103.97	42349	68.0
1962-63	2.24	91.91	40996	67.8
1963-64	2.25	104.23	46353	69.6
1964-65	2.60	121.91	46838	71.5
1965-66	2.84	123.99	43717	71.1
1966-67	2.30	92.83	40336	71.0
1967-68	2.05	95.50	40665	74.1
1968-69	2.53	124.68	49236	76.9
1969-70	2.75	135.02	49121	75.5
1970-71	2.62	126.37	48322	72.4
1971-72	2.39	113.57	47511	71.8
1972-73	2.45	124.87	50933	75.0
1973-74	2.75	140.81	51163	76.5
1974-75	2.89	144.29	49855	77.9
1975-76	2.76	140.60	50903	78.0
1976-77	2.87	153.01	53383	77.2
1977-78	3.15	176.97	56160	78.1
1978-79	3.09	151.66	49114	77.8
1979-80	2.61	128.83	49358	77.2
1980-81	2.67	154.25	57844	81.2
1981-82	3.19	186.36	58359	82.3
1982-83	3.36	189.51	56441	80.5

Table 1.5A: All India area, production and yield of sugarcane alongwith coverage under irrigation *(Contd.)*

Area - million hectares, Production - tons, Yield - kg/hectare

Year	*Area*	*Production*	*Yield*	*Area under irrigation (%)*
1	*2*	*3*	*4*	*5*
1983-84	3.11	174.08	55978	80.3
1984-85	2.95	170.32	57673	83.6
1985-86	2.85	170.65	59889	84.5
1986-87	3.08	186.09	60444	85.4
1987-88	3.28	196.74	60006	85.6
1988-89	3.33	203.04	60992	86.2
1989-90	3.44	225.57	65612	86.9
1990-91	3.69	241.05	65395	86.9
1991-92	3.84	254.00	66069	88.0
1992-93	3.57	228.03	63843	88.3
1993-94	3.42	229.66	67120	88.8
1994-95	3.87	275.54	71254	87.9
1995-96	4.15	281.10	67787	87.4
1996-97	4.17	277.56	66496	88.1
1997-98	3.93	279.54	71134	91.3
1998-99	4.05	288.72	71203	91.7
1999-2000	4.22	299.32	70935	92.0
2000-01	4.32	295.96	68577	92.1
2001-02	4.41	297.21	67370	91.6
2002-03	4.52	287.38	63576	91.3
2003-04	3.93	233.86	59380	90.7
2004-05	3.66	237.08	64752	91.2
2005-06	4.20	281.17	66928	92.5
2006-07	5.15	355.52	69022	93.2
2007-08	5.06	348.19	68877	93.5
2008-09	4.42	285.03	64553	NA
2009-10*	4.20	277.75	66099	NA
2010-11	4.86	324.91	66922	NA

* Fourth Advance Estimates as released on 19.07.2010.

Note: The yield rates given above have been worked out on the basis of production & area figures taken in '000 units.

Source: Directorate of Economics and Statistics, Department of Agriculture and Cooperation.

Table 1.6: Monthly releases of levy and free sugar

(th MT)

Year	Levy sugar	Free sugar	Total sugar	Year	Levy sugar	Free sugar	Total sugar	Year	Levy sugar	Free sugar	Total sugar	Year	Levy sugar	Free sugar	Total sugar
1980-81				*1989-90*				*1993-94*				*1997-98*			
Oct	2.69	1.68	4.37	Oct	4.32	6.00	10.32	Oct	3.92	7.00	10.92	Oct	4.16	9.00	13.16
Jan	2.71	1.00	3.71	Jan	3.32	5.00	8.32	Jan	3.51	5.75	9.26	Jan	4.00	7.25	11.25
Apr	2.57	1.25	3.82	Apr	3.32	6.00	9.32	Apr	3.31	5.45	8.76	Apr	3.71	7.25	10.96
Jul	2.37	1.80	4.17	Jul	3.32	6.00	9.32	Jul	3.36	6.00	9.36	Jul	3.71	7.50	11.21
Total	31.09	18.65	48.74	Total	41.34	70.25	111.59	Feb	42.05	71.15	113.20	Total	45.50	92.25	137.75
1986-87				*1990-91*				*1994-95*				*1998-99*			
Oct	3.63	4.50	8.13	Oct	3.33	6.25	9.58	Oct	3.80	7.00	10.80	Oct	4.08	8.30	12.38
Jan	3.13	4.00	7.13	Jan	3.33	5.75	9.08	Jan	3.78	5.75	9.53	Jan	3.72	7.50	11.22
Apr	3.32	4.20	7.52	Apr	3.33	5.50	8.83	Apr	3.37	6.30	9.67	Apr	3.71	7.25	10.96
Jul	3.32	4.30	7.62	Jul	3.33	6.25	9.58	Jul	3.41	6.90	10.31	Jul	3.72	8.00	11.69
Total	40.08	51.70	91.78	Total	40.15	71.85	112.00	Total	42.61	78.05	120.66	Total	45.30	93.30	138.23
1987-88				*1991-92*				*1995-96*				*1999-00*			
Oct	3.82	4.75	8.57	Oct	4.00	7.50	11.50	Oct	3.51	8.30	11.81	Oct	4.12	9.00	13.12
Jan	3.32	4.50	7.82	Jan	3.50	5.50	9.00	Jan	3.69	6.25	9.94	Jan	3.79	8.00	11.79
Mar	3.32	4.50	7.82	Apr	3.50	5.40	8.90	Apr	3.70	6.60	10.30	Apr	4.46	9.00	13.46
Jul	3.32	5.00	8.32	Jul	3.50	5.75	9.25	Jul	3.73	7.25	10.98	Jul	4.17	8.50	12.67
Total	40.34	56.15	96.49	Total	42.50	71.05	113.55	Total	45.16	85.10	130.26	Total	49.05	103.25	152.30
1988-89				*1992-93*				*1996-97*				*2000-01*			
Oct	3.82	5.35	9.17	Oct	3.50	7.35	10.85	Oct	3.69	8.50	12.19	Oct	4.57	10.50	15.07
Jan	3.32	5.00	8.32	Jan	3.50	5.35	8.85	Jan	4.11	6.50	10.61	Jan	4.25	8.25	12.5
Apr	3.32	4.50	7.82	Apr	3.50	6.50	10.00	Apr	3.70	7.00	10.70	Apr	2.16	10.50	12.66
Jul	3.32	5.00	8.32	Jul	3.50	6.30	9.80	Jul	3.74	7.50	11.24	Jul	2.16	10.50	12.66
Total	**40.84**	**61.15**	**101.99**	**Total**	**42.00**	**75.85**	**117.85**	**Total**	**46.59**	**90.50**	**137.00**	**Total**	**37.00**	**116.25**	**153.25**

Table 1.6: Monthly releases of levy and free sugar *(Contd.)*

(th MT)

Year	*Levy sugar*	*Free sugar*	*Total sugar*	*Year*	*Levy sugar*	*Free sugar*	*Total sugar*	*Year*	*Levy sugar*	*Free sugar*	*Total sugar*
2001-02				*2005-06*				*2009-10*			
Oct	2.43	12.50	14.93	Oct	1.96	14.00	15.96	Oct	2.35	18.50	20.85
Jan	2.26	9.00	29.26	Jan	1.83	12.50	14.33	Jan	2.09	14.30	16.39
Apr	2.17	10.00	32.17	Apr	1.61	15.75	17.36	Apr	2.02	18.00	20.02
Jul	2.16	9.50	11.66	Jul	1.55	12.00	13.55	July	2.15	14.50	16.65
Total	26.32	121.25	147.57	Total	19.77	161.25	181.02	Total	25.34	184.94	210.28
2002-03				*2006-07*				2010-11			
Oct	2.16	11.50	13.66	Oct	1.90	16.00	17.90	Oct	2.48	16.50	18.98
Jan	2.16	10.10	12.66	Jan	1.84	13.00	14.84	Jan	2.18	17.00	19.18
Apr	1.15	8.0	9.15	Apr	1.76	12.00	13.76	Apr	2.07	16.00	18.07
Jul	1.14	10.0	11.1	Jul	1.89	10.00	11.89	Jul	2.12	12.60	14.72
Total	20.5	112	132.5	Total	21.6	159.00	180.60	Total	25.99	181.70	207.69
2003-04				*2007-08*				2011-12			
Oct	2.28	11.50	13.78	Oct	2.28	16.00	18.28	Oct	2.47	17.50	19.97
Jan	1.92	10.50	12.42	Jan	1.95	14.00	15.95	Jan	2.16	14.00	16.16
Apr	2.18	14.00	16.18	Apr	1.87	17.00	18.86	Apr	2.82	15.00	17.82
Jul	2.18	13.00	15.18	Jul	1.93	120.00	13.93	Jul	2.80	17.22	20.02
Total	24.79	149.05	173.84	Total	23.44	165.00 [a]	188.4	Total	26.74	187.18	213.92
2004-05				*2008-09*				2012-13			
Oct	2.16	15.00	17.16	Oct	2.27	15.00	17.27	Oct	2.13	20.00	22.13
Jan	2.16	12.00	14.16	Jan	2.01	15.00	17.01	Jan	2.17	22.66	24.83
Apr	2.16	12.00	14.16	Apr	1.91	16.50	18.40	Apr	–	–	–
Jul	2.16	15.75	13.16	July	1.90	12.67	14.57	July	–	–	–
Total	25.69	146.25	171.69	Total	23.38	205.74*	229.12	Total	12.21	108.00	120.21

[a] Besides, a quantity of 27.5 lakh tonnes has been released by dismantling the buffer stock during May to September, 2008.

* Inclusive of 2.2 lakh tonnes out of buffer dismantling, 5.30 lakh tonnes Imported processed raw sugar and 1 lakh tonnes white imported sugar released during the season 2009-10.

Table 1.7: Wholesale free market prices of sugar*

(*Rs/qt*)

Year	*Market*	*Oct*	*Nov*	*Dec*	*Jan*	*Feb*	*Mar*	*Apr*	*May*	*Jun*	*Jul*	*Aug*	*Sep*
1975-76	Mumbai	448	430	443	431	406	424	445	436	460	481	496	480
	Kolkata	440	420	418	429	443	425	422	440	472	486	485	507
	Delhi	438	448	425	450	427	424	445	441	465	486	550	491
1980-81	Mumbai**		825	678	736	712	792	735	706	668	634	520	568
	Kolkata**			685	700	728	745		755	716	660	590	595
	Delhi**		875	725	730	735	785	755	740	710	625	590	590
1984-85	Mumbai	483	493	528	473	475	545	537	595	690	775	620	615
	Kolkata	527	537	541	505	515	552	585	613	670	772	675	615
	Delhi	480	480	490	480	500	520	550	580	660	760	660	630
1985-86	Mumbai	655	630	573	586	616	632	624	587	562	581	560	562
	Kolkata	660	640	630	610	610	600		595		610	610	608
	Delhi	640	650	575	605	605	600	620	625	610	600	580	615
1986-87	Mumbai	595	622	628	587	600	585	630	640	596	620	601	609
	Kolkata	620	620	620	624	624						632	607
	Delhi	600	590	605	610	590	590	600	590	600	620	595	595
1987-88	Mumbai	618	603	674	613	616	681	630	670	713	708	668	698
	Delhi	610		637	610	605	605	620	668	722	715	695	736
1989-90	Mumbai	893	895	788	822	807	831	773	813	775	796	826	788
	Kolkata			800	815	860	862	870	845	865	850	860	810
	Delhi				835	825	825	790	840	835	825	815	830
1990-91	Mumbai	783	780	782	850	773	798	847	844	874	865	840	878
	Kolkata	870	870	855	860	860	855	850	945	950	940	925	915
	Delhi	840	825	800	880	845	850	860	920	945	925	915	905
1991-92	Mumbai	827	780	790	852	840	822	900	897	898	915	932	921
	Kolkata	865	860	835	895	885	875	940	940	950	955	1000	990
	Delhi	860	850	790	840	830	855	900	905	960	960	950	935
1992-93	Mumbai	926	890	950	933	1060	1031	1131	1108	1040	1145	1030	@1095
	Kolkata	950	940		970	1000	980	1080	1130	1110	1150	1125	@1160
	Delhi	960	880	900	900	975	935	1020	1070	1065	1090	1090	@1130
1993-94	Mumbai	1140	1220	1285	1285	1295	1335	1440	1520	1430	1290	1368	1325
	Kolkata	1205	1240	1285	1270	1290	1320	1355	1550		1265	1360	1410
	Delhi	1130	1160	1285	1250	1250	1280	1425	1500	1450	1325	1400	1400

Table 1.7: Wholesale free market prices of sugar* *(Contd.)*

(Rs/qt)

Year	*Market*	*Oct*	*Nov*	*Dec*	*Jan*	*Feb*	*Mar*	*Apr*	*May*	*Jun*	*Jul*	*Aug*	*Sep*
1994-95	Mumbai	1261	1210	1217	1220	1210	1175	1240	1185	1210	1223	1240	1270
	Kolkata	1300		1220	1185	1225		1310	1300	1280	1240	1265	
	Delhi	1300	1230	1225	1220	1250	1270	1300	1310	1300	1290	1195	1400
1995-96	Mumbai	1290	1250	1251	1235	1270	1285	1315	1410	1265	1358	1362	1250
	Kolkata	1325	1325	1305	1370	1225	1330	1400	1450	1340	1550		
	Delhi	1370	1350	1290	1235	1250	1280	1340	1420	1290	1345	1375	1250
1996-97	Mumbai	1315	1235	1280	1230	1265	1290	1390	1418	1458	1480	1510	1463
	Kolkata	1380	1380	1280	1270	1340	1335	1480	1450	1490	1485	1515	1520
	Delhi	1310	1240	1290	1160	1220	1240	1370	1370	1420	1395	1440	1425
1997-98	Mumbai	1503		1465	1440	1435	1425	1570	1450	1458	1480	1415	1460
	Kolkata	1530	1515	1542	1535	1515	1495	1595	1582	1597	1560	1540	1510
	Delhi	1425	1425	1440	1420	1400	1400	1480	1480	1525	1535	1455	1490
1998-99	Mumbai	1471	1447	1468	1463	1423	1466	1485	1442	1420	1420	1421	1390
	Kolkata		1509	1508	1570	1552	1539	1370	1370	1420	1330	1418	1418
	Delhi	1545	1494	1467	1462	1461	1467	1535	1535	1500	1460	1505	1504
1999-00	Mumbai	1450	1385	1405	1330	1415	1480	1498	1405	1480	1490	1565	1490
	Kolkata	1375	1375	1395	1400	1403	1380	1440	1545	1550	1480	1525	1525
	Delhi	1400	1365	1365	1355	1345	1540	1565	1550	1570	1580	1660	1615
2000-01	Mumbai	1465	1425	1425	1375	1340	1440	1450	1430	1460	1412	1415	1413
	Kolkata	1525	1570	1450	1475	1475	1525	1440	1440	1420	1440	1440	1460
	Delhi	1510	1485	1450	1400	1400	1510	1500	1525	1525	1500	1500	1500
2001-02	Mumbai	1435	1410	1385	1382	1390	1413	1405	1333	1320	1310	1310	1295
	Kolkata	1460	1550	1495	1490	1490	1530	1513	1480	1450	1430	1425	
	Delhi	1540	1440	1420	1395	1425	1475	1430	1360	1340	1335	1330	1330
2002-03	Mumbai	1220	1171	1175	1171	1150	1160	1150	1147	1228	1375	1340	1336
	Kolkata				1290	1265	1275	1250	1280	1340	1420	1430	1450
	Delhi	1310	1300	1250	1240	1280	1260	1225	1230	1300	1400	1380	1410
2003-04	Mumbai	1341	1341	1286	1381	1350	1375	1500	1570	1550	1520	1574	1575
	Kolkata	1415	1415	1380	1405	1530	1470	1620	1630	1630	1630	1700	1695
	Delhi	1400	1400	1280	1380	1460	1470	1560	1575	1600	1595	1650	1630
2004-05	Mumbai	1580	1588	1879	1773	1750	1780	1777	1757	1744	1880	1837	1750
	Kolkata	1695	1695	1695	1828	1717	1800		1815	1825	1905	1895	1885
	Delhi	1630	1630	1925	1830	1850	1795	1750	1750	1800	1850	1810	1825

(Contd.)

Table 1.7: Wholesale free market prices of sugar*

(Rs/qt)

Year	*Market*	*Oct*	*Nov*	*Dec*	*Jan*	*Feb*	*Mar*	*Apr*	*May*	*Jun*	*Jul*	*Aug*	*Sep*
2005-06	Mumbai	1820	1830	1809	1891	1890	1828	1906	1898	1845	1845	1816	1780
	Kolkata	1935	1920	1880	2050	2030	1970	2060	2010	1970	1950	1880	1910
	Delhi	1870	1825	1830	2000	2000	1975	2000	1970	1885	1925	1870	1840
2006-07	Mumbai	1756	1700	1552	1490	1419	1490	1360	1295	1340	1331	1301	1335
	Kolkata	1910	1870	1775	1660	1555	1580	1475	1475	1490	1470	1495	1500
	Delhi	1800	1740	1700	1630	1500	1550	1440	1450	1435	1420	1415	1475
2007-08	Mumbai	1331	1340	1345	1410	1305	1505	1455	1442	1460	1639	1854	1735
	Kolkata	1480	1525	1525	1525	1525	1525	1525	1525	1525	1525	1525	1525
	Delhi	1510	1520	1450	1550	1515	1660	1600	1535	1525	1825	1900	1850
2008-09	Mumbai	1776	1818	1886	2041	2130	2113	2253	2385	2445	2450	2950	2930
	Kolkata	1525	1940	2070	2170	2240	2225	2276					
	Delhi	1800	1810	1965	2235	2280	2200	2425	2400	2475	2575	3000	2975
	Chennai	1797	1820	1950	2050	2200	2270	2180	2230	2360	2520	3035	2820
2009-10	Mumbai	3210	3450	3610	3880	3880	3120	2830	2720	2680	2700	2555	2625
	Kolkata	NA	3310	3750	3823	3300	3020	2830	2930	2860	2800	2730	2850
	Delhi	3200	3400	3850	4000	3520	3125	3000	2850	2800	2850	2725	2750
	Chennai	3100	3230	3700	3980	3500	3550	2830	2850	2750	2730	2660	2670
2010-11	Mumbai	2706	2961	2962	2850	2811	2781	2752	2681	2791	2771	2758	2768
	Kolkata	2850	3050	3200	2930	2928	2880	3000	2870	2870	2950	2950	2940
	Delhi	2800	3080	3100	2950	2965	3000	2940	2875	2830	2975	2950	2950
	Chennai	2750	3020	3050	2900	2925	2850	2950	2825	2850	2900	2925	2920
2011-12	Mumbai	2831	3126	2942	2872	2900	2860	2910	2922	2991	3482	3512	3600
	Kolkata	3100	3210	3000	2950	3000	2950	3100	3070	3220	3550	3630	3760
	Delhi	3075	3375	3200	3000	3000	3025	2940	3175	3125	3675	3575	3695
	Chennai	2950	–	2870	2880	2880	2850	2950	3000	3010	3600	3800	3700
2012-13	Mumbai	3442											
	Kolkata	3760											
	Delhi	3750											
	Chennai	–											

@ On 22 Sep 1992

* Prices are on Month-end basis.

** Sugar delivered to government at Rs 450/qtl

Table 1.8: Factory sugar – percentage of recovery from cane (year: November to October)

State	*1960-61*			*1961-62*			*1962-63*			*1963-64*			*1964-65*		
	Maximum	*Minimum*	*Average*	*Maximum*	*Minimum*	*Average*	*Maximum*	*Minimum*	*Average*	*Maximum*	*Minimum*	*Average*	*Maximum*	*Minimum*	*Average*
Uttar Pradesh	10.79	8.91	9.53	10.68	7.8	9.32	10.68	7.80	9.64	10.50	7.25	9.51	10.66	5.99	9.24
Bihar	9.94	8.60	9.22	10.23	8.34	9.12	10.35	8.90	9.71	10.65	9.24	10.02	10.35	8.89	9.44
Maharashtra	12.59	9.76	11.65	12.82	11.28	11.98	13.58	9.62	12.20	13.34	6.64	12.07	13.00	10.72	11.71
Gujarat	11.30	10.00	10.75	11.58	8.34	10.91	11.54	7.97	10.45	11.20	9.59	10.89	10.35	9.13	10.16
Andhra Pradesh	10.19	8.40	9.46	10.64	7.87	9.90	11.48	7.08	10.32	10.53	4.54	9.75	10.21	6.26	9.26
Madras	9.84	7.16	9.01	10.64	5.50	9.38	10.70	8.45	9.38	9.92	8.34	8.71	9.80	7.38	8.92
Punjab	9.47	8.78	8.93	9.01	7.86	8.23	9.22	6.94	8.97	9.04	7.75	8.67	8.90	8.01	8.49
Madhya Pradesh	11.09	9.03	9.25	9.97	8.88	9.41	9.94	9.22	9.62	9.51	9.32	9.46	9.60	8.66	9.00
Mysore	12.14	6.22	10.12	12.53	9.09	10.55	12.70	10.15	11.16	12.68	9.25	10.86	11.57	9.09	10.18
Rajasthan	9.53	8.81	9.19	10.27	8.46	9.30	10.30	8.64	9.46	8.36	8.23	8.30	9.54	8.00	8.94
Kerala	8.90	8.90	8.90	8.62	8.62	8.62	8.47	8.47	8.47	8.45	6.09	8.38	9.10	9.97	8.72
Orissa	9.12	9.12	9.12	8.69	8.69	8.69	8.81	8.81	8.81	8.75	7.54	8.26	8.54	8.26	8.39
West Bengal	9.85	9.60	9.66	10.36	9.66	10.18	9.55	8.94	9.44	9.60	8.67	9.54	9.39	9.39	9.39
Assam	7.89	7.89	7.89	8.60	8.60	8.60	9.69	9.69	9.69	9.17	9.17	9.17	9.07	9.07	9.07
Pondicherry	7.19	7.19	7.19	8.99	8.99	8.99	8.66	8.66	8.66	7.75	7.75	7.75	7.81	7.81	7.81
Total India	**12.59**	**6.22**	**9.74**	**12.82**	**5.50**	**9.77**	**13.58**	**6.94**	**10.28**	**13.34**	**4.54**	**10.00**	**13.00**	**5.99**	**9.66**

Table 1.8A: Number of mills of sugar by selected states

States	80-81	85-86	86-87	87-88	88-89	89-90	90-91	91-92	92-93	93-94	94-95	95-96	96-97	97-98	98-99	99-00	00-01	01-02	02-03	03-04	04-05	05-06	06-07	07-08	08-09	09-10	10-11	11-12
Andhra Pradesh	27	31	31	31	30	33	32	36	32	33	35	33	34	35	36	35	35	35	34	28	34	37	38	38	35	35	37	37
Bihar	28	23	26	27	27	28	28	25	25	23	18	19	19	11	11	10	10	10	10	10	9	9	9	8	9	9	10	11
Gujarat	13	13	12	11	11	14	14	14	14	14	16	16	17	18	17	18	17	15	17	15	17	17	18	18	18	18	19	19
Haryana							10	11	11	11	11	12	13	13	13	13	13	15	15	15	13	14	14	14	15	14	14	14
Karnataka	23	22	24	25	27	27	27	27	29	28	30	29	28	28	33	34	35	36	36	35	37	39	47	51	50	54	59	58
Maharashtra	77	88	91	90	95	96	97	99	99	97	107	109	105	95	119	123	137	135	156	138	102	142	163	172	147	143	167	170
Madhya Pradesh	7	8	8	8	8	8	8	8	8	8	9	8	7	7	7	7	8	8	6	6	7	7	8	8	9	11	13	13
Punjab	8	10	11	13	13	13	17	18	18	19	21	21	20	21	21	21	22	22	22	22	20	19	16	16	16	15	16	17
Rajasthan	3	3	3	13	2	2	3	3	3	3	3	3	3	3	3	2	2	2	1	1	1	1	1	1	1	1	1	1
Tamil Nadu*	21	24	25	25	27	30	31	33	34	34	34	36	36	37	38	39	37	36	37	35	35	36	39	39	38	42	46	45
Uttar Pradesh	90	100	101	103	103	104	105	105	107	109	109	116	117	120	115	109	100	100	101	101	106	114	133	132	132	128	125	124
Uttarakhand																	10	10	10	10	10	10	10	10	10	10	10	10
India	**314**	**341**	**353**	**356**	**366**	**377**	**385**	**392**	**393**	**394**	**408**	**416**	**412**	**400**	**400**	**423**	**436**	**434**	**453**	**423**	**400**	**453**	**504**	**516**	**488**	**490**	**527**	**529**

* Includes Pondicherry.

Table 1.9: Sectoral distribution of sugar mills

(Nos)

States	*1980-81*		*1985-86*		*1988-89*		*1990-91*		*1991-92*		*1992-93*		*1993-94*		*1994-95*		*1995-96*		*1996-97*		*1998-99*	
	Corp	*Coop*	*Corp*	*Coop*	*Corp*	*Coop*	*Corp*	*Coop*	*Corp*	*Coop*	*Corp*	*Coop*	*Corp*	*Coop*	*Corp*	*Coop*	*Corp*	*Coop*	*Corp*	*Coop*	*Corp*	*Coop*
Andhra Pradesh	15	12	15	18	13	17	16	18	19	18	19	18	19	18	19	16	18	15	18	15	22	18
Bihar	28	–	30	–	27	–	28	–	25	–	25	–	23	–	18	–	19	–	11	–	28	–
Gujarat	–	13	–	15	–	11	–	14	–	14	–	14	–	14	–	16	–	16	–	16	–	20
Karnataka	10	13	11	16	12	15	11	18	13	17	13	16	13	15	13	17	13	16	12	16	14	19
Maharashtra	10	67	11	80	4	91	6	95	5	94	4	95	3	94	3	104	3	106	–	106	5	116
Madhya Pradesh	5	2	5	3	5	3	5	3	5	3	5	3	5	3	6	3	5	3	4	3	6	3
Punjab	4	4	4	6	2	11	4	13	5	13	6	13	4	15	7	14	7	14	6	14	6	16
Rajasthan	2	1	2	1	2	1	2	1	2	1	2	1	2	1	2	1	2	1	2	1	2	1
Tamil Nadu	11	10	14	11	15	12	17	14	17	14	17	15	17	15	17	15	19	15	21	15	20	15
Uttar Pradesh	73	17	73	28	73	30	74	31	74	31	76	31	78	31	78	31	85	31	86	31	90	32
India	**166**	**148**	**173**	**187**	**159**	**207**	**174**	**229**	**181**	**229**	**189**	**240**	**189**	**237**	**189**	**240**	**184**	**232**	**180**	**232**	**206**	**259**

(Contd.)

Table 1.9: Sectoral distribution of sugar mills

(Nos)

States	1999-00		2000-01		2001-02		2002-03		2003-04		2004-05		2009-10		2009-10		2010-11		2011-12	
	Corp	Coop	Corp	Coop	Corp	Coop	Corp	Coop	Corp	Coop	Corp	Coop	Corp	Coop	Corp	Coop	Corp	Coop	Corp	Coop
Andhra Pradesh	23	18	23	18	23	18	25	11	27	15	27	15	28	15	28	15	28	15	29	15
Bihar	8	–	28	–	28	–	11	–	28	–	28	–	28		28		28		28	
Gujarat	–	22	–	22	–	22	–	19	–	22	–	22	1	22	2	23	2	23	23	2
Karnataka	18	19	19	19	22	19	21	21	25	22	26	22	40	24	39	24	39	24	43	24
Maharashtra	6	128	9	134	15	146	16	156	20	165	21	165	35	166	40	167	40	167	45	171
Madhya Pradesh	6	3	6	5	6	5	4	5	6	5	6	5	13	5	11	5	11	5	5	14
Punjab	6	16	6	16	6	17	7	15	7	16	7	16	7	16	8	16	8	16	8	16
Rajasthan	2	1	2	1	2	1	2	1	2	1	2	1	2	1	1	1	1	1	2	1
Tamil Nadu	22	15	21	16	22	16	22	16	22	16	22	16	29	16	26	16	26	16	30	16
Uttar Pradesh	96	32	97	32	91	28	76	27	92	28	94	28	128	28	129	28	129	28	129	28
India	220	273	224	282	234	297	200	296	248	316	248	316	331	320	279	325	279	325	353	328

Corp corporate sector including public sector.

Table 1.10: Capacity and production of cooperative sugar factories by states

States	Units in operation (nos)									
	96-97	97-98	98-99	99-00	00-01	01-02	02-03	03-04	04-05	05-06
Andhra Pradesh	34	35	36	35	35	35	34	28	34	37
Gujarat	17	18	17	18	17	15	17	15	17	17
Haryana	13	13	13	13	13	15	15	15	13	14
Karnataka	28	28	33	34	35	36	36	35	37	39
Madhya Pradesh	7	7	7	7	8	8	6	6	7	7
Maharashtra	106	95	119	123	137	135	156	138	102	142
Orissa	7	7	7	7	4	4	4	4	6	5
Punjab	20	21	21	21	22	22	22	22	20	19
Rajasthan	3	3	3	2	1	1	1	1	1	1
Tamil Nadu	34	35	36	37	37	36	35	34	34	35
Uttar Pradesh	117	120	115	109	100	100	101	101	106	114
Goa	1	1	1	1	1	1	1	1	1	1
Pondicherry	2	2	2	2	2	2	2	1	1	1
Total (All India)	**412**	**400**	**426**	**423**	**436**	**434**	**453**	**423**	**400**	**432**

States	Cane crushed (lakh MT)									
	96-97	97-98	98-99	99-00	00-01	01-02	02-03	03-04	04-05	05-06
Andhra Pradesh	75.6	83.2	114.8	117.2	98.7	104.7	119.8	86	92.2	123
Gujarat	90.2	83.1	98.8	100.7	102.9	97.8	118.3	97.5	74.1	107.9
Haryana	55.5	41.3	45.9	51.5	59.8	62.7	62.8	55.6	39.4	41.9
Karnataka	82.7	91.4	131.1	148.1	149.3	144.5	173	109.4	102.8	179.5
Madhya Pradesh	8.9	6.9	9.2	10.4	10.1	7.2	7.2	9.2	7.3	96.0
Maharashtra	310.2	345.8	479.0	571.0	576.4	483.9	534.0	290.8	194.6	445.8
Orissa	8.6	6.6	8.5	6.3	3.6	2.8	4.3	4.5	4.7	4.4
Punjab	69.2	36.6	36.7	46.2	51.1	62.8	60.4	40.0	32.2	36.8
Rajasthan	2.7	3.1	2.9	1.8	0.7	0.5	0.2	1.0	0.5	0.8
Tamil Nadu	117.5	145.9	195.9	186.9	184.8	191.4	166.5	92.8	114.9	231.9
Uttar Pradesh	436.3	409.1	412.7	487.9	451.4	552.1	592.7	463.5	514.7	608.1
Goa	1.4	1.1	2.0	1.5	1.6	1.0	1.4	1.1	0.9	1.2
Pondicherry	3.9	4.9	5.9	6.3	4.6	4.6	3.5	2.1	1.9	3.7
Total (All India)	**1304**	**1292**	**1576**	**1785**	**1767**	**1803**	**1943**	**1325**	**1780**	**1881**

States	Sugar produced (lakh MT)									
	96-97	97-98	98-99	99-00	00-01	01-02	02-03	03-04	04-05	05-06
Andhra Pradesh	7.7	7.8	11.1	11.8	10.2	10.5	12.1	8.9	9.8	12.3
Gujarat	9.7	8.9	10.2	11.4	10.7	10.6	12.5	10.7	8	11.7
Haryana	4.9	3.8	4.0	4.8	5.9	6.2	6.4	5.8	4	4.1
Karnataka	8.7	9.6	13.7	15.8	16.0	15.5	18.7	11.2	10.4	19.4
Madhya Pradesh	0.9	0.7	0.8	1.0	0.9	0.7	0.7	0.9	0.7	0.9
Maharashtra	34.4	38.5	53.4	65.0	67.0	56.1	62.1	31.8	22.2	52.0
Orissa	0.8	0.6	0.7	0.5	0.3	0.2	0.4	0.4	0.4	0.4
Punjab	6.1	3.3	3.1	4.2	5.0	5.9	5.9	3.9	3.1	3.3
Rajasthan	0.2	0.3	0.2	0.1	neg	neg	neg	neg	neg	0.06
Tamil Nadu	10.5	12.2	17.3	17.2	17.8	18.4	16.4	9.2	11.1	21.4
Uttar Pradesh	40.8	39.2	37.3	45.6	43.9	52.6	56.5	45.5	50.4	57.8
Goa	0.1	0.1	0.2	0.1	0.2	neg	0.1	0.1	0.1	0.1
Pondicherry	0.3	0.4	0.4	0.5	0.4	0.4	0.3	0.2	0.2	0.3
Total (All India)	**129**	**129**	**155**	**182**	**185**	**185**	**201**	**136**	**127**	**126**

Neg, negligible lakh 0.1 mn or 10^5.

Table 1.10A: Palm gur production

State	*1960–1961*	*1961–1962*	*1962–1963*	*1963–1964*	*1964–1965*
Andhra Pradesh	8	7	4	2	8
Kerala	20	8	7	7	11
Tamil Nadu	23	24	27	58	52
Mysore	7	6	6	7	6
Orissa	1	1	1	1	1
West Bengal	20	18	19	4	6
Total	**79**	**64**	**66**	**80**	**85**

Note: Total is used on actual figures.
Source: Palm Gur adviser to the government of India.

Drought in Maharashtra in 2012–2013, the country's one of the biggest sugar producing state, is likely to pull down India's overall production in the 2013–2014 sugar season to 23.7 million tons (a fall of 5% as compared to last year). In Maharashtra, sugarcane acreage is expected to fall by 12.5% in 2013–2014. This would be on top of the decline of 8% in the acreage in sugarcane in Maharashtra in 2012–2013 as it has experienced successive droughts. Sowing in 2013–2014 is also down by almost 16% in Tamil Nadu and 8% in Karnataka due to low rainfall. The drought last year in Maharashtra and other tropical regions has focused attention on the need to align sugarcane cultivation with availability and management of water in the country.

In Maharashtra, sugarcane is irrigated mainly through a canal network of dams as compared to by large rivers and higher assured rainfall in UP. Nearly 80% of Maharashtra's sugarcane is grown in acutely water-scarce areas. In Maharashtra, sugarcane cultivation, which is on less than 4% of the total cropped area of the state, takes away almost 70% of irrigation water in the state. Usage of total irrigated water by sugarcane in Maharashtra is as in Table 1.13. Total requirement of water per hectare is the highest for sugarcane. Sugarcane productivity adjusted to crop duration is as in Table 1.14. Leading to massive inequity in the use of water within the state, although the recovery rate (sugar produced after crushing 1 ton of sugarcane) is higher in Maharashtra compared to Uttar Pradesh, productivity of sugarcane in Maharashtra in terms of water usage is almost one-third. For a large scale, sustainable development of sugarcane and sugar industry, it is necessary to see that it is developed in areas which have ample water supplies, and in others like Maharashtra and Karnataka, farmers adopt irrigation technologies and farming practices that save on water. Sugarcane being a water-intensive crop, one will have to give special attention to the availability and cost of that water to remain globally competitive. Unfortunately, the current policy regime for the sugar sector does not seem to be conducive to this, and it would be a major challenge to overhaul such policies.

Table 1.11: Sugar recovery and crushing duration

State	*1970-71*	*80-81*	*84-85*	*85-86*	*86-87*	*87-88*	*88-89*	*89-90*	*90-91*	*91-92*	*92-93*	*93-94*	*94-95*	*95-96*	*96-97*	*97-98*	*98-99*	*99-00*	*00-01*	*01-02*	*02-03*	*03-04*	*04-05*	*05-06*	*06-07*	*07-08*	*08-09*	*09-10*	*10-11*	*11-12 (P)*
A. Average crushing period (days)																														
Andhra Pradesh	100	73	78	88	120	127	106	108	147	150	91	107	149	136	111	111	142	142	114	119	130	106	97	124	173	127	72	63	106	113
Bihar	116	68	53	94	102	103	101	99	115	147	82	58	123	105	90	104	108	130	103	116	125	81	82	126	145	93	59	66	96	97
Gujarat	100	140	125	154	171	202	169	166	203	162	144	148	117	203	157	131	160	169	149	152	172	151	105	150	202	187	125	150	175	137
Karnataka	129	99	96	107	129	148	134	134	155	177	132	127	182	199	130	126	171	174	159	145	158	110	99	152	187	178	96	126	169	152
Maharashtra	164	147	144	133	127	157	135	200	193	176	136	109	180	199	123	138	162	176	150	127	123	77	66	107	176	162	89	143	164	147
Madhya Pradesh	115	39	69	63	100	120	80	89	129	167	70	45	75	137	97	73	95	103	103	64	69	79	70	77	135	116	44	55	79	74
Punjab	106	74	127	132	182	128	136	145	129	129	129	91	90	178	177	87	84	105	118	147	139	90	64	78	118	136	66	54	77	102
Rajasthan	66	54	70	54	88	46	50	80	99	136	82	64	72	117	91	99	97	94	71	61	28	111	62	90	90	103	51	60	60	39
Tamil Nadu	192	142	156	192	184	182	191	175	207	205	154	171	290	249	141	172	207	185	180	194	173	111	143	234	267	214	165	148	178	172
Uttar Pradesh	148	102	102	107	166	181	138	182	160	189	129	118	148	184	142	120	117	134	129	153	161	113	117	124	158	120	72	84	103	124
All India	**142**	**105**	**107**	**116**	**141**	**153**	**133**	**158**	**166**	**173**	**123**	**111**	**161**	**181**	**130**	**123**	**141**	**152**	**139**	**140**	**141**	**100**	**96**	**126**	**174**	**149**	**87**	**108**	**136**	**137**

(Contd.)

Table 1.11: Sugar recovery and crushing duration

State	1970-71	80-81	84-85	85-86	86-87	87-88	88-89	89-90	90-91	91-92	92-93	93-94	94-95	95-96	96-97	97-98	98-99	99-00	00-01	01-02	02-03	03-04	04-05	05-06	06-07	07-08	08-09	09-10	10-11	11-12 (P)
B. Average sugar recovery (%)																														
Andhra Pradesh	10.21	9.14	9.41	9.60	9.36	9.17	10.03	9.99	9.61	9.97	10.18	9.87	9.43	9.51	10.22	9.40	9.70	10.09	10.04	10.01	10.10	10.32	10.65	10.05	9.71	10.12	9.89	9.28	9.75	9.79
Bihar	9.01	0.17	9.44	9.48	9.22	8.97	9.16	8.99	9.07	8.72	9.37	9.19	9.10	8.81	9.23	9.49	8.54	9.20	9.11	8.78	9.00	9.33	9.58	9.48	8.67	9.24	9.04	9.49	9.30	9.45
Gujarat	10.22	9.95	10.84	10.97	10.91	10.22	11.47	10.96	10.91	11.14	11.34	11.09	11.65	10.48	10.72	10.72	10.37	10.11	10.42	10.79	10.58	10.93	10.76	10.82	10.65	10.67	10.72	10.53	9.99	10.61
Karnataka	10.56	10.36	10.41	10.44	10.23	10.13	10.51	10.38	10.25	10.50	10.65	10.48	10.30	9.80	10.54	10.50	10.50	10.64	10.76	10.23	10.82	10.21	10.11	10.83	10.61	10.89	10.28	10.67	10.91	11.14
Maharashtra	11.25	11.07	11.10	11.21	10.98	10.83	11.04	10.71	10.76	11.19	11.32	11.12	10.92	10.48	11.11	11.13	11.16	11.39	11.64	11.64	11.65	10.93	11.39	11.66	11.40	11.92	11.44	11.51	11.26	11.65
Madhya Pradesh	9.29	8.40	9.32	8.97	9.20	9.30	9.56	9.78	10.01	9.65	9.87	9.21	9.55	9.11	9.75	9.89	8.98	9.90	9.26	9.89	9.90	10.15	9.80	9.76	9.43	9.54	9.63	9.40	9.66	9.38
Punjab	8.57	8.78	10.63	9.78	9.69	10.18	9.61	9.13	8.95	9.23	9.39	9.26	9.13	8.68	8.86	9.05	8.49	9.10	9.70	9.45	9.72	9.72	9.79	9.18	9.55	9.26	9.29	8.59	8.80	9.13
Rajasthan	9.23	9.49	9.85	9.32	8.99	8.35	8.86	9.24	8.44	8.74	9.44	8.58	9.06	8.91	8.76	9.55	7.99	7.56	8.76	9.45	8.43	9.53	7.64	6.85	9.04	7.05	8.82	7.80	7.73	7.66
Tamil Nadu	8.99	9.69	9.54	9.56	9.55	8.18	10.08	9.37	9.11	9.33	9.41	8.96	8.68	8.33	8.94	8.42	8.83	9.21	9.64	9.61	9.88	9.92	9.64	9.24	9.25	9.32	9.62	8.97	9.09	9.33
Uttar Pradesh	9.17	9.43	9.55	9.57	9.45	8.92	9.49	8.84	9.02	9.24	9.64	9.32	9.41	8.68	9.34	9.56	9.01	9.36	9.73	9.50	9.29	9.56	9.58	11.85	9.42	9.94	8.94	9.13	9.14	9.07
All India	**9.78**	**9.98**	**10.24**	**10.23**	**9.98**	**9.70**	**10.21**	**9.89**	**9.85**	**10.02**	**10.31**	**10.00**	**9.92**	**9.42**	**9.90**	**9.95**	**9.87**	**10.20**	**10.48**	**10.27**	**10.36**	**10.22**	**10.17**	**10.22**	**10.17**	**10.55**	**10.03**	**10.20**	**10.17**	**10.25**

P = Provisional.

Table 1.12: Production and consumption of sugarcane by states

(Lakh or 0.1 mn MT)

State	1970-71	80-81	84-85	85-86	86-87	87-88	88-89	89-90	90-91	91-92	92-93	93-94	94-95	95-96	96-97	97-98	98-99	99-00	00-01	01-02	02-03	03-04	04-05	05-06	06-07	07-08	08-09	09-10	10-11	11-12
A. Production																														
Andhra Pradesh	91	101	98	97	88	94	116	111	127	151	122	137	161	152	180	140	165	187	177	180	154	151	157	177	217	203	154	117	150	167
Bihar	62	35	37	40	36	45	54	66	78	71	60	44	57	55	58	50	51	40	40	52	46	43	41	43	60	39	50	50	128	121
Gujarat	19	44	76	65	56	60	79	91	106	102	109	102	108	105	114	118	136	141	127	125	141	127	146	146	156	152	155	124	138	142
Karnataka	85	124	134	138	140	175	184	212	210	241	225	209	331	249	233	283	347	365	432	330	325	160	143	183	287	262	233	304	396	388
Maharashtra	148	236	264	237	209	249	255	340	384	362	309	279	443	467	418	382	472	531	502	451	426	257	205	389	786	884	606	602	819	819
Madhya Pradesh	16	11	14	12	18	16	22	13	14	16	13	17	14	19	17	16	16	21	22	16	16	19	21	24	28	32	30	24	27	27
Punjab	53	39	49	51	61	58	55	65	60	69	64	47	52	86	110	72	61	68	78	92	93	66	52	49	60	67	47	37	42	47
Rajasthan	12	12	14	10	13	9	6	7	12	14	11	10	10	14	13	12	11	8	6	4	4	3	3	5	6	6	4	3	4	4
Tamil Nadu	104	186	176	200	216	210	240	233	237	252	233	277	365	329	259	302	337	351	341	326	242	177	234	351	411	381	328	298	342	393
Uttar Pradesh	547	642	717	738	860	930	893	974	1,036	1,111	1,029	1,048	1,102	1,198	1,253	1,293	1,165	1,154	1,066	1,180	1,221	1,128	1,187	1,255	1339	1247	1090	1171	1205	1288
Uttarakhand																			74	75	73	76	64	61	61	77	56	58	65	66
All India	**1,264**	**1,542**	**1,703**	**1,706**	**1,825**	**1,967**	**2,046**	**2,255**	**2,410**	**2,540**	**2,280**	**2,271**	**2,755**	**2,811**	**2,775**	**2,795**	**2,887**	**2,992**	**2,960**	**2,972**	**2,874**	**2,339**	**2,371**	**2,812**	**3,556**	**3,482**	**2,850**	**2,923**	**3,424**	**3577**

(Contd.)

Table 1.12: Production and consumption of sugarcane by states

(Lakh or 0.1 mn MT)

State	1970-71	80-81	84-85	85-86	86-87	87-88	88-89	89-90	90-91	91-92	92-93	93-94	94-95	95-96	96-97	97-98	98-99	99-00	00-01	01-02	02-03	03-04	04-05	05-06	06-07	07-08	08-09	09-10	10-11	11-12
B. Consumption by sugar mills																														
Andhra Pradesh	26	28	38	42	57	59	51	57	73	85	53	65	93	90	76	83	115	117	102	105	119	86	92	123	173	132	60	55	103	116
Bihar	32	21	15	26	32	35	35	37	46	53	35	25	43	43	39	32	30	40	29	34	45	29	26	44	52	36	24	27	41	48
Gujarat	8	33	37	51	53	57	50	60	76	68	66	74	65	108	90	83	100	107	107	106	118	98	74	108	134	128	94	113	124	94
Karnataka	19	36	42	49	60	74	67	76	92	98	80	79	119	129	83	91	131	148	160	155	173	109	103	179	252	267	161	240	338	348
Maharashtra	94	189	209	213	218	258	238	366	383	377	297	247	460	515	310	346	479	571	670	561	534	291	195	446	798	761	400	614	802	771
Madhya Pradesh	4	2	5	5	8	9	7	7	10	13	6	4	7	14	9	7	9	10	9	7	7	9	7	10	19	18	6	9	17	16
Punjab	6	6	13	15	24	20	25	32	31	42	43	34	35	73	69	37	37	46	50	59	60	40	32	37	51	58	26	21	34	43
Tamil Nadu	33	50	66	91	85	91	105	95	130	135	104	121	214	194	117	146	196	187	178	184	166	93	115	232	275	230	166	143	203	255
Uttar Pradesh	142	129	154	172	271	350	243	333	328	398	296	290	383	503	436	409	413	488	439	570	593	464	514	608	895	747	455	567	644	769
Uttarakhand																				47	52	40	40	45	56	41	24	32	32	36
All India	**382**	**516**	**601**	**686**	**852**	**939**	**856**	**1,111**	**1,223**	**1,340**	**1,300**	**983**	**1,476**	**1,748**	**1,304**	**1,292**	**1,576**	**1,785**	**1,767**	**1,767**	**1,803**	**1,943**	**1,248**	**1,887**	**2,792**	**2,499**	**1,450**	**1,855**	**2,398**	**2,570**

Table 1.13: Usage of total irrigation water by sugarcane in Maharashtra

Major crops	*Area under the crop (lakh hectares)*	*Share in GCA (%)*	*Irrigated area under the crop (lakh hectares)*	*Area irrigated under the crop %*	*Number of irrigations of 7.5 cm each*	*Total water requirement per hectare* (lakh liters)*	*Total water usage (lakh liter/hectare)*	*Share of the cropin total water usage (%)*
		*(3)=(2)*100/ total GCA*		*(5)=(4)* 100/(2)*		*(7)=(6)*7.5*	*(8)=(7)*(4)*	*(9)=(8)*100/ water usage total*
Rice	15.2	6.3	4.0	26.1	5	37.5	148.5	5.9
Jowar	40.6	16.9	3.9	9.5	3	22.5	87.1	3.4
Wheat	13.1	5.4	9.7	73.9	4	30.0	289.8	11.5
Other cereals	21.1	8.7	1.7	7.8	3	22.5	37.1	1.5
Sugarcane	**9.7**	4.0	**9.7**	**100.0**	**25**	**187.5**	**1,809.4**	**71.5**
Cotton	39.4	16.4	1.1	2.7	6	45.0	48.2	1.9
Pulses	40.4	16.8	3.8	9.4	3	22.5	85.7	3.4
Oil seeds	36.5	15.2	1.5	4.0	3	22.5	33.1	1.3

Notes:
1. The figures are for the year 2010–2011 which is the latest available.
2. 1 hectare = 10,000 square meter. For 1 cm (0.01 m) height, the volume of water required for 1 hectare would be 100 cubic meter. As 1 cubic metre of water = 1,000 liters, 1 hectare would require 1 lakh liters of water for 1 cm height.
3. The number of irrigations per crop is assumed as an average indicative figure.
4. The gross cropped area in 2010–2011 in Maharashtra was 240.69 lakh hectares.
5. Area under fruits and vegetables has not been accounted for, but since quite a bit of area under fruits (especially banana is under drip irrigation, results may not change much. The share of sugarcane may come down to roughly 66% (two-thirds).

Source: Land Use Statistics, DES.

Table 1.14: Sugarcane productivity adjusted for crop duration, recovery rates and water requirements: cases of Bihar, Karnataka, Maharashtra, Tamil Nadu and UP, 2012-13

State/variety of cane	*Crop duration (months)*	*Area (lakh hectare)*	*Relative area (% share)*	*No. of standard irrigations of 7.5 cm each) per hectare*	*Water requirements (lakh liters of irrigation) per ha. (7.5 times no. of standard irrigations)*	*Land productivity (Q./ha.)*	*Production (lakh Mt.)*	*Relative prod. (% share)*	*Normalizing land productivity for crop duration (Q/ha* month) col. (8) col. (3)*	*Normalizing land productivity for crop duration (Q/ha* month* lakh liters) col. (11) col. (7)*	*Recovery rate (%)*	*Production of sugar (Q/ha.) col. (8) *col. (13)/100*	*Water requirement (liters) of cane for production of 1 kg of sugar col. (7)/col. (14*) 100000/100*
Bihar	12.0	2.5	100.0	5.0	37.5	518.0	130.8	100.0	43.2	1.2	8.9	46.2	812
Karnataka													
Co86032	12.0	1.8	42.4	35.0	262.5	800.0	141.6	40.4	66.7	0.3	11.0	88.0	2983
Co62175	12.0	1.0	23.3	35.0	262.5	950.0	92.2	26.3	79.2	0.3	9.0	85.5	3070
CoC671	10.0	0.5	10.8	30.0	225.0	800.0	36.0	10.3	80.0	0.4	11.5	92.0	2446
Co8011	12.0	0.3	7.2	30.0	225.0	800.0	24.0	6.8	66.7	0.3	10.5	84.0	2679
Co91010	12.0	0.2	3.6	35.0	262.5	900.0	13.5	3.9	75.0	0.3	10.5	94.5	2778
Co740	12.0	0.2	3.6	35.0	262.5	800.0	12.0	3.4	66.7	0.3	10.0	80.0	3281
others	12.0	0.4	9.1	35.0	262.5	824.7	31.3	8.9	68.7	0.3	10.0	82.5	3183
Total/weighted average	11.8	4.2	100.0	34.1	255.8	840.7	350.6	100.0	71.3	0.3	10.3	87.0	2940
Maharashtra													
Adsali	17.0	0.6	6.7	32.5	243.8	965.4	60.5	10.0	56.8	0.2	12.3	118.7	2053
Preseasonal	14.5	2.5	26.7	27.5	206.3	729	181.5	30.0	50.1	0.2	12.0	87.1	2368
Suru	12.0	1.9	20.4	22.5	168.8	633.4	121.0	20.0	52.8	0.3	11.5	72.5	2327
Ratoon	11.0	4.3	46.2	22.5	168.8	558.4	241.9	40.0	50.8	0.3	10.5	58.6	2878
Total/weighted average	**12.5**	**9.4**	**100.0**	**24.5**	**183.8**	**645.6**	**604.9**	**100.0**	**51.5**	**0.3**	**11.3**	**73.1**	**2515**

Table 1.14: Sugarcane productivity adjusted for crop duration, recovery rates and water requirements: cases of Bihar, Karnataka, Maharashtra, Tamil Nadu and UP, 2012-13 *(Contd.)*

State/variety of cane	*Crop duration (months)*	*Area (lakh hectare)*	*Relative area (% share)*	*No. of standard irrigations of 7.5 cm each) per hectare*	*Water requirements (lakh liters of irrigation) per ha. (7.5 times no. of standard irrigations)*	*Land productivity (Q./ha.)*	*Production (lakh Mt.)*	*Relative prod. (% share)*	*Normalizing land productivity for crop duration (Q/ha* month) col. (8) col. (3)*	*Normalizing land productivity for crop duration (Q/ha* month* lakh liters) col. (11) col. (7)*	*Recovery rate (%)*	*Production of sugar (Q/ha.) col. (8) *col. (13)/100*	*Water requirement (liters) of cane for production of 1 kg of sugar col. (7)/col. (14*) 100000/100*
Tamil Nadu													
Co 86032 (E)	11.0	3.3	85.0	40.0	300.0	972.4	324.8	81.9	88.4	0.3	9.62	93.5	3207
Co 99004 (E)	11.0	0.2	4.0	40.0	300.0	1272.3	20.0	5.0	115.7	0.4	9.32	118.6	2530
Co 99006 (ML)	11.0	0.1	2.0	40.0	300.0	1272.3	10.0	2.5	115.7	0.4	9.38	119.3	2514
CoC 24 (ML)	10.0	0.1	3.0	35.0	262.5	1017.8	12.0	3.0	101.8	0.4	9.35	95.2	2758
CoSi 7 (E)	10.0	0.1	2.0	35.0	262.5	1526.7	12.0	3.0	152.7	0.6	9.56	146.0	1799
CoG 5 (E)	10.0	0.1	2.0	35.0	262.5	1145.0	9.0	2.3	114.5	0.4	9.29	106.4	2468
Co 94008 (ML)	10.0	0.1	2.0	35.0	262.5	1159.8	9.0	2.3	116.0	0.4	9.54	110.6	2372
Total/weighted average	**10.9**	**3.9**	**100.0**	**39.6**	**296.6**	**1010.0**	**396.8**	**100.0**	**92.6**	**0.3**	**9.58**	**96.8**	**3066**
UP													
Plantation	10.0	10.7	48.3	8.0	60.0	597.0	638.1	48.9	59.7	1.0	9.5	56.7	1058
Ratoon	9.0	11.4	51.7	7.0	52.5	583.5	666.9	51.1	64.8	1.2	8.7	50.5	1040
Total/weighted average	**9.5**	**22.1**	**100.0**	**7.5**	**56.1**	**590.0**	**1305.1**	**100.0**	**62.2**	**1.1**	**9.1**	**53.5**	**1049**

Assuming a normal monsoon and favorable weather, MY 2013/14 sugarcane planting is forecast at 5.35 million hectares, marginally higher than last year. In April 2013, the Government of India (GOI) abolished the sugar levy on mills and deregulated sale of sugar in the open market. The policy change (discussed in detail in the policy section) will help mills increase revenues and ensure timely payment to cane farmers which should encourage higher planting in MY 2013/14.

Despite higher plantings, total sugarcane production is likely to decline slightly in MY 2013/14 to 355 million tons. Cane yields in Maharashtra, India's leading sugar producing state, are unlikely to recover from last year's drought. An expected larger proportion of retune crop will reduce Maharashtra's sugarcane yields, and as a result, Indian average cane yields will shrink over last year.

India's total centrifugal sugar production for MY 2013/14 is forecast at 25.3 million tons (includes 497,000 tons of khandsari—a low recovery sugar prepared by an open-pan evaporation method). The forecast 8% decline in production over last year is mostly due to a larger diversion of cane for gur production as gur prices are expected to remain relatively strong compared to sugar prices in MY 2013/14. *Gur* (crude non-centrifugal lump sugar) production is forecast higher at 7.24 million tons compared to 5.8 million tons in MY 2012/13.

Post anticipates MY 2012/13 sugarcane production at a record 360 million tons due to higher than expected cane planting, particularly in Uttar Pradesh. However, lower sugar recovery in the drought affected state of Maharashtra is likely to bring down India's average sugar recovery to 10.5% compared to last year's 10.8%. Consequently, MY 2012/13 sugar production is estimated at 27.4 million tons, down 4% compared to last year.

The recent weakening of gur prices vis-à-vis sugar and relatively strong cane prices paid by sugar mills limited sugarcane diversion for gur production during the peak crushing season. MY 2012/13 mill sugar production as of March 15, 2013

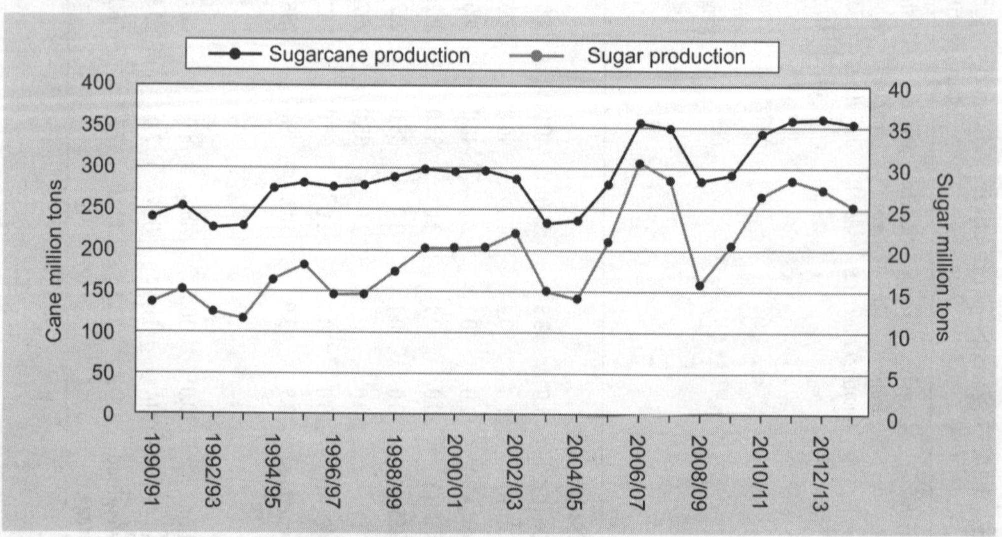

India: Sugarcane and sugar production

Source: Industry and trade sources.

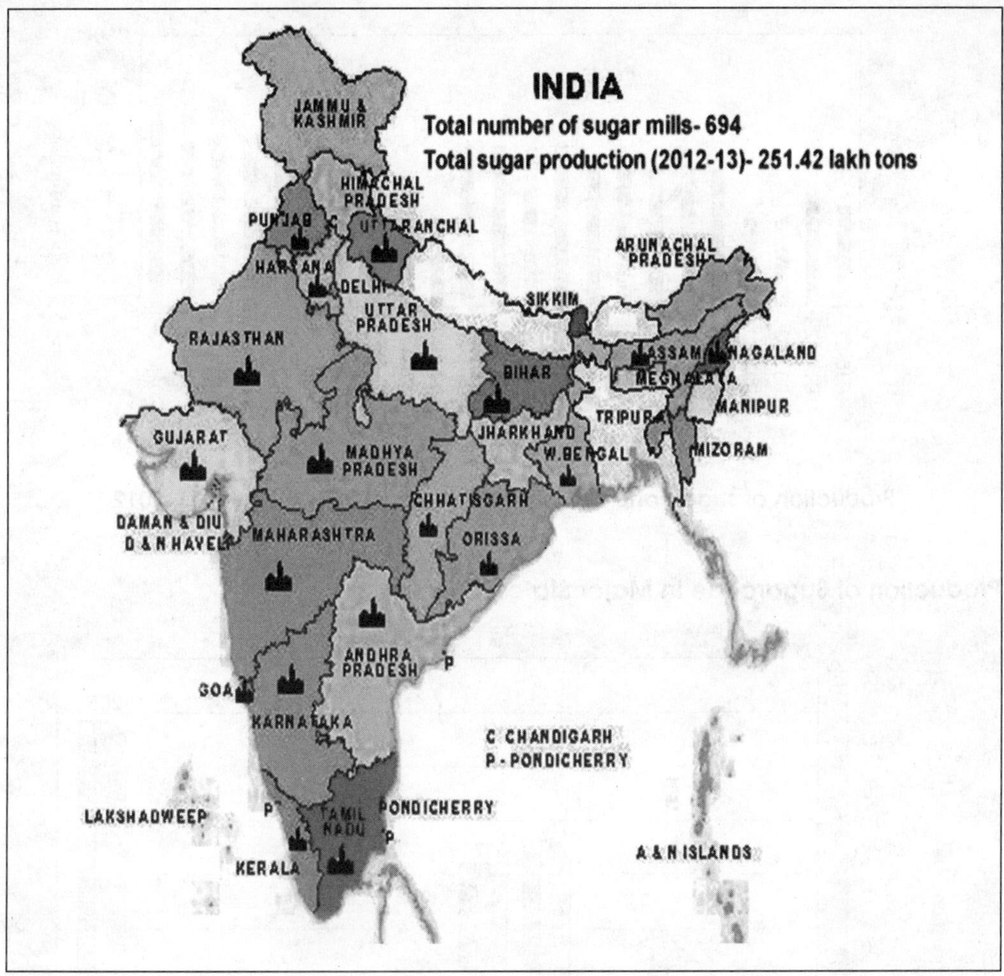

is estimated at 21.05 million tons (crystal weight basis), compared to 21.25 million tons for the corresponding period.

Consumption of sugarcane by the sugar mills (Table 1.6) shows that at the all India level it increased from 38.2 million tons in 1970–1971 to 122.3 million tons 1990–1991 and 257.0 million tons in 2011–2012. While UP is the top consumer followed by Maharashtra during 1994–1995 and 1995–1996 consumption of cane by the sugar mills was the highest in Maharashtra.

It is interesting to note from the chart that sugar and cane production have a cyclical behavior with 2–3 years upswing followed by 2 years downswing. This has happened in the past despite the fact that this sector has been heavily regulated by the government in terms of levy of sugar, monthly releases of non-levy sugar, imports and exports, and pricing of cane, etc. This causes uncertainty to farmers and millers alike with an adverse effect on fresh investments in the sector. A close look at below chart shows that the peak for the latest upward cycle was achieved in 2011–2012 and the downward cycle may be imminent.

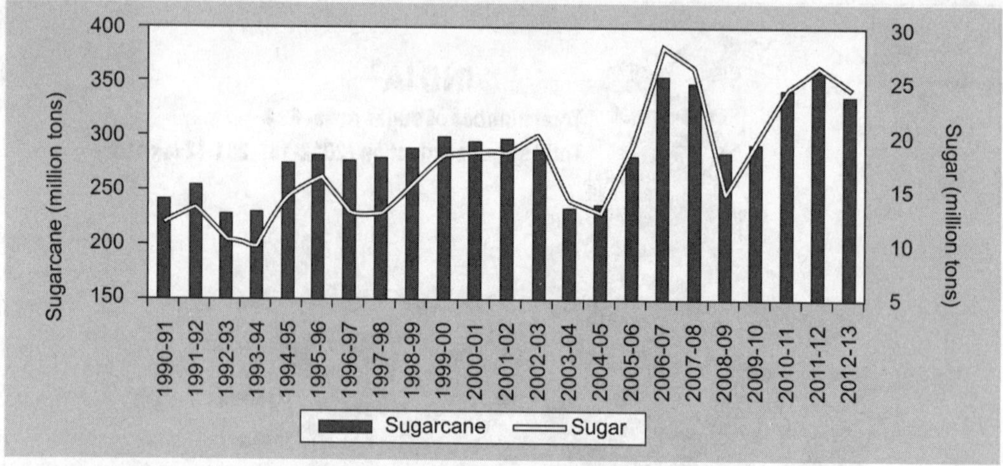

Production of sugarcane and sugar in India: 1990–1991 to 2011–2012

Production of Sugarcane in Major States of India

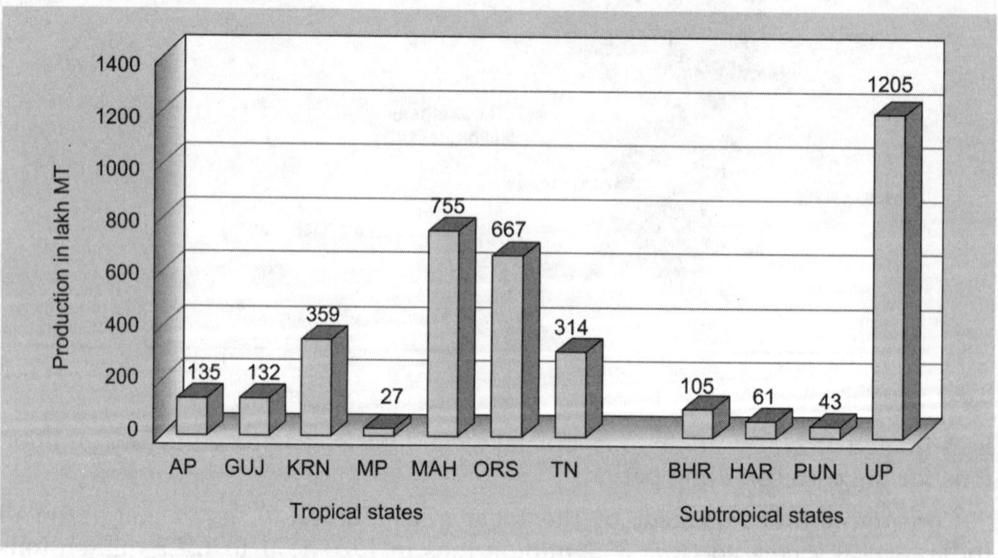

Production of sugarcane in major states of India: 2009–2010 to 2011–2012

The biggest producer of sugarcane in the country is UP (36.5% share in TE 2012–2013) followed by Maharashtra (22.0%). Other major producers of sugarcane in the country are Karnataka (10.9%), Tamil Nadu (10.8%) and Andhra Pradesh (4.6%). In terms of sugar production, Maharashtra is the biggest producer (35.9%) followed by UP (25.6%). This is partially due to the high recovery rate in Maharashtra and relatively higher diversion of cane to khandsari and gur production in UP. Over the 2000s decade, sugarcane cultivation has shown a movement from the subtropical region (Gangetic plains) to the tropical region (water scarce areas). The share of Maharashtra in sugarcane production has increased at the expense of UP. Karnataka has been a major gainer in share of sugar production largely due to its high recovery and rising profitability in the state. Over the 2000s decade, sugarcane cultivation has shown a movement from the subtropical region to the tropical region. All India trends of area, production and yield of sugarcane are as in Table 1.14 included in policy.

Sugarcane (TE 2002–2003)

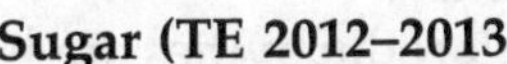

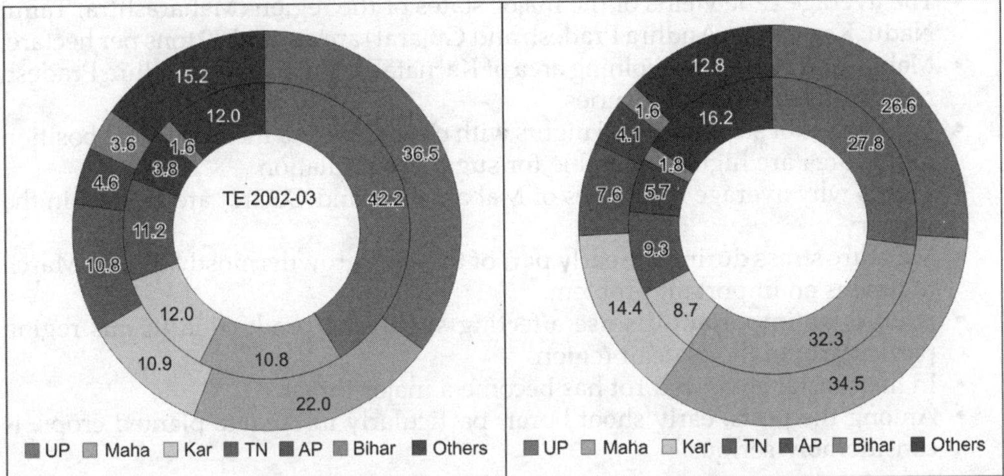

Statewise change in shares in production, sugarcane (TE 2002–2003) and sugar (TE 2012–2013)

Sugarcane Growing Regions

- Broadly, there are two distinct agroclimatic regions of sugarcane cultivation in India, viz., tropical and subtropical.
- However, five agroclimatic zones have been identified mainly for the purpose of varietal development. They are:
  1. North Western Zone
  2. North Central Zone
  3. North Eastern Zone
  4. Peninsular Zone
  5. Coastal Zone.

Tropical Sugarcane Regions

- The tropical sugarcane region consists of sugarcane agroclimatic zone 4 (peninsular zone) and 5 (coastal zone) which includes the states of Maharashtra, Andhra Pradesh, Tamil Nadu, Karnataka, Gujarat, Madhya Pradesh, Goa, Pondichery and Kerala.
- In the coastal areas of Andhra Pradesh and Tamil Nadu, there are extensive sugarcane areas with high sugarcane productivities.
- Floods, water logging diseases such as red rot are the main problems.
- In the tropical region, sugarcane gets more or less ideal climatic conditions for its growth.
- It is cultivated with better package of practices and higher irrigation levels.

- The growing season is long with more equitable and favorable conditions without serious weather extremes.
- Being a tropical country, the agroclimatic conditions of tropical India favor higher sugarcane and sugar yields.
- The tropical region contributes about 40% to the total cane production in the country.
- The productivities are higher.
- The average cane yields of the major states of the region (Maharashtra, Tamil Nadu, Karnataka, Andhra Pradesh and Gujarat) are around 80 tons per hectare.
- Maharashtra and the adjoining area of Karnataka, Gujarat and Andhra Pradesh record higher sugar recoveries.
- Long hours of sunshine, cool nights with clear skies and the latitudinal position of this area are highly favorable for sugar accumulation.
- This is why average recoveries of Maharashtra and Gujarat are highest in the country.
- Moisture stress during the early part of the cane growths mostly during March to June is an important problem.
- Smut is an important disease affecting sugarcane production in this region particularly in the plateau region.
- In the coastal areas, red rot has become a major threat.
- Among the pests, early shoot borer, particularly in the late planted crops, is considerably serious.

Subtropical Sugarcane Region

- Around 60–65% of total cane area in the country is in the subtropics. Uttar Pradesh, Bihar, Haryana and Punjab come under this region.
- Extremes of climate are the characteristic feature of this region.
- During April to June, the weather is very hot and dry.
- July to October is rainy season accounting for most of the rainfall from S-W monsoon rains.
- December and January is the very cool month temperature touching sub-zero levels in many places.
- November to March is cool months with clear sky.
- The N-W zone comprising the areas in Haryana, Punjab, Western Rajasthan and Western UP has very low temperature in December–January which often cause frost.
- During May and June, the temperatures are extremely high.
- Because of extremes of weather, the active sugarcane growth is restricted to 4–5 months only.
- In Eastern UP, Bihar, and West Bengal, sugarcane suffers due to floods and water logging during monsoon months.
- Several pests and diseases, particularly red rot and top borer and pyrilla are common and serious.
- The cane yields are lower in the subtropics due to short growing season, moisture stress, more pest and disease problem, floods and water logging and very poor ratoons.
- The average yield of the four major states (UP, Bihar, Punjab and Haryana) is around 55 tons per hectare.

Sugarcane is the most profitable crop vis-à-vis its competing crops like wheat, paddy and cotton. This has led to expansion of sugarcane in Maharashtra and Karnataka despite these states being water stressed. The drought in 2012–2013 clearly showed that something serious will have to be done in these states with regard to water management for sugarcane. Sugarcane being a very water intensive crop and the fact that per capita water availability in India is shrinking very fast and in the years to come India will be increasingly short of water, it is critical to develop sugar industry in an area that has plenty of water, and where water productivity of cane is high. But in UP and Bihar, the lopsided pricing policy of cane has the potential to jeopardize the growth of this industry. In Bihar, most of the sugar mills had fallen sick, while high cane arrears in UP do not portend well for this sector. Curiously, where the pricing policy for cane has some semblance with revenue sharing formula (as in Karnataka and Maharashtra), the sugar industry is growing despite severe shortage of water. The long-term growth of this sector in water scarce regions of Maharashtra and Karnataka will not be possible unless the farmers adopt drip irrigation (with fertigation) so that they can maximize more cane/sugar for every drop of water. This needs long-term vision of the policy makers in these states, if they want to take sugar sector to a higher trajectory.

The sugar sector of tomorrow has to be envisioned as an energy hub producing not only sugar but also ethanol from molasses and power from bagasse. Increase in ethanol pricing from Rs 27 per liter to now about Rs 33–36 per liter will help sugar sector to improve its viability and thus give a better return to farmers. In order to tap its full potential, molasses need to be fully freed from movement restrictions or reserved allocation for potable liquor. In UP, e.g. almost 20% of molasses are reserved for potable liquor and the price paid is less than one-fourth of the market price being offered by the chemical industry. It is akin to sugar sector subsidizing the potable liquor sector. Such perverse policies need to be fully overhauled. But, two issues will remain central to sugar sector's future growth: (a) how best one can align sugarcane production with better and more efficient usage of water and (b) how rationally we can align sugarcane pricing with revenue sharing formula. If these issues are tackled rationally and quickly, sugar sector can double its worth in the next 5–7 years. Else, it will remain be sieged in uncertainty, wide fluctuations and only limited growth.

Supply of sugar remains largely volatile depending on the weather condition and prices that farmers get for sugarcane. There have been surplus years of sugar production since 2010–2011 after a steep fall in production during 2008–2009 and 2009–2010 (shown in the next page charts A and B). This surplus has to be either exported or added to carry over stock for the next season. But, exports of sugar have been tightly regulated only to be freed in May, 2012. Thus, this surplus has added to the carryover domestic stocks. In 2012–2013, there has been a fall of (–) 6.4% in sugarcane production and (–) 8.0% fall in sugar production. The total sugar production in the country in the sugar season (October to September) 2012–2013 is expected to be about 24.8 million tons which is still more than the domestic consumption.

Against the demand, supply and production situation, the balance sheet of sugar showing stock-to-use ratio during 2010–2011 to 2012–2013 in Table 1.15 shows that it is about 37% during 2012–2013 which indicates a very comfortable position (excess supply) of sugar availability in the country. The higher stock to use ratio in 2012–2013 is mainly because of higher carry over stock, surplus domestic production,

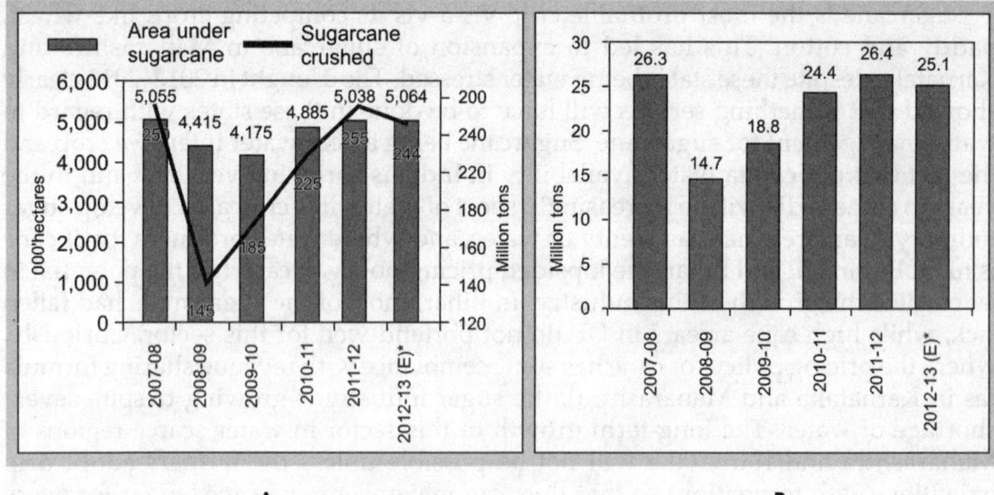

(A) Status of area under sugarcane and sugarcane crushed and (B) Sugar production

* (E) Estimated by Directorate of Sugar (upto 30th June)

Note: The years refer to sugar season.

Source: DES and Directorate of Sugar, DFPD.

imports of sugar (against nil import in 2011–2012) and lesser exports during the sugar season compared to 2011–2012. There is a global sugar surplus and international prices are depressed which has led to higher imports and lower exports. However, such higher stock to use ratio may also signal the impending crisis in the sugar industry. With about 9 million tons of estimated closing stock in 2012–2013 and likely surplus production during 2013–2014, it may result in further stock piling of sugar and increase in inventory in the sugar mills besides mounting cane arrears. The domestic prices of sugar are, therefore, expected to remain under downward pressure in 2013–2014 sugar season.

Costs and Profitability of Sugarcane During 2009–2010 to 2011–2012

It is pertinent to point that the gross value of output in the methodology of cost calculation is estimated at the prevailing market prices during harvest season in the village/cluster of villages where crops are grown and harvested. With this stipulation, an analysis of the profitability and the rate of return over costs A2+FL and C2 has been done for cane during 2009–2010 to 2011–2012, the latest years for which actual cost data is available (Table 1.16). Statewise projected cost of production (C2, A2+FL) is shown in Table 1.16A.

Intercrop Price Parity

Table 1.17 gives a picture of comparative returns on crops competing with sugarcane. It appears that sugarcane is the most profitable crop vis-à-vis its competing crops like wheat, paddy and cotton. Net rate of return (over C2) turns out to be 69% in sugarcane during 2009–2010 to 2011–2012 at all India level, compared with paddy (15%), cotton (36%) and wheat (36%). However, sugarcane is basically an irrigated

Table 1.15: Balance sheet of sugar as a percentage of its use (sugar year: october to september)

(Lakh tons, %)

S. No.	*Particulars*	*2010–11*	*2011–12P*	*2012–13E*
1.	Carry over stocks with sugar mills from previous season	51.25	62.96	66.27
2.	Less adjusted 5% due to damages/unusable stocks	2.56	0	0
3.	**Net opening stock (1–2)**	**48.69**	**62.96**	**66.27**
4.	Export allowed during the previous season but physically exported during the current sugar season	0	4.42	0
5.	**Net adjusted opening stock (3–4)**	**48.69**	**58.54**	**66.27**
6.	Production of sugar	243.5	263.43	248.00
7.	Imports	0	0	15.11*
8.	**Estimated total availability (5 + 6 + 7)**	**292.19**	**321.97**	**329.38**
9.	Estimated releases for internal consumption	208	227.25	230.00
10.	Export against ALS/AAS obligation and OGL/ bilateral agreement with Maldives	26	27.76	10.46**
11.	Estimated non-levy sales as per court order	0	8	0
12.	**Total estimated releases (9 + 10 + 11)**	**234**	**263.01**	**240.46**
13.	**Estimated closing stock on 30th september (8–12)**	**58.19**	**58.96**	**88.92**
14.	**Stock to use ratio (%) [(13/12)*100]**	**24.87**	**22.42**	**36.98**

P = Provisional; E = Estimated.

Closing balance of one season is different from opening balance of next season to account for damaged/wet sugar and sugar sold under Court orders, etc.

* It comprises 5.8 lakh tons import under OGL and 9.31 lakh tons imported under Advance Authorization Scheme (AAS).

** It comprises 1.15 lakh tons export under OGL and 9.31 lakh tons imported sugar under AAS for re-export.

Source: Directorate of Sugar, DFPD.

crop, and it needs to be compared only with fully irrigated paddy or wheat or cotton. Also, it needs to be kept in mind that sugarcane cultivation is about 13 months crop duration in Maharashtra/Karnataka (southern belt) and about 10 months in the northern one. So, it bears a longer risk cycle compared to wheat or rice which is typically 4 month crops. Since sugarcane crop cycle on an average is about three times that of wheat and paddy, the returns over A2+FL and C2 have been normalized for time duration, i.e. returns per month have been derived for these competing crops. Sugarcane being fully irrigated, it is compared to paddy and wheat grown in fully irrigated tracks of Punjab and Haryana. Hectare returns over C2 for sugarcane at all-India level stands at Rs 5,199 per month as against Rs 4,871 and Rs 5,181 for paddy grown in Punjab and Haryana, respectively and Rs 5,072 for wheat grown in Haryana. Even after taking into account these things, the intercrop parity of sugarcane will be very near to irrigated wheat and paddy.

Table 1.16: All India gross and net returns over actual cost of cultivation of sugarcane (average from 2009–2010 to 2011–2012)

State	*Cost A2+FL (Rs/hectare)*	*Cost C2 (Rs/hectare)*	*GVO (Rs/hectare)*	*Gross Returns over A2+FL Rs/hectare)*	*Rate of gross returns over A2+FL (%)*	*Net returns over C2 (Rs/hectare)*	*Net rate of returns over C2 (%)*
Andhra Pradesh	72,139	118,322	151,576	79,436	110	33,254	28
Haryana	44,838	95,294	157,789	112,951	252	62,495	66
Karnataka	52,379	91,014	177,170	124,790	238	86,156	95
Maharashtra	87,875	134,343	202,761	114,885	131	68,418	51
Tamil Nadu	89,028	114,745	188,562	99,533	112	73,817	64
Uttar Pradesh	36,618	67,211	124,210	87,592	239	56,999	85
Uttarakhand	39,492	74,735	137,626	98,134	248	62,891	84
All India wt. avg.	55,270	90,899	153,285	98,015	177	62,386	69

Notes: A2+FL cost includes all expenses in cash and kind on account of hired human labor, bullock labour, machine labor, seed, insecticides and pesticides, manure, fertilizers, irrigation charges and miscellaneous expenses including family labour. C2 cost includes A2+FL cost, imputed rental value of owned land, imputed interest on fixed capital, etc.

Source: Comprehensive Scheme (CS) for studying the Cost of Cultivation of Principal Crops, DES.

Table 1.16A: Statewise projected cost of production (C2 and A2+FL) – unadjusted for recovery of sugarcane for 2014–2015 sugar season and their shares in production in increasing order of cost

States	*A2+FL*	*C2*	*Relative shares in production (%)*
Tamil Nadu	133.18	162.93	12.19
Karnataka	105.23	176.42	13.00
Maharashtra	128.35	200.00	24.82
Uttar Pradesh	129.48	214.57	41.15
Uttrakhand	133.65	223.42	2.15
Haryana	120.55	236.56	2.22
Andhra Pradesh	150.56	245.37	5.17
All India wt. avg.	128.52	202.00	

Note: This projected cost is exclusive of cost of marketing, transportation and crop insurance premium.

The all India weighted average cost C2, adjusted at 9.5% recovery for the sugar season 2014–2015 comes to Rs 193.13/quintal. This is 8% higher than the previous years' projected cost of Rs 179.15/quintal. The cost of Rs 193.13/quintal (adjusted for recovery at 9.5%) has been derived from the unadjusted cost of Rs 202/quintal. When transportation charges and insurance premium is added, all India weighted average cost C2 comes out to be Rs 212.64/quintal.

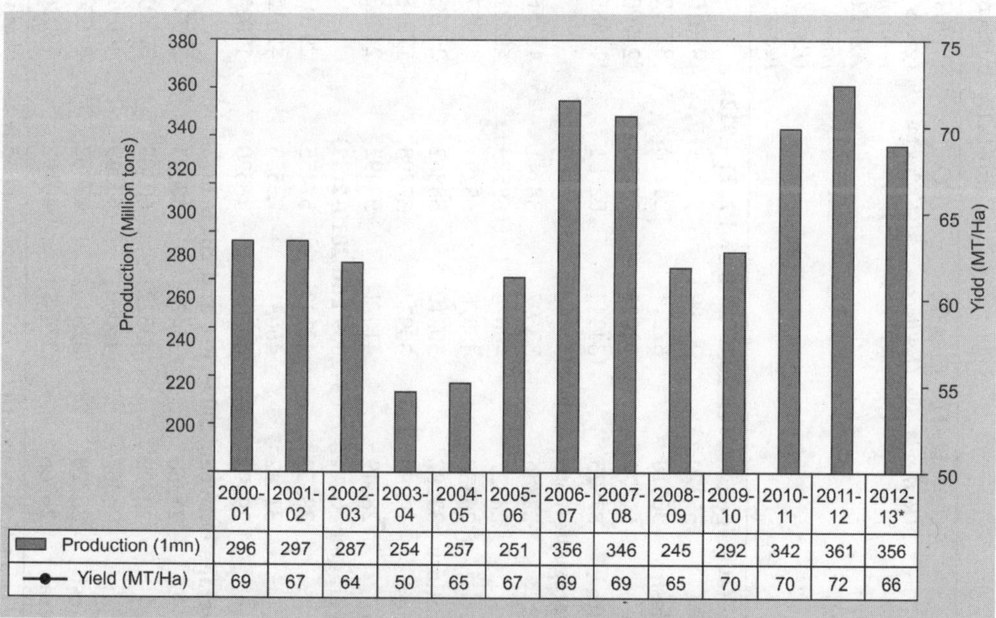

	2000-01	2001-02	2002-03	2003-04	2004-05	2005-06	2006-07	2007-08	2008-09	2009-10	2010-11	2011-12	2012-13*
Production (1mn)	296	297	287	254	257	251	356	346	245	292	342	361	356
Yield (MT/Ha)	69	67	64	50	65	67	69	69	65	70	70	72	66

Production and yield of sugarcane in India during 2000–2001 to 2012–2013

* The figures for 2012–2013 are third advance estimates.
Source: DES.

Table 1.17: Intercrop price parity in returns

Crop	*Cost A2+FL (Rs/hectares)*	*Cost C2 (Rs/hectares)*	*GVO (Rs/hectares)*	*Profits (gross returns on A2+FL basis) (Rs/28 hectares)*	*Profitability (gross returns as percentage of A2+FL)*	*Profits (net returns on C2 basis) (Rs/hectares)*	*Profitability (net returns) as% ofC2)*	*Per month returns over A2+FL (Rs/hectres)*	*Per month returns over C2 (Rs/hectaes)*
Sugarcane* (average between 2009–2010 and 2011–2012)									
All-India	55270	90899	153285	98015	177	62386	69	8168	5199
Uttar Pradesh	36618	67211	124210	87592	239	56999	85	7299	4750
Karnataka	52379	91014	177170	124790	238	86156	95	10399	7180
Maharashtra	87875	134343	202761	114885	131	68418	51	9574	5702
Paddy (average between 2008–2009 and 2010–2011)									
All India	22986	33697	38741	15756	69	5044	15	3939	1261
Punjab	28327	49074	68559	40233	142	19486	40	10058	4871
Haryana	26838	48070	68794	41957	156	20725	43	10489	5181
Andhra Pradesh	33287	50719	58862	25575	77	8143	16	6394	2036
Uttar Pradesh	19880	30924	37798	17918	90	6874	22	4479	1718
Karnataka	28849	41071	53492	24643	85	12422	30	6161	3105
Cotton (average between 2008–2009 and 2010–2011)									
All India	28352	42143	57455	29103	103	15311	36	7276	3828
Gujarat	31242	46031	73555	42312	135	27524	60	10578	6881
Maharashtra	29493	40507	46520	17027	58	6012	15	4257	1503
Wheat (average between 2009–2010 and 2011–2012)									
All India	21360	35470	48094	26734	125	12624	36	6684	3156
Punjab	22999	43522	60300	37301	162	16779	39	9325	4195
Haryana	24357	45062	65349	40992	168	20287	45	10248	5072
Uttar Pradesh	23028	37314	47082	24054	104	9768	26	6013	2442
Maharashtra	26966	37447	40192	13226	49	2746	7	3307	686

* Sugarcane as a whole is about 12 months crops and paddy as well as wheat are about 4 months crops.

Disaggregated analysis shows that productivity improvement is more pronounced in tropical region compared to subtropical region (below chart). The yield levels dipped significantly three times during last 13 years at an average periodicity of 4.3 years.

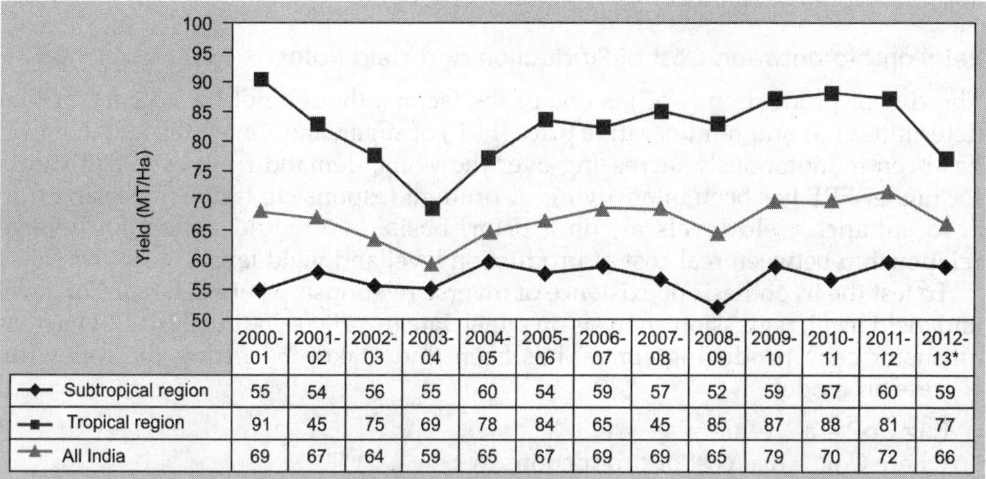

	2000-01	2001-02	2002-03	2003-04	2004-05	2005-06	2006-07	2007-08	2008-09	2009-10	2010-11	2011-12	2012-13*
Subtropical region	55	54	56	55	60	54	59	57	52	59	57	60	59
Tropical region	91	45	75	69	78	84	65	45	85	87	88	81	77
All India	69	67	64	59	65	67	69	69	65	79	70	72	66

Yield of sugarcane in tropical and subtropical regions of India during 2000–2001 to 2012–2013

* The figures for 2012–2013 are third advance estimates.
Source: DES.

The tropical region has posted higher yield levels by 44%, on an average, compared to those of subtropical region during the decade of 2000s. Based on statewise analysis, it emerges that Tamil Nadu outstrips other major cane producing states on land productivity score (below chart).

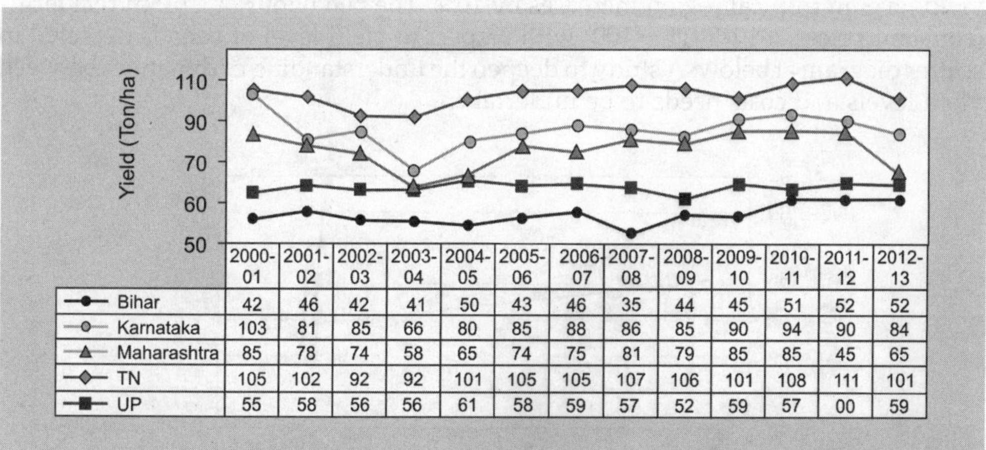

	2000-01	2001-02	2002-03	2003-04	2004-05	2005-06	2006-07	2007-08	2008-09	2009-10	2010-11	2011-12	2012-13
Bihar	42	46	42	41	50	43	46	35	44	45	51	52	52
Karnataka	103	81	85	66	80	85	88	86	85	90	94	90	84
Maharashtra	85	78	74	58	65	74	75	81	79	85	85	45	65
TN	105	102	92	92	101	105	105	107	106	101	108	111	101
UP	55	58	56	56	61	58	59	57	52	59	57	00	59

Land productivity of sugarcane in major cane producing states during 2000–2001 to 2012–2013

Note: The figures for 2012–2013 are third advance estimates.
Source: DES.

However, these land productivities are not directly comparable as crop durations vary a great deal from state to state. This needs to be appreciated, given that land use has an opportunity cost. In any case, it is a matter of further investigation to explore whether this magnitude of yield differentials can be attributed to climatic and soil conditions alone or there are some other factors that would explain this.

Relationship between Cost of Production and Yield Rates

The cost of production (CoP) is one of the factors, though not the sole factor that determines fair and remunerative price (FRP) of sugarcane. Given the fact that CoP has been monotonously increasing over the years, demand from cane cultivators for higher FRP has been intensifying. A prudent response to tackle increasing CoP is to enhance yield levels as, on a priori basis, one would expect an inverse relationship between real cost of production level and yield level.

To test the hypothesis of existence of inverse relationship between real CoP level and yield level, regression analysis on panel data (for 2000–2001 to 2010–2011 across all major cane producing states) has been undertaken by fitting the following regression model:

$$\text{Log CoP} = a + e^{*}\log y$$

where CoP = real cost of production

y = yield rate

e = elasticity

a = constant

The above regression model was tested on entire panel data and also separately on its two sub-sets viz. tropical region and subtropical region. Of these three regressions, only the regression analysis for tropical region gave the statistically significant (with 95% level of confidence) result which is presented hereunder:

$$\text{Log CoP} = 7.573331 - 0.42776^{*}\log y$$

This regression equation implies that real cost (CoP) can be decreased by 4.3% if yield level in tropical region increases by 10%. The behaviour of CoP in real terms (constant prices 2010–2011 = 100) with respect to yield level of cane is depicted in scatter diagram at below. A study to deepen the understanding of dynamics between yield levels and costs needs to be undertaken.

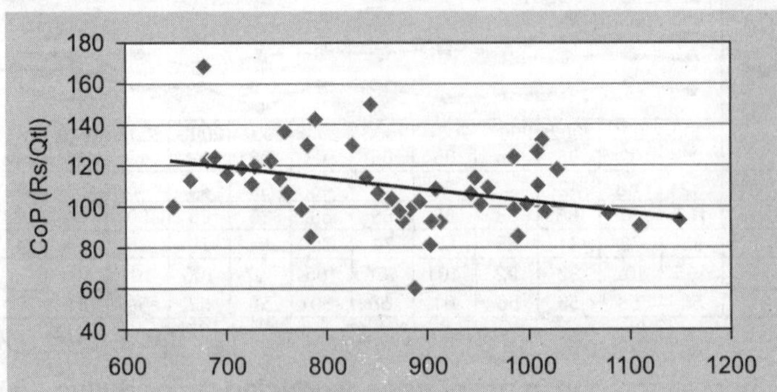

Relationship between cost of production and yield rates for tropical region (constant prices 2010–2011 = 100)

Source: DES.

Land Productivity: Adjusting for Time, Water Intake and Recovery Ratio

Land productivity is unidimensional parameter. As the duration of cane in the field varies across states, and since it requires very different quantities of water for irrigation leading to different recovery rates, need is felt to analyze other dimensions of land productivity after adjusting for the duration of the crop, its water intake, and its recovery rates. As land and water are increasingly becoming scarce in India with high opportunity costs, it is imperative that land productivity is normalized for the time duration of the crop, its water intake, and its recovery rate. With this in view, "adjusted yields" of sugarcane in five major cane producing states of Bihar, Karnataka, Maharashtra, Tamil Nadu and UP have been worked out. The summary of the results is presented in Table 1.18.

On careful perusal of Table 1.18, it is noted that Bihar is less efficient to the tune of 49% compared to Tamil Nadu when land productivity is worked out without any reference to crop duration, recovery rate of cane and water consumed in cultivation of the crop. However, when land productivity is normalized for both crop duration, and water consumption, Tamil Nadu turns out to be less efficient compared to Bihar by 73% when land productivity is measured on the basis of per lakh liter of water consumed after duly adjusting for crop duration.

On working out water requirement of cane for production of sugar, it is found that it takes 812 liters of water in Bihar and 1,049 liters in UP compared to 2,940 liters in Karnataka, 2,515 liters in Maharashtra and 3,066 liter in Tamil Nadu for producing a kilogram of sugar which implies that Bihar is more efficient by 277% compared to Tamil Nadu. It is pertinent to add here that sugar produced in Maharashtra comes from 12.5 months' cultivation of cane as compared to 9.5 months' in UP (crop duration in case of other three states lie in this range, details may be seen in Table 1.18) which is not adjusted for sugar production at factory level, although crop duration has been adjusted for cane cultivation at farm level. In any case, this analysis has high relevance for India, as sugarcane is a very water intensive crop, its long-term development must ensure that it is in line with availability of sufficient water. Given real cost of water in western/southern states is at least two to three times higher than those in Bihar/UP, it raises an issue of comparative advantage. But western India, especially Maharashtra is not blessed with natural endowment of water, as eastern UP or Bihar. Therefore, our futuristic policy needs to be aligned with natural endowment of resources.

Industrial and Other Uses of Sugarcane

- Sugarcane used for the production of white sugar, jaggery (gur), khandsari.
- In addition, sugarcane also used for chewing and extraction of juice for beverage purpose.

MANUFACTURE OF SUGAR

- Sugarcane consists of sugars as well as nonsugars, several processes such as clarification, concentration, crystallisation and purification are needed to separate sugar from nonsugars.
- The main objective of the heavy complex machinery installed in a sugar factory is to aid such separation in cane juice in the most efficient manner possible.

Table 1.18: Land and water productivity, and efficiency gaps in cane and sugar production, 2012–2013

State	*Land and water productivity*					*Efficiency gaps (%) in*				
	Land produtivity (Q/Ha)	*Normalizing land productivity for crop duration [Q/(Ha* month)]*	*Normalizing land productivity for crop duration and water [Q/(Ha* month* lakh liters)]*	*Production of sugar (Q/Ha*	*Water requirment (liters) of cane for production of 1 kg of sugar*	*Land productivity*	*Normalizing land productivety for crop duration*	*Normalizing land produtivity for crop-duration and water*	*Prodution of sugar*	*Water requirement of cane for production of 1 kg of sugar*
Bihar	518	43	1.2	46	812	49	53	0	52	0
Karnataka	841	71	0.3	87	2940	17	23	76	10	262
Maharashtra	646	51	0.3	73	2515	36	44	76	24	209
Tamil Nadu	1010	93	0.3	97	3066	0	0	73	0	277
UP	590	62	1.1	53	1049	42	33	4	45	29

Notes:

1. Efficiency gap = (1-e)*100 if e < 1, else (e-1)*100, where e = performance of a state being compared / performance of "Benchmark" state.
2. States / figures in bold symbolize "benchmark" on the corresponding parameter.

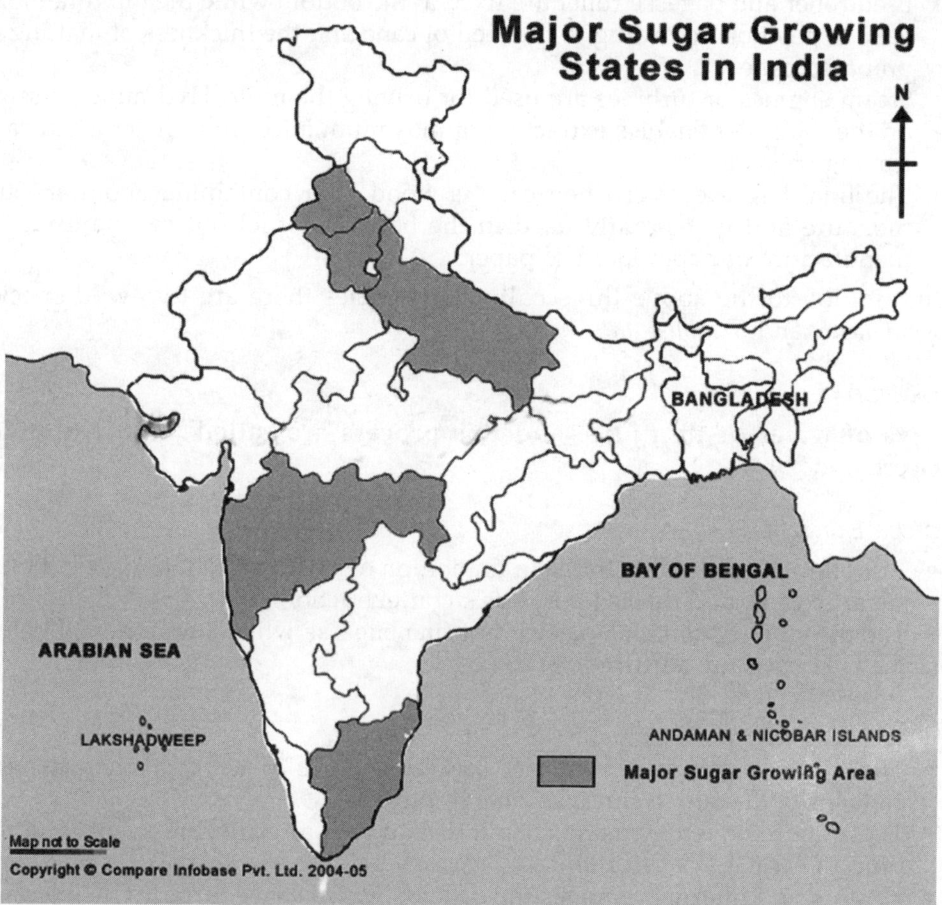

Modern Manufacturing Processes

Cane Preparation

- The cane stalks are carried in the cane carrier by two endless chains of roller type and placed at an angle.
- They are cut into chips by a set of revolving knives and are also torn into shreds by hammer mill shredders reversal of cane knives is also being adopted to improve efficiency of cane preparation.
- The shredders help shredding the cane to improve mill extraction and crushing
- Heavily grooved crusher rollers break the cane and extract the juice. Intensive preparation of cane helps in increasing the capacity and extraction of the milling plant.

Cane Crushing

- A sugar mill consists of multiple units (4–6) of three roller combination (12–18 rollers in all). In each set, three rollers are arranged in a triangular form and are called (i) cane or feed roller, (ii) top roller and (iii) bagasse or discharge roller.

- Feed roller and bagasse roller are fixed at the bottom while the top roller may vary in position according to the feed of cane and the thickness of matting of prepared cane.
- Steam engines or turbines are used for driving the mills. Hydraulic pressure on the top roller enables extraction of maximum juice from the crushed cane leaving bagasse.
- The final bagasse or crushed cane is wood fiber containing about 48–50% moisture and is generally used in the boilers as fuel but can be used for manufacture of paperboard of paper.

In addition to the above three cultivated species there are two wild species *S. spontaneum* and *S. robustum*.

Imbibition

Sprays of water or thin juice and this process are called "imbibition" or "macertation".

Sucrose Extraction

- Adoption of modern methods in imbibition enables extraction of over 93% of sugar in cane, and this is known as sugar extraction.
- The mixed juice contains particles of fine bagasse which are removed before the juice goes for clarification.

Clarification

- The juice from the mills is turbid, dark green in color, acidic in character and contains both soluble and insoluble impurities.
- These are removed by using chemicals and heat as clarifying agents and this process is called clarification.
- Heating and filtering removes the colloids which cause turbidity in juice.
- Lime treatment removes gums, pectins, organic and inorganic acid salts by precipitation.
- Colouring matter is removed by treatment with sulphur dioxide.
- The juice extracted by the mills is passed through a metal strainer to remove suspended purities. Use of clarifying agents like milk of lime and sulphur dioxide helps in precipitation non-sugars as mud gets separated from clear juice by sedimentation in classifiers and are filtered with the help of rotary drum vacuum filters.
- The precipitate from the juice is called press cake, and is used as fertilizer and in preparation of other byproducts while the clarified light juice is sent to the evaporators.
- Two processes are in vogue in clarification the more common one is sulphitition and the other is carbonation.

Sulphitition

- Milk of lime is added to the raw juice to neutralize the acidity of the juice and to keep the juice alkaline up to pH 9.0–10.5. Excess lime is neutralized by passing sulphur dioxide gas. Sulphur dioxide is used as the chief bleaching agent to make the juice brilliant and light in color.

- The juice treated with lime and sulphur dioxide is heated to boiling point so that the precipitate settles down leaving the clear juice at the top.

Carbonation

- In this process, excess of lime is neutralized by passing carbon dioxide gas resulting in precipitate of calcium carbonate.
- The lime stone mixed with coke is burnt in a special kiln to obtain burnt lime as well as carbon dioxide.
- Carbonation is a costlier process than sulphitition as the requirement of lime is high.
- The whole juice after treatments filtered using plate frame type filters. But, the latest system is to have continuous clarification in a single tray-type clarifier with vacuum filters.

Evaporation

- The clarified juice contains about 85% water, two-thirds of which is evaporated in a series of vaccum boiling cells of multiple effect evaporators thus-avoiding destruction of sugar caused by boiling of juice over direct fire or by steam in air.
- This also results in better fuel economy. These evaporator are arranged in a series and the juice is boiled in such a way that each succeeding evaporator has a higher vacuum and therefore boils at a lower temperature.
- The juice thus become more and more concentrated and in the last evaporator turn into syrup containing about 60–65% solids and the rest water.

Sugar Boiling and Crystallization

- The evaporated syrup is black in color. Sulphur dioxide is passed-through this syrup to "bleach" the coloring matter
- The sulphured syrup is then evaporated till it gets saturate with sugar.
- Seed grain is added to serve as nuclei for sugar crystals and as the water evaporates syrup is further added.
- The concentration of syrup and formation of crystals achieved in-vacuum pans.
- Pan boiling is an important skilled operation as the size and color of crystals of the fin product sugar are determined by the quality of pan boiling.
- In a boiling system, three types of massecuites A, B, C are dealt with the first grade "A" massecuite, which produced by boiling the syrup alone and other higher pure materials like melt, etc is centrifuged to separate sugar as molasses and these are called "A" sugar and "A" heavy molasses and after washing, "A" light molasses. Similarly from "B" and massecuites "B" and "C" sugars.

Diffusion

- In some sugar factories cane is prepared by two sets of cane knives and one set of mills for primary extraction of about 65–70% of the sugar content and the remaining sugar in bagasse is extracted by the diffuser.
- The bagasse contains 85% moisture which has to be reduced to about 48–50% before it can be used as fuel in the boilers.

- Slurry of prepared cane material is passed through the diffuser with conveyor. It is subjected to intensive sprays of juice of progressively decreasing concentration.
- The bagasse coming out of the diffuser contains large quantity of residual juice which is squeezed out by passing the bagasse through one or two sets of three roller mills.
- The residual juice extracted by the dewatering mills is screened and milk of lime added to bring the pH of the juice to 9.0, heated to 80°C and sent to the clarifier for settling the suspended impurities.
- Operation of the diffuser is fully-automatic with minimal manual supervision.

Centrifuging

- The massecuite from the crystallizers is pumped into a revolving, machine called "centrifuge". Washing with water and then steaming under high speed, the centrifugal force of the centrifuges is increased expelling molasses into the casing of the machine, retaining sugar crystals on the perforated sheet.
- Spinning is continued till the sugar crystals are practically free from molasses. Such separation is called "purging" or "curing".
- The use of superheated steam or wash water has eliminated the process of drying of sugar but on the other hand the sugar has to be cooled in a cooler before it is packed in jute bags.
- The final molasses which is heavy and viscous contains about one-third sucrose, one-third reducing sugars and the rest nonsugars. It serves as raw material for production of industrial alcohol and yeast and is also useful as cattle feed.

Grading

- Grading of sugar is done in sugar graders of vibrating type with different decks fitted with various meshes and the sugar from each deck is collected through separate chutes into the bags; directly.
- Grading of sugar is done according to size of grain and presently there are five grades in India viz., A1, B, C, D and E of which A1 has the biggest and "E" has the smallest crystal size.
- Sugar is classified according to color also. Presently, there are only two colors 29 and 30. The later, being superior to the former.
- With five grain sizes and two colors, there are in all 10 grades of sugar.
- Recently under new gradation, Government of India reduced the existing five grain sizes to three grades large, medium and small, the two color series remaining as they are.
- The new gradation has come into force from 1984–1985 crushing season.

Packing and Weighing

- Sugar is packed in 100 kg bags which are stitched mostly by machines.
- Sugar for export is packed in 50 kg special gunny bags having polythene lining to withstand multiple handling and transportation to long distances.

Storage

- Sugar bags are stored in pucca godowns mostly by manual labor. In many of the factories stacking is now being done by conveyor belts and stacking equipment.
- Raw sugar: A major portion of world's sugar production is from sugarcane and also from sugar beet.
- Next to white sugare "Gur" is in great demand particularly in rural India.

Refining

The extracted sugar crystals are then shipped to refineries. Raw sugar is light brown and slightly sticky because the crystals have a thin film of molasses clinging to them. Refining removes this film and produces white crystals of sugar. First the raw sugar is rinsed of its brownish film. Then, the crystals are dissolved in water and the liquid is filtered to remove impurities. The sugar is then crystallized, and the crystals are separated from the liquid by centrifuges and dried in hot air. The liquid must be centrifuged several times. Other methods of refining involve the use of milk of lime, carbon dioxide, and repeated boiling. The refined crystals are classified and stored in bins to be packaged or sent to market.

Commercial Production

The sugar from sugarcane and sugar beets is transformed into commercial sugar in two stages. First, the sugar is extracted from the plants, than it is refined. Most commercial sugar is white granulated sugar that has been processed in refineries, beet sugar factories, or cane-mill white-sugar factories. These sugars are classified according to grain size as extra-coarse, coarse, standard, fine, or extra-fine granulated. The grain size of extra-coarse granulated is larger than 0.04 inch (1.0 millimeter); that of extra-fine granulated is less than 0.01 inch (0.25 millimeter).

Other types of sugar are produced through slightly different processes than those used for white granulated sugar. Soft yellow and soft brown sugars are made by retaining some of the molasses during processing. These sugars are soft and clingy because the molasses film contains about 35 times more water than refined white sugar. Other types of sugar include english coffee sugar—large brown crystals with a characteristic caramel flavor. English coffee sugar is produced from successive boilings of refinery liquid. Candy sugar consists of very large white sugar crystals. It is slowly crystallized from very pure liquid during sugar processing and is used mainly by the brewing industry.

Liquid sugar is made from cane or beet sugar chiefly for manufacturing purposes. Cube sugar is produced by molding and pressing selected granular sugar with a sugary liquid to cement the crystals together, then drying the sugar.

Palm sugar is produced in some tropical Asian countries from the juice of date, coconut, and palmyra palms. Maple sugar is produced in Canada and the northern United States from the sap of sugar-maple trees.

From the Table 1.19, it is evident that Maharastra was top leading state tin sugar production during 2001–2002 to 2010–2011 except year 2003–2004 to 2005–2006 when UP was the leader. The fluctuation in sugar production of the country was a prominent factor during the period under review, varying from 283.61 lakh tons in 2006–2007 to ~26.91 in in the year 2004–2005. However, fluctuation in sugar production in UP is lesser.

Table 1.19: Statewise sugar production directly from cane in India for 10 years

States	*2001–2002*	*2002–2003*	*2003–2004*	*2004–2005*	*2005–2006*	*2006–2007*	*2007–2008*	*2008–2009*	*2009–2010*	*2010–2011*
Andhra Pradesh	10,48	12.10	8.86	9.82	12.36	16.80	13.35	5.93	5.15	10.06
Karnataka	15.50	18.68	11.16	10.40	19.43	26,60	29.00	16.54	25.58	36.83
Tamil Nadu	18.39	16.44	9.21	11.08	21.42	25.40	21.41	15.98	12.80	18.46
Maharastra	56.13	62.13	31.75	22.17	51.97	91.00	90.75	45.78	70.67	90.54
Uttar Pradesh	52.60	56.51	45.51	5037	57,84	84.75	73.19	40,64	5179	58,87
Bihar	3.42	4.08	. 2.74	2.54	4,22	4.51	3.36	2.14	2.58	3.85
Haryana	6.24	6.36	5.82	4.00	4.09	6.52	5.99	2.29	2.48	3.92
All India	185.27	201.40	135.46	126.91	192.67	283.61	263.56	145.38	189.12	243.94

Source: Indian Sugar-December, 2011, vol. no. LXI, issue no. 9.

Looking to the fluctuation in sugar production in the country, a critical examination with special reference to UP with regards to cane area, average yield, total cane production, total sugar production, number of factories with installed capacity and "sugar recovery" obtained during the last 11th 5 year plans is necessary.

Table 1.20 reveals that there is more than threefold increase in cane area of, the state during he span of the last 11th 5 year plans. Average yield per hectare varied from 36.43 million tons in 3rd plan to 60.76 tons in 8th plan period. Numbers of working mills was 68 in 1st 5-year plan which was raised to 132 in 11th plan period. Similarly, cane crushing capacity of mills was reported 72,327 TCD in first plan period which was raised to 7.78 lakh TCD at the end of 11th plan.

The overall impact of increase in area, productivity, number of mills and subsequent increase in crushing capacity resulted in more than fivefold increase in sugar production during the span of 1st to 11th plan period. Year-wise variation in 11th plan in cane area, productivity total sugarcane production, cane crushed, sugar recovery and and sugar production is presented below:

- Table 1.21 reveals that there appeared to be a tendency of out striping the target set for cane area probably owing to profitability of cane crop over food crops.
- Increase in average yield of sugarcane in the 11th plan period could not reach to the desired level.
- There was sufficient increase in total cane production in the terminal year of the plan.
- During last year of the 11th sugar and sugar production has shown appreciable increase.
- No definite trend in sugar recovery percentage was observed which varied from 9.79% in 2007–2008 to 8.94 in 2008–2009.
- Drawl percentage increased from 41% to 60% in 11th plan which has resulted in higher crush and higher sugar production.

Productivity of Sugarcane in Different Part of the State in 11th Plan

The existing sugarcane productivity level of UP is much below the national level. The average yield of sugarcane in UP was reported 60.76 tons per hectare. In 8th 5 year plan while Indias average yield is about 64.06 tons per hectare. In the year

Table 1.20: Plan-wise achievement with regards to cane area, average yield, cane production sugar production

S. No.	The final year of the plan	Cane area (lakh hectares)	Average yield (million tons/ hectare)	Cane product (lakh tons)	Sugar product (lakh tons)	No. of mills	Crushing capacity (TCD)	Sugar recovery (%)
1.	1st 5 year plan	7.97	40.10	319.34	10.98	68	72,327	9.69
2.	2nd 5 year plan	9.84	37.72	371.10	12.04	71	84,859	9.32
3.	3rd 5 year plan	8.26	36.43	300.80	7 .11	71	1,02,059	9.58
4.	4th 5 year plan	12.09	44.12	533.28	12.97	74	1,13,218	8.99
5.	5th 5 year plan	14.69	39.40	578.78	14.63	88	1,31,535	9.28
6.	6th 5 year plan	14.70	46.13	678.05	14.77	99	1,61,439	9.56
7.	7th 5 year plan	18.55	57.51	1,066.77	36.51	106	2,14,991	9.18
8.	8th 5 year plan	21.96	60.76	1,334.21	39.22	122	3,51,318	9.59
9.	9th 5 year plan	20.54	54.40	1,117.38	43.87	110/110	3,58,804	9.73
10.	10th 5 year plan	26.62	59.59	1,546.22	84.75	133	709,000	9.47
11.	11th 5 year plan (year 2007–2008)	28.50	56.44	1,608.59	73.19	132	761,328	9.78
	(year 2008–2009)	21.40	51.77	1,107.00	40.64	132	771,701	8.94
	(year 2009–2010)	17.88	58.80	1,051.33	51.79	128	772,365	9.13
	(year 2010–2011)	21.01	56.25	1,183.91	58.87	125	767,240	9.14
	(year 2011–2012)	22.51	58.00	1,300.00	70.00	124	763,740	9.00

Table 1.21: Physical target and achievements of 11th 5 year plan

S. No.	*Details*	*Unit*	*2007–2008*		*2008–2009*		*2009–2010*		*2010–2011*		*2011–2012*	
			Target	*Ach.*	*Target*	*Ach.*	*Target*	*Ach.*	*Target*	*Ach.*	*Target*	*Ach.*
1.	Cane area	Lakh hectare	27.00	28.50	27.00	21.40	27.00	17.88	27.00	21.01	27.00	22.51
2.	Average yield	Ton per hectare	70.00	56.44	70.00	51.77	70.00	58.80	70.00	56.34	70.00	58.00
3.	Sugarcane production	Lakh ton	1890.00	1608.59	1890.00	1107.82	1890.00	1051.26	1890.00	1183.98	1890.00	1300.00
4.	Cane crushed	Lakh ton	1226.50	747.39	1226.50	454.82	1226.50	567.34	1226.50	643.81	1226.50	780.00
5.	Sugar recovery	%	10.30	9.79	10.30	8.94	10.30	9.13	10.30	9.14	10.30	9.15
6.	Sugar production	Lakh ton	119.07	73.19	119.07	40.64	119.07	51.79	119.07	58.87	119.7	70.00
7.	Drawl	%	65	46.44	65	41.05	65	53.97	65	54.38	65	60

2011, productivity of the state can be increased up to the national average by adopting the high-yielding varietal replacement program, using improved agricultural inputs and suitable improved. Agricultural practices, use of suitable crop rotation is providing recommended dose of fertilizers and irrigation and applying plant protection measures. Tables 1.22A to D will give a picture of zone-wise average yield of plant, ratoon and sugarcane crop as a whole.

Table 1.22A: Cane area (lakh hectare)

S. No.	Year	West	Central	East	State
1.	2007–2008	7.38	12.28	8.84	28.50
2.	2008–2009	6.15	9.07	6.18	21.40
3.	2009–2010	5.28	7.78	4.82	17.88
4.	2010–2011	5.68	9.70	5.63	21.01
5.	2011–2012	5.81	11.6	5.10	22.51

Table 1.22B: Cane production (lakh ton)

S. No.	Year	West	Central	East	State
1.	2007–2008	482.80	674.60	451.19	1,608.59
2.	2008–2009	362.30	470.71	274.81	1,107.82
3.	2009–2010	348.56	458.63	244.07	1,051.26
4.	2010–2011	351.58	542.80	289.60	1,183.98
5.	2011–2012	367.00	618.77	349.95	1,335.72

Table 1.22C: Cane average yield (million ton/hectare)

S. No.	Year	West	Central	East	State
1.	2007–2008	65.39	54.94	51.05	56.44
2.	2008–2009	58.96	51.87	44.48	51.77
3.	2009–2010	65.97	58.96	50.67	58.80
4.	2010–2011	61.85	55.97	51.43	56.34
5.	2011–2012	62.95	59.48	55.79	59.35

Table 1.22D: Sugar recovery (percentage)

S. No.	Year	West	Central	East	State
1.	2007–2008	9.67	9.86	9.84	9.79
2.	2008–2009	8.83	9.15	8.89	8.94
3.	2009–2010	9.13	9.00	9.21	9.13
4.	2010–2011	8.92	9.24	9.25	9.14
5.	2011–2012	8.55	9.17	9.45	9.07

The Tables 1.22A to D depict the segregated position of cane area, cane production, average yield and sugar recovery in west, central and east UP during the 11th plan period.

The Tables 1.22A to D bring the following facts to notice:

- Table 1.22A indicates that central UP commands highest cane area. Therefore, a sincere effort is needed in the central UP to raise productivity of cane crop to achieve better average at state level.
- Table 1.22B indicates that total cane production as expected is higher in central UP. There exists possibility of more new sugar factory to come up in near future.
- Table 1.22C revels that eastern UP fetches poor yield per hectare than central and western UP. Sincere effort is needed to increase productivity level in eastern UP.
- Table 1.22D revels that contrary to general opinion, eastern UP is getting relatively higher recovery than central and western UP except with marginal fluctuation.

Productivity of Plant and Ratoon Crop in Different Parts of UP

A deeper analysis of area occupied by plant and ratoon crops and average yield obtained in different part of the state in 11th 5 year plan will help us in evolving suitable strategies for raising productivity of cane crop in state during 12th 5 year plan period (Tables 1.23A and B).

Table 1.23A: Cane area in plant and ratoon crop in different parts of up

S. No.	Year	*Plant cane area*			*Ratoon cane area*		
		West	*Central*	*East*	*West*	*Central*	*East*
1.	2007–2008	3.13	5.51	3.68	4.25	6.77	5.16
2.	2008–2009	2.36	3.54	2.00	3.79	5.53	4.18
3.	2009–2010	2.46	4.06	2.23	2.82	3.72	2.59
4.	2010–2011	2.76	5.27	3.01	2.92	4.43	2.62
5.	2011–2012	2.66	5.76	2.37	3.15	5.84	2.70

Table 1.23B: Average yield (plant and ratoon) (ton/hectare) during 11th plan period

S. No.	Year	*Plant cane area*			*Ratoon cane area*		
		West	*Central*	*East*	*West*	*Central*	*East*
1.	2007–2008	58.56	55.56	52.86	70.44	54.43	49.48
2.	2008–2009	52.56	51.52	45.08	58.96	51.87	44.48
3.	2009–2010	61.64	60.36	53.43	69.74	57.44	48.28
4.	2010–2011	57.08	57.07	53.64	66.35	54.66	48.89
5.	2011–2012	57.95	59.77	57.34	67.19	59.18	54.44

- Table 1.23A revels that some parts of state grow more than one ratoon crop. Therefore, better ratoon management is very vital for getting higher productivity.
- Table 1.23B indicates that eastern UP and central UP get poor ratoon yield than plant cane while the phenomenon is reverse in case of western UP where productivity of ratoon is much higher than plant cane. As a matter of fact, the practices of sowing sugarcane after harvesting wheat crop reduces the growth period of the plant cane as far as west UP is concerned.

Level of Production Technology in 11th Plant Period

Theoretically speaking, where recommended doses of fertilizer is applied adequate and productive irrigation is provided, quality seed cane is used and plants protection measures are applied when required, the productivity level is bound to increase. However, time of sowing is another important factor which increases or otherwise decreases per hectare of the cane crop. Achievement of 11th plan (2007–2008 to 2011–2012) with regards to distribution of fertilizer, quality seed and use of plants protection measures is given in Table 1.24.

Table 1.24 reveals that except in few years, distribution of quality seed, use of fertilizer and use of plant protection chemical were increasing year to year in 11th plan period. Ratoon management with regards to urea spray was also on rise. However, looking to the magnitude of urea occupied by ratoon crop in whole state, urea spray on ratoon crop is very meager.

Genetic variability sugarcane crop varies to a great extent sugarcane research stations located in different part of the state grow nucleus seed which is provided to different sugar mills area to raise foundation and primary nursery at farmers field to enable them to distribute more quantity of different varieties of cane seeds to the farmers. Table 1.25 gives detail account of different varieties grown in the state for the 2 year of the 11th plan.

From the perusal of the above following inferences are drawn:

- Area under total early maturing varieties was 16.60% in year 2007–2008 of the total cane area.
- Total area under midlate varieties was 78.5% in year 2011–2012.
- Total area under unsuitable varieties was highest 16.20% in year 2007–2008 which has been decreased up to 12.60% in the last year of 11th 5 year plan.

Vigorous efforts are needed to launch varietals replacement program to minimize the area under unsuitable varieties. Similarly, area under early maturing varieties has to be increased sufficiently.

Summary of Proposed Out Lay during 12th 5 Year Plan (2012–2013 to 2016–2017)

Before projecting the out lay for 12th plan following assumptions were made taking future scenario in to consideration which are likely to occur in sugarcane production technology.

Future Scenario

In future following issues are likely to occur in sugarcane production technology:

1. Limited availability of per unit area of water for irrigation.
2. Depletion of soil fertility.

Table 1.24: Production of quality seed use of fertilizer and chemical in the 11th plan

S. No.	*Programs*	*Unit*	*2007–2008*	*2008–2009*	*2009–2010*	*2010–2011*	*2011–2012*
1.	Laying out of cane seed nurseries:						
	1. Foundation	Hectare	4816	4548	4354	4342	663
	2. Primary	*	26347	28596	23005	25416	769
2.	Seed cane distribution	Lakh quintal	117.30	123.30	180.20	141.91	2.29
3.	Fertilizer distribution						
	1. Nitrozon (N)	(1,000) million tons	136.40	145.81	125.41	112.00	72.43
	2. Phosphorous (P)	(1,000) million tons	28.89	32.04	31.16	28.15	11.79
	3. Potach (K)	(1,000) million tons	6.85	8.92	8.52	11.10	5.04
4.	Nitrozon distribution per hectors	Kg/hectare	47.86	68.14	70.14	53.31	
5.	Area to be treated:						
	1. Seed treatment	Lakh hectare	0.59	0.48	0.17	0.46	0.04
	2. Soil treatment	Lakh hectare	1.71	1.81	1.36	1.50	0.81
	3. Urea spray on ratoon crop	Lakh hectare	*1.72	1.92	1.87	1.94	1.52

Table 1.25: Cane area and varietal positon in 11th 5 year plan

S. No.	Year	*Cane area (lakh hectares)*			*Percentage*			*Varietal percentage*		
		Plant	*Ratoon*	*Total*	*Plant*	*Ratoon*	*Total*	*Plant*	*Ratoon*	*Total*
1.	2007–08	12.31	16.19	28.50	43.19	56.81	100	16.60	67.20	16.20
2.	2008–09	7.90	13.50	21.40	36.90	63.10	100	14.90	69.20	15.90
3.	2009–10	8.75	9.13	17.88	48.94	51.06	100	13.30	76.80	9.90
4.	2010–11	11.04	9.97	21.01	52.53	47.47	100	10.60	77.50	11.90
5.	2011–12	10.80	11.71	22.51	48.00	52.00	100	8.90	78.50	12.60

3. Increase of prices of fertilizer germicide and pesticide chemical.
4. Price escalation of petroleum products.
5. Limited availability of farm labor.
6. Reduction in cane area due to price increase of other competitive crops.
7. Besides manufacturing of sugar, diversion of cane crops likely towards other, by-products like ethanol, etc.
8. Improvement in exiting production technology of sugarcane.
9. In the changed scenario efforts are to be made to obtain maximum out put (per unit of area) irrigation water and other inputs. It is expected that there will be increase in cane productivity and sugarcane toward gur and khandsaree will be minimized.

Future Strategies

- To raise the crush.ng capacity of sugar mills from 7.67 lakh TCD to 8.50 lakh TCD.
- To make efforts in increasing the productivity of sugarcane instead of allowing the sugarcane area to expand is the target. For that the programs relating to the development of high-yielding varieties of sugarcane and modern scientific techniques of sugarcane cultivation would have to be carried out. Arrangement for agricultural inputs for giving effect to increase the sugarcane production will be envisaged. The productivity level is proposed to be raised from almost 60 tons in 2011–2012 to 70.00 tons in 2016–2017.
- Effective implementation of publicity and propaganda work for providing knowledge of modern and scientific methods of sugarcane cultivation has also been envisaged. The brief of publicity strategies is narrated below:
  - o Making video film.
  - o Sponsoring—program through radio station.
  - o Distributing "awards to 100 growers in each year getting highest yield in cane crop competition".
  - o Cultural program.
- Giving priority to sugarcane research programs to cater the need of to ~1 seed required for seed replacement program. It is proposed that 20% plant cane area by improved seeds will be replaced every year. Total plant cane area will be replaced in the 5 years. To meet the end a rolling plan of nucleus seed required for 3 years onward will be prepared.

- Development of area of such sugarcane varieties which are high-yielding and rich in sugar for those sugar factory areas where sugarcane area as per requirement is not available as also to develop the varieties of sugarcane for the different regions according to suitability of soil and climate development of maturity wise sugarcane verities and conducting of surveys with the help of sugar mills.
- For ensuring the participation of sugar mills in the developmental programs and to engage the field staff available with the sugar factories for the development, an action plan old and unsuitable varieties will be replaced by early maturing verities so that area under unsuitable varieties is minimized.
- In western UP, sugarcane is commonly sown after harvesting wheat drop. In other part of the state, productivity level is hampered because of non-availability of productive irrigation. Strategies have been evolved to introduce technique of optimum use of limited water resources.
- Reallocation of sugar mill zone areas and providing stability to such realocated zones will be made. Intensive cane developmental programs will be carried out with the help of sugar mills in there reallocated zones.
- Arrangement for drainage for such factory areas where due to excessive rains water logging takes place. Introduction of water logging verities will be made to obtain maximum yield in adverse circumstances.
- A sizable chunk of sugarcane is diverted toward gur and khandsari. To minimize its diversion, drawl percentage is proposed to be raised from 55% to 65%, this will enable the growers to get maximum price of the maximum quantity produce.
- By strengthening cane union and making them more useful to the grower and also streamlining the activities of cane development council, a sound institutional base will be prepared to impart knowledge along with purchasing physical inputs.
- By organizing demonstration plots in the mill area as described below will be laid out.
  - o Mixed faming (potato, peas, corrigendum, wheat, etc.)
  - o Ratoon management
  - o Integrated pest management (IPM) and integrated disease management (IDM).
- By distribution of improved agricultural implements suitable strategies will be evolved to save labor.
- By introducing IPM including biological method and by introducing integrated nutrient management effort will be needed to obtain state average of 70 tons. As envisaged at the terminal year of the plan.
- Ratoon management is very much neglected in central eastern UP management of second and third ratoon will get special attention in 12th plan period.
- Heat therapy will be popularized amongst the growers to eradicate the menace of grassy shoot and other diseases.

Proposed Targets for the 12th Plan

The proposed is to keep the target for cane area at lowest possible level, i.e. the addition in area be minimum and the cane requirement of the sugar factories be met by increasing the yield per hectare and stepping up the per hectare supplies to the sugar factories. The targets for the terminal year of the 10th plan are proposed as follows (Table 1.26).

Keeping in view the propagation of different kinds of new varieties of sugarcane having higher productivity, the level in western, UP is up to the level of 75 million tons hectare. It can be achieved as in this region vast resources are available. As such with the view of developing the modern scientific techniques of cane cultivation, the target of productivity of sugarcane of the state has been proposed to the level of 70.00 million tons hectare. For achieving this target following intervention is proposed to be introduced during the 12th plan by the means district of sector and state sector.

Table 1.26: Proposed targets of area, average yield and total cane production for and of the 12th plan (2012–2017)

S. No.	*Particulars*	*Unit 2010–11*	*Year 2011–12*	*Year 2012–13*	*Year 2016–17*	*Terminal year of 12th plan*
1.	Cane area	Lakh hectare	21.01	22.51	23.00	24.00
2.	Average yield	Ton/hectare	56.34	60.00	62.00	70.00
3.	Total sugarcane production	Lakh ton	1183.98	1350.00	1426.00	1680.00
4.	Drawl	%	54	55	57	65
5.	Total cane crushed	Lakh ton	643.81	726.00	812.82	1092.00
6.	No. of sugar factory	No	125	124	126	128
7.	Crushing capacity	Lakh ton/TCD	7.67	7.70	7.80	8.50
8.	Sugar recovery	%	9.14	9.15	9.90	10.00
9.	Total sugar production	Lakh ton	58.87	70.00	80.47	109.00

Schemes Proposed in 12th 5 Year Plan

In 11th 5 year plan, following scheme were going on:

(A) Intensive cane development program:

- Improved seed production program
- Soil and seed treatment
- Ratoon management.

(B) Construction of link roads on contributed basis:

From the year 2011–2012, Rashtriya krishi vikash yojana (RKVY) started in the department and following seed production schemes were under taken:

1. Foundation seed nursery
2. Primary seed nursery
3. Seed transportation.

In RKVY, subsidy is Rs 50/quintal and Rs 25/quintal. On distribution of foundation and primary nursery seed respectively are proposed instead of plot subsidy of Rs 1,000, and Rs 500 per hectare. In district plan, this way district sector scheme and RKVY schemes created lot of differences in subsidy amount. Thus, farmers become least interested in district sector scheme. To provide the parity with RKVY scheme, subsidy in district sector scheme are also proposed to be same. The scheme, construction of link road on contributory basis was running till 11th 5 year plan. But in eastern district of the state beneficiary institution like cane society, cane development council and sugar mills even the farmers are financially poor. That is why this scheme is not giving proper result in eastern UP. So in the 12th 5 year plan, new scheme is being proposed for eastern region.

A part from the development scheme cane department has not been able to provide officers/infrastructure to the DCO and some By CC and some Dy. CC. So, 20 DCO office and 1 Dy. CC office is proposed in 12th 5 year plan.

Brief description of the above scheme and plan are given below:

(A) Improved Seed Production Program

Under this scheme foundation and primary seed nurseries are raised at cane grower farms.

I. Foundation nursery: The breeder seed is provided from sugarcane research station for foundation seed nursery. The foundation nursery holders/cane growers maintaining foundation nursery will be provided maximum 25 quintal breeder seed from sugarcane research station. After raising the foundation nursery, about 100,000 quintal seed will be available for distribution for raising primary nursery. After seed distributed from foundation nursery, maximum Rs 12,500 will be provided as subsidy to the farmers Rs 50 quintal.

The detail of the physical and financial requirement of the program is as follows:

Year	*Breeder seed availability (quintal)*	*Foundation seed produced (quintal)*	*Rs of subsidy (Rs quintal)*	*Financial requirement (lakh Rs)*
2012–2013	10,000	100,000	50.00	50.00
2013–2014	11,266	112,500	50.00	56.25
2014–2015	12,533	125,000	50.00	62.50
2015–2016	13,733	137,500	50.00	68.75
2016–2017	15,000	1,500,000	50.00	75.00
Total	**62,533**	**1,975,000**	**50.00**	**312.50**

II. Primary seed nursery: Seed producers in foundation nursery will be used for raising primary nursery. A farmer will be provided maximum 50 quintal foundation seed. Thus in primary nursery, about 10.00 lakh quintal seed will be produced for general distribution and Rs 25/quintal. Maximum upto Rs 12,500 subsidy per nursery holder will be provided.

The detail of the physical and financial requirement of the program is as follows:

Year	*Primary seed availability (quintal)*	*Rs of subsidy (Rs quintal)*	*Financial requirement (lakh Rs)*
2012–2013	1,000,000	25.00	250.00
2013–2014	1,125,000	25.00	281.25
2014–2015	1,250,000	25.00	312.50
2015–2016	1,375,000	25.00	343.75
2016–2017	1,500,000	25.00	375.00
Total	**6,250,000**		**1562.50**

(B) Soil and Seed Treatment

Under this program, insecticides, fungicides and germicide are used for controlling soil and seed borne disease, insect and pests. For encouraging germination of cane seed before sowing cane seed are treated with mercurial chemical/compound. At present is Rs 1,000 per hectare. It is required for seed and soil treatment subsidy of 50% maximum upto Rs 500 will be provided.

The detail of the physical and financial requirement of the program is as follows:

Year	*Area to be treated (lakh hectare)*	*Rate of subsidy (Rs hectare)*	*Financial requirement (lakh Rs)*
2012–2013	0.50	500.00	250.00
2013–2014	0.562	500.00	281.25
2014–2015	0.625	500.00	312.50
2015–2016	0.687	500.00	343.75
2016–2017	0.750	500.00	375.00
Total	**3.125**	**500.00**	**1562.50**

(C) Ratoon Management

About 50% area of the sugarcane is covered by ratoon crops. To improve the productivity of cane, proper management of the ratoon crop is very necessary improved management of ratoon is also required to augment the sugar recovery in ratoon management urea plus insecticides is sprayed on ratoon crop. This is very popular agricultural practice in western and central UP. Farmers generally used pesticide with urea solution. In this scheme, 50% cost of pesticides used in urea spray is to being subsidized, maximum upto Rs 150 per hectare.

The detail of the physical and financial requirement of the program is as follows:

Year	*Area to be managed (lakh hectare)*	*Rate subsidy (Rs hectare)*	*Financial requirement (lakh Rs)*
2012–2013	0.143	150.00	21.50
2013–2014	0.161	150.00	24.19
2014–2015	0.175	150.00	26.88
2015–2016	0.197	150.00	29.56
2016–2017	0.215	150.00	32.25
Total	**0.851**		**134.38**

(D) Transportation and Handling of Cane Seed

Nursery seed is to be transported from research stations for raising foundation seed nurseries and from foundation nurseries to primary nurseries. Apart from transportation careful handling, like proper seed set cutting, is also very primary seed will be subsidized in this scheme 1st year (2012–2013) about 10,000 quintal. Breeder seed will be available and be transported from research station to farmers field about 1,00 lakh. Speed are available in primary nursery all ready produced in on going scheme will be available for distribution. The detail of the physical and financial requirement of the program is as follows:

For breeder seed

Year	*Seed availability (quintal)*	*Rate subsidy (per quintal Rs)*	*Financial requirement (lakh Rs)*
2012–2013	10,000	15.00	1.50
2013–2014	11,267	15.00	1.69
2014–2015	12,533	15.00	1.88
2015–2016	13,733	15.00	2.06
2016–2017	15,000	15.00	2.25
Total	**62,533**		**9.38**

The detail of the physical and financial requirement of the program is following:

For foundation seed

Year	*Seed availability (quintal)*	*Rate subsidy (per quintal Rs)*	*Financial requirement (lakh Rs)*
2012–2013	100,000	7.00	7.00
2013–2014	112,571	7.00	7.88
2014–2015	125,000	7.00	8.75
2015–2016	137,429	7.00	9.62
2016–2017	150,000	7.00	10.50
Total	**625,000**		**43.75**

(E) Use of Biofertilizers Vermin Compost

Biofertilizers/vermin compost is an eco friendly and balance fertilizers which give all nutritional element to the crop. Importance of biofertilizers and vermin composing need no emphasis. About Rs 1,250 is the cost of biofertilizers/vermin compost per hectare. Thus, 50% subsidy upto Rs 600 per hectare is proposed. The detail of the physical and financial requirement is shown in Table 1.26A. Details for the 12th and 11th plans are in Tables 1.26B to 1.26H.

Table 26A: Area and subsidy

Year	*Area to be managed (lakh hectare)*	*Rate subsidy (Rs hectare)*	*Financial requirement (lakh Rs)*
2012–2013	0.20	600.00	120.00
2013–2014	0.225	600.00	135.00
2014–2015	0.250	600.00	150.00
2015–2016	0.275	600.00	165.00
2016–2017	0.300	600.00	180.00
Total	**1.25**		**750.00**

Table 1.26B: Proposed physical targets during 12th five year plan (2012–2013 to 2016–2017)

S. No.	*Programs*	*Unit*	*2012–2013*	*2016–2017*	*Total plan period*
1.	Cane area	Lakh hectare	23.00	24.00	117.50
2.	Productivity (average yield)	Ton/hectare	62.00	70.00	66.00
3.	Cane production	Lakh/quintal	1,426.00	1,680.00	7,873.00
4.	Laying out of cane seed nurseries				
	• Foundation	Quintal	100,000	150,000	625,000.00
	• Primary	Quintal	1,000,000	1,500,000	6,250,000.00
5.	Area to be treated				
	• Soil and aeed treatment	Hectare	50,000.00	75,000.00	312,500.00
	• Urea spray on ratoon crop	Hectare	14,334.00	22,026.00	89,587.50
6.	Transportation and handling of cane seed				
	• For breeder seed	Quintal	10,000	15,000	62,500.00
	• For foundation seed	Quintal	100,000	150,000	625,000.00
7.	Use of biofertilizer/ vermin compost	Hectare	20,000.00	30,000.00	125,000.00
8.	Construction				
	• Construction of intervillage link road	Km	334	337	1,693.00
	• Upgradation/streng-thening surface renewal of roads	Km	105	772	2,571.00

Table 1.26C: Proposed financial targets during 12th 5 year plan (2012–2013 to 2016–2017)

S. No.	*Programs*	*Unit*	*2012–2013*	*2016–2017*	*Total plan period*
1.	Laying out of cane seed nurseries	Lakh Rs			
2.	• Foundation	Lakh Rs	50.00	75.00	312.00
	• Primary	Lakh Rs	250.00	375.00	1,562.00
3.	Area to be treated	Lakh Rs			
	• Soil and seed treatment	Lakh Rs	250.00	375.00	1,562.00
	• Urea spray on ratoon crop	Lakh Rs	21.50	32.25	134.38
4.	Transportation and handling of cane seed	Lakh Rs			
	• For foundation seed	Lakh Rs	1.50	2.25	9.38
	• For foundation seed	Lakh Rs	7.00	10.50	43.75
5.	Biofertilizer	Lakh Rs	120.00	180.00	750.00
	Total		**700.00**	**1,050.00**	**4,375.00**
6.	Construction				
	• Construction of inter-village link road	Lakh Rs	4,900.00	6,000.00	27,400.00
	• Upgradation/strengthening/surface renewal of roads	Lakh Rs	1,400.00	12,500.00	38,900.00
	Total		**6,300.00**	**18,500.00**	**66,300.00**
	Grand Total		**7,000.00**	**19,550.00**	**70,675.00**

Table 1.26D: Present status: 11th plan (2007–2008 to 2011–2012)

Average cane productivity	:	56.76 Mt. ha.
Maximum productivity	:	58.80 Mt. ha. (year 2009–2010)
Average sugar recovery	:	9.30%
Maximum sugar recovery	:	9.79% (year 2007–2008)
Maximum sugar production	:	73.19 lakh Mt. (year 2007–2008)
Amount sanctioned and utilized	:	158.00 crore

Table 1.26E: Inter-state comparison 2011 (subtropical region)

S. No.	*State*	*Cane area (thousand hectare)*	*Av. yield (ton per hectare)*	*Cane crushed (lakh ton)*	*Sugar production (lakh ton)*	*Sugar (recovery %)*
1.	Uttar Pradesh	2,175	56.70	643.81	58.87	9.13
2.	Haryana	85	70.40	43.46	3.92	9.01
3.	Punjab	70	59.60	34.33	3.02	8.80
4.	Bihar	300	50.00	14.60	3.85	9.30
5.	All India	4,944	68.06	2,398.07	243.94	10.17

Source: Indian Sugar: December 2011 Vol. no. (LXI).

- Highest sugarcane area being 42.50% of the total cane area in the country.
- Highest cane area in subtropical region being 82% of the total area.
- Second in cane crushed and sugar production in the country after Maharashtra.
- Second in sugar recovery in subtropical states
- Second sugarcane department rural road net work after Maharashtra.

Vision for 12th 5 Year Plan

- Increase the cane productivity per hectare 60–70 million tons.
- Increase the area of early maturing and high-yielding varieties from 14% to 25%

Table 1.26F: Goals and priorities

S. No.	*Particulars*	*Unit*	*Upto year 2011–2012*	*Terminal year of 12th plan 2016–2017*
1.	Cane area	Lakh hectare	22.51	24.00
2.	Average yield	Ton/hectare	60.00	70.00
3.	Early maturing and high-yielding varieties	%	14.00	25.00
4.	Total sugarcane production	Lakh ton	1350.00	1,680.00
5.	Total sugarcane production	Lakh ton	726.00	1092.00
6.	Sugar recovery	%	9.15	10.00
7.	Total sugar production	Lakh ton	70.00	109.00
8.	Rural road network			
	• Intervillage link road	Km	11,700.00	13,393.00
	• Upgradation of road	Km	–	2,571.00

Table 1.26G: Major targets and monitorable targets

S. No.	*Particulars*	*Unit*	*Year 2012–13*	*Year 2013–14*	*Year 2014–15*	*Year 2016–17*	*Year 2015–16*
1.	Cane area	Lakh hactare	23.00	23.25	23.50	23.75	24.00
2.	Average yield	Ton/hectare	62.00	64.00	66.00	68.00	70.00
3.	Total sugarcane production	Lakh ton	1,426.00	1,500.00	1,575.00	1,625.00	1,680.00
4.	Sugar recovery	%	9.90	9.92	9.96	9.98	10.00
5.	Total sugar production	Lakh ton	80.47	89.28	97.11	101.29	109.00
6.	• Construction of new link road (including Poorvanchal)	Km	334.00	339.00	341.00	342.00	337.00
	• Upgradation of road	Km	105.00	499.00	545.00	650.00	772.00

- Special attention in insect, pest and disease control.
- Maintain the decreasing soil fertility.
- A suitable road network for speedy sugarcane supply according to the Marg Niti, approved by UP government.
- To reduce regional imbalance development of road network with special emphasis on eastern UP.

Table 1.26H: Sector-wise requirement for the 12th five year plan

Schemes 2012–2013	*Year*					*Total amount (in lakh)*
	2013–14	*2014–15*	*2015–16*	*2016–17*		
Intensive cane development	700.00	787.51	875.01	962.49	1,050.00	4,375.01
Construction of intervillage link road/upgradation of rural road network	6,300.00	12,200.00	13,500.00	15,800.00	18,500.00	66,300.00
Total	**7,000.00**	**12,987.51**	**14,375.01**	**16,762.49**	**19,550.00**	**70,675.01**

New Initiatives During the 12th Plan

- Instead of plot subsidy in seed nurseries, subsidy on seed distribution.
- Improved management of ratoon crop, seed and soil treatment, thus improve the productivity and sugar recovery.
- Subsidy for transportation and handling of cane seed.
- Use of biofertilizer/vermin compost.
- Emphasis on development, upgradation/strengthening of rural road network.
- Reduce regional imbalances in eastern UP.

Major Area/Schemes

Improved Seed Production Programs

1. **Foundation nursery:**
   - Further multiplication of breeder seed, foundation nursery at farmer's field.
   - Subsidy of 50/quintal after seed distribution.
   - Seed distribution of 6.25 lakh quintal and finance required Rs 312.50 lakh
2. **Primary nursery:**
   - Further multiplication of foundation seed nursery, primary nursery at field.
   - Subsidy of 25/quintal after seed distribution.
   - Seed distribution of 62.50 lakh quintal and finance required Rs 1,562.50 lakh.
3. **Soil and seed treatment:**
   - Control the soil and seed borne diseases and pests.
   - Cost of pesticide of 1 hectare about 1,000.00 subsidy of 50% maximum upto Rs 500/hectare.
   - Area to be treated 3.125 lakh/hectare.
   - Financial requirement Rs 1,562.50 lakh.

4. Ratoon management:

- About 50% area of the sugarcane covered by ratoon crop.
- Cost of pesticides of spray in 1 hectare about Rs 300 subsidy of 50% maximum upto 150 hectare.
- Area to be managed 0.891 lakh hectares.
- Financial requirement Rs 134.38 lakh.

SUGAR: TOWARD DEREGULATION

While India's original sugar policy had the government playing a very big role, ostensibly to protect farmers and ensure a sufficient supply of sugar for the public distribution system (PDS), over the years, excessive controls have led to stagnation of this sector. Decontrol and a hands-off approach by the government are expected to unleash the true potential of this large agro-based industry.

Sugar industry is the second largest agro-based industry after cotton textile industry. And India is the second largest producer of sugarcane in the world after Brazil, besides being the largest consumer of sugar. The industry supports about 50 million farmers. It is a Rs 800-billion industry with sugar mills directly paying cane farmers Rs 550 billion a year (Table 1.27).

Current Status

With around 5 million tons of sugar carryover stock and annual sugar production of 24.3 million tons in 2010–2011, India had an availability of around 29.3 million tons of sugar for 2010–2011. The current domestic consumption (for 2011–2012) is 21.7 million tons. Under the levy obligation, the government supplies around 2.7 million tons of sugar to poor families at rates much below the market price. For this, sugar mills are required to sell 10% of their output to the government at cheaper rates. Also, farmers near a particular mill cannot sell elsewhere and the mill has to buy only from them. The sugar subsidy amounts to Rs 7,000 per ton, and about Rs 19,000 million for the distribution of 2.7 million tons via the PDS (excluding supply to the Army Purchase Organization). Apparently, the industry bears the subsidy burden, but ultimately farmers bear this as the mills cannot pay the due price to farmers because of levy obligation.

The ex-factory price (the rate at which the government buys sugar from the mills) of levy sugar was raised from Rs 17.61 per kg to around Rs 19.04 between 2009–2010 and 2011–2012 which is around Rs 28.30 per kg.

The Problems

In spite of the economic reforms undertaken by the government, the domestic sugar industry is still reeling under excessive government control. The industry has no control over the raw material price or its availability. The government controls sales volumes and the selling price of sugar. PDS sugar is supplied at 40% below production cost. Stocking of sugar is an obligation on the industry. Both exports and imports of sugar are controlled by the government. Nobody has benefited from excessive state control. In fact, it has adversely affected all stakeholder farmers, consumers, manufacturers and even the government. The government's sugar policy

Table 1.27: World statistics of sugarcane

Country	*Element*	*2000*	*2001*	*2002*	*2003*	*2004*	*Average*
Argentina	**A**	280	292	294	295	305	**293**
	Y	66	65	65	65	64	**65**
	P	18400	19050	19250	19250	19500	**19090**
Australia	**A**	419	411	417	423	415	**417**
	Y	91	76	77	90	89	**85**
	P	38165	31228	32260	37968	36892	**35303**
Brazil	**A**	4846	4958	5100	5337	5455	**5139**
	Y	68	70	71	73	75	**71**
	P	327705	345942	363721	389849	411010	**367645**
China	**A**	1189	1281	1421	1433	1316	**1328**
	Y	58	61	65	64	71	**64**
	P	69299	77966	92203	92039	93200	**84941**
Cuba	**A**	1041	1007	1041	654	700	**889**
	Y	35	32	33	35	34	**34**
	P	36400	32100	34700	22902	24000	**30020**
India	**A**	4220	4316	4412	4608	4100	**4331**
	Y	71	69	67	61	60	**66**
	P	299230	295956	297208	281600	244800	**283759**
Indonesia	**A**	366	386	350	340	340	**356**
	Y	65	65	73	72	72	**70**
	P	23900	25185	25530	24500	24600	**24743**
Mexico	**A**	618	624	632	639	639	**630**
	Y	71	76	72	71	71	**72**
	P	44100	47250	45635	45127	45127	**45448**
South Africa	**A**	322	322	325	325	305	**320**
	Y	74	66	71	63	63	**67**
	P	23876	21157	23013	20419	19292	**21551**
Sri Lanka	**A**	18	18	18	17	17	**18**
	Y	59	55	55	58	58	**57**
	P	1066	1006	963	1015	1000	**1010**
Thailand	**A**	922	850	793	1121	1050	**947**
	Y	54	71	94	70	61	**70**
	P	49563	60013	74258	78170	63707	**65142**
USA	**A**	418	416	414	402	389	**408**
	Y	78	75	78	76	71	**76**
	P	32762	31377	32253	30715	27501	**30922**

A: Area '000 ha; Y: Yield MT/ha; P: Production in '000 MT.
Source: FAOStat Database 2005.

appears to be counter-productive. Also, there is no linkage between cane prices paid to farmers and sugar prices, and its by-products molasses and bagasse.

Most sugar mills are financially weak. The mills have been bearing the brunt of the government's welfare policy. The subsidy to consumers which is borne by the mills (and the farmers) is estimated to be Rs 7,000 per ton. Around 2.7 million tons of sugar is supplied to the PDS. The loss to the mills is close to Rs 19 billion. Moreover, the PDS suffers from leakages. To overcome these problems, the government is now implementing a direct transfer of the subsidy in the form of cash, to the bank accounts of the poor households. Another problem relates to arrears to sugarcane farmers. In UP alone, this stands at Rs 4,930 million (Rs 4,610 million from private mills and the rest from public sector mills).

Strengthening the Sugar Ecosystem

Experts feel that the government should remove the levy sugar obligation and buy sugar in the open market. The monthly release scheme should also be dispensed with, and the government itself should maintain strategic stocks. A stable export policy under the OGL and removal of stock limits on traders and bulk users will help the industry. The sugar industry has requested the government to increase the import duty on raw sugar from 10% to 25% to safeguard the domestic market from price distortions. Farmers seek a 20% raise in cane prices owing to the rising costs of diesel, manure and labor. Also, mills recorded profits in the last quarter of the sugar year (October–September) 2011–2012. For the year 2012–2013, they are asking for Rs 300 a quintal or even higher. The Committee for Agricultural Costs and Prices (CACP) has recommended a FRP of Rs 210 per quintal for sugarcane for the season beginning October 2013. This would be an increase of Rs 40 over the price fixed for the current season. It is said that the entire industry will benefit from the increase in FRP, as the levy sugar price is calculated on the basis of FRP for the industry, including for mills where there is a State Advised Price (SAP) as in UP, Uttarakhand, Punjab, Haryana and Tamil Nadu.

The concept of FRP was introduced in October 2009, replacing the statutory minimum price (SMP). It is fixed after taking into account the margins for cane farmers on account of risk, as well as profit on the cost of production, including transport expenses. The Commission for Agricultural Costs and Prices (CACP) also suggested creation of 4 million tons of sugar buffer stock, and use of export and import duties to reduce volatility in prices. In March 2012, the government relaxed its rules for sugar exports. Earlier, it used to allocate an export quota to every mill based on its production during the previous 3 years. The recent decision allows exports under the open general licence (OGL) VI plan. Mills are happy as the quota system has been done away with. The CACP has suggested that the government should do away with the levy quota on sugar mills as this reduces the mill's ability to adequately compensate sugarcane farmers. The Commission felt that the government should either buy sugar from the mills at market prices for the PDS or let the state government buy it and reimburse the difference between the market price and subsidized price. The idea is to transfer the subsidy burden from the mills to the government. The dual pricing regime should be dismantled. The Union Food Ministry has come up with two proposals for fixing the new retail price of sugar sold in ration shops (levy sugar) to reduce the food subsidy bill. The proposals are:

1. Allow the state governments to fix the price as per their financial resources. This means different levy sugar prices in different states/union territories.
2. The Food Ministry may fix a uniform price for the levy sugar across the country in the existing price band of Rs 13.5 per kg to Rs 25.37 per kg—the price at which the subsidy on levy sugar is nil.

The report's recommendations ensure an FRP to farmers. Thereafter, farmers would be paid 75% of the prices that mills realize for selling sugar and its byproducts—a figure that is to be recalculated every quarter. This will link farmers' remuneration to market prices. The report also advocates the freedom for farmers to sell cane to any mill, irrespective of distance. It even suggests doing away with the compulsory jute packaging. This will help the industry save Rs 10 billion, annually. The government should consider linking cane prices to the price of sugar and its by-products—the imputed value of molasses and bagasse—to help the farmers and the industry. We have to strategically manage demand-supply situation in the market to reduce volatility in the availability and price of sugar. Bagasse has the potential of generating 4,000–5,000 MW of power. Stable cane production would help in a continual and stable supply of bagasse to power producers. The country's hydrocarbon resources are limited. Most developed countries are relying on alternative fuel technologies, and allowing blending of ethanol with petrol. So India, too, should explore these options on a large scale.

The decontrol of sugar is expected to help the farmers. They will be able to negotiate with millers based on a profit-sharing mechanism linked to sugar prices. They can sell cane to the mill that offers the highest price and are likely to get prompt payments. Mills too should be happy as they will no longer have to bear the burden of levy sugar. They will also be able to export when international prices are good.

A Bitter Sugar Industry Cries for Deregulation

To save the sugar industry from death, the government should remove levy obligation immediately, buy sugar in the open market and promote a futures market. Sugar it is one of the most environment-friendly industries producing green power and also addressing the energy need of the country through ethanol. India is the largest consumer and second largest producer of sugar in the world.

Excessive Controls

Despite two decades of economic liberalization that sought to end the control era, the domestic sugar industry is still reeling under excessive government controls. For instance, raw material prices are not in industry hands; raw material availability is not in industry hands; sales volume is not in industry hands due to monthly release mechanism; selling prices of sugar are not in industry hands; supply of PDS sugar is at 40% below production cost; stocking of sugar is an obligation on the industry; cash-flow planning is not in industry hands; packaging material of sugar is not in industry hands, export-import of sugar is not in industry hands; stock limit on bulk consumers and traders is applied on domestic sugar and none on imported sugar; and other ad-hoc controls by the central and state governments. Unfortunately, sugar is the country"s only industry that has no control or say in its own fate despite supporting about 50 million farmers and generating employment for about 12% of the total rural population in nine major sugar producing states. The excessive control on the industry is even disproportionate to its impact on consumers and farmers. Sugarcane accounts for only 2.58% of total gross cropped area, and the share of sugar is just 2.4% and 1.5% of the total consumer expenditure for rural and urban India, respectively. Additionally, household consumption accounts for just one-third of the total consumption of sugar with institutions and bulk consumers accounting for the remaining two-thirds. The industry clearly defies any need for so many regulations.

Regulations Breed Cyclicality

Instead of helping anybody, the multiple controls have, in fact, adversely affected all stakeholders: farmers, consumers, manufacturers and the government. Moreover, the present structure has created a situation of "repetitive cyclicality", restricting industry's growth and its development whereby successive high cane prices induce surplus production, bring down sugar price, affect profitability and lead to cane arrears that, in turn, forces the farmer to cut down cane production. Reduced cane production leads to lower sugar production and, hence, firming up of sugar prices, leading to remunerative cane prices paid to farmers. And this "repetitive cyclicality" has become a hallmark of the industry, restricting its growth and development. It is understandable that farmers should be given remunerative and attractive cane price as incentive since cane is a longer-duration and labor-intensive crop. However, government's fixing unviable sugarcane price with no linkage to sugar prices makes it difficult to give reasonable cane price to farmers. The industry has paid around 55,000 crore in cane price in 2010–2011. This will further increase in the current year. Successive increase in cane price leads to repetitive cyclicality and even more intense government regulations on prices, open market sale, exports and imports to control prices. Thus, the industry oscillates between a deficient year and a surplus year.

Levy Sugar Obligation

The sugar industry has to bear 10% levy sugar obligation for providing sugar to the government for PDS at prices much below the cost of production. The estimated loss to the industry last year on account of this has been around 3,000 crore. If the government buys sugar in the open market for PDS, the estimated burden would be around 3,000 crore. This would be minuscule compared to the overall food subsidy bill of 70,000 crore.

Release Mechanism and Stocking

There is a regulated monthly release mechanism scheme that governs supply and sale of sugar in the market. Further, stocking of sugar as per the government norms has cost the industry around. 40,000 crore in the previous year, denting industry's margin significantly.

Export under OGL

Even during the years of surplus production, the sugar industry cannot export its surplus stock under open general licence. It has to abide by the export quota decided by the government, even during surplus years, belying any economic rationale for such an obstructive policy.

Lack of Linkage Among Prices

Curiously, there is no linkage between cane prices paid to farmers, and sugar prices and its by-products (molasses and bagasse). The government should consider linking cane prices to sugar and by-product prices—imputed value of molasses and bagasse—to help the industry and the farmer to strategically plan demand-supply in the market, and reduce volatility in availability of sugar and its prices. Bagasse has a potential of generating 4,000–5,000 mw of power. Stable cane crop production would help in continuous and stable supply of bagasse to power producers. Given the fact that hydrocarbon resources are limited, most of the developed countries are giving preference to alternative fuel technologies and allowing blending of ethanol with petrol. However, lack of a proper ethanol pricing formula is affecting its use in its blending with petrol. Considering that the country is a fast-growing economy and our energy needs are substantial and also petroleum subsidy at times of high international prices is hurting country's fiscal health, the government needs to finalize ethanol pricing formula at the earliest. Similarly, molasses have a role to play in alcohol industry and also in production of ethanol for blending with petrol.

Immediate Policy Action Needed

The industry is seeking complete decontrol and reforms of the sector in larger interest of all stakeholders. The industry needs immediate policy action to avoid building up of cane arrears and smooth operations of sugar mills in the ensuing sugar season. To begin with, the government should remove levy sugar obligation immediately and buy sugar in the open market. Monthly release scheme should also be dispensed with and the government should itself maintain strategic stock. A transparent and robust forward and futures market for sugar should be promoted. The policy should link sugarcane price with sugars' and its by-products' prices to arrive at a more realistic cane price. A stable export policy under the OGL and removal of stock limits on traders and bulk users will help the industry. Finalizing ethanol pricing formula and allowing packaging of sugar in any food grade material would be in the interest of the industry. Decontrol of the sector is the only way forward lest it gets destabilized under the excessive burden of regulations, and withers away.

Sugar Solution a Ray of Hope for Bihar Kids Battling "Brain Fever"

India is yet to identify the cause of the mysterious "brain fever" that is killing young children in Muzaffarpur in Bihar, but experts have identified a treatment—administering dextrose, a basic form of sugar. Annual outbreaks of acute encephalitis syndrome (AES) have killed hundreds of poor children in Muzaffarpur each summer for more than two decades, causing 140 deaths in June this year.

The disease kills 40–60% of the affected children with an average age of 6 years. Finally, there seems t o be a cure.

"Giving 10% dextrose (sugar) solution intravenously as soon as possible, preferably between 4 hours of the onset of symptoms, is saving lives as almost all children have symptoms of acute hypoglycemia (low blood sugar)", said Dr Jacob John, pediatrician and virologist, formerly with Christian Medical College, Vellore, who investigated deaths on the invitation of Bihar government.

"The cause is unknown, all we know is that all the children hospitalized have acutely low levels of blood glucose, as low as 10 when the healthy fasting levels are between 70 mg/dL and 100 mg/dL", said Union Health Minister Harsh Vardhan, who visited Muzaffarpur and examined medical reports of the hospitalized children. "We have tested for all viruses isolated in India, and the results are negative. We are not even sure whether it is a virus, vector (*Culex mosquito* that causes Japanese encephalitis) or an environmental toxin, such as a pesticide or something found in food or water", said Vardhan, who visited Muzaffarpur to review the situation on Saturday.

"I suspect it is a combination of factors and till the cause is identified, the treatment protocol will be symptomatic: giving intravenous dextrose infusion for low blood suger, oxygen for respiratory distress and medicine to control seizures", the toxin methylenecyclopropyl-glycine (MCPG) in lychee seed (it has not yet been analyzed in ripe or unripe fruit), use of organochlorine pesticides and intense summer heat are some of the suspected causes. But in all cases, the symptoms appear early in the morning—between 4 AM and 6 AM—after several hours of fasting, which indicates a metabolic disease", said Dr John, who has published a paper in Current Science.

Strings Attached

- The carrots interest-free loan up to Rs 4,400 crore
- Export subsidy of Rs 3,300/kg till September
- Ethanol mixing increased to 10% from 5%
- The riders
- Mills must give assurance to pay cane farmers
- Relief package only after cane arrears worth Rs 11,000 crores are paid.

Sugar Companies and Investors

The steps announced by the government to revive the sugar industry seem to have generated renewed interest in the shares of major producers while the government's steps are positive for the sector, resolution of structural issues such as linking the price of sugarcane with sugar will be important for the long-term profitability of the manufacturers. "The rally appears to be driven more by sentiment than fundamental factors", said an analyst who refused to be named. Over the next few quarters, sugar prices will depend on the monsoon.

A less-than-normal rainfall will impact sugar production next season, pushing up sugar prices, the analyst said, highlighting possible risks to the sector. The government decided to increase the import duty on raw sugar to 40% from 15%, provide additional interest-free loans to mills and increase ethanol blending in petrol to 10% from 5% at present. Ethanol is produced by sugar manufactures and its increased usage will help these companies.

The higher import duty will boost domestic sugar prices that are subdued at the moment, helping local producers, said Sanjay Manyal, sugar industry analyst at ICICI Direct. At the current sugar prices of Rs 31 per kg, many companies are making losses; they may break even after this measure. Sugar price is estimated to increase by Rs 1–2 from this measure.

"Improved access to loans should support mills' efforts to clear the mountain of sugarcane dues and improve balance sheet before the new crushing season begins", said Kamal Jain of Kamal Jain Trading Services. This will, in turn, lead to better margins. The government's intention to increase ethanol blending to 10% from 5% earlier would have limited impact on the profitability of sugar companies.

Sugar manufacturing companies have been making losses due to continued increase in sugarcane prices, even as sugar prices remained flat due to surplus production. For long-term profitability, sugarcane procurement prices may need to be linked with sugar prices.

The Rangarajan Committee appointed by the previous government had recommended a revenue-sharing formula, with mills sharing 70% of revenue from the sale of sugar and its by-products with farmers. This was expected to help to reduce earnings voltality and maintain reasonably good profits for sugar manufacturing companies.

Sugar Stocks Rally, may Gain More in Short-Term

Shares of sugar companies shot up as much as 10% on Monday after the government raised import duty on the sweetener to 40% from 15% and decided to increase the mandatory ethanol blending level in gasoline to 10% from 5% as the Center tries to revive the industry that owes farmers around Rs 11,000 crore. The positive government steps will change market perception about the sugar sector.

"Traders will find short-term investment opportunities, although a long-term investment call remains tough due to its commodity cycle", said Kunj Bansal, executive director and chief investment officer at Centrum Wealth Management. Shree Renuka Sugars surged 10.32% to Rs 29.40, Bajaj Hindusthan rallied 9.87% to Rs 29.50, Dhampur Sugar Mills jumped 7.81% to Rs 65.60 while Balrampur Chini Mills gained 7.04% to Rs 85.15 following the government announcement.

Analysts said the announcement will give respite to an industry that has had surplus output for the last 4 years. Sugar stockpiles at the end of the 2013–2014 season were estimated at 7.5 million tons. The increase in import duty will make overseas purchases nearly unviable in the world's consumer of sugar, hurting shipments from global suppliers such as Brazil, Thailand and Pakistan.

Besides, the government will extend the sugar export subsidy of Rs 3,300 per ton until September to boost output and exports, and provide additional interest-free loans to the tune of Rs 4,400 crore to cashstarved sugar mills to make payments to cane farmers.

"The government announcement has lifted sentiments about sugar companies, which have underperformed the markets over the recent past. We expect some rerating in the sector going forward", said Alex Mathews, head of research at Geojit BNP Paribas Financial Services. The government's initiative to promote ethanol blending could help it reduce the current account deficit (CAD) and boost mills' earnings.

A bigger rerating for the industry will come once sugarcane prices are linked to sugar prices, analysts said. Local sugar prices, which have been subdued due to rising stockpiles, jumped 1.5% on Monday after the announcement and are likely to rise further if monsoon rains stay subdued, said analysts. The government's steps will provide higher realisation for sugar companies.

"However, if monsoon is below normal, then sugarcane extracts can see a major decline which will be negative for the industry", said Tirthankar Patnaik, director and strategist of institutional research at Religare Capital Markets.

500 gm Sugar Added to Food Security Plan

The Narendra Modi-led government at the Center has given its nod to Delhi's plan to sweeten the food security subsidy of rice and wheat with 500 gm of sugar per beneficiary. The state has brought 37 lakh beneficiaries into the fold of the food security law so far. Delhi government hopes to add 2.5 lakh beneficiaries every month to the existing list to reach the 73 lakh target.

If assembly polls are held sometime later this year, the sugar subsidy may boost BJP's presence among beneficiaries from the low income group. The majority of this section traditionally supporters of the Congress shifted support to AAP in the Delhi assembly polls in December 2013.

The Delhi government's food and civil supplies department had written to the concerned departments under the union government about the state's plan to provide 500 gm of sugar to the beneficiaries along with rice and wheat at the subsidized rates. As of now every beneficiary gets 4 kg of wheat at Rs 2 per kg and 1 kg of rice at Rs 3 per kg under Food Security Program. Delhi now wants to add sugar to it.

The capital gets 2,900 tons of sugar from the union government as its monthly quota of rations.

Government Unveils Sops for Cash-Starved Sugar Sector

Mills are facing a cash crunch as domestic prices have slipped below the cost of production, thus negatively impacting profits. Industry fears that domestic prices of the commodity could fall further if cheaper imports are not curbed. Currently, sugarcane arrears stand at about Rs 11,000 crore across the country, with the maximum of Rs 7,200 crore being in UP—a state which is fixing higher prices due to political reasons thus "putting burden on millers". Food Minister Ramvilas Paswan, while announcing the key decisions taken at a high-level inter-ministerial meeting today, called for "a holistic view on pricing".

Paswan said that efforts would also be made to increase ethanol blending with petrol to 10%. Currently, ethanol blending is less than 2%. However, sources say the government is making plans to make ethanol blending mandatory for petroleum companies.

The decisions follow the directions of the Prime Minister Principal Secretary. The minister said the four key decisions included extension of interest-free loan given against excise duty paid by sugar mills for 5 years instead of 4 years. Paswan said the department was yet to calculate the exact interest-free loans to be provided to the industry.

In December, the UPA government had approved Rs 6,600 crore interest-free loans for the sugar industry for clearing growers' dues. It decided to give loans via banks equivalent to the excise duty paid by the mills in the past 3 years.

According to the minister, the decisions will be announced subject to the condition that mills give guarantee that they will clear Rs 11,000 crore sugarcane arrears at the earliest. "We do not have any problems to announce these incentives formally if millers are ready to make payments. If they give assurance today, we will announce incentives today itself".

Some of the decisions will be notified by ministries concerned while some require the Cabinet nod, he added. The sugar industry welcomed the announcements, assuring that it would clear the arrears as fast as possible.

The key decisions would benefit the industry and improve the liquidity of the sugar mills, which would help the industry to clear the pending payments to cane growers at the earliest. The 10% ethanol blending would save forex of $1.6–1.7 bn, which is a huge plus for the country as it would improve the revenue deficits.

Also there is a need to improve the sugar prices to allow mills to at least cover their cost of producing sugar. A 40% duty on sugar import would ensure that no sugar from other nations makes its way into the Indian markets. Though there are apprehensions that the move may see an increase in sugar prices by Rs 2–3, the industry representatives say given the excess production and losses suffered by mills due to difference between cost of production and ex-mill prices (Rs 4 in UP and Rs 1.5 in western and southern regions), the move was necessary.

We already have about 20–25 lakh tons of surplus sugar with us. This would definitely improve the market sentiments, domestic sugar prices, and better buying by the traders and wholesalers.

Prices may Go Up

- The center has announced an additional interest-free loan of up to ~4,400 crore for mills to pay arrears to cane growers.
- The government has also hiked the import duty on sugar from the existing 15–40%. The move may raise the sugar prices by Rs 2–3.

Sweet News: A Sugar that Helps Protect Hearts

A spoonful of sugar is all you need to keep your heart healthy, according to scientists who claim to have come up with a new type of the sweetener which can prevent cardiac failure.

An international team has, in fact, developed the new type of sugar—combination of sugar and seleno—that works by preventing reactive acids from damaging the heart, the "Chemical Communications" journal reported.

Our seleno-sugar compounds work by scavenging hypohalous acids, a group of highly reactive chemicals that can damage tissues when produced in the wrong place, at the wrong time or at excessive levels.

"One predictor of future heart disease in patients is the raised level of the enzyme that produces these hypohalous acids", Professor Carl Schiesser at University of Melbourne, who led the team. The team discovered their seleno-sugar compounds are able to prevent hypohalous acids from damaging the important amino acids in human plasma, a key step in stopping the development of disease.

The scientists are now working to optimize their compounds for future pharmaceutical use. "We are hoping that in the future our new chemicals will keep

State of Affairs Cost of Sugarcane Production Rs Quintal

	2005–06	*2006–07*	*2007–08*
Andhra Pradesh	96.08	88.71	106.06
Haryana	90.48	92.37	96.52
Karnataka	73.83	63.62	48.46
Maharashtra	94.91	80.15	76.29
Tamil Nadu	77.3	78.22	73.45
Uttar Pradesh	68.86	68.49	73.35
Uttarakhand	58.03	66.37	57.77

Source: Ministry of agriculture.

matters of the heart sweet. Well, at least health-wise!" Dr Corin Storkey, a team member, said.

"One way to get out of this impasse is really to expedite exports", a food ministry official acknowledged.

Corn is Ready to Sweeten Our Lives

The humble corn, mostly fed to chickens, is all set to become the Sir Galahad of India's sugar economy. Corn contains starch, which yields a thick sweet liquid called high fructose corn syrup (HFCS). This syrup can't be made into table sugar crystals we use at home. But, it is perfect for anything that needs melted sugar such as biscuits, confectionery, gulab jamuns, icecreams, cold drinks and even wines. You can even adjust the sweetness. Some HFCS concentrates are 30% sweeter than cane juice. Countries that don't grow cane, such as the US have been using fructose for 30 years. While sugarcane was cheap and plentiful, there seemed little point in India following suit. But with sugar at Rs 40 per kilo, we have crossed the Rubicon. India grows 18 million tons of corn annually and 1 kg gives 600 gm fructose. Industry watchers say, at current corn prices, the basic grade, HFCS 45%, would cost Rs 26 a kg at factory gate and can reach the wholesale market in barrels, post tax , at about Rs 32 per kg. By-products will fetch extra. Suddenly, locally-produced fructose is the smart cheaper alternative. HFCS has other advantages. Corn needs less water, nutrients and labor than cane, and grown by marginal farmers in Bihar, Karnataka and Andhra Pradesh, who could do with encouragement. More importantly, not being politically sensitive, corn enjoys a free market. Attracted by the unmistakable smell of profit, starch companies are rapidly homing in. Although corporate plans are still hush-hush , India's first HFCS factories are expected to start manufacturing within next 6 months.

"We will start with HFCS 45%. Our calculations show that local fructose will always be at least Rs 2 per kg cheaper than sugar. That would mean big saving for industrial users. Moreover, with a 30% import duty, there is no threat yet from imported HFCS", said a player in the starch industry. Even if India starts producing HFCS, would it remain a niche product or actually make a difference to our lives? That depends on how fast volumes grow. Cola companies are among Indian sugar's biggest industrial consumers. Abroad they routinely use HFCS 55%, a premium grade. But in India, fructose is still not on the agenda. To replace sugar, they need to be sure of getting reliable and ample supply at different locations across the country. That will take time.

Taste is another factor. We are used to a syrupy taste, with a full-bodied , lingering mouth feel in our cold drinks. PepsiCo gave its American consumers a nip of what we drink by introducing Pepsi and Mountain Dew Throwback versions, made with pure sugar instead of HFCS, as a 2-month promotion. So, getting Indians, especially the kids, to adapt to a new taste might be tough. But, other food companies can profit from fructose much faster. If HFCS replaces even 30% of their sugar consumption, it could be a game changer and free us from dependence on imports.

The Need for Sugar Decontrol

For years, the sugar industry was heavily controlled. Partial de-control has not led to dramatic price increases for sugar in the open market, as had been expected by those who opposed de-controlling of the sector. It now remains to be seen whether this state of affairs, with the center bearing the large burden of subsidizing sugar for PDS distribution, can be sustained in the long-term.

In a recent landmark decision, the union government has abolished the levy sugar mechanism and regulated the release mechanism to de-control the Indian sugar industry. At the same time, it has ensured that poorer sections of society continue to get sugar at the existing subsidized prices, by taking upon itself the entire financial burden of distributing sugar through ration shops. A notification in this regard has been issued on May 7, 2013.

By this landmark decision, the government has ensured that the interests of all segments of the sugar economy—be it industries, farmers, consumers and the poor are safeguarded.

For the sugar industries, this measure will give them the freedom to sell their produce without any restrictions and improve their liquidity positions. This, in turn, will ensure that millions of sugarcane farmers in India don't have to wait for their dues from sugar millers while for consumers it means increase in sugar availability in the market by as much as 10% per year.

The government has decided to reimburse the state governments for purchasing and selling sugar through the PDS below the market rate. For this, the Center will bear an additional burden of around Rs 31 billion.

The issue of de-controlling the sugar industry has engaged the attention of the government for a very long time. There were representations from sugarcane farmers' associations as well as sugar mills both major stakeholders in the sugar industry that a price sharing formula for sugarcane was long overdue.

The government, too, thought about bringing in a level-playing field where interests of the consumers on one hand and development of the sugar industry on the other could be ensured.

The demand for decontrolling the sugar industry has stemmed from the cyclic nature of sugar production in the country. This put the sugar industry at a disadvantage, almost to the point that it was no longer a viable business option, finally affecting sugarcane farmers.

Following a normal year when there are no major cane price arrears, the farmers tend to plant larger areas under sugarcane. This leads to an increase in sugarcane production with the consequent increase in sugar production, which, in turn, leads to excess stocks resulting in depressed sugar prices and building up of cane price arrears. As a result of lower returns, the farmers tend to take less care of the cane, and areas under sugarcane get reduced in subsequent years. The years of reduced sugarcane production also witness higher diversion of cane for *gur* making, a significant part of which also finds its way into the liquor industry in the unorganized sector as a substitute for molasses, which itself would be in short supply. The lower production of sugarcane and higher diversion combine to cause higher scarcity of cane for crushing in sugar mills which results in disproportionately low sugar production.

As a result, the sugar prices rise, the mills get higher returns, the arrears position is taken care of, the farmers get a good price and are encouraged to plant more, and the area under sugarcane starts rising again. In 2–3 years, this leads to another year of peak production and the cycle starts all over again.

The central government was confident of taking on the burden arising out of sugar decontrol as the country achieved an output of 26.35 million metric tons of sugar during the 2011–2012 (October–September) sugar season, which was 2 million tons more than the sugar production of 24.35 million tons during the 2010–2011 sugar season. While the seasonal variation in sugar production also started to smoothen out over the last 3–4 years, the market price of sugar remained within reasonable levels throughout the 2012–2013 sugar season.

The Rangarajan Committee appointed by the government to look into the whole gamut of issues linked to sugar decontrol had observed that a levy amounts to a cross subsidy between the open market and the PDS sugar, and it is not in the interests of the general consumer or the development of the sugar sector. Hence the committee recommended that the levy on sugar be dispensed with.

So, two crucial issues emanating from the Rangarajan Committee's report came up before the government for a decision. These were: one, whether sugar is to continue being subsidized and distributed under the PDS; and, two, does the current levy obligation on sugar mills need to be continued with or will PDS supplies be met through open market procurement?

The options available before the government were quite complex in that it not only has to take the state governments along but also look into other critical issues such as an increase in procurement costs, problems relating to market distortions including delayed payments for cane purchased by sugar mills and the subsidy burden.

It was felt that removing sugar from the PDS was not acceptable. The major decision made was that if sugar was to be continued as an item under the PDS, who would bear the extra burden for keeping the price at Rs 13.5 per kg? At present, the open market price of sugar hovers around Rs 32 per kg while the retail price through PDS is Rs 13.5 per kg which has not been revised since 2002. The government is able to provide sugar at this price by absorbing the subsidy of Rs 6 per kg after buying it from sugar mills at a levy price fixed by the government at Rs 19.50 per kg.

The decision of the government to partially decontrol sugar has not affected the sugar price in the open market, as there is enough sugar in the country with this years production expected to be around 24.5 million tons as against a requirement of 22.2 million tons.

Now, the states will also be free to purchase sugar through a transparent system at the current ex-factory price of Rs 32 per kg which has been capped for 2 years.

The government has ensured that this important decision on the partial decontrol of sugar takes care of the interests of sugarcane farmers, while also safeguarding the interests of the common man and the sugar sector.

Bitter Sugar

Sugarcane farmers in UP, Maharashtra and Karnataka were angry in 2013 because the state governments and sugar mills have not agreed to their demands regarding cane prices. Farmers in UP and Maharashtra want their governments to fix the state advised price (SAP) of sugarcane at Rs 350 and Rs 300 per quintal (or 100 kg), respectively while the governments have set it at Rs 280 and Rs 265 per quintal.

Farmers in these states say that the increase in the diesel and fertilizer prices have made the crop unprofitable. UP has not increased SAP this year; it was the same last year. The price war started in UP in early November with the onset of the sugarcane harvesting season. Of the 135 sugar mills in the state, 110 privately owned mills expressed inability to start crushing operations, saying the price of Rs 280 per quintal was too high. Represented by the UP Sugar Mills Association (UPSMA), the mill owners asked the government to reduce it to Rs 225 per quintal. They claim that sugar mills in the state are under debt and banks have denied them loans. Since the harvesting had already started in early November, the state government asked the UP Cooperative Sugar Factories Federation Limited to run its 23 cooperative mills and two corporation mills even if the private mills were on strike. They started operations on November 16 and procured sugarcane at Rs 280 per quintal.

But the deadlock in UP could not be broken, with farmers asking for Rs 350 per quintal. In November, farmers protested across the state, threatening to burn their crops. Farmer, Satyapal Singh in Lakhimpur Kheri district killed himself because he failed to repay a debt of Rs 2 lakh. He hanged himself from a tree, says the district police.

The spokesperson for the Bhartiya Kisan Union (BKU), Dharmendar Singh, says, "Rs 280 per quintal is what we agreed for the last year. In the past, one year input costs have gone up. Growing sugarcane is costing around Rs 6,000 per 0.4 hectare. The pesticides used like Corrosioin and Dentos cost Rs 1,600 and Rs 1,500 per 100 g. Farmers are once again at a loss and we will continue to protest till our demand is met". BKU is one of the largest farmer organizations in the country.

Finally, on December 1, UPSMA and the state government struck a deal that the former would procure sugarcane from farmers at Rs 280 per quintal and would pay the farmers in two installments. In the first installment, the farmers would be paid for their produce at the rate of Rs 260 per quintal within 14 days of delivery and the remaining amount, calculated at the rate of Rs 20 per quintal, would be paid at the end of the crushing season in April–May 2014. In return, the state government has agreed to waive off commission, purchase tax and entry tax for the mill owners, translating into a benefit of Rs 11 a quintal. The millers promised to start their operations by December 7 across the state.

Now Grow Sugarcane at Lesser Cost

The state government has begun encouraging farmers to cultivate sugarcane in widely spaced rows, giving room for intercropping. Experts said this would increase profit and save water. Officials are demonstrating the new technique on a 10-acre plot at the government seed farm in Raonta village in the district.

Agriculture Development Officer Dr Jaswinder Singh Brar, in charge of this 50-acre seed farm, said the seedlings of sugarcane were being planted in rows at a distance of 8 feet with 4 feet distance between the plants.

He said in the traditional cropping method, 35–40 quintals of seedlings were required to plant sugarcane on an acre against the 2 quintals of seedlings in the wide space row cultivation method. As many as 1,200–1,300 seedlings were planted on an acre in the new technique.

Dr Brar claimed the production of sugarcane was not affected in the widely spaced row cultivation method despite using lesser number of seedlings. He said that the total production of sugarcane in the traditional and the new method was 350–400 quintals.

He said apart from this, the space between the rows and plants provided the farmers a chance for intercropping of other crops such as vegetables, maize, potatoes, onions, garlic, pulses and mustard. He said farmers could also grow fodder for cattle and increase financial returns. Dr Brar further said farmers could save 80% water with this technique.

He said in the new technique, the consumption of pesticides and chemical fertilizers would also be less and labor cost would come down. This technique can motivate farmers to grow crops other than paddy and wheat.

CONSUMPTION

Indian sugar consumption is forecast to rise to 26 million tons on continued strong domestic demand. A growing population (about 1.8% per annum), coupled with forecast Indian economic growth of 6–6.7% in fiscal year 2013/14, are likely to support higher sugar consumption. Bulk consumers, which include soft drink manufacturers, bakeries, hotels and restaurants and confectionary manufacturers, account for nearly 65% of the total consumption. Most khandsari sugar is consumed by local sweet meat shops. Gur is mostly consumed in rural areas for household consumption and feed use.

The sustained increase in sugar consumption has been primarily due to the increase in population and preference of sugar over alternate sweeteners. Sugars are a major form of carbohydrates and are found probably in all green plants. They occur in significant amounts in most fruits and vegetables. There are three main simple sugars: sucrose, fructose, glucose. Sucrose is in fact a combination of fructose and glucose and the body quickly breaks it down into these separate substances. A balanced diet can (and should) come from a variety of different foods, calculated to give the desired levels of carbohydrates, proteins, fats, vitamins, and minerals. Nutritional scientists advocate that carbohydrates should provide at least 50% of our energy requirements. Of late, sustained publicity campaign is being made by the producers of chemical sweeteners against sugar consumption by attributing to it various health problems.

India is the largest consumer of sugar in the world and Indian sugar industry is the 2nd largest agro-industry located in the rural India. Currently, there are 453 operating sugar mills in different parts of the country. There are about 50 million sugarcane farmers and about 2 million skilled/semi-skilled workers involved in ancillary activities, mostly from the rural areas. The industry not only generates power for its own requirement but surplus power for export to the grid based on byproduct bagasse. It also produces ethanol, an eco-friendly and renewable energy for blending with petrol. With sugarcane cultivation in around 4.25 million hectares of land, India produces around 280 million tons of sugarcane annually. The production of sugar has witnessed a dramatic increase of around 27.00 million tons during 2010–2011 against 1.10 million tons during 1950–1960. In spite of the improvement in the production of sugar over the years, this sector has not been nourished on sound lines.

Total consumption of sugar in India increased from 2.1 million tons in 1960–1961 to 4 million tons in 1970–1971, 50 million tons in 1980–81 and 10.2 million tons in 1989–1990 to 23 million tons in 2012–1913. Corresponding per capita annual consumption figures were 4.8 kg, 7.4 kg, 7.3 kg, 12.5 and 18.3 kg. Compound growth rate during 1989–1990 and 2012–2013 was 3.76% for total and 2.05% for per capita consumption (Table 1.28). Along with sugar, India consumers gur and khandsari per capita consumption of which came down from 15.2 kg in 1960–1961 to 12.8 kg in 1989–1990 and 5.4 kg in 2002–2003 and 4.7 kg in 2011–2012. When we add to this the consumption of palm gur, India will become the top consumer of sugar.

Table 1.28: Sugar etimated annual per capital consumption

Kg

Conutries	*1960*	*1961*	*1962*	*1963*	*1964*
Argentina	29	35	39	34	38
Australia	34	53	53	53	54
Belgium	38	37	38	38	38
Brazil	36	37	38	36	34
Canada	43	44	46	45	47
Cuba	50	54	52	63	55
Denmark	59	56	57	56	56
Domnican Republic	26	25	35	35	32
Germany (East)			37	39	39
Germany (West)	33	33	34	35	33
India	5	5	6	5	5
Indonesia	8	6	6	5	5
Japan	15	17	17	18	14
Mexico	32	32	33	34	36
Sweden	46	44	46	44	45
South Africa	43	0	40	41	43
UK	55	56	54	55	52
USA	48	49	49	49	47

Notes: Figures for the year 1962, 1963, 1964 in the table have been obtained by dividing the total consumption of sugar in Table No. 46 by total population for the respective countries as indicated in the monthly bulletin of statistics of the United Nations (May, 1965 is issue).

Trends in Sugar Consumption

When we speak of sugar consumption in India, we have to consider traditional sugarcane based sweetners (gur and khandsari) as well. Thus with sugar and gur/khandsari consumption taken together the consumption stands at around 24 kg/annum.

- Per capita consumption of all sweeteners has been fairly stable at 20 kg until 1980.
- In this period, however, there has been a gradual shift from gur/khandsari to sugar.
- In 1960–1961, sugar was 4.8 kg or 25% of all sweeteners which in 1981–1982 grew to 8.2 kg or 42%.

- Between 1981–1982 to 1991–1992 total consumption grew to 24 kg with sugar at 13 kg or 55%.
- Thus, growth between 1960 and 1995 has been as under (Table 1.28A).

1960–1961 to 1981–1982	Total sweeteners steady at 20 kg sugar up from 4.8–8.2 kg
	Gur khandsari down from 15.2 kg to 11.5 kg
1981–1982 to 1991–1992	Total sweetener moved upto 24 kg
	Sugar upto 13 kg
	Gur/khandsari down to 11 kg
1991–1992 to 2011–1012	Sugar 18.3 kg, gur/khandsari 4.7 kg

Table 1.28A: Sugar consumption

Sugar year	*Per capita consumption (kg/annum)*	*Total per capita consumption (kg/annum)*	
	Sugar	*Gur and khandsari*	*Total*
2000–2001	17.75	8.72	26.47
2001–2002	18.03	8.62	26.65
2002–2003	18.46	8.50	26.96
2003–2004	19.01	8.42	27.43
2004–2005	19.68	8.40	28.08
2005–2006	20.36	8.23	25.59
2006–2007	20.89	8.19	29.08
2007–2008	21.17	8.10	29.27

The distribution of the free market segment is

Institutional	7100	78
Household	2000	22
Total household	6400	48

Thus, almost 52% or say half of the sugar produced goes in for indirect consumption, i.e. institutional segment.

Large buyers such as:

	000 million tons	*Percentage*
Soft drinks bottlers	300	4.23
Biscuit manufacturer	600	8.46
Food products	50	0.70
Confectionery	200	2.81
Pharmaceuticals	50	0.70
Hotel/restaurants	100	1.40
Sweet meat	5,800	81.70
Total	**7,100**	**100.00**

Sugar Companies

1. Bajaj Hindustan
2. Balarampur Chini Mills
3. Dhampur Sugar Mills
4. Nizam Sugars
5. Oudh Sugars and Chemicals
6. Thiru Arroran Sugars
7. Ugar Sugar Works
8. Upper Ganges Sugar and Industries.

Research to Farm

The institute has developed a short-duration sugarcane crop that matures in 10 months using tissue culture. The crops VSI-434 and VSI-435 have been successfully demonstrated in the institute and farmers have used these varieties in over 400 acres in the neighboring regions. Also, a drought – tolerant, low water-consumption sugarcane variety using molecular biology has been developed and is ready for mass multiplication. Another important variety VSI-9805 developed by the institute can provide yield comparable to Tamil Nadu crop in different climatic regions. To improve the recovery of sugar from sugarcane, the institute has developed the variety COC-671 that can give a yield of 13.5–14. All these varieties are in the laboratory scale. The sugar technologists should find methods through which the research results can reach the farm, farmers and sugar factories.

Sugar Vision 2020

Dr Kalam envisions the sugar industry by the year 2020 as follows:

1. Indian sugar industry is fully liberated from all controls both by the state and central governments and is market-driven.
2. National average production of sugar in India rises to 120 tons per hectare.
3. Average sugar recovery from Indian sugar factories is above 13%.
4. Water consumption by sugarcane producers reduces by 50% through the use of micro- and ferti-irrigation.
5. Sugarcane farmers adopt eco-farming and bio fertilization and pesticides leading to better environment.
6. Indian sugar factories achieve global standards on environment compliance compliance and plant safety.
7. Indian white sugar fully meets the international standard of 40 ICUMSA and 20% output of sugar factories is exported.
8. Ethanol production from molasses and also directly from cane supplemented with other biomass route like sweet-sorgum becomes a part of all sugar complexes, leading to energy—independent rural sector.
9. Each sugar complex with ethanol and alcohol production units is transformed into sugar PURA complexes.

Sweeteners Consumption India vs World

- Today India's per capita consumption of over 29 kg (2008–09) is higher compared to world average of 20.4 kg (Tables 1.28B and 1.28C).

- Well high above Asia average of 12.8 kg.
- Lowest is in China at 6.5 kg which distorts Asia average (alternate sweeteners basic buying high)
- Compare's well with Pakistan at 23, Sri Lanka at 24.1, Thailand at 24.9.
- But behind Philippines at 28.7 and well behind Malaysia at 39.8.
- Also substantially behind developed countries such as US, Canada, Australia, New Zealand, EC and developing countries and major sugar producing countries such as Brazil, Cuba.

Trend in Consumption Pattern

- Major increased witnessed between 1981–1982 and 2011–1012.
  - o World average 19.8–20.4
  - o Asia average 8.6–12.8
- Asia average increase is 50%. Hence we confine discussion on Asia:
  - o Japan down 10% to 21.5 kg
  - o China up 50% to 6.5 kg
  - o Thailand up 80% to 24.9 kg
  - o Malaysia up 25% to 39.8 kg
  - o Pakistan up 150% to 22.9 kg
  - o Sri Lanka up 50% to 24.1 kg
  - o Philippines up 28% to 24.4 kg
  - o India up 20% to 23.0 kg.

Sugars are a major form of carbohydrates and are found probably in all green plants. They occur in significant amounts in most fruits and vegetables. There are three main simple sugars: sucrose, fructose, glucose; sucrose is in fact a combination of fructose and glucose and the body quickly breaks it down into these separate substances. A balanced diet can (and should) come from a variety of different foods, calculated to give the desired levels of carbohydrates, proteins, fats, vitamins, and minerals. Nutritional scientists advocate that carbohydrates should provide at least 50% of our energy requirements. Of late, sustained publicity campaign is being made by the producers of chemical sweeteners against sugar consumption by attributing to it various health problems.

As per NSSO Survey (66th round), per capita consumption of sugar directly by households per month was 705 gm in rural areas and 820 gm in urban areas in 2009–2010 (July–June). Considering that 68.8% of population lives in rural areas, all India weighted average per capita direct household consumption of sugar would work out to 741 gm per month and 11.2 million tons per year for the country (for a population of 1.24 billion). As per estimates by the sugar industry the total consumption (absorption) of sugar in the country including by households, bulk buyers, and others, is about 22.5 million tons per year. Thus, considering the household requirement of 11.2 million tons per year, the balance of about 11 million tons or 50 % of the total consumption is by bulk buyers ranging from small street corner sweet shops (confectionaries) in the informal sector to large beverage companies, etc. We do not know the exact break-up between these informal sector small shops and the large beverage companies. Efforts should be made by the Directorate of Sugar to find out these consumption patterns beyond the NSSO's data on household consumption.

Table 1.28B: Sugar production and consumption in India

Years	*Total sugar production (lakh ton)*	*Total sugar consumption (lakh ton)*	*Percapita consumption of sugar (kg per annum)*
1989–1990	109.88	102.15	12.50
1990–1991	120.46	107.14	12.70
199–1992	134.04	112.70	13.00
1992–1993	106.09	118.75	13.70
1993–1994	98.33	119.60	12.40
1994–1995	146.43	122.70	13.10
1995–1996	164.51	131.26	14.20
1996–1997	129.05	138.66	14.40
1997–1998	128.55	148.39	14.50
1998–1999	155.41	150.35	14.40
1999–1900	182.00	154.19	15.40
2000–2001	185.11	162.01	15.70
2001–2002	185.29	167.81	16.10
2002–2003	201.40	183.84	17.30
2003–2004	139.95	172.85	16.00
2004–2005	130.00	185.00	16.90
2005–2006	189.59	185.00	17.10
2006–2007	282.00	210.00	18.00
2007–2008	263.00	205.00	19.30
2008–2009	147.00	220.80	19.90
2009–2010	188.00	220.00	17.90
2010–2011	243.50	210.00	17.50
2011–2012	263.43	227.25	18.30
2012–2013	240.80	**230.00**	**0.00**
CGR%	**3.48**	**3.76***	**2.05***

* Significant at 1% level of significance.
Source: Hand Book of Sugar Statistics, Indian Sugar Mills Association, Ministry of Consumer Affairs.

Table 1.28C: Per capita consumption of sugar and gur-khandsari in India

Year	*Total consumption of sugar (lakh tons)*	*Per capita sugar (kg/year)*	*Total consumption of gur and khandsari*	*Per capita gur and khandsari (kg/year)*
1960–1961	21.13	4.8	66.87	15.2
1961–1962	25.88	5.8	64.32	14.4
1962–1963	24.86	5.4	60.74	13.3
1963–1964	23.07	4.9	66.67	14.2
1964–1965	24.69	5.2	72.05	15.1
1965–1966	28.10	5.7	69.11	14.1
1966–1967	26.01	5.2	61.25	12.2
1967–1968	22.15	4.3	63.05	12.3
1968–1969	26.05	5.0	73.46	14.0
1969–1970	32.64	6.1	74.01	13.9
1970–1971	40.25	7.4	74.37	13.6

Table 1.28C: Per capita consumption of sugar and gur-khandsari in India *(Contd.)*

Year	*Total consumption of sugar (lakh tons)*	*Per capita sugar (kg/year)*	*Total consumption of gur and khandsari*	*Per capita gur and khandsari (kg/year)*
1971–1972	37.95	6.8	69.98	12.5
1972–1973	35.14	6.2	70.30	12.3
1973–1974	35.22	6.1	83.36	14.3
1974–1975	34.75	5.9	80.63	13.6
1975–1976	36.89	6.1	83.67	13.7
1976–1977	37.57	6.0	88.41	14.2
1977–1978	44.82	7.1	90.88	14.4
1978–1979	62.14	9.6	75.96	11.8
1979–1980	78.08	7.8	75.48	11.3
1980–1981	49.80	7.3	85.22	12.5
1981–1982	57.11	8.2	80.40	11.5
1982–1983	64.71	9.1	86.65	12.2
1983–1984	75.70	10.5	95.41	13.2
1984–1985	78.90	10.7	91.05	12.4
1985–1986	83.53	11.1	82.48	11.0
1986–1987	87.75	11.5	79.25	10.4
1987–1988	93.33	12.0	83.00	10.7
1988–1989	99.19	12.3	93.31	11.7
1989–1990	102.83	12.6	85.73	10.5
1990–1991	107.15	12.9	90.71	10.9
1991–1992	112.25	13.3	93.95	11.1
1992–1993	120.05	13.9	98.62	11.5
1993–1994	111.29	12.7	105.26	12.0
1994–1995	119.74	13.1	100.97	11.1
1995–1996	131.72	14.2	74.45	8.0
1996–1997	136.75	14.4	115.61	12.2
1997–1998	139.78	14.5	117.98	12.2
1998–1999	141.35	14.4	99.05	10.1
1999–2000	155.08	15.5	87.19	8.7
2000–2001	162.00	15.8	86.09	8.4
2001–2002	167.81	16.1	83.11	8.0
2002–2003	183.84	16.4	56.94	5.4
2003–2004	172.85	16.3	71.46	6.6
2004–2005	185.00	16.7	81.75	7.5
2005–2006	189.45	17.0	57.39	5.2
2006–2007	201.60	18.0	33.38	3.0
2007–2008	220.00	19.3	50.93	4.5
2008–2009	230.00	19.9	107.92	9.3
2009–2010	210.00	17.9	73.12	6.2
2010–2011	207.36	17.5	59.94	5.1
2011–2012*	227.25	18.3	56.71	4.7
2012–2013	230.00	–	–	–

* Provisional includes imported sugar.

Source: Cooperative Sugar Vol 45 (1), September, 2013.

"Sugar tax" may help fight obesity in UK Britain may soon introduce a sugar tax to curb high obesity rates in UK. The country's chief medical officer has told a parliamentary committee that sugar is addictive and a sugar tax is urgently needed. Speaking to the committee Dame Sally Davies said that she believed that "research will find sugar is addictive. She said, "we may need to move toward some kind of sugar tax. I do fear this generation of children will live less than my parents' generation". UK consumes over 5,727 million liters of sugary drinks a year. Adding a 20 pence tax for every liter would raise more than £1.1 billion. About 64% of adults in the UK are considered overweight or obese.

Can India be Self-sufficient in Sugar?

Demand in 2009–2010, it may touch a record 23 kg per person, say industry estimates. Sky high retail prices of Rs 30/kg are no real deterrent. This is partly because consumers can afford it, and partly because they have got used to paying substantially more for all food.

Moreover, sugar has no cheap alternative. But, kitchen consumption is half the story. A far bigger demand pull is from processed food factories that are buying hundreds of tons more for colas, juices, icecreams, biscuits, confectionary and ready-to-eat foods. Besides, oftener we eat out, more restaurants and fast food chains go to the market for sugar. Added to this is the change in rural diets, where refined sugar is rapidly replacing jaggery. Jaggery has become more precious as a source of molasses for local breweries that ferment it for alcohol.

Put all these together, and you know India's consumption of 23 million tons in 2009 will soon appear piffling. If each Indian eats one kilo extra in a year, we will add a million tons to that figure. Now look at supply. To meet demand over next couple of years, India needs to grow cane on at least 5.5 million hectares, with a yield of 65 tons per hectare. But, cane grows on maximum 4.4 million hectares, with an average yield of 55 ton/hectare. So, we are already short and need to boost acreage by 25% and yields 20%. Can we achieve this? Chances are slim. Sugarcane needs plenty of water and labor. Both are increasingly scarce and expensive. You could call 2009 an aberration, with 47 districts, including prime cane-growing areas, in UP officially drought affected.

But, life was already tough for about 200 sugar factories in the state, including large players Bajaj Hindusthan, Balrampur Chini Triveni, Simbhaoli, and Dhampur. UP farmers began abandoning cane even before the drought as net returns have declined despite substantial hike in procurement prices. Ditto Punjab and Haryana. Things are equally grim elsewhere. University of Agricultural Sciences, Dharwad, is advising a switch to sugar beet in Karnataka. In Maharashtra, irrigation and political support allowed even semi-arid districts that need tankers for drinking water to grow cane. But, it is unsustainable. Across India, water shortage, climate change and increased soil salinity are taking their toll. Growing cane is a luxury that India may not be able to afford much longer.

Given the sheer scale of investment by banks, taxpayers and shareholders, both government and promoters are acutely aware of the need for damage control. From drip irrigation, new varieties and monetary incentives for good growing practices to organic farming and GM cane, every option is being explored. But, the scale is still too small to significantly boost supply.

Prosperity and altered farming conditions will leave India increasingly dependent on imports. As vegetable oils have shown, that won't necessarily be a bad thing. But, it would certainly be the game changer. Consumers will have to adapt when the market rations demand with higher prices. Trade would be volatile in line with world market, and sarkari free sale quota pointless. Buffer stock norms would be history unless the government itself buys and holds sugar. Companies would have to re-jig business models to straddle cane shortages, foreign competition, and higher risk. Success will come to fastest finger first. The truly sharp ones are already seeing the 2009 crisis as a harbinger of things to come.

Sugar Addiction is Key Contributor to Heart Disease, Cancer Risk

Recently, the government has suggested that manufacturers of aerated drinks reduce the sugar content in the the products. This is certainly a welcome step that will help address the issues around sugar sweetened beverages—sodas, aerated drinks, fruit drinks, cordials, sherbets, squashes, fruit juices, pannas, thandai and iced teas. Consumption of sugar-sweetened beverages, particularly carbonated soft drinks, may be a key contributor to obesity. Excess sugar in anyone's diet can lead to coronary heart disease, obesity, insulin resistance, metabolic syndrome, polycystic ovarian syndrome (PCOS), lowered immunity, impaired brain function and increased risk to cancer. Sugar, in fact, has been found to be addictive in nature.

Sugar uses the same neurological pathways as narcotic to hit the pleasure center of the brain that send out the signal: "eat more, eat more". Individuals with a preference for binging on sweet foods tend to binge more frequently. Another effect of excessive sugar intake is change in microbial flora in the gut. In the long run, this can eventually lead to bloating, and may worsen gastrointestinal problems such as heartburn and flatulence. Abnormal gut flora has also been linked to lower immunity, allergies, skin problems like acne and eczema. Excessive sugar intake can deplete nutrients like B-vitamins, zinc and chromium.

In fact, the World health Organization has recently lowered the recommendations for sugar from 10% to no more than 5% of the total caloric intake, translating to 4–5 teaspoons / day for a 2,000 kcal diet for an average person. A single can of a sugar sweetened beverage exceeds this limit.

Children are particularly vulnerable to high and increasing consumption of sweetened drinks. It has been estimated that each additional can or a glass of sugar sweetened drink consumed everyday increases the risk of obesity by 60%.

The physiological effects of energy intake on satiation and satiety appear to be quite different for energy in solid foods as opposed to energy in fluids. Possibly because of reduced gastric distension and faster transit times, the energy contained in fluids is less well "detected" by the body and subsequent food intake is poorly adjusted to account for the energy taken in through beverages. Meanwhile, drinking an occasional can of diet soda is unlikely to hurt you. But, remember diet sodas are not silver bullets for weight loss. While they may save you calories occasionally, studies suggest that regular consumption can increase your risk of obesity and diabetes.

Everyday Foods Contain Sugar and Lead to Cavities

A recently conducted oral health survey market research firm GFK mode revealed that everyday home cooked foods pose risks when it comes to cavities. Eminent dentist Dr Ashok Dhoble, Honorable Secretary General, Indian Dental Association, further elaborates.

It is a common belief that only sugary foods and sweets lead to cavities, but interesting to know that even every day foods like dal, dalia otherwise considered healthy can cause cavities too. Cavities are a resultant from both sweet foods and everyday home-cooked foods.

The neutralization of sugar acids is the key to fighting cavities. The solution is colagate's Maximum Cavity Protection plus Sugar Acid Neutraliser TM toothpaste which is armed with a breakthrough sugar acid neutralizer technology that deactivates sugar acids and helps to prevent cavities.

Launch of Colgate Maximum Cavity Protection plus Sugar Acid Neutralizer TM is one such step in this direction. It is a technological breakthrough in dental science based on the extensive scientific research conducted over a period of 8 years. This technology works in two ways. It neutralizes the harmful sugar acids, the main cause of cavity formation, while making teeth stronger with fluoride. Various long-term clinical studies have been conducted to prove anticavity benefits of the technology.

EXPORTS

Exports of sugar from India during 1990–1991 were just 2.0 thousand tons (Table 1.29). They reached the peak (4.9 million tons) during 2007–2008. During 2012–2013, it had come to down to 2.8 million tons. Countrywise export of sugar from India during 2007–2008 to 2012–2013 (Table 1.30) shows that from among the major imports, 66.6% share was of a member of small imports UAE is the major importer with its share of 13% in 2011–2012. It was followed by Sri Lanka whose share fell down from 10.3% in 2007–2008 to 6.9% in 2012–2013.

India has also been importing sugar India in some years. While there were no imports for yours 1990–1991 to 1993–1994 million tons. In 2009–2010 when Indian production was the lowest at 14.7 million tons (Table 1.31). From among the exporting countries Brazil is the major exporter of sugar to India. Its share during 2010–2011 was 80% (Table 1.32).

India has also been importing sugar (Table 1.32). Total quantity imported during 2010–2011 was 1.2 million tons. Brazil has been the major exporter. Its share during 2010–2011 was 80.5% which increased to 99.5% during 2012–2013. A summarized position of quantity and value of exports/imports (Table 1.33) shows that while export value was the highest (5,412 crores), in 2007–2008, import value was highest (Rs 1,111.2 crores).

India Exports 8.5 Lakh Ton of Raw Sugar so far This Year

India has exported about 8.5 lakh ton of sugar including 4.5 lakh ton of raw sugar, till January 31, 2014. The country has produced about 8 lakh ton of raw sugar till January 31, 2014 and is expected to produce another 10 lakh ton of raw sugar in the remaining months of current season, said industry body Indian Sugar Mills Association (ISMA).

An ISMA release stated, "A total about 8.5 lakh tons of sugar has been exported out of the country till January 31, 2014, of which 4.5 lakh tons is raw sugar and the rest is white/refined. Another 1.2–2 lakh tons, mostly raw, are in transit for getting

Table 1.29: Export of sugar from India

Sr. No.	*Financial year (April to March)*	*Quantity ('000 tons)*	*Value (Rs crores)*	*Unit value (Rs)*
1.	1990–1991	2.00	0.91	4.55
2.	1991–1992	82.00	55.80	6.80
3.	1992–1993	365.00	316.73	8.68
4.	1993–1994	119.00	111.33	9.36
5.	1994–1995	39.35	48.88	12.42
6.	1995–1996	434.32	597.34	13.75
7.	1996–1997	667.27	860.80	12.90
8.	1997–1998	173.28	244.44	14.11
9.	1998–1999	12.74	17.36	13.63
10.	1999–2000	12.99	18.14	13.96
11.	2000–2001	338.69	430.98	12.72
12.	2001–2002	1456.45	1728.29	11.87
13.	2002–2003	1662.37	1769.49	10.64
14.	2003–2004	1200.60	1216.59	10.13
15.	2004–2005	108.69	149.53	13.76
16.	2005–2006	321.20	569.11	17.72
17.	2006–2007	1643.40	3127.47	19.03
18.	2007–2008	4684.55	5412.16	11.55
19.	2008–2009	3332.00	4448.74	13.35
20.	2009–2010	44.05	110.23	25.03
21.	2010–2011	1714.37	5419.11	31.61
22.	2011–2012	2747.35	8779.07	31.95
23.	2012–2013	2794.44	8576.60	30.69
	CGR%	**21.83***	**28.65***	**5.60***

* Significant at 1% level of significance.
Source: DGCI&S, Kolkata.

exported". Total sugar dispatches till January 31, 2014, starting from October 1, 2013 is about 79 lakh tons.

The country still has stock of 117 lakh tons as on January 31, 2014. During the current 2013–2014 season, India has produced 143.7 lakh tons sugar till February 15, 2014. It was 165.88 lakh tons during the same time last year.

The gap in sugar production over last year, during the same corresponding period, has narrowed down to 13% on February 15, from about 16% a fortnight back, that is, up to January 31, the release said. About 485 sugar mills are operational across the country as of February 15, 2014 as against 500 mills last year during the same corresponding period.

In Maharashtra, 147 mills have crushed about 454 lakh tons of sugarcane to produce about 49.80 lakh tons of sugar with 10.96% recovery, while last year when almost the same quantum of sugarcane was crushed, the average sugar recovery

Table 1.30: Countrywise export of sugar from India

Country name	*2007–08*		*2008–09*		*2009–10*		*2010–11*		*2011–12*		*2012–13*	
	Share (%)	*Unit value (Rs)*	*Share (%)*	*Unit value (Rs)*	*Share (%)*	*Unit value (Rs)*	*Share (%)*	*Unit value (Rs)*	*Share (%)*	*Unit value (Rs)*	*Share (%)*	*Unit value (Rs)*
Saudi Arab	2.00	11.39	5.82	13.56	3.38	23.76	1.75	33.80	2.88	32.62	2.59	30.70
Sri Lanka	10.34	11.56	10.21	14.73	13.39	26.96	13.03	32.32	16.61	31.49	6.88	29.53
UAE	15.21	10.87	20.75	12.62	5.20	27.62	6.86	31.80	12.43	31.00	12.98	29.31
Belgium	0.00	13.33	0.00	10.00	1.21	38.56	0.10	38.94	0.78	45.87	0.48	40.55
Kenya	1.85	11.44	2.40	13.95	1.30	21.03	0.23	32.70	3.33	35.23	0.70	31.93
Kuwait	0.40	12.41	0.42	13.46	1.26	14.77	0.51	32.49	0.28	31.73	0.55	31.17
Malaysia	4.68	10.71	4.52	12.00	17.95	26.12	6.07	30.59	4.41	29.93	4.23	29.69
USA	0.28	15.64	0.08	21.64	5.43	26.87	0.21	30.19	0.78	33.49	0.96	34.96
Maldives	0.15	11.67	0.25	15.42	16.44	25.10	0.37	32.26	0.32	34.12	0.17	36.31
Oman	0.52	11.55	0.45	14.57	1.80	18.56	0.59	30.22	1.38	32.15	0.77	32.63
Canada	0.05	15.88	0.04	17.20	3.16	26.22	0.74	30.37	0.11	30.82	0.12	37.96
Bhutan	0.02	15.09	0.07	14.69	8.73	15.43	0.21	19.89	0.08	22.80	0.07	25.30
Australia	0.01	14.01	0.02	13.06	1.31	17.52	0.05	18.73	0.06	22.91	0.03	35.25
Germany	0.19	11.70	0.04	27.77	1.53	30.90	0.03	65.60	0.05	42.76	0.06	54.36
UK	0.02	17.71	0.04	25.02	4.30	27.90	0.09	33.23	0.05	28.30	0.05	41.85
Yemen	10.13	12.18	3.25	13.51	0.50	35.43	3.20	32.76	8.53	31.52	2.70	30.30
Pakistan	5.45	11.36	0.96	15.26	5.82	20.51	29.16	30.20	1.01	30.61	0.00	00.00
Greece	0.16	17.13	0.03	13.96	0.70	30.35	0.08	34.29	0.08	31.72	0.05	30.36
Others counties	48.54	11.88	50.65	13.33	6.58	24.67	36.73	31.12	46.82	31.79	66.62	30.21
Total export (lakh million tons)	**46.41 (100)**	**11.64 (100)**	**33.32 (100)**	**13.35 (100)**	**0.45 (100)**	**24.12 (100)**	**17.14 (100)**	**32.46 (100)**	**27.47 (100)**	**32.14 (100)**	**27.94 (100)**	**30.93 (100)**

Source: APEDA, 2013.

was 10.85%. However, to-date comparison of recoveries over the last year same time, looks low, as mills have started crushing about 3 weeks late.

Till February 15, 2014, about 10 mills (four in Aurangabad zone; four in Pune zone; one on Ahmednagar and one in Nanded) have closed in comparison to 8 mills during same corresponding period last year.

UP has produced about 35.7 lakh tons, which is about 18% less than, i.e. 43.61 lakh tons of sugar produced last year, during same period. A total of 119 mills are crushing sugarcane, as against 121 mills last year.

Reported yields per hectare across UP have been lower by about 6–7% as compared to the last year. Till date, sugar recovery is 8.91%, which is higher than last year's 8.85%, if the same quantum of sugarcane crush is considered.

Table 1.31: Import of sugar by India

Sr. No.	Financial year (April to March)	Quantity (lakh tons)	Value (Rs crores)	Unit value (Rs)
1.	1990–1991	0.00	0.00	0.00
2.	1991–1992	0.00	0.00	0.00
3.	1992–1993	0.00	0.00	0.00
4.	1993–1994	0.00	0.00	0.00
5.	1994–1995	17.65	2245.85	12.72
6.	1995–1996	1.51	215.89	14.33
7.	1996–1997	0.02	3.18	14.92
8.	1997–1998	3.47	470.25	13.56
9.	1998–1999	9.00	1,111.22	12.34
10.	1999–2000	11.81	1,110.8	9.40
11.	2000–2001	0.30	31.11	10.23
12.	2001–2002	0.27	32.6	12.27
13.	2002–2003	0.41	32.83	7.92
14.	2003–2004	0.74	62.7	8.43
15.	2004–2005	9.33	976.18	10.47
16.	2005–2006	5.59	651.59	11.66
17.	2006–2007	0.01	3.49	33.17
18.	2007–2008	0.005	2.24	45.16
19.	2008–2009	3.86	583.11	15.10
20.	2009–2010	24.24	5,961.24	24.59
21.	2010–2011	11.98	2,789.54	23.28
22.	2011–2012	1.00	313.81	31.47
23.	2012–2013	11.14	3,071.70	27.57

Source: DGCI&S, Kolkata.

India's Trade in Sugar

India is currently the fourth largest exporter of sugar in the world, but is an occasional importer of sugar too, depending upon the demand and supply situation at home. During the period from 2001–2002 to 2012–2013, India has been a net exporter of sugar, except during the year 2004–2005, 2005–2006 and 2009–2010 when India was a net importer of sugar is shown in tne next page chart. During this period, India's exports of (4.7 million tons) of sugar were highest in the FY 2007–2008, whereas, India had to import 2.6 million tons of sugar in the FY 2009–2010. But in terms of value, sugar exports earned a record US$ 1.8 billion in FY 2011–2012 due to the high international prices of sugar in that year. This has been despite constant government interventions in external trade of sugar with intermittent ban on exports.

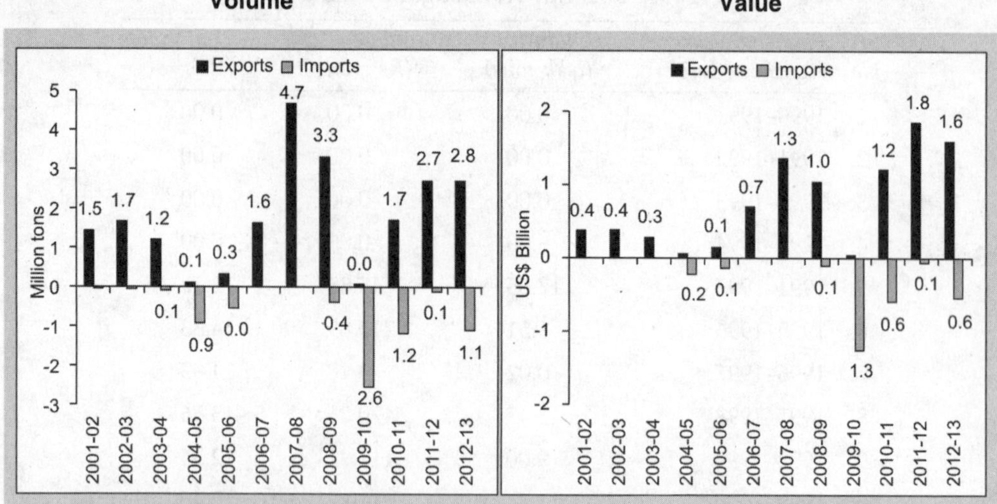

India's exports and imports of sugar, 2001–2002 to 2012–2013 (volume value)
Note: The years pertain to financial year.
Source: DGCI&S.

Exports of sugar were canalized through the notified export agencies, viz. Indian Sugar and General Industry Export Import Corporation Ltd (ISGIEIC) and State Trading Corporation of India (STC) till 15th January, 1997 when they were decentralized and permitted subject to obtaining Registration-Cum-Allocation Certificate (RCAC) from Agricultural and Processed Food Products Export Development Authority (APEDA). This requirement of issue of RCAC by APEDA was dispensed wef 1st April, 2001 and exports of sugar were allowed after obtaining the export release order from Directorate of Sugar.

Through an Ordinance, the Sugar Export Promotion Act, 1958 was repealed w.e.f. 15th January, 1997 and thus the export of sugar was decanalised. Under the decalanised regime, the export of sugar was being carried out through the APEDA, under Ministry of Commerce. Government removed the quantitative ceiling on Export of Sugar and also dispensed with the requirement of the issue of the RCAC by APEDA, w.e.f. 1.4.2001 on sugar Exports. Now, the export of sugar can be undertaken by the various sugar mills/merchant exporters, after obtaining the export Release Order from Directorate of sugar.

The export release orders in 2005–2006 sugar season were issued only to Advance License holders except that the Indian Sugar Exim Corpn. (ISEC), the joint body of Indian Sugar Mills Association (ISWMA) and the National Federation of Cooperative Sugar Factories (NFCSF), the apex organizations of sugar industry was allowed to export 1.5 lakh tons of sugar to the Trading Corporation of Pakistan. As per information received from DGFT the quantum of export obligation on account of export in 2004–2005 and 2005–2006 sugar seasons (Oct–Sept) under Advance License Scheme comes to about 21.9 lakh tons of sugar has been exported during 2005–2006 sugar season. However, to curb rise in prices of sugar in the domestic markets the Government banned export of sugar w.e.f. 22nd June, 2006 vide notification dated 4th July, 2006 upto the end of current financial year except export permitted through

Table 1.32: Country-wise import of sugar in India

Sr. No.	Country name	2010–2011		2011–2012		2012–2013	
		Quantity (lakh million tons)	*% share*	*Quantity (lakh million tons)*	*% share*	*Quantity (lakh million tons)*	*% share*
1.	Brazil	9.65	80.53	0.99	98.52	11.08	99.48
2.	Pakistan	0.00	0.00	0.00	0.00	0.05	0.44
3.	United States	0.00	0.01	0.00	0.25	0.00	0.02
4.	Japan	0.00	0.00	0.00	0.02	0.00	0.00
5.	Germany	0.01	0.11	0.00	0.09	0.00	0.01
6.	UK	0.01	0.06	0.00	0.08	0.00	0.01
7.	Canada	0.00	0.01	0.00	0.10	0.00	0.01
8.	China	0.04	0.32	0.00	0.46	0.00	0.01
9.	France	0.01	0.11	0.00	0.02	0.00	0.01
10.	UAE	0.31	2.60	0.00	0.05	0.00	0.03
11.	Singapore	0.00	0.00	0.00	0.00	0.00	0.00
12.	Austria	0.04	0.33	0.00	0.00	0.00	0.00
13.	Saudi Arabia	0.00	0.00	0.00	0.00	0.00	0.00
14.	South Africa	0.03	0.28	0.00	0.01	0.00	0.00
15.	Bangladesh	0.00	0.00	0.00	0.00	0.00	0.00
16.	Australia	0.00	0.00	0.00	0.00	0.00	0.00
17.	Indonesia	0.00	0.00	0.00	0.01	0.00	0.00
18.	Malaysia	0.15	1.23	0.00	0.00	0.00	0.00
19.	Others countries	1.73	14.44	0.00	0.10	0.00	0.01
Total import		**11.98**	**100.00**	**1.00**	**100.00**	**11.14**	**100.00**

Source: APEDA, 2013.

ISEC subject to the quantitative ceiling notified by the Director General of Foreign Trade (DGFT) from time to time. It was also provided that the ban would not be applicable for export of sugar against irrevocable letters of credit (LC) opened before 22nd June, 2006. Subsequently, the Government allowed export of sugar that has left the factory premises before 22nd June, 2006 and in port premises or in transit after verification of certain documents. Accordingly permission was given for export of 52,539 million tons of sugar.

Exports of sugar were banned w.e.f. 22nd June, 2006 because the domestic prices of sugar surged between January and June, 2006. Only exports through the ISEC, the joint body of Indian Sugar Mills Association (ISMA) and the NFCSF, were permitted subject to the quantitative ceiling notified by DGFT from time to time. Due to high production in sugar season 2006–2007, the ban on export of sugar against advance licenses was lifted wef 4th January, 2007 and then for exports under OGL w.e.f. 23rd January, 2007. Within a span of 6 months due to the cyclicality in production of sugarcane and consequently sugar, trade policy was changed from complete ban on exports to open exports through OGL. As 2007–2008 was a good production year, the requirement of obtaining export release orders from Directorate

Table 1.33: India's export and import of sugar

Financial year	*Export ("000 metric tons)*	*Export (value in Rs crores)*	*Import ("000 metric tons)*	*Import (value in Rs crores)*
1990–1991	2.000	0.91	–	–
1991–1992	82.000	55.80	–	–
1992–1993	365.000	316.73	–	–
1993–1994	119.000	111.33	–	–
1994–1995	39.350	48.88	1,765.440	2,245.85
1995–1996	434.320	597.34	150.630	215.89
1996–1997	667.274	860.80	2.131	3.18
1997–1998	173.282	244.44	346.905	470.25
1998–1999	12.735	17.36	900.471	1,111.22
1999–2000	12.990	18.14	1,181.183	1,110.80
2000–2001	338.691	430.98	30.404	31.11
2001–2002	1,456.448	1,728.29	26.578	32.60
2002–2003	1,662.370	1,769.49	41.430	32.83
2003–2004	1,200.600	1216.59	74.400	62.70
2004–2005	108.587	149.52	933.000	976.17
2005–2006	316.850	557.09	558.770	651.80
2006–2007	1,643.403	3,127.47	1.052	3.49
2007–2008	4,684.554	5,412.16	0.494	2.24
2008–2009	3,331.997	4,448.74	386.099	583.11
2009–2010	44.045	110.23	2,424.045	5,961.24
2010–2011	3,219.30	10,352.27	1,004.100	2,723.21
2011–2012	4,074.900	12,973.73	119.661	374.67

Source: DGCI & S, Kolkata [Cooperative Sugar Vol 45 (1), September, 2013].

of Sugar (except for export to EU and USA) was also relaxed w.e.f. 31st July, 2007 to be again re-introduced w.e.f. 1st January, 2009. This was done in view of the lower estimated production of sugar in 2008–2009 and 2009–2010 sugar seasons. Sugar production improved in 2010–2011 and 2011–2012 and due to comfortable sugar stocks in the country, exports of 1.5 million tons of sugar were allowed under OGL during 2010–2011 sugar season and 2 million tons during November, 2011 to February, 2012. Free exports of sugar have been allowed subject to prior registration of quantity with Directorate General of Foreign Trade (DGFT) w.e.f. 14 May, 2012.

With the development of sugar industry India has not only become self-sufficient but also an exporter of sugar exports of sugar on an organized basis commenced in 1957. In that year when the international market price of sugar was higher than that of Indian sugar, mainly because of the closure of the Suez Canal, the industry was able to export at a profit. The total exports in 1957 averaged to about 1.5 lakh tons valued at about Rs 12 crores. From the year 2008–2009 the exports of sugar in India has a downward trend; but in 2011–2012, the export has increased to 49.57 lakh tons. The impediment in the way of increasing the export of sugar is the high cost of production of sugar within the country. Production of sugar is self-sufficient at present in our country.

Import Policy

The imports of sugar were placed under OGL with zero duty in March, 1994. A basic customs duty of 5% and a countervailing duty of Rs 850 per ton was imposed on imported sugar wef 28th April, 1998 which was gradually increased from 20% w.e.f. 14th January, 1999 to 60% w.e.f. 9th February, 2000 along with continuance of countervailing duty of Rs 850 per ton (increased to Rs 950 per ton wef 1.3.2008 plus 3% education cess). In order to augment stocks for 2004–2005 and enable the Government to meet the normative 3 months consumption requirement of the country, the Advance License Scheme was liberalized for raw sugar imports, in as much as the imported raw sugar under Advance License was allowed to be processed into white sugar, sold in the domestic market, and further allowing such importers to fulfill export obligation within 24 months period or such extended period as allowed by DGFT by exporting indigenously manufactured white sugar. Such a severance of physical link between imported raw material and export product came to be known as ton-to-ton policy.

The domestic sugar production declined in 2008–2009 sugar season and so in order to augment the domestic stocks of sugar, the government allowed import of raw sugar under Advance Authorization Scheme by sugar mills at zero import duty from 17th February, 2009 to 30th September, 2009 and also allowed import of raw sugar at zero import duty under OGL w.e.f.17th April, 2009. The import duty was raised to 10% w.e.f. 13th July, 2012 in view of a declining trend in international prices of sugar to purportedly give protection to the domestic industry. This was further raised to 15% w.e.f. 8th July, 2013 due to the sluggish trend in international prices and to prevent cheap raw sugar imports.

Domestic wholesale prices of refined sugar (Mumbai) have been compared with International prices of refined sugar traded at LIFFE during the period from 2001–2002 to 2012–2013. It may be observed from the below chart that the domestic wholesale prices of refined sugar (Mumbai) have been generally higher than

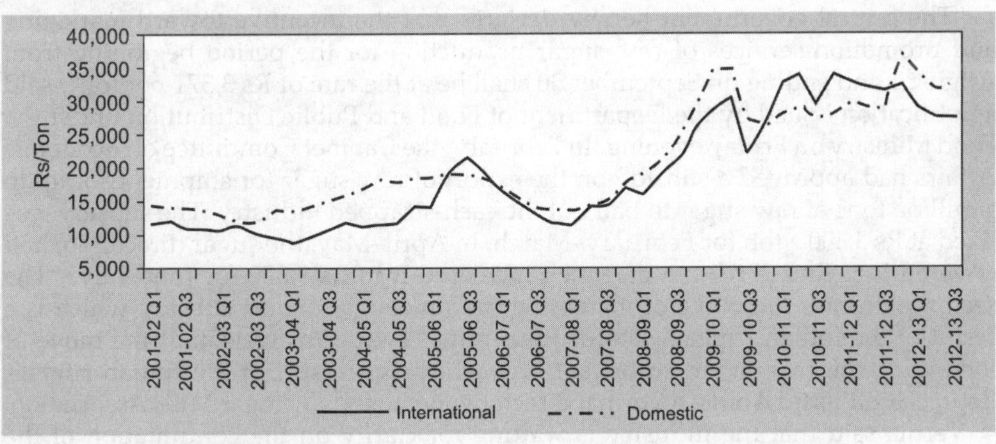

International prices versus domestic wholesale prices of sugar

Sources:

1. International refined white sugar traded at the London Futures Exchange (LIFFE).
2. Directorate of Sugar, DFPD for domestic wholesale prices at Mumbai.
3. The years pertains to sugar season viz., October–September.

international prices of refined sugar (LIFFE) during the period from 2001–2002 to 2012–2013. However, India's exports are mainly to neighboring countries like Pakistan, Bangladesh and Sri Lanka and the countries such as UAE, Yemen, Saudi Arabia, Iran, Sudan, Djibouti, Somalia, Kenya and Tanzania which are comparatively nearer to India than the main competitors like Brazil, Thailand and Australia. Because of less freight charges, it has become easier for India to export sugar to these countries.

In a nutshell, the government has broadly followed a consumer-oriented trade policy for sugar as imports were allowed at zero import duty since August 2009 (till July, 2012) while exports of sugar were tightly controlled and were subject to release orders from the Directorate of Sugar until recently. This was despite the surplus production during the years of 2010–2011 and 2011–2012. Since mid-2012, the international prices are settling to their trend level after reaching higher levels in 2010–2011 but the domestic prices of sugar are still higher. This is due to the higher cost of the raw material of sugarcane in some states, which is not linked with the prevailing prices of sugar. The government has raised the import duty to 15% recently to protect the domestic industry against cheaper imports but this may hurt the consumers. A higher import duty may just be a short-term reprieve for the industry as higher costs of domestic production are hitting the international competitiveness of Indian sugar. The solution to this muddle lies in reforming the domestic pricing policies. In terms of international trade, a stable, liberal and neutral (toward producers and consumers) trade policy with only moderate duties of 5–10% is required.

Sugar Export Subsidy Raised to Rs 3,371 Per Ton

The raw sugar export subsidy for August–September has been increased to Rs 3,371 per ton, up from Rs 3,300 in June–July after the industry lobbied for its continuation. The move comes amid criticism of the government shoring up overseas sales in violation of trade guidelines and this is being done despite companies not having paid farmers their dues as the government had asked.

"The central government hereby declares that the incentive toward marketing and promotion services of raw sugar production for the period beginning from August 1 and ending on September 30 shall be at the rate of Rs 3,371 per ton", said a notification issued by the Department of Food and Public Distribution under the Food Ministry on Friday evening. In February, the Cabinet Committee on Economic Affairs had approved a subsidy on the export of raw sugar for shipments of up to 4 million tons of raw sugar to bail out the cash-strapped industry. The subsidy was fixed at Rs 3,300 a ton for February–March. In April–May, the sugar directorate had lowered it to Rs 2,277 a ton and then increased it to Rs 3,300 for June–July. "The sector welcomes the move of increasing the raw sugar export subsidy which is a result of the Indian rupee 3,300 for June–July. "The sector welcomes the move of increasing the raw sugar export subsidy which is a result of the Indian rupee's depreciation", said Abinash Verma, director general, Indian Sugar Mills Association.

Verma said that the industry is waiting for clarity on the continuation of the export incentive scheme into the next sugar season as had been announced by the government. "This will enable industry to enter into forward contracts". The government is likely to take a call in September on whether to renew the raw sugar export subsidy for the 2014–2015 (October–September) season. However, Delhi-based independent trade analyst Tejinder Narang said the NDA government had inherited a wrongheaded policy from the previous government and it should be ended. "Why is the government doing marketing for sugar companies after decontrol while the subsidy itself is incompatible with WTO guidelines?" he said. Apart from this, food minister Ram Vilas Paswan had said in June that the government would continue the export subsidy apart from other measures only after sugar mills give a written undertaking that they would pay arrears to farmers. About 25,000 tons of raw sugar could be exported in August–September according to the sugar directorate. Till date more than 6.20 lakh tons of raw sugar has been exported with the subsidy, said government officials. Subsidy claims for more than 2.50 lakh tons have been filed, they said. Paswan told the Lok Sabha on August 8 that, as of July 31, sugar mills owed Rs 9,252 crore, or 16.2% of the total Rs 57,104 crore payable in the current sugar season. Private and cooperative sugar mills in UP owe Rs 5,741 crore, 29.61% of which is the money due for cane.

India to Boost Raw Sugar Exports

India could soon boost exports of raw sugar at the expense of top suppliers Brazil and Thailand as the government looks likely to give cash-strapped mills financial help for production so they can pay farmers. India's mills traditionally produce white sugar but a global glut has made exports difficult. A rise in sugar refining capacity in Asia and Africa has now given the country an opportunity to export raws.

But higher supplies of raw sugar from India, the world's biggest consumer and second-largest producer of the sweetener, will put further pressure on global prices, which are currently hovering at a 3 and ½-year low. Now, trade and government officials say New Delhi could announce tax breaks for mills as early as this week. "Mills can offer discounts and seal export deals if the government provides them some kind of financial support for raw sugar production", said Kamal Jain, managing director of Pune-based brokerage Kamal Jain Trading Services.

Subsidies for exports could attract the attention of the World Trade Organization (WTO) but government officials maintain that any incentives on production would not violate WTO rules. High production costs for refined, or white, sugar because of government-set prices for cane squeeze companies if they export at big discounts. Stocks, meanwhile, are piling up in warehouses at mills as farmers have produced bumper cane crops.

> India's mills traditionally produce white sugar but a global glut has made exports difficult.

In October, stocks totalled 8.8 million tons and this season, which runs to September 30, 2014, should see a fourth straight year of surplus production and falling local prices. This month in a tortuous spiral of subsidies, the government agreed to give mills interest-free loans to help pay government-set prices to cane growers.

With tax breaks, mills would produce raw sugar, cutting their white sugar output and reducing stockpiles. "Exports are unviable. Global sugar prices are falling and the rupee is becoming stronger. The government aid can make Indian raw sugar competitive in the world market", said a Mumbai-based dealer with an international brokerage.

The Indian Sugar Mills Association, the private mills platform, has maintained that paying Rs 300 quintal is out of the question. A 10% recovery, the price of cane works out to around Rs 25/kg including processing cost and incidentals, the goes up to over Rs 30/kg (Tables 1.33A and 1.34).

Table 1.33A: India: import trade matrix, centrifugal sugar, MY 2011/12

Period	*Raw sugar*	*White sugar*	*Total*
October	0	49	49
November	0	2	2
December	0	135	135
January	48,500	40	48,540
February	0	45	45
March	0	28	28
April	0	21	21
May	0	46	46
June	0	61	61
July	0	111	111
August	100,572	182	100,754
September	38,245	26	38,271
Total	187,317	746*	188,063

* Raw equivalent = 799 tons.
Note: Quantity in metric tons.
Source: Industry source.

Table 1.34: India: export trade matrix, centrifugal sugar, MY 2011/12

Period	*Raw sugar*	*White sugar*	*Total*
October	55,631	133,969	189,600
November	41,241	72,872	114,113
December	44,475	73,671	118,146
January	103,801	110,190	213,991
February	210,190	111,687	321,877
March	232,899	145,134	378,033
April	261,701	193,050	454,751
May	317,400	214,758	532,158
June	191,608	218,210	409,818
July	252,884	250,314	503,198
August	146,703	92,591	239,294
September	42,225	117,821	160,046
Total	1,900,758	1,734,267*	3,635,025

* Raw equivalent = 1,855,666 tons.
Note: Quantity in metric tons.
Source: Industry and Trade sources.

Production, Supply and Demand Data Statistics

Table 1.34A: India: centrifugal sugar (raw value basis), in thousand tons

Sugar, centrifugal India	*2011/2012*			*2012/2013*			*2013/2014*	
	Market year begin: Oct 2011			*Market year begin: Oct 2012*			*Market year begin: Oct 2013*	
	USDA official		*Old post Data*	*USDA official*		*New post Data*	*USDA official*	*New post Data*
Beginning Stocks	6,994	6,041	6,299	7,094	6,241	6,850		10,530
Beet Sugar Production	0	0	0	0	0	0		0
Cane Sugar Production	28,300	28,300	28,620	29,750	25,630	27,430		25,320
Total Sugar Production	28,300	28,300	28,620	29,750	25,630	27,430		25,320
Raw Imports	100	0	187	0	500	1,200		1,500
Refined Imp.(Raw Val)	0	0	1	0	0	100		0
Total Imports	100	0	188	0	500	1,300		1,500
Total Supply	35,394	34,341	35,107	36,844	32,371	35,580		37,350
Raw Exports	0	0	1,901	0	800	50		100
Refined Exp. (Raw Val)	1,800	2,600	1,856	2,500	1,400	500		500
Total Exports	1,800	2,600	3,757	2,500	2,200	550		600
Human Dom. Consumption	26,500	25,500	24,500	26,500	25,000	25,500		26,000
Other Disappearance	0	0	0	0	0	0		0
Total Use	26,500	25,500	24,500	26,500	25,000	25,500		26,000
Ending Stocks	7,094	6,241	6,850	7,844	5,171	9,530		0,750
Total Distribution	**35,394**	**34,341**	**35,107**	**36,844**	**32,371**	**35,580**		**37,350**

Note: Stocks include only milled sugar, as all *khandsari* sugar produced is consumed within the marketing year. virtually no centrifugal sugar is utilized for alcohol, feed, or other non-human consumption.

Table 1.34B: India: sugarcane, centrifugal, area in thousand hectares and others in thousand tons

Sugar, centrifugal India	*2011/2012*			*2012/2013*			*2013/2014*	
	Market year begin: Oct 2011			*Market year begin: Oct 2012*			*Market year begin: Oct 2013*	
	USDA official		*Old post Data*	*USDA official*		*New post Data*	*USDA official*	*New post Data*
Area Planted	5,090	5,090	5,080	5,250	5,100	5,310		5,350
Area Harvested	5,090	5,090	5,080	5,250	5,100	5,310		5,350
Production	347,870	357,670	357,670	365,000	335,328	360,000		355,000
Total Supply	347,870	357,670	357,670	365,000	335,328	360,000		355,000
Utilization for Sugar	260,000	270,000	257,000	270,000	240,000	252,000		232,000
Utilization for Alcohol	87,870	87,670	100,670	95,000	95,328	108,000		123,000
Total Utilization	**347,870**	**357,670**	**357,670**	**365,000**	**335,328**	**360,000**		**355,000**

Note: Virtually no cane is utilized directly for alcohol production. "Utilization for alcohol" in the PS&D includes cane used for gur, seed, feed and waste. "Utilization for sugar" data include cane used to produce mill sugar and khandsari sugar.

Table 1.34C: India: sugarcane area, production, and utilization

Sugarcane	*Area**	*Yield**	*Production**	*Sugar***	*Khandsari****	*Gur****	*Seed****
	Million hectare	*Tons/ hectare*	*Million*	*Million tons*	*Million tons*	*Million tons*	*Million tons*
1985/86	2.86	59.99	171.68	68.98	10.48	71.62	20.60
1990/91	3.69	65.39	241.05	122.32	13.18	76.63	28.93
1995/96	4.15	68.02	282.09	174.76	10.00	67.27	30.06
2000/01	4.32	68.49	295.60	176.65	11.00	72.48	35.47
2001/02	4.41	67.38	297.21	180.32	10.50	70.73	35.67
2002/03	4.52	63.58	287.38	194.33	9.50	49.07	34.49
2003/04	3.94	59.39	233.86	132.51	10.00	61.35	30.00
2004/05	3.66	64.74	237.09	124.77	9.50	74.37	28.45
2005/06	4.20	66.93	281.17	188.67	8.500	50.26	33.74
2006/07	5.15	69.03	355.52	279.24	7.500	26.10	42.66
2007/08	5.06	68.81	348.19	249.90	7.000	49.50	41.78
2008/09	4.40	64.77	285.00	145.00	6.500	99.30	34.20
2009/10	4.20	66.14	277.80	185.54	6.500	52.41	33.33
2010/11	4.89	70.09	342.38	240.00	7.50	53.80	41.08
2011/12	5.08	70.41	357.67	257.00	7.00	50.74	42.92
2012/13	5.31	67.80	360.00	252.00	7.00	57.80	43.20
2013/14***	5.35	66.36	355.00	232.00	8.00	72.40	42.60

* Directorate of Economic and Statistics, Ministry of Agriculture.
** Indian Sugar Mills Association except 2012/13 and 2013/14.
*** FAS/New Delhi estimate.
Note: Figures for 2012/13 and 2013/14 are FAS estimates.

Table 1.34D: India: mill sugar production by state, in 100,000 tons crystal weight basis

State	*2010/11**	*2011/12**	*2012/13***	*2013/14***
	Final	*Revised*	*Estimate*	*Forecast*
Andhra Pradesh	10.1	11.4	9.9	8.8
Bihar	3.9	4.5	4.8	7.5
Gujarat	12.4	10.0	11.9	10.6
Haryana	3.9	4.9	3.5	5.1
Karnataka	36.8	38.7	31.2	26.9
Maharashtra	90.5	89.8	79.1	58.7
Punjab	3.0	3.9	2.8	2.7
Tamil Nadu	18.5	23.8	22.1	20.5
Uttar Pradesh	58.9	69.7	77.2	84.0
Others	6.0	6.7	9.8	7.4
Total	**243.94**	**263.42**	**252.30**	**232.00**

Note: Excludes khandsari sugar, as state break-up is not available.
Sources:
* MYs 2010/11 and 2011/12 - Indian Sugar Mills Association.
** MYs 2012/12 and 2013/14 – FAS/New Delhi Estimate.

Table 1.34E: India: centrifugal sugar, price table, in rupees/metric tons (crystal weight basis)

Year	*2011*	*2012*	*2013*	*Change (%)*
January	29,500	30,000	35,400	18
February	29,650	30,000	35,710	19
March	30,000	30,250	34,500	14
April	29,400	29,400		
May	28,750	31,750		
June	28,300	32,300		
July	29,750	37,500		
August	29,500	37,200		
September	29,500	37,600		
October	30,750	38,960		
November	33,750	37,250		
December	32,000	37,360		
Exchange rate:Local currency/US $	**49.00**	**53.45**	**54.12**	

Note: Exchange rate for 2011 and 2012 refers to Indian Fiscal Years (IFY) 2011/12 (April/March) and IFY 2012/13, respectively. Exchange rate of 2013 refers to first fortnight of April, 2013.
Source: Indian Sugar Mills Association; month-end prices in the Delhi wholesale market.

WORLD SUGAR

Sugar is produced in 115 countries. It is extracted from sugarcane and sugar beet. Sugarcane is cultivated in tropical climates while sugar beet is grown in temperate regions. Around 75% of the sugar produced in the world is produced from sugarcane with beet sugar accounting for the rest. Weather conditions, crop diseases; soil quality, international trade agreements and domestic price support program—all these influence the production of sugarcane and sugar beet.

World area under sugarcane during 1961 was 8.9 million hectares (Table 1.35). It increased to 17.1 million hectares during 1990, 22.7 million hectares in 2007. Corresponding production figures were 448; 1,053.3 and 1,590.7 million tons. Global production of sugarcane, as per FAO, was 1.7 billion tons in TE 2011. Brazil is the biggest producer of sugarcane accounting for 41.4% of the world sugarcane production followed by India (17.7%). Other major producers of sugarcane are China (6.6%), Thailand (4.5%), Pakistan (3.0%) and Mexico (2.9%). Sugar beet area in the world during 1961 was 7.0 million hectares which increased to 8.9 million hectares in 1964. Having touched the highest (9.4) million hectares in 1976, it came down regularly and was just 5.2 million hectares in 2007. Corresponding production figures were 160.5, 216.2, 296.4 and 246.7 million tons (Table 1.36). Poland was having the highest area at 401 thousand hectares which increased to 444 thousand hectares in 1964–1965. Corresponding production figures were 10.3 million and 12.6 million tons. Poland was followed by United States, France and Germany. India does not figure in the major beet producing countries (Table 1.36A).

Table 1.35: Area and production of sugarcane in India and world

Area (hectare) production (tons)

Year	India Area	India Production	World Area	World Production
2007	4,900,000	355,520,000	22,724,997 A	1,590,701,770 A
2006	4,201,100	281,171,800	20,825,394 A	1,409,448,519 A
2005	3,661,500	237,088,400	20,024,720 A	1,318,844,370 A
2004	3,938,400	233,861,800	20,368,665 A	1,335,592,063 A
2003	4,520,300	287,383,200	20,786,655 A	1,375,905,539 A
2002	4,411,600	297,200,000	20,515,889 A	1,330,892,605 A
2001	4,315,700	295,956,000	19,733,362 A	1,261,133,778 A
2000	4,219,700	299,230,016	19,516,427 A	1,252,547,301 A
1999	4,054,900	295,729,984	19,204,979 A	1,267,061,236 A
1998	3,940,000	262,090,000	19,326,987 A	1,258,155,440 A
1997	4,170,000	277,560,000	19,292,772 A	1,251,603,795 A
1996	4,150,000	281,100,000	19,417,500 A	1,222,851,749 A
1995	3,870,000	275,540,000	18,577,716 A	1,172,313,285 A
1994	3,420,000	229,670,000	17,591,927 A	1,089,642,360 A
1993	3,570,000	228,030,000	17,292,800 A	1,030,379,898 A
1992	3,840,000	254,000,000	18,151,894 A	1,116,324,081 A
1991	3,686,000	241,045,504	17,783,308 A	1,089,330,376 A
1990	3,439,000	225,569,200	17,079,401 A	1,053,264,897 A
1989	3,328,900	203,036,800	16,535,904 A	1,017,998,783 A
1988	3,278,600	196,736,896	16,390,040 A	992,982,513 A
1987	3,078,700	186,089,504	16,310,476 A	990,319,251 A
1986	2,862,000	171,680,992	15,826,297 A	934,719,186 A
1985	2,953,200	170,319,200	15,947,852 A	933,213,589 A
1984	3,109,700	174,076,000	15,635,479 A	929,768,246 A
1983	3,357,600	189,505,600	15,380,802 A	903,684,353 A
1982	3,193,300	186,357,600	15,055,213 A	907,067,880 A
1981	2,666,600	154,248,000	13,686,584 A	799,604,214 A
1980	2,610,200	128,833,408	13,284,827 A	734,489,200 A
1979	3,087,800	151,655,104	13,733,150 A	770,245,178 A
1978	3,151,100	176,965,008	13,690,038 A	774,416,858 A
1977	2,866,200	153,007,008	13,029,277 A	734,858,286 A
1976	2,762,200	140,603,504	12,575,275 A	687,207,538 A
1975	2,894,200	144,288,896	12,198,454 A	655,815,792 A

Table 1.35: Area and production of sugarcane in India and world *(Contd.)*

Area (hectare) production (tons)

	India		*World*	
Year	*Area*	*Production*	*Area*	*Production*
1974	2,752,100	140,805,008	11,932,313 A	648,516,497 A
1973	2,451,600	124,866,704	11,149,211 A	600,227,145 A
1972	2,390,400	113,569,504	10,871,074 A	569,105,570 A
1971	2,615,000	126,368,000	11,055,376 A	582,105,426 A
1970	2,748,000	135,024,000	11,113,307 A	608,616,105 A
1969	2,532,200	124,676,096	10,046,924 A	538,255,737 A
1968	2,047,000	95,500,000	9,586,121 A	506,091,880 A
1967	2,301,000	92,827,008	9,949,042 A	518,890,895 A
1966	2,836,000	123,990,000	10,375,326 A	531,492,823 A
1965	2,602,900	122,077,008	10,165,125 A	531,297,486 A
1964	2,249,000	104,225,008	9,330,371 A	480,849,768 A
1963	2,242,000	91,913,008	9,038,405 A	441,722,740 A
1962	2,456,000	103,967,008	9,023,996 A	436,872,640 A
1961	2,413,000	110,001,008	8,911,879 A	447,977,522 A

A, May include official, semi-official or estimated data.

Table 1.36: Area and production of sugar beet in Asia and World

Area (hectare) production (tons)

	Asia		*World*	
Year	*Area*	*Production*	*Area*	*Production*
2007	826,816 A	33,122,001 A	5,172,671 A	246,713,216 A
2006	873,986 A	38,255,041 A	5,456,579 A	253,551,426 A
2005	852,056 A	34,366,915 A	5,413,595 A	251,582,210 A
2004	837,118 A	31,766,967 A	5,473,928 A	248,697,649 A
2003	945,921 A	31,737,769 A	5,690,226 A	229,649,014 A
2002	1,161,029 A	42,612,528 A	6,033,147 A	257,262,672 A
2001	1,106,681 A	34,323,414 A	6,027,179 A	228,057,636 A
2000	1,092,809 A	37,687,193 A	6,021,556 A	247,077,236 A
1999	1,146,407 A	38,162,353 A	6,608,270 A	260,673,285 A
1998	1,354,730 A	48,310,989 A	6,783,079 A	263,144,330 A
1997	1,366,685 A	43,924,562 A	7,041,984 A	268,043,427 A
1996	1,389,416 A	40,269,574 A	7,646,373 A	265,864,694 A
1995	1,378,695 A	36,878,234 A	7,852,829 A	264,746,777 A

(Contd.)

Table 1.36: Area and production of sugar beet in Asia and World

Area (hectare) production (tons)

	Asia		World	
Year	*Area*	*Production*	*Area*	*Production*
1994	1,501,607 A	37,146,858 A	7,975,516 A	255,073,146 A
1993	1,390,345 A	39,242,703 A	8,117,683 A	282,405,074 A
1992	1,469,930 A	43,039,482 A	8,467,816 A	282,237,910 A
1991	1,461,030 A	41,897,363 A	8,548,201 A	284,245,521 A
1990	1,309,078 A	37,154,377 A	8,657,657 A	309,186,724 A
1989	1,170,369 A	28,374,027 A	8,601,865 A	314,402,899 A
1988	1,304,423 A	32,782,521 A	8,657,643 A	293,570,876 A
1987	1,159,423 A	30,138,936 A	8,670,887 A	299,751,636 A
1986	1,139,652 A	28,585,882 A	8,667,085 A	286,334,048 A
1985	1,123,271 A	27,319,101 A	8,649,067 A	284,155,160 A
1984	1,113,186 A	28,526,795 A	8,806,714 A	296,351,939 A
1983	1,184,923 A	30,427,570 A	8,826,171 A	274,395,485 A
1982	1,131,521 A	29,182,788 A	9,055,387 A	291,773,194 A
1981	1,068,410 A	25,383,219 A	9,297,137 A	287,840,286 A
1980	963,738 A	21,214,012 A	8,865,859 A	267,856,451 A
1979	836,288 A	20,019,303 A	8,795,804 A	262,752,809 A
1978	855,724 A	19,002,837 A	9,047,772 A	282,834,069 A
1977	858,713 A	19,249,359 A	9,119,211 A	288,582,476 A
1976	886,798 A	20,940,749 A	9,431,553 A	296,408,369 A
1975	790,710 A	16,743,572 A	9,043,782 A	251,310,276 A
1974	698,676 A	14,508,409 A	8,204,662 A	234,922,029 A
1973	687,500 A	15,337,683 A	8,153,675 A	250,104,320 A
1972	658,917 A	15,652,509 A	7,967,248 A	240,336,963 A
1971	619,147 A	14,991,473 A	7,606,069 A	227,540,795 A
1970	584,462 A	13,076,624 A	7,594,912 A	224,251,952 A
1969	533,187 A	12,112,473 A	7,650,033 A	216,920,772 A
1968	526,444 A	13,124,870 A	7,787,853 A	248,856,658 A
1967	550,885 A	13,379,174 A	7,898,717 A	233,455,177 A
1966	547,154 A	11,888,391 A	7,855,161 A	212,270,253 A
1965	480,674 A	9,294,951 A	8,009,880 A	197,376,224 A
1964	450,158 A	8,862,407 A	8,344,197 A	216,206,931 A
1963	334,241 A	6,673,299 A	7,540,518 A	164,975,629 A
1962	329,397 A	5,814,410 A	6,903,028 A	149,172,711 A
1961	450,442 A	6,024,225 A	6,926,098 A	160,501,987 A

A, May include official, semi-official or estimated data.

Table 1.36A: Sugar beet-acreage and production

Countries	*Area thousand (hectares)*					*Production thousand (tons)*				
	1960-61	*1961-62*	*1962-63*	*1963-64*	*1964-65*	*1960-61*	*1961-62*	*1962-63*	*1963-64*	*1964-65*
Europe										
Austria	45	39	48	48	53	1906	1250	1544	2090	2203
Belgium	63	62	57	57	44	3063	2703	2019	2135	3114
Czechoslovakia	242	238	260	259	259	7853	6660	5811	8018	7474
Denkark*	55	39	42	69	84	2230	1397	1440	2598	3154
France	385	320	314	339	396	17990	11557	10089	12502	14831
Germany- Eastern	238	218	232	232	230	6837	4657	4970	6176	6003
Fed. Rep of**	294	260	290	301	327	12734	9295	9154	12662	13247
Hungary	133	130	125	118	133	3370	2356	2553	3434	3554
Italy	247	227	226	230	231	7530	6731	6802	7667	7711
Netherlands	93	85	77	69	79	4676	3854	2934	2691	3876
Poland	401	420	430	372	444	10262	1555	9652	10661	12574
Spain	145	158	166	116	146	3572	4423	3584	2750	3331
Sweden**	51	50	47	40	44	2414	2001	1442	1574	1731
United Kingdom	175	172	170	170	179	7331	6031	5398	5368	6318
North and Central America										
Canada	35	34	34	39	41	997	1003	1003	1166	1177
United States	387	436	446	500	565	14897	16061	16560	21163	21218
World Total	**6980**	**6850**	**6920**	**7580**	**8360**	**185070**	**159270**	**148590**	**165100**	**215120**

* Including sugar beets exported for foreign factories.
** Excluding importer sugar beets.
Source: F/O. Production year Book 1963 and 1965.

Beet Production Today

Sugarbeet, as it is known today, is unique among food plants in use throughout the world in that it is a product of breeding research, and also became a model for improving plant performance through genetics and breeding. The sugar beet plant is also unique in history by its role as a catalyst in revolutionizing agriculture. Growing sugar beets in Europe at that time changed the previous small grain monoculture and introduced the concept of crop rotation. This created the system for manuring and better soil fertility and reducing weed problem, while also supplying a source of food for livestock from beet tops, crowns and pulp.

Of the current world production of more than 130 million metric tons of sugar, about 35% comes from sugar beet and 65% from sugarcane. In the USA, about 50–55% of the domestic production of about 8.4 million metric tons derives from sugar beet. Sugar beet is grown mostly in the temperate zone from plantings made in April and harvested in the fall. Today, 11 states and two provinces within four diverse regions are involved with sugar beet production in North America. These areas include the upper midwest (Minnesota and North Dakota), the far west (California, Idaho, Oregon and Washington), the Great Plains (Colorado, Nebraska,

Montana Wyoming, and Alberta), and the Great Lakes (Michigan and Ontario; Ohio ceased production in 2005).

By 1806, cane sugar had virtually disappeared from the shelves of European shops. In 1811, French scientists presented Napoleon with two loaves of sugar made from sugar beet. Napoleon was so impressed he decreed that 32,000 hectares of beet should be planted and provided assistance to get the factories established. Within a few years there were more than 40 sugar beet factories, mostly in Northern France but also in Germany, Austria, Russia and Denmark.

Once the blockade of continental ports was removed, cane sugar reappeared and many countries stopped beet processing. By contrast, the French government supported developments in both the selection of beet varieties with higher sugar levels and improvements in sugar extraction techniques. This two-pronged approach ensured that sugar from beet became a viable option European sugar supply

The beet industry has waxed and waned over the years but today Europe produces 120 million tons of beet every year, used to make 16 million tons of white sugar. France and Germany are still the main producers but sugar is produced from beet in all EU countries except Luxembourg. Almost 90% of sugar consumed in Europe is locally grown, a feat that would have seemed incredible only 200 years ago.

There is one good news to sick sugar units. Syngenta India, a leading agri-business company has introduced tropical sugar beet in the country after tying up with a few sugar cooperatives in Maharashtra. The companies experiments of producing sugar and ethanol from sugar beet have been successful. The tropical sugar beet developed by the company gives the same quantity of sugar per unit of land in half the time and with one-third water as sugarcane. The eco-friendly nature of sugar beet is also important as it grows in saline lands.

Geographic Distribution

Sugar beet is essentially a crop of temperate region grown on 5.49 million hectares with major share (>72%) of production from Europe (Table 1.37).

Global production of sugarcane was 1.7 billion tons in TE 2011. Brazil is the biggest producer of sugarcane accounting for 41.4% of the world sugarcane production followed by India (17.7%). Other major producers of sugarcane are China (6.6%), Thailand (4.5%), Pakistan (3.0%) and Mexico (2.9%). Sugarcane and sugar beet are the two main sources of sugar. Sugarcane is cultivated in tropical and subtropical climates while sugar beet is cultivated in temperate climates. As per FAO, global production of sugar beet was 0.2 billion tons in TE 2011. EU-27 is the biggest producer of sugar beet with a share of 46.3% followed by Russia (13.0%), USA (11.3%), Turkey (7.0%) and Ukraine (5.8%). At present, it is estimated that 79% of sugar is produced from sugarcane and remaining 21% is produced from sugar beet. However, as per OECD-FAO Outlook 2013–2022, sugarcane is expected to account for virtually all the additional sugar production and to represent nearly 88% of sugar output in 2022.

Benchmarking Productivity: India vis-à-vis Other Leading Cane Producing Countries

In a globalized scenario, relative performance in yield improvement is as critical as temporal improvement in productivity levels. The role of productivity in enhancing

Table 1.37: Area, production and productivity of major sugarbeet producing countries in 2004

Continent/country	*Area (million hectares)*	*Production (million tons)*	*Yield (ton/hectare)*
Africa	0.118	7.420	62.81
Arab Magherab Union	0.059	0.456	77.41
Asia	0.857	31.626	36.89
Austria	0.045	2.934	64.60
Belarus	0.086	3.088	35.90
Belgium	0.087	6.215	70.83
Canada	0.014	0.743	52.38
Chile	0.030	2.370	78.82
China	0.190	5.860	30.84
Croatia	0.026	1.000	37.65
Czech Republic	0.071	3.579	50.34
Denmark	0.048	2.828	58.08
Egypt	0.059	2.850	48.29
Europe	3.947	179.760	45.54
France	0.386	30.554	79.13
Germany	0.440	27.159	61.65
Iran	0.180	4.900	27.22
Ireland	0.031	1.861	59.85
Italy	0.185	8.473	45.60
Japan	0.068	4.656	68.47
Latvia	0.367	0.505	36.71
Lithuania	0.023	0.904	38.83
Morocco	0.058	4.560	77.41
World	**5.497**	**249.118**	**45.31**

Source: FAO Production Year Book, 2004.

competitiveness is critical as it can reduce cost and thus prices. Therefore, it would be interesting to envision India's standing *vis-à-vis* other major cane producing countries on land productivity scale. This would help in benchmarking productivity standards, and set our targets accordingly with a view to gain greater competitiveness in production of sugar. With this end in view, India's position *vis-à-vis* other leading countries producing this crop is tracked and is presented in Table 1.38.

India is positioned second after Brazil in terms of its share in the total world production of sugarcane but stands way behind in respect of land productivity compared to that of benchmark country (Colombia). The efficiency gap of 40% exists in India's land productivity. In order to enhance the domestic productivity level, the pattern of agricultural practices of benchmark countries needs to be followed keeping in view their suitability to our country.

Table 1.38: Gap in yield level of sugarcane in India *vis-a-vis* benchmark country, TE 2011

India's rank in sugarcane production in the world in terms of		*Other leading countries (yield, share in world production*
Production	*Yield*	
2nd	11th	Colombia (113 ton/hectare, 2%); Guatemala (90 ton/hectare, 1%); Philippines (85 ton/hectare, 2%); Australia (79 ton/hectare, 2%); Brazil (79 ton/hectare, 41%); USA (74 ton/hectare, 2%); India (68 ton/hectare, 18%).

Sources: Collated from FAO.

1. Above figures are based on TE 2011.
2. Paired figures in parentheses in col. (3) indicate yield and share of production respectively in the total world production.
3. Countries with less than 1% share in total world production have not been considered.
4. Yield level for India, as given in col. (3) marginally varies from what is reported in charts 5.1 and 5.1 due to difference in reference period.

To sum up, it emerges that Bihar/UP, major cane producing states in subtropical region, are far more efficient compared to Karnataka, Maharashtra and Tamil Nadu in tropical region, when land productivity is normalized for the time duration of the crop, its water intake, and its recovery rate, especially from the point of view of water required per unit of sugar produced. In view of projection made by the International Water Resources Group (IWRG) that India will be 50% short of water by 2030 coupled with the fact that sugarcane is a water guzzling crop, its long-term development must ensure that it is in line with availability of sufficient water and its cost. It is, therefore, recommended that in states like Karnataka, Maharashtra and Tamil Nadu, sugarcane productivity needs to be maximized per unit of water and its cost. From that perspective, drip irrigation needs to be promoted which can save almost 40–50% water. Water thus saved, like any other resource, can be used for other competing crops. Also, there is need to give high priority in evolving such varieties which use less water, and get our water pricing policies right so that sugarcane crop follows a sustainable trajectory of growth with cost effectiveness.

Total world production of sugar during 1980–1981 was 87.7 million tons (Table 1.39). It increased to 114.5 million tons in 1990–1991 and 172.0 million tons by 2011–2012. This relates to total production including the one from sugar and heat. Sugar production from cane alone was 69.3 million tons in 1989–1990 and 138.9 in million tons 2012–1913.

World sugarbeet area and production are given in charts 1.1 and 1.2. Country-wise area, production and yield for beat sugar are show in charts 1.3, to 1.6. Russia had the highest area of 1.2 million hect in 2011 and Russian Federation topped in production. With regard to productivity France topped the list followed by chile and Switzerland. India does not figure any where in area, production or productivity

Table 1.39: World cane and beet sugar production and consumption

(Million MT)

Years	*Sugar from beet*	*Sugar from sugarcane*	*Total sugar production*	*World sugar consumption*
1989-90	40.65	69.31	110.01	106.82
1990-91	41.87	72.56	114.47	110.02
1991-92	38.78	78.65	117.46	113.65
1992-93	39.99	73.25	113.28	113.93
1993-94	40.16	70.85	111.06	113.47
1994-95	36.98	81.04	118.06	115.57
1995-96	37.14	86.59	123.77	117.5
1996-97	37.38	86.95	124.36	120.74
1997-98	37.99	87.51	125.54	123.3
1998-99	36.84	94.02	130.89	124.53
1999-00	36.72	99.01	135.76	127.36
2000-01	36.65	94.11	130.8	130.09
2001-02	32.59	101.81	134.43	134.34
2002-03	36.95	111.6	148.59	138.03
2003-04	34.59	107.9	142.52	138.95
2004-05	37.13	103.61	140.77	141.65
2005-06	42.58	106.81	149.43	142.94
2006-07	36.48	127.98	164.49	149.37
2007-08	32.73	130.8	163.57	150.53
2008-09	30.18	113.84	144.04	153.49
2009-10	33.39	120.01	153.44	153.45
2010-11	31.94	129.98	161.95	154.24
2011-12	38.59	133.39	172.02	158.73
2012-13	35.57	138.9	174.5	163.6

Source: USDA, Foreign Agricultural Service.

productivity of sugar beet (Charts 1.3 and 1.4). Sugarcane and sugar beet are the two main sources of sugar. Sugarcane is cultivated in tropical and subtropical climates while sugar beet is cultivated in temperate climates. As per FAO, global production of sugar beet was 0.2 billion tons in TE 2011, EU-27 is the biggest producer of sugar beet with a share of 46.3% followed by Russia (13.0%), USA (11.3%), Turkey (7.0%) and Ukraine (5.8%). At present, it is estimated that 79% of sugar is produced from sugarcane and remaining 21% is produced from sugar beet. However, as per OECD-FAO Outlook 2013–2022, sugarcane is expected to account for virtually all the additional sugar production and to represent nearly 88% of sugar output in 2022.

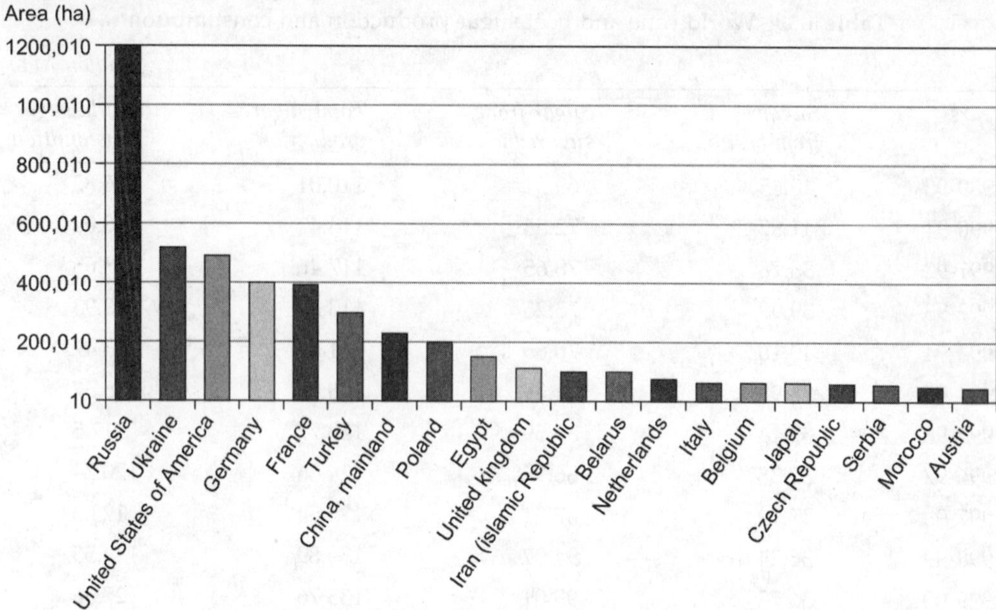

Chart 1.1: World sugar beet production by area 2011 (Ha)

Source: FAO Statistical, 2011

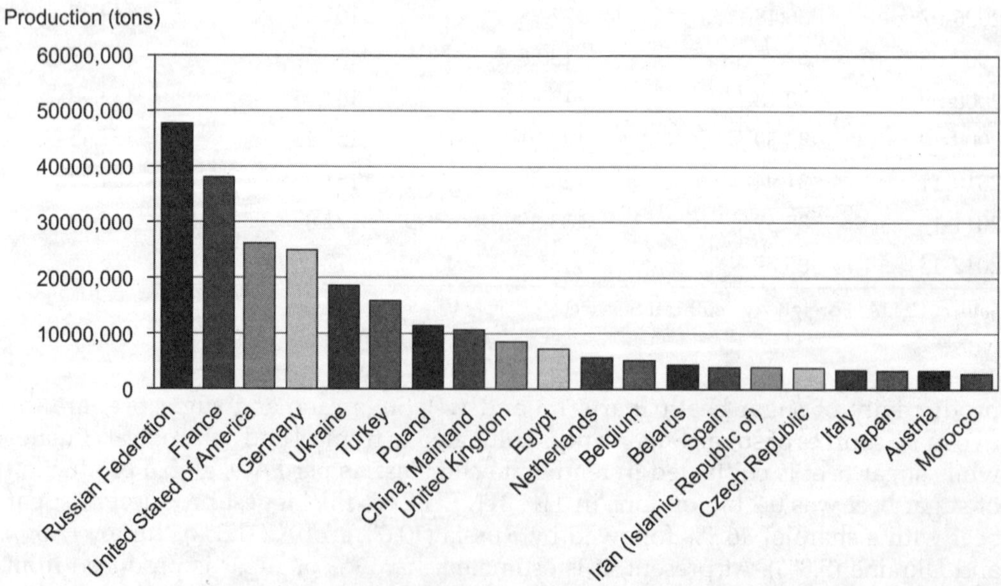

Chart 1.2: World sugar beet production by tons 2011

Source: FAO Statistical, 2011

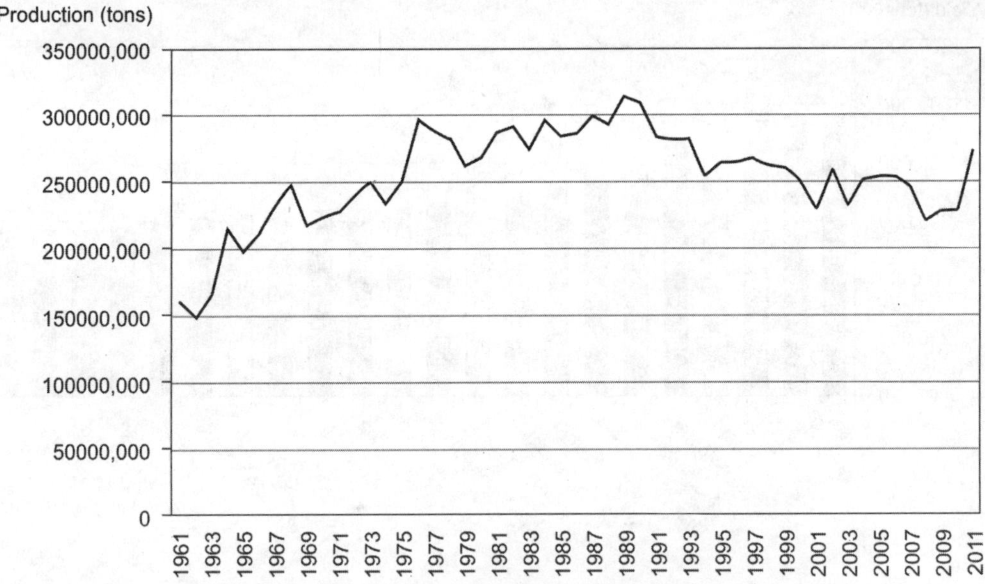

Chart 1.3: Total world sugar beet production by year

Source: FAO Statistical, 2011

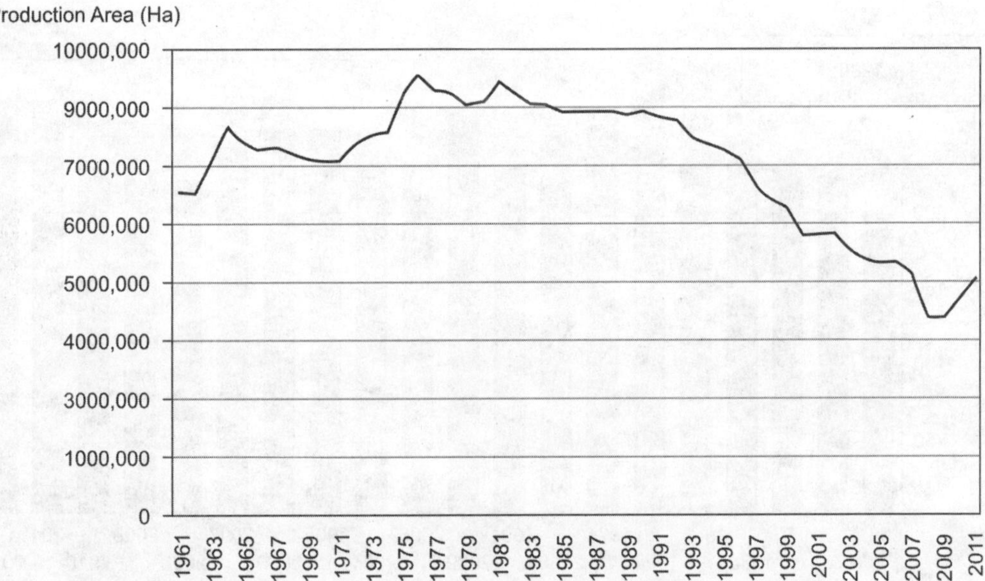

Chart 1.4: Total world sugar beet production by area (ha)

Source: FAO Statistical, 2011

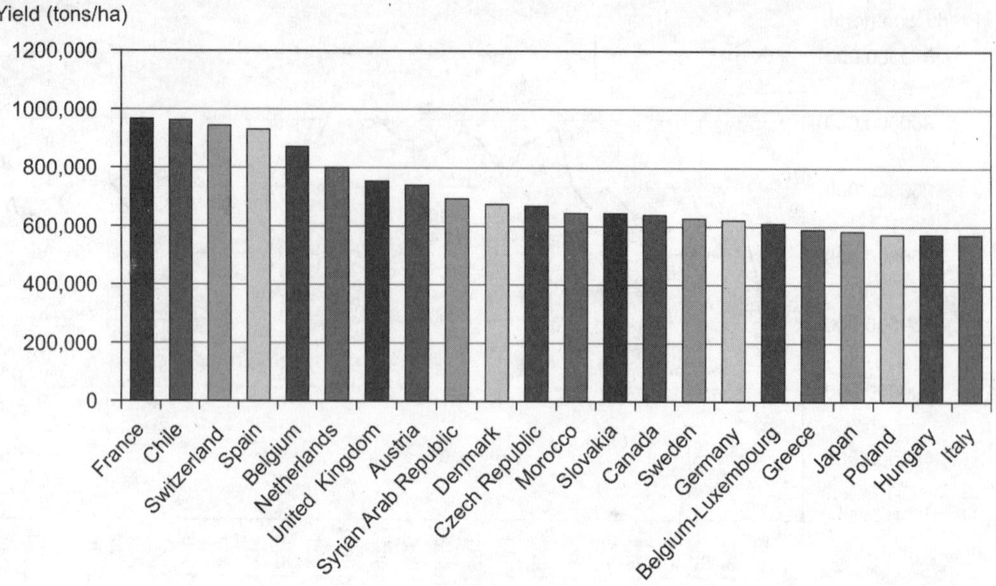

Chart 1.5: Average sugar beet yields (tons/ha by country in 2011

Source: FAO Statistical, 2011

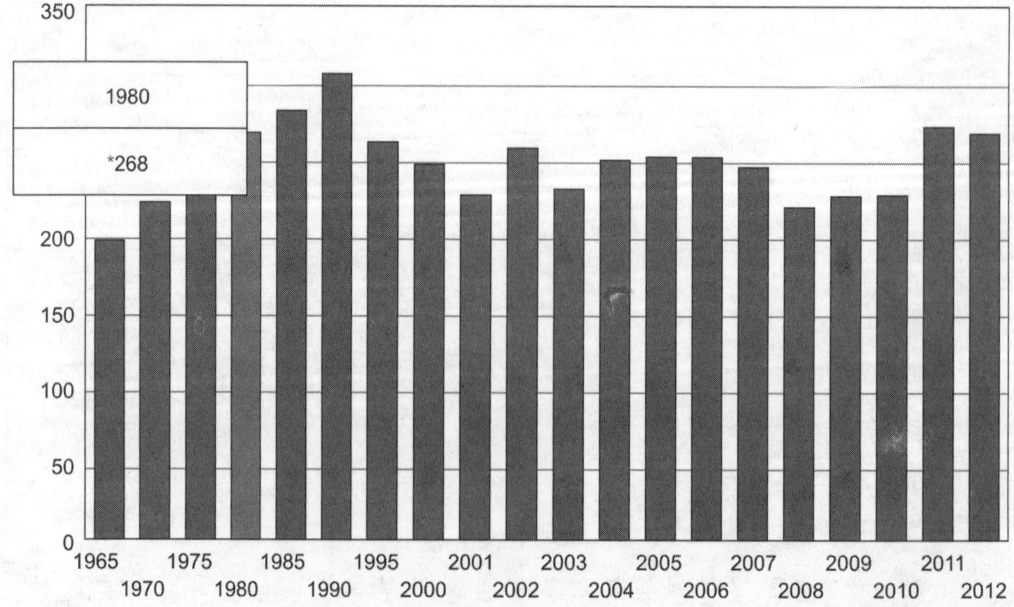

Chart 1.6: Sugar beet production worldwide from 1965 to 2012 (in million metric tons)

Source: FAO Statistical, 2011

World Sugar Cane Production from 1965 to 2012 (In Million Metric Tons)

Brazil had the highest area under sugarcane at 4.5 million hectare with a production of 304.3 million tons in 1994–1996. Corresponding figures for 2007 were 7.0 million hectare and 54.9.7 million tons Brazil is followed by India with area as 3.8 million hectares in 1994–1995 and 4.9 million hectares in 2007 with corresponding production figures of 262.1 and 355.5 million tons.

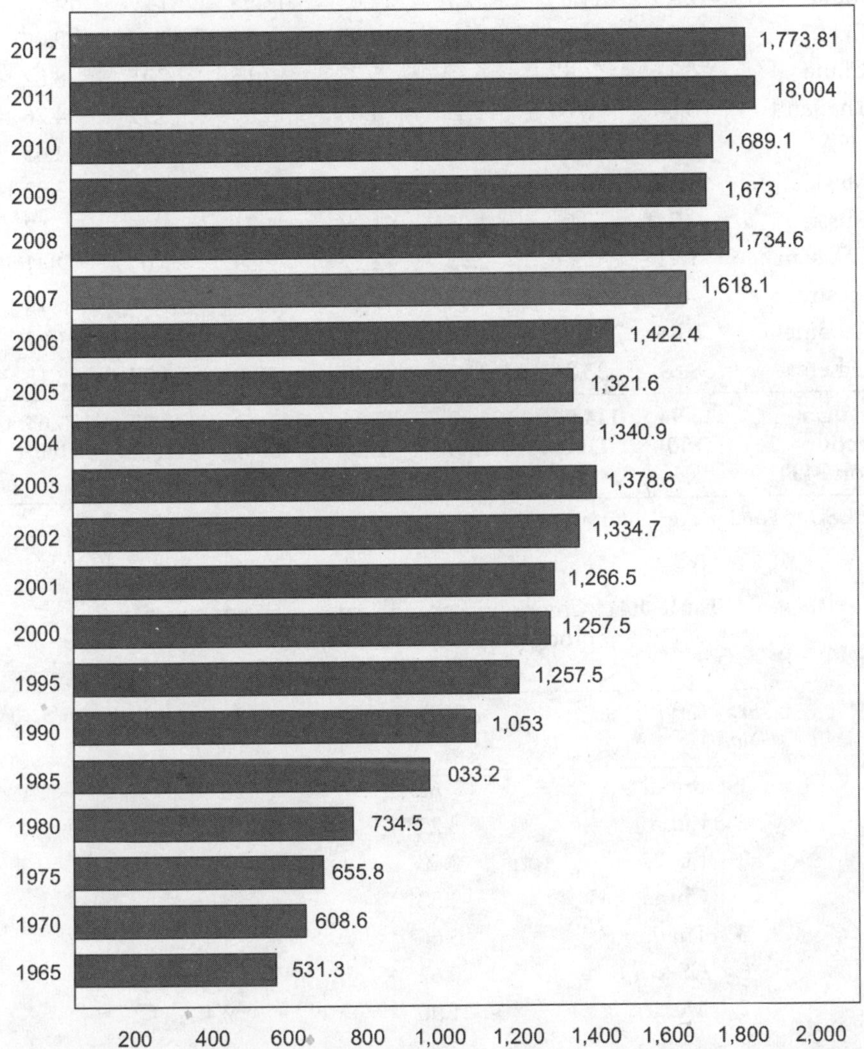

In the total world sugarcane producing countries, the share of Brazil increased from 7.3% in 1989–1992 to 22.3% in 2010–1913. While EU 27 were the top producers with 15.1% in 1989–1992, their share in 2010–2013, came down to 9.7%. As against this the share o India increased from 12.1% to 16.3% during this period (Table 1.40). Compound growth rate among the major sugar producing countries was the highest at 7.6% for Brazil followed by Guatemala (4.2%), Thailand (3.6%), China (3.5%) and India (3.2%) (Tables 1.41 and 1.41A).

Table 1.40: Major sugar producing countries in world

(Percent)

Sr. No.	Countries	1989-92	1992-95	1995-98	1998-01	2001-04	2004-07	2007-10	2010-13
		Time periods (triennium averages)							
1	Brazil	7.28	9.42	11.79	13.97	16.6	19.24	21.66	22.25
2	India	12.15	11.85	12.7	14.63	13.58	14.7	14.15	16.25
3	EU-27	15.09	15.7	14.66	14.05	12.21	13.52	10.05	9.72
4	China	6.11	6.17	6.19	5.73	7.15	7.15	8.82	7.38
5	Thailand	3.66	3.85	4.41	4.08	4.86	3.72	4.76	5.86
6	USA	5.57	6.21	5.49	5.98	5.33	4.79	4.65	4.52
7	Mexico	3.22	3.71	4	3.82	3.7	3.87	3.52	3.43
8	Russia	2.34	2.01	1.25	1.09	1.21	1.76	2.2	2.66
9	Pakistan	1.91	2.6	2.73	2.27	2.69	2.04	2.41	2.58
10	Australia	3.1	4.08	4.36	3.68	3.6	3.54	3.14	2.3
11	Gutamela	0.88	1.04	1.24	1.21	1.28	1.41	1.52	1.41
12	Others	38.69	33.36	31.2	29.49	27.8	24.27	23.13	21.64
Total sugar production (million MT)		**113.94 (100)**	**114.09 (100)**	**124.52 (100)**	**32.45 (100)**	**141.81 (100)**	**149.83 (100)**	**153.65 (100)**	**169.45 (100)**

Source: USDA, Foreign Agricultural Service.

Table 1.41: Compound growth rates in major sugar producing countries in world

Quantity

Sr. No.	Countries	CGR (%)	Estimated 't' value
1	Brazil	7.62***	26.86
2	India	3.22***	5.75
3	EU-27	–0.33	-1.13
4	China	3.52***	7.6
5	Thailand	3.66***	7.45
6	USA	0.62***	3.1
7	Mexico	1.96***	7.42
8	Russia	2.92**	2.67
9	Pakistan	2.42***	4.74
10	Australia	0.34	0.71
11	Guatemala	4.32***	17.18
12	Others	–0.71***	-5.47
	World	**1.96*****	**16.23**

** Significant at 5% level of significance.
*** Significant at 1% level of significance.

Table 1.41A: Production of sugar in selected countries

(th MT)

Country	1980-81	1985-86	1987-88	1988-89	1989-90	1990-91	1992	1993	1994	1995	1996	1997	1998	1999	2000	2001	2002	2003	2004	2005	2006	2007	2008	2009	2009-10	2010-11	2011-12
East Europe																											
- Czech Rep								563	465	550	654	648	535	420	434	484	523	521	-	-	-	-	-		-	-	
- Poland	1,134	1,109	1,797	1,825	1,895	2,174	1,566	2,201	1,503	1,734	2,380	2,112	2,242	1,968	2,104	1,626	2,038	1,912	-	-	-	-	-		1730	1649	2075
Russia/CIS							2,437	2,717	1,650	2,241	1,851	1,337	1,369	1,651	1,705	1,756	1,757	1,892	2,496	2,719	3,459	3,405	3,789	3,602	3,500	3,532	5455
West Europe																											
- EEC/EU	13,051	14,452	14,037	15,263	15,945	16,979	17,102	17,384	15,717	16,932	17,692	18,582	17,939	19,428	17,854	15,500	18,268	16,578	21,843	21,698	17,580	16,904	14,708	16,631		-	-
North America																											
- USA	4,404	5,284	5,763	5,422	5,220	5,599	6,805	7,045	6,921	7,238	6,593	6,731	3,926	8,243	8,080	7,774	6,805	7,964	7,647	6,784	7,034	7,678	6,956	6,855	7,234	7,088	7620
Central & South America																											
- Cuba	7,542	6,900	7,548	8,188	8,156	7,623	7,219	4,246	4,017	3,259	4,529	4,318	3,291	3,875	4,057	3,748	3,522	2,278	2,600	1,300	1,275	1,193	1,445	1,379	1,275	1,200	1400
- Dominican Rep.	1,069	804	759	735	636	587	593	621	579	508	670	687	409	421	438	491	516	525	529	475	487	488	492	540	-	-	-
- Mexico	2,586	4,301	3,852	3,699	3,408	3,940	3,745	4,360	3,849	4,588	4,784	5,048	5,287	5,030	4,816	5,614	5,073	5,441	5,672	5,619	5,412	5,420	5,940	5,181	5,025	5,495	5325
- Argentina	1,716	1,174	1,063	1,284	1,017	1,351	1,380	1,093	1,202	1,612	1,393	1,649	1,749	1,882	1,580	1,630	1,680	1,952	1,857	2,165	2,470	2,198	2,448	2,256	2,470	1,933	2100
- Brazil	8,547		8,458	8,582	7,793	7,835	9,925	10,097	12,270	13,835	14,718	16,371	19,168	20,645	16,464	20,336	23,567	25,730	27,290	28,135	31,622	33,199	32,291	33,455	393,775	38,127	35195
- Colombia	1,212	1,272	1,364	1,523	1,593	1,601	1,813	1,833	1,964	2,069	2,149	2,136	2,126	2,241	2,391	2,260	2,523	2,646	2,740	2,683	2,415	2,277	2,036	2,599	2,265	2,313	2340
Asia																											
- India	5,589	7,612	9,905	9,513	11,942	13,000	13,873	11,750	11,745	15,337	16,892	14,440	14,281	17,406	20,247	19,926	19,525	21,702	14,432	15,216	22,347	29,090	25,936	15,655	20,450	26,646	28500
- Indonesia	1,292	1,871	2,317	2,083	2,225	2,311	2,350	2,490	2,461	2,103	2,100	2,189	1,493	1,490	1,685	1,850	2,150	1,780	2,225	2,435	2,510	2,814	2,895	2,850	2,515	2,500	2475
- Phillipines	2,395	1,568	1,404	1,645	1,810	1,760	1,919	2,091	2,098	1,562	1,895	1,954	1,549	1,913	1,826	1,890	1,988	2,245	2,423	2,184	2,413	2,147	2,415	2,294	2,075	2,499	2245
- Thailand	1,641	2,586	2,704	4,052	3,506	4,000	5,078	3,825	4,168	5,447	6,154	6,243	4,143	5,456	6,157	5,370	6,438	7,737	7,462	4,589	5,646	7,147	7,774	7,945	7,131	10,061	10600
Africa																											
- Egypt	659	890	1,029	946	966	1,044	1,060	1,090	1,190	1,125	1,222	1,228	1,152	1,269	1,450	1,583	1,490	1,425	1,489	1,625	1,725	1,851	1,699	1,750	2,084	2,025	2000
Oceania																											
- Australia	3,419	3,294	3,510	3,755	3,844	3,612	4,363	4,488	5,222	5,119	5,618	5,883	5,085	5,514	4,417	4,768	5,614	5,315	5,530	5,393	4,729	4,627	4,619	4,523	3,503	3,512	4000
Total World	**87,696**	**97,091**	**104,290**	**105,946**	**108,861**	**113,592**	**117,335**	**111,363**	**109,622**	**117,528**	**124,217**	**125,132**	**126,694**	**134,964**	**130,004**	**130,650**	**142,090**	**148,126**	**147,285**	**141,680**	**152,347**	**166,659**	**161,571**	**149,822**	**158,838**	**165,597**	**175,054**
India's share (%)	**6.4**	**7.3**	**9.5**	**9.0**	**11.0**	**11.4**	**11.8**	**10.6**	**10.7**	**13.0**	**13.6**	**11.5**	**12.3**	**12.9**	**15.6**	**15.3**	**13.8**	**14.6**	**9.8**	**10.8**	**14.7**	**17.5**	**16.0**	**10.4**	**12.9**	**16.1**	**16.3**

Global output of sugar was 169.5 million tons in TE 2012–2013 out of which about 33.0% is traded. Brazil was the biggest producer of sugar accounting for 22.2% share of the world sugar production followed by India (16.3%) in TE 2012–2013 (see below chart). Other major producers of sugar in the world are EU-27 (9.7%), China (7.4%), Thailand (5.9%) and USA (4.5%) (Tables 1.42 to 1.44).

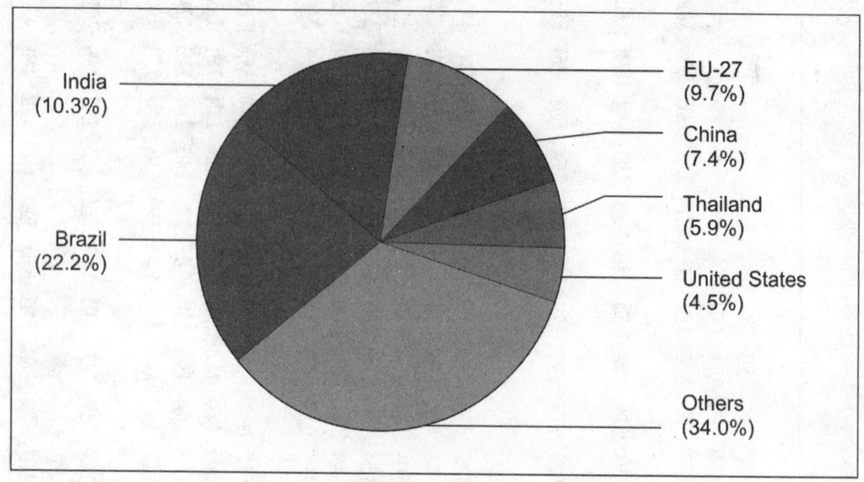

Major producers of sugar, TE 2012–2013

World Consumption

World consumption of sugar increased from 110.6 million tons in 1989–1992 to 158.9 million tons in 2010–2013 (Tables 1.45 and 1.46). Compound growth rate of sugar consumption during this period was the highest for 1.85% showed rate at 3.8 per cent followed by Indonesia (3.5%) and India (3.2%). World per capita consumption of sugar (Tables 1.47 and 1.47A) is the highest in Brazil varying from 58 kg in 2000 to 69.4 kg in 2010. Brazil is followed by Cuba 63 kg in 2000 to 57.8 kg in 2012. India is the second largest producer of sugar consumes only 20.6 kg per capita per annum. But along with sugar, it also consumes gur and khandsari where per capita consumption has fallen from 16 kg in 1860–1861 to around 8 kg now.

World Trade

World exports of sugar increased from 24.8 million tons in 1981 to 28.4 million tons in 1990. Coming back to around 24 million tons upto 1994, started rising again touching over 55 million tons during 2009–2010 are now around 53 million tons (Tables 1.48 and 1.48A).

Total global export of sugar was 56.0 million tons in TE 2012–2013 with Brazil as the biggest exporter of sugar in the world with 46.5% share followed by Thailand (13.4%) (see below charts). Other major exporters of sugar were Australia (5.2%), India (4.9%), EU-27 (3.0%), Guatemala (2.9%) and Mexico (2.5%). EU-27 is the biggest importer of sugar with a share of 7.4% closely followed by Indonesia (6.6%), USA (6.3%), and China (6.3%) in TE 2012–2013 (see below charts).

In the early period, Cuba was the major exporter in 1981 at 7.1 million tons, but continued to decline regularly coming to 0.9 million tons in 2011–2012. Brazil has been the major exporter all these years—exports increasing from 2.7 million tons in

Exports

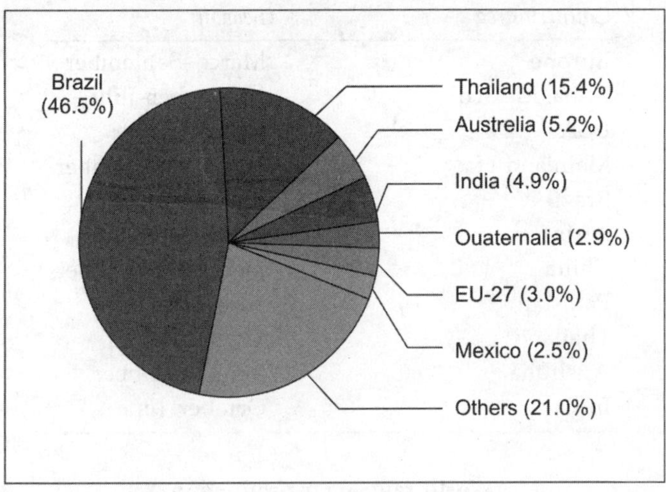

Imports

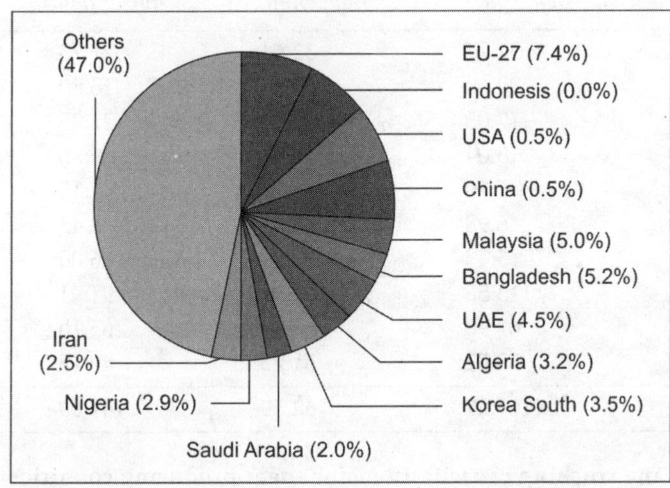

Major exporters and importers of sugar in TE 2012–2013

Source: USDA.

1981 to over 24 million tons in 2012–2013 (Tables 1.48 and 1.48A). The share of Brazil was 46.5% in world exports during 2010–2013. Although India is a minor exporter, its share increased from 0.8% in 1989–1992 to 5% by 2010–2013 (Table 1.49). Compound growth rate of major exporting countries was the highest for Brazil and a continuing declining trend for Cuba (Table 1.50). From the major importers, in share of EU-27, came down from 10.9% in 1989–1992 to 7.4% in 2010–2013, Indonesia showed the highest increase from 0.99% to 6.6% during the same period. The share of India also increased from 0.06% to 1.28% during the same period (Tables 1.51 to 1.53).

Crushing season of India vis-à-vis other countries

Country/area	*Season*
Europe	March–September
Cuba, Mexico	November–July
USA	October–June
Mainland Hawaii	January–December
Brazil	June–May
Africa	April–November
China	January–December
Pakistan	November–May
Thailand	October–April
Australia	May–December
India	October–June

World raw sugar production

(Million tons)

Country/region	*2006–2007*	*2005–2006*	*2004–2005*	*2003–2004*
Brazil	32.77	32.64	27.73	26.14
India	30.60	20.94	13.80	14.74
EU	17.05	21.94	21.95	20.20
China	13.04	9.58	9.86	10.90
USA	7.70	6.71	7.15	7.85
Thailand	6.98	5.08	5.43	7.28
Mexico	5.43	5.39	6.00	5.36
Sub-total	113.56	101.37	91.91	92.47
Total world (%)	67.90	66.40	65.10	64.30
Others	53.72	51.22	49.18	51.28
World total	**167.27**	**152.59**	**141.09**	**143.75**

Cane crushing capacity in major sugar producing countries

Country	*Average cane crushing producing countries*
Thailand	10,307
Australia	9,216
Brazil	9,168
South Africa	6,877
Mexico	4,749
Colombia	4,590
Cuba	4,229
Hawaii	4,111
Mauritius	3,195
India	2,500

Table 1.42: World sugar production, supply, and distribution including beet sugar

Country mktg year	*Beginning stocks*	*Total sugar production*	*Total imports*	*Total supply*	*Total exports*	*Total use*	*Ending stocks*
SUG - North America							
Canada							
2008/09	206	61	1,255	1,522	93	1,226	203
2009/10	203	70	1,114	1,387	37	1,150	200
2010/11	200	94	1,135	1,429	89	1,105	235
2011/12	235	130	1,103	1,468	83	1,132	253
2012/13	253	130	1,157	1,540	46	1,234	260
2013/14	260	125	1,195	1,580	45	1,275	260
Mexico							
2008/09	1,975	5,260	160	7,395	1,378	5,394	623
2009/10	623	5,115	861	6,599	751	4,875	973
2010/11	973	5,495	306	6,774	1,557	4,411	806
2011/12	806	5,351	505	6,662	985	4,653	1,024
2012/13	1,024	7,393	229	8,646	2,090	5,008	1,548
2013/14	1,548	6,890	231	8,669	2,485	5,140	1,044
United States							
2008/09	1,510	6,833	2,796	11,139	123	9,624	1,392
2009/10	1,392	7,224	3,010	11,626	192	10,075	1,359
2010/11	1,359	7,104	3,391	11,854	225	10,379	1,250
2011/12	1,250	7,700	3,294	12,244	244	10,205	1,795
2012/13	1,795	8,144	2,925	12,864	249	10,635	1,980
2013/14	1,980	8,054	3,059	13,093	227	10,691	2,175
Total SUG - North America							
2008/09	3,691	12,154	4,211	20,056	1,594	16,244	2,218
2009/10	2,218	12,409	4,985	19,612	980	16,100	2,532
2010/11	2,532	12,693	4,832	20,057	1,871	15,895	2,291
2011/12	2,291	13,181	4,902	20,374	1,312	15,990	3,072
2012/13	3,072	15,667	4,311	23,050	2,385	16,877	3,788
2013/14	3,788	15,069	4,485	23,342	2,757	17,106	3,479
SUG - Caribbean							
Cuba							
2008/09	135	1,340	23	1,498	727	669	102
2009/10	102	1,250	0	1,352	538	700	114
2010/11	114	1,150	0	1,264	577	628	59
2011/12	59	1,400	0	1,459	830	520	109
2012/13	109	1,510	0	1,619	750	720	149
2013/14	149	1,600	0	1,749	850	749	150

(Contd.)

Table 1.42: World sugar production, supply, and distribution including beet sugar

Country mktg year	*Beginning stocks*	*Total sugar production*	*Total imports*	*Total supply*	*Total exports*	*Total use*	*Ending stocks*
Dominican Republic							
2008/09	35	510	34	579	239	330	10
2009/10	10	520	77	607	261	332	14
2010/11	14	510	49	573	204	335	34
2011/12	34	553	48	635	211	380	44
2012/13	44	556	60	660	230	380	50
2013/14	50	541	40	631	212	380	39
Other SUG - Caribbean							
2008/09	132	189	459	780	170	478	132
2009/10	132	168	407	707	143	422	142
2010/11	142	187	411	740	153	459	128
2011/12	128	182	362	672	143	406	123
2012/13	123	190	394	707	127	452	128
2013/14	128	210	405	743	150	465	128
Total SUG - Caribbean							
2008/09	302	2,039	516	2,857	1,136	1,477	244
2009/10	244	1,938	484	2,666	942	1,454	270
2010/11	270	1,847	460	2,577	934	1,422	221
2011/12	221	2,135	410	2,766	1,184	1,306	276
2012/13	276	2,256	454	2,986	1,107	1,552	327
2013/14	327	2,351	445	3,123	1,212	1,594	317
SUG - Central America							
Guatemala							
2008/09	609	2,381	0	2,990	1,654	744	592
2009/10	592	2,340	0	2,932	1,815	735	382
2010/11	382	2,048	0	2,430	1,544	759	127
2011/12	127	2,499	0	2,626	1,619	750	257
2012/13	257	2,600	0	2,857	1,950	787	120
2013/14	120	2,600	0	2,720	1,850	797	73
Other SUG - Central America							
2008/09	440	2,071	0	2,511	803	1,272	436
2009/10	436	2,194	138	2,768	1,050	1,181	537
2010/11	537	2,128	0	2,665	967	1,160	538
2011/12	538	2,462	0	3,000	1,146	1,260	594
2012/13	594	2,637	0	3,231	1,247	1,366	618
2013/14	618	2,697	0	3,315	1,275	1,438	602

Table 1.42: World sugar production, supply, and distribution including beet sugar *(Contd.)*

Country mktg year	*Beginning stocks*	*Total sugar production*	*Total imports*	*Total supply*	*Total exports*	*Total use*	*Ending stocks*
Total SUG - Central America							
2008/09	1,049	4,452	0	5,501	2,457	2,016	1,028
2009/10	1,028	4,534	138	5,700	2,865	1,916	919
2010/11	919	4,176	0	5,095	2,511	1,919	665
2011/12	665	4,961	0	5,626	2,765	2,010	851
2012/13	851	5,237	0	6,088	3,197	2,153	738
2013/14	738	5,297	0	6,035	3,125	2,235	675
SUG - South America							
Brazil							
2008/09	215	31,850	0	32,065	21,550	11,650	-1,135
2009/10	-1,135	36,400	0	35,265	24,300	11,800	-835
2010/11	-835	38,350	0	37,515	25,800	12,000	-285
2011/12	-285	36,150	0	35,865	24,650	11,500	-285
2012/13	-285	38,600	0	38,315	27,650	11,200	-535
2013/14	-535	38,750	0	38,215	27,250	11,260	-295
Colombia							
2008/09	170	2,277	139	2,586	585	1,585	416
2009/10	416	2,294	185	2,895	870	1,620	405
2010/11	405	2,280	160	2,845	830	1,625	390
2011/12	390	2,270	322	2,982	876	1,771	335
2012/13	335	2,210	310	2,855	600	1,955	300
2013/14	300	2,400	290	2,990	600	2,000	390
Argentina							
2008/09	105	2,420	23	2,548	543	1,739	266
2009/10	266	2,230	0	2,496	778	1,740	-22
2010/11	-22	2,030	73	2,081	210	1,790	81
2011/12	81	2,150	5	2,236	194	1,810	232
2012/13	232	2,300	0	2,532	256	1,830	446
2013/14	446	1,800	0	2,246	220	1,840	186
Other SUG - South America							
2008/09	1,230	3,299	1,493	6,022	536	4,073	1,413
2009/10	1,413	2,954	1,679	6,046	531	4,274	1,241
2010/11	1,241	3,290	1,889	6,420	469	4,448	1,503
2011/12	1,503	3,358	1,681	6,542	478	4,487	1,577
2012/13	1,577	3,393	1,782	6,752	499	4,663	1,590
2013/14	1,590	3,403	1,724	6,717	555	4,593	1,569

(Contd.)

Table 1.42: World sugar production, supply, and distribution including beet sugar

Country mktg year	*Beginning stocks*	*Total sugar production*	*Total imports*	*Total supply*	*Total exports*	*Total use*	*Ending stocks*
Total SUG - South America							
2008/09	1,720	39,846	1,655	43,221	23,214	19,047	960
2009/10	960	43,878	1,864	46,702	26,479	19,434	789
2010/11	789	45,950	2,122	48,861	27,309	19,863	1,689
2011/12	1,689	43,928	2,008	47,625	26,198	19,568	1,859
2012/13	1,859	46,503	2,092	50,454	29,005	19,648	1,801
2013/14	1,801	46,353	2,014	50,168	28,625	19,693	1,850
SUG - Europe							
EU-28							
2008/09	3,130	14,290	3,180	20,600	1,332	17,036	2,232
2009/10	2,232	16,897	2,561	21,690	2,647	17,610	1,433
2010/11	1,433	15,939	3,755	21,127	1,113	18,040	1,974
2011/12	1,974	18,320	3,552	23,846	2,343	18,200	3,303
2012/13	3,303	16,591	3,900	23,794	1,500	18,250	4,044
2013/14	4,044	16,000	3,650	23,694	1,500	18,300	3,894
Other SUG - Other Europe							
2008/09	471	629	813	1,913	93	1,463	357
2009/10	357	719	683	1,759	122	1,270	367
2010/11	367	737	629	1,733	205	1,166	362
2011/12	362	732	677	1,771	153	1,259	359
2012/13	359	689	679	1,727	156	1,197	374
2013/14	374	684	690	1,748	156	1,218	374
Total SUG - Europe							
2008/09	3,601	14,919	3,993	22,513	1,425	18,499	2,589
2009/10	2,589	17,616	3,244	23,449	2,769	18,880	1,800
2010/11	1,800	16,676	4,384	22,860	1,318	19,206	2,336
2011/12	2,336	19,052	4,229	25,617	2,496	19,459	3,662
2012/13	3,662	17,280	4,579	25,521	1,656	19,447	4,418
2013/14	4,418	16,684	4,340	25,442	1,656	19,518	4,268
SUG - Former Soviet Union							
Russia							
2008/09	550	3,481	2,150	6,181	200	5,500	481
2009/10	481	3,444	2,223	6,148	34	5,715	399
2010/11	399	2,996	2,510	5,905	17	5,538	350
2011/12	350	5,545	510	6,405	300	5,715	390

Table 1.42: World sugar production, supply, and distribution including beet sugar *(Contd.)*

Country mktg year	*Beginning stocks*	*Total sugar production*	*Total imports*	*Total supply*	*Total exports*	*Total use*	*Ending stocks*
2012/13	390	5,000	600	5,990	200	5,515	275
2013/14	275	4,400	1,100	5,775	100	5,415	260
Ukraine							
2008/09	580	1,710	78	2,368	37	2,100	231
2009/10	231	1,382	346	1,959	1	1,878	80
2010/11	80	1,540	293	1,913	1	1,700	212
2011/12	212	2,300	12	2,524	180	1,700	644
2012/13	644	2,100	10	2,754	142	1,800	812
2013/14	812	1,700	5	2,517	100	1,800	617
Other SUG - Former Soviet Union							
2008/09	940	857	1,579	3,376	615	2,029	732
2009/10	732	937	1,784	3,453	758	1,985	710
2010/11	710	821	1,850	3,381	707	1,938	736
2011/12	736	978	1,396	3,110	706	1,697	707
2012/13	707	1,003	1,632	3,342	721	1,873	748
2013/14	748	1,013	1,684	3,445	731	1,966	748
Total SUG - Former Soviet Union							
2008/09	2,070	6,048	3,807	11,925	852	9,629	1,444
2009/10	1,444	5,763	4,353	11,560	793	9,578	1,189
2010/11	1,189	5,357	4,653	11,199	725	9,176	1,298
2011/12	1,298	8,823	1,918	12,039	1,186	9,112	1,741
2012/13	1,741	8,103	2,242	12,086	1,063	9,188	1,835
2013/14	1,835	7,113	2,789	11,737	931	9,181	1,625
SUG - Sub-Saharan Africa							
South Africa							
2008/09	227	2,350	137	2,714	1,230	1,405	79
2009/10	79	2,265	105	2,449	754	1,595	100
2010/11	100	1,985	138	2,223	400	1,665	158
2011/12	158	1,897	193	2,248	271	1,815	162
2012/13	162	2,020	222	2,404	377	1,855	172
2013/14	172	2,450	225	2,847	600	1,885	362
Swaziland							
2008/09	79	650	0	729	350	311	68
2009/10	68	658	0	726	350	316	60
2010/11	60	602	0	662	320	321	21

(Contd.)

Table 1.42: World sugar production, supply, and distribution including beet sugar

Country mktg year	*Beginning stocks*	*Total sugar production*	*Total imports*	*Total supply*	*Total exports*	*Total use*	*Ending stocks*
2011/12	21	670	0	691	315	331	45
2012/13	45	711	0	756	350	331	75
2013/14	75	750	0	825	360	351	114
Other SUG - Sub-Saharan Africa							
2008/09	1,945	4,762	4,318	11,025	1,505	7,601	1,919
2009/10	1,919	4,797	4,824	11,540	1,274	8,225	2,041
2010/11	2,041	5,142	4,915	12,098	1,645	8,437	2,016
2011/12	2,016	5,254	4,884	12,154	1,509	8,646	1,999
2012/13	1,999	5,366	5,360	12,725	1,583	9,007	2,135
2013/14	2,135	5,429	5,406	12,970	1,575	9,267	2,128
Total SUG - Sub-Saharan Africa							
2008/09	2,251	7,762	4,455	14,468	3,085	9,317	2,066
2009/10	2,066	7,720	4,929	14,715	2,378	10,136	2,201
2010/11	2,201	7,729	5,053	14,983	2,365	10,423	2,195
2011/12	2,195	7,821	5,077	15,093	2,095	10,792	2,206
2012/13	2,206	8,097	5,582	15,885	2,310	11,193	2,382
2013/14	2,382	8,629	5,631	16,642	2,535	11,503	2,604
SUG - North Africa							
Egypt							
2008/09	544	1,612	1,382	3,538	100	2,748	690
2009/10	690	1,820	978	3,488	330	2,629	529
2010/11	529	1,830	1,120	3,479	550	2,800	129
2011/12	129	1,980	1,480	3,589	389	2,850	350
2012/13	350	2,000	1,050	3,400	400	2,840	160
2013/14	160	2,020	1,200	3,380	400	2,820	160
Other SUG - North Africa							
2008/09	484	520	2,628	3,632	112	3,213	307
2009/10	307	438	2,507	3,252	132	2,818	302
2010/11	302	436	2,640	3,378	480	2,566	332
2011/12	332	440	3,234	4,006	423	3,211	372
2012/13	372	410	3,758	4,540	575	3,546	419
2013/14	419	410	3,875	4,704	585	3,700	419
Total SUG - North Africa							
2008/09	1,028	2,132	4,010	7,170	212	5,961	997
2009/10	997	2,258	3,485	6,740	462	5,447	831

Table 1.42: World sugar production, supply, and distribution including beet sugar *(Contd.)*

Country mktg year	*Beginning stocks*	*Total sugar production*	*Total imports*	*Total supply*	*Total exports*	*Total use*	*Ending stocks*
2010/11	831	2,266	3,760	6,857	1,030	5,366	461
2011/12	461	2,420	4,714	7,595	812	6,061	722
2012/13	722	2,410	4,808	7,940	975	6,386	579
2013/14	579	2,430	5,075	8,084	985	6,520	579
SUG - MiddleEast							
Turkey							
2008/09	405	2,100	5	2,510	5	2,000	505
2009/10	505	2,530	5	3,040	69	2,422	549
2010/11	549	2,274	5	2,828	75	2,291	462
2011/12	462	2,262	5	2,729	74	2,300	355
2012/13	355	2,130	5	2,490	33	2,300	157
2013/14	157	2,200	5	2,362	20	2,260	82
Other SUG - Middle East							
2008/09	2,696	819	6,622	10,137	1,043	7,635	1,459
2009/10	1,459	1,342	7,761	10,562	978	8,095	1,489
2010/11	1,489	1,106	7,639	10,234	1,580	7,085	1,569
2011/12	1,569	1,136	8,233	10,938	1,351	8,047	1,540
2012/13	1,540	1,150	9,127	11,817	921	9,324	1,572
2013/14	1,572	1,150	9,448	12,170	1,005	9,578	1,587
Total SUG - Middle East							
2008/09	3,101	2,919	6,627	12,647	1,048	9,635	1,964
2009/10	1,964	3,872	7,766	13,602	1,047	10,517	2,038
2010/11	2,038	3,380	7,644	13,062	1,655	9,376	2,031
2011/12	2,031	3,398	8,238	13,667	1,425	10,347	1,895
2012/13	1,895	3,280	9,132	14,307	954	11,624	1,729
2013/14	1,729	3,350	9,453	14,532	1,025	11,838	1,669
SUG - South Asia							
India							
2008/09	12,296	15,950	1,358	29,604	224	23,500	5,880
2009/10	5,880	20,637	2,431	28,948	225	22,500	6,223
2010/11	6,223	26,574	455	33,252	3,903	23,050	6,299
2011/12	6,299	28,620	188	35,107	3,764	23,993	7,350
2012/13	7,350	27,200	1,800	36,350	1,240	24,685	10,425
2013/14	10,425	25,450	1,800	37,675	2,000	26,200	9,475

Table 1.42: World sugar production, supply, and distribution including beet sugar

Country mktg year	*Beginning stocks*	*Total sugar production*	*Total imports*	*Total supply*	*Total exports*	*Total use*	*Ending stocks*
Pakistan							
2008/09	1,163	3,512	125	4,800	75	4,175	550
2009/10	550	3,420	1,030	5,000	70	4,100	830
2010/11	830	3,920	1,040	5,790	70	4,250	1,470
2011/12	1,470	4,520	10	6,000	350	4,300	1,350
2012/13	1,350	4,780	9	6,139	1,100	4,400	639
2013/14	639	4,970	10	5,619	440	4,450	729
Other SUG - South Asia							
2008/09	865	290	1,958	3,113	11	2,381	721
2009/10	721	255	1,998	2,974	22	2,281	671
2010/11	671	295	2,200	3,166	10	2,479	677
2011/12	677	265	2,399	3,341	10	2,639	692
2012/13	692	290	2,238	3,220	10	2,508	702
2013/14	702	290	2,263	3,255	10	2,543	702
Total SUG - South Asia							
2008/09	14,324	19,752	3,441	37,517	310	30,056	7,151
2009/10	7,151	24,312	5,459	36,922	317	28,881	7,724
2010/11	7,724	30,789	3,695	42,208	3,983	29,779	8,446
2011/12	8,446	33,405	2,597	44,448	4,124	30,932	9,392
2012/13	9,392	32,270	4,047	45,709	2,350	31,593	11,766
2013/14	11,766	30,710	4,073	46,549	2,450	33,193	10,906
SUG - East Asia							
Japan							
2008/09	454	927	1,279	2,660	1	2,100	559
2009/10	559	901	1,199	2,659	1	2,090	568
2010/11	568	700	1,331	2,599	1	2,069	529
2011/12	529	740	1,230	2,499	1	1,955	543
2012/13	543	750	1,330	2,623	1	2,072	550
2013/14	550	750	1,365	2,665	1	2,115	549
China							
2008/09	3,965	13,317	1,077	18,359	75	14,500	3,784
2009/10	3,784	11,429	1,535	16,748	93	14,300	2,355
2010/11	2,355	11,199	2,143	15,697	76	14,000	1,621
2011/12	1,621	12,341	4,430	18,392	52	14,200	4,140
2012/13	4,140	14,000	3,800	21,940	50	15,100	6,790
2013/14	6,790	14,800	2,800	24,390	45	16,000	8,345

Table 1.42: World sugar production, supply, and distribution including beet sugar *(Contd.)*

Country mktg year	*Beginning stocks*	*Total sugar production*	*Total imports*	*Total supply*	*Total exports*	*Total use*	*Ending stocks*
Other SUG - East Asia							
2008/09	554	65	2,604	3,223	305	2,264	654
2009/10	654	70	2,513	3,237	347	2,258	632
2010/11	632	70	2,621	3,323	422	2,226	675
2011/12	675	70	2,552	3,297	424	2,208	665
2012/13	665	65	2,767	3,497	408	2,383	706
2013/14	706	65	2,783	3,554	423	2,423	708
Total SUG - East Asia							
2008/09	4,973	14,309	4,960	24,242	381	18,864	4,997
2009/10	4,997	12,400	5,247	22,644	441	18,648	3,555
2010/11	3,555	11,969	6,095	21,619	499	18,295	2,825
2011/12	2,825	13,151	8,212	24,188	477	18,363	5,348
2012/13	5,348	14,815	7,897	28,060	459	19,555	8,046
2013/14	8,046	15,615	6,948	30,609	469	20,538	9,602
SUG - Southeast Asia							
Thailand							
2008/09	2,651	7,200	0	9,851	5,295	2,000	2,556
2009/10	2,556	6,930	7	9,493	4,930	2,220	2,343
2010/11	2,343	9,663	19	12,025	6,642	2,400	2,983
2011/12	2,983	10,235	0	13,218	7,898	2,510	2,810
2012/13	2,810	10,000	0	12,810	7,000	2,570	3,240
2013/14	3,240	10,900	0	14,140	8,700	2,650	2,790
Indonesia							
2008/09	590	2,053	2,197	4,840	0	4,500	340
2009/10	340	1,910	3,200	5,450	0	4,700	750
2010/11	750	1,770	3,082	5,602	0	5,000	602
2011/12	602	1,830	3,027	5,459	0	5,050	409
2012/13	409	1,970	3,570	5,949	0	5,135	814
2013/14	814	2,080	3,700	6,594	0	5,200	1,394
Philippines							
2008/09	547	2,150	23	2,720	239	1,900	581
2009/10	581	1,800	250	2,631	101	1,800	730
2010/11	730	2,520	41	3,291	507	1,850	934
2011/12	934	2,400	30	3,364	282	2,150	932
2012/13	932	2,450	35	3,417	330	2,200	887
2013/14	887	2,500	40	3,427	350	2,250	827

(Contd.)

Table 1.42: World sugar production, supply, and distribution including beet sugar

Country mktg year	*Beginning stocks*	*Total sugar production*	*Total imports*	*Total supply*	*Total exports*	*Total use*	*Ending stocks*
Other SUG - Southeast Asia							
2008/09	625	1,165	2,453	4,243	370	3,332	541
2009/10	541	1,150	2,819	4,510	368	3,578	564
2010/11	564	1,243	3,056	4,863	447	3,862	554
2011/12	554	1,273	3,036	4,863	461	3,755	647
2012/13	647	1,225	3,199	5,071	490	3,953	628
2013/14	628	1,225	3,149	5,002	488	3,886	628
Total SUG - Southeast Asia							
2008/09	4,413	12,568	4,673	21,654	5,904	11,732	4,018
2009/10	4,018	11,790	6,276	22,084	5,399	12,298	4,387
2010/11	4,387	15,196	6,198	25,781	7,596	13,112	5,073
2011/12	5,073	15,738	6,093	26,904	8,641	13,465	4,798
2012/13	4,798	15,645	6,804	27,247	7,820	13,858	5,569
2013/14	5,569	16,705	6,889	29,163	9,538	13,986	5,639
Total SUG - Oceania							
Australia							
2008/09	400	4,814	41	5,255	3,522	1,246	487
2009/10	487	4,700	78	5,265	3,600	1,252	413
2010/11	413	3,700	163	4,276	2,750	1,333	193
2011/12	193	3,683	144	4,020	2,800	1,156	64
2012/13	64	4,250	87	4,401	3,100	1,218	83
2013/14	83	4,300	90	4,473	3,190	1,218	65
Other SUG - Oceania							
2008/09	157	300	284	741	261	340	140
2009/10	140	213	261	614	184	319	111
2010/11	111	195	298	604	155	343	106
2011/12	106	235	249	590	187	302	101
2012/13	101	220	293	614	180	333	101
2013/14	101	220	313	634	180	353	101
Total SUG - Oceania							
2008/09	557	5,114	325	5,996	3,783	1,586	627
2009/10	627	4,913	339	5,879	3,784	1,571	524
2010/11	524	3,895	461	4,880	2,905	1,676	299
2011/12	299	3,918	393	4,610	2,987	1,458	165
2012/13	165	4,470	380	5,015	3,280	1,551	184
2013/14	184	4,520	403	5,107	3,370	1,571	166

Table 1.42: World sugar production, supply, and distribution including beet sugar *(Contd.)*

Country mktg year	*Beginning stocks*	*Total sugar production*	*Total imports*	*Total supply*	*Total exports*	*Total use*	*Ending stocks*
World							
2008/09	43,080	144,014	42,673	229,767	45,401	154,063	30,303
2009/10	30,303	153,403	48,569	232,275	48,656	154,860	28,759
2010/11	28,759	161,923	49,357	240,039	54,701	155,508	29,830
2011/12	29,830	171,931	48,791	250,552	55,702	158,863	35,987
2012/13	35,987	176,033	52,328	264,348	56,561	164,625	43,162
2013/14	43,162	174,826	52,545	270,533	58,678	168,476	43,379
Unrecorded							
2008/09	"	"	"	2,728	"	"	"
2009/10	"	"	"	87	"	"	"
2010/11	"	"	"	5,344	"	"	"
2011/12	"	"	"	6,911	"	"	"
2012/13	"	"	"	4,233	"	"	"
2013/14	"	"	"	6,133	"	"	"

Source: USDA, FAS, PSD online.

Table 1.43: Area and production of sugarcane

Area-'000 hectares; Production-'000 tons

	1995	*1996*	*1997*	*1998*	*1999*	*2000*	*1995*	*1996*	*1997*	*1998*	*1999*	*2000*
World	18555	19551	19367	19427	19542		1172160	1226666	1241394	1259659	1275885	
Africa	1391	1307	1347	1375	1386		73526	78180	82110	84728	83461	
Cameron	135F	135F	135F	135F	135F		1350F	1350F	1350F	1350F	1350F	
Egypt	125	126	126F	122	129F		14105	13958	13726	14353	15254	
South Africa	395	300*	311*	316*	316*		16714	20951	22155	22930	21223	
N.C. America	2701	2951	2929	2836	2800		148047	157882	165351	162339	158618	
Cuba	1050F	1245	1200F	1049	996		36000F	41300	43000F	32800	34000	
Mexico	553	569	620	631	718		42562	43352	44833	48895	45880	
USA	377	360	370	383	402		27938	26727	28751	31486	32023	
South America	5757	6055	5990	6178	6122		383112	406214	417458	429560	423805	
Brazil	4559	4827	4880	4986	4951		303699	325929	337195	345255	337165	
Asia (FMR)	8239	8779	8627	8556	8766		525426	544639	534010	540885	568701	
China	1186	1244	1103	1187	1042		70279	71260	82566	87204	78108	
India	3820	4150	4170	3940	4100		271230	282900	277250	262090	295700	
Pakistan	1009	963	965	1056	1155		47168	45230	41998	53104	55191	
Oceania	465	459	471	480	467		41951	39696	42331	42032	41247	
Australia	383	377	390	415	402		37438	35889	38633	39531	38534	

Table 1.44: Area, production, yield of sugar crops

FAO statistical yearbook 2007-2008		*Area harvested (1000 hectares)*					*Poroduction (1000 tons)*					*Yield (1000 tons)*				
Countries		*1994-1996*	*1999-2001*	*2004*	*2005*	*2006*	*1994-1996*	*1999-2001*	*2004*	*2005*	*2006*	*1994-1996*	*1999-2001*	*2004*	*2005*	*2006*
Australia	10	362	362	448	434	415	34,564	35,327	36,993	37,822	38,169	95.480	97.587	82.640	87.157	91.973
Brazil	21	4,552	4,552	5,632	5,806	6,144	304,302	335,832	415,206	422,957	457,246	66.857	73.784	73.726	72.854	74.418
China	351	1,866	1,866	1,582	1,575	1,373	83,751	84,343	96,879	95,448	110,971	44.877	45.194	61.227	60.598	80.812
Cuba	49	1,224	1,224	661	517	397	39,367	34,167	23,800	11,600	11,060	32.173	27.923	36.006	22.428	27.852
France	68	452	452	385	378	379	30,273	30,294	30,788	31,150	29,879	67.024	67.071	80.062	82.300	78.819
Germany	79	514	514	441	420	358	25,441	26,726	27,159	25,387	20,647	49.503	52.002	61.649	60.431	57.737
India		3,813	3,813	3,938	3,662	4,201	262,111	296,976	233,865	237,091	281,172	68.741	77.885	59.387	64.744	66.930
Indonesia	101	514	514	420	435	425	30,898	24,605	27,160	29,710	25,405	60.125	47.880	64.667	68.299	59.776
Iran, Islamic Republic of	102	211	211	217	216	217	6,684	7,443	10,827	10,433	10,700	31.690	35.287	49.914	48.239	49.309
Mexico	138	598	598	652	670	680	43,374	46,077	48,662	51,646	50,676	72.522	77.042	74.646	77.108	74.530
Pakistan	165	986	986	1,082	969	910	45,828	48,550	54,073	44,790	44,759	46.489	49.251	49.986	46.213	49.164
Russian Federation	185	1,083	1,083	790	759	949	16,395	14,612	21,848	21,420	30,861	15.134	13.489	27.654	28.232	32.536
Thailand	216	902	902	1,111	1,067	965	48,808	51,326	65,013	49,604	47,658	54.086	56.876	58.509	46.479	49.370
Ukraine	230	1,392	1,392	697	623	788	26,959	14,304	16,610	15,478	22,421	19.370	10.277	23.848	24.832	28.467
United States of America	231	937	937	908	876	896	53,820	59,791	53,567	49,047	57,664	57.452	63.826	58.962	55.986	64.391
World	**5001**	**26,479**	**26,479**	**25,971**	**25,544**	**25,972**	**1,424,747**	**1,506,740**	**1,585,896**	**1,569,852**	**1,642,830**	**53.807**	**56.903**	**61.064**	**61.457**	**63.254**

Table 1.45: Sugar production from cane and beet

Countries	*1960-61*	*1961-62*	*1962-63*	*1963-64*	*1964-65*
Europe (Beet)					
Austria	294	208	261	322	333
Belgium	513	453	348	367	574
Czechoslovokia	958	890	1009	1080	1009
Denmark	342	216	209	373	436
France	2727	1704	1628	2010	2401
Germany(East)	880	607	650	772	801
Germany (West)[2]	1956	1439	1488	2062	2141
Hungary	477	378	425	464	404
Italy[3]	996	975	997	917	1136
Netherlands	710	588	457	418	650
Poland	1500	1639	1329	1424	1798
Spain[3]	516	591	483	407	524
Sweden	361	302	221	240	167
UK	982	840	757	816	1025
U.S.S.R (Beet)	5717	6652	6522	6016	10223
North and Central America (Cane and Beet)					
Canada (Beet)	147	128	138	157	158
Mexico	1469	1520	1732	1932	2080
Costa Rico	70	72	91	112	100
Cuba	6767	4815	3821	4398	6051
Dominican Republic[6]	873	902	306	825	644
Haiti[7]	73	58	69	62	65
Puerto Rica	1007	915	897	898	814
United States	2795	2959	3130	3887	4024
Hawaii[6]	991	1016	999	1070	1102
South America					
Argentina[8]	850	694	798	1055	998

Table 1.45: Sugar production from cane and beet *(Contd.)*

Countries	*1960-61*	*1961-62*	*1962-63*	*1963-64*	*1964-65*
Brazil[8]	3454	3615	3304	3333	3827
British Guana	330	331	322	263	313
Peru[6, 7]	798	765	818	766	780
Africa (Cane)					
Mauritius[3, 7]	236	553	533	585	519
South Africa[15]	902	997	1083	1147	1266
Aunited Arab Republic	364	324	359	375	412
Asia (Cane and Beet)					
Burma	47	61	67	54	67
China, Taiwan	948	732	764	795	1025
India[9]	3288	2938	2348	2794	3512
Indonesia[1, 7]	678	642	589	654	650
Pakistan[9, 12]	121	208	291	267	266
Philippines	1317	1468	1555	1684	1556
Turkey (Beet)	700	470	424	514	795
Oceania (Cane)					
Australia[8, 16]	1405	1405	1880	1752	1981
Fiji Islands[8, 16]	149	146	252	304	312
World Total Centrifugal Sugar	**54980**	**51590**	**50560**	**55270**	**66240**

[1] Calender year referring to first part of split year.
[2] Includes sugar from imported beets.
[3] Year beginings July of first part of split year.
[6] Calender year referring to second part of split year.
[7] Tel Quel.
[8] Year beginings June of first part of split year.
[9] Includes sugar (raw value) refined from Gur.
[12] 1952-53.
[15] Year beginning May of first part of split year.
[16] Titrent 94(0) net

Source: FAO Production year book 1963 and 1965.

Table 1.46: Sugar consumption

(Thousand tons)

Countries	*1960*	*1961*	*1962*	*1963*	*1964 (P)*
Argentina	572	732	840	741[a]	847
Australia	349	559	578[a]	581[a]	604[a]
Belgium	349	338	353	355	357[b]
Brazil	2479	2655	2806[a]	2736[a]	2672[a]
Canada	773	807	848	859	907
Cuba	347	376	373	456	401
Denmark	272	258	264	263	260
Domnican Republic	78	79	113	116	110
Gremany (East)			600[d]	620[d]	630[d]
Germany (West)	1783	1802	1837	1929	1920
India	2053	2127	2587	2488	2336
Indonesia	715	591	585[a]	540[a]	550[a, d]
Japan	1414	1554	1602[c]	1687[c]	1310[c, e]
Mexico	1118	1156	1246	1318	1424
Sweden	343	331	346	333	342
South Africa	688		661[a]	707[a]	759[a]
UK	2895	2959	2887[f]	2974[f]	2807[f]
USA	8600	8936	9075[g, h]	9235[g, h]	8951[d, g]

(P) provisional
[a] Tel Quel]
[b] January to November,
[c] Includes Ryukyu Islands
[d] Estimate
[e] January to October,
[f] Includes Northern Islands
[g] Refined values are coverted to raw value at the present official standard rate of 93.46 to 100, except for exports which are converted to raw at the rate of 92 to 100
[h] Sugar deliveries for export in sugar containing manufactured products are included in these figures.

Sources: 1. For the years 1960 & 1961, International Sugar Council Bulletin Vol. 22 No.7.
2. For the years 1962, 1963 and 1964, International Sugar Council Bulletin (June, 1965, issue).
3. Directorate of sugar and vanaspati (figures for India).

Table 1.6.47: World per capita consumption of sugar, 2000 to 2012

(Kilograms - Raw value)

Countries	*2000*	*2001*	*2002*	*2003*	*2004*	*2005*	*2006*	*2007*	*2008*	*2009*	*2010*	*2011*	*2012*
India	16.5	17	17.3	18.1	19.4	19.6	18	18.4	19.6	20.7	19.6	18.6	20.5
USA	32	32.1	32.4	30.3	30.7	31.3	30.9	30.6	32.5	31.5	33	33.1	32.9
Cuba	63	62.5	62.4	60.8	62.3	62.3	65.9	61.4	61.6	59	57.2	57.3	57.8
Brazil	58	56.8	60.2	58	59.3	64.3	66.3	65.7	66	63.9	69.4	69.7	66.6
China	6.7	7	7.8	8.6	9	9	9.1	10.2	11.1	11.2	11.1	11	11.4
Turkey	28.6	28.8	25.6	24.3	26.6	27.1	30.3	28.3	30.4	31.9	32.8	31	33.4
Kenya	21.9	20.2	20.5	21.2	21.7	22.6	21.4	19.9	21.5	21.8	21.3	21.4	21.9
Japan	19	18.4	19.1	18.9	18.8	18.8	17.4	19.2	17.7	18.2	17.5	17.2	17.2
Mexico	46.1	47.7	49.1	51.8	50.3	46.9	47.5	46.7	47.2	47.9	41.6	39.3	40.1
Tunisia	30.8	32	32.7	33.4	33.7	33.1	35.8	36.7	33.6	35	33.8	37.2	38.5
Thailand	29.1	31	31.2	32.6	35.9	36.3	37.7	37.5	34.7	36.8	39.5	41.1	41.2
Australia	54.7	55	56	54.7	51.8	50.7	50	49.4	57.1	51.2	46.5	49.5	49.2
Pakistan	24	23.9	24.1	26.3	28.6	28.2	26.9	28.4	28	28	28.1	27.9	28.1
Indonesia	16	16.8	17.4	17.7	18	18.3	19.3	20.6	22.2	21.9	21.5	22.9	24.3
South Africa	33.3	30.3	32.5	31.5	31.9	32.9	36.3	36.7	37	37.5	38.5	39.8	40.4
Russian Federation	39.2	40.6	46.6	47.3	46.4	46	45.6	45.7	43.5	39.8	40.6	41	39.5
World Average	**21.1**	**21.6**	**22.3**	**22.7**	**23.4**	**23.4**	**23.5**	**23.9**	**24.5**	**24**	**24.1**	**23.7**	**24.6**

Source: ISO.

(Contd.)

Table 1.47A: Major sugar consuming countries in the world

(Percent)

Sr. No.	*Countries*	*Time periods* 1989-92	1992-95	1995-98	1998-01	2001-04	2004-07	2007-10	2010-13
1	India	11.13	12.11	13.06	13.64	14.38	14.02	14.87	15.32
2	EU-27	12.63	12.61	11.82	11.17	10.07	12.47	11.07	11.31
3	China	6.84	6.69	7	6.69	7.76	8.39	9.41	9.15
4	Brazil	6.44	6.71	7.03	7.19	7.2	7.38	7.62	7.28
5	USA	7.29	7.37	7.31	7.18	6.39	6.3	6.32	6.41
6	Russia	5.98	4.69	4.17	4.7	4.75	4.07	3.76	3.51
7	Indonesia	2.2	2.35	2.53	2.43	2.47	2.7	2.97	3.19
8	Mexico	3.78	3.73	3.61	3.49	3.76	3.63	3.2	2.7
9	Pakistan	2.17	2.45	2.71	2.68	2.56	2.66	2.71	2.72
10	Egypt	1.35	1.4	1.51	1.55	1.65	1.73	1.76	1.78
11	Thailand	1.05	1.2	1.37	1.36	1.4	1.42	1.36	1.59
12	Other	39.16	38.69	37.88	37.91	37.61	35.24	34.95	33.05
Total consumption (million MT)		**110.16 (100)**	**114.32 (100)**	**120.51 (100)**	**127.32 (100)**	**137.11 (100)**	**144.65 (100)**	**152.49 (100)**	**158.86 (100)**

Source: USDA, Foreign Agricultural Service.

Table 1.48: Export of sugar by selected countries

(*th MT*)

Countries	*1981*	*1986*	*1987*	*1988*	*1989*	*1990*	*1991*	*1992*	*1993*	*1994*	*1995*	*1996*	*1997*	*1998*	*1999*
Cuba	7,071	6,702	6,482	6,978	7,123	7,172	6,767	6,085	3,662	3,188	2,603	3,830	1,731	663	719
Dominican Rep.	864	480	587	528	521	369	336	301	305	306	141	353	390	216	
Brazil	2,670	2,554	2,424	1,610	965	1,576	1,614	2,273	3,008	3,602	6,299	5,309	6,586	8,675	12,467
Thailand	1,154	2,049	2,071	1,961	3,105	2,496	2,863	3,719	2,401	2,720	3,887	4,628	4,317	2,444	3,430
Mauritius	458	662	695	692	673	612	584	634	575	551	533	616	569	597	527
India	64	38					296	493	324	17	174	906	248	40	20
South Africa	736	874	1,105	909	924	833	897	255		264	346	972	984	1,087	996
Australia	2,982	2,710	2,826	2,980	3,149	3,069	2,456	2,894	3,441	4,504	4,592	4,286	4,461	4,688	4,185
Total World	**24,832**	**27,239**	**28,368**	**27,419**	**27,924**	**28,353**	**22,793**	**25,705**	**24,429**	**24,473**	**28,418**	**29,127**	**30,655**	**31,910**	**32,171**

(*Contd.*)

Table 1.48: Export of sugar by selected countries

(th MT)

Countries	*2000*	*2001*	*2002*	*2003*	*2004*	*2005*	*2006*	*2007*	*2008*	*2009*	*2008--09*	*2009-10*	*2010-11*	*2011-12*	*2012-13*
Cuba	414	343	528	307	429	NI	NI	NI	106	166	784	615	770	915	–
Dominican Rep.	203	130	116	185	165	154	152	146	143	191	–	–	–	–	–
Brazil	6,502	11,168	13,383	13,386	16,295	18,399	19,531	20,530	20,143	24,988	22,380	27,507	26,000	22,575	24,030
Thailand	4,339	3,364	4,204	5,485	4,893	3,300	2,290	4,740	5,108	5,374	5,092	5,375	6,322	7,260	7,415
Mauritius	408	614									473	485	450	400	410
India	94	57	309	324	NI	NI	1,177	2,691	4,209	NI	183	350	3,238	4,050	2,000
South Africa	1291	1040	762	804	672	859	754	623	244	498	907	820	340	300	350
Australia	3,770	3,550	3,888	4,077	4,303	4,232	4,150	3,906	3,289	3,252	3,363	3,710	2,610	2,980	3,475
Total World	**27,931**	**32,143**	**33,315**	**35,516**	**35,562**	**38,857**	**39,480**	**37,399**	**38,070**	**40,232**	**48,498**	**55,555**	**55,151**	**53,283**	**53,477**

NI : Net importer.

Table 1.48A: Compound growth rates in major sugar consuming countries in world

(Quantities)

Sr. No.	*Countries*	*CGR (%)*	*Estimated 't' value*
1	India	3.20***	26.74
2	EU-27	1.35***	5.66
3	China	3.79***	16.7
4	Brazil	2.47***	22.84
5	USA	0.92***	10.36
6	Russia	0.18	0.57
7	Indonesia	3.51***	22.83
8	Mexico	0.58**	2.2
9	Pakistan	2.54***	16.77
10	Egypt	3.32***	26.56
11	Thailand	3.16***	17.02
12	Other Countries	1.21***	17.59
World		**1.85*** **	**45.69**

** Significant at 5% level of significance.
*** Significant at 1% level of significance.

Table 1.49: Country-wise sugar exports in the world

(Percent)

Sr. No.	*Countries*	*Time periods*							
		1989-1992	*1992-1995*	*1995-1998*	*1998-2001*	*2001-2004*	*2004-2007*	*2007-2010*	*2010-2013*
1	Australia	8.04	12.8	12.04	9.57	8.72	8.48	7.43	5.15
2	Brazil	4.38	10.7	16.95	23.59	30.01	37.94	44.89	46.53
3	Colombia	1.12	1.91	2.29	2.45	2.64	2.14	1.45	1.5
4	Cuba	19.83	10.56	8.88	8.03	5	1.56	1.53	1.33
5	EU27	20.15	19.65	14.62	15.36	11.24	11.4	3.87	2.96
6	Guatemala	1.92	2.7	3.03	2.9	2.92	2.9	3.3	2.86
7	India	0.86	0.51	1.25	1.19	2.05	2.87	4.4	4.89
8	Mexico	0.65	0.27	2.42	0.85	0.34	0.78	1.93	2.54
9	UAE	0	0.42	1.51	2.13	2.75	3.26	2.17	1.68
10	Thailand	8.95	9.89	10.43	9.26	10.51	6.82	10.4	13.43
11	Others	34.1	30.59	26.58	24.67	23.81	21.85	18.58	17.13
Total export (million MT)		**33.55 (100)**	**29.85 (100)**	**36.97 (100)**	**39.22 (100)**	**45.36 (100)**	**49.17 (100)**	**48.52 (100)**	**55.95 (100)**

Source: USDA, Foreign Agricultural Service.

Table 1.50: Compound growth rate of major sugar exporting countries

(Quantities)

Sr. No.	*Countries*	*CGR (%)*	*Estimated 't' value*
1	Australia	0.22	0.04
2	Brazil	14.17***	16.24
3	Colombia	3.08***	3.18
4	Cuba	–10.30***	–11.77
5	EU27	–2.57	–0.98
6	Guatemala	4.46***	11.55
7	India	13.96**	2.64
8	Mexico	12.20**	2.32
9	UAE	4.17**	2.41
10	Thailand	3.70***	4.96
11	Others	–0.35	–1.157
Total Export		2.81***	13.17

** Significant at 5 %level of significance
*** Significant at 1 % level of significance.

Table 1.51: Major sugar importing countries in the world

(Percent)

Sr. No.	*Countries*	*Time periods*							
		1989-1992	*1992-1995*	*1995-1998*	*1998-2001*	*2001-2004*	*2004-2007*	*2007-2010*	*2010-2013*
1	EU-27	10.92	7	5.32	4.8	4.95	6.47	6.38	7.42
2	Indonesia	0.99	0.8	2.86	4.58	3.83	3.75	5.74	6.55
3	China	3.72	6.63	3.13	2	2.81	3.02	2.63	6.34
4	USA	7.66	5.56	6.85	4	3.71	5.14	6.01	6.31
5	UAE	0.33	0.93	1.95	2.4	3.23	3.89	4	4.54
6	Algeria	3.06	2.9	2.72	2.38	2.69	2.52	2.59	3.2
7	Malaysia	2.9	3.15	3.27	3.29	3.49	3.38	3.27	3.64
8	Iran	2.55	2.9	3.19	2.66	2.22	2.91	2.8	2.76
9	Bangladesh	0.16	0.25	1.73	2.11	1.9	2.25	3.07	3.22
10	Nigeria	1.56	1.56	1.72	1.96	2.38	2.67	3.04	2.94
11	India	0.06	2.38	1	1.32	0.5	1.63	2.78	1.28
12	Others	66.1	65.94	66.24	68.52	68.23	62.38	57.7	51.8
Total import (million MT)		**30.64 (100)**	**30.57 (100)**	**34.13 (100)**	**38.17 (100)**	**40.88 (100)**	**44.84 (100)**	**45.41 (100)**	**49.26 (100)**
CGR% total world import				**2.49*** **					

*** Significant at 1 % level of significance.
Source: USDA, Foreign Agricultural Service.

Table 1.52: International sugar prices in nominal and real terms

Sr. No.	Years	*World sugar prices in nominal (USD/t)* Raw sugar	White sugar	*World sugar prices in real (USD/t)* Raw sugar	White sugar
1	1990	204.04	302.31	282.6	418.71
2	1991	203.3	279.23	271.94	373.51
3	1992	211.13	273.85	275.87	357.82
4	1993	247.96	322.21	317	411.9
5	1994	305.54	396.15	382.54	495.99
6	1995	273.46	383.77	335.39	470.68
7	1996	257.32	319.27	309.69	384.25
8	1997	238.03	272.47	281.5	322.24
9	1998	155.32	216.29	181.63	252.94
10	1999	165.95	200.53	191.26	231.11
11	2000	216.09	250.32	243.76	282.37
12	2001	167.09	233.51	184.33	257.59
13	2002	176.52	221.67	191.62	240.64
14	2003	172.99	225.99	183.83	240.16
15	2004	230.62	274.99	238.32	284.17
16	2005	347.96	404.47	347.96	404.47
17	2006	257.19	328.64	249.07	318.27
18	2007	301.46	342.73	283.6	322.43
19	2008	351.45	415.98	323.56	382.97
20	2009	531.77	584.22	485.13	532.98
21	2010	595.25	650.36	537.59	587.37
22	2011	509.46	614.24	454.68	548.19
23	2012	365.42	464.14	323.1	410.38
24	2013	383.22	472.39	333.6	411.23

Source: FAO database.

Table 1.53: Wholesale and retail sugar prices
[Prices of white refined sugar in selected countries
representative prices for years 2006 to 2012 (US cents per pound)]

	2006		*2007*		*2009*		*2010*		*2011*		*2012*	
Countries	*Wholesale*	*Retail*	*Wholesale*	*Retail*	*Wholesale*	*Retail*	*Wholesale*	*Retail*	*Wholesale*	*Retail*	*Wholesale*	*Retail*
India	21.48	23.37	–	–	28.62	30.56	–	–	26.74	29.24	–	–
USA	33.1	49.58	25.06	51.48	38.1	56.36	–	–	56.22	68.3	43.38	69.41
Brazil	–	–	13.25	30.45	24.85	40.54	–	–	35.79	60.87	37.15	51.35
Turkey	46.37	63.52	52.7	65.91	50.97	64.44	53.57	66.59	50.29	62.53	49.71	63.41
Kenya	36.18	40.6	42.01	48.4	46.03	52.51	-	-	62.61	69.05	55.32	65.39
Japan	59.5	77.3	59.16	76.34	–	–	–	–	–	–	–	–
Tunisia	20.7	22.5	–	–	–	–	28.84	30.74	29.32	31.25	–	–
Mexico	27.84	47.29	27.33	52.08	28.25	51.27	–	–	–	–	26.66	70.03
Jamaica	45.39	49.13	33.9	44.4	48.79	74.99	45.45	53.83	–	–	63	91
Thailand	17.96	20.98	19.73	23.05	27.66	29.73	29.2	31.38	–	–	29.8	32.03
Pakistan	23.13	24.04	–	–	–	–	36.43	37.8	–	–	–	–
South Africa	22.98	33.6	–	–	–	46.55	–	47.52	–	47.81	–	50.74
Russian Federation	25.86	43.55	–	–	27.22	43.55	35.58	53.98	38.1	58.51	30.84	47.17

Table 1.54: Sugar production, sugar recovery and sugar yield in major countries

SP = Sugar production ('000 MT); RC = Sugar recovery (%); SY = Sugar yield (MT/ha)

Country	*Parameter*	*1990-91*	*1991-92*	*1992-93*	*1993-94*	*1994-95*	*1995-96*	*1996-97*	*1997-98*	*1998-99*	*1999-2000*	*2000-01*	*2001-02*	*2002-03*
Australia	S.P	3606	3192	4367	4412	5196	5049	5491	5650	5084	5513	4417	4768	5614
	RC	14.3	15	14.9	13.8	14.9	13.5	13.8	13.8					n.a
	SY	10.64	9.36	12.88	12.98	14.24	13.18	13.66	13.71					n.a
Brazil	S.P	7900	9200	9800	9930	12500	13700	14650	14800	19168	20645	16464	20336	23567
	RC	10.5	10.6	10.9	10.9	11.4	14.7	14.5	14.1					n.a
	SY	6.75	6.72	6.53	6.62	7.14	8.78	9.54	9.43					n.a
China	S.P	5243	6677	6650	5380	4900	5283	5685	5760	7444	7160	6904	6411	8720
	RC	9.1	9.8	9.1	8.5	8.1	8.1	8.3	8.3					n.a
	S.Y	5.2	5.74	5.34	4.94	4.73	5.15	5.44	5.43					n.a
Cuba	S.P	7620	7030	4280	4000	3300	4450	4400	4500	3291	3874	4057	3748	3522
	RC	11.3	11.3	9.1	8.7	8.5	9.8	9.8	9.9					n.a
	S.Y	5.64	5.21	3.72	3.48	2.54	3.42	3.38	3.46					n.a
India	S.P	13707	15249	12456	11660	16410	18225	14686	13650	14280	17406	20247	19906	19524
	RC	10.1	10.2	10	10	10.3	9.9	9.9	10					n.a
	S.Y	6.62	6.75	6.26	6.7	7.33	7.14	6.93	6.83					n.a
Indonesia	S.P	2120	2250	2300	2480	2450	2090	2095	2150	1493	1490	1685	1850	2150
	RC	7.6	8	7.2	7.5	8	7	7.3	7.4					n.a
	S.Y	5.81	5.84	5.69	5.98	6.05	5.23	5.17	5.44					n.a
USA	S.P	2767	3078	3068	3189	3073	3102	2880	2880	3233	3753	3658	3664	n.a
	RC	11.5	11.7	11.7	12	12.1	12	11.7	11.9					n.a
	S.Y	9.41	8.95	8.69	8.83	8.77	8.86	8.65	8.37					n.a
World Total	S.P	72401	78606	73019	70620	81092	86352	84837	85958	89643	97727	94680	97638	103007
	RC	10.2	10.4	10.1	10	10.4	10.5	10.6	10.6					n.a
	S.Y	6.2	6.32	5.97	5.94	6.3	6.65	6.74	6.76					n.a

Source: Indian Sugar, December 2003 Vol. 53, No.9.

Annexures

Annexure 1: Statewise value of output sugarcane

(Rs. lakhs)

	State/U.Ts	(At current prices) 2004-05	2005-06	2006-07	2007-08	2008-09	2009-10	2010-11	(At 2004-05 prices) 2004-05	2005-06	2006-07	2007-08	2008-09	2009-10	2010-11
1	Andhra Pradesh	97394	124026	166786	127518	62117	125297	211244	97394	121086	168085	129374	61708	56353	98918
2	Arunachal Pradesh	29	252	45	348	375	434	493	29	235	42	305	328	380	380
3	Assam	1286	1081	1228	1656	1799	1710	2230	1286	1163	1357	1320	1434	1363	1467
4	Bihar	25794	32745	36608	33205	44554	81086	112524	25794	25915	26828	25975	31242	33627	45616
5	Goa	485	447	464	476	483	576	663	485	447	464	448	394	419	393
6	Gujarat	145287	209993	171586	139564	187320	311110	252771	145287	192885	220927	193521	160356	169493	175302
7	Haryana	51551	59570	95126	86354	48430	72515	102014	51551	54257	83737	76002	33301	34351	53798
8	Himachal Pradesh	1227	1150	1396	1309	1242	1173	903	1227	1100	1270	1143	991	889	720
9	Jammu & Kashmir	62	76	76	24	4	4	4	62	76	76	24	4	4	4
10	Karnataka	121401	226538	225069	250426	261104	519329	775681	121401	207283	240575	273781	256008	273127	407948
11	Kerala	74	54	52	132	224	296	371	74	47	45	116	131	116	108
12	Madhya Pradesh	13465	17036	22518	26101	17429	24030	35385	13465	15964	20905	23691	15819	13788	18181
13	Maharashtra	204584	451675	668606	853763	559659	962385	1318521	204584	368458	629171	801183	428075	609061	777436
14	Manipur	31	13	107	108	130	46	1757	31	7	52	52	62	22	572
15	Meghalaya	9	9	15	23	25	17	17	9	9	9	14	14	9	9
16	Mizoram	112	168	161	41	202	172	179	112	131	125	25	125	131	125
17	Nagaland	143	180	259	240	774	995	774	143	169	230	192	206	245	206

Annexure 1: Statewise value of output sugarcane *(Contd.)*

(Rs. lakhs)

		(At current prices)							*(At 2004-05 prices)*						
	State/U.Ts	*2004-05*	*2005-06*	*2006-07*	*2007-08*	*2008-09*	*2009-10*	*2010-11*	*2004-05*	*2005-06*	*2006-07*	*2007-08*	*2008-09*	*2009-10*	*2010-11*
18	Orissa	5258	5922	6365	6534	3556	3590	7585	5258	5098	7080	7436	3706	2837	5732
19	Punjab	35350	45764	72010	81383	47796	42014	71933	35350	39794	54553	61654	28967	23341	36889
20	Rajasthan	1114	1821	2094	2076	1554	1965	2248	1114	1798	2067	2050	1200	1191	1206
21	Tamil Nadu	105851	271566	314254	270106	223793	273555	423403	105851	209099	243994	208475	153353	133583	181764
22	Tripura	491	435	471	545	552	710	550	491	417	426	474	471	410	470
23	Uttar Pradesh	870700	1045218	1297588	1169934	969731	1626092	1767577	870700	975537	1319788	1192289	784357	920819	1000938
24	West Bengal	1297	1264	1887	1887	1769	1684	2807	1297	1166	1602	1358	961	790	1265
25	A & N Islands	14	21	7	14	61	40	61	14	21	7	14	30	20	30
26	Puducherry	995	3412	4413	2627	1866	2843	3193	995	2571	3300	1964	1396	2126	2388
27	Jharkhand	143	123	160	232	419	858	895	143	146	146	212	367	445	454
28	Chattisgarh	270	285	305	492	280	629	328	270	329	352	476	385	612	320
29	Uttarakhand	53433	65098	88612	65513	50104	83008	64029	53433	58728	72440	53556	35986	44598	45987
	Total	**1737851**	**2565941**	**3178269**	**3122630**	**2487351**	**4138162**	**5160140**	**1737851**	**2283941**	**3099656**	**3057124**	**2001377**	**2324149**	**2858627**

Annexure 2: Statewise value of output gur

(Rs. lakhs)

	State/U.Ts	(At current prices)							(At 2004-05 prices)						
		2004-05	2005-06	2006-07	2007-08	2008-09	2009-10	2010-11	2004-05	2005-06	2006-07	2007-08	2008-09	2009-10	2010-11
1	Andhra Pradesh	64760	59012	34823	72176	154349	109849	95917	64760	55700	40752	78099	111266	71078	52237
2	Arunachal Pradesh	166	0	191	0	0	0	0	166	0	191	0	0	0	0
3	Assam	14737	13684	14508	13138	21316	27987	28398	14737	13043	15945	14639	16566	16068	16002
4	Bihar	6581	13184	26153	11141	166999	189031	230721	6581	11650	23464	9200	93027	86445	86616
5	Gujarat	114494	114453	59645	0	69111	0	0	114494	94951	39016	0	38809	0	0
6	Haryana	39144	45254	25463	21995	34376	67545	32679	39144	37430	23789	22557	24105	28471	13584
7	Himachal Pradesh	793	243	817	827	865	1216	1186	793	232	741	751	688	592	495
8	Jammu & Kashmir	0	3	3	0	0	0	0	0	3	3	0	0	0	0
9	Karnataka	38503	0	12530	0	0	158012	24960	38503	0	12988	0	0	97841	15318
10	Kerala	1787	115	104	320	5092	7949	7837	1787	115	84	192	3018	3147	3005
11	Madhya Pradesh	4401	4299	0	0	13512	0	0	4401	3646	0	0	11003	0	0
12	Maharashtra	24208	0	0	41391	402403	0	0	24208	0	0	41391	159370	0	0
13	Manipur	160	37	216	316	387	139	5662	160	37	268	273	314	113	4593
14	Mizoram	27	7	164	0	194	185	98	27	7	137	0	162	137	65
15	Nagaland	3224	3342	3327	3476	4547	3619	4524	3224	3342	3327	3476	2885	2296	2870
16	Orissa	5951	8930	9350	5938	5925	5427	10165	5951	8411	8427	4795	4098	3065	4878
17	Punjab	23054	14019	7964	14692	50539	54636	19244	23054	12416	7962	7398	25004	19259	6784

Annexure 2: Statewise value of output gur *(Comtd.)*

(Rs. lakhs)

		(At current prices)							*(At 2004-05 prices)*						
	State/U.Ts	*2004-05*	*2005-06*	*2006-07*	*2007-08*	*2008-09*	*2009-10*	*2010-11*	*2004-05*	*2005-06*	*2006-07*	*2007-08*	*2008-09*	*2009-10*	*2010-11*
18	Rajasthan	2258	4333	4759	4955	5081	6000	6538	2258	4131	5761	5299	3650	3072	3387
19	Tamil Nadu	127633	106274	140964	138779	240730	304087	275698	127633	106612	170655	140055	155875	148874	133783
20	Tripura	698	628	645	739	874	919	837	698	601	586	644	671	580	643
21	Uttar Pradesh	589361	482261	193052	267269	760366	951532	807377	589361	453379	176132	243844	549014	491973	417440
22	West Bengal	13208	21289	18605	18419	30835	29978	32442	13208	16500	16176	16588	22450	13434	14715
23	A & N Islands	95	84	42	46	0	0	0	95	84	42	46	0	0	0
24	Jharkhand	1403	1769	1769	1789	6233	12469	12951	1403	1404	1404	1420	3439	4435	4539
25	Uttarakhand	16264	6732	5344	5457	38042	43143	52570	16264	6295	5453	6146	27427	22296	25678
	Total	**1092909**	**899950**	**560437**	**622861**	**2011776**	**1973722**	**1649801**	**1092909**	**829987**	**553304**	**596814**	**1252841**	**1013177**	**806632**

Annexure 3: Statewise value of output other sugar

(Rs. lakhs)

	State/U.Ts	(At current prices)							(At 2004-05 prices)						
		2004-05	2005-06	2006-07	2007-08	2008-09	2009-10	2010-11	2004-05	2005-06	2006-07	2007-08	2008-09	2009-10	2010-11
1	Andhra Pradesh	485	426	0	0	0	0	0	485	414	0	0	0	0	0
2	Karnataka	265	272	556	293	334	421	385	265	237	563	321	321	188	185
3	Kerala	8	8	10	10	10	15	0	8	8	8	8	8	8	8
4	Rajasthan	0	0	0	0	0	1	1	0	0	0	0	0	1	1
5	Tamil Nadu	12690	13221	13528	12663	14956	21795	23906	12690	12333	12217	11522	10448	11626	11354
6	Puducherry	60	0	0	0	0	0	0	60	0	0	0	0	0	0
	Total	**13508**	**13927**	**14093**	**12966**	**15300**	**22233**	**24293**	**13508**	**12993**	**12788**	**11851**	**10777**	**11822**	**11548**

Annexure 4: Statewise value of output total sugar

(Rs. lakhs)

		(At current prices)							*(At 2004-05 prices)*						
	State/UTs	*2004-05*	*2005-06*	*2006-07*	*2007-08*	*2008-09*	*2009-10*	*2010-11*	*2004-05*	*2005-06*	*2006-07*	*2007-08*	*2008-09*	*2009-10*	*2010-11*
1	Andhra Pradesh	162639	183464	201609	199694	216465	235146	307161	162639	177200	208837	207473	172974	127432	151156
2	Arunachal Pradesh	195	252	236	348	375	434	493	195	235	233	305	328	380	380
3	Assam	16023	14764	15736	14794	23114	29696	30628	16023	14206	17302	15959	18000	17431	17469
4	Bihar	32374	45929	62761	44346	211553	270117	343244	32374	37565	50292	35175	124268	120072	132232
5	Goa	485	447	464	476	483	576	663	485	447	464	448	394	419	393
6	Gujarat	259781	324447	231231	139564	256431	311110	252771	259781	287836	259943	193521	199164	169493	175302
7	Haryana	90695	104824	120589	108349	82806	140059	134692	90695	91687	107526	98559	57406	62822	67382
8	Himachal Pradesh	2020	1393	2213	2136	2108	2389	2088	2020	1332	2011	1894	1679	1481	1215
9	Jammu & Kashmir	62	79	79	24	4	4	4	62	79	79	24	4	4	4
10	Karnataka	160169	226810	238155	250719	261438	677762	801027	160169	207521	254127	274103	256330	371155	423451
11	Kerala	1870	177	166	462	5326	8261	8208	1870	170	138	316	3157	3272	3122
12	Madhya Pradesh	17866	21335	22518	26101	30941	24030	35385	17866	19610	20905	23691	26822	13788	18181
13	Maharashtra	228792	451675	668606	895153	962061	962385	1318521	228792	368458	629171	842574	587445	609061	777436
14	Manipur	191	51	323	424	517	185	7419	191	45	320	325	376	135	5166
15	Meghalaya	9	9	15	23	25	17	17	9	9	9	14	14	9	9
16	Mizoram	139	175	325	41	396	357	277	139	137	262	25	287	267	190
17	Nagaland	3367	3522	3587	3716	5321	4613	5298	3367	3511	3558	3668	3092	2541	3077

(Contd.)

Annexure 4: Statewise value of output total sugar

(Rs. lakhs)

	State/UTs	(At current prices)							(At 2004-05 prices)						
		2004-05	2005-06	2006-07	2007-08	2008-09	2009-10	2010-11	2004-05	2005-06	2006-07	2007-08	2008-09	2009-10	2010-11
18	Orissa	11210	14851	15715	12472	9481	9017	17749	11210	13508	15508	12231	7803	5902	10610
19	Punjab	58404	59783	79974	96074	98335	96650	91177	58404	52211	62516	69052	53971	42600	43672
20	Rajasthan	3371	6154	6853	7032	6635	7967	8787	3371	5930	7828	7349	4851	4264	4594
21	Tamil Nadu	246174	391060	468746	421547	479479	599438	723008	246174	328044	426866	360052	319676	294083	326901
22	Tripura	1188	1063	1117	1284	1426	1629	1388	1188	1018	1012	1118	1143	990	1113
23	Uttar Pradesh	1460060	1527479	1490640	1437202	1730097	2577624	2574954	1460060	1428916	1495920	1436133	1333371	1412791	1418378
24	West Bengal	14504	22553	20491	20306	32605	31662	35249	14504	17666	17778	17946	23411	14224	15980
25	A & N Islands	109	105	49	60	61	40	61	109	105	49	60	30	20	30
26	Puducherry	1055	3412	4413	2627	1866	2843	3193	1055	2571	3300	1964	1396	2126	2388
27	Jharkhand	1546	1891	1928	2021	6652	13327	13846	1546	1550	1550	1633	3806	4880	4992
28	Chattisgarh	270	285	305	492	280	629	328	270	329	352	476	385	612	320
29	Uttarakhand	69697	71830	93957	70969	88146	126150	116599	69697	65024	77892	59702	63412	66894	71665
	Total	**2844267**	**3479818**	**3752800**	**3758457**	**4514427**	**6134117**	**6834234**	**2844267**	**3126922**	**3665748**	**3665789**	**3264995**	**3349148**	**3676807**

Annexure 5: Bitter-sweet: Brazilian sugar threat to Indian millers

The apex body of Indian sugar industry red flagged "challenging situation" for the sector due to falling prices of the sweetener, excess production and tightening of lending by banks that is forcing millers to sell at cheaper rates for generating cash-flow. The industry also expressed its fear of Brazil producing more sugar than ethanol because of falling crude price which may make the situation worse for them.

Raising the fear from Brazil, which could have serious implications on the international price of the sweetener, Indian Sugar Mills Association (ISMA) president A Vellayan said, "On the international front, due to the steep fall in oil prices, there is clear possibility that what might happen in Brazil is the shift from ethanol to sugar production. With the Brazilian currency falling, the price of Brazilian sugar will be so cheap that it will threaten to come into India and despite the import duty, it will be cheaper than Indian sugar".

He said government must take all possible steps to ensure that no quantity of sugar gets imported. "That's why we are demanding 40% increase in import duty and extending the subsidy for export of raw sugar so that we can export our raw sugar before the prices fall further", Vellyan said. Brazil is the biggest producer of sugar and ethanol as well.

Addressing the annual general body meeting of ISMA on Thursday, Food Secretary Sudhir Kumar said the issue of extending subsidy for exports of raw sugar in the current 2014-15 marketing year food secretary is under consideration. "There are different points of view. There are WTO implications...Whatever decision has to be taken will be taken soon. We are moving in that direction".

In February this year, the Center had announced subsidy for exports of raw sugar up to 40 lakh tons during 2013-14 and also 2014-15 marketing years (October–September) to help the cash-starved industry to clear cane arrears to farmers. However, the scheme has not been extended after September this year.

"Now, the picture is clear. Our assessment is that the opening stock (as on October 1) was 72 lakh tons and going by production and consumption estimates, this year's closing stock could be around 74 lakh tons", he said, adding that there was scope for export of some quantity of sugar.

Citing how the sugar mills in UP in particular are facing huge problem, ISMA Vice-President Tarun Sawhney said about 50% of mills in the state have not got the loans from banks for working capital requirement. The body demanded that the government should create buffer stock of two million tons, hike in sugar prices sold through ration shops and creating infrastructure for 10% blending of ethanol in petrol.

Annexure 6: More than 15,000 tons beet slicing daily capacity

	2001/02	2002/03	2003/04	2004/05	2005/06	2006/07	2007/08	2008/09	2009/10	2010/11	2011/12
Austria	–	–	–	–	–	–	–	–	–	–	–
Belgium	1	1	1	1	1	1	1	1	1	1	1
Denmark	–	–	–	–	–						
Finland	–	–	–	–							
France	11	9	13	10	9	8	12	8	6	12	12
Germany	5	5	5								
Greece	–	–	–	–	–	–	–	–	–	–	–
Ireland	–	–	–	–	–	–	–	–	–	–	–
Italy	–	–	–	–	–	–	–	–	–	–	–
The Netherlands	2	2	2	2	2	2	2	2	2	2	2
Portugal	–	–	–	–	–	–	–	–	–	–	–
Spain	–	–	–	–	–	–	–	–	–	–	–
Sweden	1	1	1	1	1	1	1	1	1	1	1
United Kingdom	1	1	1	1	1	1	1	1	1	1	1
EU-15 Countries	21	19	23	20	20	19	23	17	14	22	22
Czech Republic	–	–	–	–	–	–	–	–	–	–	–
Hungary	–	–	–	–	–	–	–	–	–	–	–
Latvia	–	–	–	–	–	–	–	–	–	–	–
Lithuania	–	–	–	–	–	–	–	–	–	–	–
Poland	–	–	–	–	–	–	–	–	–	–	–

Annexure 6: More than 15,000 tons beet slicing daily capacity *(Contd.)*

	2001/02	2002/03	2003/04	2004/05	2005/06	2006/07	2007/08	2008/09	2009/10	2010/11	2011/12
Slovakia	–	–	–	–	–	–	–	–	–	–	–
Slovenia	–	–	–	–	–	–	–	–	–	–	–
EU-25 countries	21	19	23	20	20	19	23	18	14	22	22
Bulgaria	–	–	–	–	–	–	–	–	–	–	–
Romania	–	–	–	–	–	–	–	–	–	–	–
EU-27 countries	21	19	23	20	20	19	23	18	14	22	22
Switzerland	–	–	–	–	–	–	–	–	–	–	–
EU-27 + Switzerland	21	19	23	20	20	19	23	18	14	22	22

Annexure 7: Number of beet growers

	2001/02	2002/03	2003/04	2004/05	2005/06	2006/07	2007/08	2008/09	2009/10	2010/11	2011/12	*Variation*
Austria	10316	9936	9705	9479	9318	8915	8566	8281	8069	7818	7574	–3.1%
Belgium	15170	14956	14734	14684	14301	13697	12996	8572	8342	8192	7994	–2.4%
Denmark	6104	5814	5430	4670	4370	3790	2840	1870	1590	1510	1445	–4.3%
Finland	2707	2529	2360	2300	2170	2040	1510	1060	1010	930	875	–5.9%
France	30200	30000	302200	29800	29500	29130	31000	26000	26000	26000	26000	0.0%
Germany	51995	50359	48183	46646	46676	42956	40125	34436	33256	32542	31319	–3.8%
Greece	20944	19766	16443	13423	15532	10136	5458	5015	7165	4114	2133	–48.2%
Ireland	3736	3700	3700	3706	3700	–	–	–	–	–	–	–
Italy	70000	70000	46000	46645	40000	17000	13300	9201	9362	10909	7000	–35.8%
The Netherlands	18483	17206	16397	15241	14466	13894	12350	9431	9120	8890	8457	–4.9%
Portugal	386	721	607	700	385	300	146	206	218	–	–	–
Spain	21500	21500	20000	20000	19000	16000	12700	9500	8900	8500	9722	14.4%
Sweden	4558	4435	3800	3620	3470	3170	2610	2370	2210	2150	2080	–3.3%
United Kingdom	8466	7144	7072	6970	6646	6508	4876	4566	4202	4092	3681	–10.0%
EU-15 countries	264565	258066	224631	217884	209534	167536	148477	120507	119444	115647	108280	–6.4%
Czech Republic	1002	1087	1045	935	901	866	767	718	711	730	712	–2.5%
Hungary	1071	752	795	809	809	809	679	74	114	155	173	11.6%
Latvia	–	–	–	418	386	386	–	–	–	–	–	–
Lithuania	3166	3056	2040	1800	1580	1510	1160	1000	636	593	602	1.5%
Poland			83429	77963	72790	63722	60832	40988	39986	38208	35860	–6.1%

Annexure 7: Number of beet growers *(Contd.)*

	2001/02	2002/03	2003/04	2004/05	2005/06	2006/07	2007/08	2008/09	2009/10	2010/11	2011/12	Variation
Poland			83429	77963	72790	63722	60832	40988	39986	38208	35860	–6.1%
Slovakia	–	–	472	412	387	355	225	152	180	187	186	–0.5%
Slovenia	517	470	–	–	–	–	–	–	–	–	–	–
EU-25 countries	270321	263431	312412	300211	286387	235184	212140	163439	161071	155520	145813	–6.2%
Bulgaria	–	–	–	–	20	25	–	–	–	–	–	–
Romania	–	–	39420	14311	18483	13764	5462	1555	1463	1362	1177	–13.6%
EU-27 countries	–	–	351832	314532	304890	248973	217602	164994	162534	156882	146990	–6.3%
Switzerland	7370	7197	7164	7253	7126	7017	6897	6749	6472	6153	6100	–0.9%
EU-27 + Switzerland	277691	270628	358996	321785	312016	255990	224499	171743	169006	163035	153090	–6.1%

Source: CEFS statistics, 2012.

Annexure 8: Sugar processing Industry employment during the beet processing campaign*

	2001/02	*2002/03*	*2003/04*	*2004/05*	*2005/06*	*2006/07*	*2007/08*	*2008/09*	*2009/10*	*2010/11*	*2011/12*	*Variation*
Austria	1164	1110	1067	1049	1015	872	868	858	835	794	793	–0.1%
Belgium	989	970	970	970	810	776	963	767	646	358	713	8.4%
Denmark	903	905	873	821	763	687	644	635	627	600	572	–4.7%
Finland	185	156	192	196	489	451	320	275	297	260	282	8.5%
France	8140	7963	9347	8606	8160	7683	7259	6531	6609	6645	6733	1.3%
Germany	7096	7033	6778	6517	6294	5783	5483	4813	4856	4408	4967	12.7%
Greece	2240	2177	2564	2553	2488	2263	1530	1593	1491	1350	1176	–12.9%
Ireland	–	650	650	650	325	325	325	–	–	–	–	–
Italy	7600	7100	5000	4700	5000	1700	1370	1320	1240	1240	1240	0.0%
The Netherlands	1560	1544	1492	1459	1180	1066	824	732	693	678	664	–2.1%
Portugal	268	294	283	285	246	240	173	150	156	–	–	–
Spain	3480	3400	3100	2900	2720	2190	1860	1700	1450	1490	1592	6.8%
Sweden	895	917	840	747	719	631	558	525	508	490	489	–0.2%
United Kingdom	1408	1299	1252	1264	1284	1252	1213	1000	1435	1247	1365	9.5%
EU-15 countries	35928	35518	34408	32717	31493	25919	23390	20899	20843	19860	20586	3.7%
Czech Republic	1760	1645	1603	1284	1949	1842	1238	1230	1218	1214	1371	12.9%
Hungary	1843	1585	1412	1249	1101	1101	787	223	208	202	273	35.1%
Latvia	–	–	–	–	–	–	–	–	–	–	–	–
Lithuania	1781	1702	1607	1443	1094	948	917	740	391	300	218	–27.3%
Poland	–	–	21948	14937	13532	10122	8522	5918	4848	5177	4857	–6.2%

Annexure 8: Sugar processing industry employment during the beet processing campaign* *(Contd.)*

	2001/02	*2002/03*	*2003/04*	*2004/05*	*2005/06*	*2006/07*	*2007/08*	*2008/09*	*2009/10*	*2010/11*	*2011/12*	*Variation (%)*
Slovakia	1186	1105	1248	996	980	710	550	335	304	312	435	39.4
Slovenia	–	–	–	–	–	–	–	–	–	–	–	–
EU-25 countries	42498	41555	62226	52626	50149	40642	35404	29560	27812	27065	27740	2.5
Bulgaria	–	–	–	–	350	370	–	–	–	–	–	–
Romania	–	–	–	–	1780	1780	1780	1780	1200	(1200)+	(1200)*	0.0
EU-27 countries	–	–	62226	52626	52279	42792	37184	31340	29012	28265	28940	2.4
Switzerland	393	396	388	377	372	363	353	350	347	340	346	1.8
EU-27 + Switzerland	42891	41951	62614	53003	52651	43155	37537	31690	29359	28605	29286	2.4

* The employment during the campaign includes permanent staff seasonal workers+ estimate based on previous years data.
Source: CEFS statistics, 2012.

2

Sugar Beet

The first references to the family of plants known as *beta* can be found in Greek literature around 420 BC. They were described as "versatile garden plants"; dark and light varieties are mentioned. Beet growing gradually spread throughout France and Spain, often in monasteries but also by peasant farmers. By the 15th century, beet was grown all over Europe. Originally the beet plant was grown for its leaves, which were probably the spinach or Swiss chard of their day. Later, the root became a popular vegetable, especially the red type of beet known as beetroot. In 1600, the French agronomist Olivier de Sererres reported "this choice food yields a juice like sugar syrup when cooked". At that time, nobody paid much attention to what gave the roots their sweetness.

Sugarcane provided sugar since ancient times, so why did sugar beet come into the picture? The answer involves a combination of scientific discoveries and historical events spanning three centuries. The first references to the family of plants known as *beta* can be found in Greek literature around 420 BC. They were described as "versatile garden plants"; dark and light varieties are mentioned. Beet growing gradually spread throughout France and Spain, often in monasteries but also by peasant farmers. By the 15th century, beet was grown all over Europe.

Originally the beet plant was grown for its leaves, which were probably the spinach or Swiss chard of their day. Later, the root became a popular vegetable, especially the red type of beet known as beetroot. In 1600, the French agronomist Olivier de Sererres reported "this choice food yields a juice like sugar syrup when cooked". At that time, nobody paid much attention to what gave the roots their sweetness.

The sugar beet as we know it today is derived from many years of breeding the domesticated beet (*Beta vulgaris* L.). It is said to get its name from the Greek letter *beta* because the swollen, turnip-like root resembles a Greek *B*. However, the oldest known beet type, chard, was domesticated by at least 2000 BC, and was grown by both the Greeks and Romans. Chard was originally used medicinally and for its dense foliage growth as a pot herb much like spinach or some of the Chinese leaf vegetables are used today.

The swollen, fleshy taproot familiar today was not known until the second and third century, AD. Beetroot, both red and white, were developed in Italy (thus known as the "Roman beet") by selection from the wild beets native to the seas-coasts of the Mediterranean. It was also found throughout Europe and hybridized with leaf beet types (chard) to produce the vast range of color and shape found in table beets today. It was used as a vegetable and was boiled in stews, baked in tarts, and roasted whole. White beets appear to have been more common, but less desirable than the red.

During the 18th century, the large-rooted beets, known as the mangel-wurzel, were being fed to cattle. They were introduced into England in the 1770s for use as livestock feed after being developed from early fodder beets in Germany and Holland. An unfortunate English mistranslation of the German mangold-wurzel ("beet-root") as mangel-wurzel ("scarcity root") resulted in the belief that this plant would be excellent food for the poor during periods of famine, but turned out to be better suited for cows.

A large root vegetable in 4,000-year-old Egyptian temple artwork may be a beet. Although beets have been grown as vegetables and for fodder since antiquity, their use as a sugar crop is relatively recent. As early as in 1590, the French botanist Olivier de Serres extracted a sweet syrup from beetroot, but the practice was not widely used. The Prussian chemist Andreas Sigismun d Marggraf used alcohol to extract sugar from beets (and carrots) in 1747, but the methods did not lend themselves to industrial scale production.

Beets were brought to North America by American colonists, but it is not known when for certain. They were well established by the 18th century, as mention is made of chard, and red, white, and yellow beetroot being grown in US gardens in the early 1800s. George Washington conducted experiments with them at Mount Vermon and by 1888; Burpee's *Farm Annual* offered seven different types of mangels, 12 varieties of table beets, and one variety of chard.

Developing the Sugar Beet of Today

During the mid-1700s, the German chemist Andreas Margraff discovered that both white and the red beetroot contained sucrose, which was indistinguishable from that produced from cane. He predicted then that domestic use and manufacture of sugar was possible in temperate climates, but these ideas would not be realized for another 50 years until new ways of extraction could be developed.

He began selectively breeding sugar beet from the *White Silesian* fodder beet in 1784. By the beginning of the 19th century, his beet was approximately 5–6% sucrose by weight, compared to around 20% in modern varieties. The first milestone in the history of European sugar is a remarkable discovery by the German scientist Andreas Marggraf in 1747. He demonstrated that the sweet-tasting crystals obtained from beet juice were the same as those from sugarcane. Under the patronage of Frederick William III of Prussia, he opened the world's first beet X sugar factory in 1801 at Cunern in Silesia.

The beet sugar industry in Europe rapidly developed after the Napoleoanic Wars. In 1870, the British began a blockade of France, which prevented the import sugarcane from the Caribbean. Partly in response, in 1812 Frenchman Bengamin Delessert devised a process of sugar extraction suitable for industrial application. In 1813, Napolean instituted a retaliatory embargo. By the end of the wars, over 300 sugar beet mills operated in France and central Europe. The first sugar beet mill in the US opened in 1838, and the first commercially successful mill was established by EH Dyer in 1879.

NAPOLEON TASTES BEET SUGAR

The first milestone in the history of European, sugar is a remarkable discoverd by the German scientist Andreas Marggraf in 1747. He demonstrated that the sweet-tasting crystals obtained from beet juice were the same as those from sugarcane. In 1801, the first sugar factory was built at Cunern in Lower Silesia.

Despite Marggrafs discovery, sugarcane was still the main source of sugar in the early 19th century. It took the blockage of French trade lines during the Napoleonic wars to give sugar beet the boost it needed.

In 1747, it was found that beet roots are rich source of sucrose. It took about 50 years to develop a method to extract beet root juice and its crystallization in the form of sugar. FC Achard was the first person to setup a sugar factory for processing of beet roots and making sugar out of their pulp. It was introduced in the USA as a sugar crop in early 18th century. Though sugar beet cultivation in India was initiated in 1914, its commercial cultivation started in Sriganganagar area of Rajasthan after producing first beet sugar in 1968 by Sriganganagar sugar mill.

According to another story, sugar beet is believed to have originated in the Middle East, near the Tigris and Euphrates Rivers. Cultivated form of sugar beet is believed to have evolved from wild maritime beet (*B. vulgaris* subsp. *maritima*) through selection (Cooke and Scott, 1993). Wild annual (*B. patellaris, B. webbiana* and *B. procumbens*) and perennial species (*B. trigyna, B. lomatogona,* and *B. Macrorhiza*) of beet have been found (Cooke and Scott, 1993).

Prior to this time, sugar was only obtained from the tropical sugarcane and was prohibitively expensive for most Europeans. During the early 1800s most sugar was obtained from the West Indies. After supplies were cut-off by the English blockade of continental Europe during the Napoleonic Wars, the demand for sugar grew throughout Europe. Napoleon encouraged new research with sugar beets, and between 1810 and 1815, over 79,000 acres were put into production with more than 300 small factories being built in France. After Napoleon's fall, sugar again was readily available from the tropics, and prices collapsed due to excess supplies. The majority of the factories were closed, and new development proceeded slowly. However, after the decline of slavery in the West Indies, the European industry became more competitive with the tropical source of sucrose, and by the 1850s, the industry had become well established and operating over most of the continent.

Sugar beet producing roots in first year and seeds (germs) in second year is a biennial herb grown in 45 countries of the world, and provides about 25% of world's sugar requirement in 2005. The crop is a major source of sugar in temperate countries. Beet sugar is demulcent and diuretic. The crop matures in April–May, when the cane crushing season is nearly over. Thus supply of sugar beet can extend the crushing season of mills by nearly 2 months. Original forms of sugar beet derived from white Silesian beet, which are used as a fodder, contained only 4% sugar. Repeated selection and breeding have raised the sugar content to its present level.

Beet pulp accounts for 5% (dry basis) to 30% (wet basis) of total roots, which is a good source of feed (forage/silage) for livestock. Ethanol is produced from impure sugary pulp (molasses). It is also fermented to beers. The tops with 10% digestible crude protein, form low cost substitute (forage/silage) for grain in feed concentrates. The tops contain growth stimulant "saponin". Leaves are rich in carotene (1.4–6.2%), vitamin C, E and exhibit estrogenic activity. The tops should not be fed to livestock at rates more than 25%.

BOTANICAL DESCRIPTION

Root system: The tap root forms the tuberous roots containing sucrose. There are vertical grooves along opposite side of the root from which lateral root arises. Sometimes, roots are flattened on two sides. The mature root is divided into three regions: the crown which is a convex cone, and just below is neck, which is the broadest part of the beet. The lowermost part is the root, which terminates in a long tap root.

Stem: The stem is very much reduced in size.

Leaves: The leaves arise in basal rosettes on the much condensed stem. The leaves are simple and smooth with a large blade and a petiole.

Inflorescence: The inflorescence is a terminal open panicle with spectate branches. Flowers are imperfect regular and without petals.

THINNING OR GAP FILLING

Sugar beet seed is a multigerm that produces four seedlings/glomerule. To avoid the competition, maintain single healthy plant/glomerule by plucking off the remaining ones when the seedlings develop 3–4 leaves. Thus, a uniform spacing of 20–25 cm between the plants should be maintained.

To maintain a uniform population, sometimes gap filling is required which should be done by sowing the seed instead of transplanting the seedlings because transplanting results in production of "malformed" or "frongy" roots having less weight. Gap filling should be done soon after germination.

SEED PRODUCTION

Sugar beet is propagated by seeds; hence its production is important. In India, seed production is done in Kalka (Kinnaur district) of Himachal Pradesh and Shalimar region of Jammu and Kashmir. The crop needs over wintering for seed production. Heavy snow fall in winter and 10–15 cm rainfall in summer are preferable. The seeds are produced from roots and seeds.

In seed production from roots, the matured roots are cut at the base taking away the neck, crown and leaves (called stocklings of 0.2–0.3 kg weight). The stocklings are over wintered either in covered trenches or by planting them in the field. In the field, the planted stocklings are subjected to moisture stress. After winter, the stocklings starts to regrow and produce flowers in 5–6 months and seed by end of summer.

In seed to seed crop method, the matured are allowed to pass through in the field as such (*in situ*). Thorough rouging of plants is done for maintaining purity of seed. The isolation distance must be maintained for seed production of this cross pollinated crop. It varies from 2 km in commercial to 5–6 km in foundation seed production. Nucleus and breeder seeds are produced in muslin cloth chambers. The seed yield varies from 1.6–2.0 tons/hectare. This method is ideal for areas with severe winter.

ESTABLISHING BEET FACTORIES IN THE UNITED STATES

After gaining a place in Europe, numerous attempts were made to introduce sugar beet production in the US. The first effort to grow sugar beets was in 1830 in Philadelphia but no factory was ever built, and the idea was abandoned. The first factory built in the US was at Northampton, Massachusetts in 1838, but ceased operating after 1840. Other unsuccessful attempts were made to establish factories in Wisconsin, Illinois and Michigan.

In the early 1850s, Mormon pioneers began to investigate local sugar beet cultivation and sucrose processing as a home industry to make themselves more independent. They established a factory near Salt Lake City in 1852 from machinery brought from England, and transported to Utah by covered wagon from Kansas. Unfortunately, due to a lack of knowledge of chemical processing, this attempt also was unsuccessful for producing crystallized sucrose, but it did pave the road for the future development of sugar beet culture and processing in the western US. The first successful commercial production of beet sugar in the US began in central California in 1870. By 1890, two factories were operating in Alvarado (now known as Union City) and Watsonville.

Throughout the history of the sugar beet industry in the US, many factories have been started but operated only for a short period of time. These start-up efforts often were done on a trial and error basis, moving around frequently from place to place, trying to find that right combination of factors that would result in greater long-term success. Many of the problems encountered were due to the sugar beet seed that was being imported from Europe. It was learned early by researchers with the Department of Agriculture that superior results were obtained when using home-produced cultivars, yet the industry continued to insist on using imported products. This way of thinking continued to inhibit continual success for producing beet sugar in certain areas.

SUGAR BEET AS AN ENERGY CROP

Sugar beet (*Beta vulgaris*) is a temperate crop and is mainly cultivated in the temperate countries where sugarcane cultivation is not feasible. Out of the total sugar production in the world, 22% sugar is produced from sugar beet and remaining comes from sugarcane. Some countries in tropics as well as subtropics have taken up sugar beet cultivation under the banner of TSB. Sugar beet root contains 15–20% sucrose and in the process of sugar extraction, 12–14% recovery is possible. The crop remains in the field for 5–6 months. Sugar beet being a salt tolerant crop can also be grown in saline soils where other crops fail to grow. Sugar beet is not only the source of sugar, but also provides several by-products like ethanol, cattle feed and betaine. Like sugarcane molasses, beet molasses can also be used in ethanol production as well as in the pharmaceutical industry for vitamin B production. In spite of above advantages, the sugar beet cultivation has been declining in Europe. The annual world production of sucrose is around 168 million tons, it is produced mainly for utilization in food, and nearly 45% is traded in the world market. Unlike sugarcane where sugar extraction is done through milling, the sugar from the beet is extracted by diffusion process. The beet roots are washed and cut into thin slices (cossetts). These slices are put in hot water which soaks the sugar out and forms syrup. The syrup is then purified, filtered and boiled again. Finally, it is dried to sugar, which is packaged and marketed. Once the juice has been extracted, pressed or dehydrated beet pulp provides an ideal foodstuff for cattle. Pulp can also be used to produce industrial pectin or dietary fiber contained in foods that have been "enriched with fiber". Under normal conditions processing of 100 kg fresh sugar beet can give 12–15 kg sucrose, 3.5 kg molasses, 4.5 kg dried pulp and varying amounts of filter cake and these products are utilized for various purposes including energy generation. Beet pulp is utilized for ruminant nutrition. Filter cake is used as fertilizer. Molasses are combined with beet pulp to provide animal feed, or used as feedstock in the chemical and pharmaceutical industries for fermented products such as citric acid and its esters. Sugar beet molasses are of limited value for large scale ethanol fermentation. In Europe, the sugar industry has been enabled to provide sucrose for chemical and biotechnological industries at prices similar to those of the world market. Sugar beet is an excellent source of energy for human being and animals and renewable energy source for a wide range of transportation vehicles [flexible fuel vehicles (FFV)].

The regulatory reforms to remove trade tariffs in Europe and the need for renewable sources of fuel have driven the search for more valuable by-products and the use of sugar beet as a feedstock for ethanol production. Sugar beet pulp also contains valuable polysaccharides such as a low molecular weight, arabinan or arabino-galactan-branched pectin and parenchyma cellulose that have excellent properties as emulsifiers. Additionally, a sugar beet pulp/polylactic acid (PLA) composite thermoplastic was developed with mechanical properties with less density and lower cost. A pectin-reduced sugar beet pulp was used for fermentation by *Escherichia coli* to produce ethanol following pectinase treatment. Ethanol yields were equivalent to that produced from pure cellulose even though the sugar beet pulp feedstock contained low levels of glucose and contained arabinose-rich pectin. Processing sucrose from sugar beet produces betaine as a by-product. Betaine is used in applications as diverse as sports nutrition, stabilizers and emulsifiers for food production, cosmetics and deicers for airport runways. It also has many pharmaceutical uses including the treatment of stomach problems and heart and liver disease. More outrageous products are being developed using beet, such as the production of polyester granules, polyhydroxyalkanoates (PHAs). PHAs are biodegradable plastics that can offer controlled degradation rates, so there is considerable interest in their use in medical applications such as tissue engineering, drug delivery, stent manufacturing, surgical sutures, wound dressing and endodontic material.

A. High Energy Food and Food Additives

Sugar beet is the principal sugar crop in many countries viz. USA, France, Germany, Denmark, Canada, Netherland, etc. Sugar beet contains 15–20% sucrose which is used widely as a pure high energy food or food additive. High fiber dietary food additives are manufactured from sugar beet pulp and major food processors in the US have used these dietary supplements in recently introduced new products including breakfast cereals. Unrefined sugary syrup is produced directly from sugar beet. This thick, dark syrup is produced by cooking shredded sugar beet for several hours, then pressing the resulting sugar beet mash and concentrating the juice produced until it has the consistency similar to that of honey. No other ingredients are used. In Germany, particularly the Rhineland area, this sugar beet syrup (called

Zuckerrüben-Sirup in German) is used as a spread for sandwiches as well as for sweetening sauces, cakes and desserts.

B. Livestock Feed

Sugar beet pulp and molasses are processing by-products widely used as feed supplements for livestock. These products provide required fiber and energy in rations and increase the palatability of feeds. Sugar beet tops also can be used for livestock feed. Sheep and cattle ranchers allow grazing of beet fields in the fall to utilize tops. Cattle and sheep also will eat small beets left in the field after harvest. Beet tops (leaves and petioles) also can be used as silage. Sugar beets that produce 20 tons/acre of roots also produce a total of about 5 tons/acre of *total digestible nutrients* (TDN) per acre in the tops. Tops are an excellent source of protein, vitamin A, and carbohydrates but are slightly inferior to alfalfa or corn silage for beef cattle. Tops are equal to alfalfa or corn silage for sheep. Beet top silage is best fed in combination with other feeds. Tops should be windrowed in the field and allowed to wilt to 60–65% moisture before ensiling.

C. Industrial Uses

Methane Production

Sugar production from sugar beet generates a co-product stream called raffinate, desugarized molasses or concentrated separated by-product (CSB). About 0.25 tons of raffinate is generated for every tons of sugar produced. Biogasification of raffinate at 55°C produced methane gas. Every metric tons of raffinate can generate 4,300 MJ of thermal energy from combustion of methane or about 300 kWh of electricity. Anaerobic digestion method for whole beet/ensilaged beet to produce biomethane is also an important and viable technology.

Biofuels from Sugar Crops

Present Situation and Global Players

Ethanol (C_2H_5OH) is the most used liquid biofuel, currently accounting for 86% of total liquid biofuel production. Of all ethanol produced, about 25% of global ethanol production is used for alcoholic beverages or for industrial purposes. The other 75% is fuel for transportation (World Watch Institue, 2007). Most ethanol (95%) is produced by fermentation of carbohydrates derived from agricultural crops, the remainder is synthetic ethanol. Both products are chemically identical. Another difference in ethanol that can be made is its purity. Anhydrous ethanol is at least 99% pure while hydrous ethanol contains some water and has a purity of 96%. Since gasoline and water do not mix, only anhydrous ethanol is suitable for blending. Hydrous ethanol is used as 100% gasoline substitute for cars with adapted engines. The US is still the world leader in ethanol manufacturing with more than 45 billion liters of ethanol production in 2010. At the other end of the spectrum, many developing countries including Nigeria and Malawi are turning to ethanol to boost their economies and secure their future energy needs. The Global Renewable Fuels Alliance (GRFA) in its 2010 production forecast for ethanol and the future continues to look positive for growth in the industry. Total ethanol production for 2009 was

73.9 billion liters according to data assembled by FO Licht. According to GRFA global production of ethanol in 2010 has reached 85.9 billion which will displace the need for 370 million equivalent barrels of oil globally.

The current volatility in the oil market and finite oil resources and the effect on global climate change from the addition of CO_2 to the atmosphere as a result of burning fossil fuels has increased the interest in sustainable energy generation from renewable biofuels. At present, approximately 10% of the primary global energy demand is met using biomass (Antoni et al. 2007). Some of this is from primary biofuels (i.e. unprocessed biomass) but increasingly secondary (processed biomass) biofuels are being used (FAO, 2008). Secondary biofuels often are divided into 1st generation (with a feedstock of seeds, grains, or sugars), 2nd generation (from lignocellulosic biomass) and sometimes 3rd generation (from algae and seaweed) (Nigam and Singh, 2010). Currently, only 1st generation biofuels are widely produced, with the wide adoption of 2nd generation biofuels requiring 5–10 years before the technology is available to economically produce them commercially. Because one of the main purposes of developing biofuels is the reduction of greenhouse gases (GHG), some sort of tools or sustainability metrics need to be used to compare biofuels ability to reduce GHG. Once such metric is life cycle analysis (LCA), which is an attempt to measure the total GHG effects generated from the production of a product (biofuel) including the entire process from extraction of the raw materials to the end of their use. There is a strong need to use metrics that are based on international standards, do not put developing nations at a disadvantage and focus on the global good [Food and Agriculture Organization (FAO), 2008]. The conversion of sucrose to ethanol is a simple process requiring only yeast fermentation, whereas producing ethanol from maize, wheat or other cereal grains, e.g. requires enzymes to convert starch to sugars.

However harvested sugar beet root is more difficult to store than a cereal grain. Cereal grains (primarily wheat) were feedstock to more than 50% of the 3.7 billion liters of European Union (EU) ethanol produced. Sugar beet was the next most common feedstock. Although ethanol production in Europe is growing, Brazil and the US are by far the largest producers of ethanol. The USA, Brazil and the European Union produced over 81% of the global ethanol production (FO Licht's, 2010).

On a per hectare basis, sugar beet is one of the most efficient sources of ethanol. It has been calculated that sugar beet produces between 100 and 120 liter / ton (fw) of ethanol through the fermentation process [110 liter / ton (FAO, 2008)]. The dry weight equivalent of one ton of sugar beet (fw) has been calculated to contain about 3.89 GJ of energy. Ethanol has an energy content of 21.2 MJ / liter which would give an energy value of 2.44 GJ / ton sugar beet (fw), assuming production of 115 liter / ton when converted to ethanol. FAO (FAO, 2008) calculates 5,060 liter / hectare yield for sugar beet compared with a 1,960 liter / hectare yield for maize or 952 liter / hectare for wheat, using a global estimate of average yield (46 tons / hectare for beet, 4.9 tons / hectare for maize, 2.8 tons / hectare for wheat). It has estimated that anaerobic digestion methods for whole beets to produce biomethane would produce 137% more energy than would fermentation of sugar beet to ethanol.

Bioethanol: Solutions for a Low-carbon Economy

Life cycle analysis (LCA) is one of the methods used to determine GHG effects generated from substitution of biofuels for fossil fuels. LCAs follow international standards that provide the framework for conducting these studies which are increasingly important because they are used by governmental agencies to design laws promoting or mandating the use of biofuels (US EPA 2010). Most LCA studies have indicated that 1st generation biofuels (bioethanol or biodiesel) have reduced GHG when compared to petroleum based fuels (Table 2.1) and sugarcane to ethanol route showed lowest carbon emission. Most sugar beet LCA studies have focused on conditions present in central European, where most commercial bioethanol production from sugar beet occurs (Hoffman, 2008). Bioethanol from sugar beet reduces GHG comparably to maize or sugarcane. Small amounts of nitrous oxide (N_2O), a more potent GHG than CO_2, are released from soils by agriculture. The amount released is dependent on cropping practices associated with fertilization, use of manure, or cover cropping however, it is a 300 times more potent GHG than CO_2, and, therefore monitoring its release in the atmosphere is important. Studies have concluded that sugar beet and sugarcane were effective in reducing N_2O emissions compared with maize; however, the authors stressed that management of crop nutrition, especially optimization of nitrogen fertilization was crucial in reducing N_2O emissions from the soil. Increasing resource use efficiency, where it occurs, will be critical in reducing GHG through the use of sugar beet and sugar beet co-products for biofuels in the future (Panella, 2010).

The energy derived from sugarcane is the best clean source and has irrefutable environmental advantage through its good energy balance. Sugarcane and sugar beet are small carbon emitters compared to corn, a crop which is largely used in US for ethanol production.

Table 2.1: Carbon emission in ethanol production from different crops

Crop	*Carbon emission (ton carbon/hectare)*
Sweet sorghum	1.1024
Corn	134.18
Sugar beet	1.335
Sugarcane	0.422

Biofuel Business: Future Needs and Developments

As we move into the 21 century and move away from non-sustainable fossil fuels to more sustainable biofuels, 1st generation liquid biofuels will continue to play an important part in converting away from an oil-based transport system. It is believed that sugar beet will play an important role as a feedstock in the production of bioethanol. Most of the European bioethanol production is in France, followed by Germany and Spain. However, there is interest in exploring or expanding the use of sugar beet as a bioethanol feedstock in a number of European countries, such as Ireland but especially in Eastern European nations including Slovenia and Serbia. In the Americas, Brazil (from sugarcane) and the US (from maize) are the major ethanol producers and users. Globally, there is a strong interest in Asia in the use of sugar beet as one of a number of potential bioethanol feedstocks. Because storing the harvested roots is a large impediment to using sugar beet as a bioethanol feedstock, climates where sugar beet can be cultivated both as spring or fall sown crops, will be the most attractive areas for biofuel production because the crop can be harvested daily most of the year. Biofuel production is possible where via anaerobic digestion, sugar beet could be ensiled to extend the processing will be a useful technology. Nonetheless, in the long run, even the most optimistic scenarios do not see bioethanol (especially from 1st generation feedstocks) replacing the fossil fuel now used in the transport sector (FAO, 2008). If it was possible to convert the entire US, grain yields to bioethanol that would fill only 18% of the demand for automotive fuel in the US. With rapidly expanding fleets of personal vehicles in India and China, it is imperative for the transport sector transitioning from fossil fuel to liquid biofuels and hybrid technology and then to an increasingly electric based system. In Europe, a Swedish heavy truck and bus manufacturer Scania has developed and manufactures ethanol-powered trucks and buses for urban use since the late 1980s. Currently, more than 800 Scania ethanol-powered buses are in service in various European cities, especially in the Swedish capital, Stockholm. The city is committed to replacing half its public transport fleet with vehicles powered by renewable energies by 2012.

Ethanol Summit 2011

Ethanol Summit 2011 held at Sao Paulo, Brazil (June 6–7, 2011) also stressed on a variety of new trends and uses emerging around the world, for ethanol and sugar crops. From the growing use of bioelectricity generated from burning sugarcane bagasse in high efficiency boilers, to the increased use of ethanol in the production of bioplastics and progress in the development of so-called 2nd generation ethanol, advances in flex-fuel technology for motor vehicles and in biotechnology, leading to the production of biohydrocarbon from sugarcane including diesel, gasoline, jet fuel and fine chemicals.

Sustainable Energy Technologies: Important Influences in the 21st Century

The Socioeconomic, political and environmental considerations will be the dominant factors in deciding the adoption of sustainable energy technologies in 21st century. A key factor affecting the use of sugar beet (and many other crops) is the development rate of advanced technologies (2nd generation lignocellulosic feedstocks), which is hard to predict but offers very sustainable alternatives to some of the food crops now being used as feedstocks. Another resource requirement, which is receiving increased scrutiny is the water needed (or water footprint) for bioenergy crop production. Gerbens-Leenes et al (2009) found sugar beet, and potato, are more efficient than maize and sorghum as sources for biofuels in most regions of the world. However, once sugar beet is irrigated, as it is in most areas where winter beet is grown its water footprint also grows (Gerbens-Leenes et al., 2009) and may impact regions with fast growing populations dependent on irrigated food production.

As the global population moves toward the projected 8–10 billion people in 2050 the discussion of whether to grow potential food crops for biofuels will intensify. There is serious concern that the use of crop land will both cause the grassland and forest to be brought into cropping and, thereby, both threaten food security and cause environmental damage (FAO, 2008). Although there is still uncertainty about the impacts of using abandoned agricultural land, or different cropping systems, this is a continuing dialog and a balance must be found. This is not just a challenge for biofuels if we are to feed a growing global population and maintain biodiversity in a sustainable manner, agricultural research must be focused on increasing global food production per hectare while reducing inputs—a formidable challenge!

SUGAR BEET AND BIOFUELS SCENARIO

Current technology is looking at ethanol as the primary fermentation product of sugar beet. There are, however, other choices for an end biofuel including biomethanol, biobutanol ethyl tert-butyl ether (ETBE), biomethane and biohydrogen, many of which are more energy dense than ethanol. Storage of sugar beet is a problem that could be solved by ensilage and anaerobic digestion producing a biogas, yielding more energy per hectare than bioethanol. Once 2nd generation liquid biofuels come online, there will still be niche markets for specialty fuels form locally grown crops with high conversion efficiency; sugar beet might be an excellent feedstock to produce products such as jet fuel (Kozak and Laufer, 2009). The introduction of a $30 / ton carbon tax, in the US has been predicted to reduce the beet sugar production by 87% because of the extensive use of coal to power processing factories. One solution to this cost would be using the sugar co-products – pulp and molasses (Kozak and Laufer, 2009)—to generate biomethane to provide the energy to process the sugar. There may be a trend in beet sugar processing to make the processing energy neutral—much as we see in sugarcane processing today. We may see adoption of small factory based on site energy production from renewable biofuels. In most sugar beet producing countries, in next few years economic conditions will demand a "dual purpose" sugar beet—one that may be grown as a sugar crop as well as an energy crop. However, in those areas where sugar beet is used only as biofuel feedstock, different criteria will become important. Sugar beet breeding companies have already begun or are discussing in house breeding programs for energy beets.

Around 2% of the globally produced sucrose is currently used as a source for value-added feedstock chemicals (Eggleston, 2008). Sugar beet pulp contains very little lignin, consisting of approximately equal amounts of hemicellulose and pectin. Sucrose and all of these compounds can be used as feedstocks for several important industrial chemicals; and there is tremendous potential to expand this market. As the global economy moves away from fossil fuels, sugar crops especially sugar beet will play an important role in the adoption of more sustainable energy generation; large-scale replacement of fossil fuels with renewable option is a reality in 21st century.

Current Status of Sugar Beet Research in India

Sugar beet (*Beta vulgaris L.*) is one of the three crops (sunflower and soybean being the other two) which were introduced in India around the same time. While the last two have now established themselves commercially in India, sugar beet is still awaiting to contribute significantly to the Indian agricultural scenario. None of these crops have been lacking in potential but till government push and industrial support became a reality, even sunflower and soybean were struggling to find their economic niche. Sugar beet is the last of the trio whose potential still remains untapped. It would be worthwhile to discuss the strengths of the crop and the constraints that have weighed against its acceptance till now. Sugar beet is a temperate crop, botanically known as *Beta vulgaris L.* It is a man-made crop and is the product of human selection from fodder beet for higher sugar content. The impetus for the development of sugar beet in Europe came when there was an embargo on the import of sugarcane sugar during the World War.

Sugar beet is a very efficient converter of solar energy to a form that can be utilized by men and animals. Most plants consume sugar for their own use but a few store it in the plant parts, which act as warehouse. Sugarcane and sugar beet are such plants. Sugar beet is a crop of the temperate region but its cultivation is now expanding from subtropical tracts to tropical world. Besides its conventional home in the temperate zone, it is now being successfully grown in Iran, Iraq, Algeria, Egypt, Afghanistan and Pakistan. Today, more than 25% of the world sugar requirement is met from sugar beet and beet sugar industry is well established in 45 countries spread over four continents of the world. The studies carried out in our country have established the agricultural feasibility and economic viability of sugar beet in subtropical to tropical parts of the country. The success of commercial cultivation and processing of sugar beet in Sriganganagar has further reinforced the above findings. For India, sugar beet can be an important sugar crop by supplementing sugarcane. This is mainly because of its short-duration (6–7 months as compared to 10–12 months of sugarcane), high sugar content (15–17%), high sugar recovery (12–14%) and high purity (85–90%). As such, it has good prospects for bridging the gap between present sugar production and anticipated national sugar requirement. In addition to sugar, sugar beet provides valuable by products like green-beet tops and beet molasses which are of value as cattle feed and in fermentation industry. Because of its high chemical quality, beet molasses is a priced item with potentialities for export. Hence, sugar beet is capable of occupying an important place in the sugar economy of the country.

Sugar beet is a versatile crop as it can withstand various climatic and soil conditions. Being tolerant to salinity and frost, it can help to bring several hundred hectares of uncultivable land under cultivation. The crop also can help to extend the factory season and consequently promote employment. Available in the beginning of April, sugar beet enables the factory to process both the raw materials-sugarcane and sugar beet during their high efficiency periods. It provides the added advantage of a combined agricultural and manufacturing economy.

For farmers, sugar beet is important for three main reasons. First, it is a dependable cash crop; second, it ameliorates salt affected soils with promoting soil fertility through sound farming practices and third, the by-products provide nutritious cattle feed during the hot months of the year when green fodder is not readily available.

The National Scene with Respect to Demand for Sweetener

Until recent past sugar beet was famous as a "salad" crop for table purposes in India, but it is now in semicommercial testing in subtropical parts of the country. In Kashmir valley, sugar beet is grown as a spring season crop. A beginning of commercial cultivation of sugar beet has now been made in Sriganganagar area in Rajasthan, Phaltan in Maharashtra and Tarai in Uttarakhand.

According to the vision document for 2025 of Indian Institute of Sugarcane Research and Sugarcane Breeding Institute, there is a scope for almost doubling the productivity levels due to the gap between the achievable and achieved. According to the estimates of National Commission on Agriculture (1976), the population of India may rise to 1.4 billion by 2025 AD. Then, the country will require nearly 49 million tons of sweeteners. With decreasing trends in jaggery and *khandsari* production, the country has to produce about 30 million tons of sugar. With an average sugar recovery of 10.75%, about 495 million tons of sugarcane will be required by 2025 AD (60% cane will be utilized for white sugar manufacture and 10% will go for ethanol production). The productivity requirement will have to be 100 tons/hectare, as sugarcane area may stabilize between 4.5 and 4.75 million hectares by 2025 AD.

It becomes a matter of concern when we see that the best we have achieved is about 350 million tons of sugarcane. There are increasing demographic pressures on agricultural land resulting in shrinkage of cultivable area. Therefore, unless there is a commensurate vertical increase in productivity per unit area and time, it would be difficult to meet the rising demand. This can come from better implementation of sugarcane production technology and considering options such as sugar beet and sweet sorghum to supplement sugar/ethanol production.

SUGAR SCENARIO AND SUGAR BEET ROLE

Riddled by the cycles of boom and bust in sugarcane production in India, the sugar beet crop was introduced with the object of augmenting sugar production. In 1960s, extensive exploratory trials were conducted all over the country to find out suitable areas of root and seed production. Based on the preliminary results, it was felt that sugar beet could be grown during winter in north India, while Kashmir valley and hills such as Darjeeling and Shimla were found suitable for seed production. In 1971, an All India Coordinated Research Project on Sugar beet was launched by the Indian Council of Agricultural Research with Centers at Lucknow, Pantnagar, Sriganganagar, Phaltan, Jalandhar and Kanpur. Later on, Kalyani in West Bengal, Solan in Himachal Pradesh and Mukteswar in Kumaon hills were added. At the same time, a sugarcane cum sugar beet sugar factory was established at Sriganganagar in Rajasthan.

Keeping in views, the economic importance of sugar beet in sugar and ethanol production, some subtropical countries such as India initiated sugar beet cultivation in some states under All India Coordinated Research Project (AICRP) on sugar beet during1960s. The multinational company Syngenta India Ltd had developed thermo-insensitive varieties such as HI0064, Dorotea and Posada and were grown on experimental basis in 38 sugar factories in Maharashtra. Based on experimental trials conducted at various locations, sugar beet cultivation was started in Sriganganagar, Rajasthan for sugar production and in Sundarban, West Bengal for alcohol/ethanol production. The sugar beet is the short duration and salt tolerant crop compared to sugarcane. It matures in 5–6 months and grows successfully on saline soils where other crops fail.

The 1970s and 1980s was a period of intense research activity on sugar beet. Work was carried out in germplasm evaluation, varietal development, and agronomical, pathological, entomological and agricultural engineering aspects.

Sriganganagar provided the testing ground of the production technology. India opted for self reliance for sugar beet seed and an open-pollinated, diploid Russian variety namely, Ramonskaya-06 (R-06) was found suitable for Indian conditions along with some other anisoploid varieties from Europe. The seed production of R-06 was successfully undertaken by the National Seeds Corporation in Sringagar and later on in Himachal Pradesh. The crop was a success with the farmers and the factory. It had a commercial run of over 30 years when the factory was closed due to reasons not exclusive to sugar beet. One of these, however, was the trade liberalization which closed the remunerative disposal of sugar beet molasses to a Mumbai-based pharmaceutical company. The best average root yield obtained was 39 tons/hectare and a sugar recovery of 11.32%. It may be borne in mind that this was made possible without the best available varieties. The sugar beet crop was found to be the most remunerative rabi crop as compared with wheat and mustard.

VARIETIES

Sugar beet, being a recently introduced crop into India has mostly exotic varieties. The varieties are mostly from Germany, Russia, USA, UK, Denmark, etc. Some varieties have also been evolved in the country especially from IISR, Lucknow. The important varieties are given below.

The exotic and Indian varieties of sugar beet recommended for cultivation in India.

Exotic varieties	*Indian varieties*
Hh-Monitor 212, Maribo maroepoly Maribo magnapoly, Mezzanopoly-A Ertype E, US 75, Bush E, NP poly, AJ poly, USH 6, USH 8, USH 9, US 36, MSH 102, Kawemagapoly	**Suitable for all regions** Pant S-1, Pant S-2, Pant S-3, Pant S-10, Pant composite 6, Pant composite 3
Kawegigapoly, Tribel, Ramonskava 06, US 35, Maribo Resistapoly, Triplex, BGW 674, Crimson glob, Detroit Dark Red, GWH 14, GWH 66, VSH 6, VSH 7	**Certified varieties** Pant composite 1, IIST composite 1 IISR 2, IRSR composite, Rajendra Sakarkand 35, Rajendra Sakarkand 43, Sree Bhadra and Sree Rathna
	Suitable for saline soils Pant S 1, Pant S 10, IISR composite 1 and IISR 2

Yield

A well-managed crop of sugar beet produces about 50–70 tons roots/hectare. Sugar beet roots have ~95% juice. Sugar from sugar beet roots is extracted by adopting the diffusion process. Sugar content in sugar beet ranges from 13% to 17%. The important yield attributes/by-products of sugar beet are Table 2.2.

Sugarcane production in the country has seen many ups and downs, sometimes brought about by failure of rains. In early 2000s, many southern states were reeling under consecutive droughts leading to insufficient cane supplies to the factories. At this juncture, some multinational sugar beet seed companies came out with tropicalized sugar beet varieties and a need was felt to conduct feasibility trials.

Table 2.2: The important yield attributes/by-products of sugar beet

Attributes	*Value*
Test weight of seed	20 gm
Pulp yield/ton roots	0.5–0.7 tons (wet basis); 0.08–0.1 tons (dry basis)
Molasses/ton roots	0.05 tons
Ethanol/ton sugar beet	86 liters

The ICAR responded with an AP Cess Network project in 2004. The work done at the five centers with two of these in Maharashtra showed that sugar beet could be grown successfully from October–November to April–May. The package of practices along with the suitable varieties was developed. The potential for root yield was observed to be 60–80 tons/hectare with a sugar content in the roots of 13–15%. Table 2.3 gives the performance of sugar beet varieties from diverse seed sources (IISR, Syngenta, SES Vanderhave, Iran and KWS):

Table 2.3: Performance of sugar beet varieties averaged over locations (2007-08)

S. No.	*Varieties*	*Sucrose content (%)*		*Root yield (tons/hectare)*		*Gross sugar at 180 DAS (tons/hectare)*
		*150 DAS**	*180 DAS*	*150 DAS*	*180 DAS*	
1	LK-27	13.05	14.93	78.22	67.92	10.868
2	LKC-95	12.71	14.98	76.00	65.05	11.058
3	SYT-06-07	14.26	16.40	84.79	70.99	10.807
4	SYT-06-13	14.50	16.67	75.37	69.24	10.890
5	IN-06	14.13	16.06	90.77	69.33	9.566
6	IN-07	14.28	15.76	65.27	61.32	10.248
7	PAC-60002	14.88	17.14	81.49	70.62	11.444
8	PAC-60006	13.56	16.18	72.20	66.97	11.097
9	FELICITA	13.07	15.19	84.63	80.82	11.728
10	RASOUL	13.38	14.88	64.86	55.56	9.044
11	LS-6	13.14	16.22	82.77	70.42	11.484
12	SHUBHRA	13.78	17.67	93.59	77.77	13.253
Mean		**13.73**	**16.01**	**79.16**	**68.83**	**10.957**

* DAS: Days after sowing.
Mean of four locations: Lucknow, Pune, Digraj (Sangli, Maharashtra) and Sriganganagar.

Similar to any other crop, the availability of genetically superior varieties adapted to local agroclimatic conditions is a pre-requisite for its lasting success. This explains the need for intensive efforts to breeding indigenous varieties/hybrids of sugar beet in India. In this direction 350 germplasm/varieties were evaluated for adaptation to Indian conditions. Lines with high root yield, top yield, sucrose content, and resistance to root rot, tolerance to high temperature, Bihar hairy caterpillar and salinity were identified and subsequently utilized in genetic enhancement of sugar beet under Indian agroclimatic conditions. The germplasm with male sterility and compatible restorers and maintainers are requirement for exploitation of heterosis. The sources for male sterility are being studied in available germplasm. Sugar beet is a highly cross-pollinated crop and the improved hybrids varieties have been primarily evolved by private companies abroad. For efficient domestic breeding, capable of yielding quick results, advantage of the vast experience in improvement technology and breeding advance abroad need to be taken through appropriate international cooperation. This will enable not only the availability of established in bred lines but also the germplasm, which is essential pre-requisite for plant improvement. Although, the breeding efforts made at Pantnagar and Lucknow are encouraging, appropriate strengthening of the program by way of facilities, expertize and genetic material is urgently needed.

Complete package of practices, including plant protection measures has been developed. Sugar beet cultivation research under saline soil conditions of Sunder Ban (WB) started and extended to other salt-affected soils of subtropical India Pant S-1, Pant S-10, IISR Comp-1, IISR-2 and Mezzanpoly identified as sugar beet varieties suitable for saline and alkaline soil conditions. Work on utilization of sugar beet for alcohol production initiated in Sunderban (WB).

Standardization of sugar beet seed production was done under Indian conditions at altitudes above 5000′, such as Mukteswar and Ranichauri (Kumaon Hills), Auli (Garhwal Hills), Shimla and Kalpa (Himachal Pradesh), Darjeeling (West Bengal) and Kashmir by the Lucknow (IISR Comp-1 and LS-6) and Pantnagar (Pant S-10) centers. Indigenous diploid varieties developed and recommended for general cultivation. In India, high temperature (40–45°) tolerant varieties have been identified.

Foundation seed production standardized and routinely carried out by the Kalpa center. Machines for seed polishing, core sampling for sugar determinations root digging and seed drill (Hand and Bullock-Drawn) were developed.

THE PRESENT SCENARIO

A Network Project to develop agronomical techniques for cultivation of sugar beet in India was initiated by ICAR during 2004–07, with centers at VSI, Pune, RRS, Sangli, IISR, Lucknow and Sriganganagar. The experimental findings revealed that the productivity of sugar beet grown in winter season was 60–75 tons/hectare. However, the sugar beet productivity was on 30–35 tons/hectare at farmers field. Amongst the variety, HI0064 was the best followed by the IISR, Lucknow varieties, i.e. LS-6 and IISR Comp-1. However, it is necessary to test these genotypes of sugar beet for their performance related to quality parameters, and incidence of pests and diseases under Indian conditions. Sugar beet is not only the good source of sugar, but also provides many by-products such as ethanol, cattle feed, etc. The molasses of sugar beet may be used in pharmaceutical industry for production of vitamin B_{10}

and B_{12}. The pharmaceutical companies enthusiastic to buy sugar molasses extracted from sugar beet due to better quality compared to molasses produced from sugarcane. There is need to develop sugar beet processing industry so that the farmer's should reap the better economic returns. Sugar beet may be explored as an alternative crop for sugar and ethanol production, keeping in view the trends of depleting natural resources for sugarcane production in future.

The changing biofuel scenario in the country has started looking at sugar beet with ethanol as the end-product. Several sugar factories in Andhra Pradesh, Maharashtra, Karnataka and Punjab have been keen to give sugar beet a fair trial, after having been convinced of its agronomic feasibility through in-house crop experimentation. In this, a key role has been that of the multinational sugar beet seed companies, such as Syngenta, SES Vanderhave and KWS through their Indian operations. These companies are still active in providing the know-how, seed and guidance in growing and handling of sugar beet. IISR and VSI are playing a crucial role. The SDF has financed the fabrication and setting up of a pilot plant for sugar beet processing at Samarth SSK Ltd in Maharashtra. Besides, a sugar beet-based ethanol production unit has been setup at Harneshwar (Maharashtra). While we await a feedback on these ventures, many more of such initiatives by private entrepreneurs are needed for demonstrating the economic viability of sugar beet and provide a model for others to learn from their experience.

The Need for a Stimulus

The history of sugar beet development in Europe and the USA, and also at Sriganganagar (Rajasthan) in India shows that unless there were incentives given by the government, sugar beet could not be a success. In Sriganganagar, it was the extra canal water for every acre of sugar beet that was a big attraction, and the assured purchase of sugar beet by the sugar factory. Similarly, farmers need to be attracted to the crop through such incentives. Being an industrial crop, a contract for the timely purchase of the entire produce has to be in place. Further, support for availability of seed, fertilizers and pesticides along with technical guidance in raising the crop has to be provided. The central and state agricultural extension and development machinery has to make an all out effort to be equal partners with the farmers and the factory to lend the necessary support with their active presence and postharvest management of the produce.

The Positives and Pitfalls

Sugar beet has been shown to be agriculturally feasible under Indian conditions. It has the potential to yield comparable to sugarcane in half the time with water saving of 30–40%. The suitable varieties have been identified and the production technology has been developed. The mechanization of sowing operation has been done. The ecological niches for the successful cultivation of the crop have been identified. As we go along and gain experience of growing it in specific locations, innovative refinements in crop and produce management shall be introduced by the farmers and factory personnel themselves. In fact, working models are provided by the successful cultivation of sugar beet in countries like Egypt, Morocco, Iran, Pakistan, EU and North America, which have a wide range of agroclimatic conditions and from largely manual to totally mechanized precision farming.

India is blessed with a wide range of climatic conditions which allow us to be self-reliant in sugar beet seed production. Depending on the demand, some multinationals may shift their seed production to India to reduce the seed costs. So, the availability of seed of the desired varieties has to be assured. A business model has to be developed in the form of *contract farming* where various stakeholders commit themselves to their specific role in the entire venture. This was being done at Sriganganagar among farmers, factory and seed companies. The state government has to play the role of a facilitator and observer for fair play by various stakeholders.

Thus, sugar beet can become an agricultural reality. Most of the components are already worked out and can be integrated in a mission mode with the appropriate government policy, industrial entrepreneurship and a committed agricultural department. It may also be mentioned that sugar beet has an in-built tolerance to saline and alkaline soil conditions. It has therefore the potential to bring under plough and reclaim vast tracts of salt-affected soils in the country, estimated to be around 6.7 million hectares. For integrating sugar beet with the existing cropping pattern, a lot of work has been done but still some more research may be required for the new locales. It can easily be grown as an intercrop with sugarcane to increase sugar productivity per unit time and area. The issues of the need of extraneous fuel and additional processing machinery are not insurmountable.

UNIQUE FEATURES OF SUGAR BEET AND ITS COMPARISON WITH SUGARCANE

Sucrose ($C_{12}H_{22}O_{11}$, Molecular weight 342.3) is β-D-fructofuranosyl α-D-glucopyranose, a most ubiquitous and abundantly occurring disaccharide. For sugar, its sweetness was primary but its nutritive value (calorific and others) was a secondary realization. Important sugar crops include, sugarcane, sugar beet, sugar maple, various types of palms and sweet sorghum. Sugar beet (*Beta vulgaris*), a plant belonging to the family *Chenopodiaceae*, is the second most important source of sugar (21.5% of the world sugar) after sugarcane which is grown in 57 countries. It is a biennial halophytic (as well as Na-salts scavenger) C_3 plant containing up to 20% sugar on fresh weight basis; and for its flowering (for seed production), it requires vernalization. In this plant, sugar is stored in root. The latter is composed of 90% root derived part and the remaining 10% (the crown) is derived from the hypocotyl.

Uniqueness of this sugar yielding plant are:

- It is a halophyte (can tolerate a salinity level of 9.5 m mhos/cm) as well as scavenger of sodium salts. Thus, it may be a most suitable crop to cultivate several thousand hectares of uncultivable usar lands.
- It is a C_3 plant
- Selective breeding and improved agricultural practices have improved sugar concentration in its roots from 4% to 18% on fresh weight basis and around 75% on dry weight basis, in a relatively shorter period of time.
- It is a temperate biennial plant (for a seed crop) but for the root crop it is cultivated as an annual crop.
- For flowering, vernalization is obligatory.

Leaves of sugar beet exhibit rates of photosynthesis in the range of 38–52 μmol/ m^{-2}/second, chlorophyll contents 1.20–1.75 mg/gm and carotenoid contents 3.6–7.76 mg/gm fresh weight of the leaf. Biochemically, sugar beet is a C_3 plant with

RuBP carboxylase as carboxylating enzyme with phosphoglyceraldehyde (PGAl)/dihydroxyacetone phosphate (DHAP) as primary carboxylation products. The enzyme, ribulose 5-phosphate kinase primarily regulates rates of photosynthesis. Sucrose synthesis in the leaves is primarily achieved by the activity of trans-glucosylases namely sucrose phosphate synthetase (SPS) and sucrose synthetase (SS). Sucrose translocates in the leaves through a *symplastic pathway*, however, in young and mature storage roots, it is by the *apoplastic pathway*. Sucrose is stored in vacuoles by an active uptake process and follows an ion co-transport mechanism.

With respect to its life cycle, sugar beet is a biennial plant; comprising a period of vegetative growth, cold-induced vernalization, production of upright extended flowering stem and seed production. After vernalization, bolting occurs where the stem elongates in to a tall shoot like structure. Axillary buds in the axil of the leaves on the shoots quickly develop into inflorescence (an indeterminate raceme) on which sessile flowers are borne. It is cross pollinated crop and a humidity of 75% is important for it. Warm and dry period after the pollination (during the seed development and ripening) leads to good seed setting and production of good quality seed.

Composition wise, a freshly harvested sugar beet root contains 75–76% water, 15–20% sugars, 2.6% nonsugars, and 4–6% the pulp. Processing 1 ton of fresh sugar beet roots yields are 121 kg sugar, 38 kg molasses (containing 18.2 kg sugar, 12.1 kg impurities and 7.8 kg water) and 50 kg of pulp.

Some of the physiological criteria used in selection of sugar beet are: high pulp content for high sugar, maintenance of green foliage cover during drought for drought tolerance, restricted chloride accumulation in shoots for salt tolerance, carbon isotope discrimination for improved water use efficiency, etc. Tropicalized sugar beet hybrids have been selected for heat tolerance and disease (especially the ones prevalent in tropical regions) resistance from the sugar beets growing in extreme American and European locations. These may be utilized as a valuable complimentary crop with sugarcane in tropical areas of the world.

There are differences in sugar and sugar-products derived from sugar beet and sugarcane. Sugar beet sugar/sugar products are characterized by more negative values of $^{13}C/^{12}C$ ratio and absence of theanderose.

Thus sugarcane and sugar beet, the two important sugar producing plants differ in their position in plant kingdom, process of photosynthesis, response to salinity, tissues storing sugar, process utilized for extraction of sugar, utilization of energy for their processing for sugar, mode of propagation, etc. Although they have nearly same level of sugar, sugar and sugar products from these as well as composition of their molasses in terms of carbohydrates, minerals, nonsugars and presence of vitamins.

Sugarcane and Sugar Beet Compared

A comparison of sugarcane and sugar beet is given in Table 2.4.

USEFUL PRODUCTS FROM SUGAR BEET

Sugar beet (*Beta vulgaris*), belonging to the family *Chenopodiaceae,* is the second most important source of sugar (21.5% of the world sugar) which is grown in 57 countries. It is a biennial halophytic (as well as Na-salts scavenger) C_3 plant containing up to 20% sugar on fresh weight basis; and for its flowering (for seed production), it

Table 2.4: Comparison of sugarcane and sugar beet

S. No.	*Characteristic*	*Sugarcane*	*Sugar beet*
1	Contribution to world sugar production	78.5%	21.5%
2	Cotyledonous nature of the plant	A monocotyledonous	A dicotyledonous plant
3	Crop duration	10–24 months	6 months
4	Photosynthetic characteristics	A C_4 photosynthesizing plant	A C_3 photosynthesizing plant
5	Response to salinity	Can grow only on partially reclaimed soil	Grows well/in adapted to saline soils
6	Organ and tissues storing sugar	Parenchymatous cells in the stalk (in the vacuoles and cytoplasm)	Parenchymatous cells in the concentric rings in the roots
7	Sucrose content in juice	15–20%	15–20%
8	Process for extraction of sugar (in juice)	Shredding and application of pressure	Slicing and diffusion
9	Method of propagation	Vegetative, by planting, cuttings with 1, 2 or 3 buds or even the whole cane	By true seed
10	Uniqueness of sugar and sugar products:		
	(a) Ratio of $^{13}C/^{12}C$(in sucrose)	Less negative values (–14 o/oo)	More negative values (–29 o/oo)
	(b) Theanderose (in sugar and sugar products)	Present (passes through crystallization process)	Absent
11	Source of energy for processing (for sugar)	Bagasse, a by-product of milling sugarcane is used as fuel	Has to be provided exogenously (as coal or electricity)
12	Molasses characteristics		
	Carbohydrates	Contains relatively less of sucrose (32%), more of reducing sugars (12–30%) and no raffinose.	Contains relatively more of sucrose (63%), less of reducing sugars (1%) and also 1% raffinose.
	Minerals (ash)	Relatively lesser (8.0%)	Relatively higher (11.5%, with 6% K)
	Non sugars (including nitrogenous materials)	10.0%; betaine isd absent	19.0%; contains betaine-an osmoregulant
	Vitamins	Biotin is present	Lacks biotin (vitamin H or B7)

Source: Shrivastava, 2006.

requires vernalization. The storage organ of this plant is usually called the root; of which 90% is actually *root derived* and the remaining 10% (the crown) is derived from the hypocotyl.

A freshly harvested root of sugar beet contains 75–76% water, 15–20% sugars, 2.6% nonsugars and 4–6% the pulp. Processing 1 ton of fresh sugar beet roots yields 121 kg sugar, 38 kg molasses (containing 18.2 kg sugar, 12.1 kg impurities and 7.8 kg water) and 50 kg of pulp. Out of sugar present in fresh sugar beet roots, nearly 83% is recovered as white sugar, 12.5% is lost in molasses and 4.4% is lost in some other ways. Beet roots also contain 0.3% betaine, an important osmoregulant. Molasses obtained after processing sugar beets (as percentage of dry weight) contains 66.5% sugars (sucrose 63.5, raffinose 1.5 and other sugars 1.5%), 23% other organic compounds (glutamic acid + pyrrolidine carboxylic acid 4.0%, other amino acids 3.0%, betaine 5.5%, pectins 5.0%) and 10.5% inorganic compounds with 6% K_2O. Beet pulp consists of water insoluble fibrous materials which are: pectins (2.4%), cellulose (1.2%), hemicellulose (1.1%), proteins (0.1%), saponin (0.1%) and minerals (0.1%). It has been observed that high-sugar beet roots have relatively higher amount of pulp.

After processing for sugar, sugar beet molasses, on dry weight basis, contains about 50% sugar. The latter contains predominantly sucrose, and also glucose and fructose. Its nonsugar components are salts like oxalate and chloride of calcium and potassium. Molasses also contains betaine and a trisaccharide, raffinose. These make beet molasses unpalatable for human beings. But, it is mainly used as an additive to animal feed and also as a feedstock for fermentation. In comparison to sugarcane molasses, the beet molasses lacks biotin (vitamin H or B_7).

Besides extraction of sugar, sugar beet as well as pulp and molasses obtained from its processing have been utilized for preparing some of the useful products for the benefit of mankind. Some of these are given below:

Human Food

Sucrose from sugar beets is the principal use for sugar beets in the US. Sugar beets contain from 13% to 22% sucrose. Sucrose obtained from processing sugar beets, is widely used as a high energy food as also a palatable food additive. High fiber dietary food additives have been manufactured from sugar beet pulp. In the US, these dietary supplements have been recently introduced in breakfast items.

A sugary syrup is also produced by cooking shredded sugar beet for several hours. After pressing and filtering, a honey like dark syrup is obtained. In some parts of Germany, this syrup (called *Zuckerrüben-Sirup* or *Zapp*) is used as a spread for sandwiches, to sweeten sauces, cakes and desserts. This syrup is also hydrolyzed to a product akin to high fructose corn syrup.

Health Benefits

Red beets have been allowed for their health benefits. Beets are enriched with nutrients like Mg, P, Na, K and Ca. It also contains ample of Se, Zn and Mn. The flavanoids and carotenoids present in it prevent damage to the cells. The red pigment of beets, betacyanin is effective in prevention of colon cancer. Intake of red beets also reduces high blood pressure. It helps in production of RBC in the blood and removes harmful and toxic substances accumulated in the liver. Leaves of sugar beet are known to counter bad breath. In Roman times, Hippocrates advocated use of beet leaves for healing of wounds. Sugar beets have been used to get rid of tumors and to help people with blood diseases and leukemia. It has also been used to treat and cure boils, abscesses and even acne so much so that these have earned the status of *"Beet Therapy"*.

Beverages

In many countries molasses from sugar beet is used to make a rum-flavored hard liquor like *Tuzemák* in Czech Republic and Slovakia, *Kobba Liber* in the Åland Islands and rectified spirit and *vodka* in the Czech Republic and Germany.

Feed for Livestock

Being a good source of carbohydrates, protein, fiber and minerals, sugar beet tops are used as animal feed, either as fresh or even in ensilaged form. Some of the sugar beet varieties are grown as fodder beets. Once the juice has been extracted, pressed or dehydrated beet pulp provides an ideal foodstuff for cattle. Pulp can also be used to produce industrial pectin or dietary fiber for use with foods enriched with fiber. Processing by-products of sugar beet, the beet pulp and molasses are also widely used as feed supplements for livestock. It contributes to fiber in the feed and adds to its palatability. In France, sugar beet molasses is used as cattle fodder supplement.

Pharmaceuticals

Molasses, a by-product from sugar beet processing, is widely used in the producing alcohols (ethanol and butanol), other pharmaceuticals and producing baker's yeast. A ton of molasses yields approximately 300 liters of alcohol. Alcohol derived from sugar beet is suitable for human consumption (in spirits, perfume, vinegar, pharmaceutical products, etc.) and ideal for use in household products (cleaning fluids, methylated spirits, etc.) and some other useful chemicals (solvents, etc.). For ethanol fermentation from sugar beet molasses, a new alginate-maize stem tissue matrix has been developed as a carrier for the yeast, *Saccharomyces cerevisiae*. The latter led to an ethanol production of 2.51 gm/liter/hour. Fermenting beet molasses with potassium ferro- or ferricyanide with *Aspergillus niger* produced citric acid (approximately 50% of the available sugar as sucrose). *Betaine* can be isolated from molasses, a by-product of sugar beet processing using a chromatograohic technique called "simulated moving bed". This chemical is used as osmo-protectant for commercial crops under drought conditions. *Uridine* is also isolated from sugar beet molasses. In combination with omega-3 fatty acids, use of this compound overcomes depression in rats.

Use in Agriculture

Sugar beet cultivation removes nearly 500 kg of sodium salts per hectare. Thus, its cultivation may reclaim sodic soils. Sugar beet processing generates waste lime which, if amended in the acid soils, increases soil pH. Waste lime is also a good source of nutrients like P and K. Effluent of sugar beet processing after treatment may also be used for irrigation.

Biofuel/Fuel Additives

Alcohol produced from sugar beet molasses is also used as fuels (or mixed with petrol and diesel) for automobiles in many countries. Therefore, it takes 6.22 kg of sugar beet to produce 1 kg of ethanol (approximately 1.27).

De-icing Roads

Heavy snow fall makes the road transport very difficult. Salt is used for de-icing roads during heavy snow fall. Desugared sugar beet molasses is mixed with salts in equal parts for de-icing or anti-icing products in winter control operations; and it has reduced the amount of salt on the roads as much as 30%. Sugar beet molasses, in combination with salts, is rather more effective than the road salt used alone as it reduces corrosion to some extent and also lowers the freezing point of the de-icing mixture remains and it remains more effective under such conditions. Additionally, use of this mixture, reduces the bounce and scatter of the rock salt used and decreases the time for the snow to melt.

RECENT TREND OF SUGAR BEET IN WORLD

Sugar beet (*Beta vulgaris* L.) has its origin in early 19th century from feral and fodder beets (Achard, 1979; Marggraf, 1979). Sugar beet has been specially selected and bred for sucrose production over the past two centuries (Winner, 1993). Nearly 60 countries are cultivating sugar beet in world (2011). Top fifteen sugar beet producing countries are Russian Federation, Ukraine, United States of America, Germany, France, Turkey, China, Poland, Egypt, United Kingdom, Iran (Islamic Republic of), Belarus, Netherlands, Italy and Belgium. Sugar beet is mainly produced in Europe and, to a lesser extent, in Asia and North America. During last 10 years (2000–2009), the area under sugar beet was decreasing at the rate of 0.2 million hectare per year in world consequently its production was also decreasing 1.61 million tons per year in the world. World sugar production by sugar beet has shown declining trend of 0.24 million tons per year. Roughly 20% of world sugar produced comes from sugar beet only. But, the sugar beet yield had positive linear growth with increase of 1.46 tons/hectare per year. Production does not exactly follow the same pattern as the drop in sugar beet area has been mitigated by a significant increase in yields. In recent years, world sugar beet harvested area has shown increasing trend. Among sugar beet and sugarcane, sugar beet accounts for only 16–20% area of the world where as production accounts for only 11–13% of the world. During 2011, sugar beet had 5.06 million hectare area, 272 million tons of production with yield of 53.66 in world. The sugar reforms of the European Union Common Market Organization were adopted in 2006. The reforms cover a transitional period from 2006–2007 to 2009–2010 after that the impact has shown the results. The sugar beet area in EU countries has increased from 1,546 thousand hectare to 1602 thousand hectare in recent years, during 2009–2010 to 2011–2012. One of the main goals of the reforms is to reduce sugar quota production by 6 million tons, white value, through voluntary quota reductions and through lower intervention prices. So far, in-quota sugar production has decreased by 5.8 million tons. Although duty-free access to EU markets by least developed countries began in October 2009 under Everything-But-Arms, non-preferential countries continue to face prohibitive import duties on sugar. Common Agricultural Policy of European Union (CAP) reforms continue in the EU. The sugar reforms of the EU Common Market Organization, which were adopted in 2006, were successful in reducing sugar quota production through voluntary quota reductions and lower intervention prices. To date, in-quota sugar production has decreased by 5.8 million tons (white value) just under the 6 million tons target. The EU's Renewable Energy Directive has a goal of 20% share for renewable energy in total energy consumption. In Russia (highest sugar beet producing country) also, area under sugar beet increased from 900 thousand hectares in 2009–2010 to 1190 thousand hectares in 2011–2012. In EU, sugar beet is financially more attractive than cereal, oilseed and protein (COP) crops both in terms of gross margin as well as margin over total input per hectare (before and after subsidies). In contrast with COP production, where the positive margins depend on the presence of subsidies, the greatest profitability of sugar beet depends on a system of relatively high prices (Annon., 2003).

From Agricultural Outlook 2009–2018 (Annon., 2009), the EU could emerge as the leading global sugar importer, on account of sectoral reform that has led to a huge structural contraction in sugar production and sugar beet cultivation. The majority of sugar inflows to the EU will be sourced under preferential import arrangements with the African, Caribbean and Pacific (ACP) countries in the context of new Economic Partnership Agreements (EPAs) and with Least Developed Countries (LDCs) under the Everything-But-Arms initiative, but uncertainty prevails regarding export capacity and incentives in many of these countries.

Sugar Beet: A Supplement to Sugarcane in Nontraditional Areas to Meet Future Sugar Demand

In India, sugarcane is main crop grown for processing of sugar. However, an alternative crop of sugar beet has an important role in decreasing the production cost, reducing crop period and arresting decline in factor productivity as well as sustaining crop productivity at higher level under abiotic stresses viz., water and salt stresses. In India, approximately 7 million hectare area is under saline and alkali range. Productivity in these soils are very low as compared to normal soils. Sugar beet has better alternative to bring prosperity in for these areas.

Climatic endowments, soil and water resources are the key factors for high productivity in indo-gangetic plain region. Intensified agriculture coupled with indiscriminate use of irrigation water and heavy application of fertilizers and/or plant protection chemicals to achieve maximum in production in irrigated areas has, however, led to various kinds of physical and chemical degradation of the soil. Besides, emergence of multinutrient deficiencies, the problems of soil salinity, alkalinity and waterlogging also got accentuated. These are termed as 2nd generation problems or ill-effects of green revolution. To sustain continuity of green revolution, one has to tackle these 2nd generation problems amicably. This calls for integration of technologies for conservation and management of resources *vis-a-vis* input use efficiencies while safeguarding the soil health and sustaining the productivity.

At the current level of cultivated area under sugarcane, i.e. at about 5 million hectare to meet the sugar demand of country by 2030 which is estimated at about 44.1 million tons (30 kg/capita/year and estimated population 1,470 million (Table 2.5). India would require to produce about 683.72 million tons of cane considering 10.75% sugar recovery and 60% cane drawl for crushing in 488 sugar mills. This quantity of sugarcane in future could be made available by increasing the sugarcane productivity from 62 tons/hectare to 136.7 tons/hectare (Table 2.6). Thus, our first objective should be to increase crop and land productivity particularly in subtropical region.

Table 2.5: Growing population and estimated sugar consumption in India

Year	*Population in millions*	*Sugar consumption (million tons)*		
		20 kg per capita	*30 kg per capita*	*40 kg per capita*
2010	1180	23.6	35.4	47.2
2030	1470	29.4	44.10	58.82
2050	1757	35.14	52.71	70.28

Table 2.6: Estimated growing demand of sugarcane and sugar in India by 2030

S. No.	*Item*	*Sugar consumption levels (in kg per capita per year)*		
		20	*30*	*40*
1.	Estimated population (millions)	1470	1470	1470
2.	Total sugar demand (million tons)	29.4	44.1	58.8
3.	Sugar recovery (%)	10.75	10.75	10.75
4.	Drawl of cane in sugar mill (%)	60	60	60
5.	Sugarcane required for crushing (million tons)	273.48	410.23	546.96
6.	Total sugarcane production required (million tons)	455.8	683.72	911.6
7.	Sugarcane productivity for self-sufficiency (tons/hectare)	91.16	136.7	182.3

Sugar beet performs well in clayey loam, loam or sandy-loam soils displaying neutral to slightly alkaline reaction with regard to growth and high sugar accumulation. Soils having pH 7.0–8.5 are most favorable for sugar beet crop. However, it can be grown on salt affected soils having pH range (8.0–9.6). In the Deccan tracts of Maharashtra, Karnataka, Andhra Pradesh and Tamil Nadu; sugar beet can be grown on black cotton soils. Sugar beet requires fairly cool climate, good rainfall or irrigation and bright sunshine during its growth period. Under temperate and subtropical climatic conditions, the optimum temperature for seed germination is 15–20°C and for growth and sugar accumulation is 20–25°C. The optimum temperature for germination of tropical sugar beet is 25°C and for growth and sugar accumulation is 250–35°C.

Genotypes of sugar beet are being tested for their adaptability under different agroclimatic locations. Some of the following important genotypes have been tested and grown successfully in tropical and subtropical agro-climatic regions of the country. These are HI006, Dorotea (Cauvery), Posada (Indus), IISR Comp-1 (Shubra), LS-6, R-06, etc. To obtain optimum plant population of 100,000/hectare, multigerm seed is required 10.0 kg/hectare whereas, monogerm 120,000 seeds are required for sowing in one hectare area. Field trials have indicated that a row spacing of 50 cm and intra row spacing of 20 cm gave the highest root yield of sugar beet. This spacing provided about 100,000 plants or roots/hectare. Therefore, 50 × 20 cm spacing has been found to be the best throughout India. Autumn sowing (October) was the best for obtaining higher root yield. Trials conducted to evaluate proper sowing season for sugar beet in Maharashtra have revealed that winter season (October–November) crop yielded higher than summer (January–February) and rainy season (June–July). Delay in sowing beyond October usually reduces root yields. This indicated that October month proved to be the most suitable for sowing of sugar beet.

Sugar beet responds well to fertilizers (NPK) and manures. Soils deficient in potash and boron also respond positively to these nutrients. Sugar beet requires about 100–120 kg N/hectare and 60 kg P_2O_5/hectare. Organic manures do have their favorable effect on sugar beet growth. Thus, it is desirable to apply 10–15 tons farm yard manure (FYM)/hectare before sowing, Green manuring in lieu of FYM can be taken. Nitrogen should be applied 120 kg/hectare. In loam and clayey loam soils, 40 kg N should be applied at the time of sowing as a basal dose, 40 kg N after one month of sowing and the remaining 40 kg N after 2 months of sowing. Late application of nitrogen delays crop maturity. Experiments on nitrogen doses have indicated that sugar beet responds up to 240 kg N/hectare but sucrose content in roots decreases. This suggests that application of 120 kg N/hectare is the optimum dose to harvest higher root and sugar yield. Under integrated nutrient management practice, recommended doses of NPK (120:60:60 kg/hectare) along with FYM 10.0 tons/hectare produced the highest root yields at various centers in India. For crop establishment, first irrigation is crucial because of sensitivity of seed to water. Therefore, first irrigation should be given in such a way that water should not flow over the ridges. Depending on the soil type and rainfall, irrigation scheduling is required. For convenient scheduling of irrigation to the crop, cumulative pan evaporation (CPE) method has been employed on research farms. Irrigation scheduled at 75 and 50 mm evaporation produced the highest yield of sugar beet. Under this scheduling, 10–12 irrigations are required to grow a luxuriant crop of sugar beet.

October sown crop of sugar beet starts showing signs of maturity by mid–April. Two conspicuous changes occur in the crop: (i) drying of lower leaves and (ii) sugar accumulation (15–16%) in roots and this continues till the end of May. But, by the first week of June, deterioration in juice quality starts. Irrigation should be stopped at least 3–4 weeks before the day of harvesting/lifting. However, if the soil gets too dry and hard for the harvest operation, it is, however necessary to arrange small flush irrigation for softening the soil to facilitate lifting of roots. Running of a country plough close to the rows helps in lifting roots because of loosening of soil. The roots should be detopped just below the crown portion because in this portion, sucrose content is almost negligible. If this portion is not cut, the chances of increasing impurities increase. After the harvest, unwashed roots should be transported immediately to the factory for processing. Delay at the harvest site favors microbial decomposition of roots.

Thus, if sugar beet crop is promoted by policy makers, industrialist and farmers, it has wide scope in shaping rural economy in India.

Sugar Beet a Potential New Crop for Sugar and Ethanol Production in India

Tropical sugar beet is yet to be produced in commercial scale in India and it is still considered to be toddling baby in the ethanol industry. Although few industries are claiming to be using sugar beet as feedstock for ethanol production, its growth has not reached the level expected. JK Agri-Genetics Ltd., leading seed-company of India and KWS, Germany, world leader in sugar beet breeding joined hands (JK-KWS) to introduce real tropical sugar beet hybrids to India. Nation-wide trials from 16 locations, since 3 years across India (Tables 2.7 and 2.8 give important locations list) has given some interesting insights in the sugar beet production and processing. The sugar beet growing was found to be profitable compared to the existing cropping systems in the post rainy season in Rajasthan, Punjab, Haryana, Maharashtra and North Karnataka. Farmers are willing to experiment new crop

Table 2.7: List of different industrial collaborators for sugar beet crop development in India from 2009 onward

S. No.	*Organization*	*Location*	*State*
1	Crystal Energy and Foods Ltd.	Kalanur	Punjab
2	Mohan Meakings and Breweries	Abohar	Punjab
4	Excel Crop Care Ltd.	Bhuj	Gujarat
5	Tata Chemicals Ltd.	Aurangabad	Maharashtra
6	Ugar Sugars Ltd.	Ugar	Karnataka
7	Somaiya Organics Pvt. Ltd.	Sakarwadi	Maharashtra
8	Crest Biotech Pvt. Ltd.	New Delhi	New Delhi
9	Purti Sugars Ltd.	Nagpur	Maharashtra
10	Shree Renuka Sugars Ltd.	Athani, Belgaon	Karnataka
11	Somaiya Sugars Ltd.	Sameerwadi	Karnataka

Table 2.8: List of different adaptive trials locations for sugar beet crop development in India from 2009 onward

S. No.	*Organization*	*Location*	*State*
1	Vasantdada Sugar Institute	Manjari	Maharashtra
2	Indian Institute of Sugarcane Research	Lucknow	Uttar Pradesh
3	Rajasthan Agriculture University	Sri Gagnganagar	Rajasthan
4	ARS, MPKV Maharasthra	Kasbe Digras	Maharashtra
5	Pune R and D Centre (JKAL)	Vadagaon	Maharashtra
6	Sriganganagar R and D Centre	Sadhuwali	Rajasthan
7	JK Sugars	Bareilly	Uttar Pradesh
8	JK Laxmi Cement	Sirohi	Rajasthan
9	MPUAT	Udaipur	Rajasthan
10	Chemtrol Engineering Ltd.	Belgaum	Karnataka

options looking to the profitability of the crop especially in sugarcane growing areas and saline affected areas of south Maharashtra. Sugar beet can be profitably produced in highly saline conditions or saline water irrigations as found from the experiments in Kutch area of Gujarat and Kolhapur area of Maharashtra. Growing salinity in the sugarcane areas warrants use of sugar beet as alternate crop for ethanol or sugar production. Widened cultivation window, storage experiments (indicated possibility of storing beet for 3 months) and storage possibilities of thick juice provide good scope for the enhancement of factory running period up to 10 months. JK-KWS is introducing new hybrids for India that too for wide range of sowing dates including that of August and December/January as sowings in September–November has been found to be high yielding.

Trials were aimed in identifying high yielding hybrids in different agro climatic zones, including tolerance to sclerotium, rhizoctonia, spodoptera and nematodes. The salient observations and hybrids identified for different biotic stress has been briefed below

Sclerotium: Hybrids namely 4AEO754, 7KO1, Calixta and Mangnolia showed tolerance to Sclerotium in different trials in India. In commercial farmer fields at Maharashtra and Karnataka states of India, Calixta and Mangnolia also showed tolerance to Sclerotium.

Root knot nematodes: At Pune location, 7 hybrids (Sandrina, Calixta, Mangnolia, 7KO1, 4AEO754, 8K09, 8R81) were tested for root knot nematode screening in Sick plot (400 sq m area) during August 2009. In this field, previous crop was taken tomato to create a sick plot.

In sick plot trial, very high infection of root knot was found in all the hybrids except 7KO1 and 4AEO754. Among all the hybrids, only 7KO1 and 4AEO754 hybrids survived in this trial.

At Jaipur location, screening was done in natural condition with 12 hybrids namely 4AE0754, 6GS1086, 6K73, 7K01, 8K09, 8R81, Arriba, Calixta, Capitana, Esperanza, Mangolia, and Sandrina. In natural conditions, 4AEO754, 7KO1, 8R81 and Calixta hybrids, also showed tolerance to root knot nematodes at Jaipur, Rajasthan location. Based on the two locations data, 7KO1 and 4AEO754 are found to be highly tolerant and 8R81 and Calixta to be evaluated for one more year.

Powdery mildew: Sandrina, Esperanza, Calixta showed tolerance to Powdery mildew in different trials conducted in India.

Cercospora: Hybrids namely, 4AEO754, 7KO1 and 6K73 showed tolerance to *Cercospora* infection in different trials.

Spodoptera: Among all the hybrids Clixta, Magnolia and Sandrina exhibited tolerance to leaf eating caterpillar.

High yielding hybrids with multiple tolerance level to different diseases have been identified for commercial cultivations. All the hybrids identified their important characters have been listed at the end of this article.

Srignaganagar in North and Jalgaon, Pune/Dharwad in South and West India have been identified for production of good quality beets with 90–100 tons/hectare yield and 16–24% of Brix reading (Fig. 2.1). These locations attract immediate possibilities for investments for economical ethanol and sugar production. Economics worked out with Rs 2,000 (USD 40/ton) per ton of sugar beet has been considered to be profitable to the farmers. Irrigation requirements ranged from 5–8 based on the soil conditions for the crop of 150 days. Higher yields in sugar beet depend on the plant population, which should be ideally 100,000/hectare and this can be achieved by very good land preparation at the planting time. Beet size of 1.0–2.0 kg have been found to have good sugar content and with increased size the sugar content tends to lower down.

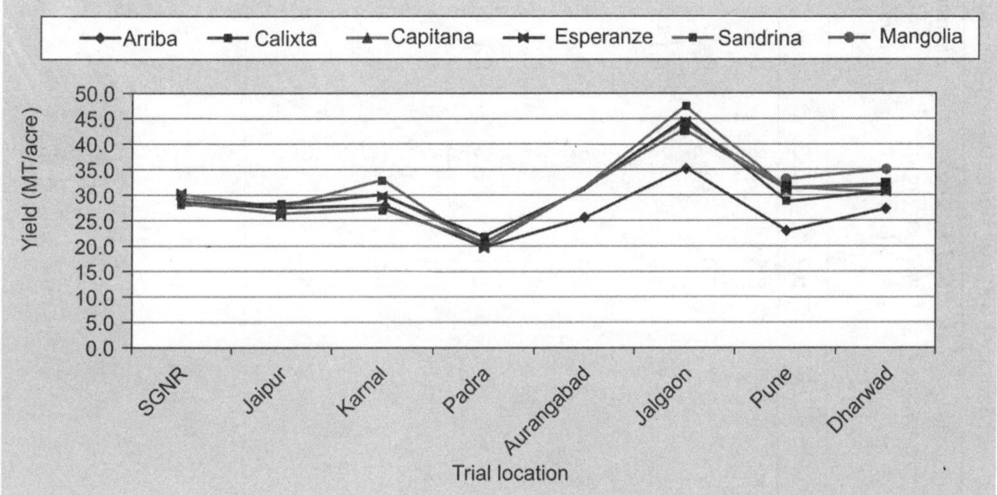

Fig. 2.1: Average yield of sugar beet JK KWS hybrids at different locations of India 2007–2011

Sugar beets are also highly suited for saline conditions; they produce highest usable biomass than any other crop in medium to highly saline conditions. Both Magnolia and Calixta were found to be highly adapted to the saline conditions (Table 2.3). Initial indications are that cultivation of sugar beet in the long run in saline condition might help in significantly improves the soil health in saline conditions.

JK Agri Genetics and KWS are working together with Sri Renuka Sugars in Karnataka and Maharashtra for commercial cultivation of the Sugar beet. Magnolia and Calixta have been introduced in the target area successfully. Crop care extension has been found to be very essential factor in improving the crop yield. Yield ranging from 16 tons to 28 tons per acre were observed in the project area. Farmers have been very happy and likely to increase the area for Sugar beet cultivation in Karnataka and Maharashtra (Table 2.9).

Large scale demonstrations were made with Somaya Sugars in Smeerwadi Karnataka, which were also found to be highly profitable. Commercialization possibility in these areas is high. We envisage very good growth will come from this area in another 2–3 years. Technology for mechanical harvesting will substantially improve the prospects of this crop in India.

The support from the government for the speedy introduction of sugar beet is essential as there is requirement of huge investment on machinery for processing, which can be exempted from the taxes and can be partly subsidized with low interest loans. There is huge scarcity of manpower for the technology transfer of the sugar

Table 2.9: Soil improvement data after sugar beet growing farmers of Maharashtra and Karnataka state season 2011–2012

Beet grower name	*Village*	*District*	*Variety grown*	*Soil testing before sowing*		*Soil testing after sugar beet harvest*		*Change in pH and EC (m mol/L) after beet crop grown*		*Beet root yield*
			JK Seeds	*pH*	*EC*	*pH*	*EC*	*pH*	*EC*	*MT/Ac*
Aryant Birnale	Mouje Digraj	Sangali	Magnolia	8.6	5.2	8.5	3.8	0.1	1.4	19.5
Murgapp Budani	Sankaretti	Belgaum	Magnolia	7.9	2.7	7.9	2.2	0	0.5	19.1
Bramhkumar Madhabavi	Darur	Belgaum	Magnolia	8.5	3.8	8.4	1.2	0.1	2.6	13.0
Kalappa Yeladgi	Shegunsi	Belgaum	Magnolia	8.5	2.7	8.5	1.2	0	1.5	13.4
Narsappa Terdal	Hulugbal	Belgaum	Calixta	8.4	4.8	8.2	4.5	0.2	0.3	10.7
Raju Terdal	Hulugbal	Belgaum	Calixta	8.5	3.7	8.4	3.3	0.1	0.4	11.2
Seetal Math	Terdal	Bagalkot	Magnolia	8.4	5.6	8.4	4.5	0	1.1	19.1
Basavprabhu Telginmani	Terdal	Bagalkot	Magnolia	8.6	3.7	8.6	2	0	1.7	18.0
Hanmanth Imanavar	Ingalgi	Bagalkot	Calixta	8.6	1.3	8.6	1.2	0	0.1	14.9

beet cultivation in India, which might require the participation of seed companies, industries and government development departments. As an incentive to promote the new crop introduction in India, an initial subsidy in crop production will help to speed up the crop introduction. This subsidy will help farmers to take initial risk of opting to grow the crop. Sugar beet hybrids seed production technology is yet be seen India, currently we are producing seed in Europe and bringing in India, this attracts more than 18% custom duty, which should be exempted to speed up the process of introduction. More machines of diverse nature to be introduced to ease harvesting process, and such machines import should also be facilitated with least customs duty. Considering fluctuation of sugarcane production and international molasses prices and sugar beet can be a profitable alternative crop for the ethanol industry. Sugar beet produces more quantity of ethanol/sugar with half time land required, half the number of irrigations, lesser nitrogen compared to sugarcane indicating the crop contributes food/water/fertilizer security of the country.

JK Agri-Genetics Ltd, Hyderabad and KWS Germany introduces following hybrids for cultivation in different agroclimatic zones of India.

Arriba

- Very high levels tolerance to rhizoctonia
- Tolerance to foliage feeders due to thick lamina
- Adaptability: North India

Calixta

- Very high levels tolerance to rhizoctonia
- Medium to high level of tolerance to powdery mildew
- Tolerance to foliage feeders
- Excellent variety for saline soil cultivation
- Adaptability: North India, South and South West India
- High yielding

Magnolia

- Very high levels tolerance to rhizoctonia
- High level of tolerance to powdery mildew
- Tolerance to foliage feeders
- Tolerance to sclerotium root rot and cercospora leaf spot
- Comparatively requires less irrigation or sustains water stress, harvest friendly
- Adaptability: North, South and South West India

Sandrina

- Very high levels tolerance to rhizoctonia
- Tolerance to powdery mildew
- Tolerance to foliage feeders
- Tolerance to sclerotium root rot and cercospora leaf spot
- Adaptability: North India

Esperanza

- Very high levels tolerance to rhizoctonia
- Tolerance to powdery mildew
- Adaptability: North India

7KO1

- Very high levels tolerance to rhizoctonia
- High level of tolerance to powdery mildew
- Tolerance to foliage feeders
- Tolerance to sclerotium root rot and cercospora leaf spot
- Adaptability: North , South and South West India
- Very high yielding.

SUGAR BEET CULTIVATION IN INDIA

This working paper is a part of the project on "economic and management aspects of sugar production from sugar beet" sponsored by the Ministry of Agriculture, Government of India, to the Indian Institute of Management, Ahmedabad. The scope of this paper is restricted to cultivation of sugar beet. After giving a brief account of achievements in sugar beet cultivation in Sri Ganganagar, we have presented a depth study of 49 cultivators (growers, dropouts and nonadopters). The various aspects covered include awareness, adoption and diffusion of sugar beet cultivation among the sample farmers, actual and recommended cultivation practices, and cultivators' experience in beet cultivation, comparative profitability of beet and other crops, and implications for its spread in North India. The study highlighted various issues related to the adoption and spread of beet cultivation and identified certain constraints. The comparative economics of bet has established its superiority over other important crops of the area. Its adoption in other areas, however, would depend on the nature of incentives and infrastructural arrangements for easy and quick disposal.

Sugar beet is an important root crop primarily cultivated in temperate countries. It became a key source of sugar in the 19th century when methods of sugar extraction from sugar beet were invented and became popular. The sugar beet roots contents 16–21% sucrose vary depending on the cultivar and climatic conditions. The sugar recovery from sugar beet used to be 3–4% higher as compare to sugarcane. The world's sugar beet production during 2011 was nearly 272 million tons with average productivity of 58.2 tons/hectare. The Russia was the largest producer of sugar beet with the annual production of 47.6 million tons followed by France, USA, Germany and Turkey in 2011–2012. The global sugar production was 174 million tons and sugar beet contributes nearly 20% of total sugar production and 10% biofuel in the form of ethanol production.

Sugar beet is a temperate crop and is mainly cultivated in cold countries where sugarcane cultivation is not feasible. Out of the total sugar production in the world, 27% sugar is produced from sugar beet. Some countries in subtropics also have taken up sugar beet cultivation. In India, growing of sugar beet was tried at Indian Institute of Sugarcane Research (IISR), Lucknow and at Padegaon in (MS) in 1960s. In 1970, the work was initiated under All India Co-ordinated Research Project (AICRP) on sugar beet. On the basis of agronomic trials conducted at various locations in India, the sugar beet cultivation was taken up in Sriganganagar area of Rajasthan for sugar production and in Sundarban area of West Bengal for alcohol production.

Sugar beet root contains 16–19% sucrose and in the process of sugar extraction, 12–14% recovery is obtained. The crop remains in the field only for 5–6 months.

Sugar beet being a salt tolerant crop can also be grown in saline soils where other crops fail to grow. Sugar beet is not only the source of sugar, but also provides several by-products like ethanol, cattle feed and B_{10}. Molasses can be used in pharmaceutical industry for vitamin B_{12}. In spite of above advantages, the sugar beet cultivation was stopped and sugar beet processing factory at Sriganganagar was closed.

Until recent past sugar beet was famous as a salad crop for table purposes in India, but it is now in semi-commercial testing in subtropical parts of the country. In Kashmir valley, sugar beet is grown as a spring season crop. A beginning of commercial cultivation of sugar beet has now been made in Sriganganagar area in Rajasthan, Phaltan in Maharashtra and Tarai in Uttarakhand.

Leading sugar refiner Shree Renuka Sugars aims to increase the processing of sugar beet, which is used in alcohol making, to 50,000 tons in the 2013–2014 marketing year starting September, from the existing 10,000 tons.

This is for the first time in India that sugar beet is being processed for use in alcohol making and farmers have benefited with additional revenue, Shree Renuka Sugars Executive Chairperson. We have successfully processed 10,000 tons of sugar beet on a trial basis this year. We will increase it to 50,000 tons next year and later to 200,000 tons. The sugar beet plant in Karnataka has a total processing capacity of 3,000 tons per day. The juice processed is directly taken to distillery for alcohol production.

"Farmers are coming forward to grow sugar beet as it gives additional revenue. The company has distillery capacity of 930 KLPD (kilo liters per day) in India. It operates 11 sugar mills globally with a total crushing capacity of 20.7 million tons per annum (MTPA). Shares of the company today closed 1.65% higher at Rs 24.65 on the BSE.

There is one good news to sick sugar units. Syngenta India, a leading agri-business company has introduced tropical sugar beet in the country after tying up with a few sugar cooperatives in Maharashtra. The company's in Maharashtra. The company's experiments of producing sugar and ethanol from sugar beet have been successful. The tropical sugar beet developed by the company gives the same quantity of sugar per unit of land in half the time and with one-third water as sugarcane. The ecofriendly nature of sugar beet is also important as it grows in saline lands.

Processing of Sugar Beet for Sugar Manufacture

Sugar beet, unlike sugarcane, cannot be processed for gur or khandsari, and can only be used for vacuum-pan sugar production. Hence its commercial cultivation is possible only around the processing units. Sugar beet roots deteriorate fast after harvesting and have to be supplied to sugar-mill within 48 hours of harvesting. Stock-piling is not possible even for a few hours and hence a well-coordinated plan of harvesting and supplying of roots is of utmost importance.

Sugar from sugar beet roots is extracted by adopting diffusion process in special diffusers based on the counter-current washing technique. It is not possible to extract juice from sugar beet roots with roller mills. The juice characteristics of sugar beet also necessitate adoption of carbonation process only for clarification, and hence carbonation with diffusers and related accessories is essential to process sugar beet in traditional sugarcane-based sugar mills in the country. Unlike sugarcane, extraneous fuel is also required for processing of sugar beet, as it does not provide bagasse for use as fuel. However, the beet-pulp and molasses produced as by-products from manufacturing of beet sugar have a good market and should be expected to more than offset extra cost on fuel in beet processing. The establishment of a profitable outlet for the by-products is, therefore, an economic necessity with this crop.

Future Needs

Efforts should be made to evolve a production technology for high yield of quality beet. As sugar beet is important for its chemical characteristics, care should be taken that sugar producing ability of the roots is not affected by cultural practices. Being a new crop in our country, it calls for foresight while planning studies leading to plant protection measures. This is important as new disease and pest problems are likely to occur with the spread of beet cultivation in the country.

The availability of efficient sugar processing technology particularly suited to our indigenous factories is essential for the successful commercial exploitation of sugar beet. Efforts are called for systematic studies resulting in definite information enabling selection of the most ideal diffusers, production of beet molasses of high chemical quality and efficient utilization of the by-products.

Critical studies on the economic aspects, needed to further confirm and preliminary findings regarding the economic viability of the crop in the country and profit ability to farm and industry, would be of great value for beet development in the country.

Future R and D could focus on the following areas:

- Adapting sugar beet to saline-alkaline soil conditions.
- Finding alternative uses of sugar beet such as jaggery, jam, etc.
- Promoting sugar beet for cattle feed.
- Technology and economics of sugar beet for ethanol production.
- Mechanization of sugar beet cultivation, particularly harvesting.
- Integrating sugar beet cultivation in the present cropping systems.
- Government policies and incentives for sugar beet industry.

Sugar Beet in Punjab

In a first for India, 10,000 farmers in Punjab are experimenting with sugar beet over 10,000 acres spread across three districts; harvest of hope for a sugarcane substitute is due in March.

Punjab is on the road to producing sugar in a new way. For the first time in the state, 10,000 acres of land have been earmarked for the cultivation of sugar beet, a crop that produces over a fifth of the world's sugar, but whose cultivation is concentrated almost entirely in Europe, the US and China.

The crop has been sown over 5,000 acres, and the area under cultivation is likely to double in the next couple of weeks. Around 10,000 farmers of Amritsar, Kapurthala and Jalandhar districts are involved in this large experiment, success for which has been predicted to hold enormous promise including that of a new "sugar revolution".

The trial is being carried out by the private Rana Sugars Ltd, based in Buttar Seviyan village, 48 km from Amritsar, with cooperation from Punjab's Agriculture and Cane Departments, Punjab Agricultural University, Ludhiana, and a Europe-based company.

Rana Gurjit Singh, Congress MLA from Kapurthala and owner of the mill, said, "we hope to bring around 12,000 acres under sugar beet this year. The mill had signed an agreement with Belgium-based SESVanderHave, the global market leader in sugar beet seeds business, for the purchase of seeds for 3 years. To encourage farmers to get out of the circle of only wheat, the mill has provided a 100% subsidy on seeds, amounting Rs 3,500 per acre. Planting and harvesting will be done by specially designed machines".

Amrik Singh, general manager of the mill, said, "we have sown sugar beet over 5,000 acres. We started sowing in mid-October in Amritsar, Kapurthala and Jalandhar districts, and an equal area will be covered by mid-December. This is a 5-month crop and we will start getting the harvest by March, and it will continue till May-end".

According to Punjab cane commissioner, the 5-month crop will be a good replacement for wheat with farmers able to earn around Rs 10,000 more per acre. "The mill offers assured buyback under a contract farming agreement on a committed price".

Jagtar Singh Brar of Mehma Sarja village in Bathinda district is one of the farmers to take up sugar beet cultivation. "I cultivated sugar beet for three years on one hectare. A company called Syngenta had supplied seeds and provided the required expertise. For 3 years, my average yield was 520 quintals per acre, which was the second highest among all nations where trials were conducted by Syngenta. The sugar extraction from my crop was the highest in the world and a certificate was awarded to me by the company. I think this crop will be successful in Punjab", he said, adding that the crop has a 3–5% higher sugar content compared to sugarcane.

The Agricultural Technology Development Agency is helping around 25 farmers start plantation on 25 demonstration plots, dedicating one acre in each block of the district. Experts said that apart from extracting sugar, the leaves of sugar beet are useful as fodder and its pulp can be used to make ethanol. The university has conducted research on sugar beet and the region's climate is found suitable for its cultivation.

ELECTRICITY FROM SUGAR

Many are not well-versed in sugar making, but the people know how to make electricity from the bagasse produced in the mill. The waste is burnt to superheat water to 515°C to produce high pressure steam. The steam is then sent to a turbo-generator: remember the contraption in the room. It rotates the generator blades, thereby producing electric current. Producing two forms of energy, electricity and heat, is called cogeneration. In the past 6–7 years, it has become the buzzword in the sugar sector. Today, 107 of the 650-odd sugar mills in the country have cogeneration plants, according to the Indian Sugar Mills Association. Most of these plants are in five sugarcane-growing states, UP, Andhra Pradesh, Maharashtra, Tamil Nadu and Karnataka. Together they are producing nearly 2,000 mw power, enough to meet the requirements of a business center as big as Gurgaon. Their maximum capacity is 2,249 mw, according to the Indian Sugar Mills Association.

For every ton of sugarcane crushed, mills get 300–350 kg of bagasse. It keeps mills afloat when sugar prices dip (see: *Sugar cycle*). The sugar business is essentially cyclical. Market sentiments change in tandem with the demand-supply equilibrium, leading to a volatile product pricing. Cogeneration and ethanol represent the much-desired byproducts providing value addition and helping soften the inimical impact of sugar cycles.

Dhampur Sugar Mills, which has the largest cogeneration capacity in the country, sold about 177 million units (1,000 units =1 mw) to Uttar Pradesh in 2007–2008. Cogeneration contributed nearly Rs 42 crore to its operating profit that year against about Rs 11 crore from sugar units. For the quarter ending March 31, 2009, EID Parry, a sugar maker in Tamil Nadu, made a profit of Rs 56.22 crore. Its cogeneration facility contributed about Rs 16.72 crore or 30% to it. The profit a company shows through cogeneration depends on the price at which its sugar unit sells bagasse to the power unit.

Big Potential

Cogeneration is happening in other sectors as well, albeit to a limited extent. A paper maker in Pallipalayam, a town in Erode district of Tamil Nadu, has increased its productivity as well as decreased its dependence on erratic power supply from the grid. Seshasayee Paper and Board is generating electricity in two of its factories. Poni Sugars, Seshasayee's sister concern located close to the paper mill, supplies bagasse. The bagasse and wood are converted into pulp for making paper. Unlike sugar mills, one of the plants uses the waste from the pulp-making process called black liquor for producing electricity.

The second cogeneration unit setup in 2005 uses a cleaner variety of coal called envirocoal, sugarcane pith and coconut shell. Together the plants have a capacity of 36.4 mw and take care of 95% of the power requirement of the paper factory. In 2004–2005, the company spent Rs 76 crore on buying and producing power. In 2007–2008, its spending came down to Rs 55 crore. Cogeneration has also provided flexibility in the company's expansion plans. "From the grid the paper plant gets only power. It still needs to setup a boiler for steam for making paper. If it can get both electricity and steam from a single source, it is economical. India has the potential of producing 7,500 mw through cogeneration in 10 industrial sectors, said a 2008 study of the International Energy Agency. Sugar is the sweetest bet because it can produce 5,100 mw of power—69% of the total cogeneration basket. If the resources and technology are cranked up to optimal levels the country can produce 10,000 mw, the study says. This is 40% of India's power deficit in 2008.

The technology for high pressure boilers was available in India. What was needed was redesigning the boilers so that bagasse could be fired inside them instead of coal.

Till the mid-90s most sugar mills used a generation system called back pressure turbines. These turbines were fitted on low pressure boilers. The steam would be sent for sugar processing and then for electricity generation; it was not condensed and recycled. The electricity produced would just about meet the captive requirement of the mills.

Around 2000 boilers producing steam at the pressure of 67 atmosphere came into play. They popularized a more efficient system called extraction and condensing turbines. It could save enough bagasse for the non-crushing crushing season. Unlike the previous technology, the new turbines took steam for sugar processing from the middle, not rear, of the turbine. A part of the steam was cooled and sent back to the boiler for reuse. With this technology one could adjust heat and power generation according to the requirement. Cogeneration plants with higher pressure (87 bar) boilers are now using an advanced version called double extraction-cum-condensing turbines. These turbines work with superheated steam (500°C). The boiler gives more flexibility in moderating heating and power requirements, and gives more electricity per tons of bagasse.

SUGAR PALM TREE: A VERSATILE PLANT

The sugar palm tree is a member of the *Palmae* family and naturally a forest species. It belongs to the subfamily *Arecoideae* and tribe *Caryoteae* Hyene reported that sugar palm has around 150 local names, indicating its multiple uses by the villagers. These names include *Arenga pinnata*, Areng palm, black fiber palm, gomuti palm, aren, irok, bagot, and kaong. In Malaysia, it is known as either *enau* or *kabung*. The sugar palm plant was originally from Assam, India, and Burma in the Indian subcontinent. It originates from an area covering South-East Asia up to Irian Jaya in the east of Indonesia. The sugar palm tree is available across the nation of Malaysia, Indonesia, and other South-East Asian countries. Its is one of the most diverse multipurpose tree species in culture.

There are several taxonomic names for sugar palm, such as *Saguerus rumphii*, *Arenga saccharifera Labill*, etc. However, in 1917, Merill, through the International Congress of Botany in Vienna, officially renamed it *Arenga pinnata*. Palms are among the oldest flowering plants in the world. For centuries, many palm species have been tapped throughout the tropical world in order to produce fresh juice (sweet toddy), fermented drinks (toddy, wine), syrup (honey), brown sugar (jaggery), and refined sugar. Redhead reported that the sugar palm tree was the first source of sugar, fresh juice, fermented drinks, and syrup. The fibers have been collected from the sugar palm tree since 1416 during the Malacca Sultanate, with several names such as aren, gomuti, and black palm fiber, and locally it is known as the ijuk fiber. The British East India Company in Penang started to plant the sugar palm tree to produce fibers owing to its high durability.

The sugar palm tree can be found at altitudes ranging from sea level up to 1,400 m a.s.l. However, Johnson stated that the sugar palm tree could grow at 1,200–1,500 m a.s.l. and in areas where the rainfall was 500–1,200 cm^3. The sugar palm tree grows in the more humid parts of the Asian tropics. Plantations are found from South Asia to South-East Asia and from Taiwan to the Philippines, Indonesia, Papua New Guniea, India, North Australia, Malaysia, Thailand, Myanmar and Vietnam.

In Malaysia, sugar palm trees can be found widely along the rivers in the rural areas of Bruas-Parit (Perak), Raub (Pahang), Jasin (Melaka), and Kuala Pilah (N. Sembilan). Generally, it can be seen throughout Malaysia, as this species grows wild in many places. In Tawau (Sabah), there are around 809 hectare of sugar palm plantation planted by Kebun Rimau Sdn Bhd; and at Benta (Pahang), there are 50 hectare of sugar palm tree plantation. However, the plantation area of this species is smaller compared with that of other palm species, such as oil palm and coconut palm, as in Table 2.10.

Table 2.10: Plantation areas of the palm family

Plantation	*Hectares*
Oil palm	1,359,691
Coconut	182,776
Sugar palm	892[a]
Sago	647
Pinang	445
Salak	41

[a]Sahari.

Applications of the Sugar Palm Tree

Among the plants of the tropics, it is difficult to find a family of plants that can produce more useful service to people than the sugar palm tree. Therefore, this family has been identified as the most versatile plant owing to its many applications such as *neera* sugar, fruits, fibers, etc.

Primary Applications

Neera Sugar

More than 3,000 palm species of the tropics and subtropics can be classified as multipurpose trees, and the sugar palm tree is considered to be one of the most diverse multipurpose tree species in culture. This is because almost all parts of the tree can be used for many important products, and it plays an important economic role for the people of rural areas. Haris also reported that the sugar palm tree can be used in various applications in the Philippines.

One of the most important products of the sugar palm tree is palm sugar, locally known as neera sugar. It is sweet and brown in color. Neera sugar is normally used as a food sweetener in traditional food. Palm sugar can be consumed freshly, or it can be allowed to ferment for a while to become palm wine. It has been reported that sugar palm was the prime source of sugar, fermented drinks and syrup.

Palm sugar can also be processed to make palm wine, vinegar, and alcohol. In Tawau (Sabah), around 809 hectares of sugar palm plantation has been planted by Kebun Rimau Sdn Bhd to produce Arengga Pinnata syrup, while at Benta (Pahang) there are 50 hectares of sugar palm plantation to produce brown sugar.

Nevertheless, in recent years the use of palm sugar has extended to another level of application—to fermentation with yeast to produce alcoholic beverages. Furthermore, advance fermentation processes can also be employed to produce bioethanol. Bioethanol is used as a raw material for the production of a variety of products such as chemical products, solvents, pharmaceuticals, cosmetics, medicines, and beverages. It can also be used for the production of biofuel as a renewable source of energy, like other bioethanol plant sources. Of more interest is the fact that sugar palm can yield the highest productivity of bioethanol (20,160 lakh hectare/year) compared with other sources such as cassava (4,500 lakh hectare/year), sugarcane (5,025 lakh hectare/year), sago (4,133 lakh hectare/year), and sweet sorghum (6,000 lakh hectare/year). Sugar palm is scattered over almost all Indonesia, with a total area of around 70,000 hectare, and in about 13 provinces in particular: Papua,

Moluccas, North Moluccas, West Sumatra, West Java, Central Java, Banten, North Sulawesi, South Sulawesi, South-East Sulawesi, Bengkulu, Kalimantan, and Nanggroe Aceh Darussalam. The large-scale commercialization of sugar palm plantations, ranging from 800,000 hectare to 4 million hectare, is going to be developed, especially in Indonesia, to make use of this potential of the sugar palm tree.

Fruits

The sugar palm tree also can produce juices from its fruits. The fruits are white in colour and are taken from its fruit bunch. They can also be preserved in heavy syrup into a product called beluluk, which is also canned, and the fruits can be cooked with sugary syrup for desserts.

Secondary Applications

Sugar Palm Fiber (ijuk)

Sugar palm fiber, known locally as ijuk, has been one of the most popular fibers among researchers over the past decade. Ijuk is black in color, and up to 0.50 mm in diameter. According to Siregar, ijuk is heat resistant up to 150°C, and its flash point is around 200°C . It has been reported that *ijuk* fiber is up to 1.19 m in length, with 1.26 kg m^{-3} density. Traditionally, *ijuk* has been used in the manufacture of ropes, filters, broom, and roofing, and in handicraft applications such as for making *kopiah*. Tomlinson reported that ropes made from sugar palm fiber have better performance than ropes made from rattan fiber (*Calamus* sp.). The main advantages of *ijuk* are its durability and good resistance to sea water. It is also unaffected by heat and moisture compared with coir fiber. Unlike other natural fibers, *ijuk* can be obtained from the trees directly without secondary processes to yield the fibers. Therefore, *ijuk* should be a good material in the development of new "green" materials.

The fiber is originally wrapped along the sugar palm trunk. The tree can grow up to 12.3 m tall and has a thick, black/brown, hairy, fibrous trunk, with a dense crown of leaves, which are white on the outside. The tree begins to produce black sugar palm fiber after about 5 years, before flowering, and the type of fiber is dependent upon the age and altitude of the sugar palm tree. The fibers that are taken after flowering will produce fiber approximately 1.4 m long. Each tree can yield about 15 kg, and around 3 kg is the very best and stiffest fiber (unpublished data, 2007). In Malaysia, black sugar palm fiber started to be used in 1,416 during the Malacca Sultanate. In 1800, the sugar palm tree was planted by the British East India Company in Penang to yield high-durability rope made from black sugar palm fiber.

The characterization (tensile and chemical properties) of single fibers from different morphological parts of the sugar palm tree, i.e. the sugar palm frond (SPF), sugar palm bunch (SPB), *ijuk*, and sugar palm trunk (SPT), has been done by Sahari. From the investigation it was found that the tensile strength of *ijuk* was 276.64 MPa, and the tensile modulus was 5.86 GPa, as shown in below Fig. 2.2. The elongation at break of *ijuk* was 22.3%, which was approximately the same as that of oil palm and coir fibers, thus showing similar physical and mechanical properties of members of the same palmae family. For the chemical analysis it was shown that *ijuk* has a high cellulose content of 52.29% (Table 2.11). Thus, the mechanical properties of sugar palm fiber are strongly influenced by the cellulose content. Cellulose was the main structural component, providing strength and stability to the plant cell walls and the fibers. Generally, *ijuk* can be used as reinforcement in composites owing to its higher tensile strength and cellulose content in comparison with other established natural fibers such as kenaf, pineapple leaf, coir and oil palm bunch.

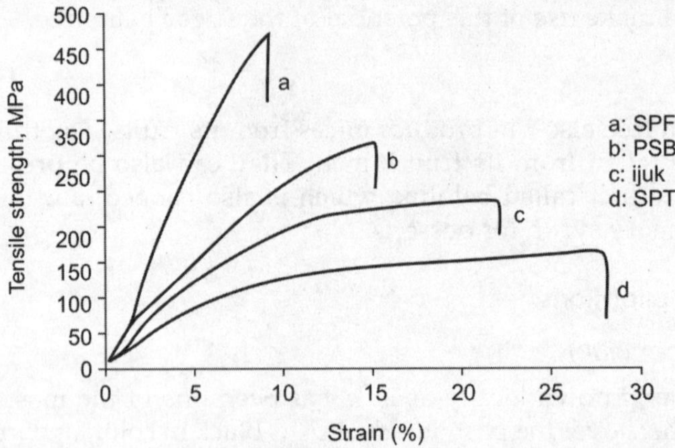

Fig. 2.2: Tensile stress-strain curve of fibers from different morphological parts of the sugar palm tree

Table 2.11: Chemical composition of fibers from different morphological parts of the sugar palm tree

Description (%)	*Sugar palm frond (SPF)*	*Sugar palm bunch (SPB)*	*Ijuk*	*Sugar palm trunk (SPT)*
Moisture	2.74	2.70	7.40	1.45
Extractive	2.46	2.24	4.39	6.30
Holocellulose	81.22	71.78	65.62	61.10
Cellulose	66.49	61.76	52.29	40.56
Lignin	18.89	23.48	31.52	46.44
Ash	3.05	3.38	4.03	2.38

Further characterization of the tensile properties of sugar palm fibers was conducted, and results are shown in Fig. 2.3. The fibers were obtained from different heights of the sugar palm tree and subjected to single fiber tensile testing. The results showed that the fibers obtained from the bottom part demonstrated inferior tensile strength, modulus, elongation at break, and toughness to fibers obtained from the upper part.

It was concluded by Ishak et al that the variation in tensile properties was due to the varying chemical composition of the fiber, which was affected by ageing, especially at the bottom part of the tree. Table 2.12 shows the chemical composition of sugar palm fiber obtained from different heights of the sugar palm tree. It was observed in this study that the cellulose, hemicellulose, and lignin contents increased with increase in tree height. As fibers at 1 m height were near to the ground, they contained a great quantity of impurities such as silica, and their ash content was found to be much higher (30.92%) compared with fibers obtained from the upper parts (5–15 m) where the ash content range was 2.06–5.84%.

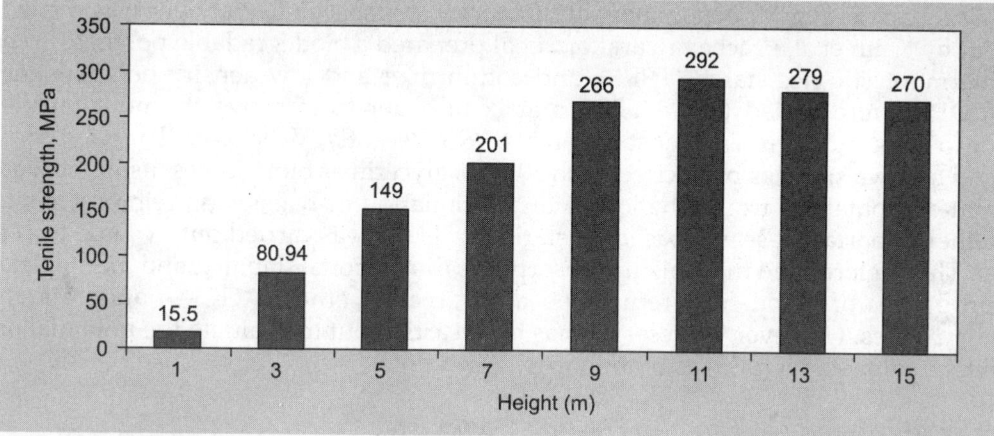

Fig. 2.3: Tensile strength of sugar palm fiber obtained from different heights of the sugar palm tree

Table 2.12: Chemical composition of sugar palm fiber obtained from different heights of the sugar palm tree

Composition (%)	*Height (m)*							
	1	*3*	*5*	*7*	*9*	*11*	*13*	*15*
Cellulose	37.3	49.36	55.28	56.55	56.8	55.75	54.42	53.41
Hemicelluloses	4.71	6.11	7.36	7.68	7.93	7.92	7.89	7.45
Lignin	17.93	18.941	20.89	20.45	23.6	22.96	24.27	24.92
Ash	30.92	14.04	5.8	4.23	2.06	4.09	3.98	4.27
Extractive	2.49	2.019	1.71	1.41	1.35	1.48	1.21	0.85
Moisture content	5.36	8.64	7.92	8.37	8.19	7.72	8.12	8.7

Sugar Palm Starch (SPS)

The sugar palm tree is one of multipurpose trees grown in Malaysia. Besides yielding neera sugar, it also provides a great variety of products such as ropes, filters, brooms, and roof materials (Mogea, 1991). Nowadays, researchers focus more on the production of bioethanol, which can be derived from neera sugar. The inner part of the sugar palm stem contains starch. It has been used as raw material for starch and glue substances. For the production of 1 ton of starch, 10–20 trees are needed, which suggests that one tree can produce 50–100 kg of starch. This accumulated starch is harvested from the trunk of matured palms and can be applied as "green" material. Starch will act as a biopolymer in the presence of a plasticicer such as water, glycerol, and sorbitol at high temperature.

In recent years, owing to the unique behavior of plasticized starch, many researchers have been using it as a biomatrix. Teixeira et al used plasticized cassava starch as a biomatrix, employing either glycerol or a mixture of glycerol/sorbitol (1:1) as the plasticicer, and combined them with cassava bagasse cellulose nanofibrils as reinforcing materials. Development of corn-starch-based "green" composites reinforced with graft copolymers of *Saccharum spontaneum L.* (Ss) fiber was carried out by Kaith et al. Prachayawarakorn et al prepared a biodegradable polymer from thermoplastic rice starch (TPRS), and cotton fiber and low-density polyethylene (LDPE) were added to the TPRS matrix in order to improve the poor tensile properties and high water absorption of TPRS. Recently, Vallejos et al applied corn and cassava starches plasticised with 30 wt% glycerin as biomatrices, using fibrous material obtained from ethanol-water fractionation of bagasse as reinforcement. Other important research based on starch materials was carried out by Duanmu et al. They determined the moisture absorption, dimensional stability, and mechanical properties of wood-fiber-reinforced allyl glycidyl ether (AGE)—potato starch composites. However, no research has been carried out to evaluate the potential of sugar palm starch (SPS) as biopolymer.

Sugar-Palm-Fiber-Reinforced Polymer Composites

Research into natural fiber has become most popular among scientists and technologists in view of environmental concerns. The need for "green" material prompts researchers to seek opportunities to develop new material on the basis of environmentally friendly criteria. This has opened up alternative ways to solving agricultural residue problems. On account of their better mechanical properties, sugar palm fibers are used as reinforcement in concrete and road construction. These fibers which are known as *gomuti* or *gomutu* and are also used as coating material in India.

The utilization of sugar palm fiber progressed one step further with its use as a reinforcing agent in polymer composites. An enormous amount of research is currently being done to study the properties of sugar palm fiber and its composites. Previous research claimed that sugar palm fiber showed promising utilization in many composite applications.

Owing to its good mechanical properties, *ijuk* fiber could be used as reinforcment material in polymer composites. The mechanical properties of *ijuk*-fiber reinforced polymer composites have been studied for cases of chopped, long, and woven *ijuk* fiber using various polymer matrices. According to Sastra et al composites made from woven fiber have much better mechanical properties than chopped and long fibers. Suriani et al studied the interfacial adhesion of *ijuk*-fiber-reinforced epoxy composites, while Leman et al studied the impact properties and water absorption of *ijuk*-reinforced epoxy composites. A small boat has also been fabricated from hybrid-woven-glass/*ijuk*-reinforced unsaturated polyester composites using the lay-up technique.

In order to enhance the interfacial properties of natural fiber composites, surface treatment of natural fibers is needed. Bachtiar et al studied the effects of alkaline treatment of sugar palm fiber on the mechanical properties of sugar-palm-fiber-reinforced epoxy composites. The results verified that the mechanical properties (tensile, flexural and impact) of the composites were improved, particularly the tensile modulus, with the treatment.

Ishak also looked into the potential of sea water treatment for surface modification of woven-sugar-palm-fiber-reinforced unsaturated polyester composites. It was interesting to note that the opposite result was obtained by Leman et al where sea water treatment resulted in a significant reduction in the tensile strength, tensile modulus, elongation at break, flexural modulus, and impact strength of composites.

The effects of impregnation modification via vacuum resin impregnation on the physical and mechanical properties of sugar palm fibers were investigated. From the investigation, the physical properties of impregnated fibers showed significant improvement when the moisture content of the fiber was dropped from 8.19% to 0.75–0.46% for impregnation with phenol formaldehyde (PF), and to 0.87–0.44% for impregnation with unsaturated polyester (UP). Meanwhile, water absorption of impregnated fiber was reduced from 116.82% to 61.64–22.52% for PF and to 63.49–23.31% for UP. It was observed that fiber impregnated with thermoset polymer resin (PF and UP) at an impregnation pressure of 600 mmHg for 5 minutes showed a notable improvement in physical properties, and that PF was superior.

Other Applications

The sugar palm tree also has many traditional applications. For example, the young leaves can be eaten fresh or cooked. However, the harvesting of young leaves will shorten their lifetime. Thus, they are taken only when really needed. The leaves are usually eaten immediately after harvesting to avoid irritation of the mouth area. Their sweet flavor when cooked is like that of young coconut. In Indonesia, young leaves, petiols, and core stems are cooked for soup or fried. Moreover, the young leaves are traditionally used for making cigarette wrappings or consumed as salads. The leaves, similarly to coconut leaves, are used for thatch, for weaving into baskets, for band matting, and for roofing.

The midribs of the leaflets are used for making high-durability brooms and fishing tools. The outer part of the stem consists of wood, which is extremely hard and durable. It can be processed for flooring, furniture, and the hand grips of tools. Its roots are useful for medicine and fishing tools. When it is boiled with water, it can break down stones within the bladder. Palm sap can be used for indigestion, rashes, and pulmonary irritation. In the Philippines, it is used to avoid tuberculosis by the fermentation process.

Conclusion

The use of "green" materials has rapidly evolved owing to health and environmental issues and the shortage of petroleum resources. This review outlines the research carried out and the significant advances made in the field of biofibers, biomatrices, and biocomposites from a renewable resource, i.e. the sugar palm tree. Nevertheless, a deeper understanding of their chemical, mechanical, and thermal properties is still needed in order to produce desirable and competitive materials derived from sugar palm fiber and sugar palm starch. The use of these unutilized materials as biofibers, biomatrices, and bicomposites will open up another avenue for the large-scale utilization of the sugar palm tree.

PALM GUR INDUSTRY IN INDIA

The making of golden palm gur with its characteristic aroma and flavor is one of the shinning traditional skills of India. The indigenous artisans, for ages, are engaged in this activity and are tapping palmyra palm and date palm to get sweet *neera* which ultimately gives *gur* or jaggery, sugar, candy and other refreshing drinks. Beside this *neera* and its diverse products and derivatives, these magnificent palms offer so much to mankind in many ways, where its roots, trunk, leaves, fibers, saplings, fruits, each in its own intrinsic way fulfil man's economic, social, educational, gastronomic and esthetic needs. Nothing in these humble palms is ever wasted, as each part serves some useful purpose.

History of Palm Gur Industry

Palm trees usually thrive in tropical and subtropical regions. In fact, there is an area designated as "Palm Belt" of the world, which extends up to 45° on both sides of the equator. This belt involves three continents covering 13 countries in Africa, ten in Asia and five in South America.

During British rule, the development of the Indian cane sugar industry under the policy of imperial preference and later tariff protection, use of vacuum pan and sulphitation processes and the government encouragement to sugarcane plantations adversely affected palm gur and palm sugar manufacture. The All India Village Industries Association, which was established in 1935, made some efforts to revive and propagate the use of palm gur. In 1937, when popular local ministries came to power in different provinces, prohibition was tried to introduce. Consequently, palm gur making was encouraged, particularly in Maharashtra and Tamil Nadu provinces, as an alternate source of employment to the displaced tappers who, earlier, used to make a country liquor (toddy) by fermenting *neera* (sweet sap from palms), and about 1,600 Palm Gur Cooperative Societies were registered in Tamil Nadu alone. However, later developments saw the fall of these ministries and with them prohibition was abandoned. This resulted in a setback to palm gur industry. After independence, a separate section was established in the Union Ministry of Food and Agriculture in 1947 to look after the development program of palm gur industry. Apart from the States namely Tamil Nadu, West Bengal and Andhra Pradesh, where palm gur making had developed as traditional industry, on account of consumer demand for it, efforts were made to develop the industry in other States also where such tradition did not exist. Training of artisans in tapping, preservation and sale of *neera*, distributing improved tools and equipment and arranging demonstrations and exhibitions for propagating *neera* and *gur* were the main facets of the development program. When prohibition was introduced in 1951 as a national policy, the organization and development of palm gur, palm sugar and other products of palm stalk, palm fiber and palm leaf as an alternative means of livelihood to the displaced toddy tappers became imperative. A Central Training School was also established to train these tappers.

Palm Gur Industry under Khadi and Village Industries Commission

The Khadi and Village Industries Commission (KVIC) took over the work of this Industry in 1957 from the All India Khadi and Village Industries Board. Technical guidance was provided to institutions and cooperatives in the Palm Gur Industry for its orientation on scientific and viable lines. The Commission's development program, among others, covered the following aspects:

1. Strengthening of the organizational base of the industry by setting up of Primary Cooperative Societies of artisans and their Federations at the State and All India levels
2. Supply of technical know-how, improved tools and equipments and other financial assistance for tapping and *gur* manufacture

3. Introduction of vacuumatic sugar and candy manufacturing techniques
4. Popularization of *neera* as a beverage with facilities for storage, transport, etc.
5. Training of artisans and other State level technical and managerial personnel.

In India, Palmyrah palm (*Borassus flabellifer* Linn.) and Datepalm (*Phoenix dactylifera* Linn. and *P. sylvestris* Roxb.) are traditionally used for obtaining various edible and nonedible products. It is estimated that there are 18 crores of palm trees in India. About 12.59 crores trees are estimated to be available for tapping, of which approximately 3.08 crores are being tapped for *neera*. If all these twelve crores of available trees are used for productive purpose, it would give employment to about 6.3 million persons and the total production would be nearly 4.20 million tons of gur and other products.

Technical Problems and Work under Palm Gur Industry

The Palm Gur Industry mainly belongs to traditional artisans who know the art of climbing tall trees and have made this hazardous work as their main occupation for livelihood. Mostly they are poor and belong to the weaker sections of the society, i.e. Scheduled Castes and Scheduled Tribes. Millions of artisans are engaged in the manufacturing activities of Palm Gur Industry in the southern part of the country. West Bengal, Orissa and to some extent in Gujarat, Maharashtra and UP, the data on total work force engaged in Palm Gur Industry is not available due to widely dispersed nature of activities. Even in the statistical publications, no where this occupation is mentioned state wise. This is a seasonal industry providing employment on an average for 150 days in a year. The manufacturing activities are carried out in small hamlets of inaccessible villages by the family members of the artisans. Under Khadi and Village Industry Sector, financial assistance has been extended to 6.64 lakhs persons. No other organised agency except Khadi and V.I. Commission has taken-up the program of Palm Gur Industry in the country (Table 2.13). The Kerala Government has created Palm Products Corporation to look after the tappers' family by providing financial assistance and marketing facilities in Kerala. Different State Governments also started financing through cooperatives and other similar bodies like District Federations and State Federations for the development of the Industry and upliftment of tapper artisans.

Table 2.13: Performance of palm gur industry during 1997–2000

Years	*Production of edible/nonedible products (tons)*	*Sales (Rs in lakhs)*	*Employment (persons)*	*Earning (Rs in lakhs)*
1997–1998	19,510.20	21,783.40	741,000	12,353.81
1998–1999	20,257.16	22,897.86	755,000	13,130.65
1999–2000	18,650.92	21,711.17	778,000	14,001.87

Objectives of the Industry

The main objectives of the Palm Gur Industry are enumerated as under:

- Strengthening organizational base for the industry by setting up primary cooperatives of artisans and District and State Level marketing cooperative federations for arranging marketing facilities for artisans' products.

- Extending financial assistance for developmental scheme and promotional assistance to the artisan's cooperatives through State Khadi and Village Industries Boards.
- Supply of technical know-how and arranging supply of improved tools and equipments to the artisans.
- Introduction of improved methods of production and its demonstration in the field.
- Conducting research and development of new area of production and elimination of drudgery in the production processes of existing schemes.
- Building up of raw materials and supplying them to artisans engaged in manufacturing of palm products.
- To utilize abundant and valuable natural resources, i.e. palm trees which are otherwise un-exploited.
- Popularizing products of Palm Gur Industry especially *neera* as beverage by various media of publicity and educating potential buyer about the nutritive value of *neera*.

Characteristics of the Industry

The characteristics of the Palm Gur Industry are enumerated as under:

- This is a traditional industry. The tapper community had taken-up various activities of Palm Gur Industry as their main occupation for livelihood in the country. Generally, no other community will accept tapping of Palms as an additional source of income due to its hazardous nature of work.
- This is a seasonal industry. It provides employment to the artisans for 150 days in a year. In addition, the industry keeps all the family members including women and children, engaged for the whole season.
- The manufacturing of palm products can be started with meagre financial investment.

Export of palm leaf articles and palm fiber

Year	*Palm leaf articles and palm fiber (Rs in lakhs)*	*Country to which exported*
1997–1998	41.83	Belgium, UK, Japan, France, Ireland, Italy, Canada, Germany, Australia, Philippines
1998–1999	80.37	
1999–2000	85.10	

Constraints of the Palm Gur Industry

- Tree climbing process for tapping palm trees still remains the most difficult and arduous task.
- Younger generation from rural areas does not find tapping occupation acceptable, as it is not adequately remunerative.
- *Neera* ferments and *gur* melts, thus both of them are having storage problems. This makes marketing efforts very risky.

Economics of single palm per year

	Raw materials	*Qty. available*	*Finished products*	*Approximate value (Rs)*
Palmyrahpalm	*Neera*	150 liters	*Gur*: 20 kg	2,250.00
	Fiber	1 kg	Brushes: 12 (no.) (No.= number)	150.00
	Eark (tender midrib)	2 kg	Baskets: 4 (no.)	60.00
	Leaf	8 (no.)	Mat: 6 (no.)	30.00
	Naar	16 (no.)	Basket: 1 (no.)	50.00
				2,540.00
Datepalm				
	Neera	100 -120 liters	*Gur*:12 kg	1,800.00
	Leaf	15 kg	Broom: 15 (no.)	300.00
	Petiole	2 (no.)	Baskets: 4 (no.)	50.00
				2,150.00

- The durability of palm leaf fancy articles is also short.
- Cost of fuel for boiling *neera* makes *gur* production uneconomical.
- Scientific methods to distinguish palm sugar from cane sugar used in areated beverages are not available to press for excise exemption on soft drinks. Thus, in the absence of this special privilege palm sugar production is discouraged.
- There is a cut-throat competition faced from the toddy tappers by those who tap palms for production of *neera* and *gur*. The toddy contractors can afford to pay higher wages whereas *neera* sales and jaggery/*gur* production do not ensure wages to that level.

Nutritive value of *Neera* (in 200 mL)

pH	7.2
Sugar (gm)	28.8
Calcium (mg)	35.4
Iron (mg)	5.5
Phosphorus (mg)	32.4
Thiamine (μg)	82.3
Riboflavin (μg)	44.4
Ascorbic Acid (mg)	12.2
Nicotanic Acid (μg)	674.1
Protein (mg)	49.7
Calories	118.3

Remedial Measures Taken

The last four decades were significant for the development of Palm Gur Industry. Initially the emphasis was on developmental and promotional activities which aimed at covering more and more artisans and upgrading their skill and efficiency. Pilot Model Demonstration Centers and Palm Gur Extension Services Centers were setup in both traditional and virgin areas with a view to transfer the improved process and techniques involved to grass root level. Later on, efforts were made to strengthen research activities in order to minimize the drudgery of artisans and elimination of basic problems pertaining to preservation of *neera* and storage and packing of jaggery ensuring better shelf life and quality of edible palm products.

As regards fuel economy, a number of highly efficient furnaces for small scale boiling have already been evolved. Recently, a very efficient furnace having multiple pan system has been evolved at Gandhigram Rural Institute, Gandhigram, Tamil Nadu. But, it is yet to be put to commercial boiling operations at Artisans level. Efforts were made to use solar energy for manufacturing of jaggery.

For enhancing efficiency and reducing risk to artisans in climbing trees, methods like aerial rope ways and bamboo ways have been introduced in the field and as a result 40% efficiency of the artisans has increased. The method of ladder counter weight system and the new implement devised by M/s Mary's Industry in automatic climbing of trees are under trial in the field and it appears that with certain modifications it could be put to commercial use very shortly in the field.

Efforts were made to diversify nonedible palm products of the industry. Visiting cards made from palm leaf are becoming popular among the people. It has very good markets due to its uniqueness.

Fiber extraction and processing were traditionally done manually by beating leaf stalk or frond of palmyrah palm with heavy wooden hammer. Recently, fiber extraction and processing machine units have been introduced. The unit can be operated by male or female artisans. By introducing the unit the efficiency and drudgery involved in fiber extraction and processing have been completely eliminated. Now, the large scale fiber production is possible in traditional and virgin areas.

Apart from the measures already introduced by this Directorate, as enumerated above, other measures pertaining to the quality and standardization of edible palm products, marketing, creating infrastructure, introduction of new schemes and products have been taken-up from time to time with a view to increase productivity, eliminate drudgery and enhance competitive capacity and increase earnings of the artisans in Palm Gur Industry.

Quality Control

The Directorate of Palm Gur Industry, by collecting the samples of palm sugar, palm gur, palm candy and palm fiber brushes from its implementing agencies like individual entrepreneur, co-operative societies, District Federations and State Federations, and by checking with the given specifications from FPO and BIS, has adopted the quality control measures for standardization of some of the products. Specifications for some products like palm gur (jaggery) and palm fiber brushes are available from the Bureau of Indian Standards, New Delhi. Other edible products like jam, squashes and jelly have been approved under Food Products Order.

Training Program

The present status of training facilities available under Palm Gur Industry is given in Table 2.14.

Table 2.14: Training program

Name of the center	*Name of the course*	*Duration of period*
Central Palm gur and Palm Products Institute, No. 39, Arul Nagar, M.M. Colony, Chennai – 600051	Palm Products Technology Course Certificate Course in Palm Sugar Making Brush Making/ Confectionery and Indigenous Sweet Meat Making/Palm Leaf Articles Making	8 months 6 months 3 months (each course)
Gajanan Naik Palm gur Technology Development Center, P.O. Dahanu, Thane District, Maharashtra – 401601	*Neera* Catering/Palm Leaf Articles Making/Brush Making	3 months (each course)
Regional Palm gur Training Center, 1-D, Beach Road, Cuddalore – 607001. South Arcot Dist. Tamil Nadu	Confectionery and indigenous Sweet Meat Making/Palm Leaf, *Agany* (part of tender palm leaf), *Naar* and *Eark* Articles Making/Brush Making/ Tappers Proficiency Course.	3 months (each course)
Dr. B.R. Ambedkar Institute of Rural Technology and Management, KVIC, Post – Trimbak Vidya Mandir, Nasik, Maharashtra – 422213	Brush Making	3 months (each course)

Government Policy Support

Some policy support measures expected from the government are:

- Taxes on palm products may be removed.
- Excise duty on palm sugar based products may be withdrawn.
- There should be a liberal approach in respect of issuance of tapping licence, fixation of rent of palm trees, local taxes and other levies.
- Establishment expenditure on State Palm Gur Federations may be met by respective State Governments.
- Monetary provisions are needed for undertaking census of palm wealth in the country.
- Palm trees on the land of local Governments/Panchayats, Central Government/Undertakings should be exclusively reserved for tapping *neera*.
- *Neera* is a nutritious and healthy drink. Concrete scientific method should be developed for preservation of *neera*, palm *gur* and other related products.

CONCLUSION

Keeping in view the nature and historical background of the Palm Gur Industry where poor tapper artisans and women from weaker sections below poverty line are mostly engaged, this Industry needs to be treated at par with Khadi Programs for which necessary policy support may be given for its survival/development. On the line of the State Government of Tamil Nadu where the palm is treated as a "State Tree", policy support also needs to be given in other concerned States where plenty of palms are available.

In consideration of the progress of technical developments in various spheres of this Industry and the existence of yet untapped vast potential for further development of this industry on a wider scale with implications in producing Wealth from Waste and offering employment to a large number of persons mostly dispersed in rural tracts all over country, this traditional knowledge based industry deserves to be propagated, promoted and encouraged.

3

Honey

Honey has a great potential not only as a healthy substitute for sugar, but also as an industry—especially as a cottage industry among villagers, tribals and small farmers. With India well placed as far as nectar and pollen resources are concerned, honey production needs to be encouragement in India.

Honey use and production has a long and varied history. In many cultures, honey has associations that go beyond its use as a food. Honey is frequently a talisman and symbol of sweetness. Honey has an indefinite shelf-life. Honey is as old as written history, dating back to 2100 BC. Where it was mentioned in Sumerian and Babylonian cuneiform writings, the Hittite code, and the sacred writings of India and Egypt. It is presumably even older than that. Its name comes from the English *hunig*, and it was the first and most widespread sweetener used by man. Legend has it that Cupid dipped his love arrows in honey before aiming at unsuspecting lovers.

Exactly how long honey has been in existence is hard to say because it has been around since as far back as we can record. *The Bible makes many references to honey, but the history of honey goes back much farther in time. Evidence shows that humans have been collecting it for 10,000 years.*

Honey is as old as written history, dating back to 2100 BC where it was mentioned in Sumerian and Babylonian cuneiform writings, the Hittite code, and the sacred writings of India and Egypt. It is presumably even older than that. Cave paintings in Spain from 7000 BC show the earliest records of beekeeping. Its "magical" properties and versatility has given honey a significant place in history. Its name comes from the English huning, and it was the first and most widespread sweetener used by man. Legend has it that cupid dipped his love arrows in honey before aiming at unsuspecting lovers.

In the Old Testament of the Bible, Israel was often referred to as "the land of milk and honey". Mead, an alcoholic drink made from honey was called "nectar of the gods", high praise indeed. The earliest record of keeping bees in hives was found in the sun temple erected in 2400 BC near Cairo. The bee featured frequently in Egyptian hieroglyphs and, being favored by the pharaohs, often symbolized royalty. The ancient Egyptians used honey as a sweetener, as a gift to their gods and even as an ingredient in embalming fluid. Honey cakes were baked by the Egyptians and used as an offering to placate the gods. The Greeks, too, made honey cakes and offered them to the gods.

The Greeks viewed honey as not only an important food, but also as a healing medicine. Greek recipes books were full of sweetmeats and cakes made from honey.

Cheeses were mixed with honey to make cheesecakes, described by Euripides in the 5th century BC as being "steeped most thoroughly in the rich honey of the golden bee". The Romans also used honey as a gift to the gods and they used it extensively in cooking. Beekeeping flourished throughout the Roman Empire. Once Christianity was established, honey and beeswax production increased greatly to meet the demand for church candles.

And, of course, bees perform the vital service of pollinating fruits, legumes, vegetables and other types of food-producing plants in the course of their business of honey production. The history of honey is a thus significant part of our history, and will have an ever-increasing role in our future. Honeybees must tap over two million flowers to make one pound of honey, flying a distance equal to more than three times around the world. The average worker bee will make only 1–12 of a teaspoon of honey during its lifetime. The famous Scottish liqueur Drambuie is made with honey.

Honey was valued highly and often used as a form of currency, tribute, or offering. In the 11th century AD, German peasants paid their feudal lords in honey and beeswax. Although experts argue whether the honeybee is native to the Americas, conquering Spaniards in 1600 AD found native Mexicans and Central Americans had already developed beekeeping methods to produce honey.

Ancient Times

Honey collection is an ancient activity. Eva Crane's *The Archaeology of Beekeeping* states that humans began hunting for honey at least 10,000 years ago. She evidences this with a cave painting in Valencia, Spain. The painting is a Mesolithic rock painting, showing two female honey-hunters collecting honey and honeycomb from a wild bee hive. The two women are depicted in the nude, carrying baskets, and using a long wobbly ladder in order to reach.the wild nest.

In Ancient Egypt, honey was used to sweeten cakes and biscuits, and was used in many other dishes. Ancient Egyptian and Middle-Eastern peoples also used honey for embalming the dead. In the Roman Empire, honey was possibly used instead of gold to pay taxes. Pliny the Elder devotes considerable space in his book Naturalis Historia to the bee and honey, and its many uses. The fertility god of Egypt, Min, was offered honey.

In some parts of post-classical Greece, like Rhodes, it was formerly the custom for a bride to dip her fingers in honey and make the sign of the cross before entering her new home. Some cultures believed honey had many practical health uses. It was used as an ointment for rashes and burns, and used to help soothe sore throats when no other medicinal practices were available.

In days of old, honey has been used not only in food and beverages, but also to make cement, in furniture polishes and varnishes, and for medicinal purposes. As bees were thought to have special powers, they were often used as emblems: Pope Urban VIII used the bee as his emblem. The bee was the sign of the king of lower Egypt during the first dynasty (3,200 BC). Napoleon's flag carried a single line of bees in flight, and his robe was embroidered with bees. In the third century BC, the bee was the emblem used on coins in the Greek city of Ephesus. The bee was the symbol of the Greek goddess Artemis. The bee was the emblem of Eros/ cupid.

Religious Significance

In Hindu tradition, babies are made to lick drops of honey and are marked by celebrations. In Hindu religion, honey enjoys the highest position along with the cow milk, when mixed together; tirth (holy / sacred nectar) is produced. The vedas and other ancient literature thousands of year old, all mention the use of honey as a great medicinal and health food. In Jewish tradition, honey is a symbol for the New Year Rosh Hashana. At the traditional meal for that holiday, apple slices are dipped in honey and eaten to bring a sweet new year. Some Rosh Hashana greetings show honey and an apple, symbolizing the feast. In some congregations, small straws of honey are given out to usher in the New Year.

In Islam, there is an entire Surah in the Qur'an called al-Nahl (the honeybee). According to Hadith, Prophet Muhammad strongly recommended honey for healing purposes. The Quran also promotes honey as a nutritious and healthy food: "and thy Lord taught the bee to build its cells in hills, on trees and in (men's) habitations...there issues from within their bodies a drink of varying colors, wherein is healing for mankind. Verily in this is a sign for those who give thought".

In Buddhism, honey plays an important role in the festival of Madhu Purnima, celebrated by Buddhists in India and Bangladesh. The day commemorates Buddha's making peace among his disciples by retreating into the wilderness. The legend has it that while he was there, a monkey brought him honey to eat. On Madhu Purnima, Buddhists remember this act by giving honey to monks. The monkey's gift is frequently depicted in Buddhist art. The Hebrew Bible contains many references to honey. In the Book of Judges, Samson found a swarm of bees and honey in the carcass of a lion (14:8). The Book of Exodus famously describes the Promised Land as a "land flowing with milk and honey" (33:3). However, the claim has been advanced that the original Hebrew (*devash*) actually refers to the sweet syrup produced from the juice of the date. In the Christian New Testament, Matthew 3:4, John the Baptist is said to have lived for a long period of time in the wilderness on a diet consisting of locusts and wild honey.

HISTORY, CULTURE AND FOLKLORE

In history, culture and folklore, honey use and production has a long and varied history. In many cultures, honey has associations that go beyond its use as a food. Honey is frequently a talisman and symbol of sweetness.

In Western Culture

The word "honey", along with variations like "honey bun" and the abbreviation "hon", has become a term of endearment in most of the English-speaking world. In some places it is used for loved ones; in others, such as the American South, it is used when addressing casual acquaintances or even strangers.

Also, in many children's books bears are depicted as eating honey, (e.g. Winnie the Pooh) even though most bears actually eat a wide variety of foods, and bears seen at beehives are usually more interested in bee larvae than honey. In some European languages even the word for "bear" (e.g. in Russian "medvéd", in Czech "medvìd", in Hungarian medve, in Croatian "medvjed") is coined from the noun which means "honey" and the verb which means "to eat". Honey is sometimes sold in bear-shaped jars or squeeze bottles.

Formation

Honey's natural sugars are dehydrated, which prevents fermentation, with added enzymes to modify and transform their chemical composition and pH. Invertases and digestive acids hydrolyze sucrose to give the monosaccharides glucose and fructose. The invertase is one of these enzymes synthesized by the body of the insect. Honeybees transform saccharides into honey by a process of regurgitation, a number of times, until it is partially digested. The bees do the regurgitation and digestion as a group. After the last regurgitation, the aqueous solution is still high in water, so the process continues by evaporation of much of the water and enzymatic transformation. Honey is produced by bees as a food source. To produce a single jar of honey, foraging honeybees have to travel the equivalent of three times around the world. In cold weather or when fresh food sources are scarce, bees use their stored honey as their source of energy. By contriving for bee swarms to nest in artificial hives, people have been able to semi-domesticate the insects, and harvest excess honey. In the hive (or in a wild nest), there are three types of bees:

1. A single female queen bee
2. A seasonally variable number of male drone bees to fertilize new queens
3. Some 20,000 to 40,000 female worker bees.

The worker bees raise larvae and collect the nectar that will become honey in the hive. Leaving the hive, they collect sugar-rich flower nectar and return.

In the hive, the bees use their "honey stomachs" to ingest and regurgitate the nectar a number of times until it is partially digested. Invertase synthesized by the bees and digestive acids hydrolyze sucrose to give the same mixture of glucose and fructose. The bees work together as a group with the regurgitation and digestion until the product reaches a desired quality. It is then stored in honey comb cells. After the final regurgitation, the honeycomb is left unsealed. However, the nectar is still high in both water content and natural yeasts, which, unchecked, would cause the sugars in the nectar to ferment. The process continues as bees inside the hive fan their wings, creating a strong draft across the honeycomb, which enhances evaporation of much of the water from the nectar. This reduction in water content raises the sugar concentration and prevents fermentation. Ripe honey, as removed from the hive by a beekeeper, has a long shelf-life, and will not ferment if properly sealed.

Honey Trivia

- Honeybees must tap over 2 million flowers to make 1 pound of honey, flying a distance equal to more than three times around the world.
- The average worker bee will make only 1–12 of a teaspoon of honey during its lifetime.
- The famous Scottish liqueur Drambuie is made with honey.

CLASSIFICATION

Honey is classified by its floral source, and there are also divisions according to the packaging and processing used. There are also regional honeys.

Floral Source

Generally, honey is classified by the floral source of the nectar from which it was made. Honeys can be from specific types of flower nectars, from indeterminate origin, or can be blended after collection.

Blended

Most commercially available honey is blended, meaning that it is a mixture of two or more honeys differing in floral source, color, flavor, density or geographic origin.

Polyfloral

Polyfloral honey, also known as wildflower honey, is derived from the nectar of many types of flowers. The taste may vary from year to year, and the aroma and the flavor can be more or less intense, depending on which bloomings are prevalent.

Monofloral

Monofloral honey is made primarily from the nectar of one type of flower. Different monofloral honeys have a distinctive flavor and color because of differences between their principal nectar sources. In order to produce monofloral, honey beekeepers keep beehives in an area where the bees have access to only one type of flower. In practice, because of the difficulties in containing bees, a small proportion of any honey will be from additional nectar from other flower types. Typical examples of North American monofloral honeys are clover, orange blossom, sage, tupelo, buckwheat and sourwood. Some typical European examples include thyme, thistle, heather, acacia, dandelion, sunflower, honeysuckle, and varieties from lime and chestnut trees. In North Africa, such as Egypt, examples include clover, cotton, and citrus, mainly orange.

Honeydew Honey

Instead of taking nectar, bees can take honeydew, the sweet secretions of aphids or other plant sap-sucking insects. Honeydew honey is very dark brown in color with a rich fragrance of stewed fruit or fig jam and is not as sweet as nectar honeys. Germany's Black Forest is a well-known source of honeydew-based honeys, as well as some regions in Bulgaria. In Greece, pine honey (a type of honeydew honey) constitutes 60–65% of the annual honey production. Honeydew honey is popular in some areas, but in other areas beekeepers have difficulty selling the stronger flavored product.

The production of honeydew honey has some complications and dangers. The honey has a much larger proportion of indigestible than light floral honeys, which can cause dysentry to the bees, resulting in the death of colonies in areas with cold winters. Good beekeeping management requires the removal of honeydew prior to winter in colder areas. Bees collecting this resource also have to be fed protein supplements, as honeydew lacks the protein-rich pollen accompaniment gathered from flowers.

Uses

Honey has a long history of human consumption and is most commonly consumed in its unprocessed state. It is taken as medicine, eaten as food, or incorporated as an additive in a variety of foods and beverages. In fact, records have it that raw honey is the most ancient sweetener and it has been in use throughout the world since several million years.

Natural honey is a sweet viscous liquid, which has a typical flavor and high nutritional value as well as immense health benefits. It is produced by honey-bees as blossom honey by secreting nectars of flowers and as honeydew honey (forest honey) by secreting the exudates of plant-sucking insects.

Honey comprises mainly sugars and water, besides several vitamins and minerals, including B vitamins. The other constituents of honey are amino acids, antibiotic rich inhibine, proteins, phenol antioxidants and some micronutrients. The sugars in honey are sweeter and give more energy than artificial sweeteners; the most abundant sugar in honey is fructose. Some of the vitamins found in honey include ascorbic acid, pantothenic acid, niacin and riboflavin; along with minerals such as calcium, copper, iron, magnesium, manganese, phosphorus, potassium and zinc.

Honey: the Sweet Troubleshooter

Honey has been in news for the wrong reasons lately. Antibiotic residues have been found in leading brands of honey—but it is a reflection on the way we produce our food.

Honey, a syrupy, sweet liquid is obtained from plant nectar by honeybees. About 80% of honey is simple sugars, mostly fructose and glucose with small quantities of other sugars like maltose, sucrose and other complex carbohydrates. Although honey is a high carbohydrate food, its glycemic index varies within a wide range from 32 to 85 depending on the botanical source.

Honey, nature's original sweetener, is being rediscovered as a natural source of energy that also offers a unique combination of nutritional benefits. In addition to being a concentrated energy source, honey contains a wide array of vitamins (vitamin B_6, thiamin, riboflavin and pantothenic acid) and minerals (calcium, copper, iron, magnesium, manganese, phosphorus, potassium, sodium and zinc).

Honey also contains several compounds that function as antioxidants, one of which is unique to honey called pinocembrin. Although relatively low in nutrients, honey contains more nutrients than refined sugars. As a rule, darker honeys contain higher amounts of minerals and are strongly flavored than lighter honeys. Honey is sweeter than table sugar as it contains more calories—one tablespoon of honey provides nearly 65 cals compared to only 46 cals provided by the same amount of table sugar.

The use of honey as medicine is mentioned in most ancient written records but even today scientists and doctors are rediscovering its effectiveness in therapeutic nutrition. Its unique composition makes it useful for treating several ailments, minor burns and scrapes including aiding the treatment of sore throats and other bacterial infections. The viscosity and the hygroscopic qualities of honey permits its even spread on a wound bed, creating a favorable environment for healing. With these properties, honey has been used as an efficient treatment of chronic wounds of the lower leg and abdomen. Thus, honey can be stated a treasure due to its following usages: honey being a rich source of carbohydrates provides a quick source of energy. The sugars in honey are primarily glucose and fructose both of which provide the body with quick energy.

Recent studies suggest that this unique mixture of sugars which occurs naturally in honey, also works best in preventing fatigue and enhancing athletic performance. Another study states that a spoonful of honey right before a workout is a good energy booster. A study presented at the annual experimental biology meeting indicated that using honey as a carbohydrate during exercise significantly improved performance and power during endurance cycling trials. It was also reported that honey reduced time to complete a 64 km time trial by over 3 minutes (compared to placebo); honey produced over 6% greater cycling power during the time trial (compared to placebo); equal performance to glucose; and it was well tolerated by all subjects. Honey consumption along with supplemental calcium enhanced calcium absorption.

Honey is an anticarcinogen. Honey containing marinades effectively limit the production of potential cancer-causing compounds called heterocyclic aromatic amines (HAAs) when marinated steak and chicken were fried. HAAs are formed when meat is cooked at high temperatures and the begins to char or blacken. Marinating meat for four hours in marinades containing 30% honey significantly reduced HAA formation. Honey exhibits resistance to microbial spoilage. Most microorganisms do not grow in honey because of its low water activity. Honey is a natural antiseptic, it helps in wounds healing, swelling goes down, and tissue grows back. Even burns heal better with honey. Honey contains appreciable amounts of plaque-fighting antioxidants and so reduces dental plaque. It also has an enzyme that produces hydrogen peroxide, which is believed to be the main reason for the antimicrobial activity of honey.

Honey had a popular use in India as a food and medicine and in the preparation of alcoholic drinks. The Hindus drank madhuparka, a mixture of honey and curds, during religious ceremonies with the toast: "I drink thee for luck, glory, power, and for the enjoyment of food".

India's Honey Regulators

- The National Bee Board, under national horticulture mission, is mandated to promote best practices. All beekeepers ought to be registered with the board to ensure honey can be traced from the form to the farm. Very few are registered.
- Agriculture and Processed Food Products Export Development Agency (APEDA) under the ministry of commerce, provides financial assistance and subsidies to honey exporters. Between 2005 and 2008, the agency was monitoring and testing honey for exports.
- Export Inspection Council (EIC), a department of the ministry of commerce, certifies safety of food products, including honey. It is recognized by EU. The council conducts tests on honey samples before it leaves for Europe and is responsible for year-long monitoring of both exporters and beekeepers.
- Ministry of Health and Family Welfare and Food Safety and Standards Authority of India implement the Prevention of Food Adulteration Act of 1954, but the act does not regulate antibiotics in honey.

Types of Honey

The color and flavor of honey depends on the nectar source, age and storage conditions. In general, darker honeys are more often used for large-scale commercial purposes while lighter-color honeys are marketed for direct consumption and demand a premium price over their darker counterparts.

Honey made primarily from the nectar of one type of flower is called monofloral honey, whereas honey made from many types of flowers is called polyfloral honey. Monofloral honey, typically, fetches better price in market due to its distinctive flavor, and includes the well-known varieties like Orange Blossom and Sourwood. However, most commercially available honey is blended to include two or more honeys, differing in floral source, color, flavor, density and geographical origin.

Honey Flavors

There are as many flavors of honey as there are flowers, since the flavor of the honey is directly influenced by the type of nectar gathered by the bees from various floral sources. Flavors can range from mild to aromatic, spicy, fragrant or medicinal and are often combined to create gourmet flavors for the discriminating palate.

Honey flavors

Acacia	Pale yellow with a delicate taste from China and California.
Alfalfa	Popular in Utah, Nevada and other Rocky Mountain states; mild, near-white, good body, good for table honey, often diluted with other honeys.
Alsike Clover	Often used for surplus honey in northern states; mild, light-colored, often mixed with honey from white clover.
Basswood or Linden	Extra-white, with a slight bite when pure, often mixed with clover honey.
Black Locust	Extra-white, high quality honey.
Black Mangrove	A Florida favorite, light with a thin body, slightly brackish taste.
Black Sage or Ball Sage	Best honey plant in California; distinctive flavor.
Blackberry	Reddish-brown or near-white in color; a bit more flavorful than clover honey.
Buckbush	Called Coralberry in the eastern US; light-amber color with good flavor.
Buckwheat	Purple to black in color; pronounced flavor; prized by food manufacturers.
Catsclaw	Popular in the southwest US; white in color.
Clover, Sweet	Clover yields massive amounts of nectar popular with beekeepers as a source; white in color and mild in flavor.
Clover, White	Most-used east of the Mississippi; color is white to extra-light amber with a mild, delicious flavor.
Cotton	Used mostly in Texas now; light in color with a mild flavor
Dandelion	Honey is yellow with a strong flavor.
Eucalyptus	Varies in color and flavor but is overall bold with a slightly medicinal aftertaste.
Fireweed	Light in color and mild in flavor.

(Contd.)

Gallberry	A Southern US favorite; light amber with a pleasant aromatic flavor; does not crystallize making it a good candidate for chunk honey.
Goldenrod	Popular in Northern US and Eastern Canada; yellow with a rich flavor.
Horsemint	White to light-amber with a minty flavor; may have a strong odor
Maple	Light amber to slightly darker; good flavor.
Mesquite	Light amber to white; usually mixed with others.
Orange and Citrus	A major source; white in color, mild flavor with delicate citrus blossom aroma.
Raspberry	White with a delicious flavor.
Saw Palmetto	Often considered the best in Florida; rich yellow in color.
Sourwood	Considered the most delicious in the eastern states; water-white with a mild, delicious flavor; sold mostly as comb honey or chunk comb honey.
Spanish Needles	Golden yellow with a pronounced flavor; can be mixed with white clover honey to obtain a mild, golden-tinted honey.

Honey Colors

Color is usually an indication of flavor concentration. Colors can range from near-white through yellow, yellow-green, gold, amber, dark brown or red to even nearly black. Usually a lighter color will indicate a milder flavor while darker honey is customarily more robust and contains more minerals. Texture can also vary from thin to heavy.

Honey Textures and Honey Products

There are also various forms of honey, including liquid, comb, cut-comb, solid (granulated or crystallized) and chunk.

- **Liquid honey,** the most widely used, is extracted from the combs by a centrifugal method and is usually filtered to remove all remnants of the comb and/or pollen.
- **Granulated or "sugared" honey** is partially or wholly solidified honey crystals.
- **Creamed honey** adds finely crystallized honey to liquid honey and has a smooth texture.
- **Comb honey** includes the honey and comb as stored by the bees and can be served as is or cut into chunks.
- **Cut-comb** is small chunks of sealed comb honey which is normally sold in pieces about 4 inches long and 1–½ inches wide, wrapped in cellophane.
- **Chunk honey** is pieces of comb honey placed into containers and covered with liquid honey.

There are over 300 unique flavors of honey in the US.

Honey Storage

Storing honey is easy. Simply keep it in a cool location away from direct sunlight in a tightly covered container. It is not necessary to refrigerate honey. In fact, it is much easier to handle if you don't. Honey may also be frozen although there is really no need. Do not be alarmed if stored honey becomes cloudy. This is called *crystallization*. It is not harmful nor is it any indication of deterioration. In fact, honey has an indefinite shelf-life thanks to its high concentration of sugar. Raw honey with high pollen content will crystallize even faster, and cold temperatures also cause crystals. Crystallized honey is one of the many forms intentionally produced for purchase by many beekeepers.

If your honey crystallizes, you can easily reliquify it by gently heating the jar in a pan of hot water, stirring while heating. Do not overheat as heat may alter flavor and color as a result of caramelization of the sugars.

HONEY AND HEALTH

Nutrition

Honey is a mixture of sugars and other compounds. With respect to carbohydrates, honey is mainly fructose (about 38.5%) and glucose (31.0%), making it similar to the synthetically produced inverted sugar syrup which is approximately fructose (48%), glucose (47%), and sucrose (5%). Honey's remaining carbohydrates include maltose, sucrose, and other complex carbohydrates. Honey contains trace amounts of several vitamins and minerals. As with all nutritive sweeteners, honey is mostly sugars and is not a significant source of vitamins or minerals. Honey also contains tiny amounts of several compounds thought to function as antioxidants, including chrysin, pinobanksin, vitamin C, catalase, and pinocembrin. The specific composition of any batch of honey depends on the flowers available to the bees that produced the honey. Typical honey analysis, fructose (38.5%), glucose (31%), sucrose (1%), water (17%), Other sugar (9%) (maltose, melezitose), Ash (0.17%), artificial sugar or artificial sweetener (3.25%) and Other (0.13%).

Honey has a density of about 1.36 kg/liter (36% denser than water). Isotope ratio mass spectrometry can be used to detect addition of corn syrup or sugar cane sugars by the carbon isotopic signature. Addition of sugars originating from corn or sugar cane (C_4 plants, unlike the plants used by bees which are predominantly C_3 plant) skews the isotopic ratio of sugars present in honey, but does not influence the isotopic ratio of proteins; in an unadulterated honey the carbon isotopic ratios of sugars and proteins should match. As low as 7%, level of addition can be detected.

Honey is composed of two main sugars: (1) levulose and (2) dextrose. These sugars do not need to be broken down by the digestive process, so honey is quickly absorbed into the bloodstream, giving a quick energy boost to the body. It also contains protein, vitamins and minerals, but no cholesterol. Darker honeys have more nutrients than light ones. Vitamin and mineral content depend on the floral source of the honey. Honey has less than 2% sodium, and as such can be labeled as a sodium-free product by Food and Drug Administration (FDA) standards.

Honey has been used in many medical applications over the years, but recent studies are now able to prove its beneficial nature in some applications, including as antibacterial topical treatment for burns and ulcers. The reason is because honey has osmotic properties; that is, it tends to withdraw water. Water molecules strongly react with the sugars in honey, leaving little water available for microorganisms. Thus, infection-causing bacteria are literally dehydrated to death by honey.

Honey nutritional value per 100 g (3.5 oz)

Energy 300 kcal	1270 kj
Carbohydrates	82.4 g
Sugars	82.12 g
Dietary fiber	0.2 g
Fat	0. g
Protein	0.3 g
Water	17.10 g
Roboflavin (Vit. B_2) 3%	0.038 mg
Niacin (Vit. B_3)	0.121 mg
Pantothenic acid (B_5)	0.068 mg
Vitamin B_6	0.024 mg
Folate (Vit. B_9)	2 mg
Vitamin C	0.5 mg
Calcium 6 mg	1%
Iron 0.42 mg	3%
Magnesium 2 mg	1%
Phosphorous 4 mg	1%
Potassium 52 mg	1%
Sodium 4 mg	0%
Zinc 0.22 mg	2%

Note: Shown is for 100 g. roughly 5 tbsp. percentages are relative to US recommendations for adults.
Source: USDA nutrient database.

Enzymatic activities of honey also produce hydrogen peroxide which generate highly reactive free radicals which kill bacteria, further contributing to its antibacterial properties.

Honey has also been used to successfully store skin graft for up to 12 weeks. Laboratory tests have shown that different types of honey have differing antibacterial sensitivities, so research continues to determine which floral sources are most beneficial.

Bee Keeping in India

Apiculture is an agro-industry in India, which uses bees as micromanipulators to harvest nectar and pollen from plant sources to produce honey and to store in beehives. Honey production and its quality as well as quantity are fundamentally related to bee species' specificity and vegetation pattern around bee colonies. In our country, we get a substantial amount of honey from *Apis dorsata*, the wild bee. However, proper beekeeping demands systematic utilization of resources through domesticated bees. Till recently, *Apis cerana* had served Indian beekeeping, but the establishment of *A. mellifera* in the country has changed the whole scenario as the species has proved much superior to the Indian bee in many regions.

As India is abundant in nectar and pollen resources, beekeeping is popular in the following regions:

- Himalayan region comprising Jammu and Kashmir, Himachal Pradesh and hills of UP.
- Plains of northern, western and central India. Punjab and Haryana are the leading producers of natural honey in the northern India. In western UP honey production has expanded fast but in Rajasthan its growth is slow. In Gujarat and the western *ghats* of Maharashtra, it is picking up. In Bihar too, there appears to be greater advancement in honey production.
- North-eastern region including West Bengal. Beekeeping with *A. mellifera* has become very popular in West Bengal and the scope in the north-eastern region is widening.
- In South Peninsula, the most promising states are Karnataka, north-eastern parts of Andhra Pradesh, Tamil Nadu and Kerala. In India, Kerala produces the largest quantity of honey. Here, tribal communities and other forest-dependent people play an important role in honey extraction. The small amount of honey collected is gathered by Girijan Service Co-operative Societies and marketed by the government agencies.

As far as marketing of honey is concerned, there are departmental marketing depots at Ernakulam in Kerala, Pune and Delhi, which are owned by *Khadi and Village Industries Commission* (KVIC). These depots purchase, process, grade and market honey. There is a chain of sales outlets throughout the country owned by KVIC depots through cooperatives/institutions. Some beekeepers' cooperative societies as well as institutions are also marketing honey, having established their own processing plants and *Agmarking* facilities. Besides, companies like Dabur, Baidyanath and Zandu are also processing and marketing honey through their own outlets. The floor price of honey is fixed on season-to-season and place-to-place basis, considering various factors.

Warning! Honey is not for Babies!

Although honey is a natural, healthy food that normally cannot support bacterial life. It is important to note that it can carry *C. botulinum* spores which may be harmful to the undeveloped immune systems of infants. The old practice of dipping pacifiers into honey to soothe crying babies should be aborted.

Infants up to 1 year of age should not be fed raw honey, as their immune systems are not yet developed enough to fend off this normally benign strain. Infection can cause a flaccid paralysis weakening the baby's muscles, causing a "floppy" baby. Other symptoms include constipation, lethargy, poor feeding, weak cry, droopy eyelids, expressionless face, drooling or swallowing difficulty, and occasionally, respiratory arrest. By the age of 1 year, most children develop enough to resist this normally benign strain of botulinum.

Infant botulism is rarely lethal, but is obviously easy to avoid in this instance. Although food manufacturers make extensive use of honey in their products, baby food manufacturers, as a rule, will not include honey in their foods recommended for those babies under 1 year of age.

It must also be pointed out that infant botulism is not exclusive to the ingestion of honey. The botulism spore can also be found in dust, soil and other uncooked foods that older children and adults are exposed to daily. The risk is minimal. Yet, it is an avoidable risk, and honey should not be fed to infants under the age of 12 months.

Honey in India

Honey is natural product that has no substitute. It is defined as a sweet liquid prepared by honeybees from nectars of plants. India has been known as land of honey. Since centuries, honey is used to treat a variety of ailments through a wide range of applications. Soulful India was supposed to be not only the cradle of humanity but also the birthplace of the bee. The latter claim was, however, contested by both Egypt and Greece. In ancient Indian scripts we find scanty information about apiculture. They allude to honey and bees more from mythological, poetical, philosophical, moral and religious viewpoints. The Rig-Veda, written about 3000 BC, often mentions honey. To the population of India honey represented everything that was sweet and beneficial. The Hindu had to turn his right side toward the beehive, as though passing a deity. God Krishna was symbolized by a bee and was called madhava, born in honey. The Hindu believed that whoever ate honey would become strong, rich, happy and wise and that it would improve not only his own look but would influence even his offspring.

In India, due to the fertility of the soil and the abundance of water and sunlight, the animals and plants are the largest on earth. The bees are no exception. *Apis dorsata*, the giant bee of India, builds enormous combs, often 6 feets square, suspended from the highest trees, hanging rocks and other inaccessible places to gain protection from man and beast. The combs are visible from a distance of miles. Special honey hunters approach the nests with ladders and ropes, usually at night time, to collect their plentiful harvest.

Despite the simplicity of technology its tremendous advantages as well as its potential of providing employment, honey production has not realized its full potential. The per capita consumption of honey in India is just 8 gm, whereas in Germany it is 1,800 gm. About 16 lakh people are directly or indirectly engaged in the bee keeping and allied activities. Major honey producing states in the country include Punjab, Haryana, Himachal Pradesh, UP, Bihar and West Bengal However, quality honey reportedly come mainly from the states of Jammu and Kashmir and Himachal Pradesh.

The All India Beekeepers' Association has made laudable contributions to the development of beekeeping and has been disseminating information about honey trade through its informative publication Indian Bee Journal. Besides, a host institution has been setup both by the government of India and the state governments to promote export of honey. Agricultural Products Export Development Authority (APEDA) under the aegis of the Ministry of Commerce and Industry, Government of India, is the nodal agency to promote exports of honey. Besides, Tribal Cooperative Marketing Development Federation of India Ltd. (TRIFED) has been playing an important role by providing training to tribals in the scientific cultivation and harvesting of wild honey. A lot of work has also been done on honey related issues like Indian bees and beekeeping by individuals, agricultural experts, agricultural colleges and institutions. The Central Bee Research and Training Institute, KVIC not only contributed to the science of bees, bee plants and beekeeping but also developed several appropriate technologies suited to Indian beekeeping.

The government of India has agreed to a proposal submitted by National Bee Board (NBB) for constituting Honeyfed in the country on the lines of Milkfed and Markfed to boost honey production in the country and has also assured 50% grant from Government of India in this regard. NBB is part of Horticulture Division of the Ministry of Agriculture. The country has 9 research Centers where qualitative and quantitative research on bee keeping is being carried out. The NBB also plans to submit a proposal for setting up a honey processing plant, lab and a bee institute. The plant would be capable of producing several products and byproducts from honey.

Exports from India

India exports natural honey to more than 70 countries in the world. The main buyers are the US, Saudi Arabia, the UAE and Yemen Republic. Total exports during 2012–2013 were 25,780.76 million tons valued at 356.28 crore rupees. The US alone purchased 86% as can be shown below.

Exports of natural honey from India in 2012–2013

Country	*Volume in million tons*	*Value in Rs million*	*Percent of share in total*
USA	22,2880.06	3097.0	86.92
Saudi Arabia	1383.55	182.8	5.13
UAE	268.00	35.8	1.00
Yemen Republic	227.00	33.1	0.93
Morocco	266.00	32.5	0.91
Belgium	228.00	32.0	0.90
Canada	127.73	22.6	0.63
Bangladesh	226.14	18.5	0.52
Nepal	159.92	15.3	0.43
Oman	73.70	13.4	0.38
Total(including others)	**25,780.76**	**3562.8**	**100**

Source: DGCIS Annual.

Associated Chambers of Commerce and Industry of India (ASSOCHAM) Study: According to a report by the ASSOCHAM, a recent decline in honey production of major exporters like China, US and Europe is proving a boon for Indian producers of honey. Further, it says that Indian honey exporters are experiencing a boon as their exports are estimated to touch 30,000 tons by 2007–2008 from the existing quantum of 20,000 tons. The beekeeping activities of countries like China, Europe and the US have been affected by the pest and viral attacks, the impact of which has been so severe and drastic that their honey exports have been virtually ruined. This has provided a great opportunity for Indian honey exporters to strengthen their position in the global market. The ASSOCHAM study is based on the growth in honey exports and feedback from various agencies under the aegis of national Beekeeping Development program launched by KVIC. Under the program, over 200 projects with an investment of Rs 2 billion are envisaged. These are expected to generate over 1 lakh jobs.

Problems

The main problems faced by the honey-producing industry in India are:

- Non-availability of infrastructure for producing genetically-superior queen bees for supply to bee- keepers
- Lack of technical knowledge for efficient management of bee colonies for higher honey yield
- Insufficient research for disease management and control
- Nonavailability of finance
- Failure in creating consumer awareness about honey and its products
- De-forestation
- Indiscriminate use of insecticides, pesticides, weedicides, etc
- Global warming and periodic changes in climatic conditions.

As beekeeping industry does not require sophisticated technology and higher capital investment, it is the right time to give attention to this industry. The industry can benefit from the great self-help potential of the rural people, tribal communities, marginal and small farmers, landless labor, etc.

The following are some opportunities in this sector, which can be easily tapped:

1. Honey has great food value and provides income
2. The demand for beeswax is increasing
3. The demand for natural honey and other products like bee-collected pollen, propolis, bee-venom and royal jelly are high, both internally and externally
4. Provides larger volume of part-time employment.

Bee-keeping Development Board, New Delhi

This is a coordinating Board to integrate the program on honeybee. The Board is headed by Secretary (Agriculture and Cooperation) with Horticulture Commissioner as the Member Secretary. The Board decides the various programs to be taken up for the development of honeybee and bee products. This Board needs to be given a separate status with functional autonomy.

Species of Honeybees

There are four species of honeybees in India. They are:

- **Rock bee** (*Apis dorsata*): They are good honey gathers with an average yield of 50–80 kg per colony.
- **Little bee** (*Apis florea*): They are poor honey yielders and yield about 200–900 g of honey per colony.
- **Indian bee** (*Apis cerana indica*): They yield an average honey yield of 6–8 kg per colony per year.
- **European bee** (Italian bee) (*Apis mellifera*): The average production per colony is 25–40 kg.
- **Stingless bee** (*Trigona iridipennis*): In addition to the above, another species is also present in Kerala known as stingless bees. They are not truly stingless, but sting is poorly developed. They are efficient pollinators. They yield 300–400 g of honey per year.

Plants Keep Bees at Bay

Collecting pollen is one of the most important tasks a bee does. Now, biologists have shown that flowers use chemical defenses to protect their pollen from bees. They secrete unfavorable chemicals which bees cannot withstand. Plants have a good reason to do so. Bees need enormous pollen to feed their young, which could be used for pollination. The pollen of several hundred flowers is needed to rear one single larvae. They also found that bees have physiological adaptation to survive on pollens of a certain flower. Denied pollen they die.

Development of Beekeeping for Improving Crop Productivity

Objectives

- To promote role of honey-bee as an agent of pollination for increasing crop productivity.
- To develop newer strains of bees for evolving disease resistant types as well as for higher production of honey.
- To encourage State/Regional level associations/cooperatives to undertake procurement, primary processing, storage, etc. of honey and its products on behalf of bee keepers to ensure maximum returns.
- To impart training to unemployed and young entrepreneurs/farmers
- Schedule caste/schedule tribe (SC/ST) aspirants in handling and managing bee colonies.
- To promote awareness and faster growth of bee keeping through mass media as well as awards at appropriate levels.

Achievements

An expenditure of Rs 46.5 million has been incurred against the 9th plan outlay of Rs 225.0 million. The significant achievements are:

- Distribution of over 0.1 million honeybees colonies
- Training of about 2,000 farmers.

The bee-keeping program will have to be implemented on a Mission Mode approach with due emphasis on crop pollination. A National Bee-keeping Development Board constituted to oversee the implementation of bee-keeping program and to coordinate the bee-keeping activities in the country need to be strengthened with statuary status having secretarial assistance for the same.

The KVIC took major initiatives for the development of bee-keeping in the country. It has an extensive network of State Khadi and Village Industries Boards, Bee-keeping Cooperative Societies and registered Institutions. The KVIC has nearly 50 years experience in extension bee-keeping. It also has a fairly developed R and D Wing and also extension system of training and education in bee-keeping. However, their thrust is on rural employment and get less focus on crop pollination. Whatever infrastructure and expertise is thus available with KVIC should be utilized. Appropriate strategies are needed for effective coordination among different agencies involved in bee-keeping and prevent duplication and overlapping of efforts.

Adequate efforts need to be made to popularize the use of honeybee both for pollination as well as for producing honey not only in the field of horticulture but also in all other areas like crop production and agro-forestry. An accurate method of registering beekeepers should be adopted so that no beekeeper come more than once in the list and no beekeeper is deleted. Registration should be done to the beekeepers on selected criteria. A person having honeybee colonies for more than 3 years or a person having more than 25 bee colonies or to whom bee-keeping and bee-keeping related activity is a full time job should be treated as a registered beekeeper.

Adequate flora for sustaining honey bee colonies is essential. Therefore, nectar bearing plants should be encouraged for plantation purposes by the agencies involved in raising of plantations. Plant species like *Plectrunthus regosus* which is available in the hills of Jammu and Kashmir, Himachal Pradesh and Uttaranchal yield finest quality of honey. Such species need to be conserved and promoted. The Rubber Board has been promoting bee-keeping as a part of their development program for tapping rubber honey.

Floral maps should be prepared in consultation with the Agricultural Universities, KVIC by the State Designated Agencies (SDA). Awareness should be created about the harmful effect of indiscriminate use of insecticides and pesticides on honeybees. The concept that honeybees are the friends of the farmers need to be promoted and the farmers advised to safeguard the honeybees.

Since information on wild bees (*Apis dorsata*) in terms of domestication and honey harvest is not sufficient, research on these bees need to be conducted. The good work on the development of bee-keeping done by the Central Bee Research and Training Center (CBRTI), Pune need to be disseminated for the benefit of the beekeepers. The Institute needs to be strengthened in terms of staff and infrastructure for addressing the emerging research and development problems on bee-keeping. ICAR may closely work with CBRTI for development of technology.

Better coordination and linkage will have to be developed with all user agencies and training facilities to be created at different levels. Suitable bee species to be identified and colonies to be distributed among farmers. It is also necessary to maintain registers of bee colony keepers. Market promotional activities require major emphasis to make bee keeping remunerative, which would finally enhance the productivity. Standard specifications for honey and other bee products have to be developed, and popularized so that proper standard are maintained.

Role of Honeybee in Agricultural Production

It is estimated a third of the food we eat solely depends on honeybees for pollination; the insect contributes about US $38 billion to the global economy. "Bees contribute to global food security and their extinction would represent a terrible biological disaster", said Bernard Vallat, director general of the World Organization for Animal Health, or OIE. The intergovernmental organization headquartered in Paris has recently prioritized research on bee mortality.

The catastrophic fall in bee numbers is not due to any single factor. Parasitic, bacterial and viral infections, exposure to pesticides and radiation from mobiles, poor nutrition and global warming are all concomitant factors that threaten the survival of honeybee colonies worldwide (see box). Since knowledge on bee diseases is insufficient, OIE has called on the international community to intensify research on how to fight the emerging and known diseases.

Agricultural economies like India are at high risk from the bee decline. Of the 160 million hectares hectares cropped area in India, some 55 million hectares depends on honeybees for pollination. Several bee research projects are underway with funding from the All India Coordinated Project on honeybees and pollinators and by institutions like Punjab University in Punjab. The researches show the bee population in India is declining, but there is no information on the extent. "The institutions do not coordinate and most focus on beekeeping, honey and wax production", said Viraktamath. "The role of bee pollination is largely ignored".

Bee Colonies Collapse

Honeybees are the most valuable pollinators of crops. In the US, the value of bees as pollinators is estimated at $15–20 billion annually. But, their numbers are declining. In 2006, beekeepers in USAs east coast reported a 31.8% decline in bee colonies. Colonies were lost as bees failed to return to their hives. This was called Colony Collapse Disorder (CCD). The collapse was linked to many factors: pesticides, parasite or pathogen attack and combination of stresses weakening immunity. In 1990s in US, insecticide Gaucho with imidacloprid as active ingredient was suspected of having harmful effects. Studies revealed that imidacloprid was toxic for bees.

Atree research organization in Karnataka, have recorded a fall in *Apis dorsata* bees in Biligiriranga hills in the state. Soliga tribals who gather their honey attributed the decline to pesticides, which bees were exposed to during their annual migration cycle to the plains. A research organization in Kerala found electromagnetic waves emitted by mobile phone towers a potential threat to bees causing death within 72 hours. The electromagnetic noise disrupts intercellular communication within bees, and they fail to find their way back to the hive.

Handled with Better Care

So far, tribals of Melghat who tap honey from wild rock bees had been destroying the honeycombs in the process. They would burn the comb, effectively depriving the forests of pollination agents. Now, they are learning to avoid the traditional methods and learning scientific skills that keep the ferocious wild rock bees tame while the villagers extract their honey.

The honey they extract is sold under the brand hunting honey and is sent on demand to Japan, from where part of it is sent to other countries. Nearly 10 quintals of hunting honey is processed and exported every year to Sitar, an Indian restaurant in Chiba, Japan. Naresh Mukut Singh, the Indian agent for Taizo Masuda's Sitar firm, regularly visits Melghat and interacts with Central Bee Research and Training Institute officials in Pune. Says Singh, "Melghat honey has become so popular that Sitar is supplying to Korea and China and we will also display the product at an exhibition later this year". For the farmer, who sells at Rs 50 a kg export earns them an additional profit around Rs 40 a kg institute officials say.

Over the years, several efforts have been undertaken to train traditional bee hunters and discourage them from destroying the honeycombs. Recently, the government launched the Scheme of Fund for Regeneration of Traditional Industries, under which 100 traditional industry clusters are taken up for development over five years. "One was extraction of honey from wild bees", said MT Wakode, director of the Pune institute. The KVIC and Coir Board are the nodal agencies for the scheme.

"We wanted to combat traditional honey collection methods that involve destroying bees and their combs by burning them", Wakode said. "Scientific procedures have been introduced that preserve the wild bees and their combs for future tappings. The United Nations Development Fund program along with KVIC took up a training project", Wakode said.

Apis dorsata, the giant bee or rock bee, has been difficult for beekeepers to manage because it does not behave like enclosed hives. It migrates during the season to follow the nectar flows, and is quick to attack. "We need no longer put the colony at risk or kill so many bees", says Benya Jambekar, a tribal in Melghat.

Armed with an easy-to-operate collection kit, including headgear with string protection, and clad in denim overalls, tribals venture out during the night to extract honey from rock bee nests. A side portion of the colony comb is cut in such a way that three quarters of the honey stored here is extracted. "The removed portion in the comb fills up within a month and is ready for another harvest", says Dhanraj Koche, secretary of the Pragati Melghat Development Society. "We have been able to train more than 700 rock bee honey collectors and curbed their migration for earning a livelihood", he said.

Once the honey is extracted from the combs, the de-honeyed pieces are melted further to get beeswax. Honey and wax are isolated and transported for marketing, Roopest Timburne at the honey processing plant at Melghat said. "This year we have been able to process 60–70 quintals of honey", Koche said. "Traditional bee hunters have now learnt that it is futile to burn the rock bee colonies. We also told them it would wipe out forests as rock bees account for pollination", Wakode said.

Duty Roster

10,000 workers in a honeybee colony.

Scouts: A few scout bees survey the area within a radius of 1 km, collect information about direction, distance and quality of food available. By performing specific dances, they pass this information on to other honeybees.

Collection: The rest fly straight to the crop for collecting nectar and pollen. The honeybees continue to visit a particular crop until its flowering withers.

Pollination: Bees' natural behavior assures fertilization of flowers. Modern beekeeping makes it possible to move a large number of bee colonies from one place to another for planned pollination of various crops.

Buzzing from Place to Place

Vivek Khalokar chose his calling after being impressed with beekeepers who came all the way from Haryana to extract honey from the hives at Amravati district's Shingnapur village, 600 km from Mumbai. "They had over 2,000 bee colonies and used to extract 80 quintals", says Vivek, a BSc in biology who went on to pursue a diploma in beekeeping at Pune's Central Bee Research and Training Institute.

Encouraged by CBRTI director MT Wakode, Vivek, 28, applied for a credit linked subsidy scheme under the Prime Minister's Employment Generation Program. The scheme is implemented in rural areas by the KVIC and the Khadi and Village Industries Board. Vivek was sanctioned Rs 10 lakh.

Within a year of beekeeping, he increased the number of bee colonies from 100–500 and got returns of Rs 10 lakh. "This year we extracted 2.5 tons of lychee honey and 1.5 tons of sunflower honey", says Vivek. The *Apis mellifera* bees will now be used in the orange crop to extract honey at Paratwada.

Vivek migrates his colonies to places such as Gorakhpur (for lychee and mustard honey), Paratwada (for orange honey) and Chikhaldara (for eucalyptus honey). He also conducted a 5 day training program and a daylong workshop on commercial beekeeping for 35 farmers and about 500 other participants. Khalokar says former president Pratibha Patil visited his beekeeping enterprises this month.

Antibiotics Prevent Disease in Bee Colonies

Beekeepers use antibiotics to prevent diseases in their bee colonies. In 1965, an Italian bee species was introduced in India by the Punjab Agriculture University since they were docile and had a much better yield. However, the bees also turned out to be much more delicate and vulnerable to disease.

Brand name	*Oxytetracycline*	*Chloramphenicol*	*Ampicillin*	*Emofloracin*	*Ciprofloxacin*	*Erythromycine*	*Number of anticides detected*
Norm	*10.0*	*ND*	*No limit*	*No limit*	*No limit*	*No limit*	
Dabur Honey	91.3	ND	26.6	88.7	ND	ND	3
Himalaya Honey	ND	ND	23.8	63.8	ND	69.7	3
Mehsons pure honey	ND	ND	ND	58.3	ND	85.0	2
Himflora Gold	ND	ND	35.5	37.7	ND	ND	2
Patanjali Pure Honey	27.1	ND	30.5	75.1	ND	186.0	4
Baidhyanath wild flower honey	ND	ND	25.2	ND	19.9	ND	2
Khadi Honey	250.4	ND	10.1	10.9	ND	ND	3
Gold Honey	57.7	4.4	ND	34.3	ND	231.3	4
Hitkari Honey	ND	ND	ND	ND	ND	ND	0
Umang Honey	ND	ND	208.1	122.1	ND	ND	2
Capilano Pure & Natural Honey	150.8	3.6	ND	144.8	ND	ND	3
Nectaflor Natural Blossom Honey	112.0	3.7	614.2	56.1	ND	280.3	5

Source: The Times of India, September 16, 2010.

Oxytetracycline, an antibiotic, is widely used by keepers to get queen bees to lay more eggs. "While no checks are prescribed for antibiotics in honey, when we procure our stock we do not know whether it contains the drugs. The industry has been aware of the problem for several years. Most big industries are not concerned with manufacturing and only sell packaged honey. It is only a question of knowing the areas where such methods of bee rearing are not used", said Nitin Malhotra, general manager, Hitkari Pharmacy, manufacturers of Hitkari Honey.

Hitkari does not have a huge honey business and only operates in the field seasonally. "We get our honey from small bee owners, those not operating commercially. They work on such a small scale that they couldn't think of using antibiotics or pesticides", added Malhotra. Narain says since there are no domestic standards, no monitoring is carried out. Honey meant for international markets, meanwhile, goes through stringent checks. "That stock which gets rejected for export since it is considered unsafe for consumption finds its way back to the domestic market. A total of seven companies own all commercial bee farms in India. The EU has rejected Indian exports on several occasions. For this, India setup export standards but doesn't seem to care about what Indians are consuming. However, we have found a lot of the honey is actually coming from China where costs are comparatively quite low", she said.

Honey in India is regulated under three legislations that include prevention of food adulteration rules, 1955, Bureau of Indian Standards and AGMARK. Anuraag Sharma, director, Shree Baidyanath Ayurved Bhavan Pvt Ltd told Times of India (TOI): "We do not manufacture honey. We subscribe to AGMARK and carry out all checks. However, no specific parameters have been set for antibiotics so we do not check for those. Checks should actually be carried out at the beekeeping level".

Bihar's Queen Bee and Her Swarm

Patiasa village in Muzaffarpur district (Bihar) is a hive of activity which spearheads a revolution of sorts. Tending honeybees in as many as 250 boxes, the women of the village harvest honey for supply to a number of firms outside the village. The buzz of Patiasa honey of the district, which is famous for its luscious shahi litchis, travelled beyond the village.

As some village women were already producing honey using desi methods, a young girl Anita decided to take it up in a more systematic manner. She also underwent training at Pusa Agricultural Institute to learn ways to produce quality honey. "The best way to judge good honey is to put a spoonful in a glass of water. If the entire chunk settles down in glass bottom, without getting even a little diluted with water, then it is the best quality of honey".

The raw materials needed for beekeeping are pollen and nectar acquired from flowering plants. Natural and cultivated vegetation, as in the case of Patiasa village, have tremendous potential of producing honey. Honey is harvested in October-November, March and June–July coinciding with cultivation of mustard, litchi and sunflower, respectively.

Buzz from Pune: Bee Colonies in Himachal Find a Savior

The honeybee population in Himachal Pradesh has come down drastically, thanks to a mite called varroa. The varroa mite that feeds on the white blood (hemolymph) of honeybees is said to have come from neighboring Nepal in 2006 and caused widespread destruction of honeybee colonies in Jammu and Kashmir and Bihar as well. The mite is also spreading to West Bengal and Haryana.

Now, there is a buzz of good news for the beekeepers from Pune. The Central Bee Research and Training Institute of India (CBRTI) has come up with a biological method to deal with varroasis. As part of this method, the parasitic mites can be separated from the bees using tobacco smoke. This smoke can irritate the mites making them fall on specialized "screened boards" kept below the hives. Armed with these boards, CBRTI made demonstrations before beekeepers in J & K and Himachal Pradesh early 2010.

The loss of bee colonies due to the mite has been tremendous in the northern belt. What was worse was that the beekeepers were unaware of the cause for a long time and could not do much about the loss". They were laying emphasis on biological methods for preventing the mite attack to ensure that the quality of honey remained pure. The CBRTI also launched training programs, and with the help of state bee keeping extension centers, generated awareness about varroasis. A special training module during April and May was also on the cards.

Bee Bacteria as Alternative to Antibiotics?

Scientists now say that lactic acid bacteria found in honeybees have shown promising results as an alternative to antibiotics in a series of studies at Lund University in Sweden. The group of bacteria counteracted antibiotic-resistant *methicillin-resistant Staphylococcus aureus* (MRSA) in laboratory experiments. The bacteria blend has already been tested on horses and healed persistent wounds. Raw honey was used to treat infections for millennia before it was processed and sold in stores.

Researchers identified a unique group of 13 lactic acid bacteria found in fresh honey, from the honey stomach of bees. The bacteria produce a myriad of active antimicrobial compounds. The bacteria were mixed with honey and applied to 10 horses whose owners had tried several other methods to no avail. All of the horses' wounds were healed by the mixture. The researchers believe the secret to the strong results lie in the broad spectrum of active substances involved.

"Antibiotics are mostly one active substance, effective against only a narrow spectrum of bacteria. When used alive, these 13 lactic acid bacteria produce the right kind of antimicrobial compounds as needed. But since store-bought honey doesn't contain the living lactic acid bacteria many of its unique properties have been lost in recent times", said Tobias Olofsson, professor of Medical Microbiology.

The study said, "today due to overuse of antibiotics and emerging antibiotic-resistant pathogens, we are facing a new era of searching for alternative tools against infectious diseases. Chronic wounds infected by pathogens are subjects for intensive research efforts because of the bacteria's ability to sustain antibiotic treatment and maintain chronic infections. "The findings could be vital both in developing countries where fresh honey is easily available".

"Honey Heals Wounds Faster than Betadine"

Dr Pillai uses a locally-manufactured ventriculoperitoneal (VP) shunt to drain out fluid from the brain. "Traditional shunts made abroad are 10 times costlier—the ones we use cost Rs 3,000 per unit", says Pillai.

In dealing with severe head injuries and disease of the nervous system, it is crucial that the pressure inside the brain be measured accurately. An intracranial catheter is inserted and the reading taken on a monitor. The catheter usually costs Rs 30,000 and the meter is worth about Rs 10 lakh.

Pillai instead inserts a simple sterilized rubber tube, filled with water, inside the brain and then connects it to any pressure monitor in the operation theater (OT). "The tube costs just a few rupees. Whenever there is an effective local option, which has been documented and proven to be safe, we try to used it", adds Dr Pillai.

In 2012, surgeons at AIIMS published a paper in the Indian Journal of Surgery, which showed that using honey (procured from beehives on neem trees) healed wounds better and faster than povidone-iodine (betadine), standard ointment used in such cases. Dr Anurag Srivastava, head of surgery at AIIMS, says that there was significant decrease in the surface area of the wound and pain in the group, where honey was used as wound dressing.

"As long as you follow basic principles of sterilization and operative technique, and provide good post-op clinical care, it is safe to use low-cost substitutes", says Dr Satish Shukla, an onco-surgeon based in Indore and president of Association of *Surgeons* of India (ASI). He further points out that although the US-FDA doesn't allow the reuse of catheters in cardiac and renal surgeries, surgeons in India safely recycle them for cost-effectiveness.

In 2003, the Indian Journal of Surgery published a paper by Dr Ravindranath Tongaonkar on the use of the mosquito net in treating adult groin hernia. Traditionally, a polypropylene mesh is used to fix the ruptured tissue but it is an expensive material. So, Dr Tongaonkar replaced it with mosquito net cloth. At the time, a meter of mosquito net cloth cost Rs 40 while the imported surgical mesh cost Rs 9,430 for a 30 × 30 cm patch. Dr Tongaonkar has used the mosquito net mesh in more than 500 hernia operations.

Similarly, instruments used in a range of expensive cosmetic procedures can be replaced with common household items once sterilized properly. Dr Shibu Thomas, a senior cosmetic surgeon who runs the inceptor cosmetic surgery and skin institute in Mumbai, uses 24-inch household electric ties (used to hold wires together) as a substitute for surgical tourniquet to put compression at the base of the breast during breast reduction surgery.

While surgical tourniquets are imported from the US and cost Rs 3,000–6,000, a pack of electric ties comes for Rs 500. He also uses a stainless steel kitchen strainer (Rs 350) to filter fat harvested for grafting instead. The medical version of the strainer can cost up to Rs 12,000.

"Most conventional surgical devices, in keeping with the US standards, are disposable. Given the cost of these devices they simply do not fit the Indian business model", says Dr Thomas. However, he also cautions that such "jugaad" should never be used as implants because that could lead to serious complications.

In Manuka Honey, Find Solution to Digestive Disorders

Honey is more than just a natural sweetener; it is known to have medicinal properties. In general, most honeys possess antibacterial, antioxidant, anti-inflammatory and prebiotic properties. Other benefits that have been attributed to honey include antitumor, antimutagenic and antiviral properties depending on the nutritional composition of the honey consumed. It is well known for its wound healing properties and as a gastrointestinal remedy. Several types of honeys are available, each with distinct properties.

The broad spectrum of anti-bacterial activity of honey is attributed to various factors including its high sugar concentration (80% sugar) and hydrogen peroxide. Nonperoxide factors include methylglyoxal (MGO), and its low pH value. Hydrogen peroxide and its high osmolarity because of high sugar concentration are the well-characterized antibacterial factors.

Certain honeys from specific plants are more effective than others. Manuka honey that comes from New Zealand Manuka bush is one such example. It has been found to be an effective therapy for digestive complaints ranging from acid reflux, gastritis, diarrhea, ulcers, *H. pylori* to fungal infections. It has been used in upper respiratory infections including chronic sinusitis, rhinitis and allergic symptoms.

All honeys contain hydrogen peroxide which imbues them with antibiotic properties. But, manuka honey exhibits antibacterial activity which is not attributed to hydrogen peroxide. It contains an exceptionally high concentration of a non-peroxide antibacterial compound MGO. MGO offers enhanced and unique antibacterial to it.

While, manuka honey also has hydrogen peroxide, polyphenols and other beneficial components, the presence of unique non-peroxide activity gives it the Unique Manuka Honey Factor (UMF). It is measured by a standard called phenol standard. For instance, UMF®5 manuka honey has the same antibacterial activity as a 5% phenol solution. Manuka honey is sold with its UMF rating; the higher the UMF factor, the greater the antibacterial potency.

How does it work? It is proposed that UMF exhibits a prebiotic effect and stimulates the growth of good bacteria (probiotics). This good bacterial growth out-competes disease-causing strains in addition to direct antibacterial effects against disease causing bacteria. This may be beneficial not only in terms of maintaining a healthy gut microbiota, but may provide some protection against the development of allergies. This may be the reason that manuka honey has also been found to reduce unhealthy bacteria in the mouth in dental plaque.

Most honeys can be used for food preservation, however, heating may lower this effect. Interestingly, manuka honey retains its antibacterial properties even on heating.

The Safe honey Comes from New Zealand Manuka Bush

Can Treat

Digestive complaints—acid reflux, gastritis, diarrhea, ulcers, *H. pylori.*

Fungal Infections

Respiratory infections—chronic sinusitis, rhinitis and allergic symptoms, unhealthy bacteria in dental plaque.

Contains

Antibiotic properties that do come from hydrogen peroxide. High concentration of a non-peroxide antibacterial compound MGO.

Sold with

Unique Manuka honey Factor (UMF) rating—the higher the UMF factor, the greater the antibacterial potency.

UMF exhibits prebiotic effect and stimulates growth of probiotics. Retains its antibacterial properties even on heating.

No Sting, Only Sweet Success with Bees

The journey of Gurcharan Singh Mann in the arena of beekeeping has been spectacular. It began with him earning a meagre Rs 2,000-odd annually in 1992 to a turnover of about Rs 4 crore, giving him an enviable standing in the panorama of state agriculture where a common farmer continues to labor without any mentionable savings.

Quitting his studies after BA-I from Government Rajindra College in 1988, Gurcharan took a loan of Rs 1.22 lakh to purchase a tractor. Ploughing his own 40-acre land at Tungwali in Bathinda, and also of others, he returned the loan amount in less than 2 years. But, it wasn't easy. He had to put in grueling hard work as the soil was sandy and underground water brackish.

In 1992, his love for agriculture took him to a 30-day course for young farmers at Punjab Agricultural University (PAU), Ludhiana, where he learnt about beekeeping, poultry, fishery and forestry. This is when life changed for this innovative farmer. He began the new venture on his farm with just two boxes, learning from his mistakes, and took his time in settling down to make his name in the competitive market which was a result of only word-to-mouth publicity. He also maintains a fish pond which is running in profit.

Besides establishing himself as one of the leading honeybee producers, 44-year-old Gurcharan made a bigger change in environment by planting trees on his farm, making use of his learning in agro-forestry. The green cover with a wide range of plants, including berries, eucalyptus, palm and mango, transformed the farm into a virtual oasis in the dry desert in the neighborhood. He transported plants on his tractor and distributed them among village residents, who contributed in changing the look of the entire village.

Gurcharan believes in a life of simplicity. He went for his wedding wearing work clothes and made sure his in-laws did not spend a single penny on the ceremony. His wife has been his greatest support and takes care of his farming ventures, particularly those related to post-produce activities like packaging.

He also setup a society for farmers, with which at least 350 farmers from Muktsar, Bathinda, Faridkot and Ganganagar were associated for a long time. A majority of them are now running individual ventures. When farmers from Harkrishanpura village put up banners saying their village was up for sale, the district administration approached Gurcharan for assistance in helping the farmers find alternatives. He goaded them to invest Rs 1 lakh in beekeeping and get Rs 1.25 lakh after one season, failing which he promised he would refund the original amount. Five farmers among them started the venture successfully.

Initially associated with the Dabur group, the Mann Farm today is supplying to bigger dealers like Kashmir Apiaries and Kejriwal, Delhi. The staff employed at the farmhouse does not make boxes merely to suffice the needs of the farm alone. These are supplied to bee farms in the entire North India, financed under a special government scheme.

Since no place grows flower for 12 months, apiary moves from one place to another. Between July and September, the farms of Bathinda and Mansa are best suited for bees. Beekeepers shift their boxes to Uttar Pradesh in September for flowers of "lauki" (gourd) and "toria" crops; to Kota in Rajasthan during October; to Ganganagar and Sangaria in Rajasthan in January; and along canals in mid-February.

This exercise involves very good public relations with the local population, particularly outside the state. One may face rigid views like in Rajasthan where village residents believe "bees would suck out all the energy out of the flowers".

Gurcharan has visited Rashtrapati Bhavan during the tenure of Dr APJ Abdul Kalam and Pratibha Patil in recognition for his innovative work. He was also awarded the Pravasi Bharti Award by the PAU in 2005, Chief Minister's Award in 2010 and NG Rangaswamy Farmers Award in 2011.

GLOBAL SCENARIO

Production, world production of honey in 2003 (Table 3.1) registered a marginal growth of 2.58% over the previous year when the same reached a level of 1,311 metric tons. China continues to be the largest producer in the world. Other major producing countries include Argenica, USA, Mexico and India. In 2003, India emerged as the 6th largest producer of honey in the world next to Mexicao. The countries showing a marginal growth in 2003 over 2002 inlcuded USA (5.13%), Iran (3.57%), Russian Federation (2.04%) and Argentina (1.87%). On the other hand, the countries witnessing a negative growth during the period comprised Canada (8.11%) and Mexico (5.08%).

Imports: Global imports of honey in 2003 (Table 3.2) registered a marginal decline of 0.65% over the previous year when the same touched a figure of 4.02 lakh tons.

Table 3.1: Global production of honey

('000 tons)

Country	*2001*	*2002*	*2003*
China	254	268	273
Argentina	80	85	85
USA	84	78	82
Thailand	60	75	75
Mexico	59	59	56
India	52	52	52
Ukraine	60	51	52
Russian Federation	53	49	50
Spain	32	36	36
Canada	35	37	34
Iran	27	28	29
World total	**1,260**	**1,278**	**1,311**

Source: Compiled from the data of FAO, Production Year book 2003, volume 57, Rome.

Table 3.2: Global imports of honey by major countries

('000 tons)

Country	*2001*	*2002*	*2003*
Germany	92.20	98.11	93.53
USA	65.75	92.01	92.15
Japan	40.19	45.04	43.79
UK	26.15	29.90	21.87
France	15.55	14.84	15.17
Italy	11.96	14.07	14.45
Spain	14.73	10.91	11.11
Saudi Arabia	7.73	4.92	9.98
Canada	5.21	8.14	9.83
Netherlands	4.55	9.50	9.38
Australia	0.77	4.49	8.80
World total	**356.94**	**404.81**	**402.16**

Source: Compiled from the data of FAO, Trade Year book 2003, volume 57, Rome.

Country-wise import trends reveal that Germany continues to be the topmost importer of honey in the world. Other major importing countries include USA, Japan, UK, France, Italy and Spain. The countries showing a steep growth during the period included Australia (95.99%) and Cananda (2076%). On the other hand, the countries showing steep decline included UK (26.86%), Germany (4.67%), Japan (2.78%) and Netherlands (1.26%).

China Leads in honey production and exports

Honey producing countries	*Produce in tons 2009*	*Export 2007*	*Production in tons 2001*	*Export 2001*
China	367,219F	65,288	254,359	106,868
Turkey	82,003	398	60,190	4,328
Argentina	81,000F	79,861	80,000	73,032
Ukraine	74,000	4,058	60,043	1,412
US	65,366	3,998	84,335	3,409
India	65,000F	12,231	52,000	3,210
World	**1,511,257A**	**409,497A**	**1,264,705**	**360,952**

A= may include official, semi-official or estimated data; F=FAO estimates, A figures in metric tons.
Source: FAO.

Exports: Global exports of honey in 2003, registered a marginal decline of 0.93% over the previous year when the same dwindled to 401.50 tons as against 405.28 tons. China continues to be the largest exporter of honey in the world. It had registered a growth of 9.95% when the same increased to 84.31 thousand tons as against 76.68 thousand tons in 2002. Other major countries showing a steep growth included Chile (105.82%), Romania (63.67%), Brazil (52.45%) and USA (41.69%). On the other hand, the countries showing a steep decline included Australia (39.29%). Canada (35.38%), Vietnam (33.56%) and Spain (21.58%).

India's Exports

India's exports of honey in 2005–2006 took a quantum jump by 74.85% when the same reached a level of Rs 116.22 crore as against Rs 66.47 crore in the previous year. India's exports of honey during the period 2002–2003 to 2005–2006 made a steady growth rising from Rs 52.90 crore in 2002–2003 to Rs 68.09 crore in the subsequent year, Rs 66.47 crore in 2004–2005 and Rs 116.22 crore in 2005–2006. In 2005–2006, USA for the first time emerged as the largest export market, putting Germany in the second rank, which happened to be India's topmost market for honey during the period 2002–2003 and 2004–2005. Accounting for a share of 65.69% of India's total exports oh honey, USA recorded a growth of 14.85% over the previous year. The other countries showing a record growth included Canada (8400%), Saudi Arabia (380.79%), UAE (9250 %) and UK (121.15%). On the other hand, the countries showing a negative growth included Germany (37.37%) and Kuwait (14.29%).

Honey and Cell Phones

Alarm bells sounded in the US at a phenomenon considered as dire as climate change: the disappearing honeybee. If the trend continues, it may spell the doom for agriculture—80% of which depends upon this humble pollinator—not to mention the environment. Amid theories about the possible reasons for the "bee colony collapse disorder" (including pesticides, disease, climate change and genetically modified crops), comes a new study that points to another culprit: the ubiquitous cell phone.

Already suffering from the colony collapse disorder (CCD) where whole colonies of bees collapsed due to various causes like the use of genetically modified crops, electromagnetic rays emitted by cell phones has now added to the woes of the honeybees. The CCD was previously attributed to viruses, parasitic mites, pesticides, genetically modified crop use and climate change. Electromagnetic frequency emitted by cell phones reduces bees' colony size and the number of eggs laid by the queen bee and changes their behavior, says a research paper published in the latest issue of Current Science.

The magnetite (a natural magnet) in their bodies that helps bees navigate is sensitive to "electro-smog" that cell phones emit into the atmosphere. For their experiment, the scientists selected honeybee colonies at the university's apiary. They exposed one set of colonies to functioning cell phones of a 900 MHz frequency band, for 15 minutes twice a day. They left the other free of the radiation. The results were unambiguous. In the colony exposed to cell phone radiation, the brood-size (comprising eggs and larvae) was just 760.19 cm^2, compared with 1975.44 cm^2 in the colony free of radiation. The queen bee exposed to radiation produced far fewer eggs a day (145) than its undisturbed counterpart (376).

And while there was no immediate exodus of bees as a result of cell phone interference, the number of pollen foragers (worker bees with pollen loads) returning to the hive declined. Consequently, the "pollen stores" (the portion of the comb containing cells filled with stored pollen) decreased in size from 246.7 cm^2 to 154.7

cm^2; and there was a dip in the number of cells containing ripe and unripe nectar. "At the end of the experiment, there were neither honey, nor pollen nor brood and bees in the colony, resulting in the complete loss of the colony", the paper says. Not too long ago, cell phone radiation was attributed to the inexplicable disappearance of another diminutive creature from Indian cities, the house sparrow.

Fall of the Bees

Population of bees, the main pollinators of food crops, is declining. This can contrain food supply, according to a UN Report.

Regions Affected

- In Europe, there has been a fall in bee colonies since 1965, unusual weakening and mortality was reported in 1998, France, Switzerland, Germany, the Spain and Italy were worst affected.
- In the US, loss of bee colonies has aggravated since 2004. During 2006–2007, 29% beekeepers in the country reported Colony Collapse Disorder, with a loss of 75% colonies.

In Asia, China, with 6 million bee colonies, has faced colony losses in the recent years due to Varroa mite attack, 25% of Japanese beekeepers have suffered the losses.

Causes of Worry

The reports says there are more than a dozen factors behind bee deaths. These include air pollution, fast-spreading fungal diseases and varieties of parasites such as the Varroa destructor, as well as the loss of habitat of wild flowers in intensively farmed areas. The increased use of pesticides, including broad spectrum and systemic pesticides, which are absorbed by plants affect bees through pollen and nectar. These pesticides combine to form a lethal cocktail that damages bees sense of direction. Because of air pollution scents that traveled 800 m in the 19th century now travel only 200 m, making it harder for bees to find plants, their food source.

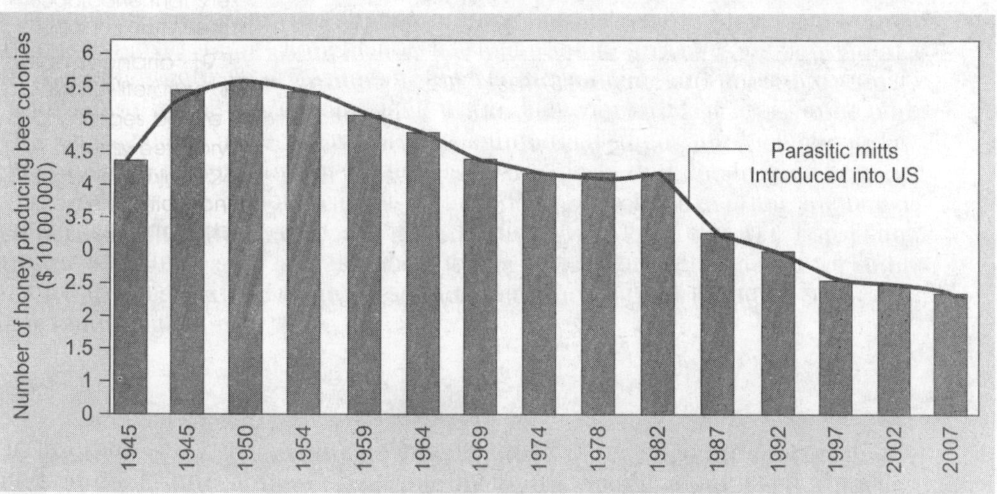

Plan to Saving Honeybees

United States of America President Barack Obama has launched a determined effort to save some of Americas busiest workers, the honeybees, crucial for the food industry and contributes a whopping $15 billion in value to agricultural crops.

Obama has created a task force comprising various agencies—to address the issue of rapidly diminishing honeybees and other pollinators, who play an integral to food security in the US.

Honeybees pollinate fruit, nuts and vegetables, and are crucial for the nation's food industry. They have declined sharply in recent years due to various factors, including pesticides, mite infestations and loss of genetic diversity.

Pollination is integrated to food security in the US, it said honeybees enable the production of at least 90 commercially grow crops in North America, Globally, 87 of the leading 115 food crops evaluated ae dependent on animal pollination, insects birds, butterflies and bats transfer pollen between plants, which allows them to make seeds and reproduce. In addition to food sustainability, honeybees boost the American economy.

Pollinators contribute more than $24 billion to the US economy, of which honeybees account for more than $15 billion through their vital role in keeping fruits and vegetables in our diets.

World Honey Production (× 1.000 tons)

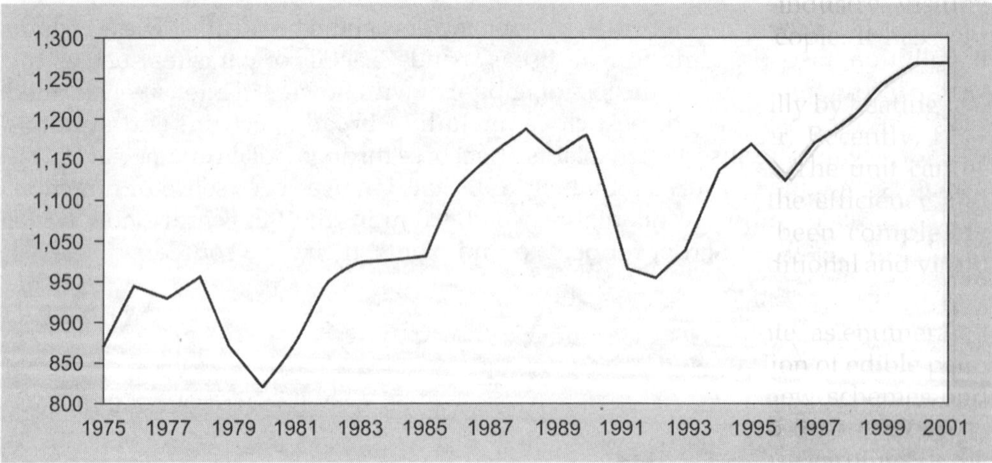

Annexures

Annexure 1A: World honey production by continent (× 1,000 tons)/production mondiale de miel par continent (× 1,000 tons)

Continents	*1991*	*1992*	*1993*	*1994*	*1995*	*1996*	*1997*	*1998*	*1999*	*2000*	*2001*
Africa	109	117	129	131	138	142	140	139	141	144	145
North and Central America	222	216	223	195	183	174	189	218	201	208	205
South America	87	87	95	97	105	100	109	109	133	141	131
Asia	334	328	326	354	365	362	402	401	435	457	465
Europe	180	182	181	291	319	278	281	291	293	286	288
Oceania	29	29	30	38	27	35	36	31	29	29	29
Total =	961	958	984	1103	1137	1091	1156	1188	1232	1265	1263

Annexure 1B

Pays/Années	*1991*	*1992*	*1993*	*1994*	*1995*	*1996*		*1997*		*1998*		*1999*		*2000*	
×	*1,000 tons*	*1,000 tons*	*1,000 tons*	*1,000 tons*	*1,000 tons*	*1,000 tons*	*1,000$ tons*	*1,000 tons*	*1,000$ tons*	*1,000 tons*	*1,000$ tons*	*1,000 tons*	*1,000$ tons*	*1,000 tons*	*1,000$ tons*
China/*Chine*	70	92	96	102	87	84	115	48	69	79	87	87	79	103	87
Argentina/*Argentina*	47	55	55	62	63	48	81	70	108	68	89	93	96	88	87
Mexico/*Mexique*	50	36 (37)	36 (35)	30	25	29	49	27	41	32	42	22	25	31	35
USA	5	10	4	4	10	5	11	4	8	5	9	5	9	5	8
Canada		11	8	8	16	10	20	8	17	11	20	15	21	15	21
Others/*Autres*	82	56	56	63	62	79	138	75	132	67	123	72	112	85	108
EU/*UE* extra	8	11	11	12	9	6		7		6		6		6	
EU/*UE* intra	18	18	22	27	29	32	(91)	29	(86)	38	(89)	40	(88)	42	(95)
Total =	280	257	252	308	301	293	505	269	461	307	458	340	430	375	441

Annexure 1C: World honey production by country / production mondiale de miel par pays (× 1,000 tons)

Countries and years/pays et années	*1997*	*1998*	*1999*	*2000*	*2001*
China	215	211	236	252	256
Former USSR	136	134	132	124	125
USA	89	100	94	100	100
UAE	106	109	117	112	111
Argentina	75	75	93	98	90
Turkey	63	67	71	71	71
Ukraine	58	59	55	52	52
Mexico	54	55	55	59	56
India	51	51	51	52	52
Canada	30	46	37	31	32
Australia	27	22	19	19	19
Brazil	19	18	19	22	20
Hungary	16	17	16	15	16

Annexure 2: If World honey importation (× 1,000 tons)

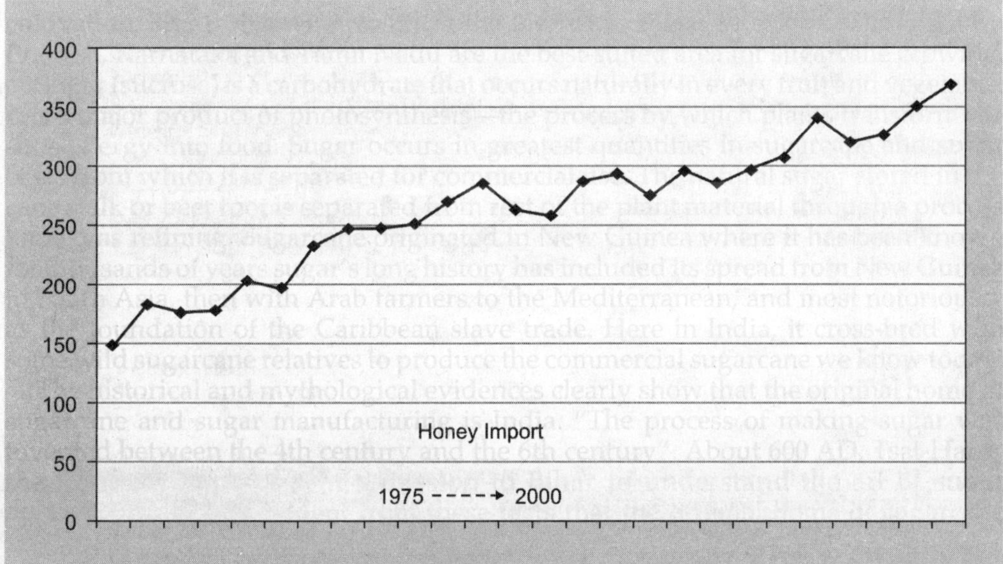

Annexure 3: If World honey exportation
(× 1,000 tons)

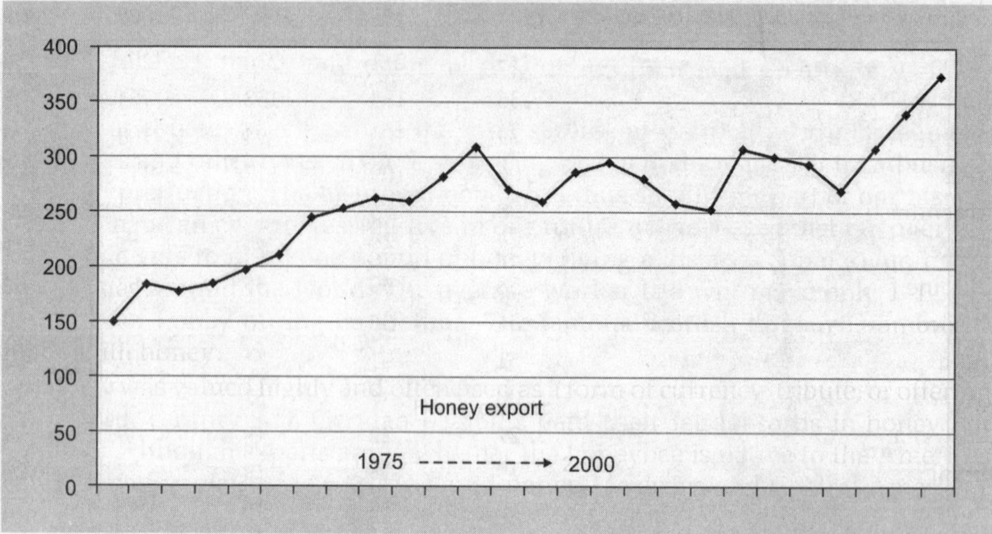

4

Sugar By-Products

FUTURISTIC VISION OF THE SUGAR SECTOR

The sugar sector of tomorrow has to be envisioned as an energy hub producing not only sugar but also ethanol from molasses and power from bagasse. Increase in ethanol pricing from Rs 27 per liter to Rs 33–36 per liter will help sugar sector to improve its viability and thus give a better return to farmers. In order to tap its full potential, molasses need to be fully freed from movement restrictions or reserved allocation for potable liquor. In Uttar Pradesh (UP), e.g. almost 20% of molasses are reserved for potable liquor and the price paid is less than one-fourth of the market price being offered by the chemical industry. It is akin to sugar sector subsidizing the potable liquor sector. Such perverse policies need to be fully overhauled. But, two issues will remain central to sugar sectors future growth: (a) How best one can align sugarcane production with better and more efficient usage of water and (b) how rationally we can align sugarcane pricing with revenue sharing formula. If these issues are tackled rationally and quickly, sugar sector can double its worth in the next 5–7 years. Else, it will remain besieged in uncertainty, wide fluctuations and only limited growth.

Sugarcane is a renewable, natural agricultural resource because it provides sugar, besides biofuel, fiber, fertilizer and myriad of by products/co-products with ecological sustainability.

- In addition to sugar, 38 value added products of commercial importance are attained.
- Sugar juice is used for making white sugar, brown sugar (khandsari) and jaggery (gur).
- The main by-products of sugar industry are bagasse and molasses. Molasses, the chief by-product, is the main raw material for alcohol and thus for alcohol-based industries in the country.
- Ethanol, a by-product of sugar, can be used as a biofuel alternative to gasoline, and is widely used in carsin Brazil.
- Sugarcane bagasse (the fibrous material leftover after crushing) is the chief source of power in the sugar mills.
- Pulp, paper-products, building materials and also as a renewable energy for power generation.
- It has been estimated that about 3,500 mw power can be generated annually without extra fuel and investment much less than required for generating the same through thermal power plants.

- Another by-product, pressmud, contains considerable amount of plant nutrients and could be an important source of organic matter, major and micronutrients.
- Sugarcane green tops are used as cattle feed. In urban areas, sugarcane juice has great demand as a thirst quencher.
- Sugarcane provides the cheapest form of energy giving food (sucrose) with the lowest unit of land area per unit of energy produced.
- It has been estimated that an average man's annual food consumption is equivalent approximately to 1 million calories.

Under present agricultural system, this is produced by 1 of 8 of an acre of sugarcane while whole wheat flour requires seven times, milk 20 times and beef over 100 times as much land to produce the same amount.

The major by-products of sugar production are **molasses**, **beet pulp**, **bagasse fiber**, and **cane wax**. Cane and beet molasses are the syrups that remain after the sugar has been crystallized out. They are used mainly as livestock feed, as is the carbohydrate-rich beet pulp, which remains after the sugar has been extracted from the beet root. Cane molasses is also used for making alcoholic drinks, particularly rum.

Sugar industry is cyclical in nature. Ethanol, a by-product of sugar, can be used as a biofuel alternative to gasoline, and is widely used in cars in Brazil. Begasse, also a by-product of sugar, can be used as a biofuel and as a renewable resource in manufacturing pulp, paper-products, building materials and also as a renewable energy for power generation. Sugar in India is a politicized industry. The center determines statutory minimum price for sugarcane. The government of most states in which sugarcane is cultivated fixes what is dubbed as the state advised price (SAP) that mills of the state have to pay to the farmers.

Bagasse is the cane fiber that remains after the sugarcane has been rolled. It is so dry that it can be used to fire the mill furnaces that heat the sugar boilers. Some of it may be baled and shipped to factories, where it is pressed into building board. Cane wax is extracted from the dried material that has been filtered out of the sugary liquid during the production of raw cane sugar. It is used in manufacturing polishes, cosmetics.

About 13% of sugarcane sap is sucrose. During harvesting, the cane stalks are stripped of their leaves and trimmed for easier handling at the cane mill or sugar factory. In the factory, the stalks are washed and cut into short lengths or shredded. The sugar is removed from the canes by a diffusion process or by milling. In the diffusion process the sugar is separated from the finely cut stalks by dissolving it in hot water or juice. In milling, the juice is squeezed from the rough pulpy mass of the stalks by pressing it between heavy rollers. These are arranged in sets of three. Each set of rollers exerts a greater pressure than the last set. While the cane is passing between the rollers it is sprayed with water to help to dissolve additional juice. The waste material, or pulp, that is left after the rolling is called **bagasse.**

The liquid extracted from the cane is a dark grayish or greenish color and is acidic. Since it contains impurities, it is necessary to use chemicals for clarification. In most instances, milk of lime is added to the raw juice. The juice is immediately heated to the boiling point and then run into settling tanks where the precipitated matter is separated from the clear juice. In order to make a white sugar directly from the cane juice, sulfur dioxide and sometimes phosphoric acid are added to the juice before the milk of lime. The same process is then followed.

Effluent water and polluted soils should not be used for growing cane for chewing and juice purposes.

The juice is evaporated into thick syrup and then concentrated by vacuum boiling in several stages. The vacuum allows the mixture to boil at a relatively low temperature to prevent scorching of the sugar syrup. The mixture is boiled until sugar crystallizes out of the liquid, forming a mixture known as **massecuite**. The raw sugar crystals are then separated from the massecuite by centrifugal machines—perforated, hollow cylinders that revolve rapidly. The syrup, called **molasses,** is forced out through the holes, but the raw sugar is left inside. Some of the raw sugar is sold as it is, but most of it goes to refineries.

GUR IN INDIA

Proportion of cane crop utilized for Gur Manufacture: The sugarcane is used for several purposes such as chewing, making white sugar, making khand, making gur and for seeds. The exact quantities of sugarcane used for these different purposes have not been ascertained but according to a rough estimate the proportion or cane crop utilized for different purposes has been as follows:

Year	*For gur (%)*	*For white sugar (%)*	*For other purposes* (%)*
1928–29	63	3	34
1929–30	64	3	33
1930–31	67	4	29
1931–32	69	4	27
1932–33	68	7	25
1933–34	67	10	23
1934–35	67	12	21
1935–36	64	16	20
1936–37	65	17	18
1937–38	63	18	19
1938–39	60	19	21
1939–40	52	27	21
1940–41	60	19	21
1941–42	63	17	20
1942–43	58	19	23
1943–44	60	20	20
1944–45	64	16	20
1945–46	64	16	20
1946–47**	62	19	19
1947–48	62	19	19
1948–49	60	20	20

* For Khandsari sugar manufacture, chewing and seed.

** Figures for the year 1946-47 and onward relate to Indian union only.

It will be seen that following the grant protection to the sugar industry in 1932, the proportion of cane crop utilized for white sugar to have stabilized at about 16–20% but the impact of this on the manufacture of gur has been small, the proportion of crop utilized for gur manufacture still remaining over 60%. The major proportion of cane is therefore still being utilized for the manufacture of gur.

History also has it that India pioneered the technique of sugar making thousands of years ago. Apparently, it was the first "spice" to be exported from India. Throughout India jaggery continues to be used extensively in cooking. Jaggery is unrefined sugar, which is widely used in Asia, Africa, Latin American and also the Caribbean countries. It is made from concentrated sugarcane juice, but here the molasses are not separated which is done in the case of sugar. There are two types of jaggery available—one that is made from sugarcane and the other one is made from Palmyra palm tree. For making jaggery, sugarcane sap from palm trees is boiled for hours and then the concentrated liquid is poured into moulds to dry and set. These moulds come in different shape which is why the jaggery available in the market comes as cylinders, round balls, cones and half spheres. Then again their color, ranging from pale gold to deep brown, will depend on the level of sweetness. My mother and others of her generation prefer the darker variety, saying that it is the purer form, well cured and therefore, has a better flavor and is sweeter.

Jaggery stores well as long as it is stored in an airtight container in a cool and dry place. Break the jaggery into smaller pieces and store, so that whenever you need to use it, you need to handle just the amount that you need. Though both Jaggery and sugar are made from the same source, there is a lot of difference in their properties and benefits. The first difference is the color. Sugar is white in color, whereas the color of jaggery can range from golden-yellow to golden brown to dark brown. The color is often dependent on two factors, namely the base ingredient used to make jaggery, and up to what extent it is cooked.

The texture of sugar and jaggery differ—while sugar crystals are solid and hard, jaggery is semi solid, soft and shapeless. This is because the molasses and other impurities are not removed from it. Most importantly the two are processed differently. Though for both initially the sugarcane juice is boiled, to make sugar the syrup it is further treated to remove unwanted particles as a result of which the end product got after condensation and crystallization is white. But in the case of jaggery, the sugar syrup is not treated neither does it undergo crystallization process. Instead the sugarcane juice is boiled continuously till it thickens and forms a paste which is then poured into moulds or blocks and allowed to set.

Their chemical composition is different too—while sugar is made only of sucrose, jaggery is made up of predominantly sucrose, mineral salts, iron and some fiber. This is why jaggery is considered healthier of the two and also recommended to those suffering from iron deficiency anemia.

Influence on human body the difference between sugar and jaggery is carried forward to their influence on the human body. Sugar which is the simplest form of sucrose is absorbed almost immediately into the blood resulting in instant energy. This is why people with diabetes should stay away from sugar. Jaggery on the other hand, is made up of longer chains of sucrose, resulting in it being digested slowly and energy being released slowly. This energy lasts longer and is not harmful. Then again since jaggery is processed in iron vessels, it is also rich source of iron. It acts as a cleansing agent and cleans the lungs, stomach, intestines, esophagus and respiratory tracts. Thus, you can see that jaggery is better than sugar as it contains iron, minerals, vitamins and sucrose. But, a word of caution for the diabetics and that is though it is better than sugar it should be consumed in moderation.

The benefits of jaggery include its ability to cleanse your body, act as a digestive agent, sweeten your food in a healthy manner, and provide good amounts of minerals. Before we go into the details of the benefits of jaggery, let me tell you that all good things do not come in nice, good-looking packages. This is true for foods as well, particularly when we talk about jaggery.

In Myanmar, the native country of jaggery, people don't bother about the color, since they have been eating jaggery since childhood and it is a mouth watering sight for most of them. Furthermore, if you hear about the way it is manufactured and stored and the standards of hygiene there, you might never think of eating it, but it is far-far better than those frozen meats and so called hygienically packed food items with chemical preservatives in them that are stored for weeks or months before reaching the consumer. In fact, in some cases, the jaggery blocks may contain some particles of sand or ash that flies in from the oven, but they are not unhygienic in any way. We eat a multitude of dust and pollutants every day while we breathe and talk. Still doubtful? Well, let us alleviate the rest of that doubt with the spectacular health benefits of jaggery.

Health Benefits of Jaggery

Sweetening agent: There are plenty of natural and artificial sweetening agents available on the market with good old white sugar right at the top. However, almost all of them are just plain sweeteners. How nice would it be if such magnificent sweeteners could add some extra burst of taste as well? The answer to that question can be found by eating jaggery. The first benefit of jaggery is that it is a colorful, taste explosion when consumed, and secondly, it is a sweetener. You can experience the difference yourself. Taste plain sugar and jaggery one after another, and it will be very clear to you. That was only the sugar cane jaggery; a single flavor. Now, you should taste the Date Palm Jaggery, Palmyra Jaggery, or one of the other flavors available.

Energy food: We know that carbohydrates, consumed in our food, give us energy upon oxidation. The simpler the carbohydrate, the sooner the energy released. On one hand, this simplicity comes as a blessing for athletes and people suffering from serious fatigue because they need instantaneous energy and can find quick relief. Therefore, sugar and glucose is the proper carbohydrate for them because they are very simple and are absorbed in the blood stream almost instantaneously to fill them with a sudden burst of energy.

But on the other hand, studies show and doctors advise that this sudden rise in sugar or energy level can be a major threat to the integrity of internal organs, particularly in the case of diabetics. In the long run, this may even give rise to diabetes, since the fluctuating sugar levels may affect the pancreas, to the point where the pancreas may lose its capacity to release large amounts of insulin at once to counter the quick increase in the body's sugar level. This sudden uplift may cause severe damage to kidneys and eyes, can raise blood pressure, and create a number of other problems in the related organ systems. Jaggery is a more complex form of carbohydrate than plain sugar. When you eat jaggery, it is digested and absorbed gradually and releases energy over an extended period of time. This can provide the eater with warmth and energy for a more extended period without harming their internal organs.

Digestive agent: This may sound strange, but in India, it is recommended to take a few grams of jaggery after a heavy meal or after eating meat because it facilitates digestion. Jaggery activates the digestive enzymes and itself changes to acetic acid in the stomach, thereby speeding up digestion and making the process go very smooth, reducing strain on the intestines and digestive tract.

Cleansing agent: You may not normally connect sweeteners and sugars with "cleansing the body", but that are actually one of the well-proven benefits of jaggery. Jaggery effectively cleans the respiratory tracts, lungs, food pipe, stomach and intestines. It pulls out dust and unwanted particles from the body while also giving relief from constipation, perhaps due to presence of fiber in it. Reducing constipation and stimulating the movement of the bowels further cleanses the body of the toxins which jaggery just cleaned out and prepared for excretion.

Source of minerals: Unlike sugar, jaggery is rich in minerals, mainly iron with traces of other mineral salts. While most of the iron in jaggery comes through its processing in iron vessels, the other minerals come directly from the sugarcane juice, since the juice does not undergo refinement or bleaching of any kind. Therefore, jaggery is a very good source of minerals for the body.

Other Benefits and Uses of Jaggery

Jaggery seasoning: Jaggery (sugarcane variety) is often used as a lining for the inner walls of earthen ovens and is meant for seasoning the materials cooked inside.

Jaggery as a building material: Even a few decades ago, jaggery was in use (and still is in use in some places) as a building material, particularly in those places where cement was not readily available. It was mixed with lime, sand and clay and used as cement for joining bricks. Jaggery, which is predominantly sucrose, upon reacting with calcium carbonate in lime and silica in clay, forms strong bonds and became very hard on drying. Some examples of such buildings can still be seen in West Bengal and in other parts of India if they are still standing.

Jaggery in toothpaste: Low-quality jaggery, mixed with the dust of tobacco, is used as tooth paste in many parts of India. It is so widely used that government earns a handsome revenue out of it. It is very popular and very addictive at the same time. Some people, who appear to have nothing to do, can be seen rubbing this stuff on their teeth the whole day and night, very lazily. It is a common sight in villages. Suffice to say, this is not a healthy or good way to treat dental health, or to pass your free time. It is not recommended as tobacco can be carcinogenic.

Jaggery for cattle feed: Jaggery of low-quality is often mixed with cattle-feed to add taste and make the cattle eat more. It also sweetens the milk of the cattle.

Jaggery used as hunting bait: There are instances where jaggery has been used as bait for hunting wild animals. It is dumped in the open so wild animals will be attracted by its smell to taste it and fall prey to the hunters. Since jaggery contains salt, besides being sweet and having a strong aroma, animals like to lick it.

Religious usage: Among Hindus, it is customary to take a bite of jaggery after attending a funeral, along with Margo leaves, crushed black pepper and to touch fire and iron, as it is said to purify. In some places, in certain religious ceremonies and rituals, small idols of jaggery, rice paste and turmeric are prepared and offered to local gods and goddesses.

Jaggery as fish bait: Jaggery is also used as fish bait. Jaggery, mixed with a number of ingredients including ant eggs, ghee, edible oils, cardamom powder, nutmeg powder, mace, poppy seeds and a variety of other things, forms an excellent bait mixture. Fishes cannot resist its smell and are pulled to the gaming spot where the hooks are waiting!

In shoty, that is the story of jaggery. It seems so simple, yet so mysterious! There are innumerable fables and folk tales in which jaggery can be found.

In some cases, jaggery is less likely to give you a bad reaction to acidity when compared to normal white sugar. There is no good explanation for this, but this is frequently seen. Even doctors suggest switching to jaggery for sweetening purposes when someone is having an unexplainable acidic reaction.

Basically, it is not too late! You should switch to jaggery today. Add it to your meals for a few days and feel the difference for yourself!

The scientists have now proved that the intake of sugar is injurious to health while consumption of gur is essential for good health. Hundred gm of gur contains 0.4 gm protein, 0.1 gm fat, 80 mg calcium, 40 mg phosphorus, 11.4 mg iron, 0.6 mg to 1 gm minerals, 168 mg carotene, 0.02 mg thymum, 0.05 mg vitamin C and 383 kilo calorie energy in the form of carbohydrates. In contrast, except carbohydrates all valuable vitamins and minerals, etc are missing from sugar. While gur has medicinal values, sugar leads to cancer, heart attack, obesity and pyorrhea.

The diet atlas of India reveals that in the case of sugar and jaggery, Punjab and Haryana top the list—on an average 85 gm is consumed per day per adult. West Bengal and Maharashtra come next with 40 gm each. In rest of the states consumption level of sugar, etc is very poor. However, the most unsatisfactory feature is that intake of jaggery declined considerably among the agricultural laborers when they started receiving wages in cash instead of traditional wages in kind and food. As a result of inadequate jaggery consumption, there is poor development of physique of the agricultural laborers and their working efficiency has deteriorated.

Now, India should concentrate on gur production instead of sugar. Due to heavy competition for food, fiber and oilseeds, there is little scope for increase in the area under sugarcane to meet the increasing demand of gur. Therefore, the only alternative left is to increase the productivity of sugarcane and gur by adopting efficient management practices for sugarcane cultivation. India sugar and gur prices in Delhi Market graph is given on the next page 298.

Research and development efforts properly organized should help to improve the yield levels throughout the country. There is more scope in this regard in the North than in the South target yield level would be 75 tons per hectare in the North and 100 tons per hectare in the South. Varieties have to be bred for gur for highest possible gur recovery.

"Gur gur reha, chela sakkar ho giya" goes the old saying but sugar has lagged far behind. Gur has always got respect in Ayurveda. The usefulness of it has now been recognized at the international level. Kudos to our gur as it has been branded as "millennium gur" and is in great demand in 23 countries, including the USA, Japan, Canada, Hong Kong, Germany, etc. In the recently concluded 88th India Science

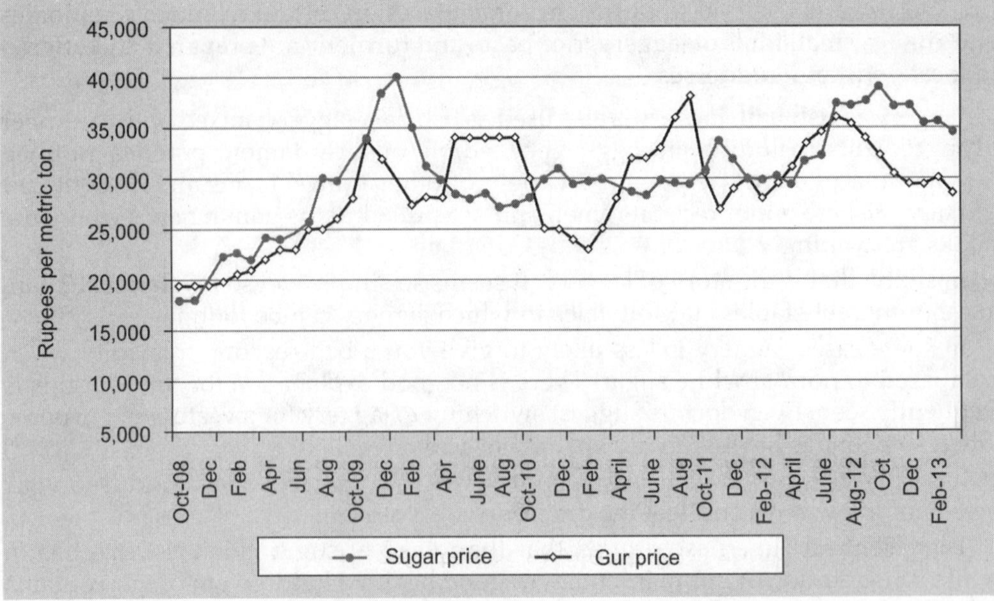

India: sugar and gur prices in Delhi market

Congress in New Delhi, the scientists impressed upon the use of new technology integrating the traditional knowledge in the preparation of gur. This will move India from the green to rainbow revolution.

The Dr Jaswant Singh of India Institute of Sugarcane Research has revealed that gur is being transformed into chocolate, liquid gur, and granulated gur for export. The technology of liquid gur has been developed at the Regional Sugarcane and Jaggery Research Institute, Kholapur, Granulated gur is manufactured at the Regional Research Station, Anaukpalli. Gur cubes would soon take the place of sugar cubes in starred hotels. This is a welcome sign for the oppressed peasantry of the country.

Sugarcane is used to make five major types of sweeteners. In the order of refinement, these are sugar, khandsari, shakkar, gur and raskat (a byproduct of the sweetener industry). Gur and khandsari are cottage industry products and do not have to deal with restrictive policies that control the sugar industry.

Gur is more nutritious than sugar, it has around 28 gm of minerals per kg as compared to just 300 mg per kg in refined sugar. Compared to gur-making, manufacture of sugar uses more chemicals such as sulphur dioxide, lime, phosphoric acid and bleaching agents. Gur is rich in iron and is useful for people suffering from anemia. Those with dry cough, indigestion and constipation also get relief with gur. According to the ancient ayurvedic text, Sushruta Samhita, gur purifies blood and rheumatism. Some recent studies have also shown that it can protect the lungs from dust and smoke in the environment.

Utilization of Gur for Various Purposes

Gur is used for different purposes such as direct consumption by human beings, for stock feeding, for refining, in milk, tea or coffee, for sweetmeat making and for other sweetening purposes. Figures for the utilization of gur for various purposes in India can only be estimated as actuals are not available. Even these figures are known only for the pre-war period.

Gur composition

Nutrition per 100 gm	
Energy	383 kcal
Protein	0.4 g
Carbohydrate	95.0
Fat	0.1 g
Minerals	0.6 g
Calcium	80 mg
Phosphorous	40 mg
Iron	2.64 mg

Source: Nutritive value of Indian foods, Gopalan et al., Natinoal Institute of Nutritional, Hyderabad 2002.

"Gur" Manufacture

- Gur manufacture is an important cottage industry from ancient times.
- Though considerable technology was developed on scientific lines from improvement in crushers for better extraction of juice to the storage of gum.
- Yet, it must be admitted that the processing of gur continues to be crude and wasteful.
- Three main operations are involved in the manufacture of gur: (i) extraction of juice from cane, (ii) purification of juice and (iii) concentration into gur.

Extraction

- Extraction of juice is done with a crusher or series of crushers.
- A six-roller hydraulic crusher, having a crushing capacity of 4 tons, has been designed by the National Sugar Institute, Kanpur, which is said to give 80% extraction and can increase the recovery of gur from 10% to 12%.

Clarification

- The juice is boiled for concentration and removal of dissolved foreign material in a circular pan made of iron or zinc sheets over a furnace.
- The suspended impurities and the gummy colloidal constituents in the Juice are removed by coagulation during the first heating, lasting about 30–45 minutes.
- Then the juice is clarified using clarificants to remove all impurities which would favor inversion of sugar. Lime is the most widely used chemical clarificants by virtue of its easy availability, begins to crystallize.
- It is stirred slowly and intermittently to avoid loss of granular structure.
- The semi-solid mass is then put into moulds.

Khandsari Industry

- Immediate substitute of sugar.
- It is sugar produced from unrefined juice.
- Competes directly with sugar due to excise duty difference.
- Good Khandsari sells at marginal discount to sugar.
- At times of low sugarcane production i.e. high molasses price, high sugar prices.
- Hence can pay for sugarcane—even more than sugar mills causing diversion.
- The word "Khandsari" is derived from the word "Khandsale" meaning sugar house with the development of the whole sugar industry, the word Khandsari came to represent the old indigenous process of white sugar manufacture.
- Khandsari sugar is yellow to whitish in color, opaque and dull in texture and either powdery or very small grained.
- It is said to have easy digestibility and better nutritive qualities.
- UP is the cradle of the Khandsain industry.
- The boiled juice called the "Rab" is taken out and filled into bags generally made of wool, these bags are placed one over the other and pressure is applied through manual labor for draining out the molasses.
- When the flow of molasses stops, the bag is emptied into special pits with brick flooring which is covered with a thick layer of the sea weed (Sewar).
- The moistened sea-weed generates heat, creating chemical reactions.
- In 3 days, all the mass of molasses is drained out and it becomes white.
- Every alternate day the upper layer or white sugar is removed and the process continued until the entire material is treated.
- The sugar is sun dried and then it becomes ready for market.
- Much of the sugar goes into the molasses and thus the recovery is hardly 5% the khandsari industry was started in UP and has now spread to many states notalogy AP, MP, Maharashtra, Punjab, Orissa and Tamil Nadu.

Uses of Jaggery

- For preparing many traditional sweets.
- For preparing country liquor (arrack)
- Thick syrup of jaggery (kakvi) consumed along with chapattis and rotis.
- Added to several culinary preparations.
- Added as one of the ingredient in some pickles.
- A component in several traditional home remedies.
- Used in preparing cattle feed
- Thick jaggery solution is fed to honey bees to prepare honey.

Quality Parameters of Jaggery

- Color (light, golden yellow color)
- Hardness (should be hard)
- Structure (crystalline structure)
- Taste (sweet without any saltishness or any other taste)
- Flavor (P\pleasant flavor)
- Shelf-life (longer keeping quality).

Quality Parameters of Juice for Getting Good Quality Jaggery

- High sucrose and high purity
- High total sugars
- High level of phosphate content
- Low level of colloidal matter, ash, mineral matter and organic nonsugar such as nitrogen (higher N produces soft Jaggery) amino acids (higher amino acid content gives dark color to jaggery), starch and gums.

How to Get Good Quality Jaggery?

- Select varieties having high sucrose content, high purity and low colloids.
- Choose early maturing, high sugared varieties (COC 671, Co 6907, CoJ64, Co 7704, etc).
- Well drained medium to light textured soils with neutral pH and less salt content are preferred.
- Calcareous soils give poor quality jaggery.
- Soils with high pH and $CaCO_3$ gives juice with more ash and colloids leads to poor quality.
- Swampy soils-poor keeping quality.
- Heavy black soils-black color to jaggery.
- Early planting is advantageous.
- Avoid late and excess manuring particularly N.
- Use more organic sources of nutrients.
- P-application useful for better clarification.
- P-application neutralize ill effects of N.
- Ammonium sulfate is better N-fertlizer over urea (since sulphur is present)
- Late application of fertlizers is deleterious.
- Irrigation with saline water gives soft and saltish-taste jaggery.
- Provide less irrigation at maturity for better sugar accumulation.
- Pest and disease infested cane give poor quality jaggery.
- Immature or over matured canes have less sugar and more non-sugars and reducing sugars leads to poor keeping quality (inversion of sucrose is a serious problem in overaged canes).
- Flowered cane should be avoided.
- There should not be pith in the cane.
- Crush the cane within 24 hours of harvest.
- Harvesting to ground level is important since, the lower internodes are rich in sucrose.
- Avoid crushing of top internodes.

Chewing

- Though no precise estimate is available about the extent of cane used for chewing and beverage purposes, it easily ranges from 1.5% to 2.0% of the total cane production.
- Varieties grown for chewing purpose are infact true officinarums.
- Chewing cane must be attractive in color, thick easy to peel and split, should be juicy, having more sugar, soft with less fiber and should have less or no wax on the rind surface.
- The rind of the cane should be less thickness and hardness.

Sugarcane for Juice

- Sugarcane juice is consumed directly.
- Cane for this purpose have higher sucrose, fructose and glucose levels are desirable.
- Also cane with higher extraction and less fiber and nonsugar component in juice and preferred.
- Besides selecting a good variety for choosing or for extraction of juice, other requirement is to ensure good soil so that cane growth is assured and thus higher juice volume.
- Salt affected soils as well as saline water irrigation should be avoided as these would affect juice taste and color.
- It is desirable to use no or less pesticides.
- Late application of fertilizers, particularly of N, should be avoided as otherwise; there could be more soluble N in juice which is undesirable.

Manufacture of Cream Jaggery

The color of gur usually ranges from yellowish to dark brown. The lighter the color of gur the better is its quality. In order to improve the color special treatment has to be given utilizing the principle of surface attraction. A process has been evolved for making gur directly from juice yielding a creamy white product. This gur has been termed cream jiggery.

Cream Jaggery: The process of manufacture of cream jiggery was evolved by the Indian Council of Agricultural Research, New Delhi. The gur produced by this process is of good quality and has cream color. It is superior to ordinary gur. Due to its fancy color there is great demand for it. Manufacture of this type of Gur was started first in the western part of UP. But now, it is gaining popularity in other parts of the country as well.

Manufacture of Neutral Gur

Neutral gur is prepared for refining purposes. It cannot be consumed directly due to its unpleasant taste. But, it contains higher percentage of sugar in it and would fetch better price than ordinary gur in the refineries.

In the manufacture of ordinary gur, there is much destruction of sugar during boiling of juice. The finished product is therefore of poor quality. The two most important causes responsible for the poor quality of gur are: (i) inversion due to acidity and high temperature and (ii) caramelization due to concentration at high temperature. In order to avoid the loss of sugar due to inversion caused by boiling an acidic juice at high temperature for a long time the juice thus neutralized is called neutral gur.

Manufacture Molassine Gur

In the Khandsari system of sugar making two straight boiling are generally practiced. The juice is boiled to first Rab and the molasses from first Rab is boiled for obtaining second sugar and exhaust molasses. During normal times a major portion of this molasses for want for adequate utilization is not easily saleable at a fair price so as to give a good return to the Khandsari. Under such circumstances the molasses is converted into gur. As the sugar per cent in exhaust molasses is very low gur prepared from it does not solidify. To make solid gur from molasses it is prepared from molasses obtained after curing first Rab. In this manufacture of 2nd sugar and exhaust molasses is eliminated and the Khandsari is saved from the problem of disposing of its exhaust molasses.

Chaku Minjha Gur

Chaku Minjha is a form of gur chiefly manufactured in the districts of Meerut. Muzaffarnagar and Saharanur. In its manufacture, the juice is boiled in the usual way after Deola clarification, but the boiled mass is struck at a slightly lower temperature than that for ordinary gur. The boiled mass which is at a temperature of 115°C is directly is directly empied into Nand and after being well stirred and cooled up to 80°C is poured by the Karigar into the Adda described below. In this way subsequent charges are poured turn by turn in other Addas of the row so that when the turn of the 1st one again comes for the next charge the previous mass has cooled down sufficiently. Successive charges one over the other are poured into the frames turn by turn till all are completely filled. After being covered with matting the gur is left over night to solidify. Next day, the block of gur in the frame is tilted on the longer side and the hessian cloth sticking to it removed completely. The block is allowed to fall on a brick placed in the middle of the frame over the hessian cloth and break slabs. In the slabs, a white line of crystallized sugar appears after every successive charge. The gur is pleasing appearance and very good in taste.

Adda: Dry bagasse is evenly spread over the ground, and mattings (chatais) are placed over it. Over the chatais rectangular frame works consisting of four well lied bundles of "Phastera" (Bajra stems) of about 6 inches diameter are placed. The length and breadth of the frame is 4 feets × 2.5. Over the whole length and breadth of the frame hessian cloth is spread.

Gur by Bugloss (Gaozaban) Clarification

Half (½) kg of Gaozaban and ¼ kg of black sajji are steeped in 6 liters of water in a bucket for a 24 hours. The mass after being well rubbed the hanks is strained through fine muslin cloth. The strained mass is again put in 3 liters of water well rubbed and restrained. To the strained liquids 1 drum of alum is added and this is boiled till. The bulk is reduced to one-fourth 3 ozs of this liquids is added to a charge 2.5 mds. Of juice in the pan after the scums has been removed. On this addition, the scums that rise to the surface are again removed. The clarified juice is then boiled to gur in the usual way.

In order to study, the quality of gur that is produced by this process comparatively, gur was also made from the same quality of juice by the usual Deola clarification. In appearance, the color of gur produced by Deola clarification was lighter than that of Gaozaban.

Andarki Gur

Andarki gur is manufactured in the districts of Saharanpur and Dehradun. The process of manufacture for this form of gur is the same as that for Chaku Minjha gur except that in this case only a single layer of cooled mass is spread over the hessian cloth in the Adda. When the mass has cooled it is cut with knives into oblong bits and collected in baskets. Sometimes, the Andarki gur is spiced with powdered ginger roots, cloves, cardamoms and shredded Copra. These are added to the boiling juice after clarification.

Shakkar

It is a kind of raw sugar directly consumed or used by Halwais for the manufacture of inferior kinds of sweets. The process of clarification and boiling is similar to that of gur except the boiling is continued a little longer than in case of Bheli gur. When the boiling mass attains the proper consistency which is at temperature of 120°C, the contents are emptied in earthen Chaks and allowed to cool. When the mass has cooled down somewhat soda dissolved I a little water is sprinkled over it and the mass well kneaded with Khurpies until it has acquired a pale yellow color. The mass is then made into a conical lump and removed to next Chak to cool down further. After 15–20 minutes the mass is rubbed violently between the hands till the powdered gur (Shakkar) is ready. The quantity of soda is about 30 gm per 24 kg of boiled mass. In order to decolorize the Shakkar and give it a good appearance Blankit (sodium hydrosulfite is also used. The blankit is added in two stages. It is first added with a little soda when the juice is boiling in the pan after clarification. In the 2nd stage, it is added dissolved along with soda to the cooled mass in the earthen Chak. The quantity of blankit added is about half that of the soda. The Shakkar so produced is pale yellow in appearance, and is taste is somewhat different.

By-products of Sugar Beet and Their Utilization

Beet-pulp, a residue obtained after extraction of sugar, is a highly valuable cattle-feed that can largely replace barley-grains in feed concentrates. Beet-pulp can be fed to cattle as fresh or in dried form. The mixing of molasses with pulp improves its palatability.

The beet molasses are used as raw material for several special fermentations and also form a rich source of lactic acid, vitamin B and other pharmaceutical preparations.

Beet-tops are a highly nutritious cattle-feed and are known to improve milk yield of cows. They, however, contain oxalic acid, and hence fresh-tops must not be fed to cattle. Sun-dried tops 100 kg + 60 g finely ground lime is a good cattle-feed.

The important findings of the sugar beet research in India led the anxiety of beet workers for practical utilization of their efforts. The thing which now needs critical examination is whether technology of sugar beet production is an economical proposition for sugar production in comparison to sugarcane, which is the traditional sugar crop. Sugar beet is par excellence in many aspects. The questions must now be posed to the sugar technologists, to the sugar industrialists and economists in the country. We have reached a stage on the agricultural technology where we say, here are the roots, we can produce them now, can you process them economically and compete with cane? Although when we conceived of the sugar beet crop, the idea was not that it would compete with sugarcane crop but that at the far end of the cane season (April onward) when sugarcane crop is difficult to harvest, and starts deteriorating; sugar beet may be processed in the same sugar factory with some modifications in the plant.

There are three major requisites for the efficient commercial exploitation of sugar beet:

1. Sufficient availability of high quality seed material with the desired genetic potentiality
2. Availability of modern beet sugar manufacturing facilities
3. Appropriate public policies.

Fuel and energy conservation: When 100 tons of sugarcane is crushed; we generate 38 tons as by-products which include 4 tons of molasses, 4 tons of filter cake and 30 tons of bagasse. With continuous adaptation of steam economy measures and installation of planetary gears and variable frequency drives, the steam and installed requirement presently is around 40% on cane and 25 kW per ton of cane per hour. The aim should be to reduce this requirement further to 30% on cane and 20 kW per ton cane per hour. This can be achieved probably by injecting steam into bagasse energy generation system. Overall energy saved can be supplied to the grid which can fetch revenue leading to reduction in the processing cost of sugar.

The processing system, in addition to producing 10 tons of sugar and 38 tons of liquid effluents, which include 35 tons of water supply externally. This surplus water has to be treated for removing the injurious products for cultivation purposes. This is the way we can create a water balance and ensure that the sugar industries give back the water to the farmer.

Medicinal Properties

The minerals present in jaggery strengthen the nervous system and relaxes the muscles.

- The selenium present in jaggery acts as an antioxidant whereas the presence of potassium and sodium helps to maintain the acid balance in the body cells and also to control the blood pressure.
- Jaggery is also helpful in curing migraine and also easing cramps during menstrual periods.
- It is generally given to new mothers soon after delivery because it helps to remove all the blood clots within forty days after the birth of a baby.
- It consists of moderate amount of calcium, phosphorous and zinc and therefore helps to purify the blood, prevent rheumatic afflictions and treat bile disorder. It is also helpful to cure jaundice.
- Culinary uses
- Jaggery is used extensively in both sweet and savory dishes across India and Sri Lanka. It is added to curries and dals in the southern states of India. A dash of jaggery when added vegetables like bitter gourd and brinjal reduces their bitterness to a great extent. The Gujaratis use it to enhance the taste in a lot of their dishes. Jaggery is also used in the preparation of toffees and some cakes.

Ethanol

What is Ethanol?

Ethanol (ethyl alcohol, grain alcohol, EtOH) is a clear, colorless liquid. It is an alcohol-based alternative fuel produced by fermenting and distilling starch crops that have been converted into simple sugars. In dilute aqueous solution, it has a somewhat sweet flavor, but in more concentrated solutions it has a burning taste. Ethanol

(CH_3CH_2OH) is made up of a group of chemical compounds whose molecules contain a hydroxyl group, (-OH), bonded to a carbon atom. Ethanol made from cellulosic biomass materials instead of traditional feedstocks (starch crops) is called *bioethanol*.

The word alcohol derives from Arabic al-kuhul, which decnotes of fine powder of antimony produced by distilling antimony and used as an eye makeup. Alcohol originally referred to any fine powder, but medieval alchemists, later applied the term to the refined products of distillation, and this led to current usage.

The fermentation of sugar into ethanol is one of the earliest biotechnologies employed by humans. The intoxicating effects of ethanol consumption have been known since ancient times. Ethanol has been used by humans since prehistory as the intoxicating ingredient of alcoholic beverages. Dried residue on 9,000-year-old pottery found in China implies that Neolithic people consumed alcoholic beverages.

The earliest known scientific identification of ethanol was from the Persian polymath, Rhazes, in the 9th century. Although distillation was well known by the early Greeks and Arabs, the first recorded production of alcohol from distilled wine was by the School of Salemo alchemists in the 12th century. The first to mention absolute alcohol, in contrast with alcohol-water mixtures, was Raymond Lull.

In 1796, German-Russian chemist Johann Tobias Lowitz obtained pure ethanol by mixing partially purified ethanol (the alcohol-water azeotrope) with an excess of anhydrous alkali and then distilling the mixture over low heat. French chemist Antoine Lavoisier described ethanol as a compound of carbon, hydrogen, and oxygen, and in 1807 Nicolas-Theodore de Saussure determined ethanol's chemical formula. Fifty years later, Archibald Scott Couper published the structural formula of ethanol. It was one of the first structural formulas determined.

Ethanol was first prepared synthetically in 1825 by Michael Faraday. He found that sulfuric acid could absorb large volumes of Coal gas. He gave the resulting solution to Henry Hennell, a British chemist, who found in 1826 that it contained "sulphovinic acid" (ethyl hydrogen sulfate). In the 1828, Hennell and the French chemist Georges-Simon Sérullas independently discovered that sulphovinic acid could be decomposed into ethanol. Thus, in 1825 Faraday had unwittingly discovered that ethanol could be produced from ethylene (a component of coal gas) by acid-catalyzed hydration, a process similar to current industrial ethanol synthesis.

Ethanol was used as lamp fuel in the United States as early as 1840, but a tax levied on industrial alcohol during the Civil War made this use uneconomical. The tax was repealed in 1906. Use as an automotive fuel dates back to 1908, with the Ford Model able to run on gasoline or ethanol. It remains a common fuel for spirit lamps.

Ethanol intended for industrial use is often produced from ethylene. Ethanol has widespread use as a solvent of substances intended for human contact or consumption, including scents, flavorings, colorings, and medicines. In chemistry, it is both a solvent and a feedstock for the synthesis of other products. It has a long history as a fuel for heat and light, and more recently as a fuel for internal combustion engines.

- Ethanol as derived from molasses is a byproducts from sugar production
- It is used as a solvent in scents, flavorings, colorings and medicines.
- Denatured or chemically altered ethanol is used as a fuel or an industrial solvent.

Bidders for blending program this year

State	*Quantity*
Maharashtra	15.61
Uttar Pradesh	10.74
Karnataka	9.59
Haryana	5.32
Punjab	4.85
Andhra Pradesh	4.72

Selling ethanol at Rs 27/liter is naturally not affordable now. Ethanol has been made since ancient times by the fermentation of sugars. All beverages, ethanol and more than half of industrial ethanol are still made by this process. Simple sugars are the raw material zymase, an enzyme from yeast, changes the simple sugars into ethanol and carbon dioxide. The fermentation reaction, represented by the simple equation $C_6Hi_2O_6$! $2CH_3CH_2OH + 2CO_2$ is actually very complex, and impure cultures of yeast produce varying amounts of other substances including glycerine and various organic acids. In the production of beverages, such as whisky and brandy, the impurities supply the flavor. Starches from potatoes, corn, wheat, and other plants can also be used in the production of ethanol by fermentation. However, the starches must first be broken down into simple sugars. An enzyme released by germinating barley, diastase, converts starches into sugars. Thus, the germination of barley, called malting, is the first step in brewing beer from starchy plants, such as corn and wheat.

Ethanol melts – 114.1°C, boils at 78.5°C, and has a density of 0.789 g/mL at 20°C. Its low freezing point has made it useful as the fluid in thermometers of temperatures below – 40°C, the freezing point of mercury, and for other low-temperature purposes, such as for antifreeze in automobile radiators.

Ethanol can be produced from any biological feedstocks that contain appreciable amounts of sugar or materials that can be converted into sugar such as starch or cellulose. Sugar beets and sugar cane are examples of feedstocks that contain sugar. Corn contains starch that can relatively easily be converted into sugar. A significant percentage of trees and grasses are made up of cellulose which can also be converted to sugar although with more difficulty than required to convert starch.

The ethanol production process starts by grinding up the feedstocks. So, it is more easily and quickly processed in the following steps. Once ground up, the sugar is either dissolved out of the material or the starch or cellulose is converted into sugar. The sugar is then fed to microbes that use it for food, producing ethanol and carbon dioxide in the process. A final step purifies the ethanol to the desired concentration. Ethanol is also made from a wet-milling process. Many larger ethanol producers use this process, which also yields products such high-fructose corn sweetener.

Ethanol is used as an automotive fuel by itself and can be mixed with gasoline to form what has been called "gasohol' fuel ethanol—the most common blends contain ethanol (10%) and ethanol (85%) mixed with gasoline. Over 1 billion gallons of ethanol are blended with gasoline every year in the United States. Because the ethanol molecule contains oxygen, it allows the engine to more completely combust the fuel, resulting in fewer emissions. Ethanol is one of the best tools to fight vehicular pollution, contains oxygen (35%) that helps complete combustion of fuel and thus reduces harmful tailpipe emissions. It also reduces particulate emissions that pose a health hazard. Since ethanol is produced from plants that harness the power of the sun, ethanol is also considered as renewable fuel. Therefore, ethanol has many advantages as an automotive fuel.

Most industrial ethanol is denatured to prevent its use as a beverage denatured ethanol contains small amounts, 1 or 2% each, of several different unpleasant or poisonous substances. The removal of all these substances would involve a series of treatments more expensive than the federal excise tax on alcoholic beverages (currently about $20 per gallon). These denaturants render ethanol unfit for some industrial uses. In such industries, undenatured ethanol is used under close federal supervision.

The Clean Air Act Amendments of 1990 mandated the sale of oxygenated fuels in areas with unhealthy levels of carbon monoxide. Since that time, there has been strong demand for ethanol as an oxygenate blended with gasoline. In the United States each year, approximately 2 billion gallons are added to gasoline to increase octane and improve the emissions quality of gasoline.

Blends of at least ethanol (85%) are considered alternative fuels under the Energy Policy Act of 1992 (EPAct). E85, a blend of ethanol (85%) and gasoline (15%), is used in flexible fuel vehicles (FFVs) that are currently offered by most major auto manufactures. FFvs can run on gasoline, E85, or any combination of the two and qualify as alternative fuel vehicles under EPAct regulations. In some areas, ethanol is blended with gasoline to form an E10 blend [ethanol (10%) and gasoline (90%)].

Ethanol-Blended Petrol to Cut Import Bill By Rs 18K Crore

The NDA government is pushing for ethanol-blended petrol to become a reality which could bring down India's oil import bill by an estimated Rs 18,000 crore a year.

Blending of ethanol with petrol will help bring down India's growing dependence on crude oil imports, which costs the country $150 billion or Rs 9 lakh crore per annum. The government can save anywhere up to $3 billion (Rs 18,000 crore) a year, by blending ethanol (10%) with petrol. The government believes that sugarcane farmers are likely to benefit from the move as ethanol is a by-product of sugarcane. Farmers also feel that it could get them a good price for their crop. In 2008, the government announced the National Policy on biofuels, mandating a phased implementation of blending ethanol with petrol in various states. However, the process has been delayed due to over-pricing and procurement issues.

In recent tenders floated by oil companies for procuring ethanol, they were not willing to pay the benchmark price and insisted on a delivered cost of Rs 44 a liter, against the cost of Rs 46 per liter of ethanol.

Mandatory blending of ethanol (10%) with petrol, this would mean procuring over 2 billion liter of ethanol every year, an oil company. State government has been asked to expedite clearances to ease the availability of ethanol for blending. Ethanol is also used by the chemical, alcohol and spirits industries. Its cost to these also determines its cost to oil firms.

Physical Properties

Ethanol is a volatile, colorless liquid that has a slight odor. It burns with a smokeless blue flame that is not always visible in normal light. The physical properties of ethanol stem primarily from the presence of its hydroxyl group and the shortness of its carbon chain. Ethanol's hydroxyl group is able to participate in hydrogen bonding, rendering it more viscous and less volatile than less polar organic compounds of similar molecular weight, such as propane. Ethanol is slightly more refractive than water, having a refractive index of 1.36242 (at ë = 589.3 nm and 18.35°C). The triple point for ethanol is 150 K at a pressure of 4.3×10^{-4} Pa.

Solvent Properties

Ethanol is a versatile solvent, miscible with water and with many organic solvents, including acetic acid, acetone, benzene, carbon tetrachloride, chloroform, diethyl ether, ethylene glycol, nitromethane, pyridine and toluene. It is also miscible with light aliphatic hydrocarbons, such as pentane and hexane, and with aliphatic chlorides such as trichloroethane and tetrachlorethylene.

Ethanol's miscibility with water contrasts with the immiscibility of longer-chain alcohols (five or more carbon atoms), whose water miscibility decreases sharply as the number of carbons increases. The miscibility of ethanol with alkanes is limited to alkanes up to undecane, mixtures with dodecane and higher alkanes show a miscibility gap below a certain temperature (about 13°C for dodecane). The miscibility gap tends to get wider with higher alkanes and the temperature for complete miscibility increases.

Ethanol-water mixtures have less volume than the sum of their individual components at the given fractions. Mixing equal volumes of ethanol and water results in only 1.92 volumes of mixture, mixing ethanol and water is exothermic, with up to 777 J/mol being released at 298 K.

Mixtures of ethanol and water form an azeotrope at about 89 mole percent ethanol and 11 mole percent water or a mixture of about 96 volume percent ethanol and 4% water at normal pressure and T = 351 K. This azeotropic composition is strongly temperature- and pressure-dependent and vanishes at temperatures below 303 K.

Hydrogen Bonding in Solid Ethanol at 186°C

Hydrogen bonding causes pure ethanol to be hygroscopic to the extent that it readily absorbs water from the air. The polar nature of the hydroxyl group causes ethanol to dissolve many ionic compounds, notably sodium and potassium hydroxide, magnesium chloride, calcium chloride, ammonium chloride, ammonium bromide and sodium bromide, sodium and potassium chloride are slightly soluble in ethanol. Because the ethanol molecule also has a nonpolar end, it will also dissolve nonpolar substances, including most essential oils and numerous flavoring, coloring, and medicinal agents.

The addition of even a few percent of ethanol to water sharply reduces the surface tension of water. This property partially explains the "tears of wine" phenomenon. When wine is swirled in a glass, ethanol evaporates quickly from the thin film of wine on the wall of the glass. As the wine's ethanol content decreases, its surface tension increases and the thin film "beads up" and runs down the glass in channels rather than as a smooth sheet.

Flammability

An ethanol-water solution that contains 40% ABV (alcohol by volume) will catch fire if heated to about 26°C (79°F) and if an ignition source is applied to it. This is called its flash point. The flash point of pure ethanol is 16.60°C (61.88°F), less than average room temperature.

The flash points of ethanol concentrations from 10% ABV to 96% ABV are shown below:

- 10%—49°C (120°F)
- 12.5%—about 52°C (126°F)
- 20%—36°C (97°F)
- 30%—29°C (84°F)
- 40%—26°C (79°F)
- 50%—24°C (75°F)
- 60%—22°C (72°F)
- 70%—21°C (70°F)
- 80%—20°C (68°F)
- 90%—17°C (63°F)
- 96%—17°C (63°F)

Alcoholic beverages that have a low concentration of ethanol will burn if sufficiently heated and an ignition source (such as an electric spark or a match) is applied to them. For example, the flash point of ordinary wine containing 12.5% ethanol is about 52°C (126°F).

Sugar mills produce around 260 liters of ethanol from each tons of molasses, depending upon the technology employed while crushing. But, a major part of the molasses is supplied to alcohol manufacturers who procure the raw material at a high price of around Rs 6,000 a ton. Even a mandatory 5% blending of ethanol with petrol, as committed by government 3 years ago to protect the environment 3 years ago, would be difficult to meet because of a fall in sugarcane output. India needs around 600 million liters of ethanol a year for 3 years to meet the 5% blending norm. If this is increased to 10%, the country would need 1,200 million liters of ethanol.

Corn as Source of Energy

Why and how do we plant corn and harvest energy? It is known that average yield of 5 tons/hectare of corn grain can give more than 80,184,256 kJ plus 105,505,600 kJ from corn plant residues. This energy is equal to 4,430 kg petroleum or 6,156 kg cola. Corn is the most important and abundant crop produced in Yugoslavia. Corn, as we usually think of it, is primarily a feed and food grain. However, there are many uses and think of it, is primarily a feed and food grain. However, there are many uses and application of corn. When we talk about corn from energy point of view two of many corn applications are the most important. First of all, the widest application of corn is an animal feeding and for the industrial preparation of animal feed. The second one is the application of corn for ethanol production.

The best way of energy comparison among cereals is the total carbohydrate and fat production. Corn is very competitive as a high carbohydrate yielding plant. Table 4.1 shows energy comparison among cereals and fats. This comparison is based on metabolished energy, the energy that can be used by animal. The data indicate that the metabolished energy, the energy that can be caused by animal. The data indicate that the metabolished energy of corn is the highest among cereals followed by sorghum, wheat, ray, barley and oats. In addition, there are at least 25 different types of feedstuff that can be made from corn. At least 25, different processes are applied in preparation of these feedstuffs. For example, gluten with (65%) protein is a by-product of wet milling and used as high protein feedstuff, corn oil can be produced from corn germ by both dry-and wet milling and used as the high energy source, green plant of corn and corn silage are used as soft feed; dextrose is a product of starch hydrolysis that is completely digested and so on. The second important application of corn, from energy point of view, is the use of corn in ethanol production. Interest in corn as an ethanol-producing crop was renewed during the 1970s because of the energy crisis. Table 4.1 presents the ethanol yield per hectare for different cereals. Ethanol produced from corn promised a renewable source of fuels for cars and other engines with environmental advantages. Only the carbohydrate portion of the grain is converted into ethanol, all else can be recovered as a valuable by product called distillers dried. Grains which are sold as feedstuff. The most important quality criterion for this type of use is the starch content in the grain which should be over 70% in dry substances in order to obtain 37 up to 40 liters of pure alcohol from 100 kg of corn. Corn can provide the carbon and energy source for virtually any fermentation.

Both wet dry milling process are alternative methods for concentrating the starch component of corn. The dry milling can produce a substrate of a higher starch content than whole corn about 80%. The we-milling process produces a purified starch that can be almost completely converted to ethanol.

Starch is a polysaccharide composed exclusively of D-glucose and is one three most abundant organic compounds found on the earth. Two major components of starch are amylase and amylopectin. Amylose is essentially a linear macromolecule

Table 4.1: Metabolished energy values for cereals and fat feedstuffs

Cereal	*Metabolized energy (kJ/kg^{-1})*	*Fat*	*Metabolized energy (kJ/kg^{-1})*
Corn	14,110	Animal fat	29,760
Sorghum	13,810	Lard	33,150
Wheat	13,350	Soyabean oil	38,680
Barley	11,800	Tallow	26,370
Oats	11,130	Fatty acids from soyabeen	34,110
Rye	11,970	Lecithin	28,170

Cereal	*Ethanol yield (liters/1,000 kg)*	*Yield grain tons/hectare*	*Ethanol (liters/hectare)*
Corn	360	5.4	1,950
Wheat	340	3.1	1,054
Barley	250	2.5	625
Rice	430	5.0	2,200
Sorghum	350	3.7	1,300
Oats	240	2.4	580

of D-glucose units linked alpha-1 to 4 to each other. Amylopectin is a branched macromolecule of D-glucose units linked alpha-1 to 4, with 5% alpha-1 to 6 linkages in branched points. Four different enzymes are used in starch conversion: beta-amylase (liquefying), alpha-amylase, glucoamylase and pullulanase (sacccharifying). The role of alpha-amylase enzymes in the initial steps of conversion is to decrease the viscosity of a gelatinized starch. This thinning and liquefaction activity produces only dextrins as the reaction products. Saccharifying enzymes hydrolyze the starch and dextrins to glucose or maltose.

Advantages

It is hard to find any negatives about bio-fuels. They are green farmer-friendly, appeal to every politician's desire to reduce import dependency, allow governments to give subsidy to growers of cereals, oilseeds and sugarcane, and generate industrial investment. All this makes biofuels very palatable to everyone across the political and economic spectrum. It is India that has a future in ethanol, mainly because it is derived from a by-product molasses, instead of cane juice. In Brazil, ethanol is part of debate whether the country should use sucrose, which is in demand, to make food or as a fuel. In India that debate is irrelevant in so molasses are concerned.

Some of the advantages of ethanol as an automotive fuel are that it is 100% domestic, it gives distinct environmental benefits with respect to CO, ozone-farming potential, total CO_2 and total potency weighted toxics. Refueling is akin to that of gasoline or diesel, and it is applicable for both light and heavy duty vehicles. It has more energy density compared to gasoline with optimized compression ratio, and maintenance required is more or less identical to that of conventional fueled vehicles.

The main benefit of ethanol is that it made from agricultural crops like sugarcane or corn. Other benefits include its higher octane number, higher flame speed, lower CO, HC, NO_x emissions, usage of lean mixture and better volumetric efficiency. Ethanol may be a good fuel for spark ignition engines especially in warm climates.

Comparison of ethanol with other fuels

Property	*Ethanol*	*E85*	*Methanol*	*Gasoline*
Chemical formula	C_2H_2OH	—	CH_2OH	C_4-C_{12}
Octane no.(R + M)/2	98-100	96	100	86-94
Lower heating value (Btu/lb)	11,500	12,500	8570	18,500
Liter equivalent	1.5	1.4	1.8	1
Km/liter*	70%	72%	55%	100%
Fuel tank size	1.5	1.4	1.8	1
RVP (psi)	2.3	6.12	4.6	8–15
Air fuel ratio	9	10	6.45	14.7
Excess vehicle Power*	5% more	3.5%	4% more	Standard

Ethanol had emerged as sustainable, renewable and viable alternative to the fast depleting no-renewable fossil duels. It is also a comparatively environment friendly energy source. Massive use of ethanol, as one of the options, can help India meet its commitment to curb it greenhouse gas emissions. The use of ethanol as an alternative to conventional fuels reduces carbon dioxide (CO_2) emissions by 25%. Each tone of sugarcane used to produce ethanol absorbs 0.17 ton of CO_2 from the atmosphere.

It is estimated that carbon monoxide is reduced by 15–60% and hydrocarbons/volatile organic compounds (VOC) by 5–20%. It also reduces nitrogen oxides in the emissions. *Methyl tertiary-butyl ether* (MTBE) is also used as an oxygenate but the requirement of MRBE is double that of ethanol for the same oxygen content. The blending of ethanol also reduces the temperature of the engine, combustion chamber and engine carbon deposits improves the startability of the engine and reduces engine knocking and thus improves engine life. Many countries are now replacing petroleum-based oxygenates like MTBE with ethanol.

Certain issues arise in the use of ethanol in motor vehicles fuel. The fuel issue is that ethanol contains approximately 28–33% less energy than an equivalent volume of gasoline. This implies that the mileage obtained from automobiles run on ethanol blends would be lower than gasoline powered cars. Data on theoretical energy contents of gasoline and ethanol blends show that for ethanol blended gasoline with oxygen (2%) content, v/v ethanol (5.7%) is required, leading to a decrease of 1.7% energy content. On the other hand, a 3.5% oxygen level requires ethanol blend (10%), resulting in a decrease of 3% in energy content. However, the Oxygen in ethanol improves the combustion characteristics of the fuel and increases the octane number, thereby working to increase the mileage. On the whole, due to a lack of proper field tests, there is no clear-cut evidence of either an increase or decrease in mileage. Available evidence shows that a lot depends on the age and type of vehicle, and on the average there is no change in mileage in the case of 5 or 10% ethanol blend as compared to gasoline.

With the increase in the number of ethanol-driven vehicles all over the world, the compatibility of ethanol as an automotive fuel raised questions.

Relative equivalent CO_2 emissions of fuels

Fuel	*Eqv. CO_2 emissions*
Diesel	368.0
CNG	302.2
LNG	499.7
LPG	384.2
Ethanol	229.1
Methanol	400.9
Hydrogen	389.0
Battery (lead acid)	307.7
Fuel cell	207.5
Hybrid (Pb acid-CNG)	304.6

Usage of Ethanol

The demand for ethanol stems from three quarters—the alcoholic beverages industry, the chemical industry and the transport sector. At present, roughly 50% of the ethanol consumption is by the alcoholic beverages industry followed closely by the alcohol-based chemicals industry. All other uses, including that for automotive fuel, constitute a miniscule fraction of total consumption in India (Tables 4.2 and 4.3). This is despite the general belief that ethanol which is a biofuel is green and farmer friendly. It has great potential as an environmental friendly fuel. It has also a wide application in various fields like perfumeries, beverages and pharmaceutical industries, it can be used to run automobiles without any modification in engines. It is claimed that corn ethanol is almost as efficient as petrol. On an average, it produces 95% as much energy as petrol.

Among the major countries in the world in bioethanol production, Brazil is a front runner, and introduced a program to produce ethanol for use in automobiles in order to reduce oil imports as early as 1931. Brazilian ethanol is made mainly from sugarcane. Pure ethanol (100%) is used in approximately 40% of the cars in

Table 4.2: Demand for alcohol—view point of alcohol manufactures

Year	*Alcohol consumption*			
	Alcoholic beverages industry	*Industrial alcohol*	*Other*	*Total*
1995–96	5,197	4,951	442	10,590
1996–97	5,882	4,641	535	11,058
1997–98	4,782	4,630	347	9,759
1998-99	4,894	4,688	351	9,933
1999–2000	5,009	4,746	355	10,110
2000–01	5,127	4,805	356	10,291
2001–02	5,247	4,865	363	10,475

Table 4.3: Demand for alcohol—view point of chemical manufacturers

Year	*Alcohol consumption for*				
	Alcoholic beverages industry	*Industrial alcohol*	*Other*	*Total*	
				Six states	*All India*
1995–96	2,857	4,792	243	7,892	8,578
1996–97	3,056	4,587	204	7,848	8,530
1997–98	3,472	3,910	259	7,641	8,305
1998–99	3,757	4,721	199	8,677	9,432
1999–2000	5,002	4,347	155	9,503	10,329
2000–01	4,935	4,052	181	9,169	9,966
ROG (% p.a)	11.6	–3.3	–5.7	3.0	3.0

Note: All India values are worked out from 6 states data based on assumption that these six states (Uttar Pradesh, Maharashtra, Karnataka, Tamil Nadu and Andhra Pradesh account for 92% of country's production of sugar and molasses.
Source: State Excise Commissioners as quoted by Department of Chemical and Petrochemicals

Brazil. The remaining vehicles use blends of ethanol (24%) with gasoline (76%). Brazil consumes nearly 4 billion gallons of ethanol annually. In addition to consumption, Brazil also exports ethanol to other countries. Sweden has used ethanol in chemical production for many years. As a result, Sweden's crude oil consumption has been cut in half 1980. During the same time period, the use of gasoline and diesel for transportation has also increased. Emissions have been reduced by placing catalytic converters in vehicle exhaust systems which decrease carbon monoxide, hydrocarbon, and nitrogen oxide emissions. To a address global warming concerns, the amount of carbon dioxide produced while burning fossil fuels must be reduced. Ethanol-blended gasoline and ethanol diesel are being considered as viable alternatives to further lower emissions levels.

USA uses corn as the main sources of bioethanol. Thailand uses sugarcane as well as cassava for ethanol. Japan, Germany, Canada, Australia, Indonesia, South Africa and Sweden are the other leading countries using ethanol blends. Bio-diesel is also being used in USA, Austria, Finland, Greece, Czech Republic, Ireland, Italy and Spain. The main sources of bio-diesel in these countries are rapeseed, sunflower, olive oils. Prompted by the increase in oil prices in the 1970s, ethanol is produced in France from grapes that are of insufficient quality for wine production.

Recently the international price of sugar crossed 18.5 cents a pound, the highest in the past 25 years. Not that there was a sudden jump in the consumption of sugar or that the sugar production had suddenly plunged. It was simply that sugarcane was diverted to production of ethanol which is used as a substitute for gasoline to power cars. The largest producer of ethanol from sugarcane is Brazil. In 2005, it produced 14 billion liters. Most cars on Brazilian roads are run on flexible-fuel. They use ethanol, gasoline or a blend of the two. Ethanol can be produced not only from sugarcane but also from corn, wheat, tapioca, sweet sorghum, palm oil, etc. only from sugarcane but also form corn, wheat, tapioca, sweet sorghum, palm oil, etc. Other countries are either producing and using ethanol in large quantities or are providing incentives to expand ethanol production and use. Sweden is using large quantities of ethanol as a fuel. Some Canadian provinces promote ethanol use as a fuel by offering subsidies or up to 45% gallon of ethanol.

US is the second largest producer of ethanol based largely on maize. It has capacity to produce 15 billion liters annually and the US Energy Policy Act of 2005 requires that production is increased to 28 billion liters by 2012. No wonder, President Bush in his State of the Union message complained of Americans' addiction to oil in preference to available alternatives.

It is the sharp increase in the price of oil that has attracted greater attention to ethanol as an oil substitute. Commercial viability of ethanol will, however, depend on the price of the food product from which ethanol is derived and the price for which it is a substitute. In the case of sugarcane, for instance, the diversion to ethanol raised the international price of sugar from 10 cents to 18.5 cents a pound and would delay further diversion since it would make ethanol far too costly.

Even today, in Brazil, substitution is possible because it is subsidized by the government. India imports nearly 70% of its oil consumption, a part of which can be substituted by ethanol. With the price of oil at about $60 and no prospects of its dropping below $50, it may be worthwhile to go in for ethanol substitute. No doubt, production and supply of ethanol have been on the agenda for some time though the progress has been slow. In Brazil, more than half of the cane production is used to produce ethanol which replaced 40% of its gasoline demand. With some support from the government, it should be possible for us to reach 20% substitution in the next 5 years.

It has been mentioned earlier that the USA and Brazil, the two large agro-based countries have evolved a sizable ethanol program, which has helped their economies to a great extent. The ongoing programs have virtually overhauled the Brazilian sugar and fuel economy. The program has met with success due to sizable Government support (in fact, in USA, the support continues even today). In Brazil, with massive investments, ethanol program is making rapid progress based on market economy and consumer preferences. Like Rome was not built in a day, the Brazilian program also took three decades to come to this shape.

Prospecting for Green Diesel

The Energy and Resources Institute (TERI) based in New Delhi, over 80% of passengers and 60% of the freight were moved by road. The Government estimates that the country's diesel requirements in 2011–2012 could be more than 66 million tons, one and a half times higher than in 2001–2002. TERI estimates that India's diesel needs would cross 100 million tons by 2020 and 200 million tons by 2030.

Today most diesel is produced by refining petroleum, but it is worth remembering that Rudolf Diesel designed his revolutionary compression engine to run on vegetable oils. Even now, certain types of diesel engines can readily run on vegetable oils efforts have led to popularize the substitution of oil from seeds of the tree *Pongamia pinnata* (known as "Honge" and "Karanja") for diesel in village power-generation sets and irrigation pumps.

Europe makes bio-diesel from sunflower and rapeseed oil, US from soybean oil, Thailand from palm oil, and recently a bio-diesel factory opened in the Philippines that would use coconut oil. But since India does not produce enough edible oil for its culinary needs, a Planning Commission Committee on development of biofuel, which submitted its report in 2003, noted that bio-diesel in this country would have to be made from nonedible oilseeds.

Several plants found in India, including *Pongamia pinnata*, neem, rubber, and castor bear seeds with nonedible oils that can be used to produce bio-diesel. But the plant that is arousing great enthusiasm for this purpose is *Jatropha curcas*. "Jatropha is the first choice since it can be grown in both saline and alkaline soils, arid and semiarid conditions, low slopes of hilly areas, and degraded and abused soils".

The Planning Commission Committee on biofuels estimated that producing 20% blends by 2011–2012 would require over 13 million tons of bio-diesel, which, in turn, would require Jatropha to be cultivated on over 11 million hectares.

Limited Availability

Plantations of Jatropha and Pongamia are just being established in States such as Andhra Pradesh, Tamil Nadu, Madhya Pradesh, Chhattisgarh, Uttaranchal, and Gujarat. It would be 2–3 years before these plantations began yielding sizeable quantities of oilseeds to be turned into bio-diesel, he pointed out.

Even supplying the market with 5% bio-diesel blends is currently not proving easy. In October 2005, the Union Government gave permission for public sector oil marketing companies to purchase pure bio-diesel that met quality standards. The oil companies could then use this bio-diesel to produce 5% blends. The government fixed the purchase price for bio-diesel at Rs 25 per liter.

However, bio-diesel is not currently available at that price, says an oil company official. If Jatropha seeds cost Rs 6–7 per kg, then bio-diesel can be produced at Rs 27–32 per liter, estimates Dr Ghosh. But right now, there is a "mad scramble" to purchase Jatropha seeds in order to start plantations and the seeds are expensive, he says.

Bio-diesel can be produced within the country cheaper than the current market price of conventional diesel but not at Rs 25 a liter, insists K Radhakrishna, a director of Hyderabad-based Southern Online Bio-Technologies Limited. The company's German-made bio-diesel plant is expected to go into operation in July this year and produce 10,000 tons of bio-diesel annually. The company is setting up networks to collect nonedible oilseeds from farmers and tribals. It is encouraging farmers to plant Jatropha and Pongamia and offering buy-back agreements for the oilseeds. The company has also made arrangements with a Malaysian company to import alternative feedstock such as palm oil if required.

Converting vegetable oils into bio-diesel is not particularly complicated, but the efficiency of the process, the ability to use different types of vegetable oils, and maintaining quality are key issues. The Central Salt and Marine Chemicals Research Institute at Bhavnagar in Gujarat has filed an international patent for its process that can accommodate a range of vegetable oils and oilseeds. The process is able to efficiently extract oil from the seeds and convert it into bio-diesel that can meet exacting European quality standards, says PK Ghosh, director of the Institute. The Indian Institute of Chemical Technology at Hyderabad, another Central Government laboratory, too is getting ready a technology for turning a wide variety of seeds and oils into high-quality bio-diesel. The Institute was also working on catalysts that would reduce the effluents produced, according to RBN Prasad, head of its Lipid Science and Technology Division.

Several trials have now been undertaken in the country running cars, buses, and even trains on pure as well as blended bio-diesel. Two C-Class Mercedes-Benz cars were driven across India using unblended bio-diesel, traveling over 8,000 km in diverse conditions from the high humidity of the South to the high temperatures of North India and even going to Leh in the Himalayas. "We got very good results in terms of emissions", says Suhas Kadlaskar, DaimlerChrysler India's director for Corporate Affairs and Finance. The soot emissions from these cars were down by almost two-thirds without any perceivable loss of power.

The Tatas are plying 40 company buses in Pune on 10% blends of bio-diesel provided by the Indian Oil Corporation (IOC). Some 20 of the Haryana State Road Transport Corporation's long-distance buses are run on pure bio-diesel supplied by IOC. Southern Railways' Tiruchi division is using a 10% blend of bio-diesel to run six trains daily; the bio-diesel is produced at the Perambur Loco Works in Chennai.

After the first oil shock of the early 1970s, a group at Indian Space Research Organization's Vikram Sarabhai Space Center in Thiruvananthapuram came up with a technology to turn nonedible oilseeds into what it called "space crude". The liquid fraction of the crude could be used to produce petrol, kerosene, diesel, and lube oils and the gaseous fraction turned into cooking gas. While the technology appeared promising, large-scale production foundered because of problems of securing large quantities of oilseeds at a reasonable price.

Before them is the enviable example of Brazil. Brazilian cars and even apparently its small aircraft have been shifting to either pure ethanol (also known as ethyl alcohol) or ethanol-petrol blends. The use of ethanol stabilized fuel prices in Brazil, saved the country some $50 billion that it would otherwise have spent importing oil over the last 30 years or so and created an estimated one million rural jobs, points out the World Watch Institute in its State of the World 2006 report. Combined with increased domestic oil production, Brazil is expected to become self-sufficient in energy this year.

India: Gur, price table, in rupees/metric tons (actual weight basis)

Year	*2010*	*2011*	*2012*	*Change (%)*
January	24,000	30,000	29,500	–2
February	23,000	28,000	30,000	7
March	25,000	29,500	28,500	–3
April	28,000	31,000		
May	32,000	33,500		
June	32,000	34,500		
July	33,000	36,000		
August	36,000	35,500		
September	38,000	34,000		
October	30,500	32,500		
November	27,000	30,500		
December	29,000	29,500		
Exchange rate: Local currency/US $	49.00	53.45	54.12	

Note: Exchange rate for 2011 and 2012 refers to Indian Fiscal Years (IFY) 2011/12 (April/March) and IFY 2012/13 respectively. Exchange rate of 2013 refers to first fortnight of April, 2013.
Source: Indian Sugar Mills Association; month-end prices in the Delhi wholesale market.

5

Sugar Substitutes

A *sugar substitute* is a food additive that duplicates the effect of sugar in taste, but usually has less food energy. Some sugar substitutes are natural and some are synthetic. Those that are not natural are, in general, referred to as *artificial sweeteners.* An important class of sugar substitutes is known as *high-intensity sweeteners*. These are compounds with sweetness that is many times that of sucrose, common table sugar. As a result, much less sweetener is required, and energy contribution often negligible. The sensation of sweetness caused by these compounds (the "sweetness profile") is sometimes notably different from sucrose, so they are often used in complex mixtures that achieve the most natural sweet sensation.

If the sucrose (or other sugar) replaced has contributed to the texture of the product, then a bulking agent is often also needed. This may be seen in soft drinks labeled as "diet" or "light", which contain artificial sweeteners and often have notably different mouthfeel or in table sugar replacements that mix maltodextrins with an intense sweetener to achieve satisfactory texture sensation.

In the United States, six intensely-sweet sugar substitutes have been approved for use. They are saccharin, aspartame, sucralose, neotame, acesulfame potassium and stevia. There is some ongoing controversy over whether artificial sweetener usage poses health risks. The US Food and Drug Administration (USFDA) regulates artificial sweeteners as food additives. Food additives must be approved by the Food and Drug Administration (FDA), which publishes a Generally Recognized as Safe (GRAS) list of additives. To date, the FDA has not been presented with scientific information that would support a change in conclusions about the safety of the six approved artificial sweeteners. The safe conclusions are based on a detailed review of a large body of information, including hundreds of toxicological and clinical studies.

There is also an herbal supplement, stevia, used as a sweetener. Controversy surrounds lack of research on stevia's safety and there is a battle over its approval as a sugar substitute.

The majority of sugar substitutes approved for food use are artificially-synthesized compounds. However, some bulk natural sugar substitutes are known including sorbitol and xylitol which are found in berries, fruit, vegetables, and mushrooms. It is not commercially viable to extract these products from fruits and vegetables, so they are produced by catalytic hydrogenation of the appropriate reducing sugar. For example, xylose is converted to xylitol, lactose to lactitol, and glucose to sorbitol. Still other natural substitutes are known, but are yet to gain official approval for food use.

Some nonsugar sweeteners are *polyols*, also known as "sugar alcohols". These are, in general, less sweet than sucrose, but have similar bulk properties and can be used in a wide range of food products. Sometimes the sweetness profile is "fine-tuned" by mixing high-intensity sweeteners. As with all food products, the development of a formulation to replace sucrose is a complex proprietary process.

FOOD INDUSTRY USAGE OF ARTIFICIAL SWEETENERS

The food and beverage industry is increasingly replacing sugar or corn syrup with artificial sweeteners in a range of products traditionally containing sugar.

According to market analysts Mintel, a total of 3,920 products containing artificial sweeteners were launched in the US between 2000 and 2005. In 2004 alone, 1,649 artificially sweetened products were launched. According to market analysts Freedonia, the US artificial sweetener market is set to grow at around 8% per year to $189 million in 2012.

Aspartame is currently the most popular artificial sweetener in the US food industry, as the price has dropped significantly since the Monsanto Company patent expired in 1992. However, sucralose may soon replace it, as alternative processes to Tate and Lyle's patent seem to be emerging. According to Morgan Stanley, this can mean that the price of sucralose will drop by 30%.

Alternative sweeteners are highly consumed in America. According to research studies explained by the American Journal of Clinical Nutrition in 2003–2004, Americans 2 years of age and older consumed 585 g per day of beverages and 375 g per day of foods with caloric sweeteners. More than 66% of Americans consumed these beverages with alternative sweeteners and 82.3% of Americans consumed foods with added caloric sweeteners. On the other hand, 10.8% of Americans in 2003–2004 consumed noncaloric alternative sweetener flavored beverages and 5.8% consumed noncaloric alternative sweetener flavored foods.

Some commonly consumed foods with alternative sweeteners are diet sodas, cereals, and sugar-free desserts such as icecream. Alternative sweeteners are found in many products today due to their low or noncaloric characteristics. This can be used as a method of advertisement for dieters or those conscious of their sugar intake. Those with diabetes can greatly benefit from alternative sweeteners that do not affect their blood sugar levels drastically. This aids in maintaining low insulin use in the body and blood sugar levels. Alternative sweeteners such as xylitol and saccharin have many positive research results that show qualities of dental decay prevention.

REASONS FOR USE

Sugar substitutes are used for a number of reasons including:

To assist in weight Loss: Some people choose to limit their food energy intake by replacing high-energy sugar or corn syrup with other sweeteners having little or no food energy. This allows them to eat the same foods they normally would while allowing them to lose weight and avoid other problems associated with excessive caloric intake.

Dental care: Sugar substitutes are tooth friendly, as they are not fermented by the microflora of the dental plaque. An example of a sweetener that can benefit dental health is *xylitol.* Xylitol works to prevent bacteria from adhering to the tooth surface, thus preventing plaque formation and eventually decay. The carbohydrates and sugars consumed usually adhere to the tooth enamel. Bacteria can feed upon this food source allowing them to quickly multiply. As the bacteria feed upon the sugar, they convert it to acid waste that in turn decays the tooth structure. Xylitol cannot be fermented by these bacteria, so the bacteria have difficulty thriving, thus helping to prevent plaque formation.

Diabetes mellitus: People with diabetes have difficulty regulating their blood sugar levels. By limiting their sugar intake with artificial sweeteners, they can enjoy a varied diet while closely controlling their sugar intake. Also, some sugar substitutes do release energy but are metabolized more slowly, potentially allowing blood sugar levels to remain more stable over time.

Reactive hypoglycemia: Individuals with reactive hypoglycemia will produce an excess of insulin after quickly absorbing glucose into the bloodstream. This causes their blood glucose levels to fall below the amount needed for proper body and brain function. As a result, like diabetics, they must avoid intake of high-glycemic foods like white bread, and often choose artificial sweeteners as an alternative. Avoiding processed foods—individuals may opt to substitute refined white sugar with less-processed sugars, such as fruit juice or maple syrup (See list of unrefined sweeteners).

Cost: Many sugar substitutes are cheaper than sugar. Alternative sweeteners are often low in cost because of their long shelf-life and high sweetening intensity. This allows alternative sweeteners to be used in products that will not perish after a short period of time.

CONTROVERSY OVER HEALTH

A 2005 study by the University of Texas Health Science Center at San Antonio showed that increased weight gain and obesity were associated with increased use of diet soda in a population-based study. The study did not establish whether increased weight gain leads to increased consumption of diet drinks or whether consumption of diet drinks could have an effect on weight gain.

Animal studies have indicated that a sweet taste induces an insulin response in rats. However, the extension of animal model findings to humans is unclear, as human studies of intragastric infusion of sucralose have shown no insulin response from analogos taste receptors. The release of insulin causes blood sugar to be stored in tissues (including fat). In the case of a response to artificial sweeteners because blood sugar does not increase there can be increased hypoglycemia or hyperinsulinemia and increased food intake the next time there is a meal. Rats given sweeteners have steadily increased calorie intake, increased body weight, and increased adiposity (fatness). Furthermore, the natural responses to eating sugary foods (eating less at the next meal and using some of the extra calories to warm the body after the sugary meal) are gradually lost.

Artificial sweeteners do nothing to help weight loss and could actually cause us to pile on that scientists have found the pounds. Research suggests that our bodies are unable to distinguish between the calories—free sugar substitutes widely used in the food industry and the real thing. Artificial sweeteners behave in a similar way to sugar, by activating sensors in the gut which are key to the absorption of glucose. So, the body processes extra sugar—and all the calories that go with it. For the dieter, it means little or no weight loss. Over time, it could even lead to gaining weight. Researcher Soraya Shirazi—Beechey of Liverpool University says, "If someone wants to lose weight, I don't think artificial sweeteners are going to help. My recommendation is to eat natural foods, but to eat less of them".

Shirazi-Beechey studied the processes in the small intestine by which the sugar or glucose from food is absorbed into the bloodstream. She identified specific cells which detect sugar, releasing hormones essential for its passage through the lining of the gut and into the blood, where it is either burned off or is converted into fat. Crucially, these cells release the hormones when confronted by artificial sweeteners. This primes the gut to absorb real sugar. Artificial sweeteners can also activate the glucose sensor and increase the capacity of the intestine to absorb more sugar.

Five intensely: Sweet sugar substitute are commonly used in artificial sweeteners. Here is what they are and what they contain.

MAJOR SUGAR SUBSTITUTE

Cyclamate

Corn syrup and honey have long been used as substitutes for sugar, and in the US sorghum syrup is sometimes used for the same purpose. In the 20th century, artificial sweeteners such as saccharin, cyclamates, aspartame, and dulcin, or sucrol, became popular substitutes for sugar. Artificial sweeteners were originally used as sugar substitutes for diabetics and others forced to restrict their intake of sugar, but they became increasingly popular in soft drinks and other foods for people who wished to restrict their intake of calories to control their weight. In general, artificial sweeteners have no food value; they are not metabolized by the body and are excreted unchanged.

In the US, the USFDA banned the sale of cyclamate in 1970 after laboratory tests in rats involving a 10:1 mixture of cyclamate and saccharin indicated that large amounts of cyclamates causes bladder cancer, a disease to which rats are particularly susceptible. The findings of these studies have been challenged and some companies are petitioning to have cyclamates reapproved. Cyclamates are still used as sweeteners in many parts of the world, and are used with official approval in over 55 countries.

Saccharin was discovered in 1879. It has about 500 times the sweetening power of cane sugar. Although its safety was the subject of intense controversy during the 1970s, it is still used as a sugar substitute. Cyclamates were developed in 1937 and marketed in 1949. They have about 30 times the sweetening power of sucrose. They were banned in 1969 when tests showed them to be potentially harmful to laboratory animals as well as humans, but further investigations did not substantiate the original conclusions.

Saccharin

Saccharin was the first artificial sweetener and was originally synthesized in 1879 by Remsen and Fahlberg. Its sweet taste was discovered by accident. It had been created in an experiment with toluene derivatives. It has about 500 times the sweetening power of cane sugar. A process for the creation of saccharin from phthalic anhydride was developed in 1950, and, currently, saccharin is created by this process as well as the original process by which it was discovered. It is 300–500 times as sweet as sugar (sucrose) and is often used to improve the taste of toothpastes, dietary foods, and dietary beverages. The bitter aftertaste of saccharin is often minimized by blending it with other sweeteners.

Fear about saccharin increased when a 1960 study showed that high levels of saccharin may cause bladder cancer in laboratory rats. In 1977, Canada banned saccharin due to the animal research. In the US, the FDA considered banning saccharin in 1977, but Congress stepped in and placed a moratorium on such a ban. The moratorium required a warning label and also mandated further study of saccharin safety.

Subsequently, it was discovered that saccharin causes cancer in male rats by a mechanism not found in humans. At high doses, saccharin causes a precipitate to form in rat urine. This precipitate damages the cells lining the bladder ("urinary bladder urothelial cytotoxicity") and a tumor forms when the cells regenerate ("regenerative hyperplasia"). According to the International Agency for Research on Cancer, part of the World Health Organization, "Saccharin and its salts was downgraded from Group 2B, possibly carcinogenic to humans, to Group 3, not classifiable as to carcinogenicity to humans, despite sufficient evidence of carcinogenicity to animals, because it is carcinogenic by a non-DNA-reactive mechanism that is not relevant to humans because of critical interspecies differences in urine composition".

In 2001, the US repealed the warning label requirement while the threat of an FDA ban had already been lifted in 1991. Most other countries also permit saccharin but restrict the levels of use, while other countries have banned it, outright.

Aspartame

Aspartame was discovered in 1965 by James M. Schlatter at the GD Searle company (later purchased by Monsanto). He was working on an antiulcer drug and spilled some aspartame on his hand by accident. When he licked his finger, he noticed that it had a sweet taste. It is an odorless, white crystalline powder that is derived from the two amino acids aspartic acid and phenylalanine. It is about 200 times as sweet as sugar and can be used as a tabletop sweetener or in frozen desserts, gelatins, beverages, and chewing gum. Its chemical name is L-alpha-aspartyl-L-phenylalanine methyl ester and its chemical formula is $C_{14}H_{18}N_2O_5$. Though it has no bitter aftertaste as saccharin, its drawback is that it might not taste exactly like sugar because it reacts with other food flavors. When eaten, aspartame is metabolized into its original amino acids and has a relatively low food energy.

Initial safety testing suggested that aspartame caused brain tumors in rats; as a result, the additive was held up in the US for many years in the FDAs approval process. In 1980, the FDA convened a Public Board of Inquiry (PBOI) consisting of independent advisors charged with examining the purported relationship between aspartame and brain cancer. The PBOIs conclusions were unclear as to whether aspartame causes brain damage, and recommended against approving aspartame at that time, citing unanswered questions about cancer in laboratory rats. In 1981, FDA Commissioner Arthur Hull Hayes, newly appointed by President Ronald Reagan approved aspartame as a food additive. Hayes cited data from a single

Japanese study that had not been available to the members of the PBOI as his reason for approval.

Since the FDA approved aspartame for consumption, some researchers have suggested that a rise in brain tumor rates in the United States may be at least partially related to the increasing availability and consumption of aspartame. Some research, often supported by companies producing artificial sweeteners, has failed to find any link between aspartame and cancer or other health problems. Recent research showed a clear link between this substance and cancer; leading some experts to call for the FDA to pull aspartame from the market. This research has led the Center for Science in the Public Interest to classify aspartame as a substance to be avoided in its Chemical Cuisine Directory. However, the European Food Safety Authorities (EFSAs) press release about the study, published on 5 May 2006, concluded that the increased incidence of lymphomas/leukemia's reported in treated rats was unrelated to aspartame, the kidney tumors found at high doses of aspartame were not relevant to humans, and that based on all available scientific evidence to date, there was no reason to revise the previously established Acceptable Daily Intake levels for aspartame.

Several EU countries approved aspartame in the 1980s, with EU-wide approval in 1994. The European Commission Scientific Committee on Food reviewed subsequent safety studies and reaffirmed the approval in 2002. The EFSA reported in 2006 that the previously established Adequate Daily Intake was appropriate, after reviewing yet another set of studies.

It has also been investigated and approved by the Joint Expert Committee on Food Additives of the United Nations Food and Agricultural Organization and World Health Organization.

Sucralose

Sucralose is a chlorinated sugar that is about 600 times as sweet as sugar. It is produced from sucrose when three chlorine atoms replace three hydroxyl groups. It is used in beverages, frozen desserts, chewing gum, baked goods, and other foods. Unlike other artificial sweeteners, it is stable when heated and can therefore be used in baked and fried goods. Sucralose is minimally absorbed by the body and most of it passes out of the body unchanged. The FDA approved sucralose in 1998.

Most of the controversy surrounding Splenda, a sucralose sweetener, is focused not on safety, but on its marketing. It has been marketed with the slogan, "Splenda is made from sugar, so it tastes like sugar". Sucralose is a chlorinated sugar prepared from either sucrose or raffinose. With either base sugar, processing replaces three oxygen-hydrogen groups in the sugar molecule with three chlorine atoms.

The "Truth about Splenda" website was created in 2005 by the Sugar Association, an organization representing sugar beet and sugar cane farmers in the US, in order to provide its view of sucralose. In December 2004, five separate false-advertising claims were filed by the Sugar Association against Splenda manufacturers Merisant and McNeil Nutritionals for claims made about Splenda related to the slogan, "Made from sugar, so it tastes like sugar". French courts ordered the slogan to no longer be used in France while in the US the case came to an undisclosed settlement during the trial.

Safety concerns pertaining to sucralose revolve around the fact that it belongs to a class of chemicals called organochlorides, some types of which are toxic or carcinogenic; however, the presence of chlorine in an organic compound does not in any way ensure toxicity. The way sucralose is metabolized may suggest a reduced risk of toxicity. For example, sucralose is extremely insoluble in fat and thus does not accumulate in fat as do some other organochlorides; sucralose also does not breakdown and will dechlorinate only under conditions that are not found during regular digestion (i.e. heavy heat applied to the powder form of the molecule).

Lead Acetate

Lead acetate (sometimes called *sugar of lead*) is an artificial sugar substitute made from lead that is of historical interest because of its widespread use in the past, such as by ancient Romans. The use of lead acetate as a sweetener eventually produced lead poisoning in any individual ingesting it habitually. Lead acetate was abandoned as a food additive throughout most of the world after the high toxicity of lead compounds became apparent.

Dulcin or Sucrol is no longer used because of its toxic effects. Aspartame, marketed under the trade name NutraSweet, received FDA approval in the early 1980s. Although its components (phenylalanine, aspartic acid and methanol) occur naturally in foods, aspartame itself does not, and its safety has been the subject of controversy.

Neotame: Neotame is rapidly metabolized completely culminated, and does not accumulate in the body. However, its breakdown releases poisonous methanol and should be consumed in trace amounts.

Acesulfame potassium: This calorie-free artificial sweetener is commonly used in carbonated drinks along with sucralose or aspartame. Acesulfame has been shown to stimulate insulin secretion in rat's possibly aggravating reactive hypoglycemia (low blood sugar attacks).

Drugs which control the sugar sensor cells, leading to more or less entering the bloodstream, could help to treat disease such as diabetes and obesity.

List of Sugar Substitutes

The three primary compounds used as sugar substitutes in the US are saccharin (e.g. *Sweet'N Low*), aspartame (e.g. *Equal, NutraSweet*) and sucralose (e.g. *Splenda, Altern*). In many other countries xylito, cyclamate and the herbal sweetener stevia are used extensively.

Natural Sugar Substitutes

1. Adenylic acid or adenosine monophosphate (AMP)
2. Brazzein—Protein, 800 × sweetness of sucrose (by weight)
3. Curculin—Protein, 550 × sweetness (by weight)
4. Erythritol—0.7 × sweetness (by weight), 14 × sweetness of sucrose (by food energy), 0.05 × energy density of sucrose
5. Glycyrrhizin—50 × sweetness (by weight)
6. Glycerol—0.6 × sweetness (by weight), 0.55 × sweetness (by food energy), 1.075 × energy density, E422
7. Hydrogenated starch hydrolysates—0.4 × –0.9 × sweetness (by weight), 0.5 × –1.2 × sweetness (by food energy), 0.75 × energy density
8. Insulin
9. Isomalt—0.45 ×– 0.65 × sweetness (by weight), 0.9 × –1.3 × sweetness (by food energy), 0.5 × energy density, E953

10. Lactitol—0.4 × sweetness (by weight), 0.8 × sweetness (by food energy), 0.5 × energy density, E966
11. Luo Han Guo—300 × sweetness (by weight)
12. Mabinlin—Protein, 100 × sweetness (by weight)
13. Maltitol—0.9 × sweetness (by weight), 1.7 × sweetness (by food energy), 0.525 × energy density, E965
14. Maltooligosaccharide
15. Mannitol—0.5 × sweetness (by weight), 1.2 × sweetness (by food energy), 0.4 × energy density, E421
16. Miraculin—Protein, does not taste sweet by itself, but modifies taste receptors to make sour things taste sweet temporarily
17. Monatin—naturally-occurring sweetener isolated from the plant *Sclerochiton ilicifolius*
18. Monellin—Protein, 3,000 × sweetness (by weight)
19. Pentadin—Protein, 500 × sweetness (by weight)
20. Sorbitol—0.6 × sweetness (by weight), 0.9 × sweetness (by food energy), 0.65 × energy density, E420
21. Stevia—250 × sweetness (by weight)-extracts known as rebiana, Truvia, PureVia; mainly containing rebaudioside A, a steviol glycoside
22. Tagatose—0.92 × sweetness (by weight), 2.4 × sweetness (by food energy), 0.38 × energy density
23. Thaumatin—Protein, 2,000 × sweetness (by weight), E957
24. Xylitol—1.0 × sweetness (by weight), 1.7 × sweetness (by food energy), 0.6 × energy density, E967.

Artificial Sugar Substitutes

Note that because many of these have little or no food energy, comparison of sweetness based on energy content is not meaningful.

E number	*Common name*	*Max permitted level*	*Sources*	*Application*
E950	Acesulfame potassium	0.05% (w/w)	Standard 1.3.1-Food Additives (Australian)	Liquid milk products and flavored liquid milk
		N/A	N/A	N/A

STEVIA (Mau Tulasi)

[*Stevia rebaudiana* (Bertoni) Hemsl.]

Family: Asterac

Stevia is a subtropical perennial that produces sweet steviol glycosides in the leaves for which it also known as "Cheeni Tulsi" or "Mou Tulsi". Plants grown at higher latitudes actually have a higher percentage of sweet glycosides. The plant can be utilized as a source for the production of a natural sweetener (food) as a source of chlorophyll (non-food, oral-hygiene product, medicine) as a source of phytosterols (non-food).

Medicine: Raw stuff for the synthesis of oral contraceptives, cholesterol suppressing medicine, antitumor activity against prostrate tumors and activity against rheumatism), the sweetener can be converted in gibberellins by fermentation (non-food—agrochemicals), the vegetative residue can be used as animal feed and the stalks can be used as a source of cellulose (non-food: cellulose industry).

Its medicinal uses include regulating blood sugar, preventing hypertension, treatment of skin disorders, and prevention of tooth decay. The compound obtained from stevia is considered to be the best alternate source for diabetes sufferer. The added value for this new crop can go up to a considerable extent. Market opportunity appears great. Statistics indicate that in some countries upto 30% of their needed sugar is replaced by stevioside-like sweetness products.

Soil and Climate

Stevia prefers a well-drained fertile sandy loam or loam soil, high in organic matter with ample supply of water. It prefers acidic to neutral (pH 6–7) soil for better growth. It requires a consistent supply of moisture, but not waterlogged. Too much soil moisture can cause rot. It is a semihumid subtropical plant that shows higher leaf production under high light intensity and warm temperature. Day length is more critical than light intensity. Long spring and summer days favor leaf growth. Short days trigger blossoming. Stevia prefers partial shade during considerable summer sunshine.

Varieties

There are three named varieties developed by Sunfruits Pvt Ltd, Pune viz.

1. SRB-123: It can be harvested 5 times in year. The glycoside content is in between 9% and 12% found suitable for South.
2. SRB-512: It is suitable for Northern India and the glycoside content is in between 9% and 12%.
3. SRB-128: Highest stevioside content upto 21%. Found suitable for Northern India.
4. Material that yields stevioside in the range of 9–12% or above can be used as good material for commercial cultivation and should be maintained by vegetative propagation only.

Propagation

Stevia is usually propagated by stem cuttings, which root easily. Sweetness in leaves varies with varieties. Therefore, for propagation cutting should be obtained from a source, which is high in stevioside and low in associated bitterness. Rooting can be enhanced by using commercial rooting hormones. Cutting should be 2–4 inches long, from leaf axils of current year growth with at least two leaf buds above ground. All the lower leaves are removed keeping 2 or 3 small leaves. Treatment with paclobutrazol 100 ppm has been found to induce the root initiation in short-time. Effective outcome of this treatment can be obtained when the cuttings are planted during the month of February–March. Propagation can be done in other period also with varying success.

Plant Protection

No serious pest and diseases have been observed. Neem oil diluted in water may be sprayed against aphids if appear. Deer and rabbits are fond of stevia due to sweet taste. Fencing is necessary.

Harvesting

Time of harvesting depends on land type, variety and growing season. The first harvest of the crop can be had in 4 months after planting and subsequent harvest once every 3 months. Generally, it can be scheduled for mid to late September when plants are 50–70 cm in height. Short days induce flowering. Optimum yield (biomass) and stevioside quality and quantity is best obtained just before flowering. The easiest harvesting technique is to cut the branches off with pruning shears before stripping the leaves. The tips of the stems can be clipped off and added to harvest yield, as they contain as much stevioside as do the leaves. On an average three commercial harvests can be obtained per year.

It is better to cut the plants leaving about 10 cm stem portion from the ground. This will facilitate new flushes to emerge, which can be harvested as the next crop.

For domestic use leaves may be used fresh for tea or may be combined with mint leaves.

Drying

Immediately after harvest the herb is dried. This can be accomplished on a screen or net. The freshly harvested plants can be hung upside down and dried in shade. It can also be dried using simple drying racks inside transparent poly house or transparent glass roofing or by passing dry air just above room temperature.

Drying of the stem and soft green leaf material is completed immediately after harvesting utilizing a drying wagon or a kiln or done naturally in case of large-scale production. Depending on weather conditions and density of loading, it generally takes 24–48 hours to dry stevia at 400–500°C. The drying process does not require excessive heat; more important is good air circulation. On a moderately warm fall day, stevia can be quick dried in the full sun in about 12 hours (longer drying time will lower the stevioside content of the final product). A home dehydrator can also be used although sun drying is the preferred method. After adequate drying, the leaves are stripped of the stems/twigs and packed and stored in cool, dry place. For large-scale commercial production artificial drying and threshing of the dry herbs to separate leaves may be employed.

Yield

About 15,000 kg/hectare of green herb is obtained which on drying gives about 4,166 kg/hectare. After separating stems this yields about 3,000 kg/hectare in the first year. Yield goes on decreasing from 3rd year of planting and hence terminated.

Replacement and Replanting

From the subsequent years some plants will die off due to various reasons, these gaps should immediately be filled up by well-developed seedlings raised in large size poly bags. Depending on soil type and management the productivity will decline after 2–3 years and this should be replaced with new plantation.

Stevia can be grown either in pots on balcony or any sunny spot. It does well in "container gardens". A 10–12 inches diameter container filled with a lightweight growing mix is an ideal size for each plant. A little mulch on the top will help retain the moisture in the shallow root zone.

Nature's Zero Calorie Sweetener—Stevia

Stevia shrub (*Stevia rebaudiana*), a member of the sunflower family native to Paraguay, contains stevioside, which is 300 times sweeter than sugar. The government is not approving stevioside, which is natural and safe, and allowing artificial sweeteners despite insufficient data to prove them safe. India being the diabetes capital of the world, demand for low-calorie sweeteners is high. An estimated 10–20% people in India have diabetes; the market for low-calorie sweeteners is at least 25% if one combines the obese and weight conscious consumers with diabetics.

Unlike FSSAI, other departments are interested in using stevia's potential. The National Medicinal Plant Board (NMPB) gives 20% subsidy to farmers who cultivate it. Stevia can be harvested three to four times a year. Farmers can earn Rs 70–120 per kg of stevia leaves and it is exported at Rs 200–250 a kg. Stevia is cultivated in over 1,800 hectares (hectare) in different states under NMPB schemes. According to Sun Fruits Ltd, a company that cultivates stevia commercially, the sweetener can play an important role in all products that need sucrose—food, beverage, agriculture, medicine, animal feed and skin care products.

At present, stevia accounts for just 1% of the global sugar-substitute market, though its value in the US market is expected to grow to $2,000 million by end of 2011, from $21 million in 2008. The Indian market for sweeteners can shift towards stevia if it gets a boost from the government. Stevia is cheaper than sugar. The average sugar yield from a 0.4 hectare sugarcane field is four tons; average yield of stevia extract that equals sweetness of sugar is over 60 tons from 0.4 hectare. The market for stevia in India is limited because there are no processing units. The government-run Institute of Himalayan Bioresource Technology at Palampur in Himachal Pradesh is planning to setup the country's first patented ecofriendly stevia processing unit near Delhi (The unit's capacity won't be high—300 kg leaves a day).

Why Ban Stevia?

Stevia is a natural sweetener for diabetics and patients of phenylketonuria (genetic disorder). It is non-fermentative and flavor-enhancing. People of Paraguay have been using stevia for hundreds of years while China has been using the sweetener commercially for the past two decades. None of them has reported any harmful side-effect—the human body metabolizes the sweetening agents of stevia just like any other glycoside. The national health inspection authorities in China have approved stevia as a food additive, and in Australia, it is listed as therapeutic goods. In 2004, the Joint Expert Committee on Food Additives of the World Health Organization allowed using stevia as a food additive. Despite extensive use of stevia, why has the Food Safety and Standards Authority of India banned it? It must provide a scientific basis for notifying that stevia is not a food item.

Stevia: A Better Alternative to Sugar and Artificial Sweeteners

Most medical experts would agree that one of the best ways to improve your health is to reduce your sugar intake. Doing this can help to decrease one chance of getting diabetes and being overweight or obese both epidemics in this country with adults and children alike. Consider these facts:

- Since 1985, childhood diabetes has increased ten-fold. The Centers for Disease Control predicts that if this trend continues, one out of every three children born beginning in 2000 will develop diabetes in their lifetime.
- About two-thirds of US adults are overweight or obese; while up to 30% of children are overweight, compared to 4% in 1982. In the past 25 years, obesity in children has more than doubled, affecting at least 15% of school-age children!

The average American ingests over 150 lbs of sugar annually! That represents a whopping 305 lb bags of sugar each year! In reality, much of this sugar is in the form of high fructose corn syrup prevalent in foods because it is much cheaper than sucrose, common tabletop sugar.

While some might think that artificial sweeteners are the best solution to curb our love affair with sugar, others disagree. Artificial sweeteners do eliminate the high calories and carbohydrates associated with sugar, however many believe that these alternatives are unsafe and are actually worse than sugar. So is there yet another alternative available?

If there were an all-natural sweetening ingredient that's been used safely for over 30 years in other parts of the world for food applications and diabetes management with no ill effects, would you be interested? Well, such a substance does exist and it is called stevia.

Using stevia, an all natural alternative to sugar and artificial sweeteners, is gaining increasing popularity worldwide. *Stevia rebaudiana*, its botanical name, is derived from a plant in the chrysanthemum family grown primarily in South America and Asia. The plant's intense sweetening qualities are complex molecules called steviosides that are glycosides made of glucose, sophorose and steviol. These are what make stevia up to 300 times sweeter than sugar and non-caloric. These glycosides do not get absorbed into the body; rather simply pass through leaving no calories. The Japanese have used stevia in food applications from soft drinks to soy sauce since the 1970s and recent reports indicate that stevia commands up to an incredible 50% share of Japan's commercial sweetener market. Moreover countries like Brazil use stevia for the treatment for diabetes.

The advantages to stevia are numerous, so the following are the most frequently cited. In its pure form, it is non-caloric and doesn't affect glucose levels, an advantage for diabetics and hypoglycemics. Also, it has no carbohydrates or fat, so it is great for dieters, especially those watching carb intake. Unlike artificial sweeteners, high quality stevia has little aftertaste when measured properly. It has no known side effects like some chemical sweeteners and has been safely consumed around the world for decades. Actually, stevia's original medicinal uses date back centuries ago with the Paraguan Indians who mixed the herb in teas for its healing properties. Since stevia is sugar-free, candida sufferers can use it. Health conscious consumers take advantage of stevia to avoid sugar and help to prevent diabetes and obesity. The website www.ncbi.nlm.nih.gov, under the direction of the National Institutes of Health, National Library of Medicine and National Center of Biotechnology

Information, offers abstracts from stevia studies that indicate it may also aid in lowering blood pressure and regulating glucose levels.

The average consumer may not have heard about stevia until recently because of its current FDA approval as a dietary supplement, not as a sweetener or food additive. Numerous studies worldwide tout its overall safety and health benefits. As of this writing, about 10 countries, including Japan, Paraguay and Brazil have approved stevia as a sweetener and/or food additive. The FDA approved the use of stevia only as a dietary supplement since 1995. This means stevia companies must maintain a fairly low profile, thereby limiting its distribution and marketing potential. For instance, health food stores and natural grocers must place stevia in the supplements section, not with the natural sweeteners for fear of the FDA mandate. The stores cannot promote the "sweetening" qualities of stevia, even though that is why it is purchased.

Stevia can be used as a healthy substitute in most sugar applications, including baking and cooking since it is heat stable. The average conversion rate of sugar to stevia is one cup of sugar per one teaspoonful of pure stevia extract. Clearly very little stevia is needed to replace sugar. When used in beverages, stevia dissolves quickly and easily and, depending on your taste preference, only a pinch is needed. The real challenge to using stevia effectively is knowing what ingredients to use in a recipe to make up for the volume and consistency lost with the elimination of sugar, especially in baked goods. That is why it is a good idea to find stevia cookbooks with proven recipes when you are starting out. You can also find some free recipes online. Finally, stevia is not appropriate in recipes that require sugar caramelizing or browning like meringues.

Stevia is available in many forms including liquid, teas, plants/leaves, pure white and green powdered extract and powdered blends with different fillers. In baking, the pure extract is used primarily and, in some cases, the liquid variety. Stevia can be purchased at health food stores, natural grocers, food coops and online. Currently, a big push is underway to expand distribution into grocery stores, vitamin shops and drugstores.

Due to the number of factors that can influence your stevia purchase experience, the following guidelines provide some good advice:

- You often do get what you pay for; don't buy based solely on price; taste and quality matter.
- Higher percent of stevioside doesn't necessarily make the stevia better; you can find excellent tasting stevia with this key plant composition at even 80%.
- If you purchase the green powder for its slightly higher health benefits, it will usually have more aftertaste than the white powder.
- The product's country of origin doesn't matter; it's farming, manufacturing and processing experience and techniques do.
- At this time, stevia production is not standardized, so taste and strength do differ depending on brand.
- Use a minimal amount; can be overwhelming if you add too much initially; add more lately if needed.

Widespread use of sugar and artificial sweeteners are at dangerous levels. The negative side effects and controversial studies regarding their proposed safety suggest that another alternative is desirable and necessary. Stevia may be a welcome option for those who want to ingest more natural ingredients with no known side effects, no calories, no carbs, no fat, no affect on glucose levels and no sugar or artificial sweeteners. Stevia may also be advantageous in the prevention and treatment of diabetes, obesity and other health conditions. Check with your doctor before including stevia to your diet. If he/she doesn't recommend it, politely ask why to see if the reason is satisfactory to you.

For more information on stevia or to try free stevia recipes, visit the web or www.steviadessert.com and cookbooks like Sensational Stevia Desserts by Lisa Jobs, $19.95 retail price, Healthy Lifestyle Publishing LLC, Copyright ©2005. The book is available at various online sites including www.steviadessert.com, Amazon, Barnes and Noble, health food stores or you can order it at your favorite bookstore.

Market Potential

The government is not approving stevioside which is natural and safe, and allowing artificial sweeteners despite insufficient data to prove them safe. India being the diabetes capital of the world, demand for low-calorie sweeteners is high. An estimated 10–20% people in India have diabetes; the market for low-calorie sweeteners is at least 25% if one combines the obese and weight conscious consumers with diabetics. Unlike Food safety and standards Association of India FSSAI, other departments are interested in using stevia's potential. The National Medicinal Plant Board (NMPB) gives 20% subsidy to farmers who cultivate it. Stevia can be harvested three to four times a year. Farmers can earn Rs 70–120 per kg of stevia leaves and it is exported at Rs 200–250 a kg. Stevia is cultivated in over 1,800 hectares in different states under NMPB schemes.

According to Sun Fruits Ltd, a company that cultivates stevia commercially, the sweetener can play an important role in all products that need sucrose—food, beverage, agriculture, medicine, animal feed and skin care products. At present, stevia accounts for just 1% of the global sugar-substitute market though its value in the US market is expected to grow to $2,000 million by end of 2011, from $21 million in 2008. The Indian market for sweeteners can shift toward stevia if it gets a boost from the government. Stevia is cheaper than sugar. The average sugar yield from a 0.4 hectares sugarcane field is 4 tons; average yield of stevia extract that equals sweetness of sugar is over 60 tons from 0.4 hectares.

The market for stevia in India is limited because there are no processing units. The government-run Institute of Himalayan Bioresource Technology at Palampur in Himachal Pradesh is planning to setup the country's first patented ecofriendly stevia processing unit near Delhi (the units capacity won't be high—300 kg leaves a day).

Safe Limit

Food safety authorities in several countries have approved steviosides as food additive. These include Brazil, China, Japan, Australia and New Zealand. The USFDA has categorized steviosides as generally recognized as safe. Some countries have fixed an average daily intake for it which is the safe daily intake limit for a substance over a life-span. In 2008, a joint committee on food additives of FAO and WHO fixed the upper limit for steviosides at 4 mg/kg of body weight. The EFSA has fixed the limit for it at 4 mg/kg body weight.

Research

Stevia industry in India is yet to make headway. Due to the absence of research on stevia plants in India, clonal material is perhaps imported and tissue culture plants are raised. The cost of such plants can be high unless the government subsidizes it. The Japanese have been using stevia for over 40 years and countries like China, Korea, Taiwan, Thailand and Malaysia are following suit. Japan has even banned use of synthetic sweeteners.

There are no processing facilities for stevia leaves. This might be a limiting factor in increasing the area under cultivation—around 1,800 hectares, at present. Big companies like Zydus Cadila that claim stevia has a leafy after-taste need to check with Japan, China and several other countries how they manage. Have they ascertained the quality standards of these countries and can they not import their technology? The India Stevia Association needs to pressure the government to recognize the high value stevia has for several patients.

A New Sweetener

Cough syrups and diet drinks could soon become more tastier as scientists have found a new compound which they say blocks taste buds' ability to detect bitter flavors. The discovery of the compound called GIV3616 which is tasteless and prevents tart tastes being sensed by the tongue could be added to foods and beverages to make them more palatable, said the researchers. Ioana Ungureanu of the research team that developed the compound at Givaudan Flavors Corporation in Cincinnati, Ohio, said, "A lot of people are very sensitive to bitter taste in medicines, calorie-free sweeteners and foods".

"We had like to be able to make their diets more enjoyable by masking the off-putting flavors of bitterness", Ungureanu was quoted as saying by LiveScience. "Blocking these flavors we call 'offnotes' could help consumers eat healthier and more varied diets. It could encourage them to switch to noncalorie soft drinks and help children and seniors swallow bitter-tasting medications". The researchers, who presented their findings at the annual conference of the American Chemical Society in Anaheim, California, said GIV3616 is not the first compound capable of masking bitter tastes from the tongue.

That honor belongs to GIV3727, which improves the taste of artificial sweeteners such as saccharin and sucralose. But, the bitterness blocker GIV3616 is more potent than its predecessor and dissolves more quickly in food and beverages, Ungureanu said. As people have become more concerned about the amount of salt, fat and sugar in processed foods, interest in flavor blockers has jumped according to the American Chemical Society.

Instead of masking bad or bitter flavors with salty, fatty ingredients, food manufacturers are interested in using chemicals that interfere with the taste receptors on the tongue, leaving them temporarily unable to detect unpleasant flavors.

Sugar Miracle

Synsepalum dulcificum or "miracle berry" as it is commonly referred to in West Africa where it grows, is quite prized by the locals for an amazing property: it makes sour things taste spectacularly sweet. As it is consumed, a rogue protein in it called miraculin attaches itself to the tongue's sensory receptors and then the magic starts.

Till up to an hour later when the tongue subsequently comes in contact with acids found in sour foods, the protein acts as a miraculous sweetness inducer, changing the subjective taste experience totally. Tart citrus then tastes like candy, sharp cheeses like cheesecake and bitter beer like milkshake. In fact, people are known to have developed serious gastric problems overdosing continuously on lemons. Curiously, the little berry itself has a low sugar content and is only mildly tangy which brings us to the fox in the fairytale who, after his humiliating episode with the unsour grapes, had fortunately chanced upon a lemon tree in the same thicket and immediately plucked a few of its low-lying produce and proceeded to scoff them. And as we all know, he was last overheard by the crow muttering loudly how sweet those face-saving fruits tasted.

Like the fox, a lot of us also have a form of miraculin in our minds that temporarily alters the truth. Overdosing on that perception, however, has no lasting value and can ultimately cause ulcers of self-deceit. More importantly, if taste is only on the tongue of the partaker, what does it say about beauty being in the eye of the beholder?

6

Sugar Policy

India is the second largest producer of sugar after Brazil in the world. The sugar industry occupies an important place in the Indian economy. Nearly 7.5 million people across the country are directly or indirectly employed in the industry. Over 50 million eke out their livelihood from growing and supplying sugarcane. The sugar industry contributes annually around Rs 50 billion by way of excise duty, cess, value-added tax (VAT), entry tax and octroi.

The sugar industry is the second-largest agro-based industry next to textiles in India. Sugar is produced from sugarcane and sugar beet. Approximately 70% sugar is produced from sugarcane and 30% is produced from sugar beet. Sugarcane is grown in semitropical region while beet is grown in temperate climate.

Policy of sugar industry: The Department of Food and Public Distribution monitors and implement various policies of the government and development of sugar industries, vegetable oil vanaspati industries. It also takes stock of the indigenous production, internal requirement, allocation of sugar, vanaspati and edible oils. It comprises of two administrative bodies, that have described at below.

SUGARCANE PRODUCTION AND PRICING POLICY

The Government of India (GOI) supports research, development, training of farmers, transfer of new varieties, and improved production technologies (seed, implements, pest management) to growers in its endeavor to raise cane yields and sugar recovery rates. The Indian Council of Agricultural Research (ICAR) conducts sugarcane research and development at the national level. State agricultural universities, regional research institutions, and state agricultural extension agencies support these efforts at the regional and state levels. Central and state governments also support sugarcane growers by ensuring finances and input supplies at affordable prices.

To increase the area of cultivation and production in the country, the GOI has implemented the "Sustainable Development Fund of Sugarcane Based Cropping System Area under Macromanagement Mode of Agriculture" program in various sugarcane growing states. Additionally, under Rashtriya Krishi Vikas Yojaana (National Agriculture Development Program), State Governments have been given flexibility to choose their priorities for the formulation of crop development projects including sugarcane.

The GOI collects Rs 240 ($5.60) per ton of sugar produced by mills in support of the Sugarcane Development Fund (SDF) which is used to support research, extension, and technological improvement in the sugar sector. The SDF is also used to support sugar buffer-stock operations, provides a transport subsidy for sugar exports, and provides an interest subsidy on loans for the installation of power generation and ethanol production plants. In March 2008, the GOI enacted the SDF (Amendment) Bill, 2008, enabling the government to include the use of SDF funds for debt restructuring and soft loans to sugar mills.

The GOI establishes a minimum support price (MSP) for sugarcane based on recommendations by the Commission for Agricultural Costs and Prices (CACP) and consultations with State Governments, sugar industry and cane grower associations. Four years ago, the GOI announced a new fair and remunerative price (FRP) system that links cane prices with miller's sugar price realization. Several state governments augment the MSP/FRP, typically by 30–40% due to political compulsions rather than market pricing. Sugar mills are required to pay the "state advised price (SAP)" to sugarcane farmers irrespective of the market price of sugar. A forecast of a smaller cane crop normally encourages sugar mills to pay higher cane prices, resulting in prices exceeding the MSP/FRP in most of the growing states.

SUGAR MARKETING POLICY: GOVERNMENT APPROVES PARTIAL MARKET DECONTROL

On April 4, 2013, the Cabinet Committee on Economic Affairs, Chaired by Prime Minister Manmohan Singh, abolished the sugar levy on mills and deregulated the sale of sugar in the open market. Under the sugar levy, mills were obligated to sell 10% of their sugar production at below-market prices to the GOI. The GOI distributed this sugar at subsidized rates to poor consumers through the public distribution system (PDS). Under the new system, the GOI will continue to supply subsidized sugar for the poor by procuring sugar from the open market through open tenders. The difference between the open market price and PDS sale price will be borne by the GOI. The sugar industry will continue to be subject to production controls by state governments including sugar industry licensing, specified cane procurement areas for sugar mills, and cane pricing. Decontrol of sugar marketing will be reviewed in 2 years after assessing its effect on farmers and market prices [for more information please refer to Global Agriculture Information Network (GAIN) report IN3036]. An official notification on sugar levy reform is expected to be out soon.

On March 26, 2013, prior to the partial decontrol of the sugar industry, the GOI decided to release 10.4 million tons of sugar as non-levy quota for open market sale between April and September, 2013. The sale and delivery period for the above quota is specified without intermonth restrictions.

The non-levy quota will be apportioned and released only among those sugar mills which have submitted online production returns at the time of release. Mill-wise quota apportionment will discount the entire non-levy quota released for the period of October, 2012 through March, 2013. Any quantity left unsold will not be available for sale during the period of April, 2013 to September, 2013. There will be no conversion of unsold non-levy quota into levy quota during the period of current release, i.e. April to September, 2013.

Enforcement of Regulated Release Mechanism

In order to safeguard, the interests of sugarcane growers, the producers of sugar and the general public to stabilize the open market price of sugar and to obviate intervention in the "regulated release" mechanism, the Essential Commodities Act, 1955 was amended in June, 2003. "The Essential Commodities (Amendment) Act, 2003" incorporates the provisions of Clauses 4 and 5 of the Sugar (Control) Order, 1966 in the Essential Commodities Act, 1955 through insertion of subclause (3D) and (3E). As per this amended Act, no producer, importer or exporter of sugar shall sell or otherwise dispose of or deliver any kind of sugar except under and in accordance with the direction issued by the government.

Futures Trading in Sugar

Sugar was approved for futures trading in May, 2001. At present, three national exchanges, viz. National Commodity and Derivative Exchange Ltd. (NCDEX), Mumbai, Multi Commodity Exchange Ltd. (MCX), Mumbai, National Multi-Commodity Exchange (NMCE), Ahmedabad and E sugar India Ltd., Mumbai and E-Commodities Ltd., Delhi have been given recognition for future trading in sugar. Except, E-Commodities Ltd., Delhi, trading in sugar is taking place in all other exchanges. Bulk of the futures trading in sugar takes place at NCDEX.

Levy Sugar Supply under PDS

The population base for supply of levy sugar under the PDS was changed from 1991 census population to the projected population as on March 1, 1999 with effect from March 1, 2000. With effect from February 1, 2001, the population base for supply of levy sugar under the PDS has been changed to the projected population as on March 1, 2000. In order to ensure better targeting, levy sugar supply under the PDS has been restricted only to the Below Poverty Line (BPL) families in all States/UTS except the North Eastern States, Hill States and Island Territories with effect from 01.02.2001.

The minimum per head per month quantum of levy sugar allotted under the PDS was increased from 425 gm to 500 gm with effect from February 1, 2001. The Monthly levy quota under the PDS for various States/UTs (Union Territories) with effect from 01.02.2001 is 2.16 lakh tons.

Release of Non-Levy Free Sale Sugar

160.20 lakh tons of non-levy free sale sugar was released for sale in the open market during 2005–2006 sugar season as compared to 146.00 lakh tons during the previous sugar season 2004–2005.

Sugar Prices

Under the provision of sub-section 3(c) of section 3 of the Essential Commodities Act, 1955, the ex-factory prices of the levy sugar requisitioned from the sugar mills is fixed having regard to:

a. The minimum price, if any, fixed for the sugarcane by the Central Government.
b. The manufacturing cost of sugar.
c. The duty or tax, if any, paid or payable thereon
d. The reasonable return on the capital employed in the business of manufacturing sugar.

Sugar mills are paid the levy sugar price on zonal basis. However, the Central Government also determines the average all India levy sugar price. For the sugar season 2003–2004, the average all-India levy sugar price has been determined at Rs 1,305.92 per quintal as against Rs 1,259.99 for the preceding sugar season.

The Cost Study for the determination of levy sugar prices for 2004–2005 to 2006–2007 was entrusted to the Cost Accounts Branch (CAB) of the Ministry of Finance. The government has since received the report of the CAB which is under consideration.

Retail Issue Price of Levy Sugar under the PDS

The retail issue price of levy sugar under the PDS has been fixed at Rs 13.50 per kg with effect from March 1, 2002 which is continuing.

UTTAR PRADESH SUGAR INDUSTRY'S FATE AGAIN HANGS IN BALANCE

After facing the ire on law and order issues, Uttar Pradesh (UP) government might face the closure of its sole and the largest agriculture based Rs 35,000 crore sugar industry. UP sugar industry, the second largest in the country, has for the second time since the commencement of the sugar season 2013–2014, decided to declare a shutdown, this time for a whole year, if their demand for rational cane price is not met. The sugar industry of the state, which houses noted names such as Bajaj Hindustan, Dhampur Sugar, Dalmia Sugar among others has complained that due to lack of a definite cane price linkage formula, the industry is in no position to pay "unreasonably decided cane price".

The industry executives said that out of all the incentives announced by the central government, none will come to their rescue. "Of the Rs 4,400 crore interest-free loan announced by the center on Monday, only 30%, i.e. Rs 1,300 crore will fall in the kitty of the state. Others like ethanol blending is no financial aid and export subsidy is for sugar exporting state Maharashtra", said a senior sugar industry executive.

The cane payment arrears in the state have touched Rs 7,000 crore and the industry fears that it would cross the Rs 10,000 crore mark by season end. "Under these circumstances, when our own State Government is not appreciative of the problems faced by the industry, and assurances given are not fulfilled, there seems to be no other alternative but to suspend crushing operations of our sugar factories during 2014–2015 sugar season", said the letter written by UP Sugar Mills Association (UPSMA) to the chief secretary, government of UP. The letter reviewed by ET said that during 2011–2012 and 2012–2013 sugar seasons alone, the industry has lost around Rs 4,000 crore only because there has been a total mismatch between the sugar prices fixed by UP Government and the revenue realization by the mills.

The state advised cane price for this season is Rs 280 per quintal, against the demand of the industry to keep it at Rs 240 per quintal or imply the Rangarajan formula for cane price linkage to market rate of sugar. Other sugar producing states such as Maharashtra and Karnataka have already adopted linkage formula for cane price wherein farmers share the revenue generated by the mills.

A UP sugar industry executive requesting anonymity said that since the close of the last sugar season in September 2013, at least 40 FIRs have been issued by the state government to the millers on non-payment of dues to the cane farmers. "We

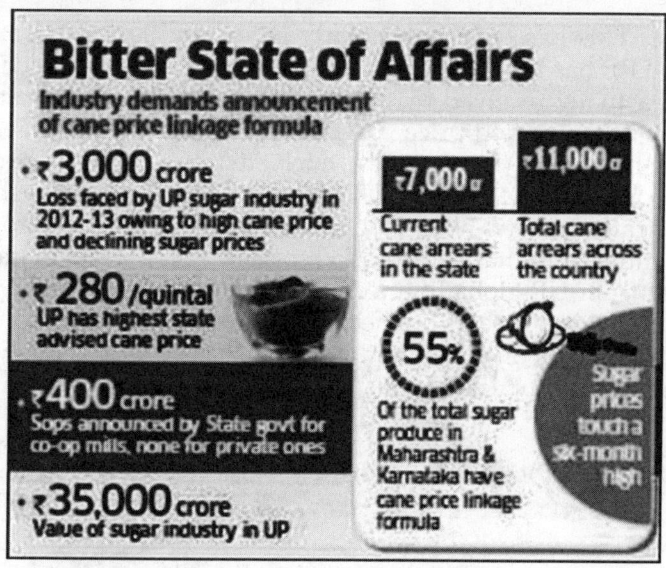

had cautioned the state government that the arrears would touch Rs 10,000 crore, then there is no need for such coercive action. We are opened for providing suggestions and advice in the larger benefit of the industry", said a sugar industry executive. "We cannot help it if the cane price is beyond our payment capacity. Incentives might help now, but the same situation would arise in the next season We need a definite solution in form of a cane price formula", said the executive.

The UP sugar industry has recommended sharing of 75% of revenue realization with the farmers. "This would translate into a cane price of around Rs 240–250 per quintal", said UPSMA executive. Notably, in the state budget announced last week, around Rs 400 crore was allocated to the cooperative mills recently to pay the cane farmers.

"The cooperative millers get a discount of Rs 80 per quintal on the cane price and we get none. The private millers are producing 90% of the State's sugar and are asking for just Rs 40 per quintal relief on cane price", said a UP based private miller. Sugar prices have been on a downslide, since the commencement of current sugar season, touching the lowest in 5 years in January this year. The announcement of financial sops cheered the industry and market.

The spot price at NCDEX for the Kolhapur mandi was at Rs 31.85 per kg for Kanpur mandi it increased to Rs 33.60 per kg. The retail price of sugar in both Mumbai and Delhi has already touched a 6-month high at Rs 38 and Rs 38.12 per kg, respectively.

Wholesale Price of Non-Levy Sugar

The range of wholesale prices of non-levy sugar in the four metropolitan cities (Delhi, Mumbai, Kolkata and Chennai) during 1998–1999 to 2006–2007 (upto 30th November, 2007).

Since 2009–2010 sugar season, when the concept of Statutory Minimum Price (SMP) was replaced by Fair and Remunerative Price (FRP), there has been a gradual effort to align FRP more closely to the value of sugar and its by-products from one quintal of cane. This has been particularly so during 2012–2013 and 2013–2014 seasons, when FRP has been increased by 17.2% and 23.5%, respectively. But, the prices that are actually received by cane farmers are SAP as in states like UP, or some sort of final "negotiated price" based on "surplus sharing" mechanism as in case of Maharashtra sugar cooperatives which are much higher (Chart 6.1). For the 2012–2013 season, the cane price in UP is higher than in Maharashtra despite a lower recovery rate (9.1% vis-à-vis 11.4%) and a shorter duration crop (9.5 months *vis-à-vis* 13 months in Maharashtra). No wonder, rising costs of cane has made domestic sugar from UP globally uncompetitive, creating a glut of sugar on one hand and mounting cane arrears on the other. The situation has become precarious, despite 15% import duty on sugar, and indications are that it is likely to worsen as global prices remain at subdued levels.

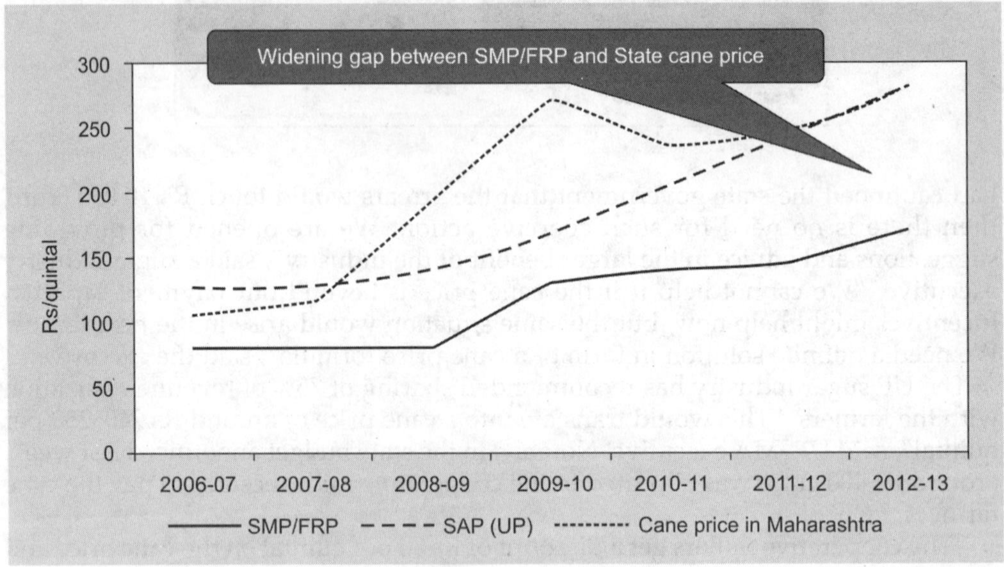

Chart 6.1: SMP/FRP vs state cane prices
Source: Directorate of Sugar, DFPD and Cane Commissioner, Pune

The lack of alignment between the cost of main raw material (sugarcane) and then recovered price of the processed product (sugar) has led to record cane arrears in 2012–2013. The cane price arrears for 2012–2013 sugar season touched a record Rs 11,990 crore by 15 April, 2013 amounting to 21.2% of the total cane dues. Similar situation was earlier witnessed in 2007–2008 when these cane arrears were even higher at 22.9% of price payable (Chart 6.2). A sharp fall in cane production was experienced, thereafter, in 2008–2009 and 2009–2010 which should alert us for an impending downward cycle in the sugar sector. The prices announced by some State Governments, most notably UP in 2012–2013, do not reflect any rational linkage either with the cost of production of sugarcane or the value of sugar and its by-products recovered from a quintal of cane. While farmers consider SMP/FRP to be on the lower side, the SAP in UP seems on the higher side compared to what the sugar factories can afford, given the prices of sugar. And a proof of that lies in

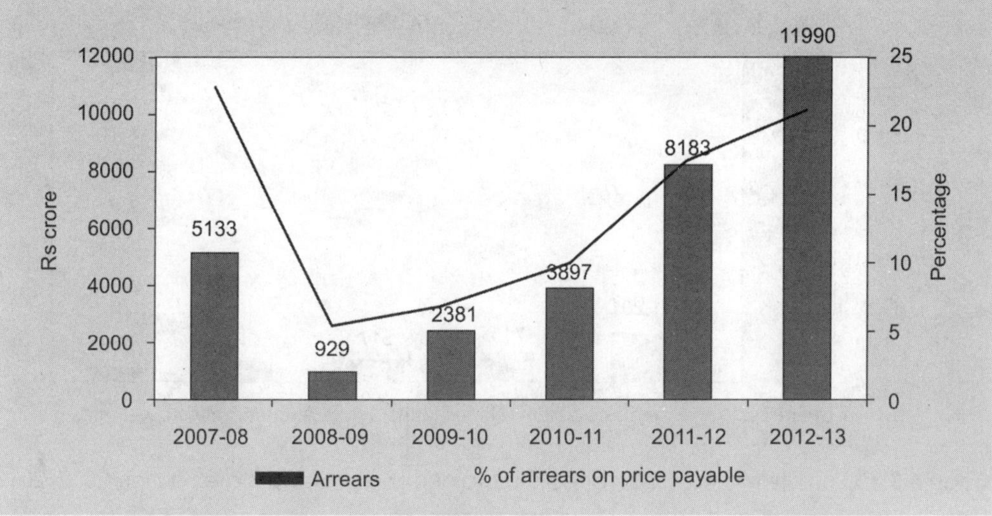

Chart 6.2: Cane price arrears during 2007–2008 to 2012–2013

Note: The arrears are as on 15th April of the sugar season.
Source: Directorate of Sugar, DFPD.

mounting cane arrears. If we have 1 or 2 years more like this in a row, in all likelihood, several sugar factories will start closing down their production lines as no one would like to incur losses on continuous basis. The solution to this problem obviously lies in having the pricing of cane based on revenue sharing formula.

UP is the largest producer of sugarcane, alone accounts for around two-thirds of the total arrears at Rs 7,840 crore (Chart 6.3). The State Government of UP, in the backdrop of severe criticism by the Allahabad High Court, has decided to issue Recovery Certificates (RCs) against mills that have defaulted in payment to sugarcane farmers and has threatened to file FIRs against mills that do not pay farmers at least 90% of their dues by 31st July, 2013. It may be noted here that UP has increased its SAP by an average rate of 19.3% during the last three sugar seasons (2010–2011 to 2012–2013), while the ex-mill sugar prices have increased by only 2.6% per annum during the same period. This disconnect between the two prices has led to the precarious financial position of sugar mills leading to accumulation of cane arrears. This would become unsustainable in the long run and lead to financial sickness and ultimately demise of the sugar industry as had happened earlier in Bihar. It must be realized that sugar sector cannot run sustainably on arbitrary pricing of cane without taking into account the revenue realization from its main products, and certainly not by court orders. In this context, it should also be realized that with gradual evolution of FRP, the rationale of SAP is no more justified. If any state wants to give some extra support to its cane farmers, an investment subsidy or income support policy would be better and not the price policy which distorts the markets.

Inherent Bias in the Current FRP System

As an illustrative example, for 2013–2014 sugar season, for UP, if the ex-factory sugar price stays around Rs 33/kg, the revenue sharing formula would suggest a

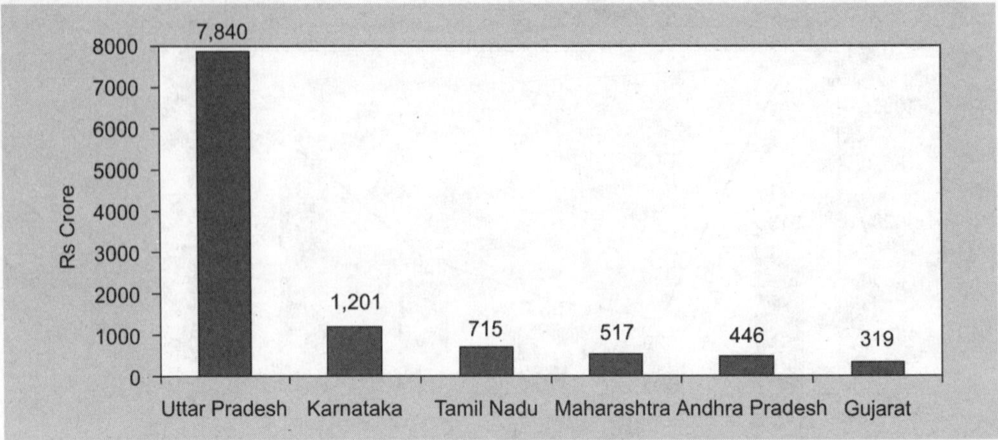

Chart 6.3: Cumulative cane price arrears in major cane growing States during 2012–2013

Note: The arrears are as on 15th April of the sugar season.
Source: Directorate of Sugar, DFPD.

price of the cane to be at 75% of the value of sugar from 1 quintal of cane assuming a minimum recovery ratio of 9.5%. This would amount to Rs 235 per quintal (Rs 33 × 9.5 × 0.75), even if the recovery ratio is below 9.5%. For Maharashtra, assuming that the recovery ratio is around 11.5% and ex-factory sugar price is around Rs 30/kg, the corresponding cane price through revenue sharing formula will be Rs 259 per quintal (Rs 30 × 11.5 × 0.75). The announced FRP of Rs 210 per quintal at 9.5% recovery ratio will mean Rs 210 per quintal for UP, but Rs 254 per quintal for Maharashtra [Rs (210/9.5) × 11.5]. If the FRP is increased to Rs 235 per quintal (as determined by revenue sharing in UP), then the corresponding price for Maharashtra would be Rs 284 per quintal [(235/9.5) × 11.5]. This cane price in Maharashtra would amount to 82.4% share of farmers in the value of sugar [= 284 × 100/(30 × 11.5)] which would price out the sugar industry. The purpose of this illustration is to show that the existing FRP formula at 9.5% recovery rate cannot do full justice simultaneously to the two main States producing sugar which have a wide variation in their recovery levels. Therefore, it would be in the best interest of both the states to adopt revenue sharing formula, as it would bring in rationality, certainty and stability in the system and would surely give them better price than FRP. But if they go by SAP, as UP is doing, and announcing a much higher price for cane than what could be given based on the value of sugar and its by-products, then the sugar sector would soon run into trouble which will not be in the interest of either the farmers or millers.

Partial Decontrol

The Central Government has partially decontrolled the sugar sector in line with the recommendations of the Rangarajan Committee. The dismantling of the levy obligation (for 2 years) and the deregulated sugar release mechanism will lead to a more competitive, efficient and profitable sugar sector, thereby benefiting all stakeholders—the growers, the millers and the consumers. Removal of the burden of levy sugar will give the industry an annual savings of about Rs 3,000 crore, whereas abolition of regulated release mechanism will reduce inventories and ensure better cash flows. Increase in ethanol prices through competitive bidding will also benefit the sugar industry. These much awaited reforms will improve liquidity with millers which, in turn, will ensure better and timely payment of cane price to farmers. But, pricing of cane remains central to the sugar sector, and unless that is put on a scientifically sound and transparent principle, by linking sugarcane prices to end-product prices, sugar sector will remain victim of instability, and thereby cannot realize its true potential. This has to be recognized by all cane growing states, especially UP.

Hybrid Pricing Formula

As in respect of any other produce, the revenues realized from the sale of all the products and by-products should be equitably shared among producing stakeholders, and consumers too should get a competitive price. Based on this premise, Rangarajan committee had carefully estimated the relative share of costs incurred by farmers and millers and recommended sharing of 70% of the revenue from sale of sugar, molasses, bagasse and press-mud produced from a quintal of cane, to rationalize pricing of cane. Loading the value of by-products on value of sugar, this pricing formula worked out to about 75% of the ex-mill value of sugar produced from a quintal of cane. Under the revenue sharing formula, sugarcane growers will, in the first place, be paid some Minimum Fair and Remunerative Price (MFRP) as fixed by the Commission, with the balance paid at a later stage after realization of revenues 5. Rationalizing sugarcane pricing along these lines will help in reducing volatility in sugar production and farmer income. This is a practice followed throughout the major sugar producing nations, and 75% of the value of sugar produced from 1 quintal of cane would perhaps be one of the highest prices of cane offered anywhere in the world. The Commission's calculations show that this will not only ensure a fair and stable return to farmers, but also assure mills a reasonable return on their investments. Karnataka has already decided to adopt a revenue sharing formula which deserves credit. The Commission is given to understand that Maharashtra is also moving in that direction, and hopefully they will also adopt this formula. It is high time that the states in the north, especially UP, also make a note of this and start moving in that direction in the overall interest of this sector's growth with stability.

EFFICACY OF PRICING POLICY

The Commission as mandated, has been recommending the prices for sugarcane (SMP/FRP) keeping in view the cost of production of sugarcane, return from alternative crops, availability of sugar at fair price, recovery of sugar from sugarcane, realization made from sale of by-products, reasonable margins for sugarcane growers, etc. The Central Government decides about the SMP/FRP for sugarcane based on the recommendation of the Commission, which is expected to be adopted by all sugarcane growing states after due adjustments to recovery rates. However, in reality, there is wide variation in the cane prices paid to farmers by different states. For instance most of the states in the subtropical belt, especially UP, announce their own SAPs which are some sort of "negotiated prices". In certain years, these SAPs turn out to be much higher (as in 2012–2013) in relation to the prices of sugar and its by-products being produced from cane, leading to large cane arrears. In the tropical belt, especially of Maharashtra, Karnataka, etc. cane pricing has some semblance with revenue sharing formula, albeit not very transparent and explicit. The effect is evident with two-thirds of the cane arrears concentrated in the subtropical states, especially UP.

If we analyze the SMP/FRP at all-India recovery rate as a proportion of total value of sugar (Table 6.1), we find that on an average over 5 years, the value comes to be only around 50%. In recent years, there has been a gradual effort to align FRP more closely to the value of sugar and its by-products from 1 quintal of cane. This has been particularly so since 2011–2012, as the cane price has been increased by 44.8% in 2 years. In 2013–2014 season, the FRP of Rs 210 per quintal gives a 70% share of the value of sugar at the all India level and to the farmers in UP (at an ex-factory sugar price of around Rs 33/kg) and 74% in Maharashtra (with recovery ratio at 11.5% and ex-factory sugar price of around Rs 30/kg). However, it needs to be appreciated here that SMP/FRP, customarily, has to be kept toward a lower side as sugar prices can go up or down but FRP may not be revised downward.

As noted earlier, UP announces its own SAP. An attempt is made in Table 6.2 to compare the farmer's share (in terms of cane price paid) in the total value of sugar derived from 1 quintal of cane in UP to the Revenue Sharing Formula recommended by Rangarajan Committee. It is observed that over a period of 5 years, the average share of farmers in the sugar value obtained by farmers has been 74% in UP. This is very close to the 75% share recommended by the Rangarajan Committee. But on a

Table 6.1: SMP/FRP as a percentage of value of sugar

Sugars	*All India ex-mill sugar prices (Rs/qtl)*	*All India recovery rate (%)*	*Total sugar value from one quintal of cane of cane (Rs/qtl)*	*SMP/FRP (Rs qtl)*	*SMP/FRP at all India recovery rate*	*SMP/FRP as percentage of value of sugar (%)*
(1)	*(2)*	*(3)*	*(4)=(2)*(3)*	*(5)*	*(6)=(5)*(3) basic recovery rate*	*(7)=(6)* 100/(4)*
2008–09	2,127	10.05	213.76	81.18	90.65	42.41
2009–10	2,980	10.20	303.96	129.84	139.41	45.86
2010–11	2,659	10.17	270.42	139.12	148.93	55.07
2011–12	3,070	10.27	315.29	145.00	156.75	49.72
2012–13	3,150	10.27	323.51	170.00	183.78	56.81
2013–14 (E)	3,150	10.27	323.51	210.00	227.02	70.18

Notes:
1. Basic recovery rate was 9% till 2008–2009 and 9.5% years thereafter.
2. The recovery rate for 2012–2013 and 2013–2014 is assumed to be the same as 2011–2012 which is the latest available.
3. The ex-mill price for 2013–2014 is assumed to be similar to 2012–2013.
4. E: Estimated.

Source: Directorate of Sugar, Ministry of Consumer Affairs, Food and Public Distribution and State Replies.

Table 6.2: A comparative analysis of cane price paid to farmers as a percentage of value of sugar *vis-à-vis* rangarajan committee formula of revenue sharing in UP

Sugar season	*Ex-mill sugar price*	*Cane price paid to farmers (SAP)*	*State recovery rate (%)*	*Total sugar value from one quintal of cane*		*Farmer's share in total revenue (cane price paid to farmers/total sugar value)* 100*		*Cane price payable to farmers under revenue sharing formula of Rangarajan Committee (75% of total sugar value from 1 quintal of cane*
				At state recovery rate	*At 9.5% recovery rate*	*At state recovery rate*	*At 9.5% recovery rate*	*At 9.5% recovery rate*
(1)	(2)	(3)	(4)	(5)=(2)*(4)	(6)=(2)*9.5	(7)=(3)*100/(5)	(8)=(3)*100/(6)	(9)=0.75*(6)
2008–09	2,230.83	140.00	8.91	198.77	211.93	70.43	66.06	158.95
2009–10	3,121.67	165.00	9.13	285.01	296.56	57.89	55.64	222.42
2010–11	2,806.67	205.00	9.15	256.81	266.63	79.83	76.88	199.98
2011–12	3,076.46	240.00	9.09	279.65	292.26	85.82	82.12	219.20
2012–13	3,335.94	280.00	9.09	303.24	316.91	92.34	88.35	237.69
Average						**77.26**	**73.81**	

Notes:
1. The ex-mill price for 2012–2013 is up to May, 2013.
2. Annual ex-mill sugar price has been calculated on the basis of monthly averages of price range provided by Directorate of sugar.
3. Basic recovery rate was 9% till 2008–2009 and 9.5% years thereafter.
4. Rangarajan Committee assumes a basic minimum recovery rate of 9.5%.
5. The recovery rate for 2012–2013 is assumed to be the same as 2011–2012 which is the latest available.

Source: Directorate of Sugar, Ministry of Consumer Affairs, Food and Public Distribution and State Replies.

yearly basis, farmer's share fluctuated widely from 58% in 2009–2010 to 92% in 2012–2013. This uncertainty in the share, to the farmers and the millers, hampers fresh investments and adoption of new technology. Therefore, the Commission feels that Rangarajan Committee recommendation of revenue sharing formula would be more effective, transparent and rational as was also recommended in its Report last year.

It is, therefore, essential that an appropriate pricing formula is devised so as to ensure a fair sharing of the value created in the cane sugar value chain by protecting the interest of both farmers and millers. To bring in greater certainty, stability and transparency into the sugar industry, and to rationalize the pricing of sugarcane, Rangarajan Committee has recommended for sharing the revenue pot of value created in the sugarcane value chain between the farmers and millers in the ratio of their relative costs and has suggested that 70% of the value of sugar and each of its three major by-products, namely bagasse, molasses and press mud (all ex-mill), be fixed as the cane dues payable to the farmer. Loading the value of by-products on sugar value, this amounts to roughly 75% of the ex-mill value of sugar alone produced from a quintal of cane. The Rangarajan Committee however has also recommended moving towards the hybrid formula, i.e. revenue sharing principle dovetailed with some sort of a minimum FRP, keeping in view of the fact that sugar prices are quite volatile.

The Commission is of the view that in order to keep pace with best international practices and to avoid uncertainty and volatility in sugar prices and sugar cycles, India needs to move from the existing system of fixed pricing of cane toward hybrid pricing by adopting the recommendations of the Rangarajan Committee early.

RECOMMENDATIONS FOR PRICE POLICY

The CACP formulates its price policy for sugarcane within the scope of its mandate and the terms of reference given to it under the Sugarcane (Control) Order, 1966 issued under the EC Act, 1955. Prior to 2009–2010 sugar season, the Central Government was fixing the Statutory Minimum Price (SMP) of sugarcane and farmers were also entitled to share profits of a sugar mill on 50:50 basis. The sharing provision was introduced in the Control Order as Clause 5A in September, 1974 with a well-intended purport to empower farmers to equally share the dividends of the mills. However, it remained virtually unimplemented mainly on account of delays in the announcement of profits by the mills. The Sugarcane (Control) Order, 1966 was amended vide notification 22.10.2009 and the concept of SMP was replaced by the FRP of sugarcane. For this purpose of working out FRP, a new item "reasonable margins for growers of sugarcane on account of risk and profits" was inserted in Clause 3(1) vide notification dated 22.10.2009 and made effective from 2009–2010 season.

Clause 5A relating to sharing of profits between sugar factories and farmers was thus deleted.

As per the amended provisions of Clause 3(1) of the Sugarcane (Control) Order, 1966, "*The Central Government may, after consultation with the authorities, bodies or associations as it may deem fit, by notification in the official Gazette, from time to time, fix the* ***Fair and Remunerative Price*** *of sugarcane to be paid by producers of sugar or their agents for the sugarcane purchased by them, having regard to:*

a. *The cost of production of sugarcane*
b. *The return to the grower from alternative crops and the general trend of prices of agricultural commodities*
c. *The availability of sugar to the consumers at a fair price*
d. *The price at which sugar produced from sugarcane is sold by producers of sugar*
e. *The recovery of sugar from sugarcane*
f. *The realization made from sale of by-products viz. molasses, bagasse and press mud or their imputed value (inserted on 29.12.2008)*
g. *Reasonable margins for growers of sugarcane on account of risk and profits (inserted on 22.10.2009)".*

Accordingly, the Commission is required to pay due regard to the statutory factors listed in the Control Order. It may be worth emphasizing that this includes taking into account not only the recovery and pricing of sugar, but also its by-products namely molasses, bagasse and press mud. Thus, revenue sharing of sugar factories is expected to be reflected in sugarcane pricing. As detailed in the Commission's earlier report for the marketing season 2013–2014, the current system of FRP has not proved to be very effective. The share of FRP in the value of sugar for the sugar season 2012–2013 comes out to be only 56.0% for UP and 58.3% for Maharashtra. This is at least 20% points less than the 75% share of cane price in sugar value realized devised by the Rangarajan Committee. On the other extreme, in UP, in 2012–2013, the SAP has led to a 92.3% share of farmers in the value of sugar. No wonder, it has led to mounting cane arrears in UP, and brought the sugar mills on the brink of a financial crisis. One or two such years in a row can start a downward spiral of shutting down of sugar mills, a beginning of the downfall of sugar sector in UP. In Maharashtra, the cane price paid has a share of 79.5% which is relatively closer to the Rangarajan Committee estimate. But, the problem with these SAPs is that they are not based on any transparent or scientific basis and lead to wide fluctuations in returns to farmers. The solution to this lies in evolving a hybrid approach dovetailing FRP with revenue sharing as recommended by the Rangarajan Committee, and phasing out SAP.

For the sugar year 2013–2014, already FRP of sugarcane is announced at Rs 210 per quintal at minimum 9.5% recovery level. Indications on sugar prices are that they are not likely to improve compared to what prevailed in 2012–2013. They could even go down, given the surplus sugar at home and globally in 2013–2014. For Maharashtra, this FRP of Rs 210 per quintal would turn out to be Rs 254 per quintal [(210/9.5) × 11.5], assuming a recovery ratio of 11.5%. At a sugar price of Rs 30/kg, this would amount to roughly 74% of the value of sugar produced from a quintal of cane, very close to what would work out under revenue sharing formula (75%). But the SAP of cane in UP, if increased further from the existing Rs 280/qtl in 2012–2013 to a higher level in 2013–2014, and if sugar prices remain where they are, this can spell disaster in the sugar sector, and needs to be avoided in the long-term interest of the sugar sector. Even the existing SAP is unsustainable in the face of current sugar prices, and rising cane arrears is a signal that trouble is brewing up in the sugar sector.

The stock-to-use ratio at about 37% at the end of 2012–2013 sugar season indicates a very comfortable position (excess supply) of sugar availability in the country. With about 9 million tons of estimated closing stock in 2012–2013 and likely surplus production during 2013–2014, there is going to be excess supply, putting downward pressures on sugar prices unless rupee depreciates further or international market improves.

The Commission has carefully examined the projections of domestic and international agencies for sugar prices in 2014–2015, and believes that the prices of sugar may be within a broad range of Rs 30 to Rs 34 per kg in the domestic market. NCDEX futures show that domestic prices of sugar (Grade M crystal sugar) would remain stable in the range of Rs 3,050–3,070 by the beginning of sugar season 2014–2015. On the international price front, markets are adjusting to a third consecutive year of a global sugar surplus. The international price of refined sugar as given in OECD-FAO Agricultural Outlook for 2013–2022, inequivalent rupee terms (with exchange rate assumed at 1US$ = Rs 60) is forecast at Rs 30 per kg for 2014–2015 season.

The projected cost of production (C2) of sugarcane at all India level (weighted average), adjusted at 9.5% recovery is Rs 193.13 per quintal. As regards intercrop price parity it is evident that at all-India level net return as percentage of C2 during the period 2009–2010 to 2011–2012 comes to 69% and net returns in absolute terms, Rs 62,386 per hectare. It is clear that sugarcane is the most profitable crop vis-à-vis its competing crops like wheat, paddy and cotton. Even when it is compared to the fully irrigated tracts of Punjab and Haryana, it is still found that returns on sugarcane are higher than paddy and wheat.

After having analyzed the factors in all their aspects, the Commission recommends that FRP of sugarcane for the year 2014–2015 be fixed at Rs 220 per quintal linked to basic recovery of 9.5% (an increase of 4.8%). It may be noted that the FRP during the last two sugarcane seasons has already been increased by 44.8%. For each 0.1% increase in recovery over and above 9.5%, the FRP would be increased by Rs 2.32 per quintal. All India average recovery rate being 10.27% achieved in 2011–2012, the FRP recommended would come to Rs 237.83.

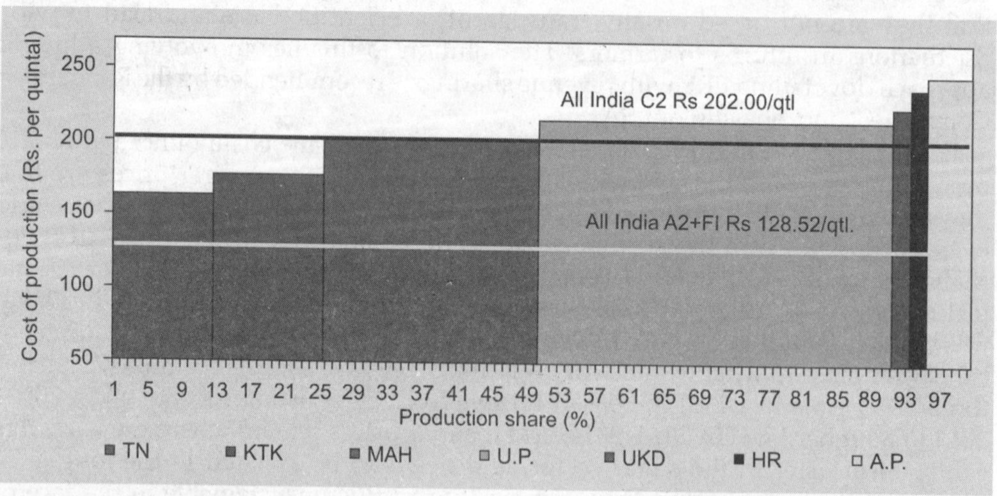

Recent Initiatives

SAP differs from state to state. Hence, the industry has urged the union agricultural ministry to fix market-driven prices so that mills could pay uniformly to cane farmers across the country. Uniform cane prices will also enable mills to produce sugar at uniform cost.

The center allowed sugar mill—which had imported raw sugar under the advanced licence scheme (ALS)—to fulfill their re-export obligations till March 2011, thus withdrawing the option of paying the applicable duty instead. About a million tons of sugar was imported in 2004–2005 on a ton-to-ton basis. Under ALS, mills are allowed to import raw sugar at zero duty against a future export commitment.

In August 2010, the government decided to relax sugar stockholding norm for bulk users such as icecream and beverage-makers by allowing them to keep the sweetener for 90 days of their usage from the current 15 days. The industry had been demanding that the stockholding limit on bulk users be relaxed to discourage them from buying imported sugar on which there is no such restriction.

Sugar companies have been asking the government to levy duty on cheap imported sugar. For instance, even a 20% import duty on sugar will give a landed cost of approximately Rs 29 per kilogram which is close to the domestic price and will therefore help to stabilize it.

On March 15, 2011, government raised the price sugar mills must pay to cane growers from the season starting October 2011. For the current season (up to September 2011), the minimum cane purchase price had been fixed at Rs 1.39 per kg. The new price is about 4.2% higher at Rs 1.45 per kg. Of course, this is a welcome step though mills have been paying much higher than the minimum price. It is hoped that higher minimum price would encourage growers to plant cane in larger areas. This would result in higher production in 2011–2012. The ISMA is in favor of allowing more quality of sugar for exports under open general licence (OGL) to take advantage of high global prices and pass on the benefit to cane growers as sugar prices fell recently. This would help trim huge opening stocks.

The ethanol program has been re-launched. The 5% blending (with petrol) has been re- started from October 2010, with a provisional price of Rs 27 per liter. About

India: Sugarcane price table, in rupees per ton

	2010/11	*2011/12*	*2012/13*
Minimum support price (MSP) or fair remunerative price (FRP)			
Wheat	11,200	12,850	13,500
Rice (Grade A)	10,300	11,100	12,800
Sugarcane	1,391.2	1,450.0	1,700.0[a]
State advised Price (SAP) for Sugarcane, by State			
Uttar Pradesh	2,050–2,100	2,350–2,500	2,750–2,900
Haryana/Punjab	1,900–2,200	2,200–2,310	2,350–2,760
Southern States[b]	1,750–2,300	1,800–2,050	2,200–2,500

Notes:

[a] FRP for 2012/13 at 9.5% recovery, subject to a premium of Rs 1.79 for every 0.1 percent increase in recovery above 9.5%.

[b] Sugar mills pay market price.

In 2011/12, Tamil Nadu government was paying Rs 100 in addition to SAP as transport cost

Exchange rate:

2011/12 (April-March) 1 US$ = 53.45 Indian Rupees

2012/13 (April-March) 1 US$ = 54.12 Indian Rupees

Source: Indian Sugar Mills Association.

India: monthly release of sugar for 2009/10 through March, 2012/13

Month	*2009/10*	*2010/11*	*2011/12*	*2012/13*
October	1.99	1.90	2.00	4.40
November	1.56	1.62	1.92	
December	1.69	1.71	1.91	7.63
January	1.59	1.92	1.62	
February	1.79	1.54	1.46	
March	1.80	1.54	1.46	
April	1.80	1.81	5.21	10.4
May	1.92	1.76		
June	1.91	1.86		
July	1.47	1.47	5.42	
August	1.92	1.93		
Sept	1.60	1.73		
Total	**21.03**	**20.77**	**21.39**	**22.43**

Note: Quantity in million metric tons weight basis.
Source: Indian Sugar Mills Association.

600 million liter has been contracted for supplies, and supplies of 100 million liter have been made up to February 2011. There has been opposition from some groups, but the government, oil companies and sugar industry are committed to the success of the program. Recently, the center has increased sugar stock-holding limit to 500 tons from 200 tons. This is to encourage procurement from sugar mills. The empowered group of ministers has also extended the order which authorizes states to impose stock limit on sugar by 6 months from April 1, 2011. The increased stock holding will enable traders to procure more sugar from millers and replenish their pipelines. The group also allowed exports of 500,000 tons of sugar under OGL.

Costs, Profitability and Inter-crop Price Parity

For pricing of sugarcane, i.e. in arriving at a fair and remunerative price (FRP), the Commission considers not only the cost of production but also the demand supply situation of both sugarcane and sugar, trends in market prices of sugar in domestic as well as in international markets, and the price realized from sale of sugar and its by-products, viz., molasses, bagasse and press-mud produced from a quintal of sugarcane. Apart from these factors, allowance is made for profit and risk margins in arriving at FRP as per the mandate given under sugarcane (control) order, 1966.

As part of this exercise, the commission uses the cost of cultivation/production estimates generated under the comprehensive scheme (CS) being implemented by the Directorate of Economics and Statistics (DES). These estimates are normally received with a lag of 2–3 years. The latest estimates are available for the year 2011–2012 for major sugarcane growing states of Andhra Pradesh, Haryana, Karnataka, Maharashtra, Tamil Nadu, UP and Uttarakhand.

In order to arrive at the projected cost of production of cane for the year 2014–2015 for its FRP recommendation, the Commission has used the actual data for latest three years, from 2009–2010 to 2011–2012, and projected each one of them for the year 2014–2015, for each sugarcane growing state, based on specially constructed input price index. Thus, there are three estimates of projected costs for each state each one based on 2009–2010, 2010–2011 and 2011–2012 respectively, which are then averaged. In this exercise, the construction of input price index is most critical. This is based on input prices data for the latest years, and projected for 2014–2015.

The Commission takes into account latest input price data for various inputs from different sources, viz., Labor Bureau, Shimla, replies from State governments, Office of the Economic Adviser (OEA), Ministry of Commerce and Industry, Fertilizers Association of India (FAI), National Seeds Corporation (NSC), etc. The all India paid out cost including family labor (A2+FL) per quintal and overall C2 cost per quintal are arrived at by taking weighted average of respective state specific estimated costs, weights being shares of production of each state in absolute quantity in total production.

Despite best methodology and assumptions, projections could turn out to be different from the reality which will be known only when actual costs are available usually after 3 years. Therefore, Commission also incorporates a "correction factor" (CF) based on the difference between actual and projected costs for latest three years data in a rolling fashion in its projections to arrive at more accurate projections. These projected cost estimates are then presented for various states.

Costs and Profitability of Sugarcane During 2009–2010 to 2011–2012

It is pertinent to point that the gross value of output in the methodology of cost calculation is estimated at the prevailing market prices during harvest season in the village/cluster of villages where crops are grown and harvested. With this stipulation, an analysis of the profitability and the rate of return over costs A2+FL and C2 has been done for cane during 2009–2010 to 2011–2012, the latest years for which actual cost data is shown in the next page 352.

During the period 2009–2010 to 2011–2012 at all-India level, gross returns over A2+FL cost is Rs 98,015/hectare, the highest level is for Karnataka at Rs 124,790/hectare and lowest for Andhra Pradesh at Rs 79,436/hectare. The rate of return over C2 cost during this period stands at 69% at all India level, and ranges from 28% in Andhra Pradesh to 95% in Karnataka. Two major sugar growing states of UP and Maharashtra (with 41% and 25% share respectively in all India production) show a sharp difference in profitability, with UP showing profitability at 85% and Maharashtra at 51% over C2. The sharp difference in profitability in these two states is attributed to proportionately higher cost of cultivation (C2) for Maharashtra relative to that of UP, despite its yield level higher than that of UP.

Labor and Input Price Movement

The Commission has made an assessment of average daily wage rates for agriculture labour, based on the data furnished by the Labor Bureau, Shimla for which the latest data available is up to May, 2013. Compared to the corresponding month of previous year, the wage rate has increased by 20% at all India level, with highest for Karnataka by 30.2% followed by Bihar, Maharashtra, Madhya Pradesh, UP and Rajasthan all greater than 20% (All India level of percent hike in wage rate) and lowest for Odisha by (–) 4.5%. In absolute terms, Kerala has the highest wage rate at Rs 489.16 per day, followed by Punjab at Rs 272.78 per day and lowest for Gujarat at Rs 130.93 per day during the month of May, 2013 (latest month wage rate reported

All India gross and net returns over actual cost of cultivation of sugarcane
(average from 2009–2010 to 2011–2012)

State	*Cost A2+FL (Rs/ hectare)*	*Cost C2 (Rs/ hectare)*	*GVO (Rs/ hectare)*	*Gross returns over A2+FL (Rs/ hectare)*	*Rate of gross returns over A2+F L (%)*	*Net returns over C2 (Rs/ hectare)*	*Net rateof return over C2 (%)*
Andhra Pradesh	72,139	118,322	151,576	79,436	110	33,254	28
Haryana	44,838	95,294	157,789	112,951	252	62,495	66
Karnataka	52,379	91,014	177,170	124,790	238	86,156	95
Maharashtra	87,875	134,343	202,761	114,885	131	68,418	51
Tamil Nadu	89,028	114,745	188,562	99,533	112	73,817	64
Uttar Pradesh	36,618	67,211	124,210	87,592	239	56,999	85
Uttarakhand	39,492	74,735	137,626	98,134	248	62,891	84
All India wt. avg.	55,270	90,899	153,285	98,015	177	62,386	69

Notes: A2+FL cost includes all expenses in cash and kind on account of hired human labor, bullock labor, machine labor, seed, insecticides and pesticides, manure, fertilizers, irrigation charges and miscellaneous expenses including family labor. C2 cost includes A2+FL cost, imputed rental value of owned land, imputed interest on fixed capital, etc.
Source: Comprehensive Scheme (CS) for studying the Cost of Cultivation of principal Crops, DES.

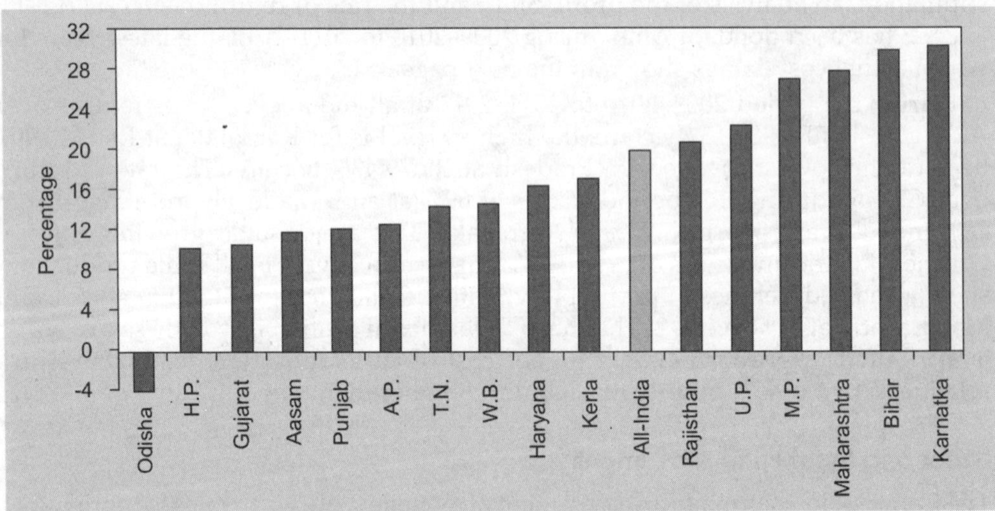

Statewise and all India rise in agriculture labor wage rate (Rs/day) (In May, 2013 over May, 2012)

by Labor Bureau). Chart 6.1 represents the increase in wage rate at All India level and by states in May, 2013 over May, 2012.

The Commission observes the price trends of farm inputs to assess how they impinge on cost of production. Wholesale price index (with base year 200,405 = 100) for major farm inputs during the period May, 2012 to May, 2013 has shown an upward trend, except light diesel oil (LDO) (with decrease of 9.7%). As per the above index, fertilizer prices have escalated by 7.1%, electricity for irrigation by 36.2%; pesticides by 3.0%; tractors, by 3.9%; lubricants, by 7.1%; high speed diesel oil (HSDO) by 21.2%; fodder by 18.5%; cattle feed by 19.3%.

Import Duty on Sugar Up at 25%; may Impact Prices

In a move that could lead to increase in sugar prices, the government hiked the import duty on both raw and refined sugar to 25% from the existing 15% on 13 August 2014. The increase in duty would make imports unviable and may lead to some jump in domestic sugar prices that could cause burden on consumers but would help to revive the business of cash-starved mills who owe farmers around Rs 6,800 crore. India has been importing sugar in small quantities taking advantage of lower global prices.

According to a notification issued by the Central Board of Excise and Customs, import duty has been raised to 25% on raw sugar and refined or white sugar. The higher duty will also be applicable to bulk consumers who import raw sugar, the government said, adding that this has been done in public interest. The Food Ministry had recommended increase in import duty on sugar to 40%. "However, the Finance Ministry has hiked the duty marginally, considering inflationary concerns and to give some relief to domestic millers", a senior Food Ministry official said.

Currently, domestic sugar prices are ruling stable in the range of Rs 34–40 per kg in view of surplus stocks, as per the data maintained by the Consumer Affairs Ministry. Sugar mills are facing a cash crunch as domestic prices have slipped below the cost of production, hurting their profits. Mills in UP are selling sugar at Rs 30.50 per kg while the cost of production remains at Rs 37 per kg. Similarly, mills in Maharashtra are selling the commodity at Rs 28.50 per kg as against the cost of production of Rs 31.

Industry Body Indian Sugar Mills Association (ISMA) hailed the decision saying this will improve cash-flow of millers and help clear cane arrears. "We welcome the decision. At current global prices and rupee-dollar exchange rate, this increase in duty will check all sugar imports, which will certainly improve the domestic market sentiments", ISMA Director General Avinash Verma said. Currently, sugarcane arrears stand at about Rs 6,800 crore across the country with the maximum of Rs 5,000 crore in UP, he added.

The government has announced several measures to improve liquidity of millers. Earlier in 2014 the government had rolled out a scheme of Rs 6,600 crore interest-free loan to mills for making cane payments to growers. It is also giving export subsidy.

Mills Owe Rs 6,800 Crore to Farmers

- The increase in duty would make imports unviable and may lead to some jump in domestic sugar prices
- It would help to revive the business of cash-starved mills who owe farmers around Rs 6,800 crore
- The higher duty will also be applicable to bulk consumers who import raw sugar
- Sugar mills are facing a cash crunch as domestic prices have slipped below the cost of production.

Cane Arrears and Closed Mills

Sugar factories in Karnataka want more time to pay up farmers' dues. This is an annual issue in every sugar-producing state, with no permanent solution in sight. Although some sort of sugar and cane price linkage has been suggested, no one is willing to take a call. Meanwhile, the net result remains the same: past dues mount and mills keep shutting or seeking relief. Statewise and sectorwise numbers of installed sugar factories are given below: *

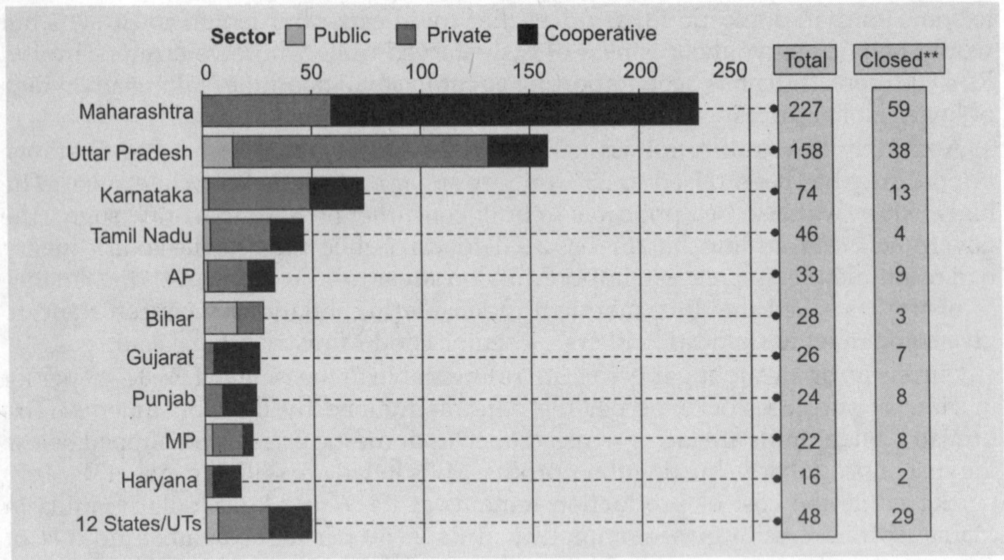

* As of 30.9.2014
** Closed during the current sugar season 2013-14 (up to 30.06.2014, provisional figures)
Source: Parliament questions.

As Debt Rises, Sugar Mills Seek Export Subsidy Sop

The sugar industry has made a fresh pitch for extending the controversial export subsidy on raw sugar citing a threefold jump in its debt burden from Rs 11,400 crore in 2008 to Rs 33,600 crore in 2013.

While the Cabinet is expected to raise the subsidy to Rs 4,000 a tons from Rs 3,371 next week, the powerful sugar lobby also wants a fresh loan-restructuring package despite managing to extract major concessions on bank loans earlier. During bumper harvests, the industry typically cites its inability to pay cane arrears to pressurize the government into doling out concessions such as export and loan subsidies.

This time, however, the export subsidies have been questioned at the WTO, where Australia, Brazil and the US have alleged the subsidies aren't compliant with global trade rules. The Indian Sugar Mills Association said this is probably the first time that the mills are unable to even pay the Centrefixed fair and remunerative price to the farmers.

Ethanol trade

State	*Export duty*	*Import duty*
UP	1	0
Delhi	0	2
Gujarat	0	3
MP	0	1
Maharashtra	1.5	1.5
Punjab	0	2
Rajasthan	0	1
Uttarakhand	0	1.10

State Duty on Ethanol Curbs its Availability

You can get ethanol-blended petrol in Noida or Ghaziabad in UP, but not in Delhi. This is because Delhi charges Rs 2 as "import duty" whereas UP levies Rs 1 as "export duty" on per litre of ethanol. This is not peculiar to this part of the country. Another eight states either charge some import or export duty or both on movement of ethanol.

The list of states includes some of the major sugarcane producing states such as Maharashtra, Gujarat, Haryana and Punjab. The practice is on despite the UPA and now the NDA pushing for more blending of ethanol in petrol. Ethanol is a cheaper and cleaner fuel.

Sources said road transport minister Nitin Gadkari, who is pushing for more use of ethanol including introducing vehicles that can run on 85% and 90% blending of ethanol, is keen to resolve the prevailing "duties" across different states.

Sugar Industry Seeks Financial Restructuring

Reeling under the "worst financial crisis ever" coupled with problem of plenty, the sugar mills' body, Indian Sugar Mills Association (ISMA), is demanding financial restructuring of the sector. The association wants paddy / wheat-like regulation for the sugar industry. As per the industry, there should be just one support price fixed by the Centre—Fair and Remunerative Price (FRP)—as it is called for sugarcane farmers.

The states, if they want to further incentivise the farmers, should pass on extra benefits (higher than FRP) through their own budget, it said today, pleading for financial assistance from the Centre.

"We are unable to pay anything extra because of mounting arrears and crashing sugar prices. Ex-mill sugar prices are at its lowest in the past 3 years and the mills across the country are struggling to pay even the FRP", ISMA president A Vellayan said.

The surplus sugar stocks further add to the industry's woes. Though opening up of exports is a short-term measure, the industry demands permanent solution—a structural review of the way FRP and the SAP are fixed.

Due to high sugarcane price fixed by the government, the cost of sugar production in India is among the highest in the world, making Indian sugar uncompetitive in the international market. According to the association, cane price arrears in last sugar season in March-April 2014 crossed Rs 13,000 crore and with current season's sugarcane prices either at the same level or higher and ex-mill sugar prices being substantially lower than what was in last year, it is feared that cane price arrears will be higher than last season if the situation is not rectified.

The industry says that India is producing surplus sugar continuously for the past five seasons. During the current sugar season also, the industry will produce more than what is required domestically.

Demands of Sugar Mills

Continuation of the incentive scheme on raw sugar production and exports of 25 lakh tonne sugar Incentives over and above Fair and Remunerative Price fixed by the Centre to be borne by the states from their own budget Debt burden of the sugar industry has more than tripled from Rs 11,443 crore at the end of 2007-08 to Rs 36,601 crore in the past 5 years. At present, ex-mill sugar prices are the lowest in the past 3 years.

Subsidy for Sugar Exports Increased

The Cabinet on Thursday approved a higher subsidy of Rs 4,000 a tonne for exports of raw sugar, a decision that could support local prices by reducing excess supplies as India stares at a glut in production.

The export incentive will be given for 1.4 million tonnes of raw sugar in the 2014–15 season, which began on October 1. The subsidy is given for specific periods and it was most recently Rs 3,371. Food minister Ram Vilas Paswan had in the last week of January cleared the increase in subsidy to help the cash-starved industry pay arrears to sugarcane farmers.

India, the biggest sugar producer after Brazil, has an annual domestic requirement of 24.8 million tonnes. But, this season's production is pegged at 25 million tonnes and the country also has a carryover stock of 7.2 million tonnes. "Even if we keep 6 million tonnes for 3 months' requirement, we have enough stock and hence can export", the minister had said.

Indian Sugar Mills Association welcomed the move. "Sugar mills will need to gear up to produce the 1.4 million tonnes of raw sugar in the balance 1–1.5 months of crushing period remaining. At the current global and domestic prices, raw sugar exports from India is just about viable with the incentives", it said in a news release.

As per ISMA's estimates, there is a surplus of around 2.5 million tonnes and therefore the industry will require incentives for another 1-1.5 million tonnes. "This is the only way forward for the industry to pay cane price even at the FRP (fair and remunerative price) level this season, otherwise the cane price arrears which are at Rs 12,300 crore will very soon cross Rs 13,000 crore recorded in last season", it said.

> Sugar mills will need to gear up to produce the 1.4 of raw sugar in the balance 1.1.5 months of crusing period remaining. At the current global and domestic prices, raw sugar exports from India is just about viable with the incentives.

According to the food minister, the long-term solution for sugar mills is upgrading their units and using more of their by-products such as ethanol and bagasse. The export subsidy was introduced in February last year at Rs 3,300 per tonne. It was increased to Rs 3,371 for August and September 2014.

Annexure

Annexure 1: Sugar output to see 30% rise year-on-year; prices seen depressed

While Maharashtra, the top sugar producer of the country is all set to produce a historical output, the industry—under pressure from excess sugar and depressed prices—is only to see more problems. The state is likely to produce over 10 MT (metric ton) of sugar, an increase of 30% over the last year's sugar production and more than 5% as compared to the estimate of industry body Indian Sugar Mills' Association (ISMA).

Maharashtra produced 77 LT (lakh ton) sugar during the season in 2013-14. The state had initially estimated to produce 93 LT sugar in the current 2014-15 season, which it revised upward to 97 LT. However, last week, the state's sugar commissionerate revised it to 100 LT. "We now expect to crush 875 LT sugarcane and produce 100 LT sugar", said Vipin Sharma, commissioner (sugar), Maharashtra.

ISMA, in its January estimates has pegged country's sugar output at 26 MT while the central government has put it at 26.5 MT. According to ISMA, Maharashtra is expected to produce 95 LT sugar and it will not take a call on revising the estimates now as the crushing season is at its fag end. Factors like increase in area under sugarcane, increase in the area of the high-yielding sugarcane variety of Co-265, and better crop care by the farmers as sugarcane is the only crop, which is giving good returns to the farmers when prices of all other commodities have been depressed.

The area under cane in the state increased by about 12.5% from 9.37 LHa (lakh hectares) last year to 10.54 LHa this year while the area under Co-265 variety increased from 25% to 35%. "The overall yield of cane has increased from 80 tons per hectare to about 95 tons per hectare", said a state government official, requesting anonymity. Though the state government has pegged sugar production at 10 MT, industry sources say the production can be 105 LT. If the state records this production, it would be higher than the ISMA's estimate by about 4%.

With the world market flooded with cheaper sugar mainly from Brazil, Indian exporters and millers are waiting for the Brazialian surplus to get over which would create demand for the Indian commodity. Indian exporters claim that Indian sugar is not competitive despite the subsidy of 4 per kilogram due to a fall in global sugar prices.

Sugar–coated Problems

10 MT estimated produce by Maharashtra in Fy 16.

30% jump in sugar out over last fiscal.

5% higher produce estimated ISMA's prediction.

12.5% increase in area under cane harvest this fiscal.

9.37 hectares area under cane harvest in 2013-14.

10.54 hectares area under cane harvest in 2014-15.

10.54 hectares area under cane harvest in 2014-15.

77 lakh tons sugar output by Maharashtra in 2013-14.

100 lakh tons sugar output estimate by Maharashtra in 2014-15.

875 lakh tons sugarcane to be crushed this fiscal.

26 MT estimated sugar output for current fiscal.

Rs 4/kg subsidy for Indian sugar.

Rs 2,600 cr accumulated cane price arrears by Maharashtra sugar mills.

Out of 177 sugar mills have paid FRP to farmers.

35% area under Co-265 cane variety for this fiscal.

80 tons/hectare overall yield of cane in 2013-14.

95 tons/hectare present yield of cane.

Index

T

U

W